DECISION SUPPORT SYSTEMS
IN THE
TWENTY-FIRST CENTURY

George M. Marakas

Kelley School of Business
Indiana University

 Prentice Hall, Upper Saddle River, NJ 07458

**This book is dedicated to Marti and Jim,
the two teachers in my life.
Thank you both for your love.**

Acquisitions Editor:	David Alexander
Assistant Editor:	Lori Cardillo
Editorial Assistant:	Keith Kryszczun
Editor-in-Chief:	P. J. Boardman
Marketing Manager:	Nancy Evans
Production Editor:	Marc Oliver
Managing Editor:	Dee Josephson
Manufacturing Buyer:	Lisa DiMaulo
Senior Manufacturing Supervisor:	Paul Smolenski
Manufacturing Manager:	Vincent Scelta
Design Manager:	Patricia Smythe
Cover Design:	Joan O'Connor
Cover Illustration/Photo:	Tom Collicott
Composition:	Impressions Book and Journal Services, Inc.

 Copyright © 1999 by Prentice-Hall, Inc.
A Simon & Schuster Company
Upper Saddle River, New Jersey 07458

Library of Congress Cataloging-in-Publication Data

Marakas, George M.
    Decision support systems in the twenty-first century : DSS and
data mining technologies for tomorrow's manager / George M. Marakas.
        p.   cm.
    Includes bibliographical references and index.
    ISBN 0-13-744186-X
    1. Decision support systems. 2. Database management. 3. Data
mining. I. Title.
    HD30.213.M36 1998
    658.4'038'0285574—dc21
                                           98-44575
                                         CIP

Prentice-Hall International (UK) Limited, London
Prentice-Hall of Australia Pty. Limited, Sydney
Prentice-Hall Canada, Inc., Toronto
Prentice-Hall Hispanoamericana, S.A., Mexico
Prentice-Hall of India Private Limited, New Delhi
Prentice-Hall of Japan, Inc., Tokyo
Simon & Schuster Asia Pte. Ltd., Singapore
Editora Prentice-Hall do Brasil, Lida., Rio de Janeiro

Printed in the United States of America

10 9 8 7 6 5 4 3 2

Brief Contents

Contents

Preface

Decisions are activities we face every day. The really good news about making decisions is that the majority of the ones we encounter in our daily lives are both routine and relatively clear-cut. Deciding what clothes to wear, what to have for breakfast, what movie to watch on television, or what food to buy at the grocery are all typical of the day-to-day decisions that confront us. The bad news, however, is that while important, these decisions are not the type that we must face in the course of pursuing our chosen occupation. We will not get paid for being able to decide what to wear to work. As managers, we establish our worth with our organizations by being able to cope with decisions such as whether to invest in an emerging technology that could create significant competitive advantage for the firm, or how we can best deploy the limited human resources available for a given project, or what mix of products is the best one for the current and future market conditions. In other words, the really important decisions are often difficult to make and require both a great deal of information and an increased level of decision support. That is what this book is all about: making and supporting managerial decisions.

CONCEPT AND PURPOSE

This text was written to provide a foundation for teaching the subject of decision support systems (DSSs) from a cognitive processes and decision-making perspective. The content concentrates on issues emphasizing managerial applications and the implication of decision support technologies on those issues.

Gorry and Scott Morton (1989) are often given credit for the classic definition of a DSS:

> Decision support systems couple the intellectual resources of individuals with the capabilities of the computer to improve the quality of decisions. [They comprise] a computer-based support system for management decision makers who deal with semi-structured problems. (p. 60)

I have always found it somewhat counterintuitive that the definition of the subject is written from a user's perspective, yet the texts available to teach the subject to students in business schools tend to be written from a designer's perspective. In response to this, I have written this text to place strong emphasis on helping the student thoroughly understand the "support" aspect of a DSS. The content is focused on a distinctly "real world" orientation with an emphasis in all topic areas on application and implementation over design and development. The manager of tomorrow does not need to understand DSS *design* for that is the domain of the computer scientist and the systems analyst. Rather, the skills necessary are those that relate to the effective and strategic *application* of decision support technologies to advance the quality of problem identification and the associated solutions. Taking a multidisciplinary user/manager approach, this text looks at decisions and technologies necessary to support those decisions in the twenty-first century. The coverage of decision making and cognitive processes includes such topics as models of decision-making, biases and heuristics, creativity enhancement, decision strategies, simulation, and discovery. This book reflects an incorporation of the best components of the leading texts on decision support while additionally providing coverage of topics not previously broached (most notably, data visualization and mining).

In short, this book was motivated by my belief that there exists a significant need to integrate our knowledge of decision making with the application of decision support technology. Application and understanding of use are, and will continue to be, more important to our managers of today and tomorrow than design.

WHO SHOULD USE THIS BOOK

This book is directed to business school students who aspire to a career in management with a firm that is a significant user of technology or is a member of a technology-driven industry—in others words, all students in business school. The primary course targets for this text are upper-level undergraduate or graduate DSS electives. These types of courses are regularly offered at four-year universities as well as many community colleges. Ideally, students should have completed an introductory MIS program and possibly a semester of systems analysis and design before moving on to a focus on DSSs. In addition, the further students are in their business curriculum, the more relevant the decision-making perspective of the text will become. In addition to being directed to students, many of the chapters in this text were written to provide a good reference for practitioners to use in the course of their daily decision-making activities.

ELEMENTS OF PEDAGOGY

The text makes appropriate use of many traditional pedagogical features commonly found in top business school curricula. The writing style is intended to strike a useful balance between a professional and conversational approach. Extensive use of graphics and examples of each concept introduced is made throughout. Each chapter contains an introductory minicase targeted toward the concepts introduced in that chapter. The end-of-chapter structure contains a summary of the key concepts introduced, review questions and problems, and references and additional support readings. A brief description of each of the pedagogical features of the text is listed below.

Chapter Learning Objectives

A statement of learning objectives for each chapter is presented in both performance and behavioral terms. In other words, the objectives state what the student should be capable of *doing* and *understanding* as a result of reading the chapter.

Chapter Minicase

The minicases are all derived from actual situations and have been selected to allow the student to have a point of reference for the material about to be presented in the chapter. In addition, each minicase makes specific reference to each of the key players in the scenario so that additional investigation using a variety of research tools could be conducted by either an individual student or a student team to further explore the situation presented.

Figures and Tables

Clear, carefully designed figures and tables have been included to aid in the student's understanding of the material. Wherever possible, the diagrams contained in each chapter are not only referenced in the body of the text but are positioned in such a way that they serve as a repeated visual reference for the textual discussion.

Narrative Vignettes

To further the explanation of some of the concepts associated with the process of making a decision, the technique of *narrative vignette* is employed. Here, a situation using a fictitious cast of characters is presented to allow the student not only to see how the particular technique under discussion is applied but also to relate it to a set of circumstances or a context in which it might be considered relevant or applicable.

Key Concepts

Immediately following each chapter summary is an outline of the key concepts presented in the chapter in order of their appearance. This section can aid the student in reviewing the material contained in the chapter in preparation for class discussion or examination.

Questions for Review

Each chapter contains a list of ten to twenty questions intended to allow the student to test his or her retention and understanding of the material contained in the chapter. Each question is phrased in such a manner that the answer can be readily found in the chapter and that a detailed and precise answer can be provided. Sample responses to each question are available in the instructor sections of the World Wide Web (WWW) site for the text.

Further Discussion

Several questions are provided at the end of each chapter that expand upon the material presented to allow the student to engage in a richer thought process and discussion than would occur using the review questions. Each of the discussion questions can be used to engage students in an open class discussion and many of them can be easily expanded into individual or team miniprojects.

World Wide Web Site

The WWW site for this text is located at http://www.prenhall.com/marakas. This extensive resource contains over four thousand direct links to DSS-related Internet sites. To further enhance the learning process, the links are organized in the same manner as the text and are categorized according to their direct relevance to a particular section within each chapter. As such, each section of each chapter can be expanded as necessary by using the Internet resources associated with that section to allow for exploration or greater focus on a particular subject.

Note to the Student

The student accessible links on the text's Web site can be accessed by using the key created from the access program contained on the diskette shipped with each text. Each access key will allow student access to the chapter-specific sections for eight months from the date of the first access and registration. In addition, once you register on the site, you will be able to use the automatic response feature of the site, which allows you to work through any exercises or homework assigned to you by the instructor and submit your responses directly to the instructor via electronic mail. This feature will also create a duplicate copy of your homework response and e-mail it to you for your records if you provide a usable e-mail address during your registration process.

Note to the Instructor

The instructor accessible sections of the Web site contain a number of useful support elements and materials. Animated PowerPoint slide files are provided for each chapter that include not only all the tables and figures contained within the chapter but also additional slides sequenced in the order of the material to be used as desired in preparing a multimedia presentation or lecture. Accompanying the slides are brief teaching notes for each chapter intended for use in preparing in-class lectures and exercises.

Sample responses to each chapter-end review question are also provided so that review quizzes or test items can be easily graded and evaluated. In addition, several data sets and sample software packages are either stored or linked in the instructor section of the site. These resources can be used to create projects of any length or complexity as well as in-class demonstrations of actual DSS-related software applications.

The instructor accessible sections of the Web site are available only to current text adopters and are available for eight months following the first access. To acquire a valid user ID and password you simply need to register yourself as the instructor of the course by going to the Web site and completing the initial instructor registration process. In this process, you will be asked to supply the name and e-mail address of your Prentice Hall book representative. Upon completion of the process, your registration request will be forwarded to your sales representative for validation. If you are a current adopter of the text, the sales representative will supply you with an authorization key to be typed into the authorization field located in the instructor authorization screen on the Web site. Once this is saved, you will be able to access the instructor sections of the site. If you have any problem with your authorization, please contact your Prentice Hall sales representative.

CHAPTER DESCRIPTIONS

Chapter 1—Introduction to Decision Support Systems

The first chapter introduces the concept of a DSS and explains each of the commonly associated component elements. Also included is a brief history of the evolution of the DSS to the present day. Additionally, the chapter includes a discussion of the various types and categories of DSSs that are currently available and in use.

Chapter 2—The Decision Maker

This chapter focuses attention on the decision makers and positions them as an integral part of the DSS environment. Issues such as decision styles, effectiveness of decisions, and the types of support that can be provided by a DSS are discussed.

Chapter 3—The Process of Making a Decision

Here the focus turns to the concept of a decision and the process by which it is made. Basic decision theory is introduced and related issues including bounded rationality, biases and heuristics, and fundamental cognitive processes are discussed. In addition, the student is introduced to the concepts of effectiveness and efficiency with a discussion that focuses on comparing and contrasting these often confused characteristics of a decision.

Chapter 4—Decisions in the Organization

The fourth chapter focuses on the organization. Because it is in this environment and context that most managerial decisions will be made, it is important to understand the basic concept of an organization and to explore many of its facets including culture, power and politics, and the types of "organizational level" decisions that might be encountered.

Chapter 5—Modeling Decision Processes

Chapter 5 introduces the various common techniques employed in the modeling of decision processes. Several examples of common decision model structures are introduced. Also in this chapter is a discussion of probability and methods for forecasting probabilistic events that may be associated with a complex managerial decision.

Chapter 6—Group Decision Support and Groupware Technologies

This chapter begins a series of chapters that each focus on a particular aspect of decision support technologies. We begin with a thorough exploration of the process of group decision making and conclude with identification and explanation of various types of multiparticipant decision-making technologies.

Chapter 7—Executive Information Systems

Continuing the focus on specific DSS technologies, this chapter looks at the domain of the executive and the application of DSS technology to the development and application of an executive information system (EIS). Coverage includes a definition of EIS technology, a brief history of its evolution, the unique characteristics of executive-level decisions and decision makers, as well as issues related to the successful introduction of an EIS into an organizational environment.

Chapter 8—Expert Systems and Artificial Intelligence

A brief overview of the concept of expertise begins this chapter. A thorough discussion of the elements of artificial intelligence and expert systems follows. The chapter concludes with a look at the issues associated with designing, building, and evaluating an expert system. Appended to chapter 8 is a chronological synopsis of expert system technologies.

Chapter 9—Knowledge Engineering and Acquisition

Chapter 9 extends the discussion of expert systems by focusing on the concept of knowledge and the methods by which it is acquired and codified in an expert system's knowledge base.

Chapter 10—Machines That Can Learn

The newest members of the world of artificial intelligence and decision support systems are the focus of this chapter. The concepts of fuzzy logic and linguistic ambiguity are introduced in detail as a precursor to a discussion of artificial neural networks and genetic algorithms. Appended to chapter 10 is an overview of two popular software applications within this realm. Following this, a mathematical derivation of the most popular artificial neural network learning algorithm is provided.

Chapter 11—The Data Warehouse

This chapter and the next introduce the hottest topics in decision support systems today: the data warehouse and data mining. Chapter 11 thoroughly covers the basic concepts of data warehousing and discusses several commercial data warehousing products.

Chapter 12—Data Mining and Data Visualization

Extending the concepts introduced in chapter 11, this chapter looks at the realm of data mining and complex pattern extraction. The concept of on-line analytical processing (OLAP) and its variations is introduced. In addition, the chapter contains a discussion of the techniques used to mine data, their current limitations, and their application in data visualization contexts.

Chapter 13—Designing and Building Decision Support Systems

The topic of decision support, even in its most applied sense, would not be complete without a discussion of the strategies and tools necessary to bring the system to life. This chapter is the first of a two-part focus on the issues associated with the design and development of a modern DSS.

Chapter 14—Implementing and Integrating Decision Support Systems

Chapter 14 concludes our focus on DSS development issues by looking at the activities necessary to effectively implement, integrate, and evaluate an organizational DSS.

Chapter 15—Creative Decision Making and Problem Solving

As we begin to close our in-depth focus on decision making and problem solving it becomes necessary to include a discussion of one of the most elusive yet critical elements to successful managerial decision making: creativity. This chapter looks at the concept of creativity and the various methods of enhancing it. Following this is a discussion of a related topic, intelligent agents.

Chapter 16—Decision Support in the Twenty-First Century

This capstone chapter provides a look at the DSS of tomorrow. By reviewing where we have been to date, the chapter guides us into a brief glimpse of what the future holds for DSSs, expert systems and artificial intelligence, and executive information systems.

ACKNOWLEDGMENTS

In this, my first effort at writing a textbook, I have learned a great deal and have stumbled a great deal in the process. Without the constant help of a number of people correcting my mistakes, answering my questions, contributing to the vast amount of required labor, and reassuring me in the myriad times of self-doubt, I do not believe this book would have come to pass. What follows is a brief, but nonetheless heartfelt, expression of my deepest gratitude and dedication to those people who were instrumental in the development of this project.

First and foremost, I wish to thank my biggest supporters, my parents, George and Joan Marakas. Thank you for the many sacrifices you have made over the years to get me to this point in my life and to allow me the opportunity to experience this adventure.

To my daughter, Stephanie, who throughout her entire life has always insisted that her Dad can fix anything, even his own mistakes. Stephanie, thank you for never being shy about expressing your pride in me.

To my best friend and companion, Debra Herbenick, who quite literally found herself constantly having a stack of papers thrust under her nose accompanied by the request that she provide her editing talents and her constructive suggestions. Without her help, I would not have been able to create a readable manuscript and my message would not have been as clearly delivered. Thank you, LB, for holding my hand. Your devotion is reflected on every page.

To my army of assistants—Yu-Ting "Caisy" Hung, Ji-Tsung "Ben" Wu, Han-Chieh "Harry" Jiang, Yu-Lin "Emily" Lin—who invested endless hours in the final compilation of this text and its supporting Web site. You will be a part of this book, and whatever contribution it makes, forever.

To my mentors, Dan Robey and Joyce Elam. You have given of yourself to teach me how to teach others. Without your wisdom and guidance I would be lost.

To Beth Spencer and JoAnn DeLuca, from Prentice Hall, whose combined contagious energy and excitement gave me the courage to submit a proposal for this text and without whom this text would surely not exist.

I must express my deepest appreciation to my editors, David Alexander and P. J. Boardman. Between the two of them, they provided me with the energy to press on during some tough times. David's constant coercion, I mean encouragement, brought me to the successful end of this project and, possibly, to the threshold of another.

I am also indebted to a number of people who reviewed the manuscript, offering their praise and suggestions for improvement. While many of them I have never met, I hope to change that in the near future: William R. Bruyn, DeVry Institute of Technology; Ranjit Bose, University of New Mexico; Fatemeh Zahedi, University of Wisconsin; Jerry Fjermestad, New Jersey Institute of Technology; Madjid Tavana, LaSalle University; B. S. Vijayaraman, The University of Akron; Bradley C. Wheeler, Indiana University; Russell K. H. Ching, California State University, Sacramento; Tom Wichser, DeVry Institute of Technology; and Gustav Lundberg, Duquesne University.

In closing this rather lengthy, but quite necessary, acknowledgement, I would be remiss if I failed to thank my good friends and colleagues Brad Wheeler and Steven Hornik. Both of you have given me energy with your friendship and comfort with your faith.

Finally, my sincere thanks goes out to all my students who attended my classes and assisted me in my development of ideas, examples, explanations, and content. You are my true motivation and I will always remember you.

ABOUT THE AUTHOR

George M. Marakas is an assistant professor of information systems for the Kelley School of Business at Indiana University in Bloomington. His teaching expertise includes systems analysis and design, technology-assisted decision making, managing IS resources, behavioral IS research methods, and data visualization and decision support. In addition, Marakas is an active researcher in the area of systems analysis methods, data mining and visualization, creativity enhancement, conceptual data modeling, and computer self-efficacy.

Marakas received his Ph.D. in Information Systems from Florida International University in Miami and his MBA from Colorado State University. Prior to his academic career, he enjoyed a highly successful career in the banking and real estate industries. His corporate experience includes senior management positions with Continental Illinois National Bank and the FDIC. In addition, Marakas served as president and CEO for CMC Group, Inc., a major RTC management contractor in Miami, for three years.

During his tenure at the University of Maryland and now at Indiana University, Marakas has distinguished himself both through his research and in the classroom. He has received numerous national teaching awards and his research has appeared in the top journals in his field.

Beyond his academic endeavors, Marakas is also an active consultant and has served as an advisor to a number of organizations including the Central Intelligence Agency, the Department of the Treasury, the Department of Defense, Xavier University, Professional Records Storage, Inc., and United Information Systems, among many others. His consulting activities are concentrated primarily on workflow reengineering, CASE tool integration, and organizational system conversion to Lotus Notes. He is a Novell Certified Network Engineer and has been involved in the corporate beta testing program for Microsoft Corporation since 1990. Marakas is also an active member of a number of professional IS organizations and is an avid golfer, a PADI-certified Divemaster, and a member of Pi Kappa Alpha fraternity.

CHAPTER

1

Introduction to Decision Support Systems

Learning Objectives

■ Understand the definition of a decision support system (DSS) based on three common themes: problem structuredness, decision outcome, and managerial control

■ Understand the benefits and limitations of DSS use

■ Be familiar with the history of DSSs

■ Grasp the five basic components of a DSS

■ Learn the roles of data and model management systems

■ Learn the functionality of a DSS knowledge base

■ Learn the importance of the user interface in a DSS

■ Learn the user roles and patterns of DSS use in a DSS

■ Gain an understanding of the categories and classes of DSSs that are essential in determining the best approach to designing or implementing a new system

Mervyn's Department Stores

Faced with increasing competition from discounters, department stores have had to reconsider the best way to secure and maintain a competitive advantage. Mervyn's, a leading clothing retailer with over 280 stores in the United States, is using a sophisticated decision support system (DSS) to provide its analysts with information to identify trend-right products and facilitate quick decisions.

Although existing systems at Mervyn's provided large amounts of data, the challenge was to construct a system that would effectively integrate and distill that data into mission-critical information for decision making. Inadequate data access and analysis capabilities in these earlier systems prevented managers from exploiting the wealth of information buried in Mervyn's transaction data.

Compounding this problem was Mervyn's need for quick access to 300 to 700 gigabytes of data. Performing sophisticated analyses within a reasonable time frame on a data set of this size was beyond the scope of most existing decision support technologies. The solution required query performance optimization and various parallel software schemes new to decision support.

Mervyn's also needed to standardize business analyses for more meaningful comparisons. Sue Little, manager of Merchandising Planning and Logistics Systems at Mervyn's, says, "We've never had data where units and dollars matched. Buyers looked at everything from a dollar perspective and Inventory Management saw everything from a unit perspective. There was never anything that tied the two kinds of numbers together easily."

To solve these problems, MicroStrategy, a manufacturer of DSS development software, and Mervyn's used DSS Agent, a development application manufactured and sold by MicroStrategy, to develop The Decision Maker's Workbench (DMW). This DSS application allows for trend, performance, and inventory stock analyses. Analysts can see, by ad zone, how product sales peak and valley over seasons, or how they vary from region to region. This helps them decide when and where to peak or deplete inventory. Through its use of symmetric multiprocessing hardware and parallel query processing technology, DMW reduced the time required to perform this task from an hour to less than a minute, helping Mervyn's realize its strategic aim of securing a competitive advantage through timely decision making.

Sue Little comments, "DMW let us look at different types of merchandise together, on-line, at the atomic level, in either dollars or units. We're finally comparing apples with apples, and we're now spending only 10 percent of our time gathering data and 90 percent acting upon it, rather than the other way around."

The DMW application incorporates features such as data surfing, drill down, intelligent agents, and alerts. Mervyn's application includes maps that display geography-based exception reporting and executive views that summarize business trends and exceptions in a newspaper-like interface. Decision Maker's Workbench includes forecasting capabilities, enabling end users to develop "what-if" scenarios by performing ad hoc analyses on query results.

The study of decision support systems (DSSs, for short) is not about computers. Although they play an integral role in the DSS world, computers are just one part of the picture. The study of DSSs is really about people—about how people think and make decisions, as well as how they act on and react to those decisions. The DSS field is one of the few information systems (IS) fields that can lay claim to having both identifiable roots and a clear focus. Decision support systems are designed, built, and used to assist in the activity that they are named for: supporting the decision-making process. Mind you, they are not intended to make the decisions themselves, although we will see examples of DSSs that do almost exactly that. The real purpose of a DSS is to provide support to the decision maker during the process of making a decision. Therefore, when you study DSSs, you study people, decisions, and how those decisions are made.

1-1 DSS DEFINED

Common Characteristics

This section offers a definition of *decision support system,* but first we need to look at some characteristics common to most, if not all, DSS applications. Table 1-1 contains a list of those attributes.

As you can see, the typical DSS serves many functions; thus, arriving at a simple but comprehensive definition of a DSS is more difficult than it may first appear. In fact, there are probably as many definitions as there are books about the subject. The good news, however, is that the various definitions address some common themes, and a focus on those themes should yield a good working definition of the concept.

Table 1-1 Common DSS Characteristics

- Employed in semistructured or unstructured decision contexts
- Intended to support decision makers rather than replace them
- Supports all phases of the decision-making process
- Focuses on the effectiveness of the decision-making process rather than its efficiency
- Is under control of the DSS user
- Uses underlying data and models
- Facilitates learning on the part of the decision maker
- Is interactive and user-friendly
- Is generally developed using an evolutionary, iterative process
- Provides support for all levels of management from top executives to line managers
- Can provide support for multiple independent or interdependent decisions
- Provides support for individual, group-, and team-based decision-making contexts

The first of those themes is the dimension of *problem structuredness*. This dimension focuses on the degree to which a decision or decision-making situation displays certain structural characteristics. A traditional view of this dimension sees the decision situation to be *highly structured* when the objectives of the decision are easily determined without conflict, alternative courses of action are few or clearly defined, and the effects of the decision are certain. Conversely, a *highly unstructured* decision is one where the objectives of the situation are often conflicting, the alternatives available to the decision maker are difficult to isolate, and the effect of a particular course of action or selection of an alternative carries with it a high degree of uncertainty. The role of the DSS in this is to provide support to the decision maker on the "structurable" portions of the decision, thus freeing the decision maker to focus his or her cognitive resources on the truly unstructured portions of the problem—those portions that, given the limits of technology to execute the complex problem-solving strategies contained in human memory, are better left for resolution by the human decision makers(s). The decision processes employed in addressing the unstructured portions of a decision situation can be thought of as the human processes we do not yet understand well enough to effectively simulate via automation. More on that later.

A second theme found in most definitions of a DSS is that of decision outcome. The information-rich environment of today's organization is where the DSS is commonly found and where it performs much of its work. Because a key element of a technology that is intended to *support* the process associated with making a decision is the decision itself, we will spend a great deal of our time considering just exactly what decisions are and why we need technology to support us in making them. The *effectiveness* of a given decision, or degree to which the decision succeeds in reaching its objectives, is an essential element in the decision-making process. Therefore, our definition of a DSS must take into account the role the system plays in supporting the realization of decision objectives.

A third theme present in definitions of a DSS is that of *managerial control*. The ultimate responsibility, and accountability, for the outcomes associated with decisions lies with the manager. When you stop to think about it, the *decision* can be argued to be the most powerful tool in a manager's arsenal of weapons. The decision is the vehicle by which all of the organization's resources are deployed or structured at any given moment. It is the primary mechanism used by management to reach the organization's strategic objectives and to fuel its successes in its chosen field of endeavor. Whether the decision is thought of as a *choice,* a *course of action,* or a *strategy,* it manifests itself as an activity that culminates in the selection of, and commitment to, one of multiple alternatives. The control of this final selection must reside with the decision maker(s). To that end, the DSS must provide support to the selection process but, ultimately, must be positioned to allow the final selection to be made by those managers directly responsible and accountable for the outcomes.

Given these three common themes, a formal definition of a DSS can be advanced that will serve as a foundation upon which a more detailed understanding of the construction, application, and use of DSSs can be built. A *decision support system* is a system under the control of one or more decision makers that assists in the activity of decision making by providing an organized set of tools intended to impart structure to portions of the decision-making situation and to improve the ultimate effectiveness of the decision outcome.

What It Can and Cannot Do

The DSS is clearly a powerful tool and is rapidly becoming an integral component of managerial work. The speed with which today's information becomes yesterday's news is increasing at a staggering rate. Tomorrow's manager will confront an ever-narrowing window of opportunity within which effective decisions will need to be made. Deadlines will be measured in days, hours, and minutes rather than in quarters, months, and years. The leveraging of technology intended to allow for tomorrow's manager to be effective in such a high-speed environment is what decision support is all about. To meet the demands of managerial work a DSS must be able to provide the decision maker with certain key elements vital to his or her success. The benefits to be derived from using a DSS are not realizable in all decision situations or by all decision makers. Such realization depends on the degree of fit between the decision maker, the context of the decision, and the DSS itself. Assuming the fit is there, however, we can, in general, expect several potential benefits from using a DSS. In addition, we must acknowledge and understand the limitations of using a DSS. Table 1-2 contains a list of such potential benefits and limitations.

As you can see, the DSS is expected to serve the decision maker by extending his or her capacity to process the mountain of information encountered during the course

---

Table 1-2 Benefits and Limitations of DSS Use

Benefits
- Extend the decision maker's ability to process information and knowledge
- Extend the decision maker's ability to tackle large-scale, time-consuming, complex problems
- Shorten the time associated with making a decision
- Improve the reliability of a decision process or outcome
- Encourage exploration and discovery on the part of the decision maker
- Reveal new approaches to thinking about a problem space or decision context
- Generate new evidence in support of a decision or confirmation of existing assumptions
- Create a strategic or competitive advantage over competing organizations

Limitations
- DSSs cannot yet be designed to contain distinctly human decision-making talents such as creativity, imaginativeness, or intuition
- The power of a DSS is limited by the computer system upon which it is running, its design, and the knowledge it possesses at the time of its use
- Language and command interfaces are not yet sophisticated enough to allow for natural language processing of user directives and inquiries
- DSSs are normally designed to be narrow in scope of application, thus inhibiting their generalizability to multiple decision-making contexts

---

of making a decision. Further, many components of a decision situation, although structured, are nonetheless highly complex and time-consuming. The DSS can solve those portions of the problem, saving the decision maker cognitive resources and, more important, large blocks of precious time. Because of this, using a DSS can be expected to decrease the overall time associated with reaching a complex, unstructured decision.

Additional benefits can be found in the areas of innovation and creativity. Simply using the DSS can provide the decision maker with avenues to explore that might otherwise go unnoticed or be deemed too complex and difficult to pursue. The tools within the DSS can stimulate the problem solver to reach innovative insights regarding solutions and their associated outcomes. In addition, the output of the DSS may often justify the position of the decision maker(s)—thus facilitating consensus among a large group of potentially affected stakeholders. Finally, given the shrinking window of opportunity associated with the pace of business, the DSS may provide the competitive advantage to advance the organization past its competitors or to at least allow it to stay abreast of the marketplace. To achieve some or all of these potential benefits, however, the manager must understand not only the appropriate application of a particular decision support tool but also its limits.

No matter how well a DSS is designed, its value is constrained by certain limitations. To begin with, the DSS, like any other computer-based system, contains only the "knowledge" it has been given by its designers and possesses only the "skills" associated with its tool set. Although we will explore the concept of a DSS that can "think" in chapter 8, and of one that can "learn" in chapter 10, the DSS is nonetheless limited by its design and its designers.

Other drawbacks of the DSS include limits on its ability to perform reasoning processes that require distinctly human characteristics such as creativity, intuition, or imagination. Such cognitive activities still belong to the domain of human experience and do not lend themselves well to automation or machine simulation. Further, the DSS must be designed to communicate its information to its user in a manner that is readily understood and useful within the context of the decision situation. Although humans can adapt their methods of communication readily to the needs or constraints of a given situation, computer systems such as DSSs cannot. As such, the methods by which we communicate with a DSS and those by which it responds may serve as limitations to effective use. We will explore these issues of interface and interaction in chapter 13.

Finally, and maybe most important, is the understanding that a "universal DSS" does not exist and probably never will. A typical DSS is designed to be useful within a relatively narrow scope of problem-solving scenarios. Thus, to effectively solve a complex problem or reach a decision of significant magnitude may require the use of several DSSs. In that case the decision maker is faced with the task of coordinating multiple systems that may require output from one as input to another. The integration of multiple DSSs therefore becomes, in and of itself, a decision of some complexity and uncertainty.

In summary, decision support systems can make the decision process more effective and bring it within the capabilities of the human decision maker. They cannot, however, overcome or prevent the actions of a poor decision maker. The user ultimately controls the process and must, therefore, possess an understanding of when to use a DSS, what DSS(s) to use, and, most important, to what degree to depend on the output and information obtained from such use. The manager must see the DSS as a valuable tool in the decision process rather than as a mechanism that itself makes the decision.

1-2 HISTORY OF DECISION SUPPORT SYSTEMS

The Evolution of the DSS

The roots of the DSS grew from the efforts of managers to apply quantitative models to the daily problems and decisions they faced in an organizational environment. The concept was born in the early 1970s and is generally attributed to two articles written during that time. The first, written by J. D. Little (1970), was entitled "Models and Managers: The Concept of a Decision Calculus." Little observed that the biggest problem with management science models was that managers rarely used them. He described the concept of a decision calculus as a "model-based set of procedures for processing data and judgments to assist a manager in his decision making," (p. B470). Little suggested that for such a system to succeed it must be simple, robust, easy to control, complete on issues of importance, adaptive to the needs of its user, and easy to communicate with.

The second article, "A Framework for Management Information Systems," was written by Gorry and Scott Morton (1989), and it is here that the term *decision support system* was coined. Gorry and Scott Morton developed a two-dimensional framework for the provision of computer support to managerial activities (see table 1-3). Each of these dimensions is assumed to be continuous rather than composed of discrete components. The vertical dimension is a classification of decision structure as originally proposed by Simon (1960). Simon suggested that decisions be categorized according to the degree to which they are *programmed* (repetitive, routine, and com-

Table 1-3 Gorry and Scott Morton Framework for Decision Support

Type of Decision	Management Activity			Support Needed
	Operational Control	*Management Control*	*Strategic Planning*	
Structured	Inventory control	Load balancing for production lines	Physical plant location	MIS, quantitative models
Semistructured	Securities trading	Establishing marketing budgets for new products	Analysis of acquisition of capital assets	DSS
Unstructured	Determining the cover photo for a monthly magazine	Hiring of new managerial personnel	Determination of research and development projects	Human reasoning and intuition

monplace) or *nonprogrammed* (novel, unique, and consequential). The horizontal dimension of the framework represents the levels of managerial activity proposed by Anthony (1965). Here, it is conceived that all activities of managers can be categorized into three unique classes: (1) *strategic planning,* where decisions related to the objectives of the organization are made, (2) *management control,* where decisions related to the effective and efficient procurement and deployment of the organization's assets are made, and (3) *operational control,* where decisions relating to the day-to-day tasks and activities of the organization are made. By combining the approaches of Simon and Anthony, the framework serves as a guide for the allocation of IS resources where the greatest payoff, or return on investment, may be found. From this framework, the concept of the decision support system was born.

The evolution of the DSS from its conception in the 1970s to the present day has seen numerous extensions of the original notion. The modern day study of DSSs must include a focus on conventional model-based systems, knowledge-based systems, artificial intelligence, expert systems, executive information systems, group support systems, data visualization systems, and organizational decision support systems. Each of these areas will be explored in depth in later chapters.

A Brief Glimpse of the Future

If the number and types of DSSs and associated applications are any indication, then the DSS may very well be the most successful of all computer-based information systems. Today's organizations are rapidly realizing the need for embracing information technology as an integral tool in their store of strategic weapons. Tomorrow's organization will employ computer-based IS in virtually every aspect of its operation—from the development and marketing of its product or service to the coordination of its employees, processes, and activities worldwide. The role of the DSS in tomorrow's organization cannot be overstated. Managers will rely on the availability of more powerful and useful DSS applications in the conduct of their daily activities. The DSS of the twenty-first century will serve as the primary vehicle for keeping up with the seemingly exponential growth in the size, complexity, and speed with which business will be conducted. In chapters 15 and 16, we will explore the various applications and uses for DSS technologies in the global marketplace of tomorrow.

1-3 INGREDIENTS OF A DSS

Basic DSS Components

It should be clear to you by now that a DSS is not a simple system with common, identifiable characteristics and a singular or common purpose. As we have seen, simply defining a DSS requires consideration of a number of factors including its intended purpose, the context within which it will be used, and the outcome objectives of its use. Describing or classifying a DSS in terms of its components poses an equally challenging task. Once again, before we can construct a generalized component structure for a DSS we need to look at the various methods of classifying DSSs by their component parts.

An early classification by Alter (1980) divided the DSS components into seven categories depending upon the degree of direct influence each component part could have on the decision at hand. Figure 1-1 shows the classification scheme proposed by Alter along with a mapping of the various components to common problem-solving and decision-making tasks. Originally, Alter's classification assumed that each category could be thought of as a separate and distinct system rather than as a functional component within a larger system. As shown in figure 1-1, however, we can see that the seven separate components can be logically grouped into a simpler classification scheme of either model-oriented or data-oriented systems. We will soon see that this simple dichotomy is in harmony with more modern classification methods for DSSs.

Another approach to isolating and defining individual components of a DSS focuses on the nature of the language provided by the DSS to manipulate data and/or models and the degree to which the language used is *procedural* or *nonprocedural*.

The concept of *language procedurality* is relatively simple and is unique to the design and application of DSSs. Basically, the user of a DSS should be able to specify the information he or she wants from that DSS, as well as whether that information exists in a database, must be derived or computed by one or more models contained within the DSS, or must be computed by a model that is constructed by the DSS from other models stored specifically for that purpose. Languages that are highly procedural require the user to be very specific with regard to how the data are to be obtained, from where they are to be obtained, and exactly how a particular model or set of models is to process that data. Nonprocedural languages simply require the user to specify the information that is needed and the DSS takes care of the rest. Somewhere between these two extremes we find a degree of procedurality that affords users a means of providing parameters to prespecified data retrieval operations or a predetermined set of models. As you can see, the degree of procedurality of the language system allows for a wide variety of configurations and designs.

Building upon the two classification methods discussed, the components of a DSS can generally be classified into five distinct parts:

1. The data management system
2. The model management system

FIGURE 1-1 Alter's Classification of DSS Components

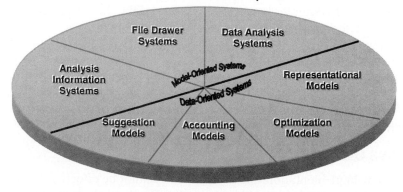

3. The knowledge engine

4. The user interface

5. The user(s)

The Data Management System

The *data management* component of a DSS is where the various activities associated with retrieval, storage, and organization of the relevant data for the particular decision context are managed. Additionally, the data management system provides for the various security functions, data integrity procedures, and general data administration duties associated with using the DSS. These tasks are carried out within the data management component by several subsystems. Among these subsystems are the *database(s), database management system, data repository,* and *data query facility.* Each of these elements is discussed in greater detail in section 1-4.

The Model Management System

Similar to the role of the data management system, the *model management* component performs the retrieval, storage, and organizational activities associated with the various quantitative models that provide the analytical capabilities for the DSS. Within this component are the *model base, model base management system, model repository, model execution processor,* and *model synthesis processor.* A detailed review and comparison of this component to the data management system is performed in section 1-4.

The Knowledge Engine

The *knowledge engine* is where activities related to problem recognition and generation of interim or final solutions, as well as other functions related to the management of the problem-solving process, are performed. The knowledge engine is the "brains" of the outfit. The data and the models come together here to provide the user with a useful application that supports the decision context at hand. We will look at the knowledge engine in greater detail in section 1-5.

The User Interface

As in any other computer-based information system, the design and implementation of the *user interface* is a key element in DSS functionality. The data, model, and processing components of the DSS must be easily accessed and manipulated if the DSS is to provide the necessary support to the decision context without getting in the way of the task at hand. Furthermore, the ease with which the user can communicate with the DSS, whether it be for the specification of parameters or the early investigation of the problem space, is tantamount to the successful use of a DSS. These responsibilities, among many others, fall to the user interface and will be discussed in section 1-6.

The DSS User

The design, implementation, and use of a DSS cannot be effective without considering the role of the *user.* Issues related to user skill set, motivations, knowledge domain, patterns of use, and role(s) within the organization are considered essential elements in the successful application of a DSS to a decision context. Remember, one of the essential characteristics of a DSS is its being under the *control of the user*. Without considering the user as a part of the system, we are left with a set of computer-based systems that, by themselves, provide no useful function at all. We look at the user more closely in section 1-7 and again in chapter 2.

1-4 DATA AND MODEL MANAGEMENT

The Database

More organizations each day are realizing the importance of data as a corporate asset that must be managed. Because of this, the processes by which data are collected, stored, and disseminated have undergone vast improvements in recent years. This increased focus on the value of data to the organization is particularly relevant to the study of decision support systems because the quality and structure of the *DSS database* component largely determine the success of the modern DSS.

A *database* is an integrated collection of data, organized and stored in a manner that facilitates its easy retrieval. The structure of a database should correspond to the needs of the organization and should allow for access by multiple users and, when appropriate, for use by more than one application. The concept of a database organizes data into a logical hierarchy based on the degree of aggregation or granularity of that data. This hierarchy consists of four elements:

1. Database
2. Files
3. Records
4. Data elements

Figure 1-2 shows how the various elements of the hierarchy are logically integrated in a typical database.

Just as the database is a collection of integrated data organized into files, the *file* serves as a collection of data organized into *records* that all relate to a particular information focus. For example, a particular data file may contain information regarding sales transactions during a specific period, say for an organization's last fiscal year. Or a similar data file may contain historical sales volume information for an entire industry over the last five years. Regardless of the nature of the data, it must all be related to a common subject and must be organized so that various useful aggregations of the data within that file can be created and compared.

Although data within files are organized into a common structure, the sources of the data contained within the files may be quite diverse. The files may include data generated from internal transactions, external sources, and individual users of the DSS.

Internal data normally come from an organization's transaction processing systems in the course of conducting the daily affairs of the organization. Payroll and salary data, sales transactions, production level and throughput, as well as other transactions generated by the various business units of the organization, are all examples of internal data sources that may appropriately contribute one or more files to a typical

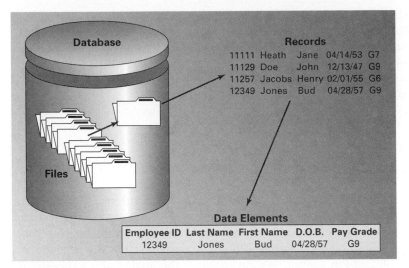

FIGURE 1-2 Hierarchy of Data

DSS database. Transaction-level data are a major source of information regarding the operations of an organization or business unit. Depending on the problem context in which the DSS is operating, this data may be all that is necessary for the DSS to provide the necessary level of decision support. Oftentimes, however, an internal data source is only one contributor of information to the DSS database.

External data sources are as broad as the imagination allows. They may include targeted collections of data for a particular industry, market research data, employment information for a particular geographic region, rate schedules or cost tables for particular products or product classes, geopolitical economic or census data, or a historical list of all court cases within a particular legal jurisdiction, such as the Supreme Court. The list is literally endless. It is a safe bet that if a source of data generation exists, then a database containing that data also exists. The good news for DSS designers and users is that most of the imaginable external data can be gotten with relative ease and at little or no cost. The bad news is that there is so much of it, and with more being made available each day, just figuring out where to look can be a monumental task. Fortunately, however, developments such as the Internet and World Wide Web have made access to external data much easier than in the past. In addition, data delivery services such as Mead Data Central's LEXIS-NEXIS, Dow Jones News Retrieval, CompuServe, and a myriad of others have made the downloading, integration, and analysis of external data a relatively common occurrence in the corporate DSS environment.

Regardless of the source, the data contained within the files in the DSS database are organized into homogenous structures, or subunits, called *records*. In turn, the data contained within each record are organized into a series of *data elements,* or *fields.* The data element is the smallest unit of decomposition within the logical hierarchy and cannot normally be broken down further. Each record is constructed so that it contains a set of data elements related to a *specific instance* of the type of information contained within the file. An example of this might begin with a file containing data about the sales of various items in an organization's product line. Information such as product code, product name, date and time of sale, quantity or amount of sale, location of sale, and other specific pieces of data concerning the transaction may be organized and stored within a data record. Once these records are stored, they can be retrieved individually based on a unique piece of data, such as invoice number, or they can be retrieved as a unique subset, such as all records containing a particular product code. More important, they can be combined with other sources of organized data within the DSS database to allow for extensive analysis of relationships that might otherwise go unnoticed by the DSS user. This ability to combine data records from multiple sources gives the DSS a powerful, and virtually infinite, repository of data from which the user can draw during the decision-making process.

One additional source of data that may be contained within the typical DSS database is referred to as *individual-level* or *private data.* Each instance of use of a DSS generates data about the decisions made, the questions asked, and the various combinations of data constructed for that particular problem context. In addition, individual *heuristics,* or rules of thumb, used by various DSS users may also be stored in the DSS database. These individual-level data elements and records often serve to create a unique personality for the DSS, thus tailoring the system to the needs of a specific user or group of users within its defined problem context. Information such as an individual's personal assessment of specific data or past situations, a heuristic stating that "during December sales of Product A can be expected to be 37 percent of the sales of Product B," or simply a library of past queries or data source integrations may all be stored as individual-level data in the DSS database.

The Database Management System

The multitude of data that can be organized into files and databases must be managed, and this important role falls to the *database management system (DBMS).* The DBMS has two main responsibilities:

1. The coordination of all tasks related to storing and accessing information in the database and disseminating information to the community of DSS users

2. The maintenance of logical independence between the data contained in the DSS database and the DSS application

Modern DBMSs possess a wide variety of capabilities and are generally managed by a skilled *database administrator* assigned specifically to that task. Commercial DBMS packages from Sybase, Oracle, IBM, and others provide powerful foundational applications from which the DSS database can be managed. Recent DBMS developments include the facilitation of the process of integrating a large number of unrelated, or disparate, data sources into a single, accessible database known as a *data warehouse.* Data warehouses provide large amounts of data to the DSS in a form and manner that is more conducive to DSS use. They will be discussed in greater detail in chapters 11 and 12.

The first responsibility of the DBMS—the coordination of tasks related to the storage, access, and dissemination of database information—involves several activities and functions. These include updating (in the form of adds, deletes, edits, or changes) data records and elements as transactions occur, facilitating the integration of data from various sources, and retrieving data from the database for queries or report generation. In addition, the DBMS performs many administrative functions related to DSS operation such as data security (control of unauthorized access, database error recovery, data integrity, and concurrency issues), the creation of personal or temporary databases for individual user experimentation and analysis, and the tracking of DSS usage and data acquisition, among others. Many of these activities are performed in the background and are intended to be invisible to the DSS user. Nonetheless, they are essential to the successful use of a DSS in a problem-solving context.

The second main responsibility of the DBMS, that of maintaining logical independence between the data and the DSS application, is also of extreme importance to the success of a DSS. The typical DSS scenario involves one or more users making decisions that are largely based upon information taken from a large pool of constantly evolving data. The DBMS must manage the *physical* organization and structuring of this data within the database and its associated files without constraining the *logical,* or apparent, arrangement of the data to either the DSS application or the DSS user(s). The same data may need to be presented in one form, such as a graph or table, under one set of circumstances and in a completely different manner, say as input to an analytical model, in another situation. In addition, as new sources of data are made available to the DSS, the DBMS must manage the integration of these disparate sources so that they appear to be all neatly organized in a common structure and location even when they are not. By maintaining independence between physical data structure and DSS applications, the DBMS allows for a much broader use of a single database, either by multiple DSS applications, multiple user groups, multiple problem contexts, or any combination thereof. Table 1-4 describes the various functions of a typical DBMS.

The Model Base

A *model* is a simplification of some event or process constructed for the purpose of studying that event and thus developing a better understanding of it. The important characteristic of a model is that it is a simplified form of reality. It is intended to resemble the actual process or event as closely as possible but normally does not contain the same level or kind of detail as the phenomenon itself. In many cases, we can ascertain many characteristics of a process or event. Moreover, we can often predict the nature or outcome of that event under certain conditions without having to actually experience or recreate the event under study. The value of this capability can be found in the reduced cost, effort, and time derived from studying a model rather than the event itself. Imagine the effort (and risk) necessary to remain inside a hurricane for its duration to predict its path or its strengthening. Imagine the costs associated with having to build an airplane to see how fast it will fly, or if it will fly at all. Imagine the time it would take to determine how popular a new product or service is going to be if you had to ask everybody's opinion about it before you began selling it. In each of these cases, modeling can be an effective source of information for the decision process. Although the underlying models contained within a DSS are the essence of

Table 1-4 General Functions of the DBMS

Data Definition
- Provides a data definition language (DDL) that allows users to describe the data entities and their associated attributes and relationships
- Allows for the interrelation of data from multiple sources

Data Manipulation
- Provides the user with a query language to interact with the database
- Allows for capture and extraction of data
- Provides rapid retrieval of data for ad hoc queries and reports
- Allows for the construction of complex queries for retrieval and data manipulation

Data Integrity
- Allows the user to describe rules (integrity constraints) to maintain the integrity of the database
- Assists in the control of erroneous data entry based on the defined integrity constraints

Access Control
- Allows identification of authorized users
- Controls access to various data elements and data manipulation activities within the database
- Tracks usage and access to data by authorized users

Concurrency Control
- Provides procedures for controlling simultaneous access to the same data by more than one user

Transaction Recovery
- Provides a mechanism for restart and reconciliation of the database in the event of hardware failure
- Records information on all transactions at certain points to enable satisfactory database restart

the concept of decision support, the degree to which these models are designed and constructed to resemble the real thing is normally dependent upon the needs of the decision maker using them. Nonetheless, without the presence of one or more models associated with the problem context under investigation, a DSS becomes limited in its contribution. We will focus on the various types of models and their construction in detail in chapter 5.

The *model base* in a DSS is the modeling counterpart to the database. Just as the DSS database stores the data used by the DSS, the model base contains the various statistical, financial, mathematical, and other quantitative models the DSS uses to perform a variety of analyses. The model base is what differentiates a DSS from other computer-based information systems. The ability to run individual or combined models or to construct new models makes the DSS a powerful support tool in the problem-solving environment.

Managing the Models

The underlying models in a typical DSS can range in number, size, and complexity much like the data stored in a DSS database. To manage this contingent of analytical tools the DSS uses a *model base management system (MBMS)*. Table 1-5 contains a list of the basic functions of the MBMS.

Two very important responsibilities of the MBMS are the *execution and integration* of the models available to the DSS and the *modeling of user preferences*. The user is normally required to provide data as input to a model or to provide certain parameters that may affect the model's execution. The MBMS takes care of this process by providing the user with easy access to the various models as well as facilitating entry of important parameters and data to the models.

Often the execution of one or more models requires the user to provide specialized syntax or commands to initiate the process. The MBMS generates the necessary command structure and locates the models for the DSS. The specific formatting requirements for data or parameter entry are also handled by the MBMS subsystem. Finally, the need to combine or integrate several individual models into a more complex one occurs regularly in DSS use. The MBMS facilitates this process of integration by providing the necessary links between the models as well as controlling the order of model sequencing and execution.

The *modeling of user preferences* is the process of collecting, organizing, and integrating the preferences, judgments, and intuitions of the individual DSS user into the modeling operation. Decision makers and decision contexts both have constantly changing and conflicting preferences. The MBMS, where appropriate, must provide a mechanism to incorporate the individual user or problem context preferences into the analytical process so that the outcomes represent not only the quantitative, or stochastic, results but also the more qualitative, or context-specific, conditions and constraints. In short, the MBMS plays an important role in facilitating the decision support process through a DSS application. We explore this issue of user characteristics and preferences in chapters 2 and 3.

Table 1-5 General Functions of the MBMS

Modeling Language
- Allows for the creation of decision models from scratch or from existing modules
- Provides a mechanism for the linking or chaining of multiple models to allow for sequential processing and data exchange
- Allows the user to modify models to reflect specific preferences

Model Library
- Stores and manages all models and solver algorithms for easy access and manipulation
- Provides a catalog and organizational schema of stored models along with brief descriptions of their individual functions or applications

Model Manipulation
- Allows for management and maintenance of the model base with functions similar to those found in a DBMS (i.e., run, store, query, delete, link, etc.)

1-5 DSS KNOWLEDGE BASE

No decision or problem-solving context is devoid of the need for reasoning. A decision that can be made without reasoning is really not a decision at all. Admittedly, the more structured a decision context is, the less reasoning necessary for a successful outcome. It follows that we can envision a point where the reduction in required reasoning converges with the increase in problem structure. At this intersection we find those decisions that are so structured that no reasoning is required to make them. By default this must be the point where no decisions exist.

It is important at this stage that we are clear as to what exactly reasoning is. *Reasoning* is the process by which new information is derived from a combination or combinations of existing, or previously derived, information. In its simplest form, reasoning allows us to rely on information as facts, even though we haven't specifically verified that information personally. For example, if we know for a fact that a particular company has a current ratio (current assets to current liabilities) of 2.6 and a quick ratio (liquid assets to current liabilities) of 1.7, we know two isolated facts about this company. Through the process of reasoning, however, we also can "know" that the liquidity of the company is generally sound. No one told us this, nor did we personally verify it, but we know it nonetheless. There are many forms of reasoning used in problem solving and decision making, and we will explore them in greater detail in chapters 8, 9, and 10. At this point, however, our definition is sufficient to aid in our understanding of yet another component of a DSS: the *knowledge base.*

The *knowledge base* is where the "knowledge" of the DSS is stored. By knowledge, we mean the rules, heuristics, boundaries, constraints, previous outcomes, and any other "knowledge" that may have been programmed into the DSS by its designers or acquired by the DSS through repeated use.

The information contained within the knowledge base component of a DSS bears unique characteristics that differentiate it from information contained in either the database or the model base components. First, the knowledge base contains information that is generally *problem domain–specific;* that is to say, it is knowledge that is applicable or relevant within only a narrow problem-solving context. Conversely, the database and model base components store a wide range of domain-related elements. The database or databases associated with a DSS are not limited to a particular problem-solving domain. The models contained within the model base are likewise not constrained by the defined problem-solving context within which the DSS resides. The knowledge base, however, generally does not contain anything that is not directly relevant, or directly derived from, the problem-solving context. Think of it this way: Knowledge is a domain-specific construct whereas data and models are useful across several domains or tasks.

So what exactly is contained in the DSS knowledge base? All kinds of knowledge that might be used by a domain expert: descriptions of various objects or entities and their relationships, descriptions of various problem-solving strategies or behaviors, domain-related constraints, uncertainties, probabilities, and so on. The knowledge contained in the knowledge base can be categorized into two simple groups: facts and hypotheses. The *facts* represent what we know to be true at a given time. The *hypotheses* represent the rules or relationships that we believe exist between the facts.

Let's assume that we have a simple knowledge base that contains a select number of variables that are deemed by experts to be most important in evaluating a potential borrower's creditworthiness:

1. Number of years of credit history (a numerical fact)
2. Quality of the credit history (a ranking fact, *perfect, almost perfect, very good, good, not good, awful*)
3. Job description of the borrower (a category fact, *doctor, lawyer, computer operator, college professor*)
4. Number of years of employment in this job area (a numerical fact)
5. Total income of the borrower (a numerical fact)
6. Total debt obligations of the borrower (a numerical fact)
7. Amount of money the borrower wants to borrow (a numerical fact)

Now, in addition to these facts, our knowledge base also contains the relationships among them. In other words, we have also stored the manner in which one or more facts are related to each other. Figure 1-3 graphically illustrates the relationships between the facts contained within our knowledge base.

In this case, our objective is to make a decision regarding whether we should lend money to a *specific* person. Notice, however, that the relationships between the

FIGURE 1-3 Examples of Credit Rule Combinations

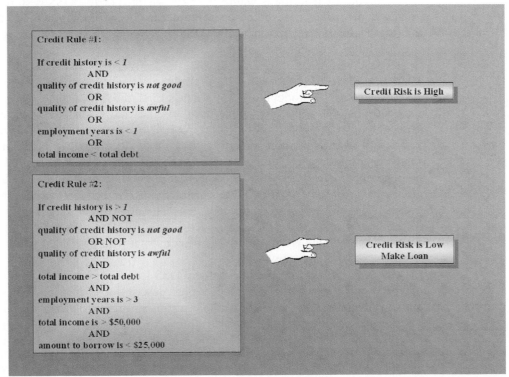

facts are not focused on any particular person but rather are simply stated in the form of rules. One rule may state the relationship between fact 1 and fact 2, another rule may state the relationship between fact 5 and fact 6, and so on. Although these rules can be thought of as a series of models, they are unique in that they can be combined in any manner and in any order to produce a decision outcome. Figure 1-3 shows two such combinations. For example, let's say the borrower has a short credit history (high risk), but the history that exists is perfect (extremely low risk). She has a good job and has been employed in this job area for a long time (both low risk). However, her debt is extremely high compared to her income (high risk) and the amount of money she wants to borrow is also extremely large (high risk). In this case, the knowledge base combines the facts we have presented with the relationships among those facts (relationships, by the way, that we programmed into the DSS) and might "conclude" that we should decide against making the loan to the borrower. Bear in mind that this example is a simple one and, when compared to the types and sizes of typical knowledge bases, a somewhat trivial one as well. It demonstrates, nonetheless, just how the knowledge base of a DSS fits into the whole scheme.

Knowledge Acquisition

By now, you should be wondering where all this knowledge and all these rules come from. If the user of the DSS already knows this stuff then why do we need a DSS? Well, that's the point! The typical user of a DSS does *not* know this stuff. The DSS user relies on the integrity of the data in the data base, the quality and accuracy of the models in the model base, and the merit and reliability of the facts and relationships in the knowledge base when using the DSS during a decision-making activity. So how *does* all that knowledge get into the DSS?

From experts, that's how! One or more people called *knowledge engineers* (KEs) interview the domain experts and gather the information necessary for the knowledge base. Knowledge engineers are specially trained to interact with domain experts for the purposes of acquiring all of the knowledge the expert has in a particular domain and all of the relationships among that knowledge. A variety of knowledge acquisition techniques such as interviewing, protocol analysis (thinking out loud), and modeling, among many others, are used to get the information out of the experts' minds and into the knowledge base. The process of knowledge acquisition is a daunting task, indeed. We will focus on the different techniques associated with acquiring and organizing the knowledge of experts in chapters 8 and 9.

Knowledge Retrieval

Once we have the facts and relationships collected and into the knowledge base we need a method of getting them back out in an organized and useful fashion. The *inference engine* (IE) is that part of the knowledge base component that facilitates this process. The IE is a program module that activates all the domain knowledge that has been gathered and performs *inferencing,* or basic reasoning, to work toward a solution or conclusion based upon the values for the facts given and the relationships or rules associated with them. The inference engine must be supplied with rules on how to apply the rules, with strategies for conflict resolution in the event there are two rules in opposition to each other, and in many cases, with methods of determining the probability that a conclusion derived from a set of facts and rules is reliable. We will discuss IEs in depth in chapter 8.

It should be clear that the knowledge base component of a DSS, when combined with the capabilities of modern DBMS and MBMS facilities, creates a potent tool for supporting the complex decisions made by today's and tomorrow's managers. These three components by themselves, however, can accomplish little. They need to be made accessible to the DSS user in a manner that truly supports the decision-making process and facilitates their individual and combined use with a minimum of effort. What we need is an *interface*.

1-6 USER INTERFACES

An *interface* is simply a component of a system that is specifically intended to allow the user to access the internal components of that system in a relatively easy fashion and without having to know specifically how everything is put together or how it works together. The easier it is for a user to access the system the better the interface. Also, the more common the interface, the less effort and training it takes for a user to move from one system to another. The essential concept behind programs such as Microsoft Windows and the software applications written for it is that of a *common interface*. Saving and retrieving files in one Windows program is the same basic process as in all other Windows-based applications. The concept of the common interface is not limited to computer-based systems, however. The modern automobile has achieved an almost universal set of characteristics in its interface. This is why you don't have to get a license to drive a particular car or type of car. Unless you try to drive something radically different in its interface, such as a semitrailer or school bus, you need just one license to drive. The interfaces are so similar that if you know how to drive one car, you know how to drive them all.

As you might expect, however, the world of DSSs does not yet enjoy the benefits of a universal, or common, interface. Not that it doesn't want to, mind you. It's just not so easily accomplished. Remember, DSSs are not generic applications intended to be used by a variety of users in a variety of settings. On the contrary, a DSS is a domain-specific application that is normally designed to be used by a small group. As such, the design and implementation of a common user interface is just not easily attained. There is good news, though: Because of the limited user base for a particular DSS, a common interface is not so very important. Since the system is essentially "custom designed" for the user(s), the interface is also designed for the specific user or users of the system.

Interface Components

The DSS interface is responsible for all interaction and communication with the user(s). Given this level of responsibility, the interface must not only include software components (such as menus and command languages) and hardware components (such as multiple monitoring or input facilities), but must also deal with factors relating to human interaction, accessibility, ease of use, user skill level, error capture and reporting, and issues relating to documentation, among many others. Because of this breadth and depth of responsibility, DSS experts generally regard the interface as the single most important component in the system. Without a good user interface, the power and functionality of the DSS remains forever inaccessible. Think of it this way: As far as the user is concerned, the interface and the DSS are one and the same. Poor interface equals poor system. In the past, lack of support for many DSS implementations has been linked to a poor user interface that served only to discourage use rather than facilitate it. Table 1-6 contains the basic components of a DSS interface along with many of the factors that must be considered in its design.

Throughout this book we will explore the details of interface design as it relates to a specific DSS application context such as executive information systems, expert systems, or group decision support systems. For now, you can think of the DSS interface as having two components: the communication language and the presentation language.

The Communication Language

The *communication language,* or *action language,* component deals with activities associated with the user's direct dialog with the DSS. The various modes of data entry are included in this component. Data can be entered into the DSS by conventional methods such as keyboard, mouse, trackball, or touchpad. More recently, however, the communication component has been expanded to allow for a variety of not-so-common data entry mechanisms. Virtual reality devices such as biophysical input gloves, retinal scanners, and head position monitors are becoming common input methods. In addition, DSS applications using joysticks, voice recognition, and optical scanning devices are also being developed. Essentially, anything that can serve as potential input and can be captured as input is fair game for the communication language component of the interface. Figure 1-4 contains examples of common input devices that could be used with a typical DSS.

Table 1-6 General Functions of the DSS Interface

Communication Language
- Allows for interaction with the DSS in a variety of dialog styles
- Identifies the form of input to enter requests into the DSS
- Provides support for communication among multiple DSS users
- Can be effected in a variety of formats including menu driven, question/answer, procedural command language, or natural command language
- Can capture and analyze previous dialogs so that future interactions can be improved

Presentation Language
- Provides for the presentation of data in a variety of formats
- Allows for detailed report definition and generation by the DSS user
- Allows for the creation of forms, tables, and graphics for data output
- Can provide for multiple "windows," or views, of the data to be available simultaneously,

FIGURE 1-4 Common Input Devices

Probably the most common aspect of the communication language is the *menu*. Menus provide the user with an organized and intuitive method of selecting among the many functions, alternatives, commands, or outcomes available through the DSS. Properly organized and logically designed, menus can serve as guides for the inexperienced DSS user and as efficient vehicles of navigation for the DSS expert. Poorly designed menus, however, can render an otherwise powerful DSS unusable. As stated previously, we will explore the details of good interface design throughout the course of the book.

The Presentation Language

The *presentation language* component of the DSS interface is where all the action is. This is what the user actually sees, hears, or experiences during DSS use. Output devices such as printers, plotters, display monitors, audio monitors, and voice synthesizers are all part of this component. On-screen methods such as multiple windows, graphs, tables, charts, icons, messages, and audio triggers or alerts are also part of the presentation language. Just as the communication language component serves as the basis for the user to transmit information and commands to the DSS, the presentation language component serves as the vehicle for the DSS to communicate with the user. These two components must be designed to work together in seamless harmony if the DSS is to be considered *user-friendly*.

Research has shown that the method by which information is presented to a user can have a dramatic effect on how valuable that information is perceived to be and how accurately it is interpreted. The presentation language component must be designed so that a wide variety of presentation methods can be either preselected as a preference or selected "on the fly" by the DSS user while viewing various stages of output. Various graphs, tables, charts, and combinations must be easily selectable by the user so that the output can be viewed from as many perspectives as possible. This ensures that the output is appropriate for the many different users of the DSS as well as for the range of problem contexts and decisions to be supported by the system. As with the communication language component, we will discuss issues of presentation in greater detail throughout the book within the context of specific DSS applications.

1-7 THE DSS USER

No DSS can be considered functional or complete without the user. Unlike many other computer-based information systems, in the DSS the user is as much a part of the system as is the hardware or software. The *user* is commonly defined as the person, or persons, responsible for providing a solution to the problem at hand or for making a decision within the context the DSS was designed to support. The DSS user is often the most involved person or group in the entire life cycle of the system. Users may be involved in the conception of a DSS, in its logical and physical design, in its testing and implementation, and, of course, in its use.

User Roles

The user as defined above, however, may not actually ever "use" the DSS. Alter (1980) classifies DSS users into one of five basic roles. He further classifies the various user roles into one of four basic patterns of use. Figure 1-5 shows the relationship between the defined user roles and their patterns of use.

In Alter's classification, the *user* is defined as the person who communicates directly with the DSS regardless of method or intention. The *decision maker* is the person who ultimately makes the decision based, in whole or in part, upon the output from the DSS. An *intermediary* is a particular type of user who serves as a filter or interpreter of the output from a DSS. The intermediary may work closely with the decision maker to assist in interpreting the DSS output during the various stages of the decision-making process. The *maintainer,* or *operator,* is responsible for the daily operational aspects of the DSS such as keeping the system and its data up-to-date and in operational condition. Finally, the *feeder* provides data to the DSS but might not ever directly use the DSS as a decision support tool. The role of feeder may be filled by one or several people or groups that regularly generate data relevant to the problem context the DSS was designed to support. In some cases, all the user roles may be simultaneously occupied by a single person, or, in other cases, they may be managed by several different people or groups. Alter suggests that the fewer people involved in the various user roles, the simpler the DSS becomes to implement and use. As you can see, however, the realm of the DSS has many users that may never actually "use" the system to make a decision.

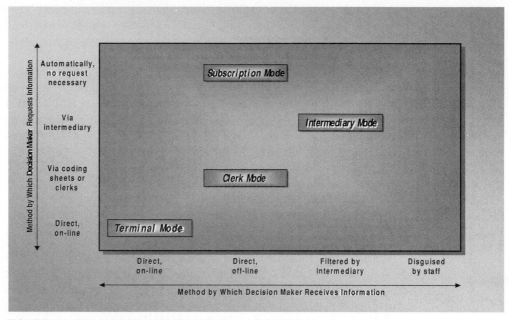

FIGURE 1-5 Alter's Decision Maker Patterns of Usage

Patterns of DSS Use

The patterns of use described by Alter are beneficial in understanding how various users may interact with the DSS. In the *subscription mode* the decision maker typically receives *scheduled reports.* Such reporting is generally preformatted and generated on a regularly scheduled basis. The reports are often generated automatically by the DSS and require no inquiry (other than the original one) on the part of the user. Moreover, these reports are usually generated through consolidation of existing information submitted from several sources throughout the organization and are received either through off-line methods such as hard copy or, increasingly, through asynchronous electronic methods such as e-mail or file transfer. An example of subscription mode usage would be the periodic receipt of a budget variance report.

In the *terminal mode,* the decision maker interacts directly with the DSS in an on-line manner. In this mode, the user determines and provides the input, directly manipulates the models in the model base, and directly receives and interprets the output. The terminal mode user may use the received output to either make the final decision or determine the need for additional or more refined interaction with the DSS. An example of a typical terminal mode access would be the use of a DSS in analyzing or determining optimum stock portfolio combinations for a particular brokerage client.

A DSS can also be used in a *clerk mode.* Here, the decision maker is using the system directly but is not interacting with the DSS in an on-line, real-time manner. Instead, the inputs, parameters, and requests are formed off-line and submitted via input coding forms or other electronic batch submission processes. While the decision maker awaits a response from the system, he or she can work on other activities of a more timely nature. Situations where a large number of users need access to a DSS but do not need on-line interactions are most compatible with clerk mode usage. Such systems can handle a large number of requests efficiently and can perform many complex analyses before returning the answers to the various clerk mode users. A common example of this type of system usage would be a DSS that is used to determine renewal rates for insurance customers or custom quotations for highly specialized service industries.

The fourth DSS usage category is the *intermediary mode.* Here the decision maker interacts with the DSS through one or more intermediary users. In this mode, the intermediaries are necessary due to the complex nature of either the analysis or parameter input process. In an extreme case, the DSS is positioned as a tool to be used by the intermediary in the preparation of his or her final report to a decision maker. This mode of usage frees the decision maker from having either to interact with the "automated beast" or even know how the system works. A common example of this mode of use might be an organizational pricing structure that is predicated on multiple analyses by several divisions but ultimately must be consolidated by a human decision maker. The days of the intermediary usage mode are numbered, however. The windows of opportunity normally associated with typical managerial decisions are becoming ever smaller and more temporally demanding. Because of this, the time spent "interacting" with the technology through intermediaries may be prohibitive for most narrow windows of opportunity. Tomorrow's decision maker must have direct access to the support technology and must be skilled in its deployment and use. Furthermore, the designers of tomorrow's decision support technologies must be ever mindful of the speed with which these technologies must be employed and with which the answers must be obtained. For now, however, suffice it to say that each of the four patterns of use has its place and when properly applied provides the necessary utility for the particular problem-solving context at hand.

1-8 CATEGORIES AND CLASSES OF DSSs

There exist a variety of proposed methods for classifying and categorizing decision support systems. Methods based on the type of support offered by the DSS; decision situation; degree of user guidance or procedurality; orientation toward data, text, rules, or models; and focus on individual versus multiple decision makers are all used in classifying the myriad of DSSs in existence or under development. For the moment, however, it is enough to understand that the unique characteristics of a particular DSS that serve to classify it may be important in determining the best approach to the design or implementation of a new system. We will explore these issues in greater depth in chapters 13 and 14.

Data-Centric and Model-Centric DSSs

Building upon Figure 1-1 (page 9), figure 1-6 contains a classification scheme for DSSs suggested by Alter. In this method, two primary support orientations for a DSS are used. The *data-centric* orientation is focused primarily on data retrieval and analysis

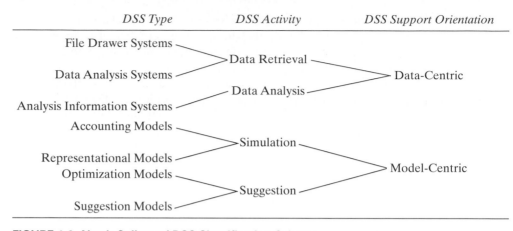

FIGURE 1-6 Alter's Collapsed DSS Classification Scheme

support activities. The *model-centric* orientation includes activities such as simulation, maximizing or optimizing scenarios, and those DSS outputs that generate suggested actions based upon embedded rules or models. Within these two basic categories, a broad spectrum of DSS types can be positioned.

Formal and Ad Hoc Systems

Donovan and Madnick (1977) proposed a method of DSS classification based upon the attributes of the problem-solving context. The *formal,* or *institutional,* DSS is designed to focus on decisions that are periodic, or recurring, within an organization. Such decision contexts require regular interaction with a DSS to ensure consistent and effective decision outcomes. Examples of this kind of system are found in periodic pricing scenarios typical of the petroleum industry or in dynamic decision contexts such as portfolio management or seasonal inventory control. The formal DSS tends to be very stable in its design and evolves over a period of years into a highly refined, reliable support mechanism.

In contrast, the *ad hoc* DSS is designed to focus on a very narrow problem context or set of decisions that is usually not recurring or easily anticipated. In these DSSs, the nature and immediacy of the decision situation become the drivers for design and implementation considerations. A typical scenario for an ad hoc DSS might be the need to make decisions regarding a pending hostile takeover or corporate merger. Historically, the cost of developing ad hoc DSSs was prohibitively high, thus limiting their availability and usefulness to only those decision situations of an extreme nature. However, the advent of DSS generators (generalizable software development environments that provide basic DSS functionalities such as DBMS, MBMS, and knowledge management)[1] has made the ad hoc DSS a feasible, cost-effective method of providing high-quality decision support to those situations where "custom" applications are the order of the day.

---

[1] DSS generators and their application will be discussed in chapter 13.

Directed versus Nondirected DSSs

Silver proposed a method of classifying DSSs by the degree to which the system provides *decisional guidance*—that is, the manner in which a DSS guides its users in constructing and executing decision-making processes by providing assistance in choosing and using its operators. Silver defines *operators* as those elements of the DSS (menus, buttons, models, algorithms, tools) that can, or must, be manipulated by the user in the course of the decision-making process. This method of classification suggests that users may benefit from such guidance "imposed" upon the process by the DSS. Figure 1-7 illustrates a two-dimensional matrix of decisional guidance used to classify various decision support methods.

Silver's classification initially categorizes a DSS by the type of guidance provided: *mechanical* versus *decisional. Mechanical* guidance is the more common form of directiveness in a DSS and generally consists of assisting users with the "mechanics" of the operating system's features such as menus, buttons, and commands. In contrast, *decisional* guidance assists the users in dealing with the various decision-making

FIGURE 1-7 Silver's Classification of Decisional Guidance

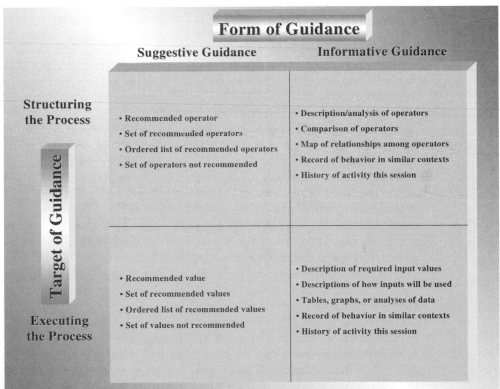

Source: Reprinted by special permission from *MIS Quarterly,* Volume 15, Number 1, March 1991. Copyright 1991 by the Society for Information Management and the Management Information Systems Research Center at the University of Minnesota.

concepts relevant to the problem context. This category can be broken down further into guidance intended to assist in the *structuring* or *execution* of the decision-making processes. Finally, each decisional guidance subcategory can be classified by the form the guidance takes: *suggestive* or *informational*. The former manifests itself as proposed courses of action to the user. Examples of suggestive guidance would be a suggestion from the DSS regarding which operator to invoke in the next step or a recommended starting value as input to a chosen algorithm. The latter provides users with information relevant to the situation at hand but does not indicate how the user should proceed based on that information. Silver contends that the type of guidance used is likely to have a significant effect on how the system is used and on the decision outcomes made with the system.

Procedural and Nonprocedural Systems

As discussed in section 1-3, *procedurality* refers to the degree to which a user of a DSS can specify whatever information he or she wants from that DSS in whatever form he or she wants it. In a method of classification similar to Silver's approach, the various DSSs can be positioned on a continuum according to their degree of procedurality. For example, a DSS using a highly procedural data retrieval language such as COBOL would require the user to provide detailed specifications regarding how the data is to be retrieved and precisely how each of the necessary computational subroutines is to be performed. The slightest deviation from a set of rigid syntactical rules such as a missing parenthesis or comma or a particular variable specifier out of order would result in an unrecognizable command to the DSS, or worse, a command that while recognizable may produce some highly unpredictable results. This system would be positioned at the extreme procedurality end of the spectrum.

Systems using less procedural languages, such as those written in typical fourth-generation languages such as Oracle or Smalltalk that employ a structured query language (SQL), allow the user to use less of a procedural approach to the construction of commands or requests for information. These systems tend to fall near the middle of the procedurality spectrum. The nonprocedural command structure, though easier to understand and construct, nonetheless requires the user to follow a set of rules regarding sequence and syntax that is somewhat foreign to the way one naturally thinks and converses. The bottom line is that the user needs to learn a new vocabulary and grammar to use a command-oriented DSS effectively.

Recently, a trend toward *natural language* command languages has emerged. These systems, written in modern development environments such as Lotus Notes, provide the user with a command syntax that closely resembles natural English language sentences. An extension of the concept of nonprocedurality, the natural language command processor accepts commands and instructions in the form of commonly structured English sentences that are sequenced and constructed at the convenience of the user rather than at the convenience of the command language. When we speak or write to each other, our sequence of words, punctuation, spelling, and grammar are all important factors in conveying meaning, but we can live with some fairly significant deviations from the rules without losing the essence of the meaning. In written form, if a comma is missing or a word is misspelled, we can often still understand the message being conveyed. In a command-oriented language, regardless of procedurality, a missing comma or a command parameter out of order can render the message uninterpretable by the command processor. The natural language DSS is more tolerant of these issues and can actually be designed to "learn" the user's intentions over time. That is, the command processor can interpret the meaning of a new command within the context of the previous commands or requests made by the user. Additionally, natural language systems can be easily adapted to alternative forms of input such as voice recognition or even visual pattern matching. This means that commands may be given to the DSS by simply speaking them or by making a specific motion or expression to a camera connected to the system. Despite the obvious advantages of a natural language command processor, however, the emergence of this type of DSS is in its infancy. Technology still has a long way to go toward providing users with machines they can interact with in a natural, humanlike manner. We will explore some of these issues in chapters 8 and 16.

Hypertext Systems

Yet another method for classifying DSSs focuses on the technique used by the system to provide the necessary knowledge management for the problem context. One such technique is the document-centric *hypertext* system. Such systems support the decision process by keeping track of a large and often disparate knowledge base that is primarily document or text based. Activities including document creation, revision, searching, grouping, merging, indexing, and forwarding, among others, are typically found in a text-based DSS. Using the concept of hypertext, the text-based DSS can facilitate the user's exploration of a particular flow of ideas through a group of documents. Various pieces of text within a document can be linked to related pieces of text in other documents so that a particular thread or train of thought can be explored. The most common example of this concept is found on the World Wide Web (WWW).

A user can begin at one Web site and by using hypertext links travel through literally millions of documents, or Web pages (see figure 1-8), investigating a particular flow of ideas. At any time, the user can restructure the investigation to explore a new twist or turn or simply abandon the search and start over. This natural sojourn through related documents and pieces of text is driven entirely by the user and closely resembles the way human beings think and make associations among myriad concepts. Hypertext systems support the decision process by relieving the user of the significant effort it takes to relate and remember things. Computers are far superior to humans at those tasks. The user is thus free to perform the decision process activities related to thinking and evaluating. These activities are still best performed by a human problem solver for most of the typically unstructured problem-solving contexts faced in daily life.

Spreadsheet Systems

Another technique DSSs use for knowledge representation is the *spreadsheet* system. This simple, yet powerful, method of representing relationships through the use of a matrix of rows and columns allows the user not only to create and represent relationships in the form of mathematical or locational links but also to directly manipulate those linkages and see the end result. Application packages such as Microsoft Excel or Lotus 1–2–3 are powerful spreadsheet environments that can serve as a foundation for sophisticated and complex decision support systems. More recently, the concepts of hypertext representation and spreadsheet systems have been integrated into com-

FIGURE 1-8 Example of WWW Page with Hypertext Links

Source: DSS Research Resources Home Page, © 1997. Used by permission of Daniel Power.

mon development environments such as Lotus Notes. Using this approach, the DSS designer can incorporate spreadsheet representation of knowledge within a hypertext-constructed document so that the user can manipulate the data using a combination of the techniques as he or she sees fit.

Individual and Group DSSs

Probably the most widely used method of classifying a DSS is by focusing on its ability to provide support to a single decision maker or to a group of decision makers. In the modern business world, it is unrealistic to assume that decisions of consequence are going to be made by a lone decision maker. Rather, they are made by a collective or through the consensus of multiple decision makers. As such, the concept of a *group decision support system* (GDSS) serves as a unique identifier for a system and suggests that the design, implementation, and use of such systems is different than that of DSSs intended for use by a single decision maker or problem solver. We will explore the similarities and differences between these two types of systems in chapters 6 and 7.

1-9 CHAPTER SUMMARY

This chapter introduces you to the world of decision support and DSSs. By using the basic definitions and classification frameworks covered here you will be able to focus on the complexities and details of each type of DSS presented in the remaining chapters, and, in addition, you will be able to relate the use of a particular DSS to its appropriate, and often inappropriate, problem context.

A DSS is truly a dynamic system that requires knowledge beyond that of the typical IS professional. The decision makers of tomorrow will rely on this technology to support their daily activities and to assist them in managing the ever growing knowledge base necessary to make informed and effective decisions. Although this book cannot possibly serve as a single source of knowledge for computer-based decision support, it can and will provide you with a solid foundation for understanding, interacting with, and effectively using the decision support technologies of tomorrow.

Key Concepts

- Definition

  A decision support system (DSS) is a system under the control of one or more decision makers that assists in the activity of decision making by providing an organized set of tools intended to impart structure to portions of the decision-making situation and to improve the ultimate effectiveness of the decision outcome.

- Benefits/limitations of the DSS

  The manager should see the DSS as a valuable tool in the decision process rather than as a mechanism for the making of the decision itself.

- The components of a DSS

  The data management system

  The model management system

  The knowledge engine

  The user interface

  The user(s)

- Categories and classes of DSSs

  Data-centric DSS versus model-centric DSS

  Formal DSS versus ad hoc DSS

  Directed DSS versus nondirected DSS

  Procedurality

  Hypertext management systems

  Spreadsheet systems

  Individual versus group DSS

Questions for Review

1. What are some of the common characteristics of a decision support system and how are they related to the decision-making process?
2. Why is a DSS a powerful tool for decision makers?

3. Is a "universal DSS" possible? Why or why not?

4. Why is the concept of procedurality important to the design and implementation of a DSS?

5. List and briefly describe the five basic components of a DSS.

6. What is a database? What are the possible sources of data collected in a database? Why is the ability to combine data records from multiple sources so important to DSS users?

7. What is a DBMS? Explain its two main responsibilities and how they contribute to the functionality of a DSS.

8. What is a model? How can a model base support decision makers in the problem-solving process?

9. Describe the two main responsibilities of the MBMS and the role of an MBMS in a decision support system.

10. What is reasoning? Why is reasoning important to the decision-making process?

11. What is a knowledge base? What is its role in a DSS?

12. How does knowledge get into the DSS? How can it be retrieved and organized into useful information?

13. What must be present in order for the user to be able to communicate well with the DSS?

14. Explain the roles of the various types of users of a DSS.

15. Describe and give an example of each pattern of DSS use.

16. Compare and contrast data-centric versus model-centric systems, formal versus ad hoc systems, and directed versus nondirected systems. What are the advantages and disadvantages of each type?

17. Compare the benefits and limitations of highly procedural languages and less or non-procedural languages.

For Further Discussion

1. Analyze a DSS application in the market. Describe its main components and summarize its functionalities.

2. Observe the decision-making processes in an organization that you are familiar with. Discuss how a decision support system can help in the process. Decide which category of DSS can fit with the characteristics of those decision-making processes.

3. Compare a DBMS and an MBMS. What is common to both? What are the differences between them?

4. The admissions office at the University of Maryland needs a decision support system for evaluating applications. They have to build a database for the DSS. Specify the data sources and data that could be found for the admissions office to use.

5. Interview a member of an organization that is using a DSS. Specify the roles of the users and find their patterns of use.

6. DSS experts generally agree that the interface represents the single most important component in the system. Why is the user interface such an important component in a decision support system? Which kinds of interfaces are considered user-friendly?

2

The Decision Maker

Learning Objectives

- Understand the elements and framework of the decision-making process

- Be familiar with the classification of decision makers

- Based on decision makers' cognitive complexity and value orientation, understand the classification of decision styles and the three related factors: problem context, perception, and personal values

- Understand the interactions between problem context and decision styles in order to design systems that provide appropriate support

- Comprehend the definition of a good decision and the forces acting upon the decision makers during the decision process

- Learn the common types of support that can be provided by decision support systems

Disaster at Tenerife

Experts in cockpit resource management will study the worst tragedy in aviation history for its many lessons. The Canary Islands, situated off the coast of Morocco, are a popular tourist site, but Los Rodeos airport, on the island of Tenerife, was particularly busy on the day of March 27, 1977. Las Palmas airport, located in the Canary Islands capitol, had been rocked by a bomb early in the afternoon and inbound traffic had been diverted to Los Rodeos. The airport on Tenerife did not have the capacity of Las Palmas, so aircraft were squeezed in on its ramp. Among those diverted to Los Rodeos that day were Pan Am Flight 1736 and KLM (Royal Dutch Airlines) Flight 4805, both Boeing 747s laden with passengers. The Pan Am flight had arrived after the KLM jet and was parked behind it on the apron, just short of the departure end of runway 12.

On the flight deck of the KLM aircraft, Captain Jacob van Zanten, a highly regarded training captain, was anxious to get back in the air as his duty hours for his crew were running low. When the tower radioed that Las Palmas had reopened, van Zanten decided that, instead of refueling at Las Palmas, which would undoubtedly be busy with the reopening, he would refuel while waiting on the ramp at Los Rodeos. It was now Pan Am 1736's turn to depart, but the only way to reach the departure end of the active runway, runway 30, was to enter runway 12 and backtrack. Unfortunately, KLM 4805 had only just begun refueling and there was no way the Pan Am airliner could taxi around it with the limited space at Los Rodeos. Pan Am's First Officer Bragg called the KLM crew, asking how long it would take to refuel, to which they replied, "About thirty-five minutes." There was nothing the crew of flight 1736 could do but wait. While flight 4805 was refueling, fog was moving onto the airport and by the time it had finished, visibility had decreased to as little as 900 feet in some areas. The KLM crew finally started their engines and prepared to take off. As they taxied to the beginning of runway 12, the tower instructed flight 4805 to "taxi straight ahead . . . ah . . . for the runway . . . make . . . ah . . . backtrack." At this point, Pan Am 1736 had also started its engines and was holding short of the runway. The visibility now prevented the tower from seeing either the runway or the two aircraft. Bragg then called the tower for instructions and flight 1736 was told to "taxi into the runway and . . . ah . . . leave the runway third . . . third to your left."

Apparently the pronunciation was unclear to Pan Am's Captain Grubbs who said, "I think he said first," to which Bragg replied, "I'll ask him again." Meanwhile the tower called flight 4805, instructing the crew, "at the end of the runway make one eighty and report . . . ah . . . ready for ATC clearance." After this communication, Bragg called back and said, "Would . . . you confirm that you want us to turn left at the *third* intersection?" The tower replied, "The third one, sir . . . one two three . . . third one." The crew of flight 1736 was still having difficulty sorting out the taxiways as they rolled down the runway. At this point, flight 4805 had reached the end of the runway and was making its 180-degree turn. As the aircraft finished the turn, van Zanten opened the throttle and the plane began to move forward. First Officer Meurs said, "Wait a minute . . . we don't have an ATC clearance," to which van Zanten said, "No, I know that. Go ahead and ask" as he held the brakes. Meurs called for the clearance and as he was reading it back, van Zanten again opened the throttles, saying, "Let's go, check thrust." After repeating the clearance, Meurs, in an attempt to let the controller know what was happening, said, "We are now at takeoff." The tower controller apparently took this to mean they were ready for takeoff, saying, "OK . . . stand by for takeoff . . . I will call you." On the flight deck of the Pan Am aircraft, the crew was obviously anxious about the implications of the transmission from flight 4805, Braggs saying, "We are still taxiing down the runway!" to which the tower replied, "Roger, Pan Am 1736, report the runway clear." Unfortunately, this first transmission blocked the tower's transmission to flight 4805 so all the KLM crew heard was, "OK." The transmission from flight 1736 troubled flight 4805's Flight Engineer Schreuder, prompting him to say, "Did he not clear the runway then?" Van Zanten, now focusing on the takeoff, replied with only "What did you say?" Schreuder repeated himself, saying, "Did he not clear the runway then, that Pan American?" to which both van Zanten and Meurs replied, "Yes, he did." Flight 1736 was still creeping down the runway, trying to find the proper turnoff, but obviously now concerned about KLM 4805's transmissions. Grubbs said, "Let's get the hell right out of here," to which Bragg replied, "Yeah . . . he's anxious isn't he?" A few seconds later, Grubbs spotted the lights of flight 4805 coming at them through the fog and said, "There he is . . . look at him! Goddamn . . . that son-of-a-bitch is coming!" He opened all four throttles in an attempt to swing the aircraft off the runway as Bragg yelled, "Get off! Get off! Get off!" Van Zanten saw flight 1736 still in the runway and pulled back, attempting to climb off the runway before impacting the aircraft. The nose gear managed to clear flight 1736, but the rest of the aircraft slammed into the Pan Am plane's starboard side. Flight 4805 remained airborne for a few more seconds before slamming into the ground and exploding. Pan Am 1736 was crushed and quickly caught fire as well. Everyone on board KLM 4805 was killed. The flight crew of Pan Am 1736 all survived uninjured, having just missed being hit by flight 4805's engine. Amazingly, 66 others survived from the Pan Am aircraft. Unfortunately, 583 people died that day on Tenerife in what is still today the worst aviation accident in history.

The biggest question on the minds of investigators was why van Zanten, a highly experienced training captain, would make the decision to begin a takeoff without a takeoff clearance from the tower. Meurs was still copying the en route clearance when van Zanten began advancing the throttles. It seems clear that van Zanten was aware that the clearance hadn't been received when Meurs checked him and he replied, "No, I know that. Go ahead and ask." It is likely that van Zanten was in a rush to get to Las Palmas because of the delay on the ground and his crew's lack of extra duty hours. However, even after the en route clearance was given, the tower instructed KLM 4805 to "standby for takeoff," which the crew failed to hear as well as the clear indications that Pan Am 1763 was still on the runway. In addition, Meurs did nothing to enlighten van Zanten that they were not cleared for takeoff after his initial comment. It is possible that Meurs was not comfortable challenging van Zanten due to his experience level. To exacerbate the situation further, the efforts of the crew of flight 1736 were hampered by the low visibility. They had only a small diagram of the airport and the third taxiway led backwards from their intended taxi direction—a turn of 135 degrees, which would be extremely challenging in a 747. They apparently believed that the fourth taxiway, which was at a 45-degree angle in the proper direction, was the one the tower intended for them to use, so they proceeded past taxiway 3. None of the taxiways at Los Rodeos were marked. A final consideration was the difficulty with English of the tower controller and the KLM (Dutch) crew. With the weather as bad as it was, relying solely on radio communications was already a dangerous practice, but the nonstandard communications of both parties led to a breakdown of situational awareness. The Dutch investigation team placed the blame firmly on the controllers at Los Rodeos, while the American investigation team found the actions of Captain van Zanten to be the primary cause of the accident.

Can you decide?

2-1 DECISION MAKERS—WHO ARE THEY?

In chapter 1, we explored the component parts and essential elements of a DSS from the inside out. We began with the DBMS, MBMS, and knowledge base and proceeded to weave our way out of the mechanical insides of the system to the user interface. Finally, we found our way to the user. The purpose of that inside out investigation was to lay the groundwork for understanding what a DSS is and what it is not. There is much to discuss on these two subjects but because every discussion must begin somewhere, this one will begin with you—the decision maker.

Chapter 1 briefly touched on the subject of objective, or purpose, regarding the design and use of a DSS. It is really quite simple: We know we *need* to make decisions but we don't know exactly *how* to make them. In this context, "how" does not always mean procedure or method, although a DSS can be extremely valuable in that part of the decision-making realm. Rather, we are referring to the "how" part of decision making that deals with the processing of large volumes of seemingly disparate data and the managing of a myriad of models of reality that can serve to "predict" certain key outcomes. This chapter begins by focusing on the reason why we have decision support systems at all: the decision maker. Were it not for the need of human problem solvers to be supported in certain phases of the often lengthy and complex process of semistructured decision making we wouldn't have DSSs and, as such, we wouldn't need to talk about them. Happily, for us at least, decision makers need support and a DSS is just the ticket. We begin, therefore, by exploring just who these decision makers are and what makes each of them unique.

Profile of a Decision

One last point of order remains before focusing directly on the decision maker. We need to have a working model of what the decision maker, in the generic sense at least, is trying to accomplish during the making of a decision.

The literature on the subject contains many theories about how decisions are made, the steps within the decision-making process, the motivations for making the decision, the steps within the steps, and on and on and on. All of this attention is not bad, mind you. It's just way too much for a manager to absorb and understand. Here we are going to focus on one or two theoretical frameworks for the decision process and use them to guide our investigation of both the process and the people involved in it.

Figure 2-1 shows a profile of one of the many ways that a decision is made. The reason this model must be described that way is that in the real world of decision making, a decision is rarely, if ever, made in exactly the order suggested by the model or even by using all of the steps contained in the model. Moreover, the process depicted is a static representation of a distinctly dynamic operation. The specific conditions and circumstances of the problem to be solved will ultimatcly dictate the way in which the decision is made. Nonetheless, we can use the model in figure 2-1 as a basis for understanding what should be going on in a typical decision context.

The decision maker plays a somewhat schizophrenic role in the process of making a decision. Not only is he or she considered an element, or step, in the process (as shown in figure 2-1) but the decision maker is also a participant, in varying degrees, in all of the steps in the process. In chapter 3, we will see how this dual role complicates

FIGURE 2-1 Example of a Decision-Making Process

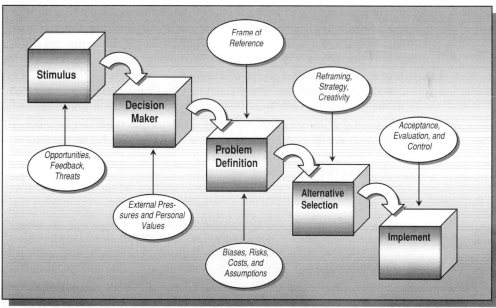

Source: Adapted from Rowe, A. J. and Boulgarides, J. D., (1994), *Managerial Decision Making,* Englewood Cliffs, NJ: Prentice-Hall. Used by permission, © 1985, all rights reserved.

the process of decision making and, further, adds complexity to the management of the process. For now, however, let's simply look at each element in the process and see how this all fits together.

Stimulus

The first step in the process is the presence of some externality or force that causes the decision maker to perceive that one or more problems exist that require one or more decisions to be made. A *problem* is defined simply as the perception of a difference between the current state of affairs and a desired state of affairs. If a decision maker thinks things need to change or conditions need to be altered then a problem is perceived to exist. This perception of a problem context is caused by one or more stimuli. These stimuli can come in many forms and can be perceived differently by different decision makers. In other words, what is perceived by one decision maker as a problem may not be viewed as a problem by another member of the same organization. This disparity of perception may occur because a problem really *doesn't* exist and the decision maker is misinterpreting existing facts or information or because a problem really *does* exist and one or more members of the organization fail to recognize it. Complicated, isn't it?

The form the stimuli take can often affect the perception of a problem. Often, a problem doesn't manifest itself as a problem per se. It manifests itself as a series of symptoms that indicate the presence of an underlying problem. We will explore the difference between problems and symptoms in chapter 3. For now, suffice it to say that something has to "happen" to trigger the decision-making process.

The Decision Maker

The example in figure 2-1 shows the decision maker as one part of the process. Throughout our discussion, however, we posit the decision maker as a participant in the process. We will focus on the participant role in the next few chapters. Here the decision maker is defined as simply the next step or event following the onset of a stimulus.

The decision maker is truly a "black box" in every sense of the word. Metaphorically, we can fit everything we truly "know" about what goes on inside the mind of a decision maker into a thimble. Some would argue that the thimble is really a basket and that we really do know a great deal, but, regardless, we just don't know nearly as much as we want to about the DSS user. This is an area of research that has much to contribute to the manager of tomorrow.

Problem Definition

As stated above, problems often manifest themselves as a series of symptoms that all relate to the real problem or are the results of it. Regardless of this situation, however, the problem solver must define the problem before any effective investigation of alternative solutions can be conducted. This phase is crucial to the successful outcome of the decision-making process. If the right problem definition is formulated then the right problem will be solved. If, however, the problem definition is flawed by an incorrect reading of the true nature of the problem at hand then a potentially great solution to the wrong problem will be offered. Worse yet, it may also be implemented. Hopefully, the DSS will provide guidance in the elimination of potential problem definitions and the identification of the correct one.

Alternative Selection

This is the heart of the decision-making process and the portion of it where a DSS is often most useful. The selection of an effective solution from a set of feasible alternatives is the essence of decision making. It is the decision itself. The DSS can be used to provide quantitative approaches to the analysis of the set of feasible alternatives and to assist the manager in choosing the best available solution to the problem at hand. We will see in chapter 3, however, that this selection process is the part we are least naturally equipped to perform and, thus, the one in which we must most rely on the DSS to assist us.

Implementation

Once the user settles on the most effective solution from the set of alternatives the work has really just begun. The decision process triggers actions and events within the organization that are focused on implementing the solution and, thus, solving the problem. These actions include creating consensus and acceptance, negotiation, strategizing, politicking, and intense planning. The greatest solution in the world is worthless if it is not effectively implemented. A DSS can be of limited support in assisting with decisions directly related to issues of implementation; this is the phase where the decision maker him- or herself becomes the most important player. The success or failure of implementing a solution ultimately rests with the decision maker. We will explore this aspect of the process in greater detail in chapter 4.

Classes of Decision Makers

Now that we have a model of the decision process to help us understand what is going on we need to focus our attention on the decision maker. The reason there are so many different types of DSSs is that there are so many different types of problem contexts. There are also many different types of decision makers that must be supported. See figure 2-2 for a model of the different decision-maker classifications.

Individual

The *individual* decision maker, as the name implies, stands alone in the final decision process. This class of users essentially works alone during the decision process in the sense that the analysis of information and the ultimate generation of a final decision rests solely in their hands. Because an individual decision maker is, by definition, an individual his or her unique characteristics with regard to knowledge, skill set, experience, personality, cognitive style, and individual biases come to bear in the decision-making process. Each of these traits has both a direct and an interactive effect on how the decision maker is ultimately going to decide and on what types of support are needed during the process. This is one reason why the design of a DSS is often so complex. To be truly effective, a DSS intended for use by an individual problem solver must

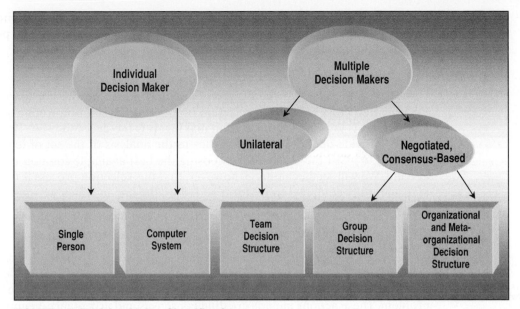

FIGURE 2-2 Decision Maker Classification

be designed to account for his or her unique characteristics and needs. If more than one individual decision maker is to use the DSS, then the design must reflect the unique characteristics and support needs of each of the intended users. The combinatorial nature of this problem should be readily apparent. Designing a DSS for individual use is a complex and difficult activity. We will see just how these complexities and difficulties manifest themselves and how they are addressed in chapters 13 and 14.

Multiple

This class of decision makers is made up of *multiple* individuals interacting to reach a decision. We differentiate between multiple decision makers and group or team decision makers (see the next section). Here, the *multiple* decision makers are those who each has a stake in a particular decision outcome and thus is motivated to reach eventual agreement and common commitment to a course of action. Each member of this class may have unique motivations or goals and may approach the decision process from a different angle. Furthermore, each may use a common DSS or a variety of systems as support for his or her contribution to the decision-making process. Finally, it is often the case that multiple decision makers do not possess equal authority to make a particular decision, nor do any of them possess enough authority to make the decision alone. In these problem contexts, multiple decision makers do not necessarily meet in a formalized manner or conduct open forums or discussions as a unit. Instead, the institutionalized patterns of communication and the various levels of authority within the organization structure the interaction among the participants in such a way that eventually a "decision" is reached and implementation begins. The best way to conceptualize this class of users is as a dynamic union of users who act as individual decision makers in reaching a decision or solution to a particular problem context.

Group

In contrast to the multiple decision maker, a *group* decision maker is characterized by membership in a more formal structure where each member of the group has a similar vested interest in the decision outcome and has an equal say in its formation. Group decision makers generally work in a formal environment that consists of regular meetings devoted to working through the decision process, formal schedules and agendas focusing on specific portions of the process, and often deadlines by which the decision must be finalized and operationalized. Common examples of group decision makers are those who make up organizational committees and juries. Each participant is involved in the making of a decision based on consensus of the group, but none has any more input or authority to make the decision than any other. Because the formalization of the decision process serves as the primary characteristic that differentiates the group decision maker from the multiple decision maker the unique nature of the group process must be understood if support is to be provided by a DSS. We explore these issues in depth in chapters 6 and 7.

Team

Yet another class of decision maker is called the *team* decision maker. This class can be thought of as a combination of the individual and group classes. Often, an organization's structure is such that although the authority to make a particular decision rests with an individual manager, he or she is supported by several assistants who are working toward the same goal(s). In the team context, decision support may come from several individuals empowered by the key individual decision maker to collect information and/or make certain determinations regarding a portion of the intended decision outcome. Also, support may come from one or more DSSs being used by any combination of key or assistant team members. In this context, the team produces or "manufactures" the final decision, but the formalization of that decision and authority to make it rests with the individual decision maker. Figure 2-3 illustrates the differences between the individual, multiple, group, and team classes of decision makers.

One unique difference between decisions made by a group and those made by a team is the type of decisions made. In the group class, decision outcomes are often *negotiated* outcomes. This is because external forces often determine the need for the formation of a group in the first place and, in such scenarios, the choices facing the group are often controversial. The group decision makers, therefore, tend to seek alternatives that permit the attainment of the group's original objectives while serving as a compromise among all of the concerned parties. In the team class, however, decisions are normally *unilateral* in nature. Only one decision maker has the authority and responsibility to make a unilateral decision, even though many people can be said to have influenced that decision's final form. This type of decision is the most basic and generally possesses many characteristics similar to those decisions made by the individual decision-making class.

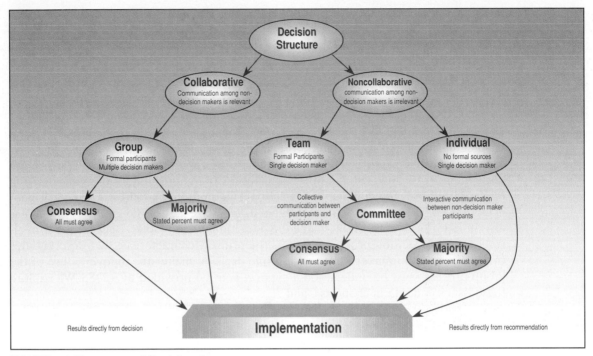

FIGURE 2-3 Taxonomy of Decision Structures

Organizational and Metaorganizational

Over fifty years ago, Chester Barnard, a noted expert on management as a science, offered a definition of an *organization* as "a system of consciously coordinated activities of two or more persons" (Barnard 1938, 73). Although a lot has changed since Barnard's definition was first printed it remains viable today. The glue holding the organization together is the purposes and goals shared by its members. Using this definition, we can easily conceive of organizations within organizations: groups and teams that consciously coordinate their activities for the purpose of reaching a commonly held objective or goal. Decision makers at the organizational level are those who are empowered with the authority and charged with the responsibility of making decisions on behalf of the entire organization. The characteristics of those decisions and the processes used in arriving at them, by definition, bear strong similarities to those made by individual, team, and group class decision makers. This being the case, why do we need to identify a unique class of decision makers at the organizational level?

One reason is the breadth and depth of information needed by the organizational decision maker. This class of users is embodied by the most senior level of management: the CEO. As we will see in chapters 6 and 7, a special type of DSS has been developed for use at this level. We call these special DSSs *Executive Information Systems (EIS)*.

Another reason why we differentiate between the team or group classes and the organizational class is that the decisions made by this class of users generally require support from the entire organization if they are to be successfully implemented. A classic example of this type of decision making is found in most Japanese organizations. The concept, called *nemawashi,* uses a central decision maker following a prescribed set of consensus-building conventions at all levels of the organization until a global agreement is reached concerning what the final decision should be. Organizational decision makers generally do not have the resources to implement large-scale decision outcomes without support from the vast majority of their subordinates. As such, these decision makers have special support needs that differ from those at the individual, group, or team levels and are appropriately categorized separately.

There exists yet another class of decision maker beyond the organizational level. All of the world's organizations together make up the system of enterprise. Decisions made by users operating at this level tend to be oriented toward social welfare, quality of life, allocation of controlled or limited resources, social order, or civil justice. In other words, decision makers in this class are not principally oriented by economics as are the decision makers within the system of enterprise. They are, rather, focused on decisions that affect the establishment of social order. Because organizations exist within the social economic system, all decision makers, and their respective decisions, must account for the decisions made at the *metaorganizational* level. More important, as with all other classes of decision makers, metaorganizational decision makers require special support and, thus, special systems of support.

2-2 DECISION STYLES

To further our understanding of just who this person, the decision maker, really is we need to better understand those things that directly affect his or her behavior. One such area of focus is decision style. *Decision style* is a term used to describe the manner in which a manager makes decisions. The manager's design style is reflected in the way he or she reacts to a given decision-making context—what is believed to be of value or importance, how the information is interpreted, how the externalities and forces are dealt with. The ultimate effect of a particular individual's decision style on a decision outcome is dependent on factors such as problem context, the perceptions of the decision maker, and the personal set of values that he or she brings to the situation. The good news is that mechanisms exist to measure and categorize decision styles, and the results obtained from these measures can be used to inform the design and implementation of a DSS. More on that later.

Context, Perception, and Values

The three factors of *context, perception,* and *values* intertwine in their relationship to decision style. The problem *context* involves factors relating to the forces acting on the decision maker in the course of making the decision. Organizational and environmental forces such as government regulation, new technologies, market competition, and internal power struggles all affect the problem context. Forces of a more individual nature such as skill set, energy, motivation, and perceived abilities, among others, can also shape the problem context. The totality of these forces must be balanced and managed by the decision maker during the problem-solving process.

Another factor affecting decision style is *perception*. Decision makers bring personal biases into the problem context that often serve to "convert" the facts so that they better match their own reality. It has been demonstrated that managers tend to perceive a problem situation and its potential solutions in relation to their personal goals rather than a strict set of realities. Because of this, perceptual biases interact with the problem context to determine a particular decision maker's approach to solving a problem and whether that approach is effective. We focus in depth on the effects of individual biases on decision outcomes in the next chapter.

Last, but not least, the personal *values* of the decision maker are important in determining his or her decision style. Values are those world views or global beliefs that guide individual actions, judgments, and desired outcomes. An individual's values are not tied to any particular object or situation and are generalizable across all modes of conduct. Moreover, values are acquired beginning at birth and tend to remain strong throughout a person's lifetime. Because of this, individual values form a permanent framework that influences a person's behavior and the manner in which he or she makes decisions.

The complexity with which these three factors intertwine in the formation of decision style is significant. Using established measures of decision style, however, we can build a classification scheme for decision styles that serves us in the design of DSSs intended for use in specific problem contexts by users possessing certain decision style characteristics. Let's begin by looking at the basic classes of decision style and their associated characteristics.

Figure 2-4 shows a decision style classification scheme derived from the work of noted psychiatrist Carl Jung. The classification scheme is the basis for many measures of decision style including the popular Myers-Briggs Type Indicator test (Myers 1962) and the Decision Style Inventory developed by Alan Rowe.[1] As can be seen in the figure, decision style is classified using two component parts: cognitive complexity and value orientation. Using these two dimensions four distinct categories of decision style can be identified.

Directive

The *directive* decision style combines a high need for structure in the problem context with a relatively low tolerance for context ambiguity. Decision makers possessing these characteristics tend to focus on decisions of a technical nature and often do not require large amounts of information or consider multiple alternatives. They are generally considered efficient managers but require visible levels of both security and status. Finally, directive-style decision makers tend to function best when they communicate verbally rather than through writing or other multichannel media.

Analytical

This style demonstrates a much greater tolerance for context ambiguity and tends toward the need for greater volumes of information and the consideration of large sets of alternatives. *Analytical-style* decision makers are best at coping with new, often unexpected, situations and problem contexts. They simply enjoy solving problems! In contrast to the directive style, analyticals prefer written communication and are not quick

---

[1] The complete Decision Style Inventory measure can be found in appendix A.

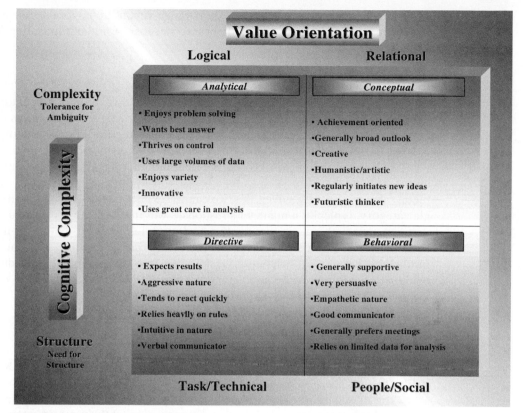

FIGURE 2-4   Decision Style Model

Source: Adapted from Rowe, A. J. and Boulgarides, J. D., (1994), *Managerial Decision Making,* Englewood Cliffs, NJ: Prentice-Hall. Used by permission, © 1985, all rights reserved.

to reach a decision or solution. Their orientation toward detail often results in protracted investigations of the problem context before a final decision is made.

Conceptual

Much like the analytical decision maker, the *conceptual* manager demonstrates a high tolerance for ambiguity but tends to be much more of a "people person." Conceptuals display an openness with their subordinates and tend to be driven by an idealistic emphasis on values and ethics. This type of decision maker is a long-term thinker and is generally strongly committed to the organization. In addition, this type is very achievement oriented and values accolades and organizational recognition. Their management style is commonly one of participation and loose control. As implied by their name, conceptuals are thinkers rather than doers.

Behavioral

The fourth category of decision style is low on the cognitive complexity scale. Nonetheless, *behavioral* types display a deep commitment to the organization and are very employee oriented. This style requires a relatively low amount of data input and, as such, tends to display a relatively short-range vision. Behaviorals are conflict-averse by nature and tend to rely on meetings and consensus for communicating to and organizing subordinates.

So What?

The four classifications of decision style in the Rowe typology provide us with a method of categorizing decision makers according to the characteristics of their particular style, but we need a method of operationalizing this knowledge into the design process for a DSS. To accomplish this, a few key points must be addressed.

To begin with, one must recognize that human beings are complex and no simple method of classification, such as the Decision Style Inventory, is going to reflect completely this complexity. Given this, we cannot expect managers to fit neatly into a single category. Typically, a manager's responses will indicate the presence of a dominant decision style with one or possibly two backup styles. Thus it is better for us to think of a manager's decision style in terms of *style patterns* rather than a distinct and highly predictable set of rigid behaviors. Despite this, knowing an individual's dominant and backup decision patterns can yield a great deal of information useful in the design of interfaces and levels of procedurality or directiveness.

Context/Decision Style Interaction

Table 2-1 gives us a number of style-situation comparisons and behavior outcomes regarding the four classifications that can serve to inform the design of a DSS for a particular type of decision maker.

The key issues in our focus on decision style as it relates to DSS design and use are the decision maker's specific reactions to stress and the method in which problems are generally solved. If we use our knowledge of these characteristics in the design of a DSS intended for use by a known decision style we may be able to provide support that is in harmony with the user's preferred approach. Conversely, if we ignore decision style or fail to provide appropriate support for a particular style, the DSS may actually inhibit the success of the process and reinforce certain biases or weaknesses in the decision maker's approach to solving the problem. Some simple examples may better illustrate this point.

Table 2-1 Common Characteristics of Decision Style Behaviors

Basic Style	Behavior under Stress	Motivations	Problem-Solving Strategy	Nature of Thought
Directive	Explosive, volatile	Power and status	Policies and procedures	Focused
Analytical	Focuses on rules	Challenge	Analysis and insight	Logical
Conceptual	Erratic, unpredictable	Recognition	Intuition and judgment	Creative
Behavioral	Avoidance	Peer acceptance	Feelings and instincts	Emotional

Source: Adapted from Rowe, A. J. and Boulgarides, J. D., (1994), *Managerial Decision Making,* Englewood Cliffs, NJ: Prentice-Hall. Used by permission. © 1985, all rights reserved.

Let's say we know the primary user of a proposed DSS possesses a dominant decision style in the *analytical* category. We know this style displays a high tolerance for ambiguity, uses considerable data in reaching a conclusion, strives toward optimization of the solution, is creative, and prefers a structured, rule-oriented environment. This type of user would be able to function effectively in a procedural DSS environment and would require access to a wide variety of data sources and models during the course of using the DSS. Systems that are designed to allow for innovative and counter-intuitive analyses and model combining would be most useful to the analytical-style manager.

The opposite situation would be the pairing of a particular decision style with a system that is designed in opposition to the salient characteristics of that style. Consider a system that is highly procedural and directive being used by a manager whose dominant decision style is highly *directive*. The directive type has a low tolerance for ambiguity and is not good at coping with stressful situations. He or she has a need for control and power and would require an interface that allows for such control to be exercised in the operation of the system. The tedious nature of constructing an exact and semantically accurate query or command to the DSS would soon wear thin on a directive decision maker. Also, recall that the directive type is primarily a verbal communicator. This would suggest that output requiring visual analysis for interpretation would not be utilized as well by a directive as would a simple, concise, table or narrative response from the DSS. In sum, designing the system to complement the user's decision style can provide additional support to the decision-making process and failing to do so can inhibit the success of the process.

2-3 DECISION EFFECTIVENESS

What Makes a Good Decision a Good Decision?

There is an old saying in the used car business that a "good deal" is the deal you just agreed to. This approach makes the assumption that the buyer would never knowingly agree to a "bad deal" and therefore, if he or she agreed to it, it must be good. We can think of agreement to a deal as a decision and can assume that the decision to agree is viewed by the buyer as a good decision. But how do we really know if a decision is a good one?

Given the fact that decision making is at the heart of managerial activities and that good decisions are significantly related to the long-term success of an organization, one would expect to find a wealth of knowledge regarding the profile of a good decision and the determinants of successful decision outcomes. Unfortunately, this is far from the case. While a number of studies have investigated the factors relating to successful decisions, few if any offer any useful prescriptions for improving the chances of decision success. We are faced, then, with defining a good decision and then using that definition to judge whether or not a good decision has been made.

The following definition of a "good" decision is offered: A *good decision* is one that results in the attainment of the objective or objectives that gave rise to the need for a decision within the boundaries and constraints imposed by the problem's context. In other words, if we reach our goal given the limitations of our situation then we have made a "good" decision. Another way of looking at it is that if by our decision we solved the problem at hand without causing any new problems, then our decision must have been a good one. The problem is that we don't really know whether a decision is a good one until after it is made. We are, therefore, faced with analyzing our intended decision in terms of the intended ends that will be accomplished by the designated means available to us. This is one reason why decisions are often hard to make. We will explore this more in the next chapter when we look at the various theories associated with decision making. In the meantime, we need to better understand the various forces that shape the problem context and, thus, both the decision process and its outcome.

Decision Forces

Several models have been proposed to explain the variety of potential forces and constraints that can act on a problem context, and thus on a decision maker, during the course of making a decision. Each of these models suggests that the decision maker must balance the forces acting upon the process and must contend with the dynamics of the forces in formulating and implementing a final decision. Figure 2-5 illustrates these forces. Although each problem context is unique, it is not unusual for the majority, if not all, of the forces listed to present themselves in one form or another during a typical decision-making process. Let's briefly review each of the major categories of forces and constraints found in a typical decision process.

FIGURE 2-5 Forces Acting upon a Typical Decision Maker

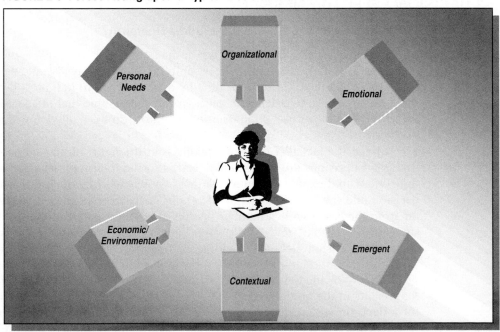

Personal and Emotional

The decision maker does not live in a vacuum and is not without typical human needs. As such, the conditions that relate to his or her feelings, health, security, rewards, frustrations, anxieties, and maybe most important, cognitive limitations can all be of consequence during the process of selecting the appropriate alternative. Each of these *personal forces* can serve to either reinforce or debilitate the manager's ability to make a sound decision. Because of this, the personal forces acting upon the decision process must be given careful consideration by the decision maker during the formulation of a decision strategy.

The human mind has often been referred to as infinite in its capacity and power. However, the practical nature of our understanding of human cognitive processes suggests we are limited in our present ability to store and process knowledge. Compared to the rate at which knowledge is advancing, we possess only a modest amount of knowledge relative to all that is known. Moreover, studies have shown that we are limited in our capacity for processing the knowledge we do possess. Miller (1956) has suggested the concept of "the magic number seven, plus or minus two." We typically are not capable of processing more than from five to nine distinct pieces of knowledge at a time. We will see in chapter 3 that the use of certain strategies for decision making can overcome this and other cognitive limitations, but suffice it to say cognitive limits are a significant force in the decision-making process.

Economic/Environmental

Forces and constraints in this category include limits on resources, governmental regulation, societal values such as views on the moral or ethical nature of the decision being considered, competitive pressures of the marketplace, the demands of the consumer, the needs and demands of the individual stakeholders potentially affected by the decision outcome, and the emergence of new technology. Individually or in combination, these forces require the decision maker to respond in a manner that results in the alteration of the final decision to account for, or control for, their effects.

In 1994, Intel discovered a bug in its new Pentium processor that caused the results of certain calculations to be inaccurate (see figure 2-6). The basic problem was that simple division requiring accuracy to sixteen significant digits was affected. Intel executives decided to inform their consumers about the problem but maintained that it was so minor in nature that it would occur only once every 25,000 years for the typical user and that it required no recall by the manufacturer or action on the part of the consumer. Intel failed to consider certain market forces, however, in the making of this decision. IBM was a major consumer of Intel processors and had a significant inventory of 486-class machines in its warehouses. The market was excited about the new Pentium processor and as a result had stopped buying 486 machines in anticipation of the Pentium. When IBM heard of the Pentium bug, it began a public campaign to discredit Intel's claims. IBM claimed that the problem was much larger than Intel was suggesting, arguing that it could occur once every twenty-four days and that the typical user would most surely be affected. Although neither side was able to provide substantive evidence to support its claims, the public began to lose their enthusiasm for the Pentium and reverted to purchasing 486-class machines—something that certainly pleased IBM. Had Intel simply offered to replace the processors when the original announcement was made, the counterattack by IBM would not have had much effect on the consumer. Because Intel failed to account for the environmental forces associated with its competition and with the introduction of new technologies, it lost the momentum created by the hype over the new Pentium processor in addition to suffering a $475 million fourth-quarter loss. The dust has since settled and Intel has more than recovered from their "bad" decision. Nonetheless, this serves as a classic example of the need to account for *economic/environmental* forces.

Organizational

Within the manager's own organization forces and constraints exist that must be accounted for in the process of making a decision. Policies and procedures, issues of group conformity, organizational culture, and coordination of staffing and other resources can affect the nature of the decision process. The degree to which the manager interacts with his superiors and subordinates combined with the overall policy structure of the organization can significantly alter a decision process, and thus, its out-

FIGURE 2-6 Excerpt of E-mail Posting of First Observed Intel Pentium Division Problem

```
FROM: Dr. Thomas R. Nicely
Professor of Mathematics Lynchburg College
1501 Lakeside Drive Lynchburg, Virginia 24501-3199
Phone: 804-522-8374 Fax: 804-522-8499
Internet: nicely@acavax.lynchburg.edu

TO: Whom it may concern
RE: Bug in the Pentium FPU
DATE: 30 October 1994

It appears that there is a bug in the floating point unit (numeric coprocessor) of many, and perhaps
all, Pentium processors. In short, the Pentium FPU is returning erroneous values for certain
division operations.

For example, 1/824633702441.0 is calculated incorrectly (all digits beyond the eighth significant
digit are in error). This can be verified in compiled code, an ordinary spreadsheet such as Quattro
Pro or Excel, or even the Windows calculator (use the scientific mode), by computing

                    (824633702441.0)*(1/824663702441.0),

which should equal 1 exactly (within some extremely small rounding error; in general, coprocessor
results should contain 19 significant decimal digits). However, the Pentiums tested return
0.999999996274709702 for this calculation. A similar erroneous value is obtained for x*(1/x) for
most values of x in the interval 824633702418 <= x <= 824633702449, and throughout any interval
obtained by multiplying or dividing the above interval by an integer power of 2 (there are yet other
intervals which also produce division errors). The bug can also be observed by calculating 1/(1/x)
for the above values of x. The Pentium FPU will fail to return the original x (in fact, it will
often return a value exactly 3072 = 6*0x200 larger).

The bug has been observed on all Pentiums I have tested or had tested to date, including a Dell P90,
a Gateway P90, a Micron P60, an Insight P60, and a Packard-Bell P60. It has not been observed on any
486 or earlier system, even those with a PCI bus. if the FPU is locked out (not always possible),
the error disappears; but then the Pentium becomes a "586SX", and floating point must run in
emulation, slowing down computations by a factor of roughly ten. I encountered erroneous results
which were related to this bug as long ago as June, 1994, but it was not until 19 October 1994 that
I felt I had eliminated all other likely sources of error (software logic, compiler, chipset, etc.).
I contacted Intel Tech Support regarding this bug on Monday 24 October (call reference number
51270). The contact person later reported that the bug was observed on a 66-MHz system at Intel, but
had no further information or explanation, other that the fact that no such bug had been previously
reported or observed...
```

Source: Courtesy of Dr. Thomas R. Nicely and Lynchburg College.

come. Consider an organizational climate that tends to discourage new or innovative thinking and prefers to reward conformance to existing policy and procedures. A decision maker in this organization will soon become frustrated with constantly being turned down when suggesting new or innovative decision outcomes. Over time, the omission of creativity from the organization's decision process will become institutionalized, and the decisions made by its managers that remain will be constrained by an organizational culture characterized by lack of vision and foresight.

Contextual and Emergent

A significant source of constraint and consequence to the decision process is the problem context itself. Within this category are found issues relating to skill inventory, time requirements, motivation to reach a decision, and the perception of importance by the decision maker. Probably the most important and noticeable of these is time requirements. Even if all other forces acting upon the situation are effectively dealt with, time limits can create severe pressure and stress on the decision maker and, if left unattended or ignored, can significantly increase the probability of error or poor-quality decision outcomes. Cognitively demanding activities are often classified as such not because the activity itself is demanding but because the time limitations associated with each decision in the activity make it so. Consider the multitude of decisions an airline pilot must make. Activities associated with deciding to ascend or descend, turn left or right, or increase or decrease power are in and of themselves not necessarily cognitively demanding or stressful. But when those decisions have to be made by a pilot traveling at 350 miles per hour while approaching another aircraft traveling at a similar speed the time limitations completely change the nature of the decision process. The two or three seconds allowed for these decisions may preclude the consideration of all relevant information or the consideration of multiple decision strategies. Bear in mind that this type of situation is not out of context for a discussion of managerial decision making. The pilot's office is the cockpit and his job is to make these types of decisions on behalf of his organization. In a relative sense, many of the decisions faced by managers on the ground have a time limitation that can induce the same levels of stress found by the airline pilot facing a collision situation.

2-4 HOW CAN A DSS HELP?

This entire book is devoted to answering the question of how a DSS can help, but it is appropriate at least to begin to list the ways in which a DSS can assist in the decision process with respect to the various forces we just discussed.

Recall from chapter 1 that a DSS, while useful, is not a universal solution with regard to supporting all that needs to be addressed in the course of making a decision. The DSS is not intended to replace the decision maker. Rather, it is intended to provide him or her with focused support for one or more activities within the decision process. Because of this limitation, we must become aware of the nature of available support a DSS can offer. Then we can see the need to incorporate DSS technology in those problem contexts where it is appropriate. Table 2-2 lists the basic types of support that a DSS can provide.

Table 2-2 Common Types of Support Provided by a DSS

- Explores multiple perspectives of a decision context
- Generates multiple and higher quality alternatives for consideration
- Explores and tests multiple problem-solving strategies
- Facilitates brainstorming and other creative problem-solving techniques
- Explores multiple analysis scenarios for a given decision context
- Provides guidance and reduction of debilitating biases and inappropriate heuristics
- Increases decision maker's ability to tackle complex problems
- Improves response time of decision maker
- Discourages premature decision making and alternative selection
- Provides control over multiple and disparate sources of data

The types of support listed are not always mutually exclusive nor are they always appropriate for a particular problem context. This is what makes the design, implementation, and application of a DSS so challenging and unique from all other information systems. Properly applied, however, a DSS can become an essential element in the creation of a "good" decision.

2-5 CHAPTER SUMMARY

This chapter has demonstrated that while all people may be created equal all decision makers are not. Decision makers come in many different forms. Some are individuals, others come in groups, yet others are part of teams or organizations. Each type faces unique problem contexts and each requires unique sources and kinds of support to reach a particular decision. The unique characteristics associated with different types of decision makers combined with the unique nature of the problem contexts faced by each type reinforce the reasoning behind the statement that a generic DSS does not, and probably never will, exist. In the next chapter we begin to examine the process of making a decision and various models of decision making in use.

Key Concepts

- Profile of a decision (2-1)
  Stimulus
  The decision maker
  Problem definition
  Alternative selection
  Implementation
- Classes of decision makers (2-1)
  Individual

Multiple

Group

Team

Organizational

Metaorganizational

- Factors intertwine in the formation of decision styles (2-2)

Problem context

Perception

Personal values

- Decision styles (2-2)

Directive

Analytical

Conceptual

Behavioral

Context/decision style interaction

- Definition of a good decision (2-3)

A good decision is one that results in the attainment of the objective, or objectives, that gave rise to the need for a decision within the boundaries and constraints imposed by the context in which the decision was made.

- Decision forces (2-3)

Personal and emotional

Economic/environmental

Organizational

Contextual and emergent

Questions for Review

1. List the major components of the decision-making process.
2. Define stimulus and describe its place in the decision-making process.
3. Depict the dual roles of a decision maker in the decision-making process.
4. In which portion of the decision-making process is a DSS most helpful for decision makers? Why?
5. List and briefly describe the classes of decision makers.
6. Define individual decision makers and describe the various traits that affect the way they make decisions.
7. Specify the unique differences between decisions made in a group environment and a team environment.
8. Identify the characteristics of decision makers at the organizational level. What is the special type of DSS developed for them?
9. Describe the three forces that affect a particular individual's decision style.

10. Briefly describe the classifications of decision styles based on the nature of problem context, cognitive complexity, and value orientation.

11. Why is the understanding of decision makers' decision styles important to the design and implementation of a DSS?

12. What makes a good decision a good decision?

13. List and briefly describe the forces that can act on a problem context and on a decision maker during the course of making a decision.

14. How do personal and emotional forces act upon the decision process?

15. How do organizational forces and constraints influence the decision process?

16. What is the role of a DSS in relation to a decision maker?

For Further Discussion

1. In the decision-making process, which element do you think is most important? Please state your reasons.

2. Discuss the nature of multiple and group decision makers. Give an example for each of them. What are the differences between them?

3. Observe a decision maker in an organization that you are familiar with. Based on the nature of the problem context, and personal perception and values of the decision maker, specify his or her decision style(s).

4. We all understand that designing the system to complement the user's decision style can provide additional support to the decision process and failing to do so can inhibit the success of the process. Find a case that can support this dictum.

5. Analyze a good decision made by an organization. Discuss the reasons why you think it was a good decision. How did the decision maker(s) make it?

3

The Process of Making a Decision

Learning Objectives

■ Understand the difficulties of decision making from different angles such as problem structuredness, cognitive limitations, uncertainty of decision outcomes, and alternatives and multiple objectives

■ Learn the classification of decisions and understand the role of these typologies in the design of decision support systems

■ Understand Simon's model of problem solving

■ Learn the theory of rational decision making

■ Gain an understanding of Simon's "satisficing" strategy and bounded rationality

■ Clarify the confusion between a symptom and a problem

■ Become familiar with the process of choice

■ Understand the decision maker's cognitive process and its effects on decision making

■ Learn four of the most common heuristic biases and their impacts on decision making

■ Distinguish between effectiveness and efficiency

Phillips Petroleum Product Pricing

Phillips 66 Company is a wholly owned subsidiary of Phillips Petroleum Company. Between November 1984 and June 1985, Phillips Petroleum was the object of two hostile takeover attempts: one by T. Boone Pickens and the other by Carl Icahn. During that same period, Phillips Petroleum shed over $2.2 billion worth of assets and assumed $8.8 billion worth of debt, raising its debt ratio from 20 to 80 percent.

To respond to the financial crisis, Bob Wallace, the president of Phillips 66, downsized and delayered the organization, cutting management and staff by 40 percent. Recognizing that improved access to information was essential to managing the company through the transition, Wallace championed the development and implementation of an executive information system (EIS) that would enable more focused and timely delivery of information to managers at all levels of the company.

Wallace knew that one of the decision-making activities of the new DSS that would benefit the company the most is the process of product pricing. Pricing is probably the most critical and time-valued business process in the oil and gas industry. Managers face market conditions that call for them to make detailed product pricing decisions on a daily basis. Prior to the implementation of the EIS, pricing was executed and controlled both centrally and, more important, manually. Field sales representatives literally drove through their sales districts, looked at the competition's pump prices, and then called these figures in to the central pricing group, which used this information to set the prices for the three major regions of the country. All local service stations within a region used the same price. It regularly took three to four days to put a price into effect in all locations and, in many cases, the new price was based on incorrect or even missing information from the field. Setting the price just one penny too low could result in a loss of up to $40 million in annual profits. This decision-making activity was mission critical for Phillips, and Bob Wallace knew that if something wasn't done to improve the support for this process, a big, and probably costly, mistake was likely to be made.

Wallace also knew that the decision makers in the pricing division were some of the best in the industry and that improving upon their skills was not a likely scenario. The only way to improve the efficiency and effectiveness of the pricing decision process was through the strategic deployment of computer and communication systems to support the decision makers. Enter the DSS. The new system was integrated with daily pricing information on competitors' prices in each local area and the daily spot prices on the commodity market. Local pricing information on Phillips 66's prices from each individual service station was automatically drawn by the EIS on a daily basis. The information was then analyzed and displayed in a series of graphs that provided an easily understood and highly accurate report on Phillips 66's and local competition's pricing to the decision maker.

Through the EIS, Phillips' managers got the necessary information and analytical tools to enable them to formulate their pricing strategies and coordinate the pricing activity on a daily basis with increased accuracy and speed. In addition, managers had the necessary communication support to assure that the pricing information could be communicated throughout the company quickly, reliably, and accurately.

By changing the previously centralized approach to pricing, the EIS completely changed the way Phillips ran its business. Under the new system, liquid propane gas was now priced locally at each of the company's eighty-two individual pipeline terminals. This allowed the individual managers to assume control of the pricing activity and to respond much more quickly to changes in specific markets. Customers now feel that Phillips 66 is more responsive, and their competitors seem confused by the new pricing structure and are having trouble reacting.

Charlie Bowerman, vice president of Marketing, conservatively estimates the system has generated increased profits of better than $20 million because of its responsiveness to customer needs and changing market conditions. More important, through the support of information technology, the decision makers at Phillips 66 Company improved the outcome of their critical decisions and, in doing so, led their organization through a time of crisis and successfully headed off other hostile takeover attempts.

—Yu-Ting "Caisy" Hung

3-1 WHY ARE DECISIONS SO HARD?

How is it that we often seem to know in advance that a decision is going to be hard to make? When you think about it, our ability to size up many decision situations rather quickly in terms of classifying them as easy or hard is quite spectacular. Faced with the responsibility of deciding whether to spend the day at the beach with friends or stay at home and mow the grass, almost immediately we sense that this decision will not be a very hard one to make. Conversely, if we bear the responsibility of adopting a new technology into our organization that will decrease operational costs while simultaneously improving product quality, but will mean the layoff of up to a thousand employees, we also seem to know intuitively that this decision will be no day at the beach. The real question is how do we know whether a decision will be easy or hard when we haven't even begun to gather information about it or to make it?

The answer depends on a variety of structural, psychological, physical, and environmental factors. The difficulties (or lack thereof) associated with making a decision can be the result of innumerable combinations of complexity, uncertainty, organizational and environmental pressures, and individual decision-maker limitations. In this chapter, we will explore four key areas that can individually or collectively determine the relative difficulty of a pending decision: structure; cognitive limitations; uncertainty; and alternatives and multiple objectives.

Structure

Recall from chapter 1 that Simon (1960) proposed to classify problems on a continuum from *completely structured* to *completely unstructured.* Figure 3-1 illustrates this classification and contains examples of decision structures that would exist at each end of the continuum.

Simon distinguished between the two ends of the spectrum by discussing the degree to which a decision is programmed:

> Decisions are programmed to the extent that they are repetitive and routine, to the extent that a definite procedure has been worked out for handling them so that they don't have to be treated *de novo* each time they occur. Decisions are nonprogrammed to the extent that they are novel, unstructured, and consequential. There is no cut-and-dried method of handling the problem because it hasn't arisen before, or because its precise nature and structure are elusive or complex, or because it is so important that it deserves a custom-tailored treatment. . . . By nonprogrammed I mean a response where the system has no specific procedure to deal with the situations like the one at hand, but must fall back on whatever general capacity it has for intelligent, adaptive, problem-oriented action. (pp. 5–6)

In other words, programmed decisions are easy because we have immediately available to us all the parts necessary to make the decision; we have a "program" to make the decision. Nonprogrammed decisions are hard because, in addition to gathering the necessary information and making the decision, we must also "write the program," or design the process by which the decision is made. In applying Simon's classi-

FIGURE 3-1 Continuum of Decision Structures

Stable context   *Volatile context*
Commonplace   *Atypical, unique*
Recurrent   *discrete*
Programmable   **DSS Domain**   *Intuitive, creative*
Easily accessible information   *Problematic access to information*
Decision criterion understood   *Decision criterion unclear*
Focused decision strategy   *Multiple decision strategies*

Structured   **Semistructured**   **Unstructured**

fication method to the realm of the DSS, Keen and Scott Morton (1978) chose to refer to the ends of the continuum as *structured* and *unstructured*, and we will adopt this convention as well.

As can be seen in figure 3-1, the degree of *structuredness* of a decision is determined by a variety of factors. Decisions that are made repeatedly during the normal course of activity tend to be (or become) structured. An airline pilot frequently makes decisions about takeoffs and landings, routing, and passenger comfort such as whether or not to turn off the seatbelt sign. Such decisions, due to their commonplace and repetitive nature, are relatively structured. If, however, the pilot is faced with deciding to land her aircraft with one engine out at an airfield with which she is not familiar or does not have maps for, the decision becomes much more unstructured.

Cognitive Limitations

We just can't know everything. Sometimes we can't even handle all that we have to know for the situation at hand. Even worse, occasionally we can't even summon forth into our conscious mind information we have previously encountered and stored. Worse yet, when we do successfully retrieve previously stored information, it is often not completely accurate. While the human mind is a marvelous (and theoretically infinite) reasoning, computational, and storage mechanism, our present understanding of it suggests that we are indeed limited in our ability to process and store information and knowledge.

One of the most famous and oft-cited investigations into cognitive limitations is the work of Miller (1956). His research has long stood as an example of the *cognitive limits* of the human mind. Through a series of experiments using a large sample of human subjects, Miller determined that the immediate field of awareness of the human mind is limited to the manipulation of between five and nine distinct pieces of information. In other words, at any given moment, we can only consciously keep track of "the magic number seven plus or minus two" active items of knowledge during the processing of a decision. Miller introduced the term *chunk* to describe an "organized unit of information" stored in the working memory. In essence, Miller's conclusions suggest that the brain's capacity to handle information is constrained by the number of chunks in the receiving stimulus. He also demonstrated that humans tend to develop ways of organizing information into larger chunks according to past experience, with experts being more proficient at *chunking* information than novices in a given knowledge domain. Although we have developed many methods of aggregating information in an attempt to mitigate this limitation, the basic conclusion of Miller's work remains true. Because decision making is very much a cognitive exercise, the cognitive limitations of the individual decision maker can substantially increase the degree of difficulty of making a particular decision. We will explore the issue of cognitive limits in more detail later in this chapter.

Uncertainty

The concept of "20/20 hindsight" is a good way to develop an understanding of *uncertainty*. When one looks back at the outcome of a decision and the process by which it was made, one can see with complete certainty what the outcome of that decision process was. If we could predict the outcome of a particular decision with the same degree of certainty, all decisions would be easy to make.

Total *certainty* implies that there exists complete and accurate knowledge regarding the outcome of a pending decision. Genuine *uncertainty* suggests that the outcome of a pending decision cannot be determined even within the confines of a probabilistic framework. The bad news is that we are generally faced with some degree of uncertainty in a decision-making situation and that total certainty seldom exists. The good news is that genuine uncertainty is almost equally as uncommon. Usually, the decision maker can assign some subjective probability to the expected decision outcome so that some degree of certainty is assumed. In most cases, the accuracy of such subjective probabilities is based upon the degree of completeness and accuracy of the information used to assign them. Implicit in all this is that most decision outcomes contain an element of risk on the part of the decision maker. In chapter 5, we will look at a variety of methods developed to assist the decision maker in assigning high-quality subjective probabilities to decision outcomes as well as techniques that can be used to reduce the degree of uncertainty in a given decision context. For now, let's assume the axiom that the more uncertain a decision outcome is to the decision maker, the more difficult the decision becomes to make.

Alternatives and Multiple Objectives

Regardless of the context in which a decision is being made, the objective of the exercise is to produce a desired outcome. We can characterize an outcome or a result as the product manufactured during the decision process. In fact, regardless of whether the decision is made by an individual, a team of individuals, or at the level of the organization, the objective remains the same: to choose from a selected set of alternatives the one that will produce the greatest number of desirable outcomes with the least number of undesirable consequences. Because we don't know with certainty that any of our outcomes will actually occur we must carefully consider each of the possible outcomes associated with a given decision strategy to ascertain whether the desired effect will be achieved.

It is here that the complexity or difficulty of a given decision can be significantly increased by the presence of multiple alternatives or objectives. Each new alternative needs to be thoroughly analyzed and compared to the other alternatives. It becomes clear that the inclusion of an additional alternative to the selection set creates a significant combinatorial increase in the difficulty of the decision. To further exacerbate this problem, the decision maker may have more than one objective or goal at any given time. As such, the selection of one alternative that, by itself, satisfies the criteria of the decision objective may also impede the progress of another related goal. Now the process is compounded by the shared values and goals of the decision maker in addition to the combinatorial issues of multiple alternatives.

One method commonly used by managers to cope with this situation is to discard the marginally acceptable alternatives early in the choice process. By doing so, the decision maker can devote energy to concentrating on those remaining alternatives that appear to be better suited to produce the desired outcome. Although this process of elimination intuitively appears to be a fruitful method of making the correct choice, we will see later in this chapter that this may not be true. In fact, this very method may actually serve to eliminate the possibility of ever selecting the best alternative in light of the objectives and constraints.

3-2 A TYPOLOGY OF DECISIONS

Decisions, decisions, decisions. No two are completely alike. The myriad of decisions facing a manager in his or her lifetime is staggering. In fact, the typical day of a manager can be jam-packed with a seemingly nonstop stream of decisions. The kind of support needed for one decision may be entirely different from the support required for the next decision. We need a method of reducing the vast number of possible decision contexts into a more manageable set of categories.

There are many different methods of classifying decisions. We could classify them according to managerial level, for instance: *line-level* decisions versus *middle manager* decisions versus *senior management* decisions. Or we could classify them according to their focus, say *strategic* versus *administrative* decisions. What about classifying them according to the strategy used to make the decision: *computational* versus *judgmental?* You can see that decisions can be logically categorized by a variety of notions. Regardless of the method employed, however, if we are to design and implement successfully a support technology for a given decision context we must be able to classify (or better yet, isolate) those decisions for which the DSS can be expected to be useful and those for which it cannot. We need a typology. Figure 3-2 illustrates one example of a typology of decisions based on a combination of several methods found in decision-making and DSS literature. Let's focus for a moment on the classification schemes contained in the figure.

FIGURE 3-2 Typology of Decisions

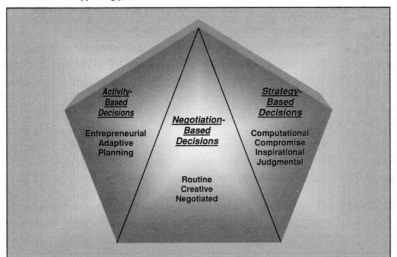

Negotiation-Based Decisions

Delbecq (1967) proposed a three-point classification scheme based on the notion of negotiation:

1. *Routine decisions.* The decision maker or makers are clear on the desired goal or objective and the policies, procedures, and technologies that exist to achieve the goal. Routine decisions can be thought of as analogous to Simon's programmed decisions.
2. *Creative decisions.* Novel approaches are needed to handle the complexity of these decisions. An agreed-upon strategy or method is lacking and the outcome is uncertain due to incomplete knowledge or absence of a known strategy. These decisions can be thought of as analogous to a nonprogrammed or semistructured decision.
3. *Negotiated decisions.* There exists conflict in either goals or approaches to the decision at hand. As such, the various opposing factions must confront each other in an effort to resolve the differences. In these decisions the manager may not be the decision maker at all but rather a participant in the decision-making process.

Activity-Based Decisions

Mintzberg (1973) proposed a typology of decisions that focuses attention on the activity with which the decision is most associated:

1. *Entrepreneurial activities.* This type of decision is generally characterized by high levels of uncertainty. The selection of alternatives is motivated primarily by proactive considerations and is typically focused on near-term growth over long-term issues.
2. *Adaptive activities.* Also characterized by high levels of uncertainty, these types of decisions are typically motivated by reactive considerations and are focused more on the short-term issues at hand.
3. *Planning activities.* This decision environment is characterized by high risk and the decisions made are motivated by both proactive and reactive considerations. The focus here is more on growth and efficiency over the long term.

As can be seen from Mintzberg's approach, the support necessary for decisions classified in this manner would be determined primarily by the environment in which the decision was being made rather than by the actual structure of the decision itself. In this regard, Mintzberg's classification suggests a differentiation based on decision strategy rather than decision structure as with Simon's or Delbecq's approaches.

Strategy-Based Decisions

Yet another division in our typology of decisions is represented by the approach taken by Thompson (1967). His classification scheme differentiates decisions based upon the primary strategy used in making the final choice:

1. *Computational strategies.* Considerable certainty exists with regard to outcomes and cause/effect relationships. Strong preferences exist for possible outcomes.
2. *Judgmental strategies.* Preferences for possible outcomes are quite strong but outcomes and cause/effect relationships are highly uncertain.

3. ***Compromise strategies***. High certainty exists regarding the outcomes and cause/effect relationships, but the preferences for possible outcomes or alternatives are weak or unclear.

4. ***Inspirational strategies.*** Preferences for possible alternatives or outcomes are weak or unclear and a high degree of uncertainty exists regarding cause/effect relationships.

In Thompson's approach we find two dimensions in which the strategy is formed: *certainty* and *outcome preference*. In this case, necessary support would be determined based upon which strategy would appear most fruitful given the decision being undertaken.

Despite the method of classification employed, it can be seen that all methods have certain characteristics in common. As shown in figure 3-1, they can all be further classified into one of two categories—those of a *routine*, recurring nature with high certainty and those of a *nonroutine*, nonrecurring nature with high uncertainty. Using this metaclassification approach we can reduce the complexity of determining what type of support may be warranted given the basic characteristics of the decision type being faced. In other words, by gaining a better understanding of the classification of the decisions being faced in a given context we might better be able to determine what specific features of a DSS would be useful in support of that context.

3-3 DECISION THEORY AND SIMON'S MODEL OF PROBLEM SOLVING

If we are to understand what is actually going on in the "black box" world of the decision maker, we need some point of reference or "lens" through which to view the various manifest behaviors and begin to explain their relationships. This lens is usually found in the form of a theory of the process. Numerous theories have been advanced that attempt to explain the process of decision making. Keen and Scott Morton (1978) proposed a categorization of decision-making theory that attempts to organize the myriad of decision theories into five main perspectives. Table 3-1 contains their taxonomy of decision-making perspectives and provides a brief description of each.

Regardless of the theoretical approach we embrace, it is important to realize that the development of a good *prescriptive* approach to decision making—such as the design and implementation of a DSS—is rooted in the development of a workable and sound *descriptive* theory. For our purposes, we will explore and build upon the work of Simon and his colleagues by investigating the decision-making process as a process of *rational behavior*.

Figure 3-3 illustrates Simon's (1960) three-phase model of problem solving.[1] Though elegantly simple in construction, Simon's model has withstood the test of time and, even today, serves as the basis for most models of management decision making. Notice that the model depicts the problem-solving process as a flow of events that can

---

[1] Although Simon's model was constructed within the realm of problem solving, decision making can be thought of as a special type of problem solving. In making a decision, we include events that focus on opportunities as well as on the selection of an effective solution to a problem. In addition, Simon's original model did not contain an implementation phase. This step was added later by Sprague and Carlson (1982).

Table 3-1 Keen and Scott Morton Classification of Decision-Making Perspectives

Rational Manager Perspective
- Classic conception of decision making
- Assumes rational, completely informed, individual decision maker
- Favored by proponents of cost-benefit analysis
- Requires analytic definition of decision variables
- Requires precise, objective criterion for choice

Process-Oriented Perspective
- Focuses on how decision maker can effectively function with limited knowledge and skills
- Emphasizes heuristics and search for solutions that are "good enough"
- DSS design goal is to assist in improving existing solution, not to seek the optimum

Organizational Procedures Perspective
- Seeks to understand decisions as output of standard operating procedures
- Design goal is to determine which of these procedures might be supported or improved
- Stresses identification of organizational roles
- Includes focus on communication channels and relationships

Political Perspective
- Decision making is viewed as a personalized bargaining process between business units
- Assumes that power and influence determine the outcome of any decision
- Design goal focuses upon the decision-making process rather than the decision itself

Individual Differences Perspective
- Focuses on individual problem-solving behaviors
- Design is contingent on the decision-making style, background, and personality of intended user

---

proceed in either a linear or iterative fashion. That is, at any point in the process, the problem solver may choose to return to the previous step(s) for additional refinement. Let's look at each phase of the process in more detail.

Intelligence

The process begins with the *intelligence* phase. During this phase the decision maker is "on the lookout" for information or knowledge suggesting the presence of a problem or the need for a decision. This scanning activity may be either periodic or continuous in nature. Problems tend to manifest themselves as a noticeable (real or perceived) difference between a desired state and the present state. Often problems are detected simply as a result of the scanning activity taking place during the intelligence phase of the process. Implicit in the "activation" of the problem-solving process is the detection of a problem that can be "owned" by the problem solver.[2] If the deci-

---

[2] *Ownership* in this sense means the problem is within the domain of the problem solver's ability to solve it. A problem can be perceived but not ownable in this sense.

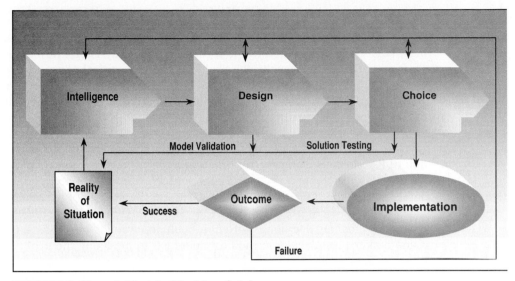

FIGURE 3-3 Simon's Model of Problem Solving

sion maker or his or her organization *cannot* solve the problem, then it cannot be owned and therefore does not trigger the next phase of the process. Instead, such conditions tend to be classified as constraints or conditions that may be necessary to consider when solving problems that can be owned. An example of this can be found with environmental conditions such as taxes or interest rates. A decision maker may perceive the tax rate imposed on his imports or exports to be excessive. Nonetheless, this perceived difference between the current state and the desired state is beyond his direct control. As such, the "problem" must be classified as a constraint or externality that must be considered when solving other "ownable" problems.

Problems within the scope of the decision maker generally manifest themselves during the scanning activity. For example, a daily review of a production log may reveal a condition suggesting the need for maintenance. Another example can be found in the cockpit of a commercial airliner. There is an old adage among pilots that describes flying as "hours of boredom occasionally interrupted by stark, raving terror." Most activity in the cockpit of an aircraft consists of scanning the multitude of instruments that provide the pilot with feedback about the aircraft and the environment in which the aircraft is flying. The pilot has developed an expectation of the value of each of these bits of information under a variety of conditions. When one or more of the instruments does not conform to this expected range of values, a problem is detected and the pilot must move on to the next phase of the problem-solving process.[3]

---

[3] I must explain my regular reference to airplane cockpits. They are the "offices" of the managers (pilots) that fly them. Additionally, they offer a fertile environment for a variety of decisions ranging from highly structured with few constraints to seemingly unstructured with multiple constraints (most notably: time). While the majority of readers will not move on to "manage" a commercial airliner, the lessons learned from studying the many problems faced will be easily generalizable to an office located on terra firma.

Design

Once the problem has been identified and formally defined, the decision maker must begin activities related to the formation and analysis of alternatives intended to serve as potential solutions to the problem. This is a critical phase in the process. The host of potential solutions to the problem must be explored and reduced to a workable subset. Each potential solution must be carefully analyzed and compared to all others with regard to expected outcome, cost, probability of success, and any other criteria deemed critical by the decision maker.

Another critical activity performed during this phase is the analysis and selection of a problem-solving strategy. Determining the range of feasible solutions is one thing, but determining how to go about actually selecting an acceptable solution and implementing it is quite another. As you can see, the process of problem solving sometimes involves *decisions within decisions* and *problems within problems*. This is one reason why making decisions is often difficult and fraught with risk and error. The decision maker must decide on the best approach to modeling the problem, identifying the key factors or variables to be contained within the model, and the relationships among those variables. Finally, decisions must be made regarding what analytical tools are most appropriate for testing the integrity of the chosen model and its possible outcomes. During this phase, the decision maker may find that he or she needs more information regarding the problem at hand and may return to the intelligence phase in an attempt to satisfy that need before returning to design further phase activities and proceeding to the third phase of the process.

Choice

Intuitively this phase should be the most clear-cut of the three in terms of associated activities; however, we will soon see that it is exactly the opposite. This is also where the concept of decision making as a rational behavior will be explored in detail.

In this phase, the decision maker selects one of the available solution alternatives generated and analyzed in the previous phase. Once again, we find complexity as a result of decisions within decisions. For instance, before the decision maker can select a feasible solution to the problem a secondary scanning of the internal and external environment must be conducted to ensure that the solution about to be implemented is still the best choice given the constraints at hand. Although many decisions can be made in environments of reasonable stability and expectation, in some cases the dynamics of a decision-making environment are so fluid that solutions cannot be selected based upon conditions that exist at the moment but must be based upon the expected or estimated conditions at the time the solution will be physically implemented. The petroleum industry is a perfect example of this. Recall the problems facing Phillips Petroleum in this chapter's minicase. The decision regarding the price of oil and refined petroleum products must be made in an environment of constant flux. An error of a single penny per gallon can cost the company millions of dollars in future revenues. In addition, the decision as to pricing (the solution) must be made for a future period, thus requiring an estimation of the market conditions some time in the future.

This dichotomy of environmental conditions (stable versus fluid) often requires a return to the previous design phase for further refinement of the selection strategy and definition of the feasible solution subset. In addition, implicit in this dichotomy is the need for a decision regarding what constitutes an acceptable solution. Does the situation require an "optimal" solution or will an "acceptable" one suffice? What level of risk are we willing to assume in the selection of a solution alternative? The stability or fluidity of the decision context can serve to determine the answers to these questions and thus the selection of a decision-making strategy. Table 3-2 identifies several modeling and analysis strategies associated with our decision either to optimize or to satisfy.

3-4 RATIONAL DECISION MAKING

Before we go any further, let's take a closer look at our two strategic alternatives.[4] The concept of *optimization* suggests that the decision maker will choose the alternative that is clearly the best possible one providing the best overall value and outcome. Such an optimal solution may manifest itself as the lowest cost, the highest goal attainment, or the highest ratio of goal attainment to cost. Regardless of the structure of the outcome, the optimal solution is the "best of all possible solutions." The problem is, how do we know what "all the possible solutions" are? Back to that shortly.

In many circles, particularly the disciplines of economics and management science, optimization is considered *rational behavior.* In other words, it is rational to make a decision that, after review of all possible alternatives, brings the maximum satisfaction or utility to the decision maker. "The end of rational behavior, according to economic theory, is the maximization of profits in the case of business firms and the maximization of utility in the case of people in general" (Katona 1953, 313). Most normative economic theory, such as laws of market equilibrium or supply and demand, is built upon the assumption that man is distinctly rational in behavior and will always seek the optimal solution to a problem.

Table 3-2 Modeling and Analysis Strategies

Satisficing strategies	*Optimizing strategies*
Simulation	Linear programming
Forecasting	Goal programming
"What-if" analysis	Simple queuing models
Markov analysis	Investment models
Complex queuing models	Inventory models
Environmental impact analysis	Transportation models

Note: Techniques such as Markov analysis and queuing are advanced methods of determining probabilities of events. For a detailed explanation of such methods the reader is referred to any good management science text.

---

[4] A variety of decision-making strategies exists in the literature including focused approaches such as analytic hierarchy process (Saaty 1987), elimination-by-aspects (Tversky 1972), incrementalism (Lindblom 1959), and Etzioni's (1967) mixed scanning approach, among many others. For the purposes of simplicity and clarity, however, this text will focus on the two general strategic categories as discussed.

Despite the attractiveness of optimization as a decision-making strategy, its practical application in managerial decision-making contexts is problematic. A number of conditions exist in the realm of management decisions that make optimization difficult, if not impossible, to operationalize. First, many decisions faced by managers are distinctly qualitative in nature and thus do not lend themselves to the quantitative approaches associated with optimization. For example, the decision faced by General Motors in 1984 regarding the location for its new 4 million-square-foot Saturn manufacturing facility was one of a complex, qualitative nature. Admittedly, issues of a quantitative nature such as cost of land, cost of labor, transportation and shipping issues, availability of necessary resources, and taxes were relevant to the final decision. However, other issues such as quality of life afforded for the employees, quality of available education, and other life-sustaining services were equally relevant. While the quantitative issues could be accurately measured the relevant qualitative issues could not. As such, optimization is of little value in this scenario.[5]

A second problem with optimization as a viable solution strategy is identified by Simon (1960). He makes the point that it is just not feasible to attempt to search for every possible alternative for a given decision. The cost of doing so is easily seen as enormous. Furthermore, the ability of humans to keep track of all possible alternatives and to effectively compare them to one another is limited by our cognitive capacity (remember, seven plus or minus two). In the next section, we will look at a more narrowly defined and more realistic approach to rational decision making that does not suffer from these impracticalities and seems to be a more accurate model of what is occurring in that "black box" between our ears.

3-5 BOUNDED RATIONALITY

Once again, we must look to Nobel Prize–winning scholar Herbert A. Simon for a more practical theory of problem-solving behavior than the rational model. Simon can be credited for his "demolition" of the rational, economic man. In his early work, he questioned the concepts of maximization and optimization as they were applied to normative economic models. Simon suggested that were the concept of man as a profit-optimizing entity tenable, there would exist no price tags. Think about it: If man truly wanted to maximize profit, then each transaction would be a negotiation for the highest possible price. While some buyers would obtain the product at a lower price than the last buyer, others might be willing to pay much higher prices. This would, over time, theoretically result in optimized profits. So why doesn't the "economic" man do this?

It's much too hard, that's why! Simon argued that the cognitive limitations of man make it impractical to consider all possible alternatives to a particular problem. And even if we could review all relevant alternatives, we would not be able to assimilate all the information so that we could make an appropriate decision. Instead, Simon suggested that we tend to "simplify reality" by focusing our energy on finding a solution that meets our preconceived notion of what an acceptable solution looks like.

[5] Saturn headquarters was finally located in Spring Hill, Tennessee.

When we find such a solution, we immediately adopt it and stop looking for a better one. In the case of our price tag example, we decide upon an acceptable margin of profit and then we openly price our product to reflect that margin. Although this may not result in optimal profits it does satisfy our criterion of profiting from our sales. And it is a whole lot easier than negotiating each sale into a quantifiable end. Simon used the term *satisficing* to refer to this search-limiting strategy. Further, because decision makers are bounded by the cognitive limitations of all human decision makers, they actually do make rational decisions that are bounded by often uncontrollable constraints. Simon referred to this as *bounded rationality*.

Problem Space

Simon's concept of bounded rationality can best be understood by an example. Figure 3-4 contains a graphical representation of a typical *problem space*.

Assume that the graphic on the left represents the boundary of the identified problem at hand and all possible solutions to that problem: good ones, bad ones, great ones, OK ones, and so on. In addition, the problem space contains the "best" or optimal solution to the identified problem. The rational model of decision making suggests that the problem solver would seek out and test each of the solutions found in the problem space until all solutions were tested and compared. At that point, the best solution would be known and identifiable.

Simon argued that this is not what really happens in a typical decision making scenario. The graphic on the right illustrates his approach. What the decision maker actually does is develop a model of what an acceptable solution to the problem looks like. Then he or she searches the problem space for a sufficient match to that preconceived solution model. When such a match is found, the search ends and the solution is implemented. Thus, the decision maker will most likely not choose the optimal solu-

FIGURE 3-4 Problem Space and Search Space

tion because the narrowed search of the problem space makes it improbable that the best solution will ever be encountered. Using this approach, the decision maker settles for a satisfactory solution to the given problem rather than searching for the best possible solution.

So how does this relate to the design and use of a DSS? To begin with, we can see that a human decision maker is not likely to expend the energy necessary to gather all relevant information available regarding a particular decision. Next, we can assume that even if all information were available the decision maker probably could not assimilate it and thus would not use it. Finally, given the concept of bounded rationality, it appears that left alone the typical decision maker preconceives the structure of a desired solution before the search for a solution even begins. All this suggests the need for guidance and structure in the identification of a problem and the selection of a satisfactory alternative. Thus, the need for a DSS.

A secondary issue of some importance to this discussion is the strategy used by the decision maker in exploring the problem space and selecting the final alternative. There must be a method to "measure" each alternative encountered against the preconceived model. Simon suggests that decision makers tend to develop a set of *heuristics,* or "rules of thumb," to manage their search. These heuristics arise from experience, perception, opinion, intuition, bias, and training. These search rules, while intended to improve the efficiency of the search process, often reduce the decision maker's effectiveness rather than improving it. We will explore this issue in detail in the last section of this chapter.

Problems versus Symptoms

One aspect of bounded rationality that can have a debilitating effect on the decision-making process is the typical decision maker's confusion between a symptom and a problem. Not understanding and consciously distinguishing between the two can lead to disastrous results.

As defined previously, a problem represents the difference between a perceived condition and a desired condition. If you have a headache (the perceived condition) and you really don't want one (the desired condition) then you believe you have a problem. So, then, what exactly is a symptom?

The notion of symptom is rooted in the concepts of cause and effect. Let's go back to the headache example as a rather simple but effective method of understanding the differences. The headache is perceived as undesirable and therefore is classified as a problem. We determine the situation to be undesirable and wish to "solve the problem" by taking action to eliminate the headache. This results in a trip to the doctor. Here is where the difference between symptoms and problems begins to become clear.

If the doctor chooses to classify the headache as a problem then he will prescribe some medication, let's say aspirin, and before long the headache goes away. Everything seems OK until we sit down the next day in class and begin taking notes on the material being presented on the blackboard. Suddenly, the headache returns. We have learned of a desirable relationship between the headache and aspirin so we take some and the headache, once again, goes away. Unfortunately, the next day it comes back. So what's the problem?

The "problem" is that our bounded rationality is allowing us to become temporarily satisfied with "treating the symptom" rather than "treating the disease." The headache is simply a manifest condition of a more deeply rooted phenomenon: We need eyeglasses! Therein lies the distinction between symptoms and problems. A symptom is evidence of a problem but not necessarily the problem itself. Think of a symptom as simply a deviation from the norm. Defined this way, a symptom does not necessarily have to be bad to be a symptom. If during the review of a periodic budget versus actual report the reviewer notices that costs for a particular item have exceeded estimates, then a perception of a problem immediately manifests itself. Further review shows that sales for the product manufactured with that high-cost item are way up in a certain region. That sounds good. Would that "favorable variance" trigger the perception of a potential problem? Probably not, but it should. In both cases, the variance was a deviation from the expected norm. At the very least, these deviations should result in a more detailed review. Although they may seem unrelated or rooted in completely different areas, they may in fact be highly related and point to a deeper problem. Suppose the higher-than-expected sales in a particular region were due to an overzealous marketing manager reducing the price of the product severely below market simply to increase sales. Without a reasonable short-term strategy for increasing market share or competing with a local vendor, this price reduction is unacceptable. Moreover, this sudden increase in sales also accounts for the sudden increase in costs associated with the material necessary to make the product. If each variance were treated as a core problem then the real problem would not be solved. Moreover, depending upon the method used to treat the symptoms, they may simply disappear, thus masking the problem from further investigation.

It should be clear that distinguishing between a problem and its related symptoms is of extreme importance to successful decision making. We can define a symptom as a *manifest effect of an underlying cause*. The real difference lies in the results associated with the symptom's elimination. The treatment of a symptom normally results in the elimination of the symptom (effect) but does not result in the removal of the associated problem (cause). The reverse, however, is not true. If we take the time and energy to fully identify and define the root problem, we will be able to craft a solution that will result in not only the elimination of the problem but of its associated symptoms as well. We will explore how a DSS can assist in sorting through the symptoms to get to the problems in chapter 5. For now, just remember that if we get eyeglasses, we see better *and* we don't have a headache. If we simply take aspirin, we get rid of the headache for a little while, but we never will be able to see clearly.

3-6 THE PROCESS OF CHOICE

In a sense, the *choice* phase of the problem-solving model stands at the zenith of the decision-making process. Simon suggests:

> The decision itself is the culmination of the process. Regardless of the problem, the alternatives, the decision aids, or the consequences to follow, once a decision is made, things begin to happen. Decisions trigger action, movement, and change. . . .

All of these images have a significant point in common. In them, the decision-maker is . . . at a moment of choice, ready to plant a foot on one or another of the routes that lead from the crossroads. All of the images falsify decision by focusing on its final moment. All of them ignore the lengthy, complex process of alerting, exploring, and analyzing that precede that final moment. (1960, 1)

In other words, if we expend all of our energies focusing on the choice phase as our goal, we will not do justice to the entire process and will, most likely, not make a good decision. This is simply Simon's way of pointing out the importance of identifying the problem before trying to solve it.

The choice phase is principally focused on those decisions of the semistructured to unstructured type. Again, if a decision is highly structured, it's not much of a decision at all. Where there is true choice, there is uncertainty. The decision maker is faced with the selection of an alternative derived from a primarily judgmental decision strategy. Quantitative models can be used to compare and evaluate the alternatives and, in some cases, can reduce the level of uncertainty facing the decision maker. Nonetheless, in the end, the uncertainty is always present and the decision maker must make a choice in the face of it.

Normative versus Descriptive Choice

It is important to understand the difference between the *normative* and *descriptive,* or *behavioral,* approaches to decision making. In the normative approach, choice is a theory in and of itself, whereas in the behavioral approach, choice is simply a step within a process. This distinction is crucial to the successful design and use of a DSS. Theories of choice make the assumption that future consequences are predictable to a degree of certainty and that the decision maker has to make a guess concerning the future preference of one of those consequences. Theories of choice address uncertainty simply by assigning a probability distribution to each of the future consequences. What these theories do not address, however, are the activities associated with framing, developing alternatives, determining goals and objectives, and implementing the decision once it has been made. Despite this seemingly narrow focus on the process, we must have a thorough understanding of the tools developed to assist in a normative decision-making approach because the use of a computer decision aid is implicitly a normative perspective. This does not suggest that a DSS cannot support a behavioral decision process, because it most certainly can. What it means is that the majority of the support within the capabilities of a modern DSS is distinctively normative in nature. Many of the other activities associated with a behavioral approach must often be supported by means other than the DSS itself. We will explore the advantages and limitations of these normative support approaches in greater detail in chapter 5.

Measurable Constraints

Another aspect of the choice phase that we must consider in the design of a DSS is that choice challenges the decision maker with a number of measurable constraints. Table 3-3 lists a number of characteristics that are generally associated with models of choice. Obstacles such as cognitive limitations, incomplete or inaccurate information,

Table 3-3 Common Characteristics of Models of Choice

- *Unfamiliarity.*   Degree to which decision task is foreign to decision maker
- *Ambiguity.*   Degree to which decision task is unclear to decision maker
- *Complexity.*   Number of different components to decision task
- *Instability.*   Degree to which decision components change during or after choice
- *Reversibility.*   Degree to which choice can be reversed if outcome appears undesirable
- *Significance.*   Importance of choice to both decision maker and the organization
- *Accountability.*   Degree to which decision maker is culpable for choice outcome
- *Time/Money.*   Constraints on decision process and solution set
- *Knowledge.*   Amount of relevant knowledge possessed by decision maker
- *Ability.*   Degree of intelligence and competence of decision maker
- *Motivation.*   Desire of decision maker to make a successful decision

Source: Adapted from Beach and Mitchell (1978).

time limitations, and cost restrictions all serve to bound the possible solution set during the choice phase. In addition, the decision maker is further constrained by his or her own psychological makeup. Stress, perceived commitment to a course of action, fear of failure or reprisal, and personal biases further exacerbate the constraints of the choice process. "There can be little doubt that human frailty pervades the act of choice and renders the entire decision-making process amenable to scrutiny and question at virtually every point" (Harrison 1995, 58).

3-7 COGNITIVE PROCESSES

We have touched on many *cognitive processes* so far but need to focus a bit more on several of them. Remember, one of the primary reasons a decision maker needs a DSS in the first place is because the cognitive processes of human decision makers are limited in many ways. The successful design and implementation of a DSS depends to a great extent on our complete understanding of the cognitive processes in place during decision-making activities.

Cognitive Limitations

Table 3-4 contains a list of many of the psychological factors that have been determined through research to contribute to the cognitive limits of the human decision maker.

As can be seen from the list of factors, the decision maker faces a formidable task if he or she is to overcome, or at least compensate for, these cognitive limitations. It appears that the typical decision maker uses many techniques that do not fall within the normative concept of choosing an ideal alternative. Probably the most important technique associated with attempting to overcome cognitive complexity is the natural tendency to strive for *simplification*.

Any constraint on an activity, no matter what the context, serves to increase the complexity of the activity and can normally be expected to increase the effort neces-

Table 3-4 Factors Contributing to Cognitive Limitations

- Humans can retain only a few bits of information in short-term memory.
- Decision makers display different types and degrees of intelligence.
- Decision makers that embrace closed belief systems tend to inordinately restrict information search.
- Decision makers that employ a concrete thinking approach tend to be limited information processors.
- Propensity for risk varies among decision makers. Risk takers require less information than risk avoiders.
- Decision maker's level of aspiration is positively correlated with desire for information.
- In general, older decision makers appear to be more limited than younger ones.

Source: From Harrison (1995).

sary to complete it successfully. Cutting a large tree down in the middle of a forest or a pasture is significantly easier than cutting the same tree down next to a house. The very existence of the house serves as a significant constraint with regard to how one might go about cutting down the tree. If knowledge and analysis prevail, then the tree will come down only if there is a feasible method of preventing any damage to the house. Otherwise, the tree stays put. In most cases, a method can be designed to reach the objective within the confines of the situation, but that method may radically depart from the normal, and probably easier, method. If knowledge and analysis do not prevail, however, the tree may still come down, but the chances of damage to the house are large. In this case, the decision maker may attempt to relieve some of the cognitive pressure associated with the problem by simplifying the situation. In essence, he or she may simply "wish" the house away.

The previous example is not as far-fetched as it may seem. Cognitive limitations can often cause a decision maker to seek a way to simplify a decision context until it displays a reasonable and more manageable level of complexity. One method of accomplishing this is to create a *simplified model of reality*. Once this model of reality is constructed, the decision maker can focus attention on solving the problem represented by the model rather than the one represented by reality. If the simplified model accurately represents the salient characteristics of the problem then this strategy should result in an acceptable decision. If, however, as is often the case, this simplified model of reality has been constructed in such a way that several subtle, yet salient, factors have been left out, then the probability of a successful outcome markedly decreases. At this point, one might wonder how any rational person could ignore a house that stands in the way of a falling tree. In section 3-8, we will see exactly how this seemingly irrational behavior can take place. For the moment, believe that it can, and does, happen.

Perception

Perception is a special kind of cognitive limitation. Decision makers tend to act upon what they can "see." This form of "selective discrimination" applied to the structure of a particular decision context may effectively limit the decision-making process. It is, however, through perception that the degree of constraint or limitation imposed by an internal or external force gains its significance.

Perception is key to the decision-making process because it is the "filter" through which all facts must pass. Once the facts pass through the perception filter, they emerge as much more aligned with the decision maker's version of reality. In other words, reality is what one perceives it to be. This filtering of facts can result in a decision that is based on the perceived reality of a problem context rather than its true structure. Depending upon the degree to which the decision maker "filters" reality, the perception of a given problem-solving context may be significantly distorted. When this happens, successful decision outcomes become questionable.

A number of factors go to make up a decision maker's perceptual filter. The most common factor is simply the uniqueness of the decision maker him- or herself. Perception is the cumulative result of experience, personal frame of reference, goals, values, beliefs, motivations, and instinctive biases. In addition, a person's cognitive limitations often extend to his or her inability to accurately perceive a situation at all. These *perceptual blocks* can serve as filters that are almost impermeable to the facts. Table 3-5 lists several perceptual blocks.

One of the most common perceptual blocks is the inability of the decision maker to isolate the problem at hand. Often the complexity of the symptoms makes it difficult to identify the underlying problem. Without a structured approach to the collection and organization of symptoms the problem may likely go undetected. If we can't isolate the problem, we can't solve it.

Bounded rationality is another form of perceptual block. In attempting to make the problem conform to a preconceived notion of reality a decision maker can blind him- or herself to potential solutions to the problem that deviate from the expected solution. This perceptual block is often referred to as "thinking inside the box." Adams's (1979) classic nine-dot puzzle serves as an excellent vehicle for demonstrating this. Figure 3-5 shows the initial layout of the puzzle.

The problem is to find a solution whereby, *without lifting your pencil from the page,* you draw no more than four straight lines that connect all nine dots. At the end of this chapter you will find the "standard" solution to this problem as well as a number of extremely creative solutions collected by Adams over the years.

So what does this puzzle have to do with perceptual blocks and DSS design? Decision makers often impose constraints or rules on a problem that do not exist in reality. In doing so, they create artificial boundaries on the solution set and the range of

Table 3-5 Common Perceptual Blocks

- Difficulty in isolating the problem
- Delimiting the problem space too closely
- Inability to see the problem from various perspectives
- Stereotyping
- Cognitive saturation or overload

Source: From Clemen (1991).

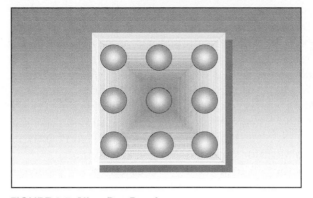

FIGURE 3-5 Nine-Dot Puzzle

Source: J Adams, *Conceptual Blockbusting,* (pages 24 and 25). © 1986 by James L. Adams. Reprinted by permission of Addison Wesley Longman.

potential solutions becomes severely limited. As you can see by the common solution offered to this problem, one must be sure not to create tacit or unspoken constraints if the problem is to be effectively solved. DSS design must acknowledge the common propensity of the user to impose artificial constraints and must be designed so that real constraints are recognized and artificial or self-imposed constraints are questioned. Chapter 15 will focus more on this topic.

Yet another perceptual block is the practice of *stereotyping*. We all do it to some degree and it acts as a barrier to seeing the true facts of any situation. Suppose, for instance, that you are a passenger in the first-class cabin of a commercial aircraft. You are sitting quietly reading a magazine, enjoying a refreshment, and occasionally gazing out the window at the serenity of the clouds and sky above and below you. You haven't a care in the world and you feel quite safe knowing the pilot is a professional and highly trained individual. In fact, you recall being impressed with how smooth the takeoff and climb to cruising altitude were compared to other flights you have taken.

Suddenly, you look up and notice the cabin attendant speaking with a man chewing on a toothpick dressed in blue jeans and a tee shirt. His hair is shoulder length and he is wearing two hoop earrings on one earlobe. The attendant appears to be focused on his every word and smiles respectfully as he opens the door to the flight deck and disappears. Your curiosity takes over. You immediately motion to the flight attendant and inquire as to the man's identity. "Why that's Captain Conway," replies the flight attendant. "He is one of our most experienced pilots. It's always a delight to be assigned to his crew," he continues. Just what are you thinking and feeling at that moment?

The true facts of the situation are that Captain Conway is an experienced pilot and his demonstration of that ability up to that moment was truly exemplary. So what's the problem? The problem is that the persona of Captain Conway is not what you expected it to be and, because of this single incident you begin to question all of the facts associated with the pilot. Granted, a commercial airline pilot is expected to be in uniform and well-groomed, but the fact that he isn't doesn't change the reality of the situation; you are under the care of a highly skilled, professional aviator. Stereotyping is simply a self-imposed perceptual barrier to reality.

Judgment

Although numerous strategies exist with regard to the comparison and evaluation of solution alternatives, *judgment* often appears to be the most favorable. Using judgment, the decision maker makes a choice based upon experience, values, perception, and intuition. One reason for its favor is that when compared to detailed analysis, judgment is much faster, more convenient, and less stressful. When properly applied in harmony with other selection strategies, judgment is a meaningful and useful tool in the choice process and can contribute significantly to decision quality. When applied in isolation, however, judgment is nothing more than a guess.

One of the primary reasons judgment cannot be used exclusively in the choice process is that it relies heavily on the decision maker's recollection and recognition of events. If the situation allows for accurate recall of experiences and a factual identification of the current set of events with those experienced in the past then judgment will be effective in determining the appropriate choice. If, as is more often the case, recollection is "blurred" by cognitive limitations then judgment becomes flawed and other analytic strategies must be employed to confirm or deny the decision maker's judgment. Table 3-6 lists several ways that cognitive limitations can affect judgment.

In the next section, we will explore various biases and heuristics that are often inherent in a decision maker's strategies and that can contribute to "errors" in perception and/or judgment.

3-8 BIASES AND HEURISTICS IN DECISION MAKING

Heuristic Search and the "Rule of Thumb" Approach

No matter what the situation, no matter who we are, no matter how well-trained we become in decision making and problem solving, we have certain "rules of thumb" that we rely on in making decisions. "It never rains here on the 4th of July," or "Only buy stocks with a price/earnings ratio of less than 9," or "Professors never cover anything important on the first day of class" are all examples of rules of thumb that we use when making decisions. Another term for such "rules" is *heuristics*. The word *heuristic* comes from the Greek word for "discovery." This derivation is appropriate because heuristics are often developed through trial-and-error experience that, over time, is subjected to a wide variety of analysis and experimentation. If a heuristic is

---

Table 3-6 Ways in Which Cognitive Limitations Can Affect Judgment

- Judgment is more dependent on preconceptions and bias than relevant new information
- Intuitive judgments are often misleading
- Availability is an intuitive judgment about the frequency of events or proportion of objects (see section 3-8)
- Representation attempts to classify concepts and is often illusory
- Judgmental fixation describes the anchoring of an individual regarding consequences

Source: From Clough (1984).

well tested and thought out it can serve as a reliable tool for reducing the search process to more manageable levels. This approach is referred to as *heuristic search* or *heuristic programming.* This type of search process tends to follow a series of steps based upon the "rules" known to the decision maker until a satisfactory solution is found. Such searches are often less costly and more efficient than a completely blind search where all alternatives are tested in the order of discovery. Moreover, several researchers, such as Zanakis and Evans (1981), have shown that heuristic searches can provide solutions very close to those produced by a comprehensive blind search. Table 3-7 lists the major advantages associated with the use of heuristics as well as situations where the use of heuristics may be more appropriate than an optimization strategy.

A common problem used to demonstrate combinatorial complexity also serves as an excellent example of a heuristic solution strategy: the problem of the traveling salesman.

The nature of the problem is rather simple. A traveling salesman must visit customers in several cities across the country. Because of policies relating to efficiency and cost restriction for travel he can only visit each city once during his trip and he must visit all the cities along his route before returning to his home base. Because his costs are primarily associated with the total distance traveled, the solution should be one where the policies of the company are followed and the route taken is the shortest possible route. Sounds simple enough, doesn't it?

Figure 3-6 depicts the cities in which the salesman has customers and the distances between each city.

The complexity of the problem increases as the number of cities increases. If we assume a route to go only in a single direction (because of the rule of not visiting the

Table 3-7 Advantages and Appropriate Uses of Heuristics in Problem Solving

Advantages of Heuristic Use
- Simple to understand
- Easy to implement
- Requires less conception time
- Requires less cognitive effort (human) or less CPU time (computer)
- Can produce multiple solutions

Appropriate Uses of Heuristics
- The input data are inexact or limited
- The computation time for an optimal solution is excessive
- Problems are being solved frequently and repeatedly and consume unnecessary time
- Symbolic rather than numerical processing is involved
- Simulation models are oversimplified when compared to problem complexity
- A reliable, exact method is not readily available
- The efficiency of an optimization process can be improved by good starting solutions
- The optimization is not economically feasible

Source: From Zanakis and Evans (1981).

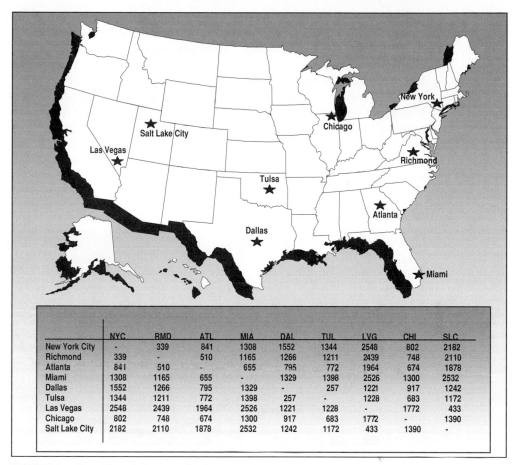

	NYC	RMD	ATL	MIA	DAL	TUL	LVG	CHI	SLC
New York City	-	339	841	1308	1552	1344	2548	802	2182
Richmond	339	-	510	1165	1266	1211	2439	748	2110
Atlanta	841	510	-	655	795	772	1964	674	1878
Miami	1308	1165	655	-	1329	1398	2526	1300	2532
Dallas	1552	1266	795	1329	-	257	1221	917	1242
Tulsa	1344	1211	772	1398	257	-	1228	683	1172
Las Vegas	2548	2439	1964	2526	1221	1228	-	1772	433
Chicago	802	748	674	1300	917	683	1772	-	1390
Salt Lake City	2182	2110	1878	2532	1242	1172	433	1390	-

FIGURE 3-6 Traveling Salesman Problem — Cities to Visit

same city twice) then the total number of unique routes can be determined by the following formula:[6]

$$\text{number of unique routes} = 0.5 \, (\text{number of cities} - 1)!$$

If the number of cities is 9, as shown in the figure, then the total number of routes is 20,160. If we increase the number of cities by 1 to 10 cities, the number of routes jumps to 181,440. Adding only 1 additional city raises the total to over 1.8 million and with 12 cities the number jumps to just under 20 million possible routes. Even with a computer the solution to this problem becomes time consuming and difficult. One method of finding the solution is a quantitatively based method known as *branch and bound*.[7] This

---

[6] Note that "!" indicates a factorial mathematical operation. $5! = 5 \times 4 \times 3 \times 2 \times 1 = 120$.

[7] Branch and bound is a general search method. The method starts by considering the original problem bounded by a feasible region. A search for an optimal solution continues by repeatedly subdividing the originally bounded region into bounded subregions until either a solution is found or all possibilities have been exhausted.

method, although effective, is not necessarily efficient for combinations of any significant magnitude. This problem can be satisfactorily solved by following a heuristic. One heuristic might be the following: "Starting from your home base, go to the closest city. Continue going to the closest city until the last city is visited. Then return to your home base." Figure 3-7 shows the solution derived from following this heuristic.

As you can see, the solution seems to be relatively reasonable and acceptable although we do seem to "pass by" cities we have already visited (see the routes from Miami to Chicago or Salt Lake City to New York City, for instance). What if we modify our heuristic to the following: "Always follow an exterior route so that a connection between two cities is never crossed and no backtracking is performed." Figure 3-8 shows the derived solution based on this modification.

FIGURE 3-7 Initial Heuristic Solution

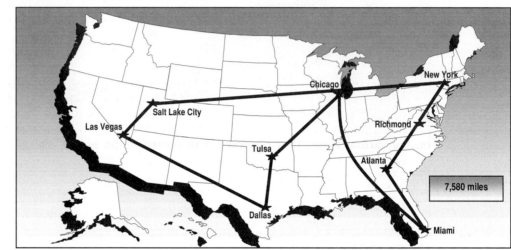

FIGURE 3-8 Modified Heuristic Solution

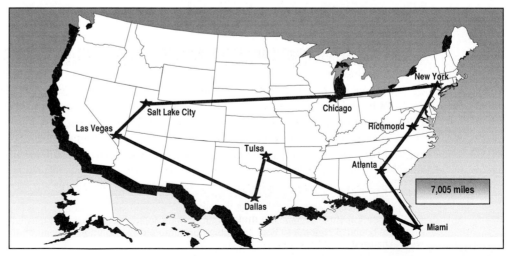

With a single modification we have improved upon our first solution by 575 miles. More important, we didn't have to test all 20,160 solutions to find an acceptable one. This is but one example that, when employed properly, heuristics are a valuable problem-solving tool.

Heuristic Bias

In some situations, however, the use of heuristics can be detrimental to finding an effective solution. Geoffrion and Van Roy (1979) explain:

> Commonsense approaches and heuristics can fail because they are often arbitrary. They are arbitrary in the choice of a starting point, in the sequence in which assignments or other decision choices are made, in the resolution of ties, in the choice of criteria for specifying the procedure, in the level of effort expended to demonstrate that the final solution is in fact best or nearly so. The result is erratic and unpredictable behavior—good performance in some specific applications and bad in others. (p. 117)

The bottom line seems to be that the typical decision maker develops a set of simplified models of reality in the form of decision heuristics and then relies upon that set of rules to make the decisions at hand. If the rules are arbitrarily developed, as suggested by Geoffrion and Van Roy, then less than stellar solutions will result.

In the early 1970s Tversky and Kahneman published a series of papers focusing on the various biases they observed with regard to the use of arbitrarily developed heuristics. Their results show that decision makers tend to rely on a limited set of heuristic principles that often lead to severe and systematic errors in their thinking. Table 3-8 contains a description of common biases demonstrated by individual decision makers.

Of the extensive list of biases and heuristics developed by Tversky and Kahneman four of the most common categories are: (1) availability, (2) adjustment and anchoring, (3) representativeness, and (4) motivational. Each of these categories is relevant to the design and use of an effective DSS.

Table 3-8 Common Biases of Individual Decision Makers

- They tend to overestimate low probabilities and underestimate high probabilities
- They appear to be insensitive to the true sample size of their observations
- They adjust their first estimate incrementally based on additional evidence
- They tend toward overconfidence in their ability to estimate probabilities
- They tend to overestimate the ability of others to estimate probabilities
- They tend to compare pairs of alternatives rather than a whole list
- They tend to minimize reliance on explicit trade-offs or other numerical computations
- They often exhibit choices that are inconsistent
- They tend toward viewing mutually exclusive events

Source: Adapted from Harrison (1995).

Availability

The *availability bias* is the result of the typical individual's inability to accurately assess the probability of a particular event occurring. Individuals tend to assess an event's probability based upon past experience, which may not be representative. In other words, we tend to judge the probability of an event occurring according to the ease with which we can recall the last time it occurred. Before Hurricane Andrew hit in August of 1992 (see Figure 3-9), most individuals (including myself), and even most insurance companies, grossly underestimated the probability of total devastation of the magnitude that Andrew produced. I would have estimated that the probability of losing everything I owned was very small. And it very well might have been. Despite my low probability estimate I insured my house and belongings to their fullest value. The day after Andrew struck I realized that the chances of losing everything had suddenly risen to 100 percent! The insurance companies suddenly realized it, too, much to their dismay. The point is that all of the estimates were based upon the recollection of the last time a storm of that magnitude had occurred. In my case, it was never. Even in the case of most native Floridians it was never. Nonetheless, it did happen and only a very few were close to being prepared.

A subset of the availability bias is the bias of *illusory correlation.* In this case, an individual decision maker inappropriately assumes that because two events appear to have occurred frequently in relation to each other, then they must be strongly correlated. During late 1996 and early 1997 a large number of black churches were the sites of apparent arson. It seemed obvious that these fires were all related, yet after a thorough investigation no evidence of relationship could be established. Several individuals were apprehended and judged to be guilty of the crime of arson, yet no relationship among them could be demonstrated. In fact, several of the fires were later determined not to be the result of arson at all. In other words, the evidence suggested that the fires were not correlated, at least not in the sense that they were set by the same person or group of people. Illusory correlation can serve to bias a search process for an appropriate solution.

Reduction of the availability bias can be effected through a structured review and analysis of objective data. In the absence of such data, a decision maker can at least attempt to honestly assess the potential bias in his or her recollections and then adjust the estimate up or down accordingly. In any event, support for a decision process must include provisions for the identification and control of availability and illusory correlation wherever reasonable.

Adjustment and Anchoring

People often make estimates by choosing an initial starting value and then adjusting this starting point up or down until they arrive at a final estimate. Unfortunately, people have a tendency to underestimate the need for adjustments and to remain biased, or *anchored,* to their original starting estimate. For example, an individual might estimate the number of people in attendance at an event to be 22,000. This starting value may be based upon observation or logic such as knowing how many seats exist at the location and then estimating the percentage of empty seats. Or it may be based on a number that appeared to the decision maker to be representative

FIGURE 3-9 Damage Caused by Hurricane Andrew in August 1992.

of the number of people in attendance. In either case, any change in the estimate will be made in the form of an increase or decrease from that initial starting point, or 22,000, and will tend to be biased toward it. Because of this tendency to underadjust, most subjectively derived probability distributions are too narrow and fail to estimate the true variance of the event.

One method a DSS might employ to minimize error from this bias is to require the user to assess the intervals associated with more than one point. Instead of assessing the variability from a single point, say the mean, a DSS asks the user to assess an interval from the 0.05 fractile to the 0.95 fractile.[8] Implicit in this single estimate is the fact that the true value may lie outside the ends of the interval. Then the DSS asks the user to estimate the quartiles (0.25 to 0.75).[9] The combination of these estimates is then used as a method of determining a midpoint of final estimate. Accuracy can be improved in this manner by assisting the user to avoid anchoring on a central value where possible.

Representativeness

A third common heuristic bias, *representativeness,* is quite similar to the bias of illusory correlation. Decision makers often attempt to ascertain the probability that a person or object belongs to a particular group or class by the degree to which characteristics of the person or object conform to a stereotypical perception of members of that group or class. The closer the similarity between the two, the higher the estimated probability is of one being associated with the other. Tversky and Kahneman offer a simple problem as evidence of the effect of representativeness. Consider the following:

> "Tom W. is of high intelligence, although lacking in true creativity. He has a need for order and clarity, and for neat and tidy systems in which every detail finds its appropriate place. His writing is rather dull and mechanical, occasionally enlivened by somewhat corny puns and by flashes of imagination of the sci-fi type. He has a strong drive for competence. He seems to have little feeling and little sympathy for other people and does not enjoy interacting with others. Self-centered, he nonetheless has a deep moral sense."
>
> The preceding personality sketch of Tom W. was written during his senior year in high school by a psychologist on the basis of projective tests. Tom W. is now a graduate student. Please rank order the following nine fields of graduate specialization by the likelihood that Tom W. is now a graduate student in each of these fields:
>
> (a) Business Administration (b) Computer Science
> (c) Engineering (d) Humanities and Education
> (e) Law (f) Library Science
> (g) Medicine (h) Physical and Life Sciences
> (i) Social Science
>
> (Adapted from Tversky and Kahneman 1973)

The usual classification for Tom W. is based on the subjective assessment that he is a "nerd." As such, most people tend to classify him either in Computer Science or

---

[8] An *interval* is the mathematical distance between any two points on a line or numbers in a list. A *fractile* is an interval defined as a fraction or proportion of a list.

[9] The first *quartile* of a list is a number such that one-quarter of the numbers in the list are below it. The third quartile has three quarters of the numbers below it and the second quartile (also referred to as the median) has half the numbers above it and below it.

Engineering. If, however, we use a different method of determination, say the base rates of graduate students in a particular discipline, we might come to a completely different conclusion. The fact is, despite the popularity of the two fields mentioned above, there are many more graduate students in Humanities and Education or Social Science than in either Computer Science or Engineering. Simply stated, the probability of Tom W. being in either field (d) or (i) is greater than for fields (b) or (c). Failing to consider base rates in favor of representativeness can have a detrimental effect on a decision outcome.

Another form of this bias is commonly referred to as *gambler's fallacy* or *insensitivity to sample size*. In this case, individuals draw conclusions of probability from highly representative small samples despite their extreme sensitivity to statistical error. Take the case of the man standing next to the roulette wheel at a casino. You approach the table and the man turns to you and whispers, "Put everything on black!" You ask why you should do this, and the man replies, "Listen friend, I have been standing here for the last half hour and red has come up fifteen times in a row. C'mon man, black is due!"

His mistake is twofold. First, our friend is failing to realize that the spin of a roulette wheel (assuming it is fair) is an event independent from either the previous or subsequent spins. Given this, the number of times red has come up in a row has nothing to do with the probability of either red or black occurring again. Second, he is basing a probability estimate on a small sample size. We know from the laws of probability that if the roulette wheel is spun a large number of times the true probabilities of each occurrence will be manifest. Small samples can be highly biased above or below their true mean.

Yet another form of representativeness bias is failure to recognize *regression to the mean*. Tversky and Kahneman relate an anecdote to illustrate this bias. They recall a flight instructor who always made it a point to praise a student for a good landing and to reprimand a student for a poor landing. The instructor began to notice that when a student was praised, the next landing was not as good. When, however, a student was reprimanded the next landing was much improved. The instructor concluded that a reprimand was an effective form of feedback whereas a compliment was not.

The instructor's conclusion was clearly in error. When a phenomenon is random, then extreme examples tend to be followed by less extreme ones. This is because the true mean lies somewhere between the two examples and the laws of probability suggest that given enough trials the true mean will be realized. So an extremely good landing will probably be followed by one that is not so good and an extremely bad landing (not too bad, we hope) will tend to be followed by a better one.

Motivational

So far, the biases discussed have been related to each other by their cognitive roots. They are all rooted in the way an individual processes information received during the course of problem solving. There is, however, a noncognitive bias that can have dramatic effects on solution outcomes. Incentives, either real or perceived, often lead the decision maker to estimate probabilities that do not accurately reflect his or her true beliefs. These are referred to as *motivational biases*. The estimates derived under the conditions of a motivational bias often reflect the personal interests of the decision maker who is providing them. Such estimates can also come from an information provider that is thought to be an expert in a particular field. In that case, the decision maker must be aware of the potential for motivational bias and must decide how much credence to give the expert's estimates.

Motivational biases can manifest themselves in a number of scenarios. For example, a salesperson may be required to provide a monthly sales forecast indicating expected sales productivity. A motivational bias may cause the saleperson's estimate to be lower than reality so that when the forecast is exceeded it looks like the salesperson performed exceptionally well. In another example, evidence suggests that weather forecasters tend to report that the chances of rain are slightly higher than the true probability. This bias has been shown to exist primarily at the subconscious level. It is thought that weather forecasters subconsciously would rather prepare people for bad weather and have them be pleasantly surprised by the sunshine than have them expect good weather and be disappointed.

This type of bias may be the most difficult to address through the design of a DSS. One possible method would be to have the DSS solicit a number of estimates from similar sources both related to and unrelated to the problem context. Given enough information, the user may be able to detect motivational bias in a trend associated with estimates obtained from related parties that does not exist from unrelated sources. While this approach is not foolproof, it may heighten the awareness of the decision maker to the potential of motivational biases.

3-9 EFFECTIVENESS AND EFFICIENCY

In chapter 1, we learned that a major goal of a DSS is to improve the effectiveness of decision outcomes. This is probably the most important claim in the entire body of DSS literature. A close second is the desire to improve the efficiency of the decision-making process for a given context. These two concepts, although complementary in nature, are nonetheless distinct and often are in conflict with each other in the design and implementation of a DSS. Distinguishing between the two concepts is imperative to fully understand their impact on the usefulness of a DSS.

Effectiveness in decision making is focused on *what* should be done, whereas *efficiency* is focused on *how* we should do it. To be effective requires careful consideration of the various criteria influencing the decision at hand. If we are to design a DSS that can assist in increasing the decision maker's effectiveness, we must uncover his or her perception of the decision context. In contrast, improving efficiency implies focusing only on issues that will minimize completion time, cost, or effort. Often a tension exists between the two goals because an increased focus on one can result in a reduction of the other. Keen and Scott Morton provide a good example of the distinction between effectiveness and efficiency:

> A company's computer center . . . proudly boasts of its efficiency: it generates more output—management reports—than almost any other center in the country. The computer downtime is low and the machine is fully utilized, with minimal idle time. Inputs are quickly processed and outputs are delivered promptly. Un-

fortunately, the reports produced are not seen as useful by their recipients. Managers instruct their secretaries either to file the hundred-page summary of last month's operations unread or to throw it in the wastebasket. The center is *efficient* in its pursuit of an *ineffective* goal [emphasis added]. (Keen and Scott Morton 1978, 7)

Table 3-9 shows some outcomes from the use of a DSS categorized by their contribution to *efficiency* and *effectiveness*.

The primary difference between the two goals is that effectiveness requires constant adaptation, learning, and rethinking, often at the risk of slow progress and many false starts, whereas efficiency simply focuses on more economical ways of doing the same thing. A good example of the tension between the two can often be seen in the research and development (R&D) function in an organization. R&D can be argued to be a grossly *inefficient* expenditure of resources for the purpose of providing future effectiveness. R&D could be eliminated because it is not needed to perform any current operational tasks, and its elimination would have a significantly favorable impact on the current year's profits. If the scale is tipped in favor of efficiency then this argument is virtually irrefutable. If, however, effectiveness is the goal, then the elimination of R&D could be the death of the organization. In the interest of effectiveness, efficiency must often be sacrificed. It becomes a significant task for the DSS designer to create the appropriate balance between these two, often conflicting, goals. Heuristically speaking, the more unstable the environment, the more the focus is on effectiveness. If the environment is stable, then a company can focus its attention on performing next year's operation more efficiently than it did this year's. In the years to come managers will find their focus increasingly favoring effectiveness over efficiency. And the DSS will become a primary tool in support of that focus.

3-10 CHAPTER SUMMARY

This chapter discusses the processes involved in making a decision. The difficulty in programming a decision bears a relationship to its structuredness. Easy (structured) decisions involve repetitive and routine procedures. On the other hand, a decision is

Table 3-9 Contributions to Effectiveness and Efficiency from DSS Use

Effectiveness
- Easier access to relevant information
- Faster and more efficient problem recognition and identification
- Easier access to computing tools and proven models to compute choice criteria
- Greater ability to generate and evaluate large choice sets

Efficiency
- Reduction in decision costs
- Reduction in decision time for same level of detail in the analysis
- Better quality in feedback supplied to the decision maker

difficult, or unstructured, when cognitive limitations and relative uncertainty cloud the decision-making process. When random factors lead to an indeterminable outcome, the accuracy of the pending decision is often askew.

Decisions can be classified by type: activity-based, negotiation-based, or strategy-based. Activity-based decisions are decisions that focus attention on the activity with which the decision is most associated. Negotiation-based decisions are classified into three types based on the notion of negotiation. Finally, strategy-based decisions are differentiated based on the primary strategy used in making the final choice.

The process of making a decision is complex and often unclear to even the most proficient decision makers. Being aware of the natural barriers to effective decision making can help to improve both the process and its associated outcomes.

Key Concepts

- The difficulties of decision making (3-1)

  The difficulties associated with making a decision lie in a variety of structural, psychological, physical, and environmental areas:

    Problem structuredness

    Cognitive limitations

    Uncertainty of decision outcomes

    Alternatives and multiple objectives

- A typology of decisions (3-2)

  By gaining a better understanding of the classification of the decisions being faced in a given context, we can better determine what specific features of a DSS would be useful in support.

  Negotiation-based decision

    Routine decisions

    Creative decisions

    Negotiated decisions

  Activity-based decisions

    Entrepreneurial activities

    Adaptive activities

    Planning activities

  Strategy-based decisions

    Computational strategies

    Judgmental strategies

    Compromise strategies

    Inspirational strategies

  Metaclassification

    All decisions can be further classified into one of two categories:

Decisions of a routine, recurring nature with high certainty

Decisions of a nonroutine, nonrecurring nature with high uncertainty

- The design and implementation of a DSS is rooted in the development of a workable and sound descriptive theory. (3-3)

Simon's problem-solving model (3-3)

Intelligence

Problem perception and definition process

Design

Alternatives formation and analysis

Problem strategy selection and analysis

Choice

Alternatives selection process

- Optimization is considered a rational decision-making behavior that suggests that the decision maker will choose the alternative that is clearly the best one providing the best overall value and outcome. (3-4)

- Satisficing strategy (3-5)

Decision makers tend to find the first acceptable solution that meets their preconceived notion instead of looking for the optimal one.

- Bounded Rationality (3-5)

Bounded by their cognitive limitations, decision makers make rational decisions that are bounded by uncontrollable constraints.

The confusion between a symptom and a problem, one issue of bounded rationality, can have a debilitating effect on the decision-making process. The difference between a problem and its related symptoms lies in the results associated with its elimination: (3-5)

The treatment of a symptom results in the elimination of the symptom but does not result in the removal of the problem.

The elimination of the root problem results in not only the removal of the problem but the exclusion of its associated symptoms.

- One of the primary reasons for a decision maker needing a DSS is because the cognitive processes of human decision makers are limited in many ways: (3-7)

Perception

Perception is the cumulative result of experience, personal frame of reference, goals, values, beliefs, motivations, and instinctive biases. Common perceptual blocks include difficulty in isolating the problem, bounded rationality, and stereotyping.

Judgment

Using judgment, decision makers make a choice selection based upon experience, values, perception, and intuition. When judgment is applied in isolation, it is nothing more than a guess with often little basis in reality.

- Decision makers tend to rely on a limited set of heuristic principles when making decisions. Biases will be introduced if these rules of commonsense approaches and heuristics are arbitrarily developed. Four of the most common heuristic biases are: availability, adjustment and anchoring, representativeness, and motivational. (3-8)

- It is a significant task for DSS designers to create a balance between the two, often conflicting, goals of a DSS: (3-9)

   Effectiveness

   With constant adaptation, learning, and rethinking, decision makers focus on the improvement of decision outcome.

   Efficiency

   By using more economical ways, decision makers focus on the improvement of the decision-making process for a given context.

Questions for Review

1. State the difficulties of decision making from the perspective of problem structuredness.
2. Why is the understanding of a decision typology so important to the design of a DSS?
3. Describe the activity-based typology of decisions. Give an example of each class.
4. Briefly describe the components of Simon's problem-solving model.
5. Is it possible to make an optimal decision? Why or why not?
6. What is satisficing?
7. Why is the concept of bounded rationality important to the decision process?
8. What is the difference between a problem and a symptom?
9. What is the impact of confusing a problem and a symptom during the decision-making process?
10. What are the dangers associated with simplifying a decision context?
11. Describe the effect of a decision maker's perception decision making.
12. What is the effect of a decision maker's judgment on decision making?
13. What are the benefits of using a heuristic search (heuristic programming) approach?
14. Define heuristic bias.
15. List and briefly describe the four most common heuristic biases.
16. Compare and contrast the concepts of effectiveness and efficiency.

For Further Discussion

1. You are about to buy a car. Using Simon's problem-solving model, list your activities in each phase.
2. Assume that you are going to make a decision about the price of a new product. Use the typologies described in this chapter to classify this decision. State any assumptions if needed.
3. Give an example of the concept of bounded rationality from your own experience.
4. Analyze a problem you have encountered recently. List the symptoms and classify the cause(s) of these symptoms. So what exactly was the problem?

5. Analyze the cognitive limitations you experience during your decision making. Can a DSS help? If yes, how can it help?

6. Make a list of heuristics that are used regularly by someone in your family, school, or company.

7. Analyze a bad decision made by an organization. Discuss the reasons why it failed. Was the failure related to the cognitive limitations or heuristic biases of the decision maker?

Answers to Nine-Dot Problem

The common solution to the puzzle is shown in the figure on the left. The figure on the right shows an alternate three-line solution.

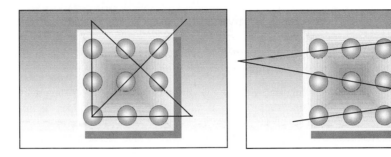

Other solutions that have been collected by Adams include the following:

- Fold the paper so that the dots line up in a row. Then a single straight line can be drawn through the dots.
- Roll up the paper and tape the ends together so that a spiral can be drawn through all the dots.
- Cut the paper into strips and tape them together so that the dots are in a single row.
- Draw very small dots close together in a square pattern and then draw a single fat line through all of them at once. This solution was provided by a 10-year-old girl.

Source: J Adams, *Conceptual Blockbusting,* (pages 24 and 25). © 1986 by James L. Adams. Reprinted by permission of Addison Wesley Longman.

CHAPTER

4

Decisions in the Organization

Learning Objectives

■ Learn the definition of an organization and the decision-making activities within an organization

■ Be familiar with the five dimensions of organizational decisions: group structure, group roles, group process, group style, and group norm

■ Understand the need for different types of support systems at different organizational decision levels

■ Comprehend the meaning of organizational culture and its influence over decision-making activities within an organization

■ Understand the relationship between organizational culture and the organization's ability to change

■ Learn the influence of power and politics on decision-making activities within an organization and comprehend their impact on the design and implementation of DSSs. Be familiar with the functionality of organizational decision support systems (ODSSs)

The Cuban Missile Crisis

On October 16, 1962, American aerial photoreconnaissance revealed that the Soviet Union had begun to construct missile bases and to place both medium-range (one thousand miles) and intermediate-range (two thousand miles) missiles on the island of Cuba, some ninety miles from the border of the United States. Still smarting from his administration's foreign policy fiasco at Cuba's Bay of Pigs, and fearing that unchecked Soviet interference in the Western Hemisphere would demolish American credibility worldwide, President John Kennedy resolved to respond strongly. After a week of intense secret discussions with his most trusted advisers, Kennedy issued an ultimatum to the Kremlin. The missiles, he demanded, must be removed immediately or the United States would impose a naval blockade to prevent the delivery of more missiles. Furthermore, the United States would dismantle the existing missiles in Cuba by force. This announcement alarmed both the nation and world. Never before had two superpowers appeared to be on a direct course toward a nuclear war. U.S. Secretary of State Dean Rusk reported, "We're eyeball to eyeball." The U.S. military advanced plans for the invasion of Cuba; however, the decision was made to resolve the crisis peacefully.

According to Soviet Premier Nikita Khrushchev's memoirs, in May 1962 he conceived the idea of placing intermediate-range nuclear missiles in Cuba as a means of countering an emerging lead of the United States in developing and deploying strategic missiles. He also presented the scheme as a means of protecting Cuba from another U.S.-sponsored invasion, such as the failed attempt at the Bay of Pigs in 1961.

After obtaining Fidel Castro's approval, the Soviet Union worked quickly and secretly to build missile installations in Cuba. On October 16, President Kennedy was shown reconnaissance photographs of Soviet missile installations under construction in Cuba. After seven days of guarded and intense debate in the U.S. administration, during which Soviet diplomats denied that installations for offensive missiles were being built in Cuba, Kennedy, in a televised address on October 22, announced the discovery of the installations and proclaimed that any nuclear missile attack from Cuba would be regarded as an attack by the Soviet Union and would be responded to accordingly. He also imposed a naval quarantine on Cuba to prevent further Soviet shipments of offensive military weapons.

During the crisis, the two sides exchanged many letters and other communications, both formal and "back channel." Khrushchev sent letters to Kennedy on October 23 and 24 indicating the deterrent nature of the missiles in Cuba and the peaceful intentions of the Soviet Union. On October 26, Khrushchev sent Kennedy a long rambling letter seemingly proposing that the missile installations would be dismantled and personnel removed in exchange for U.S. assurances that it or its proxies would not invade Cuba. On October 27, another letter arrived from Khrushchev, suggesting that missile installations in Cuba would be dismantled if the United States dismantled its missile installations in Turkey. The American administration decided to ignore this second letter and to accept the offer outlined in the letter of October 26. Khrushchev then announced on October 28 that he would dismantle the installations and return them to the Soviet Union, expressing his trust that the United States would not invade Cuba. Further negotiations were held to implement the October 28 agreement, including a U.S. demand that Soviet light bombers also be removed from Cuba, and to specify the exact form and conditions of U.S. assurances not to invade Cuba.

Following is Khrushchev's letter of October 24 to President Kennedy:

His Excellency
Mr. John F. Kennedy President of the United States of America
Washington

Dear Mr. President,

Imagine, Mr. President, what if we were to present to you such an ultimatum as you have presented to us by your actions. How would you react to it? I think you would be outraged at such a move on our part. And this we would understand.

Having presented these conditions to us, Mr. President, you have thrown down the gauntlet. Who asked you to do this? By what right have you done this? Our ties with the Republic of Cuba, as well as our relations with other nations, regardless of their political system, concern only the two countries between which these relations exist. And, if it were a matter of quarantine as mentioned in your letter, then, as is customary in international practice, it can be established only by states agreeing between themselves, and not by some third party. Quarantines exist, for example, on agricultural goods and products. However, in this case we are not talking about quarantines, but rather about much more serious matters, and you yourself understand this.

You, Mr. President, are not declaring a quarantine, but rather issuing an ultimatum, and you are threatening that if we do not obey your orders, you will then use force. Think about what you are saying! And you want to persuade me to agree to this! What does it mean to agree to these demands? It would mean for us to conduct our relations with other countries not by reason, but by yielding to tyranny. You are not appealing to reason; you want to intimidate us.

No, Mr. President, I cannot agree to this, and I think that deep inside, you will admit that I am right. I am convinced that if you were in my place you would do the same.

. . . This Organization [of American States] has no authority or grounds whatsoever to pass resolutions like those of which you speak in your letter. Therefore, we do not accept these resolutions. International law exists, generally accepted standards of conduct exist. We firmly adhere to the principles of international law and strictly observe the standards regulating navigation on the open sea, in international waters. We observe these standards and enjoy the rights recognized by all nations.

You want to force us to renounce the rights enjoyed by every sovereign state; you are attempting to legislate questions of international law; you are violating the generally accepted standards of this law. All this is due not only to hatred for the Cuban people and their government, but also for reasons having to do with the election campaign in the USA. What morals, what laws can justify such an approach by the American government to international affairs? Such morals and laws are not to be found, because the actions of the USA in relation to Cuba are outright piracy. This, if you will, is the madness of a degenerating imperialism. Unfortunately, people of all nations, and not least the American people themselves, could suffer heavily from madness such as this, since with the appearance of modern types of weapons, the USA has completely lost its former inaccessibility.

Therefore, Mr. President, if you weigh the present situation with a cool head without giving way to passion, you will understand that the Soviet Union cannot afford not to decline the despotic demands of the USA. When you lay conditions such as these before us, try to put yourself in our situation and consider how the USA would react to such conditions. I have no doubt that if anyone attempted to dictate similar conditions to you—the USA, you would reject such an attempt. And we likewise say—no.

The Soviet government considers the violation of the freedom of navigation in international waters and air space to constitute an act of aggression propelling humankind into the abyss of a world nuclear-missile war. Therefore, the Soviet government cannot instruct captains of Soviet ships bound for Cuba to observe orders of American naval forces blockading this island. Our instructions to Soviet sailors are to observe strictly the generally accepted standards of navigation in international waters and not retreat one step from them. And, if the American side violates these rights, it must be aware of the responsibility it will bear for this act. To be sure, we will not remain mere observers of pirate actions by American ships in the open sea. We will then be forced on our part to take those measures we deem necessary and sufficient to defend our rights. To this end we have all that is necessary.

Respectfully, /s/ N. Khrushchev
N. KHRUSHCHEV
Moscow 24 October 1962

4-1 UNDERSTANDING THE ORGANIZATION

Up to this point, the focus has been on two fairly microlevel concepts: the decision and the individual decision maker. Without a thorough understanding of these building blocks, no useful macrolevel perspective can be derived. In this chapter, the emphasis will shift from the micro to the macro perspective of decision making: the *organization*. Looking at the process from the top down allows us to see a distinctly different set of facets to the activities and characteristics of decision making and problem solving.

Textbooks on organizations abound with a variety of definitions for the term. Most formulations include some mention of *systematic patterns of interaction among various social entities with the intention of achieving some common purpose or goal.* The definition used in this text includes these common characteristics but has been broadened to include issues of structure, resources, politics, and the environment. For our purposes, an organization can be thought of as *a unified system of resources defined and structured by a collective of functional and political subsystems bound by a set of stated goals and functioning within a set of loosely defined environments.* Implicit in this definition is the assumption that the whole of an organization is greater than the sum of its parts; it thus allows its members collectively to pursue and achieve greater goals than they could by acting individually. Using this definition, we will look at the various aspects of decision making and decision support necessary for the operationalization of this implied synergy.

A "Nexus of Decisions"

Stohr and Konsynski (1992) suggest that it is useful to view an organization as a "nexus of decisions." The organization's purpose is to make decisions within a business environment; it is defined by its decision opportunities, authorities, and responsibilities. In this perspective, decisions and decision making are the true essence of the organization and serve as identifiers of its boundaries, policies, procedures, customs, and theater of operations. Note, however, that this view is independent of the physical manifestation of the individual decision makers that make up the organization. Here, the organization can be made up of a complex network of individuals, teams, groups, and computerized decision support systems. How this all fits together is the subject of this chapter.

Dimensions of Organizational Decisions

If we dissect the definition of organization offered above, several factors can be identified. Figure 4-1 depicts five dimensions that can affect both the kinds of decisions made in the organization and the methods necessary to make them effectively.

Group Structure

We discussed briefly in chapter 2 the concept of decision-making structure. In this sense, we are focusing on the relationships between the point of decision (the person or persons who ultimately make the decision) and the participants in the decision-making process. If the decision maker acts alone and does not work with any formal participants other than independent or third-party information sources then the structure can be thought of as *individual.* If the decision maker retains sole responsibility and authority to make the decision at hand but employs a formal group of people with defined roles who act in harmony to provide information and/or services to the decision maker, then the structure is more representative of the *team* approach. Finally, if a formal group of individuals is charged with the responsibility and authority to make a decision, but no single member of the assemblage has any more or less decision-making authority than any other, the structure is most representative of a true *group*

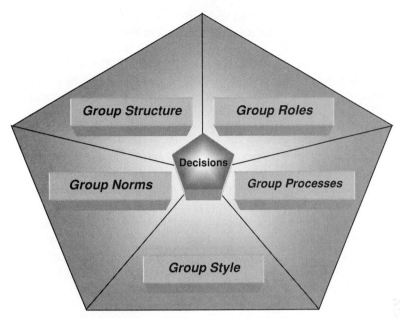

FIGURE 4-1 Factors Affecting Organizational Decisions

structure. Given the unique nature of these three decision structures it can be easily seen how the types of decisions made, as well as the methods employed, can vary significantly. Chapter 8 will focus on these various structures as they relate to specific DSS design requirements.

Group Roles

Each member of a decision-making body will have one or more specified roles. In the individual structure, all necessary roles are assigned to the sole decision maker: information gatherer, analyzer, DSS user, and so on. As the structure evolves toward a team or group structure, however, the necessary roles are spread among the various members so that each participant becomes a more realized component of the process. Depending upon how the organization has defined these roles (and who has been assigned them) the nature of the decision strategy employed as well as the scope of decision types assigned can be materially changed.

Group Processes

Using a kind of "chicken and egg" analogy, the process employed by a decision-making body can have a dramatic impact on the type of decisions that can be effectively made by that body, which can decidedly affect the method or process that must be used to make those types of decisions. Implicit in this seemingly circular problem is that the concepts of decision process and decision type must be in harmony with the decision-making body's perspectives. If a particular multiparticipant structure is employed, then certain decision processes no longer become relevant or effective for that group. For example, in the United States the final decision to go to war rests with a single person: the president. Although the president must formally request Congress for a declaration of war, the decision to do so, nonetheless, lies with a single decision maker. The reason for this is that the framers of the Constitution realized that this type of decision would not be best made by assemblage. The need for multiple sources of informed advice and knowledge is clear but the need for consensus seeking, which is typically associated with a group, is clearly not. If the time ever comes to make such a decision, it is best left to a decision process employed by one person.

Group Style

In chapter 2, we also visited the concept of decision style. In any decision-making context, the various interpersonal relations with stress, consequences of outcome, power and politics, and like-mindedness can determine both the method and type of decision best assigned to a particular decision-making body. As was discussed previously, the decision maker's style can affect the process, his or her behavior under specified conditions, and the quality of outcome. For example, a decision-making context such as whether to declare war on a foreign country would not be best suited for a diverse group of individuals with equally diverse views on the concept of war. Such a decision is better placed in the hands of a group of individuals that share similar beliefs regarding the salient concepts and can make the necessary decision based only on the information presented rather than on personal beliefs or political stances. Organizations must be cognizant of these components and must strive to create decision-making bodies that possess the best combination of ingredients for the given decision situation.

Group Norms

This final dimension is probably the most important. The social psychology of decision making is a powerful force affecting the activities of any decision-making "body" from individual to metaorganizational. Issues relating to shared meaning among the constituents, individual and collective social pressures, genres and prescriptions regarding behavior, personal beliefs, and potential sanctions, among others, can all serve to shape the decision-making environment within an organization.

Viewing all five of these factors in relation to each other we can see decision making within the organization as a continuous process. That is, the factors are "fluid elements that change based on their independent dynamics . . . constantly out of adjustment and seeking equilibrium, yet never quite in balance with each other in spite of a leader's best efforts" (Gore 1964, 26–27). Here is more evidence of the futility of optimization and the reality of satisficing with respect to the set of decisions being made within a particular organization. To complicate this discussion further, we must also recognize that this balancing act occurs in not two but three dimensions: (1) number of participants, (2) structure and roles of the participants, and (3) positioning of the participants within the organizational hierarchy.

Organizational Decision Levels

An organization, when viewed from a decision-making perspective, can be thought of as a hierarchy having three discrete levels: (1) operations, (2) tactical, and

FIGURE 4-2 Hierarchy of Organizational Decision Levels

(3) strategic (see figure 4-2). Within these three levels, all organizational decisions can be positioned.

The decision makers in an organization are a large and diverse population of individuals. At the foundational level, *operations,* the line personnel make decisions regarding day-to-day activities relating to production or services while the line supervisors deploy available resources and make decisions necessary to meet assigned quotas or schedules. The *tactical* (or planning) level implements decisions made at the highest level of the organization as well as decisions involving the acquisition of resources necessary to maintain desired capacities and outputs at the operations level. Most decisions relating to the internal administration of the organization are made at this level as well.

The members of the *strategic* decision-making hierarchy of an organization include the senior executives of the largest industrial and service firms in the world, the top administrators of the largest government agencies, and the generals and senior officers in the military. This elite group of decision makers, though the smallest of the three in number, represents the principal decision makers in our society. Theirs are usually the most far-reaching of all the decisions made across the three levels.

The level at which a decision is made within the organization must be taken into consideration when designing and implementing a DSS. Different types of systems are generally associated with different levels of the organization. One problem facing the designer of a DSS for a particular organizational level is the fluidity and diversity of skills and competencies found at each level. As workers in one level are promoted to a higher one, they must change many of their decision-making perspectives and strategies and assimilate new roles and assignments. Old habits sometimes persist, however, and often these necessary changes do not occur. Here the DSS designer must account for a phenomenon referred to as the *Peter Principle,* which suggests that an individual will eventually be promoted to his or her level of incompetence (Peter and Hull 1969). When this occurs, the skill set and competency expected by the DSS designer may not exist, and thus the effectiveness of the applied decision aid becomes questionable. We will focus on this issue in more detail in chapters 13 and 14.

4-2 ORGANIZATIONAL CULTURE

So What Is This Culture Thing, Anyway?

The term *organizational culture* is ubiquitous in the literature on organizational behavior, theory, structure, and management. There appears to be no shortage of offerings with regard to a definition for the term. A brief perusal of the literature reveals examples such as *dominant values espoused by an organization* (Deal and Kennedy 1982), *the philosophy that guides organizational policy toward employee and customers* (Pascale and Athos 1981), *the basic assumptions and beliefs that are shared by the members of an organization* (Bowers and Seashore 1966), or "just the way things are done around here." Regardless of the sources of the definitions, however, they all seem to have a common denominator: *shared meaning.* For our purposes, we will adopt the definition offered by Edgar Schein (1985), a noted organizational theorist, who defines organizational culture as a *system of shared meaning consisting of beliefs, symbols, rituals, myths, and practices that have evolved over time.* Through his definition we will explore this facet of the organization and its relationships to the decisions being made within.

Organizational culture is not an abstract milieu with no well-defined elements. Research has shown that organizational culture has an extremely powerful influence over the activities, including decision making, of an organization. Robbins (1990) identifies ten elements that when mixed together define a particular organization's culture. Table 4-1 lists these ten characteristics of organizational culture.

Table 4-1 Ten Characteristics of Organizational Culture

1. *Individual initiative.* The degree of responsibility, freedom, and independence that individuals have.
2. *Risk tolerance.* The degree to which employees are encouraged to be aggressive, innovative, and risk seeking.
3. *Direction.* The degree to which the organization creates clear objectives and performance expectations.
4. *Integration.* The degree to which units within the organization are encouraged to operate in a coordinated manner.
5. *Management support.* The degree to which managers provide clear communication, assistance, and support to their subordinates.
6. *Control.* The number of rules and regulations and the amount of direct supervision that are used to oversee and control employee behavior.
7. *Identity.* The degree to which members identify with the organization as a whole rather than with their particular work group or field of professional expertise.
8. *Reward system.* The degree to which reward allocations (i.e., salary increases, promotions) are based on employee performance criteria in contrast to seniority, favoritism, and so on.
9. *Conflict tolerance.* The degree to which employees are encouraged to air conflicts and criticisms openly.
10. *Communication patterns.* The degree to which organizational communications are restricted to the formal hierarchy of authority.

Source: Organization Theory, 3/E by Robbins, S. P., © 1990. Reprinted by permission of Prentice-Hall, Inc., Upper Saddle River, NJ.

Note that the characteristics are not limited to strictly structural issues. They also include several dimensions of behavior. It is important to note that an organization's culture is an evolutionary product of both the historical structure and the various courses of action of its members.

Relationship of Culture to Performance and Change

Performance

In chapter 2 we said that individual decision style affects decision strategy and quality of outcome. Decision style can also influence the way individuals act within an organizational environment. In some environments individuals are supportive of others; in others there is a pervasive struggle for control. Some organizations appear to be rigid and inflexible with regard to novelty or change while others encourage innovative thinking and approaches to problems. Because of this, the DSS designer must become aware of the influence of organizational culture on the types of decisions made and the appropriateness of various strategies employed within a particular cultural climate.

One method of viewing the relationship between organizational culture and decision making is by focusing on the concept of *cultural fit*. Successful organizations tend to display a "good fit" between their culture and their external and internal environments. A good *external fit* suggests a culture that is shaped to both the organization's strategy and its marketplace. For instance, market-driven strategies tend to be more successful in environments that are fluid and dynamic. Such climates emphasize conflict tolerance, individual initiative, risk taking, high departmental integration, and horizontal communication channels. The types of decisions and their associated strategies made in this culture will tend to be unstructured with a focus on effectiveness, novelty, and creativity, and will require a broad range of information sources. As such, certain DSS functions that tend to support these types of decisions and strategies will need to be emphasized and available in the firm's support technologies. In contrast, organizations that tend toward a product-driven approach to the marketplace often focus on high efficiencies, function best in more stable climates, and tend to promote a culture that is high in control and low in conflict and risk propensity. The decisions made in this environment will clearly fall toward the structured end of the continuum, and the decision support technologies employed in such an organization will need to be highly structured in their underlying model base and analytical tools. It is important to note, however, that one approach is neither right nor better than another. If the culture fits with the external climate, then the organization has a better chance of succeeding.

Internal fit is another key element in organizational success. It refers to the match between an organization's culture and its primary technologies. Cultures that tend to minimize individual initiative and risk taking, such as those of a product-driven orientation, also tend to adopt more routine technologies that provide additional stability to the organization. Such technologies take the form of well-developed control mechanisms, automated assembly machinery, and common back-office processing mechanisms. In addition, because these types of technologies are generally well-developed and require little individual intervention they also tend to support a more centralized decision-making emphasis where operating procedures, policies, schedules, and the like are all prescribed from a central authority. In cultures where initiative, creativity, and risk taking are supported and/or rewarded, nonroutine technologies that require adaptability are more prevalent. It is in these climates that DSS technologies are likely to be found as an integral part of the problem-solving activities. Putting DSS technology in the wrong organizational culture is the technological equivalent of trying to fit a square peg into a round hole—it may fit but it won't work very well.

Change

Another important aspect of organizational culture is that it often determines a firm's ability to change or adapt to changes in environmental conditions. Axiomatically speaking, survival equals ability to change. Organizations with cultures that do not allow for flexibility and change will fail to maintain their market position and will often fail to survive altogether. Cultures that promote the status quo and demonstrate a passion for stability will find it difficult, if not impossible, to respond to flux in the environment. In their book *In Search of Excellence,* Peters and Waterman (1982) identify eight characteristics of excellent companies. Table 4-2 contains a list of these hallmarks of excellence.

Note that each of the characteristics identified by Peters and Waterman is action oriented. Decisions made and strategies employed under these conditions tend to be highly diverse and to support a wide variety of support technologies and methods. In contrast, the more bureaucratic-type organization tends to use the "boardroom decision strategy," where a centralized control system is operationalized and managed, thus eliminating the need for individual or group DSS technology within the organization. Culture is important!

4-3 POWER AND POLITICS

It's a fact of life in most organizations: Power and politics are integral parts of the myriad of decisions that are made on a daily basis. While the term *power* is often thought of in a pejorative sense, Zaleznick (1970) recognizes it as an important, positive element in effective decision making:

> Whatever else organizations may be, problem-solving instruments, sociotechnical systems, reward systems, and so on, they are political structures. This means that

---

Table 4-2 Characteristics of Excellent Companies

- They have a bias for action.
- They stay close to and understand the customer.
- They provide autonomy and encourage entrepreneurship.
- They recognize that productivity is based on people.
- They are hands-on and value driven.
- They "stick to their knitting."
- They display a simple form and a lean staff.
- They maintain simultaneous loose-tight controls.

---

organizations operate by distributing authority and setting a stage for the exercise of power. It is no wonder, therefore, that individuals who are highly motivated to secure and use power find a familiar and hospitable environment in business. (p. 47)

As with many of the other concepts of organizations discussed so far, there are a variety of definitions for organizational power. Given our focus on decision making and support, we can identify power as being composed of five basic factors. Table 4-3 contains an outline of these five factors along with several subcategories.

We can think of power as it relates to decision making as a multifaceted capacity of one person or group within an organization to prevent another from reaching a desired goal. In addition, it includes the potential of one person or group to influence another to act or change in a particular direction. *Authority, informal power, influence,* and *politics* are all contributing forces to the effect of power on decision making in organizations.

Managerial decision-making power within an organization can manifest itself in a multitude of scenarios. Such power is broad in scope and its support must often come in the form of control or constraints to such power. Harrison (1995) has identified twelve significant elements of managerial decision-making power:

1. The power to decide the kind and quantity of jobs made available.
2. The power to decide (within legal limits) where, when, and how the operations of the organization will be conducted.
3. The power to decide what services, supplies, or raw materials to buy from other firms or subcontractors, and the power to decide (within legal limits) how, where, and when to purchase them.
4. The power to decide the service to be provided or the product to be produced.
5. The power (within legal limits) to set and administer prices.
6. The power to decide the amount of new investment and how, where, and when to invest it.
7. The power to shape and temper the value systems of the nation's population through sponsorship of the mass media.

Table 4-3 Five Factors of Power

1. *Power sharing.* Determines how a manager exercises authority and whether he or she wishes to exercise the power available to them.
2. *Authority.* The legitimacy a manager has for activities that come under his or her domain and direct supervision.
3. *Informal power.* The set of relationships that permit the accomplishment of interdependent tasks and coordinated activities.
4. *Influence.* The result of direct or indirect intervention in which the manager's preferences are the basis for arriving at a decision.
5. *Politics.* Related to negotiation, consensus formation, assertion of influence, or devious practices employed toward achieving a specific objective.

Source: Adapted from Rowe and Boulgarides (1994).

8. The power to influence the administration of existing legislation and the preparation and passage of new legislation by supporting candidates for political offices and lobbying.

9. The power to influence the general health and welfare of entire communities and of the general population through the use of technology and processes that produce noxious and irritating emissions.

10. The power to pay or withhold dividends.

11. The power to decide the amount of resources (if any) to be given to educational and philanthropic institutions and how, where, and when to make such gifts.

12. The power to withhold power.

As can be seen from the above list, decision making and power go hand in hand. Each of the twelve manifestations would require a completely different type of decision support mechanism than the others. Furthermore, within each of the twelve categories a multitude of subcategories of decisions can be found. For example, within the power to decide the amount of new investment lies a variety of problem-solving contexts and needs for decision support. Different investments will require different analyses using different models and different heuristics. Each of these subcategories of decisions would require a DSS designed specifically to meet the needs of its decision-maker(s). The point is that while the design and implementation of a DSS is primarily dependent on the context in which it is to be used, the bigger picture of the organization and its power centers must also be taken into consideration if effective support is to be provided.

Politics

Although they exist in a somewhat symbiotic relationship, power and politics can be thought of as distinct and thus can permeate the decision-making processes within an organization in different manners. More important, politics is an essential element in the formation of decision-making strategies.

Patz and Rowe (1977) describe *politics* as a process that "increases certainty in an organization, based on reducing the effect of factors contributing to uncertainty." In this sense, politics is related to decision-making through negotiation, formation of consensus, and influence. Each of these forces can have a material effect on a decision strategy or outcome and it is clear that there is a need for political competence in any given problem-solving context. Skill and competence in the political aspects of decision-making can result in measurable benefits to an organization that might otherwise go unrealized.

Mintzberg (1985) observes that organizational politics in decision making are not automatically dysfunctional to the organization but can instead be beneficial:

1. Politics may correct deficiencies in other more legitimate systems of influence and provide for certain forms of flexibility not otherwise available.

2. Politics can act in a Darwinian sense to bring the strongest members of an organization into the most critical decision-making roles.

3. Politics can often serve to ensure an objective hearing of all sides of an issue when no other reasonable means are available.

4. Politics can often help to promote necessary organizational change blocked by more traditional means.

5. Politics can facilitate the decision-making process, particularly the effective implementation of choices to serve particular interests.

In the design, implementation, and use of a DSS in an organization, the political environment in general and the direct political influences on the decision context in particular must all be given careful consideration. The politics of a given decision require the decision maker to be fully aware of the various relationships among the stakeholders involved in the choice outcome. Such political factors can include the probability of a stakeholder group supporting or rejecting a particular choice strategy or it might include information about certain constraints imposed by one political unit upon another that might impede the implementation of a certain choice set. For example, a decision involving the merging of two, previously autonomous, organizational units into one for the purpose of reducing common costs may involve political issues such as conflicting authority over certain organizational resources or processes, differing or opposing policies of conduct, or even lack of a shared vision of the mission for the new, combined departments. Regardless of the level at which the decision is being made—individual, team, group, or organization—power and politics will serve to shape and mold the decision context and thus the type of decision support required.

4-4 SUPPORTING ORGANIZATIONAL DECISION MAKING

Although organizational decision support systems (ODSSs) will be covered in chapters 6 and 12, it is important to our discussion of organizational decision making to briefly introduce the concept here. This section describes the boundaries of this level of decision support.

An ODSS can be thought of as a support technology that focuses on decisions involving many people. This conceptualization enlarges upon the notion of group decision support (GDSSs will be covered in detail in chapter 7), where a small group of individuals is provided support in making decisions of mutual interest and importance. The characteristic that sets an ODSS apart from a GDSS is managerial control. In an ODSS environment, the support technology is designed and deployed so that the organization's division of labor with regard to decision making is defined and controlled to a certain extent by the technology. While traditional decision-making structures have tended toward a conventional hierarchical arrangement and have often resembled the organization's formal authority configurations, the more modern organization acknowledges that many decisions have a tendency to cut across conventional lines of authority. When this situation occurs (and it does with great frequency), the need for temporary or virtual decision-making functions becomes necessary. In these contexts, the need for a decision may actually manifest itself as a set of related decisions distributed across a set of decision makers in such a manner that not all decisions are the province of an individual or a group. Despite this distribution, however, these decisions are assumed to be related and thus there exists a desire to coordinate them. When such distributed decision scenarios arise, the need for the design of an ODSS to support them presents itself. Culnan and Gutek (1989) suggest four fundamental activities that create the need for organizations to gather, store, and use information through an ODSS. Table 4-4 contains these four activities along with a listing of several types of ODSS functions that may be relevant in support of the activities.

Key Concepts

- The definiti[o]

  Assuming th[e]
  allows its me[mbers]
  dividually, a[nd]
  tured by a c[...]
  functioning [...]

- Five dimens[ions]

  Group struc[ture]

    Given the [...]
    seen how [...]

  Group roles

    Each mem[ber]
    upon how [...]
    ture of th[e]
    materially [...]

  Group proce[ss]

    The conc[ept]
    making b[...]
    create de[...]
    decision s[...]

  Group norm[s]

    The socia[l]
    decision-[...]

- Organizatio[n]

  Operations

    Most deci[...]
    vice by de[...]

  Planning

    Most deci[...]

  Strategic

    Decisions [...]
    three leve[l]

    The level [...]
    tion wher[...]

for or;

enhar
the su
work
conce
exists
area c
fits of
of dec
ety of
interc
their
in cha

4-5 CHAPTER S

In ch
decisi
also i

maki

 Tabl

- .
- .
- .
- .

C H A P T E R

5

Modeling
Decision Processes

Learning Objectives

■ Learn how a fully formed problem statement is developed using three key components: the current state of affairs, the desired state of affairs, and the objective(s)

■ Learn to identify the problem scope

■ Understand the three fundamental components of problem structuring: choice, uncertainty, and objective

■ Be familiar with two decision-modeling tools: influence diagram and decision tree

■ Based on an understanding of the problem structure components and tools, learn the common decision structures and their variations

■ Be familiar with various types of decision models, either abstract or conceptual, which will be the foundations for the decision maker's analysis and subsequent forecasts and prediction

■ Understand the three requirements of probability

■ Gain an understanding of different types of probabilities: long-run frequency, subjective probability, and logical probability

■ Learn the estimation and forecast of probabilities of the identified uncertainties using direct probability forecasting, odds forecasting, or comparison forecasting

■ Recognize the techniques of estimating measurable liability (calibration), analyzing sensitivity (sensitivity analysis), and evaluating information costs (value analysis)

 ■ 110 ■

What Were the Odds of This Happening? The *Exxon Valdez*

At four minutes past midnight, on March 24, 1989, the *Exxon Valdez,* loaded with 1,264,155 barrels of North Slope crude oil, ran aground on Bligh Reef in the northeastern portion of Prince William Sound, Alaska. About one-fifth of the total cargo, 11.2 million gallons, spilled into the sea. After three days of calm weather and smooth seas, strong northeasterly winds arose and dispersed the oil beyond any hope of containment. Much of the oil was converted by wind-driven mixing of the oil and sea water into an emulsion known as mousse, which will not burn and which is very difficult to remove from the surface of the sea or from shore. The spilled oil, now in the form of thin sheets and thick mousse, continued to spread to the southwest. The oil came ashore along an approximate 750-kilometer (470-mile) trajectory that ran from Prince William Sound to the southern Kodiak Archipelago and Alaska Peninsula. Scientists estimated that 35 percent of the spilled oil evaporated, 40 percent was deposited on beaches within Prince William Sound, and 25 percent entered the Gulf of Alaska where it either became beached or was lost at sea. Field surveys conducted in the summer of 1989 identified 790 miles of shoreline within Prince William Sound that had been oiled, over 200 miles of which were classified as heavily oiled. In the Kenai Peninsula–Kodiak region, more than 2,400 miles of shoreline were found to be oiled.

The response effort involved the unloading of unspilled cargo, vessel salvage, booming of sensitive areas, beach surveys and assessments, overflights to track the floating oil, skimming of floating oil, cleanup of oiled beaches, wildlife rescue, waste management, logistics support, and public relations. Major cleanup operations were conducted each spring and summer from 1989 to 1992. Thousands of workers were involved in the cleanup and logistics support operations that included hundreds of vessels, aircraft, and a substantial land-based infrastructure. In 1989, cleanup efforts involved more than 11,000 people and 1,400 marine vessels. This multiyear cleanup cost more than $2 billion. Techniques used to remove or clean oil included burning, chemical dispersants, high-pressure/hot water washing, cold water washing, fertilizer-enhanced bioremediation, manual and mechanical removal of oil and oil-laden sediments. Some interesting statistics include the following:

The oil recovered by skimming operations in 1989 accounted for only about 8.5 percent of the original spill volume.

Cleanup operations on the beaches during the first four summers led to the recovery and disposal of approximately 31,000 tons of solid oily wastes, which were estimated to account for 5 to 8 percent of the original spill volume.

About 90 percent of the oil in surface (< 25 centimeters) beach sediments was removed by natural processes (storm erosion and biodegradation) during the 1989–90 winter, whereas only about 40 percent of the deeper oil was removed.

By 1992, the combination of natural processes and cleanup activities had eliminated nearly all of the surface oil, though small amounts persisted along many shoreline segments in the Sound.

The federal on-scene coordinator, Admiral Ciancaglini, released a letter officially concluding the shoreline cleanup on June 10, 1992. The cleanup for the *Exxon Valdez* oil spill took three years and exceeded $2.1 billion in costs. In subsequent investigations, it was determined that Aleyeska, the consortium of oil companies responsible for constructing and maintaining the Alaska pipeline, had adopted an oil spill contingency plan that was totally inadequate to protect against a spill of such magnitude. Investigators found evidence of a gross underestimation of probabilities of risk associated with various oil spill scenarios, including one such as the *Exxon Valdez.* It was further determined that had the plan been more realistic regarding the probability of disaster, more resources would have likely been appropriated and would have been on-hand when disaster struck.

5-1 DEFINING THE PROBLEM AND ITS STRUCTURE

Recall that the key to the many functions of a DSS and the variety of forms that a modern computer-based DSS can take is one or more underlying models that can be used to study the problem at hand and to derive specific information about it. In this chapter, we will focus on the various problem definition and decision models available to the DSS designer.

Problem Definition

No matter how hard you try, you can't possibly know how to get where you are going unless you know where you are. This adage becomes a virtual law in the world of problem solving and decision making. As much as you desire to solve the problem and arrive at a choice decision, you can't be successful if you don't take the time first to identify and define the problem fully. This may sound simplistic or trivial but the typical decision maker, more often than one might imagine, fails to identify the problem at hand formally and concisely before beginning the process of solving it. Remember the headache problem from chapter 3? Failing to identify and define the problem fully results in a solution that may look like a great idea but that does not solve the problem.

In chapter 2, a *problem* was defined as *the perception of a difference between the current state of affairs and a desired state of affairs.* If we can identify and describe the current state of affairs and the desired state of affairs, we can develop a fully formed problem statement. This statement should contain three key components: (1) the current state of affairs, (2) the desired state of affairs, and (3) a statement of the central objective(s) that distinguishes the two. The value of these components can be better understood by looking at a typical problem statement and analyzing its content.

A common error in the formation of a problem statement is a premature focus on the choice set of solutions for the problem rather than the problem itself. When this happens, bounded rationality "kicks in" and the problem space becomes limited to those alternatives that appear to match the preconceived one embedded in the problem statement. The decision maker is left not with a fully formed problem statement but rather a statement of a solution looking for a problem to solve. For example, let's analyze the following statement using the three components of a fully formed problem statement outline above:

> Should there be a death penalty for convicted murderers?

The statement actually represents a solution looking for a problem. To begin with, the problem statement isn't a *statement* at all—it is a *question.* When the statement is formed this way, the answer becomes either an affirmation or denial of the solution provided in the question. If the answer is yes, then the problem is solved by invoking a death penalty. If the answer is no, then the problem is solved by abolishing the death penalty. In neither case, however, is any real problem being stated—thus no real problem will be solved. One way to determine what the real underlying problem might be is to explore the reasons why a particular choice alternative is under consideration:

> Why should convicted murderers be put to death?

Exploring the first statement from this perspective refocuses our attention on a reason for the choice rather than the choice itself. The answer to this question moves us closer to a statement containing the three necessary components:

> Many convicted murderers are being released back into society and are committing murders again. A determination must be made regarding how to prevent this from occurring.

By stating the problem in terms of the current situation, desired situation, and objective, a clear definition is provided and a path toward a solution is discovered.

Problem Scope

Once a problem statement is fully formed and stated, the decision maker must examine the scope of the problem. Upon examination, it may be determined that the problem is definitely worth solving but that the scope of it, as stated, is beyond the available resources, cognitive limitations, or time constraints. In such cases, the scope of the problem must be reduced to a focus that allows for successful deployment of the available resources toward a solution set. Generally speaking, the scope of the problem will be determined by the priorities of the decision maker.

To limit the scope of a problem one must first identify its breadth. One method of doing this is to begin to identify details about the problem through a series of questions. How many people are affected? How much does it currently cost? When did this first begin? What has been tried before? Who else knows of this problem? Who else is working on a solution to this problem? What is the true magnitude of this problem? Questions such as these can help the decision maker determine the breadth of the problem and thus determine a reasonable scope to focus on.

Problem Structure

The design of a problem structure is very similar to the design of any other structural entity, such as a car, a building, a landscape, or even a work of art. In each case, the basic approach remains the same: Detailed thought and analysis must occur simultaneously with regard to (1) final appearance, (2) elemental details, and (3) the relationships between those elements. This type of design process is often iterative and can, at times, become quite complex. Many times the designer must revise a decision made at one point in the process to account for a change made at another. This constant movement continues until the designer is satisfied with the equilibrium created among the three dimensions.

Regardless of the decision context, a problem structure can be described in terms of three fundamental components: (1) choices, (2) uncertainties, and (3) objectives. Using these three components, we will explore the basic problem-structuring tools, common structural configurations, and issues of model selection based on the problem at hand.

Choices

Implicit in the concept of *choice* is the existence of multiple alternatives. If only one alternative exists then there exists no choice and, thus, no decision. One way of thinking about this need for at least two alternatives is to assume that all decisions have as one alternative to simply "do nothing." While this approach will not solve the problem, it is nonetheless a viable alternative that can and often should be considered. We will assume that all problems and decisions have this alternative of inaction and will not include it in the models we construct. Just don't forget that it exists and should at least be given early consideration in any problem analysis.

One of the most common methods of modeling a problem structure is the *influence diagram.* Using this approach, the three components of a problem structure are represented by specific shapes that are combined and connected to represent the problem being modeled. Another common approach is the *decision tree,* which focuses on the choice set and the expected outcomes. We will cover these modeling techniques in greater detail later in this section but will begin using them now to illustrate the three components. Figure 5-1 illustrates the shapes used for each structural element in both techniques and an example of a choice tree with four alternatives.

Uncertainties

If one were able to determine all events in a problem context with certainty (meaning a 100 percent probability of occurrence) then making complex decisions would become child's play. Also, the process of decision making would be far less interesting and would not need to be studied. Fortunately for teachers of problem-solving techniques and students (such as yourself) who are interested in the subject, this is not the case. All problem structures contain *uncertainties* that must be accounted for by the decision maker. It is important to note that the primary difference between choices and uncertainties is the probability of occurrence. With a choice, there is a 100 percent probability of at least one alternative being selected and there is an equal probability of any particular one being selected. This is true because by the

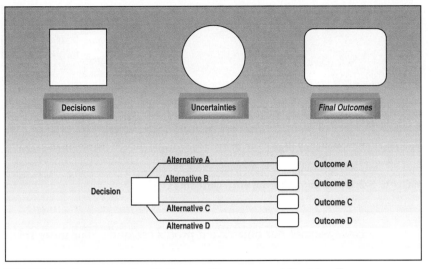

FIGURE 5-1 Components of Influence Diagrams and Decision Trees

time a set of viable alternatives has been identified, each has been placed in the set after the various uncertainties have been identified and accounted for. Thus, the selection of an alternative "branch" on the structural tree is under the complete control of the decision maker. With regard to uncertainties, however, the same is not true. By definition, uncertainties are situations that are beyond the direct control of the decision maker, and their individual probability of occurrence is only estimable within a certain range of possibilities at best. Because of this, the occurrence of one uncertain event may require a complete restructuring of all future events. This is where the real complexity of problem solving begins and where the real value of problem structuring can be found. By diagramming each of the uncertainties and including the expected probability of each one occurring, the decision maker can visualize the various paths of future events and can more easily compare one possible scenario to another. This is the basic approach used to create complex computer-based simulations. We'll look at these types of models in section 5-2. Figure 5-2 illustrates the modeling of an uncertainty with three possible outcomes and their associated probabilities.

Objectives

Once the last of the uncertainties has been resolved and the myriad of choices have been analyzed and selected, the destiny of the decision is set: An outcome will occur. At this point, we need to model how that outcome, whatever it may be, is to be evaluated with respect to its desirability or degree of success. *Objectives* provide us with a method of establishing the criteria that can be used to measure the value or desirability of a particular outcome. The closer the outcome matches the criteria, the more desirable it is. Examples of objectives include specific reductions in disease, specific percentage increases in market share, and specific increases in revenues or decreases in costs, among many others. Note that a well-formed objective must allow for a quantifiable comparison. An objective such as "to increase profits" is difficult to

FIGURE 5-2 Uncertainty Model with Outcomes

evaluate. Have we met our objective if profits are one dollar more this year than last? According to the way the objective is stated, we have. Most likely, however, this was not the intention of the decision-making activity. A more fully formed objective such as "to increase profits by 10 percent over last year" or "to improve profits by $50,000 over the prior period" would better reflect our intent. Decisions can have multiple objectives to evaluate outcomes, but to be a fully modeled decision at least one measurable objective must be identified.

Structuring Tools

Influence Diagrams

An *influence diagram* is a simple method of graphically modeling a decision. The three components of a decision (as illustrated in figure 5-1) are included, as appropriate, and are linked with arrows to model the relationships between them. Figure 5-3 contains several simple influence diagrams along with a legend for the various shapes and line types used in their construction.

As shown in the figure, there are two types of arrows (referred to as *arcs*) used to connect the *nodes* (the component elements of the decision model). The solid arrows will always point to uncertainties and objectives and represent a relationship of relevance. In other words, when a solid arrow is used it indicates that the predecessor is relevant for assessing the value of the succeeding component. In the lower left of the figure, notice that Decision A is related to Event B using a solid arrow. This indicates that Decision A (the predecessor) is relevant in the determination of the probability of Event B occurring. For instance, the chance of a student receiving an A for a particular exam is dependent to some extent on whether he or she chose to study. Also notice that Event A is related to Event B by a solid arrow (upper left of the figure). In this case, the probability of Event A occurring is relevant to the probability of Event B occurring. For example, the probability of getting caught in a rainstorm and getting wet partly depends on the probability of rain occurring.

Dashed arrows are used only to point to decisions and indicate that a decision was made with knowledge of the outcome of the predecessor node. Thus, the relationship between Event A and Decision B suggests that the decision maker made Deci-

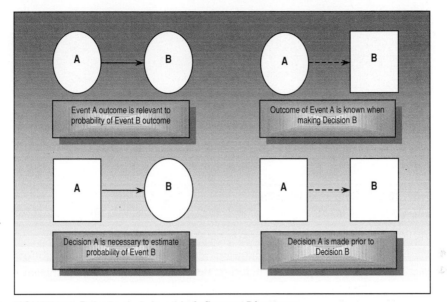

FIGURE 5-3 Relevance Arrows in Influence Diagrams

sion B with full knowledge of the *outcome* of Event A (upper right in the figure). Another way of looking at this is that a decision maker makes a decision with full knowledge of what has occurred prior to the decision being made. If a dashed arrow is used to connect one decision event to another (lower right) it means that the first decision was made before the second decision was made. In this way, we can depict the sequential ordering of decisions in the diagram by the path through the various nodes.

One additional characteristic of an influence diagram is that, when properly constructed, it has no cycles; regardless of where you start in the diagram there is no path that will lead you back to the starting point. The arrows form a path that is one-way. Once a node is left behind, there is no path that will allow a return to it. This rule for construction is in keeping with the reality of decision making and problem solving. Once a decsision is made, it is made. We cannot go back to a decision at a later time and "unmake" it.

Decision Trees

Although the influence diagram is an excellent tool for modeling the structure of a particular decision context, it does not allow for the depiction of many of the details associated with the decision at hand. Another structuring tool that can be used to complement the influence diagram is the *decision tree*. In this diagram, only choices and uncertainties are modeled. The two components are connected by lines referred to as *branches*. The branches extending from a choice node represent the items contained in a choice set available to the decision maker. The branches radiating from an uncertainty node represent the possible outcomes from a particular event. The value of each outcome is attached to the end of each outcome branch. Figure 5-4 contains an example of a simple decision tree.

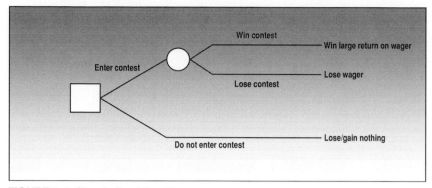

FIGURE 5-4 Simple Decision Tree

Much like an influence diagram, a decision tree can be thought of as similar to a railroad. It is typically constructed to be read beginning on the left and continuing to the right until an outcome is reached. In addition, several "rules" must be followed in its construction to assure that the diagram clearly represents the details of the decision context.

First, the branches extending from a choice node must be constructed so that the decision maker can choose only one option. No branch can be modeled as a combination of choice options. Second, the branches radiating from an uncertainty node must represent a set of outcomes that are both *mutually exclusive* and *collectively exhaustive*. The first condition, mutually exclusive, means that only one of the possible outcomes can occur. An example of this would be an uncertainty node with two branches representing success or failure. In this case, the rule is followed because a project can either succeed or fail but not both. The second condition, collectively exhaustive, means that the branches represent all possible outcomes; no other possibilities exist. Together these two conditions require that when the uncertainty is resolved, one and only one outcome will prevail.

The third rule of decision tree construction is that all possible paths that can be followed over time by a decision maker are fully mapped in the tree, including all possible choices and uncertainty outcomes. It can easily be seen that as a decision context becomes more complicated, the size of the decision tree will increase exponentially. For example, if we start with a choice node with three branches, each with two outcomes, we have a total of six possible outcomes. If, however, we add one additional choice node with three alternatives after each uncertainty in the model we increase the total number of possible outcomes from six to eighteen. This exponential growth is often referred to as "the tree getting bushy."

Finally, the decision tree must be constructed to depict an accurate chronology of events over time. This is best accomplished by strictly adhering to the left-to-right construction of the tree. From left to right, a typical decision tree begins with a choice node and either other choice nodes are encountered or uncertainties must be resolved until all possible paths have been accounted for.

Common Decision Structures

There is no debate concerning whether all decision contexts are unique; they are. Nonetheless, as with many other situations faced in our lives, decision contexts have certain characteristics and patterns in common. In this section, we examine decision structures that occur quite frequently during the course of daily managerial activities. By understanding these common structures, a decision maker can more quickly identify the probable structure of a new decision context.

Basic Risky Decision

Many problems faced by a decision maker necessitate a choice selection in the face of some uncertainty. In the *basic risky decision* structure, a successful decision is a function of both the correct selection from the choice set and the outcome of an uncertainty. See figure 5-5 for an example of how this decision structure could be used to model a decision to buy stock. Here is another example:

> Product manager Stephanie Essington is considering a sales promotion for her company's new soft drink, Blaster. She would like to focus on consumers that regularly go to the beaches during the summer. The campaign would be called "Blaster's Fun in the Sun Summer" and would promote the new soft drink with miniconcerts, giveaways, beach volleyball, and other such events. The rationale for the beach setting is that when people play in the sun they often enjoy a cool, refreshing drink to quench their thirst. If this summer proves to be a particularly hot one, Blaster and Stephanie could both become quite successful. If, however, it rains a great deal this summer in the beach areas, then both Blaster and Essington will be "all wet."

In the example above, the decision context is modeled with three components: (1) *choice*—whether or not to run the promotional campaign, (2) *uncertainty*—whether it will be sunny or rainy, and (3) *objective*—to make Blaster successful. As can be seen, the objective of making Blaster successful is a function of both the choice

FIGURE 5-5 Basic Risky Decision

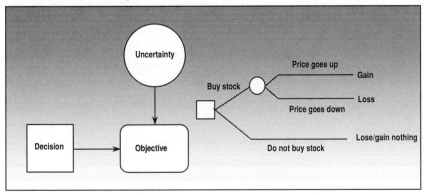

to run the campaign and the amount of rain at the beaches. The basic risky decision structure can be used to describe a variety of common situations faced in a managerial setting. There are, however, two variations of this common structure that can be encountered as well: the *basic risky policy* and the *basic risky decision with multiple objectives.*

As shown in figure 5-6, the *basic risky policy* variation describes a problem context where the choice made from the set of alternatives has a direct influence on the probabilities of an uncertainty as well as on the objective. Consider this example:

> Stephanie Essington's summer beach campaign for Blaster was a remarkable success and the new product is off and running. Essington is still the product manager but her bonus check allowed her to buy a new Corvette. Now she is working on a new campaign intended to increase sales even further while still building upon the beach theme established during the product's initial rollout. Stephanie believes that the packaging for Blaster could be redesigned to be more "outdoor friendly." She is proposing a package that has a built-in, resealable spout and is more heavily insulated than a typical soft drink container. Introducing this new packaging could serve to greatly increase market share. However, the new packaging would be more expensive than conventional methods and would also decrease profits to a certain degree.

This problem is still modeled with three components but their relationship differs slightly from the *basic risky decision* structure. Here, both the choice (whether to

FIGURE 5-6 Variations of Basic Risky Decision Model

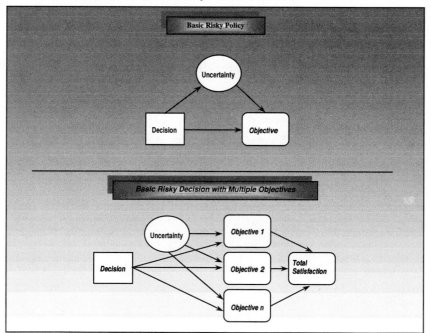

repackage the product) and the uncertainty (market share) have a direct influence on the objective (profits). In addition, however, the uncertainty associated with the probability of a given increase in market share is also directly affected by the choice. If Stephanie doesn't repackage the product then the probability of increased market share as a result of repackaging will be reduced to zero.

In the second variation, the *basic risky decision with multiple objectives,* the decision maker is faced with making a trade-off between objectives in order to manage the uncertainty present in the decision context. The best solution will be the one that results in the greatest measured success. Our soft drink example demonstrates this variation:

> Blaster has become the number one soft drink at all of America's beaches and is fast becoming a big seller throughout the country, no small thanks to the "Super Steph" as she is now affectionately referred to by her colleagues. The company has given her carte blanche to move Blaster into the international arena. Because of this, Essington has to increase the size of the product management team. She has considered several different configurations for her team that mainly differ by the number and location of the new team members. The more new team members, the greater the market coverage is for Blaster, but the greater the overall cost of managing the product.

Here, the choice (which team configuration to select) is directly related to more than one objective (market coverage and management cost). The uncertainty (sales) is also directly related to the multiple objectives. In addition, the choice will also affect the probability distribution of the uncertainty.[1] If one objective is maximized then the other will suffer. The decision maker must strike a suitable balance between the multiple objectives by selecting the appropriate alternative from the choice set.

Certainty

A second common decision structure involves those situations where the trade-off among the various objectives and risk is not a significant consideration. In this structure, the *multiple objective, no risk decision,* the degree of measured success or satisfaction with the final choice is based on the creation of an appropriate trade-off among the objectives of the various stakeholders. A variation of this structure is the *multiple objective/multiple approach, no risk decision.* This structure manifests itself in situations that are so broad and complex that a single approach would not resolve the problem completely. This situation is common when dealing with issues of public policy such as drug abuse, crime, unemployment, or homelessness. In business, managers face this situation with problems of employee morale, new product development, and issues of improved efficiency or effectiveness. In most cases, these situations are so complex that designing a single decision-structure model is untenable. To accomplish the analysis, the decision maker must decompose the problem context into more manageable submodels. At this point, the decision maker must determine the

---

[1] This particular decision structure is a variation of a variation. It is referred to as a basic risky policy with multiple objectives.

degree of emphasis to be placed on each submodel and then select the alternative available from the choice component of each one. Let's get back to Stephanie and see how Blaster is doing:

> The new Blaster product management team has been in place for quite some time and its success has been overwhelming. Senior management has repeatedly given Stephanie raises and promotions based on the successes of her team, and she has done the same for her team members. Now, however, the company wants Stephanie and her team to "do it again," so to speak, with a new product introduction. Since Team Blaster is so well respected by senior management, Stephanie has been given the authority to design as well as market the new product. To begin this process, she must assign the various team members to new roles based on their individual strengths and weaknesses, she must determine which market niche to target based on recent consumer survey data, she must schedule the testing and rollout for the new product, and she must create an initial budget for the research and development effort. Each of these decisions, while somewhat affected by the others, is basically individual in nature and fairly complex in total.

Here the element of risk, while arguably present to some degree in each of the choice scenarios, is not of major importance. The focus is on combining the individual objectives so that the largest measurable degree of success can be expected.

Sequential

Decision processes do not always manifest themselves so that a clear beginning and a clear end can be structured. More often, conditions change over time and a choice made earlier may no longer be appropriate or deemed useful. Furthermore, an alternative that was not viable at a particular time in the past may now appear more desirable based on the new set of conditions present. The *sequential* decision structure is a series of *basic risky decisions* in successive time periods with arrows used to indicate the relationships between each temporal choice set. Figure 5-8 illustrates this type of decision structure.

FIGURE 5-7 Multiple Objective, No Risk Decision

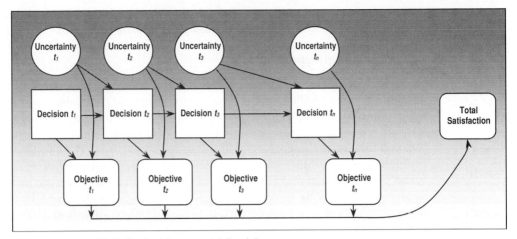

FIGURE 5-8 Multiple-Period Sequential Decision

As you can see, a decision made in one time period affects the degree of total measured success across all time periods as well as the measured success in that same time period. In addition, the decisions in the following time periods (and possibly the prevailing conditions) are affected to a degree by the decision(s) made previously. Using a sequential structure model, the decision maker explicitly acknowledges the links between decisions with a common objective made over time. The opportunity to change course at some point in the future leaves open the possibility that a somewhat riskier strategy could be pursued in one time period and, if not successful, could be followed by a more conservative approach to mitigate the damage from the prior period. Also, this modeling structure allows the decision maker to see the future so that a decision to defer action until a period sometime in the future may also be made.

5-2 DECISION MODELS

In addition to the arsenal of analytical models contained within the model base of a typical DSS and used to solve a particular problem or problem type, the decision maker must also be concerned with the structure of the problem context. In this sense, a problem can be thought of as a set of subsystems that are functionally decomposable at the desire of the decision maker. Each of these subsystems can be modeled so that an accurate representation of that part of the problem context is symbolized. Once this simplified representation of reality is in place, decision makers can use these models as a foundation for their analysis and subsequent forecasts and predictions. In this section, we look at the various classes and types of decision models and their applications to specific problem types.

Decision models can be classified in a number of ways. One common high-level classification is to divide the models in terms of their explicit inclusion of time as an element. Models that do not explicitly acknowledge time are called *static models* and those that do are referred to as *dynamic models.* Another widespread method of classification is by the technique's mathematical or logical focus.

Abstract Model Types

An *abstract decision model* focuses on the mathematical precision with which various outcomes can be predicted. This type of model can, theoretically, assist in determining which alternative should result in the most favorable outcome. Based on this prediction, a decision maker can develop a strategy for implementing the proposed alternative and thus solve the problem. This all sounds good; however, as each subsystem of a problem context is modeled and further decomposed, some detail of the information is lost to the decision maker. This loss of information is built into the modeling process because we are trying to create a *simplified* representation of reality, and to achieve this simplification we eliminate certain pieces of information from the abstraction. The decision maker is constantly faced with creating a balance between models that capture the complexity of the problem with models that are simple enough to analyze and solve. This balance is never completely in equilibrium and thus the decision maker must always be aware of the "credo of humility" for mathematical modeling: All models are wrong; some models are useful (Golub 1997). This caveat notwithstanding, mathematical abstractions are useful when their limitations are known and acknowledged by the decision maker.

In keeping with the concept of functional decomposition, abstract models can be divided into four subsystems, each displaying unique characteristics (see table 5-1).

Deterministic Models

A *deterministic model* is one in which no variable can take more than one value at any given time. In this model type, the same output values will always result from any given set of input variables. Most of the traditional models of normative economic theory are deterministic as are many of the common models used in financial analysis. These model types are found to be particularly useful when a problem structure contains a large number of elements and complex relationships. Common deterministic models include *linear programming, nonlinear programming,* and *differential equations.*[2]

Table 5-1 Decision Model Classification

Deterministic. Optimization, linear programming, financial planning, production planning, convex programming.
Stochastic. Queuing theory, linear regression, logit analysis, path analysis, time series.
Simulation. Production modeling, transportation and logistics analysis, econometrics.
Domain-specific. Normative economic models, economic-order-quantity, constraint modeling, behavior modeling, technology diffusion, meteorological models.

---

[2] Each of these modeling techniques is beyond the scope of this text to explore fully. Any good management science textbook can be used as both guidance and reference when applying one or more of these mathematical tools.

Stochastic Models

In a *stochastic model,* at least one of the variables is uncertain and must be described by some probability function. These model types are often referred to as *probabilistic models* because they explicitly incorporate uncertainty into their structure. When constructing a stochastic model, the decision maker distributes the input value of one or more variables around some mean value and the output variables take the form of a frequency distribution rather than a discrete set of values. In general, a stochastic model that has the same number of elements as a deterministic model is more difficult to manage and becomes more complicated to solve, ceteris paribus.[3] Common stochastic modeling techniques include *game theory, queuing theory, linear regression, time series analysis, path analysis,* and *logistical regression* or *logit analysis.*

Simulation Models

Unfortunately for most decision makers, problem structures do not often readily fall into either a strictly deterministic or probabilistic realm. More often, some of the subsystems of a problem context are deterministic, some are stochastic, and some are a combination of both. One technique developed to allow for this combined complexity in problem structures is the *simulation model.* A simulation can be thought of as a technique for conducting one or more experiments that test various outcomes resulting from the combining of modeled subsystems into a dynamic environment. Simulation is intended to imitate reality rather than simply model it. Simulation modeling is commonly applied in areas where the cost of a full-scale changeover to determine the best alternative is prohibitive. Other areas where simulation has proven to be valuable include proof of concept testing—where new ideas are tested using a minimum of resources or time—and the study of current processes and operations in order to gain a better understanding and to explore methods of improvement. The following scenario illustrates a situation where simulation modeling would be an appropriate problem-solving technique:

> Postmaster Steve Hornik has been at his new location for a little more than a year now and many of the operational deficiencies that existed when he arrived have been corrected. The customers of the postal facility seem to be generally pleased with the level of service provided by the employees and business has increased since Hornik's arrival. One situation that continues to trouble the new postmaster, however, is the regular occurrence of long lines at the only two service windows at various times of the day. Although the clerks seem to be serving each of their customers as effectively and efficiently as possible, Steve wonders if more windows and a defined procedure for staffing the windows would improve service even more and reduce the waiting times associated with the long lines. After much thought, Postmaster Hornik has narrowed his focus to one of four possible strategies:
>
> **1.** Add one window for parcel pickup and delivery only. Staff this window full-time with one employee to handle both drop-offs and pickups.

---

[3] The term *ceteris paribus* is used to qualify a comparison and freely translated means "all other things remaining equal."

2. Use the same strategy as in strategy 1 except use two employees: one for drop-offs only and one for retrieving customer parcel pickups.

3. Add two windows and staff them with clerks that can handle any type of service request including parcel pickup. These windows would be open during all regular business hours.

4. Use the same basic strategy as in strategy 3 but only open the additional windows during peak business hours.

Hornik believes that one of the four strategies he has designed will solve the problem effectively. The problem is that he doesn't know how to determine which one and he can't very well keep tearing up the post office to build new windows to find out.

In this situation, the problem cannot be analyzed effectively with static, abstract models. Many of the variables in the model are not only dynamic but vary in relation to the time of day, the day of the week, and probably the season. Furthermore, physically investigating each of the scenarios would not only be expensive and time consuming but would negatively disrupt the environment that currently exists at the post office. Using simulation modeling, however, these various scenarios can be compared against each other and can be tested over days, weeks, or even years in a matter of a few hours. The decision maker can easily design a series of simulations that account for the time of day, the expected frequency of various service requests (parcel pickup, drop-off, postage purchase, etc.), the distribution of arrivals and departures, number of windows, speed of execution of each service request, and so on. Based on the comparative results of the various simulation runs, the decision maker can then determine the most desirable alternative and the best balance among the stated objectives.

Despite its attractiveness, simulation modeling is not without disadvantages. First, an optimal solution is not guaranteed by a simulation model. The model will only inform the decision maker of the probabilistic outcome and allow for a comparison of modeled scenarios (remember bounded rationality?). Second, the construction of a simulation model, while often the most cost-effective solution to a problem analysis, is nonetheless time consuming and costly. Third, the results obtained from a simulation model are distinctly context specific and are not generalizable to other problem domains. Finally, simulation is an attractive and entertaining method to managers. Because of its "glitz" other analytical solutions that could yield equal or even better or more accurate results are often overlooked. When its limitations are understood and acknowledged, however, simulation is a powerful abstract analytical modeling technique that can provide positive results when properly applied.

Domain-Specific Models

The fourth type of common abstract model is the *domain-specific model*. The sciences have evolved to the point where the need for highly specific types of decision-making techniques and contexts has emerged. In these cases, each discipline has developed its own set of abstract mathematical modeling techniques to serve its needs. Models of supply and demand are unique to the toolbox of economists. Other well-known domains such as operations research, sociology, ecology, medicine, and meteorology have each developed its own unique abstract modeling techniques. In the design of a DSS for a specific problem domain, the designer must become aware of any domain-specific models available for inclusion in the model base.

Conceptual Model Types

Despite the variety of abstract mathematical models to choose from and their individual and combined power to assist in problem structuring, there are times when a formal mathematical approach to a problem may not be the most appropriate strategy. Examples include problem contexts where abstract models may oversimplify the structure or the mathematical modeling process may be too time consuming or too costly. Another example is when the decision maker is so familiar with the problem context that an abstract representation would yield no gains. In these cases, a *conceptual model* becomes the more appropriate method of forecasting the outcomes associated with various choice alternatives.

Conceptual models can be thought of as analogies to the problem context. Implicit in this perspective is the notion that while all problems are unique, no problem is completely new. Experience from a past problem context can be used to assist in forecasting events and outcomes in the new context. Using this method, decision makers can recall and combine a variety of past experiences and contexts to create an accurate conceptual model of the current situation and to assign probabilities to those event components that remain uncertain.

Conceptual modeling is often criticized as being overly subjective and individually biased toward the beliefs of the decision maker. Although this argument certainly has some merit, we must also recognize that the choice of a particular abstract modeling approach is also a subjective decision and is dependent on the decision maker's expertise in the chosen technique. Furthermore, abstract models are based on equally subjective mathematical assumptions of how things are related. Suffice it to say that both methods allow for the injection of individual biases and assumptions in their construction and use. Both the designer and user of a DSS must be fully aware of the appropriateness (or lack thereof) of a particular technique when applying it in a given problem context. The use of conceptual modeling and analogical reasoning will be explored in greater detail as it applies to artificial intelligence and knowledge engineering in chapter 9. Returning to our post office problem, we can see an example of conceptual modeling in action:

> Postmaster Steve Hornik has completed his simulation of the four customer service scenarios and the results proved to be effective in improving the long lines. Because of his demonstrated success with the redesign of the mail lobby, Hornik has been selected to design and test a drive-up mail window proposed by the postmaster general. Five different locations have been given the resources to test this new concept and each has been told to be creative and to experiment where applicable. Steve is excited about this opportunity but is struggling with exactly how to implement it. Because the post office serves a relatively small community, the bulk of the customer traffic arrives on foot. Those that arrive by automobile usually park down the street at the main parking garage for the business district and then walk to their desired destinations. Hornik is wondering whether this is because of the convenience associated with the central parking facility or because

no previous alternative such as the drive-up facility existed. He creates three scenarios to identify the uncertainties:

Strong acceptance. Postal customers will use the new drive-up facility extensively because it will be easier than hand-carrying large packages and bulky mail in addition to other parcels the customer may have.

Poor acceptance. Postal customers will avoid using the new facility because it will require them to "schedule" their trip to the post office either before parking for shopping or after completing their shopping.

Moderate acceptance. Some of the elderly customers will find the availability of the new facility to be beneficial. Overall, the drive-up window will fill a void in the range of services provided and will prove to be moderately useful.

Hornik reasons that, of the three possible scenarios, the strong acceptance scenario is the least compelling, and the moderate acceptance outcome is the most compelling. He therefore assigns the following probabilities to the three outcomes: $P[\text{Strong}] = 10$ percent, $P[\text{Moderate}] = 60$ percent, $P[\text{Poor}] = 30$ percent.

Howard's Test of Clarity

Whether a decision maker chooses to employ abstract techniques, conceptual approaches, or a combination of both, the final step in the structuring process is ensuring that all components of the context model are clearly defined. Howard (1988) proposed a useful method for determining when the conceptualizations of variables and outcomes have been identified and defined sufficiently:

> Imagine a clairvoyant who has access to all future information. . . . Would the clairvoyant be able to determine unequivocally what the outcome would be for any event in the structure diagram? No interpretation or judgment should be required of the clairvoyant. (quoted in Clemen 1991, 55)

Given the above scenario, could the events at every node of the model be fully determined without interpretation? The decision model passes the clarity test when this question can be answered affirmatively. There should be no room for interpretation or misunderstanding regarding the basic components of the decision structure. Applying the clarity test to a structuring model is an iterative approach to the refinement of each individual component. Only after all elements have been fully refined should the decision maker move on to considering selection of a solution strategy.

5-3 TYPES OF PROBABILITY

It should be clear by now that a decision is not much of a decision unless there is some uncertainty present. If all things are crystal clear then the decision becomes mostly a mechanical process where logic and common sense are the primary tools. The important point here is that virtually all decisions contain elements of uncertainty and for a decision to be made with any degree of success, those uncertainties must be quantified in some manner. This is where the importance of understanding the concept of probability enters the picture.

A central tenet of modern decision analysis is that we can symbolize any kind of uncertainty through an appropriate application of basic probability. Despite the obvious appropriateness of probability theory for describing uncertainties it is probably the most misused and misunderstood tool of decision making. Properly applied, probability theory can be invaluable in the structuring, resolution, and choice selection of a given problem context. Improperly applied, however, it can lead to decisions that are perfect in all respects except for their outcome. In the next few sections, we will explore the fundamentals of probability theory and will focus on various methods of estimating and forecasting the probabilities of uncertain events.

The Three Requirements of Probability

No matter what the scenario the proper application of probability theory requires that three conditions be met. Table 5-2 contains a list of these requirements.

The first requirement implies that all probabilities are positive and that no event can have less than a 0 percent chance of occurring. Conversely, it makes perfect sense that no event can have greater than a 100 percent chance of occurring either.

The second requirement imposes a mathematical constraint on the probability of multiple outcomes to a particular event. Assuming that the outcomes are *mutually exclusive*—that is, if one can happen, then the other cannot—then the probability that one of them occurs must be equal to the sum of their respective probabilities. If there is a 25 percent chance that a new policy in a company will boost employee morale and a 35 percent chance that morale will stay the same despite the implementation of the new policy, then the probability that morale will either increase or stay the same is 60 percent. (What might the probability of morale going down be?)

The third requirement is probably the most important to successful decision making. If we know the complete set of outcomes for a given event, at least we know what cannot happen: An outcome that is not contained within the set of all possible outcomes cannot happen. If a baseball game is played, we do not know who will win, but we do know that the only possible outcomes are that one of the two teams will win or lose. Because the rules do not allow for a tie, we know that the probability of this occurring is 0 percent. Once we know the set of mutually exclusive outcomes for an event, we are said to have a set that is *collectively exhaustive*. The sum of probabilities for this set of all possible outcomes must equal 1. In other words, if we know all possible outcomes for an event that must occur then the probability that one of them will occur is 100 percent. If the uncertainties contained within a decision context are mod-

---

Table 5-2 The Three Requirements of Probabilities

1. All probabilities must lie within the range of 0 to 1.
2. The probabilities of all individual outcomes of an event must add up to the probability of their union.
3. The total probability of a complete set of outcomes must be equal to 1.

---

eled within these three qualifying factors, then the probabilities will be appropriate. Once we have established the appropriateness of our probabilities we can focus our attention on the degree of accuracy of the various estimations. We will cover the accuracy issue in detail in the following sections.

Types of Probability

Regardless of whether a problem context is modeled via an abstract approach or a more conceptual method we will eventually be faced with estimating the probabilities of the identified uncertainties. To this end, there are three different ways that probability can be expressed: (1) *long-run frequency,* (2) *subjective,* and (3) *logical.*

Long-Run Frequency

Most introductory texts in statistics and probability begin their presentation with probability viewed as a measure of *long-run frequency.* This approach relies on the so-called "law of large numbers," which states that if an event or an experiment is repeated a large number of times, the observed frequency of a particular outcome of that event will be a good estimate of the true probability of that outcome. The most common example used to demonstrate the long-run frequency approach is the flip of a coin:

> Take a coin from your pocket or purse and flip it into the air. Let the coin fall to the ground and lay flat. What is the probability that the coin will land heads up?

The answer to this question should pose no measurable debate or require significant thinking to determine. There are two possible outcomes to the event: *heads* or *tails.* We assume the coin is fair and that the two possible outcomes are mutually exclusive. Given this, each possible outcome has a 50 percent probability of occurring. Note that this simple analysis also satisfies the three requirements for probabilities. If we repeat this "experiment" a large number of times we will find that each outcome occurs approximately 50 percent of the time.

Advocates of a long-run frequency approach are often referred to as *frequentists.* The frequentist approach advocates the estimation of probability through experimentation and repetition. There are times, however, when thinking about probabilities in terms of long-run frequencies is either impractical or untenable. Consider the need to estimate the probability of a major nuclear accident at a power plant nearing completion. Let's narrow the scope of the problem to the probability of a nuclear accident within the next fifteen years. It would be impractical to run a repetitive set of experiments to estimate the probability (nor would we want to even if it were practical). Nonetheless, we must make such estimates all the time and we must have a reasonable sense that we can rely on such estimates. To accomplish this we have to think of probability in another way.

Subjective Probability

Consider the following questions:

- What is the probability that the coin flipped at the beginning of the 1986 Super Bowl game between the Chicago Bears and the New England Patriots came up heads?

- What is the probability that James Knox Polk was the president of the United States in 1843?
- What is the probability that Button Gwinnett, Caesar Rodney, William Whipple, and William Williams were all signers of the U.S. Declaration of Independence?

If the answers to the above questions do not come readily to mind, don't worry. In every case, the event has taken place and the true probability of the event is known. Nonetheless, if you do not know the answer, you are uncertain. Let's go back to our coin flip example:

> Using the same coin you used in the previous example, flip the coin into the air. This time, however, catch the coin before it lands and slap it onto the back of your other hand. Do not look at the coin. What is the probability that the coin is heads up?

If you are like most people your initial reaction is to argue that the probability of heads in this experiment is exactly the same as the last one: 50 percent. You reason that knowing that the coin was flipped did not provide you with any new information regarding the outcome and that slapping it on your other hand does not change the probability of the outcome. Thus, the probability remains at 50 percent. Your initial reaction fails, however, to correctly identify the probability in question. In this experiment, your uncertainty lies not with the randomness of the coin but, rather, with your uncertainty of the outcome. Your probability estimation was made after the fact. The uncertainty is completely within your own mind. In this case, the probability estimation is not a measure of the outcome itself, but is a measure of your uncertainty of the outcome. From a frequentist perspective, the answer to the question is either 100 percent or 0 percent; you just don't know which.

Situations like these require a perspective that is different from the classical long-run frequency approach. The *subjective probability* approach views probability as the "degree of belief" an individual has that a particular outcome will occur. To adopt this approach is more than just allowing for probability estimations that are "acts of faith." Implicit in its acceptance is a set of underlying assumptions that, if satisfied, infer a set of numbers that can describe our degree of belief and, more importantly, conform to the requirements for probabilities such that they can be combined to infer the probabilities of other related uncertainties. Several researchers have successfully undertaken the development and formalization of such assumptions (e.g., de Finetti [1964] and Savage [1954]). Table 5-3 contains these *axioms for probability* that allow us to estimate probabilities subjectively.

Shared Meaning and the Need for Numbers   While on the subject of subjective probability estimation, we need to briefly revisit the concept of *shared meaning* introduced in chapter 4. If I use a particular term or phrase to describe something and you understand it in the same way as I do, we are said to have a shared meaning with regard to that phrase. If you don't understand my meaning, then I need to rephrase or restate myself. When it comes to probability estimation, the concept of shared meaning becomes extremely important. We can describe the probability of an event with words such as "common," "rare," "infrequent," "regular," and "typical," among many others. The problem with using this approach, however, is that it requires a shared

Table 5-3 Axioms for Subjective Probability Estimation

- For any two uncertainties, A is more likely than B, or B is more likely than A, or A and B are equally likely.
- If A_1 and A_2 are any two mutually exclusive events, and B_1 and B_2 are any other mutually exclusive events; and if A_1 is not more likely than B_1, and A_2 is not more likely than B_2; then (A_1 and A_2) is not more likely than (B_1 and B_2). Further, if either A_1 is less likely than B_1, or A_2 is less likely than B_2, then (A_1 and A_2) is less likely than (B_1 and B_2).
- A possible event cannot be less likely than an impossible event.
- Suppose $A_1, A_2, \ldots A_n$ is an infinite decreasing sequence of events; that is, if A_n occurs, then A_1 occurs, for any n. Suppose further that each A_n is not less likely than some other event B, again for any n. Then the occurrence of all of the infinite set of events:

$$A * n = 1, \ldots, \infty, \text{ is not less likely than } B.$$

- There is an experiment with a numerical outcome such that each possible value of that outcome, in a given range, is equally likely.
- If an individual is able to, or wishes to, express his or her judgments of likelihood according to these axioms, then numbers must exist that describe his or her perceptions of the uncertainty of any event that satisfy the rules of the probability calculus. Conformity to these rules is our definition of what it means to be rational in evaluating uncertainty.

Source: Watson, S. R. and Buede, D. M., *Decision Synthesis: The Principles and Practice of Decision Analysis.* Cambridge University Press, © 1987.

meaning between us if we are truly to communicate. Research in the field of cognitive psychology suggests that different adjectives or phrases can mean different things to different people in different contexts. Beyth-Marom (1982) studied the relationship between certain descriptive phrases and the specific probability estimations associated with them. Subjects given the phrase "There is a non-negligible chance . . ." provided specific probability estimations ranging from below 0.36 to more than 0.77. In addition, we can change our subjective estimations based upon the context in which we are estimating them. Consider this: The statement "There is a slight chance of rain later this evening" arguably carries with it a completely different subjective probability estimation (and a different connotation) than the statement "There is a slight chance of a category five hurricane later this evening." Shared meaning is important in probability estimation and numbers make it happen. Section 5-4 contains several methods for eliciting numerical estimations of subjective probability.

Logical Probability

Use of the third type of probability is most often confined to those situations where accuracy is tantamount to success and the probability of a probability is involved. The concept of *logical probability* suggests that even though a probability may be derivable, its accuracy may not be acceptable under any circumstances. The following example serves to illustrate the concept:

> Betty Boggess has just received some distressing news from her doctor. Based on the results of a recent set of chest X rays the doctor has determined the existence of a small tumor in one of her lungs. The doctor explained to her that the tumor is either benign or malignant. If it is benign then there is no danger to her health and there is no need to have it removed. If, however, the tumor is cancerous then

it must be removed immediately or it will prove fatal. Ninety percent of the time, tumors of this type are not malignant. The doctor then picked up the telephone and scheduled Betty for immediate surgery. Why?

The doctor's decision to schedule immediate surgery may, at first glance, appear to be both counterintuitive and precipitous. Surely a biopsy procedure would be able to determine the nature of the tumor and would clearly be less intrusive to the body than major surgery. This being the case, why wouldn't the doctor perform a biopsy before performing surgery?

The answer to this question lies with the concept of logical probability. Although the biopsy procedure could determine the condition of the tumor, the accuracy of the procedure is not 100 percent. If the pathologist extracts lung tissue directly from the tumor and the results indicate malignancy, then immediate surgery will be indicated. If, however, the pathologist extracts lung tissue that is not a part of the tumor (even one cell outside the actual tumor boundary) then the test for malignancy will be negative and the need for surgery will appear moot. The problem lies not with the accuracy of the test itself but with the logical probability of performing it correctly. The location of the tumor is such that the slightest margin of error is intolerable. Because the doctor cannot be 100 percent certain that the tissue tested was from the actual tumor he has no *logical* choice but to perform surgery. Situations where logical probability is applicable usually manifest themselves in a manner that suggests that a probability estimation of less than 100 percent is the same as zero.

5-4 TECHNIQUES FOR FORECASTING PROBABILITIES

If we accept the notion that all probabilities, regardless of their type, must be represented by numbers, then we are faced with developing a set of acceptable methods for eliciting them. Techniques for forecasting probabilities using a long-run approach such as *statistical regression, time-series analysis,* or *network optimization* are numerous and entire libraries could be devoted to their description and application. As such, discussion of these techniques is beyond the scope of this text and we will not focus on them here. This section will concentrate on techniques for eliciting *numerical subjective probability estimations* that can then be combined with other estimates using the laws of probability. Three such approaches are covered here: (1) *direct forecasting,* (2) *odds forecasting,* and (3) *comparison forecasting.*

Direct Probability Forecasting

The *direct* method is the simplest of all techniques for eliciting subjective probabilities. It is as straightforward as its name implies: The decision maker or expert is simply asked to estimate the probability of an outcome for a particular event. If the source is highly skilled and experienced at providing such quantitative forecasts, such as a professional meteorologist, then the potential for obtaining an accurate estimation is high. If, however, the source is not sufficiently experienced then the accuracy of the estimate is suspect and its usefulness becomes severely limited. Nevertheless, properly obtained direct estimates can be both useful and efficient methods of assigning numerical values to subjective probabilities.

Odds Forecasting

The second common method for eliciting subjective probability estimations focuses on a gambling perspective. The goal of *odds forecasting* is to find specific amounts of money to win or lose such that the decision maker is willing to accept either side of the bet. Once these amounts are determined, they can be transformed into odds and from there into estimates of probabilities. This is the basic concept behind the setting of odds for such things as sporting events.

If an oddsmaker sets the odds for a particular sporting event at 2 to 1, implicit is the oddsmaker's perception of each team's chance of winning. Odds are simply another method of expressing a subjective probability. The oddsmaker in the above example believes that the favored team (the one with the greater odds) is twice as likely to win as they are to lose. Given this, the oddsmaker is indifferent to which team you bet on. If you take the favorite and they win, you win even money. If they lose, you lose your bet. If, however, you take the underdog and they win, you win double your money; if they lose you simply lose your bet. In either case, the expected value of the bet is the same regardless of which side is taken. Consider the following:

> The Miami Heat have had their best season ever. They have played so well that they have advanced to the second round of the NBA playoffs. They must now face the four-time champion Chicago Bulls in a best of seven series. Although the Heat have never won a playoff series from the Bulls they were the only team to beat the Bulls twice in the regular season, once on the Bulls' home court. The decision maker is faced with two possible bets:
>
> > Win $X if the Bulls win the series.
> > Lose $Y if the Bulls lose the series.
> >
> > Lose $X if the Bulls win the series.
> > Win $Y if the Bulls lose the series.

The amounts for X and Y can be thought of as amounts of money placed into a pool. The winner gets all the money in the pool and the loser gets nothing. The two bets can be referred to as *symmetrical* since they are simply mirror images of each other. Figure 5-9 contains the decision tree for this example.

If the amounts for X and Y are set so that the decision maker is indifferent to which side of the bet to take, we can represent them in the following mathematical form:

$$X * P(Bulls\_Win) - Y * [1 - P(Bulls\_Win)]$$
$$= Y * [1 - P(Bulls\_Win)] - X * P(Bulls\_Win)$$

From this, we can derive the following:

$$2\{X * P(Bulls\_Win) - Y[1 - P(Bulls\_Win)]\} = 0$$

If we divide both sides through by 2 and expand the left side of the equation we get the following:

$$X * P(Bulls\_Win) - Y + Y * P(Bulls\_Win) = 0$$

FIGURE 5-9 Decision Tree for Odds Forecasting Method

Now, by collecting terms:

$$(X + Y) * P(Bulls\_Win) - Y = 0$$

The above equation reduces to following:

$$P(Bulls\_Win) = \frac{Y}{[X + Y]}$$

All we need to do now is determine the values of X and Y and we can calculate a subjective probability estimate. Assume the decision maker is willing to win $100 if the Bulls win and lose $225 if the Bulls lose. His subjective probability estimate can be calculated as follows:

$$P(Bulls\_Win) = \frac{225}{[100 + 225]} = \frac{225}{325} = 0.6923 \approx 0.70$$

Based on this estimate the odds for the bet are 7 to 3 in favor of the Bulls.

Procedure for Establishing the Indifference Bet

Finding the amounts for which the decision maker is indifferent to the bet involves a simple iterative process known as *bracketing*. Begin establishing values that are highly favorable to one of the two bets and ask which side of the bet is preferred. Depending upon the response, vary the amounts so that the opposite bet becomes favorable. Continue this process of gradual adjustment until no particular bet appears more favorable than the other to the decision maker. At this point, the indifference amounts are established and a subjective probability estimation can be calculated.

Comparison Forecasting

Similar to the odds forecasting method, the *comparison* approach (sometimes referred to as the *lottery forecast*) presents the decision maker with a choice between participating in one of two lottery-like games. The two games are constructed in such a way that one is an *uncertain event* and the other is a *reference game* with a known probability of winning. The idea is to determine a probability of winning so that the decision maker is indifferent as to whether the uncertain game is played or the reference game is played. The uncertain event is usually constructed in the form of winning a big prize or losing a small amount of money; such as winning an all-expense-paid European vacation or losing $100. The reference game is often structured in the form of a partially shaded wheel of fortune where the shaded area represents a winner and the unshaded area represents a loser. Figure 5-10 illustrates the decision tree for this method and the structure of the two lotteries.

As with the odds forecasting method, the probability of winning the reference lottery is repeatedly adjusted slightly upward or downward until the decision maker is indifferent as to which game to play. The assumption is that if the decision maker is indifferent, it is his or her subjective probability estimation of winning the uncertain game that creates this indifference.

Decomposing Complex Probabilities

The example problem contexts we have seen so far have been fairly straightforward in that they have not contained uncertainties that were dependent on other uncertainties. In practice, however, many situations arise where the difficulty in estimating a probability lies in its dependency on one or more other uncertain events. Such a situation can also manifest itself as a dependency on a sequence of prior events or even on any of various sequences of prior events. Under these conditions, the phrase "That depends . . ." is often used to preface a request for a subjective probability estimation.

When faced with a complex decision structure containing *conditional probabilities,* the decision maker must use a technique known as *decomposition.* In this approach, we rely on the rules of probability to determine the probabilities of each possible outcome in the problem structure and then determine the probability of the event in question using a formula for calculating total probability. The following example illustrates this approach:

FIGURE 5-10 Decision Tree for Comparison Forecasting Method

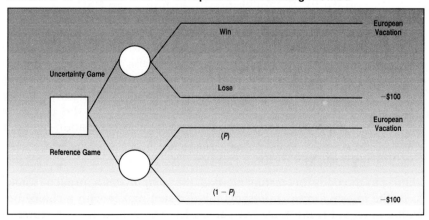

LB Industries, a regional New England–based firm, manufactures a heat recovery unit called HeaTrap for use on both electric and gas forced-air residential furnaces. HeaTrap uses a patented method of recycling lost heat and can result in energy savings of up to 30 percent annually. Vice President of Sales Debra Herbenick is trying to determine the probability that sales for HeaTrap will exceed 25,000 units for the forthcoming winter sales period. She needs to notify the production division of her estimates so that they can plan for the necessary production schedules. She knows from past years that sales of HeaTrap are dependent to a large extent on the winter conditions in their regional market area. She estimates the probability that sales will exceed 25,000 units to be 0.80 if winter conditions prove to be severe and 0.50 if conditions are moderate. Currently, the probability of severe winter conditions is forecast to be 0.70 and for moderate conditions, 0.30. Herbenick has to make a decision fast.

In order to determine the probability of an event conditioned by one or more other outcomes we need to determine the probabilities along each branch of the decision tree. In this example, to determine the probability of sales exceeding 25,000 units ($P[A]$) three additional probabilities must be identified: (1) the probability of severe winter conditions ($P[B]$), (2) the probability of sales exceeding 25,000 units if conditions are severe ($P[A|B]$), and (3) the probability of sales exceeding 25,000 units if conditions are moderate ($P[A|B']$).

Debra has set up the decision tree (figure 5-11) necessary to solve the problem and determine the answer to her question. She uses the following formula for total probability to solve for the probability of sales exceeding 25,000 units:

$$P[A] = P[A|B] * P[B] + P[A|B'] * P[B']$$

By using the probability estimations known to her, she calculates the probability that sales will exceed 25,000 units for the forthcoming winter sales period and contacts production with her estimate:

$$P[A] = 0.80 * 0.70 + 0.50 * 0.30 = 0.71$$

FIGURE 5-11 Decision Tree for LB Industries Decomposition Problem

Incorporating Forecasting Techniques into a DSS

It should be becoming clear that the majority of probability forecasting techniques, either objective or subjective, can be easily included in the model base of a typical DSS. The real question facing the designer is which ones to include and under what circumstances to offer them to the user.

In practice, there is no set of rules or "absolute truths" regarding the selection and application of an appropriate forecasting technique. Research has shown that the set of tools selected by a decision maker is not necessarily based on any particular unique insight but is rather a function of which tools and techniques he or she is most comfortable with. Given this, the burden of educating the user as to the appropriateness and limitations of each of the available techniques falls to the DSS designer. Although the choice is not always clear-cut, there are several factors that can influence the selection of one technique over another. Table 5-4 contains a list of these elements that can affect the choice of method.

Although each of the factors listed in the table can affect the selection of a forecasting technique, the application of the most appropriate technique for the problem context solves only half of the problem. Even if the correct technique is being used, the source of the estimation must be skilled enough to provide an estimate of measurable reliability. This becomes most important when a technique such as direct estimation is deemed appropriate. The last section in this chapter addresses this problem.

5-5 CALIBRATION AND SENSITIVITY

Being Well Calibrated

In most situations we don't really need to know the exact probability for a particular outcome or event. In fact, even if we could know the exact probability of an event occurring it is *still just a probability*. A probability is just a specialized way of specifying an average and an average simply means that given enough time the event will occur this often. Although averages are useful descriptors they can also be misleading. Take, for example, the man who places his left hand in a vat of boiling oil (497.2°F) and his right hand in vat of liquid nitrogen (−300° F). On the "average," he should be quite comfortable (98.6°F). Although this is a little exaggerated you still see the point. We need more information than simply a probability estimation if we are to make an informed decision.

Despite the skill of the estimator and the accuracy of the estimate, accidents do happen and things do not always go as smoothly as we would like. Rather than a single

---

Table 5-4 Factors Affecting the Selection of a Forecasting Technique.

Problem structure	Complexity	Problem size
Precision	Availability	DSS designer preference

Source: From Davis (1988).

probability estimation we might benefit from an estimation of the worst-case scenario and the best-case scenario. Properly constructed, we can say that the actual probability estimate lies somewhere between these two values. This range of values is referred to as a *confidence interval.* A decision maker might indicate with 90 percent confidence that the probability of the event outcome will fall between the values estimated for best-case and worst-case scenarios. With this additional information we can more reliably move forward in making our decision. Or can we?

Simply because an estimate has a stated confidence interval does not necessarily make it reliable. The ability of the decision maker or expert to make such an estimate will have a significant effect on reliability. To test this, we might have the decision maker make ten independent estimates for the same subjective probability. Assuming 90 percent confidence, nine out of the ten estimates should contain the true value for the probability. If this occurs, the decision maker is said to be *well calibrated* with regard to that type of estimation and we can assume that the estimator is well aware of his or her predictive abilities. If, on the other hand, the number of correct estimates is less than nine out of ten, the decision maker is *overconfident* in his or her knowledge and ability to provide useful estimates in this domain.

A well calibrated source requires years of experience and feedback to develop. This is one reason why (despite evidence on any given weekend to the contrary) professional meteorologists have been found to be generally well calibrated. They have to make the same set of estimations day after day and year after year. Each of their estimations gets direct feedback in the form of what weather actually occurred. Over time, they become highly skilled at making such estimations and their confidence interval becomes narrower.

Most decision makers, however, are not well calibrated even in areas of general knowledge. The confidence intervals we assume in making our general knowledge estimations are often too narrow, suggesting we are generally overconfident in our basic knowledge of the world around us (recall the biases of *anchoring* and *adjustment* discussed in chapter 3). Try your hand at the list of questions in table 5-5 to see how well calibrated you are in general knowledge.

Sensitivity Analysis

Once the estimations have all been made, the decision maker can now begin the process of selecting the most desirable alternative given the information at hand. Assuming the models are accurate reflections of reality and each of their underlying assumptions are valid and appropriately modeled, the decision maker should be in a reasonable position to make an informed choice. The problem remaining is that the "assumptions about the assumptions" must be valid or the success of the entire process becomes questionable.

Simply because a model suggests a particular direction or course of action does not necessarily make it the only choice. Even if the underlying assumptions in the model appear reasonable there may exist other sets of assumptions that would be equally as reasonable. *Sensitivity analysis* is a method used to determine the degree to which the alteration of an underlying assumption has a material effect on the results obtained from the model. Another common name for this method is *what-if analysis*

Table 5-5 Calibration Test for General Knowledge

For each question provide a 90 percent confidence interval for your answer. The answers to some questions may be quite familiar to you, whereas others may not. Vary your confidence interval accordingly.

1. What is the percentage of U.S. citizens over fifteen years of age that is considered literate?
2. What is the present life expectancy for the total U.S. population?
3. How many stripes are on the American flag?
4. How many televisions were owned in the United States in 1993?
5. How many airports are there in the United States?
6. How many terms of office did Theodore Roosevelt serve as U.S. President?
7. What NBA team set a record in the 1980s for the most consecutive losses to start a regular season?
8. What is considered to be the most popular activity in the Catholic Church besides Mass?
9. Who quit as PTL chairman on October 8, 1987?
10. What state was former White House Chief of Staff John Sununu governor of for three terms of office?

Note: Answers are at the end of this chapter.

because the decision maker is interested in the change in the various outcomes "if" this changes or that changes.

Performing sensitivity analysis on a model or model set can accomplish a number of useful objectives. Models that have large swings in output values based on minor changes in inputs can be identified and adjusted if necessary. Variables known to be sensitive to minor change can be tested for range of stability. Models can be adjusted to reflect the real-world sensitivity to change within the problem context. Regardless of the objective, the sensitivity of a model to change is as important to the success of a decision scenario as the accuracy of the model's construction.

Although many methods exist to guide the decision maker in performing sensitivity analysis, all follow the same basic process. The first step is to set all variables within the model to their nominal or expected state. Then choose a variable to study and vary it within, and external to, its assigned range of values while recording the associated outcomes. If a small change in the variable of interest causes a measurable change in the outcome then that variable is said to be *highly sensitive* or *significant* and its inclusion in the model is both necessary and appropriate. If, on the other hand, varying a particular variable over its expected range produces only a minor change in the outcome, it is said to be relatively *insensitive* or *insignificant* and it can either be removed from the model entirely or fixed at a nominal value, thus removing one variable from affecting the set of possible outcomes:

> A state variable may become fixated either because it has an important influence on the worth per unit of its range, but an extremely small range, or because it has little influence on the worth per unit of its range, even though it has a broad range. (Howard and Matheson 1968, 719)

You can easily see that as the model contains more variables the combinations of potentially sensitive interactions become quite large. This is another area where automated decision support can be invaluable to the decision maker. Chapter 6 will cover the most common type of what-if analysis tool, the spreadsheet, in greater detail.

Value Analysis

One final consideration before making a choice selection is the determination of whether there is enough information of sufficient reliability to make a successful decision. Because many of our daily decisions must be made in the face of uncertainty we often ponder whether we could improve our knowledge of an uncertain event. If the outcome of an uncertainty could be known with certainty then we could say we possess *perfect information* about that event. If, however, we possess information that allows us to estimate the probability of an uncertain event and we could get additional information that would allow us to better refine that estimate but not reach certainty, we are said to possess *imperfect information*. The question becomes how much we can afford in time or money (essentially the same thing) to acquire additional imperfect information and further our chances of success.

One method of answering this question is by using the concept of *expected value* to determine the relative costs of various pieces of information. An approach known as the *expected value of perfect information* (EVPI) can be employed to determine whether or not we should spend additional resources to acquire additional imperfect information.

Assume we could consult a clairvoyant (remember Howard's Test of Clarity?) regarding the true outcomes of each uncertain event in our decision tree. In that case, the decision maker would know exactly what was going to happen before it happened and could, therefore, make a decision with 100 percent success. This would result in the expected value of making a decision to be equal to its true value. In other words, if the expected value of a decision is $1 million and we can make it with 100 percent certainty of success, then the true realizable value is also $1 million and thus the two values are equal. Because we know we cannot make such a decision with 100 percent confidence, we must calculate an expected value based on the various probabilities for each possible outcome contained within our model. Consider the following example:

> Councilman Doug Peters is still a little uncomfortable about voting to commit the city to a consortium of other city governments formed to negotiate the forthcoming cable television franchise with Televiz Cable Corporation (TCC). He still isn't sure whether the $50,000 membership fee to the consortium will result in a significant gain over negotiating the franchise agreement with TCC independently of the consortium. He decides to do an EVPI calculation to identify how much it is worth.

Assuming perfect information, the expected payoff associated with the consortium is $375,000. The expected value of the uncertain scenario is $200,000. Thus, the EVPI cost becomes $175,000. Since the cost of joining the consortium is significantly less than the EVPI, the correct decision is to vote in favor of joining.

5-6 CHAPTER SUMMARY

Decision and problem modeling is a fundamental skill for effectively studying a problem context, and more importantly, for deriving and organizing the necessary information about it. It is vital that a model be clearly defined and formulated to solve a problem successfully. This chapter has focused on identifying and explaining the numerous problem modeling and definition techniques available to the DSS designer to refine the DSS model base.

In addition to understanding how to formulate the problem, a DSS designer must also understand the available pathways the problem could follow. The modern computer-based DSS is capable of taking many forms, but its essence is always the presence of an underlying model base. No underlying model, no DSS.

Key Concepts

- Failing to fully identify and define the problem results in a solution that may look like a great idea but doesn't solve the problem. By developing a fully formed problem statement, a statement stating the problem in terms of the current situation, the desired situation, and the objective, decision makers can get a clear definition of problem. (5-1)

Once a problem statement is fully formed and stated, the decision maker must examine the scope of the problem, which must be reduced or limited to a focus that allows for successful deployment of the available resources toward a solution set.

- Regardless of the decision context, problem structure can be described in terms of three fundamental components: (5-1)

Choices

Implicit in the concept of choice is the existence of multiple alternatives. Influence diagram and decision tree are two common methods of modeling a problem structure of multiple alternatives.

Uncertainties

All problem structures contain uncertainties that must be accounted for by the decision maker. By diagramming each of the uncertainties and including the expected probability of each one occurring, the decision maker can visualize the various paths of future events and can more easily compare one possible scenario to another.

Objectives

A well-formed objective that allows quantifiable comparison provides decision makers the criteria that can be used to measure the value or desirability of a particular outcome. The closer the outcome matches the criteria, the more desirable the outcome is.

- Structuring tools (5-1)

Influence diagram

An influence diagram provides a simple method of graphically modeling a decision. The relationship between the three components (choice, uncertainty, and objective) can be modeled by linking them with solid and dashed arrows.

Decision tree

In this diagram, only choices and uncertainties are included in the model. They are connected by lines referred to as branches. By following the construction rules, the details of the decision context can be represented clearly.

- By understanding the common decision structures, a decision maker can more quickly identify the probable structure of a new decision context. Common decision structures include the following: (5-1)

Basic risky decision

In this structure, a successful decision is a function of both the correct selection from the choice set and the outcome of an uncertainty. There are two variations of this common structure:

Basic risky policy

The basic risky policy variation describes a problem context where the choice made from the set of alternatives has a direct influence on the probabilities of an uncertainty as well as on the objective.

Basic risky decision with multiple objectives

In this variation, the decision maker is faced with making a trade-off between objectives in order to manage the uncertainty present in the decision context. The best solution will be the one that results in the greatest measured success.

Multiple objective, no risk decision/certainty decision

This decision structure involves those situations where the focus is on the trade-off among the various objectives and risk is not a significant consideration. The degree of measured success or the satisfaction with the final choice is based on the creation of an appropriate trade-off among the objectives of the various stakeholders. A variation, multiple objective/multiple approach, no risk decision, describes a situation in which the problem context is so broad and complex that a single approach would not resolve the problem completely. The focus is on combining the individual objectives of the decomposed submodels in such a way that the largest measurable degree of success can be expected.

Sequential decisions

The sequential decision structure is a series of basic risky decisions in successive time periods with arrows used to indicate the relationships between each temporal choice set. A decision made in one time period affects the degree of total measured success across all time periods as well as the measured success in that same time period. In addition, the decisions in the following time periods are affected to a degree by the decision(s) made previously.

- Decision makers can use decision models, the simplified representation of reality, as a foundation for their analysis and subsequent forecasts and predictions. (5-2)

Abstract decision model

An abstract decision model focuses on the mathematical precision with which various outcomes can be predicted. This type of model can assist in determining which alternative should result in the most favorable outcome. When using abstract models, decision makers should create a balance between models that capture the complexity of the problem and models that are simple enough to analyze and solve.

Abstract decision model types

Abstract decision models can be divided into four subsystems, each displaying certain unique, identifiable characteristics:

Deterministic models

A deterministic model is one in which no variable can take more than one value at any given time. That is, the same output values will always result from any given set of input variable.

Stochastic/probabilistic models

In a stochastic model, at least one of the variables in the model is uncertain and must be described by some probability function.

Simulation models

Simulation is a technique for conducting one or more experiments that test various outcomes resulting from the combining of modeled subsystems into a dynamic environment. Based on the comparative results obtained from the various simulation runs, the decision maker can then determine the most desirable alternative and the best balance among the stated objectives.

Domain-specific models

In some special domains, each discipline has developed its own set of abstract mathematical modeling techniques to serve its needs. In the design of a DSS for a specific problem domain, the designer should be aware of any domain-specific models available for inclusion in the model base.

- Conceptual decision model (5-2)

Conceptual modeling can be thought of as an analogy of problem context. Experience from a past problem context can be used to assist in forecasting events and outcomes in the new context. Using this method, decision makers can recall and combine a variety of past experiences and contexts to create an accurate conceptual model of the current situation and to assign probabilities to those event components that remain uncertain.

- Howard's Test of Clarity (5-2)

Ensuring that all components of the context model are clearly defined is the final step in the problem structuring process. There should be no room for interpretation or misunderstanding regarding the basic components of the decision structure. Only after all elements have been fully refined should the decision maker move on to considering selection of a solution strategy.

- We can symbolize uncertainty of any nature through an appropriate application of basic probability. Properly applied, probability theory can be invaluable in assisting a decision maker in the structuring, resolution, and choice selection of a given problem context. Improperly applied, however, it can lead to decisions which are perfect in all respects except for their outcome. (5-3)

- The three requirements of probability (5-3)

All probabilities must lie within the range of 0 to 1.

The probabilities of all individual outcomes of an event must add up to the probability of their union.

The total probability of a complete set of outcomes must be equal to 1.

- Type of probabilities (5-3)

Long-run frequency

Based on the "law of large numbers," the observed frequency of a particular outcome of an event will be a good estimate of the true probability of the outcomes if that event or experiment is repeated a large number of times.

Subjective probability

The subjective probability approach views probability as the "degree of belief" an individual has that a particular outcome will occur. Implicit in its acceptance is a set of underlying assumptions that, if satisfied, infer a set of numbers that can describe the degree of belief and, more important, conform to the requirements for probability such that they can be combined to infer the probabilities of other related uncertainties.

Logical probability

The concept of logical probability suggests that while a probability may be derivable, its accuracy may not be acceptable under any circumstance. Situations where logical probability is applicable usually manifest themselves in a manner that suggests a probability estimation of less than 100 percent is the same as zero.

- Techniques for forecasting probabilities (5-4)

Direct probability forecasting

The decision maker or expert is simply asked to estimate the probability of an outcome for a particular event.

Odds forecasting

The goal is to find the specific amount of money to win or lose such that the decision maker is willing to accept either side of the bet. Once these amounts are determined, they can be transformed into odds and from there into estimates of probabilities.

Comparison Forecasting

When faced with a complex decision structure containing conditional probabilities, the decision maker must use the technique of decomposition. In this approach, the probabilities of each possible outcome in the problem structure are determined by relying on the rules of probability. Then, the probability of the event in question can be determined using a formula for calculating total probability.

Research has shown that the set of forecasting techniques selected by a decision maker is not necessarily based on any particular unique insight but is rather a function of which tools and techniques are most comfortable to the decision maker.

- In addition to the proper selection and application of forecasting techniques, well calibrated sources of estimation are needed so that an estimate of measurable reliability with a narrow confidence interval can be provided. (5-5)

- Sensitivity analysis (5-5)

Sensitivity analysis is a method used to determine the degree to which the alteration of an underlying assumption has a material effect on the results obtained from the model.

- Value analysis (5-5)

One of the final considerations before making a choice selection is the determination of whether there is enough information of sufficient reliability to make a successful decision. By using the concept of expected value, the relative costs of various pieces of information can be determined.

Questions for Review

1. What are the three key components of a fully formed problem statement?
2. List and briefly describe the three fundamental components of a problem structure.
3. Is it true that all decisions have at least two alternatives? Please explain.
4. Compare the two common methods of modeling a problem structure: influence diagram and decision tree. What are the focuses of each?

5. What is the primary difference between choices and uncertainties?

6. What is the purpose of setting up objectives when modeling a decision?

7. Explain why an influence diagram should have no cycles.

8. List and briefly describe the rules that must be followed in the construction of decision tree diagrams in order to assure that the details of the decision context are clearly represented.

9. Describe the basic risky decision structure and its variations.

10. Briefly describe the multiple objective, no risk decision structure and its variation.

11. What is the sequential decision structure? State the possible relationships among prior, current, and future decisions.

12. Explain the concept of abstract models.

13. List and briefly describe the types of abstract models.

14. Briefly describe the disadvantages of simulation modeling.

15. What is the purpose of Howard's Test of Clarity?

16. State the three rules of probability.

17. List and briefly describe the various types of probabilities.

18. Explain how shared meaning and the need for numbers are important to subjective probabilities estimation.

19. Compare the main concepts of odds forecasting and comparison forecasting.

20. Define sensitivity analysis and state its value to the decision maker.

21. What is the main purpose of value analysis?

For Further Discussion

1. Tiberon Foods, a $5.5-billion beef, seafood, and frozen foods producer, relies on timely and accurate reports to develop sales and operational plans. However, physically mailing reports to their field sales force was not an efficient process. By the time the reports were in the hands of decision makers, they were often over a week old. Therefore, Tiberon management decided to adopt a platform that would support more timely collaborative analysis and remote access that would leverage their current data warehouse. Based on this description, describe the problem using a fully formed problem statement.

2. Assume that you are the chief information officer (CIO) of Tiberon Foods. Identify the problem scope based on the resources available. Make assumptions if needed.

3. Alice is a senior student at the University of Maryland. She has decided to pursue her master's degree after graduation. Now she is faced with deciding which schools to apply to. Model her decision using either an influence diagram or a decision tree. Specify the choice, uncertainty, and objective(s) in the model. Make assumptions if needed.

4. Discuss the benefits and limitations of using decision models.

5. Study a decision made in an organization that you are familiar with. Describe the decision using decision models. What type of model did you choose and why?

6. Try to predict the probability of your favorite sports team winning in a coming game using the techniques of direct, odds, or comparison forecasting. Explain your forecasting results.

7. To be, or not to be, that is the question:
Whether 'tis nobler in the mind to suffer
The slings and arrows of outrageous fortune
Or to take arms against a sea of troubles,
And by opposing end them. To die—to sleep—
No more; and by a sleep to say we end
The heartache, and the thousand natural shocks
That flesh is heir to. 'Tis a consummation
Devoutly to be wished. To die—to sleep.
To sleep—perchance to dream: ay, there's the rub!
For in that sleep of death what dreams may come
When we have shuffled off this mortal coil,
Must give us pause. There's the respect
That makes calamity of so long life.
For who would bear the whips and scorns of time,
The oppressor's wrong, the proud man's contumely,
The pangs of despised love, the law's delay,
The insolence of office, and the spurns
That patient merit of the unworthy takes,
When he himself might his quietus make
With a bare bodkin? Who would these fardels bear,
To grunt and sweat under a weary life,
But that the dread of something after death—
The undiscovered country, from whose bourn
No traveller returns—puzzles the will,
And makes us rather bear those ills we have
Than fly to others that we know not of?

Hamlet, Act III, Scene 1

Hamlet is faced with a major decision. Had he had some of the decision modeling tools outlined in this chapter he may have been better equipped to make the decision. Identify Hamlet's choices and his perceptions of risk and use a decision tree and influence diagram to model his decision.

Answers to General Knowledge Calibration Test

1. 97 percent
2. 75.9 years
3. 13 stripes
4. 218 million television sets
5. 13,363 airports
6. 2
7. Miami Heat
8. Bingo
9. Jerry Falwell
10. New Hampshire

6

Group Decision Support and Groupware Technologies

Learning Objectives

- Understand the concept of multiparticipant decision maker (MDM), the basic MDM structures, and the basic types of communication networks

- Understand the different types of problems with groups

- Be familiar with the basic concepts and definitions of MDM support technologies

- Learn two different classes and types of MDM support technology classifications by features and by technology

- Be familiar with the six types of groupware

- Understand the common MDM coordination methods

- Comprehend the meaning of the virtual workplace

Plano Police Department

With criminals using every resource at their disposal to evade the law, police departments are always looking for ways to upgrade their own technology to share information in better ways. The round-the-clock efforts of law enforcement—involving multiple shifts in different departments and interaction with agencies in other jurisdictions—can make trying to share information a near-impossible task.

The Plano, Texas, police department is now better organized to bring in lawbreakers—and is breaking down day-to-day communications barriers within its ranks—thanks to some powerful tools created with Lotus Notes. And the results are particularly satisfying to the developer behind the project—a man who once wore a badge.

"A couple of years ago I saw an article about the Boston Police Department using Lotus Notes to track gang activity," says Randy Rogers, an ex-cop who now runs Technology Helps Company (THC), a company specializing in the development and sale of software applications for law enforcement.

"As a district sales manager for Lotus, and also as a former deputy sheriff, I was interested to see if Notes could have the same impact on law enforcement as it had on the corporate world by organizing information and improving communications. So I got the code that was codeveloped by Lotus and the Boston Police Department and put in the public domain, started developing applications, then gave them to police departments."

Rogers, who lives in Plano, decided his hometown police department would be a good place to use Lotus Notes to develop additional networked applications that could provide an integrated tracking tool for all areas of police work.

He began with a database for gang activities that let officers track details of gang members with physical descriptions, method and areas of operations, and even photos. Soon, gang-activity databases were also installed in neighboring cities in north Texas. The early results were rewarding, and within a few months the database proved its usefulness by helping officers identify drive-by shooting and burglary suspects. But Rogers knew he needed to offer more applications than just tracking gang activities.

"I expanded the system to include a wide range of activities, such as robbery, burglary, forgery, auto theft, sex crimes, and internal affairs complaint tracking," Rogers said. "It gives the department a much more integrated approach to cross-checking files and data. It also streamlines internal administrative tasks. For example, a captain can now review a complaint against an officer electronically and act on it almost immediately, instead of waiting for a piece of paper to make its way through the department."

Rogers said an additional benefit of using Notes in a police department setting was the easy replication and sharing of information by other municipal law enforcement agencies. Currently Plano is linked with four other police departments via direct dial-up connection, but that is expected to expand to a dozen or more in the near future.

"We're extremely pleased with the results," said Bruce Glasscock, chief of police of Plano, which has a population of about 190,000. "One of the most important features of the Notes system is it lets us network all of our investigative units, so investigators can quickly identify if other units are working on the same individual."

Glasscock added that Notes is very easy to use for officers, who only need to "pick up a mouse and click." He said the flexibility of Notes paid off recently when a new law affected how certain materials in personnel files needed to be filed. A standards unit in the police department was able to create a database with parameters to meet the new regulations within a couple of hours.

Rogers, who also used Notes to develop a national case tracking system for the National Network of Children's Advocacy Centers, agreed with Glasscock's assessment. "It's a great platform for creating applications, databases, workflow platforms, and messaging systems, including communicating over the Internet," he said.

"Law enforcement had been working much the same way for 200 years," Rogers noted. "Investigators would get on the phone and say, 'Have you ever heard of this guy?' It was like dialing for dollars—you try to get lucky. With our Notes database, this changes everything. The communications barriers aren't there anymore. It's going to make police work a lot more effective."

askibm@vnet.ibm.com

6-1 GROUP DECISION MAKING

Up to now, we have focused on the processes associated with decision making from an individual perspective. Although a large proportion of the daily decisions faced by a typical manager must be made by an individual, many of the decisions faced in today's workplace are made by *groups of individuals.* Groups bring several advantages to the choice process: the addition of multiple sources of knowledge and experience, a wider variety of perspectives, and the potential synergy associated with collaborative activity. They also bring with them several disadvantages that, when unattended, can result in decision outcomes ranging from problematic to catastrophic.

A common cliché used to describe groups is the description of a camel as "a racehorse designed and assembled by committee." Despite the improbability of this statement the point is nonetheless clear: Too many decision makers results in either a bad decision or no decision at all. Many senior executives have become so jaded with the concept of group meetings that they condemn and avoid them. The problem, in most cases, lies not with the use of multiple decision makers or participants itself, but rather with the inappropriate marriage of the problem context and the structure of the assembled participants. In this chapter we explore the structures and problem contexts of group decision making, the advantages and disadvantages associated with groups, and the decision support technologies that exist in support of the group effort.

So What Makes a Group a Group?

Let's begin with some definitions. Until recently, the literature on group processes and decision making had not put a great deal of effort into establishing clear definitions of various collections of individuals brought together in a problem-solving context. Groups were defined as simply a *collective entity* that is independent of the properties of its members. In other cases, the group was characterized as a *set of individuals* the combined properties of which serve to define the properties of the group. In still other cases, the structure of the problem context served to define the group. As you can imagine, this lack of attention to just what constitutes a group has led to some confusion and much debate.

Holsapple (1991) took a giant step toward reducing the confusion by suggesting the term *group decision maker* be replaced with the term *multiparticipant decision maker* (MDM). This approach eliminated the confusion associated with the term *group* and allowed for a system of classification of various MDM structures. As these various structures were established, the unique characteristics of each emerged. Research has begun to focus on the various interactions among the participants as well as on the conditions under which a particular structure is appropriate.

For our purposes, we will build upon the work of Holsapple and others to provide a definition of multiparticipant decision making. Here, we define multiparticipant decision making to be *an activity conducted by a collective entity composed of two or more individuals and characterized in terms of both the properties of the collective entity and of its individual members.* Using this definition, we can construct a taxonomy of MDMs based upon structure and decision context. Figure 6-1 contains a hierarchical approach to MDM classification (introduced briefly in chapter 2) proposed by Marakas and Wu (1997).

As shown in the figure, the differences among the various structures are significant and clearly defined. Using this taxonomy, the structure of a particular MDM can be readily identified and a determination as to its appropriateness for a given problem context can begin. Each of the MDM types has a specific structure of interaction among the decision maker and the participants. Figure 6-2 illustrates each of the basic MDM structures contained in the taxonomy.

Using the taxonomy from figure 6-1 we can identify the unique characteristics of each of the three main MDM structures. The *group structure* is classified as a collaborative structure, whereas both the *team* and *committee* structures are classified as non-collaborative. These classifications are based on the degree of relevance of non–decision maker interaction to the final product. The differences between the team and the committee structures are also based on participant interaction. Using this approach, we can associate a specific set of criteria with a specific MDM structure.

Communication Networks

The structure of an MDM is primarily based on the interaction and flow of communication among the various members. In this sense, *communication* can be thought of as

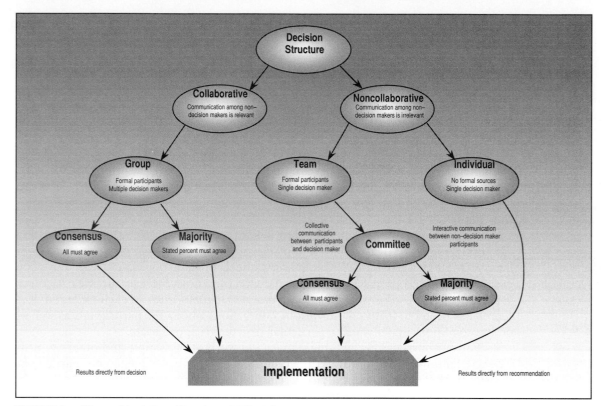

FIGURE 6-1 Hierarchical Classification of MDM Structures

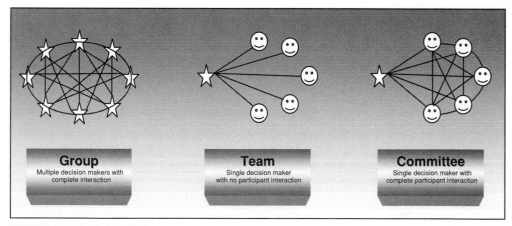

FIGURE 6-2 Basic MDM Structures

any means by which any type of information is transmitted to one or more members of the MDM. Implicit here is the establishment of two dimensions of communication: (1) the direction of the information stream and (2) the structure of the information stream. Using figure 6-2, we can see evidence of both dimensions in each of the classifications.

Early research into group interactions (see Bavelas 1948; Leavitt 1951) established four basic types of communication networks: (1) *the wheel,* (2) *the chain,* (3) *the circle,* and (4) *the completely connected network.* It can be seen from figure 6-3 that each classification of MDM can be mapped onto one of these four basic types of networks. By doing this, we can classify MDMs in terms of the *degree of centralization* exhibited by each of the four network structures.

The Wheel Network

This communication network is considered to be the most structured and hierarchical of the four types. In our MDM taxonomy, it is best represented by the *team* structure. In a wheel network, each participant can communicate with the decision maker at the center but cannot interact with any of the other participants. The decision maker can communicate with any or all participants depending upon his or her specific needs. Any communication between two or more participants is the result of the decision maker "passing along" information from one to the other. In general, wheel networks are most appropriate when routine or recurring decisions are being made and tend to result in high-quality decisions in contexts where time and cost are priorities. These networks, however, are generally unsatisfying to all participants other than the decision maker given the limitation of interaction built into the structure.

FIGURE 6-3 Basic Communication Network Structures

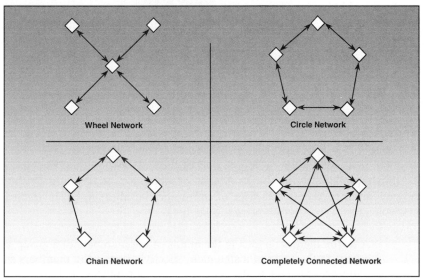

The Chain Network

The chain network is similar to the wheel in terms of focus on the decision maker and lack of free interaction among the participants. This type of network can be thought of as a formalized relay system where each participant receives information from one participant and sends it to another. The end participants provide their information to the middle participants who combine the information with their own and communicate the result to the decision maker. The decision maker makes a decision and sends it back through the relay participants to the end members. Given a five-person chain, the decision maker is, directly or indirectly, in contact with all participants, whereas the middle members communicate with two persons and the end members with only one. As such, the chain network is generally less satisfying to the end members than the middle ones and is most satisfying to the decision maker. Like the wheel, the chain displays a high degree of centrality and is appropriate for routine or recurring decisions with high-probability outcomes.

The Circle Network

In contrast to the previous two communication networks, the circle network provides all members an equal opportunity for communication. In this structure each participant receives the sum of all prior information and serves as a decision maker. Research has shown that this structure provides higher satisfaction to its members regarding their roles than the wheel approach offers to its peripheral members. This network serves as the model for the *group* and *committee* MDM structures and is often employed in situations where negotiation or consensus must be the basis for the final decision.

The Completely Connected Network

Inherent in this network structure is the complete lack of restriction on communication and interaction among the members. Because it offers such freedom it is generally the most satisfying to the members in terms of their roles. On the other hand, because of the greater potential for interactions in the completely connected network, information takes longer to convey and the possibility of error and message distortion is much higher than in other network forms. This communication network is the basis for the true *group* structure. Table 6-1 lists the four network structures and classifies them according to their degree of centrality.

Group Behaviors and Norms

According to our definition of an MDM, the collective entity bears the characteristics of each of its individual members *and* of the unit as a whole. Because of this, MDMs establish certain *norms,* or standards of behavior, that guide the decision-making process and represent "the price of continued membership" (Harrison 1995). Homans (1950) characterizes group norms as such:

> A norm, then, is an idea in the minds of the members of a group, an idea that can be put in the form of a statement specifying what the members should do, ought to do, are expected to do, under given circumstances. (p. 123)

Table 6-1 Principal Characteristics of Network Structures

Highly Centralized—Wheel, Chain
- They are efficient for routine and recurring decisions
- They tend to strengthen the leadership position of the central members
- They tend to result in a stable set of interaction among the participants
- They tend to produce lower average levels of satisfaction among the participants

Highly Decentralized—Circle, Completely Connected
- They tend to produce higher average levels of satisfaction among the participants
- They facilitate nonroutine or nonrecurring decisions
- They promote innovative and creative solutions

In most cases, the "social standing" of MDM participants is measured largely by their adherence to the established norms of the group. The behavior of the MDM members and the processes under which the MDM operates are continually guided by a comparison against the desired behavior as dictated by one or more norms. It is here that the concept of *norm sending* becomes important. Through this process, the participants in an MDM structure let each other know whether a given behavior is considered acceptable. Norm sending can be accomplished through such activities as definition by example (the leader sets an example of appropriate behavior), peer review (periodic assessment of each member's past actions and behaviors), or sanctioning (reward or punishment as a result of conformity or nonconformity). Regardless of the method, once the norms are established and sent, a process of internalization driven by education and enforcement must occur that ensures constant adherence to the standards of behavior set forth. Of utmost importance to the success of the MDM is the fit between the structure, norms, and problem context. In designing a support mechanism for a particular MDM-based scenario, the DSS designer is, once again, faced with obtaining a delicate balance among several salient forces. We will focus on these forces in greater detail in section 6-2.

Deciding How to Decide

As discussed previously, each MDM structure carries certain advantages and disadvantages and, when properly employed, can result in decision outcomes with high probabilities of success. The choice of which method to use must be based upon several factors associated with the decision context. Vroom and Yetton (1973) have identified the various factors that must be considered when faced with determining an appropriate decision structure (see table 6-2).

Using these factors, a set of heuristics can be derived to guide the manager in marrying the appropriate MDM structure to the decision context. Table 6-3 contains a matrix composed of the Vroom and Yetton factors and the various MDM structures proposed by Marakas and Wu.

Let's look at a couple of examples. Selection of the *individual structure* suggests that the following conditions apply to the decision to be made: it is relatively unimpor-

Table 6-2 Factors Used in Determining Decision Structure

- The importance of the quality of the decision
- The extent to which the decision maker possesses the knowledge and expertise to make the decision
- The extent to which potential participants have the necessary information
- The degree of structuredness of the problem context
- The degree to which acceptance or commitment is critical to successful implementation
- The probability of acceptance of an autocratic decision
- The degree of motivation among the participants to achieve organizational goals
- The degree of potential conflict among the participants over a preferred solution

Table 6-3 Matrix for MDM Structure Selection

Factors	Individual	Team	Committee	Group
High importance		✔	✔	
Decision maker expertise	✔			✔
Participant expertise		✔	✔	✔
High structuredness	✔	✔	✔	
Acceptance critical			✔	✔
Acceptance probable	✔	✔		
Participant motivation				✔
Potential for conflict			✔	

tant and highly structured; the information necessary is directly available to the decision maker without any need for formalization of the information source(s); and the expertise of the decision maker is critical. Typical of these types of decisions are those dealing with subordinate hiring, routine task assignments, or decisions involving individual purchases. In these cases, the manager can make the decision quickly and effectively without the need for consultation or formal division of decision-making labor.

Conversely, the selection of the *committee structure* implies the need for some degree of consensus. It assumes that the decision maker does not possess sufficient information, expertise, or possibly time to make the decision alone. He or she requires subordinate expertise along with acceptance and commitment by various organizational members or constituencies. Problems addressed by this approach would include independent intraorganizational investigations involving issues of conduct or impropriety (such as a Senate hearing to determine misconduct in campaign spending), determination of adoption of an infrastructure support technology (such as the decision to adopt a particular e-mail package or database platform), or decisions requiring the need for widespread commitment and support (such as the appointment of a new department head or division president). As can be seen from these examples, the marriage of structure and context is tantamount to a successful decision outcome. In section 6-3, we will look at various types of DSS technologies that can be provided to the

MDM structures in our taxonomy. Before we can do that though, we must look at the problems faced by the DSS designer when providing support to an MDM environment.

6-2 THE PROBLEM WITH GROUPS

The one thing we know for sure about groups is that some unique processes occur when a group of individuals get together; however, we just don't know what all those processes are. Despite widespread research into MDM and various group processes, there is less than widespread agreement regarding the relative effectiveness and benefits associated with managers making decisions as individuals versus as members of an MDM. Much literature can be found that praises the relative virtues of consensus and collective decision making. On the other hand, strong support for the significant disadvantages associated with the MDM approach also can be found. In this next section, we focus on these issues as additional preparation for our discussion of specific methods of support for MDM contexts.

Size

The number of members of a particular MDM structure is probably the most widely studied and consequential component of group decision making. One reason is that, when compared to individual decision making where the number of participants is fixed at one, MDM structures can involve from two to an indeterminable large number (consider the size of the MDM structure that elects the president of the United States every four years).

MDM size is strongly related to a number of behavioral phenomena. Studies have shown that as the size of the group increases, individual satisfaction tends to decrease. One reason for this is that the size of an MDM is tied to the relative amount of participation available to its members. As the size increases, the less active members tend to become noticeably less productive. Further, logic suggests that the management of a large MDM requiring consensus or majority is easier when the size is small (five to seven participants) as opposed to large (twenty-five or more participants).

Another reason that size is a significant factor in MDM success is that as MDM size increases member cohesiveness decreases. Studies have shown that when membership is high, subgroups and internal coalitions tend to form that serve to redirect the focus of the participants away from the common goal of the collective and toward the local interests of the coalition. In some cases, the power of a subgroup within a larger MDM can become significant and must, therefore, be recognized and accounted for when decisions are being made. Boards of directors for large corporations often face this issue when several members of the board band together to form a minority coalition. Political parties also regularly face issues surrounding the formation of subgroups within the context of a large MDM. Shull et al. (1970) found that the ability for each individual member to view the other participants as individuals tends to fall off fairly rapidly after the size reaches six or seven, and the identification of the group goals becomes progressively more difficult.

Another issue related to MDM size is the increased likelihood for certain members of large MDMs to feel threatened or reluctant to participate because the size imparts a sense of impersonality to the problem context. Generally speaking, the larger the membership, the more likely a particular member is to receive negative feedback. This situation tends to exacerbate the likelihood of coalitions forming and of members becoming dissatisfied. Table 6-4 contains a comparative synopsis of the primary effects associated with MDM size.

Despite the apparent drawbacks, sometimes a large MDM structure provides benefits specific to the unique nature of the problem context. For example, in situations where quantitative judgments must be made, the larger the membership of the MDM, the more likely the results of the judgment will reflect the general population. We know this from our understanding of statistics. Consider the need for the Internal Revenue Service to estimate the impact of a new regulation involving a particular tax write-off. It would be beneficial to assemble a large MDM comprising a wide variety of IRS personnel experienced in this particular area of taxation.

Regardless of a specific MDM's structure, the number of its participants is a factor that must be given careful consideration in its formation and that can significantly influence both the design and degree of effectiveness of any decision support mechanisms employed.

Groupthink

Irving Janis, a noted social psychologist, was one of the first to identify a phenomenon uniquely associated with multiparticipant decision making. He coined the term *groupthink* to refer to "a mode of thinking that people engage in when they are deeply involved in a cohesive *ingroup,* when the members' striving for unanimity overrides their motivation to realistically appraise alternative courses of action" (Janis 1982, 9). Groupthink results in a deterioration of the collective mental efficiency, the propensity to test reality, and the overall moral judgment of an MDM. Harrison (1986) expanded upon Janis's definition of groupthink by suggesting that "the more friendly and cooperative the members of a group, the greater the likelihood that independent critical thinking will be suspended in deference to group norms and in observance of group cohesiveness" (p. 184). Groupthink results in a relative ineffectiveness of the MDM at best, and a generally unfavorable set of outcomes at worst. Table 6-5 summarizes the unfavorable outcomes associated with groupthink.

The "agreement-at-any-cost" mentality one finds in groupthink has been blamed for a wide variety of unfavorable decision outcomes, most notably in the public sector.

Table 6-4 Effects Related to MDM Size

- Participant interaction tends to decrease as size increases.
- Affective or emotional relationships tend to decrease as size increases.
- Central, dominant leadership tends to increase as size increases.
- Conflict is resolved with political rather than analytical solutions as size increases.

Table 6-5 Potential Consequences of Groupthink

- Tends to preclude a complete and open-minded analysis of opportunities in the development of objectives
- Inhibits a meaningful search for information and tends to bias any searches toward a self-fulfilling selectivity
- Limits the participants' ability to appraise alternatives impartially
- Often results in a complete failure to consider possibilities associated with cost of failure, which, in turn, tends to result in choice selections that are more risky than is warranted by the payoff.
- Tends to eliminate the formation of contingency or fallback positions

For example, many researchers and historians agree that groupthink was evident in the Nixon cabinet and was a contributing factor to the Watergate scandal and the resulting resignation of a U.S. president in 1974. The debacle associated with the Iran hostage rescue attempt in 1980 has also been attributed to groupthink. More recently, several researchers have suggested that groupthink was evident in decisions made just prior to the Challenger space shuttle disaster in 1986. It is clear that the design of any tool intended to support decision making in an MDM structure must be able to address and mitigate the problems associated with groupthink.

Other Sociological Issues

Conflict

Several additional issues related to MDM structures and member behavior bear mention. The quest for consensual support often brings with it a number of social liabilities. For example, as with groupthink, the desire to be viewed as a "good" member and to be accepted by the other participants often leads to conflict avoidance. While conflict is inherent in most human endeavors (and managerial decision making is certainly no exception), avoidance of conflict is generally associated with a withdrawal from the source of the confrontation. If that source becomes a salient issue to the decision outcome or even the MDM structure itself, the resultant weakening of the effectiveness of the MDM is inevitable. The principal problem with conflict avoidance or suppression is that such actions only conceal the basic issues of disagreement rather than resolve them. Natural group dynamics such as the struggle for power, individual role dissatisfaction, personality attributes, and divergence in goals can all result in some form of conflict (or conflict avoidance) and a reduced effectiveness of MDM choice outcomes.

Anonymity

One common method used to control sources of potential conflict and to support other MDM processes is *participant anonymity*. Most group support technologies provide for individuals to express their opinions, offer analyses, and vote—all anonymously. When the identity of an individual is divorced from his or her proposal, then the merit of the proposal can be evaluated without regard to the status of its author.

Moreover, the "safety" associated with being able to express oneself without fear of retribution or conflict can result in more equal participation among MDM members and allow for more open contributions to be made. In many cases, anonymity can result in more and better information being generated and, thus, better decision outcomes.

Gender Differences and Similarities

There was a time during the early stages of the industrial revolution when women were not commonly involved in managerial decision making. Women had been assigned certain distinct social roles that essentially precluded them from any meaningful participation in the day-to-day managerial functions of an organization. At the dawning of the digital revolution, however, the role of women changed dramatically. Today, women constitute over 40 percent of the U.S. workforce and their enrollment worldwide in MBA programs continues to rise astronomically. As a result of this rise in the number of women in positions of consequential managerial authority, a proliferation of research into issues related to *gender* has evolved. Most notably, issues related not to how men and women may actually differ but rather to how people *think* they differ have become a topic of increased focus. The perceived differences associated with gender appear to have a marked effect on issues related to decision making in both the individual and MDM realms.

Numerous writings have focused on perceived gender differences in a variety of social settings. Studies have shown that men tend to accept risk more readily than women. In general, studies have found females to be more participative than males in MDM decision-making contexts and to demonstrate significantly different values than males (values are an important component in all decision-making contexts as discussed in chapter 2).

Several studies have revealed gender-related value differences such as females placing a higher value on issues including *ability, ambition, skill, cooperation,* and *flexibility.* Females have generally been found to place the highest value on *ability,* whereas males tend to consider *achievement* as most important. Contrary to common stereotypes, women have been generally found to be more career-oriented than men. In other studies, females were found to be more apt to award financial assistance based on merit, whereas males favored the awarding of financial aid based on need. Regardless of the situation, however, two important issues need to be noted: (1) differences in decision making related to gender must be categorized as either inferential or actual (the two categories are distinctly different in their effect on decision outcomes) and (2) differences in decision making related to gender are more often than not a source of strength rather than weakness in an MDM setting. The point here is not to rank the differences related to gender but simply to note them as their degree of discernability suggests a measurable effect on decision processes and outcomes. It is important to note that most studies focusing on measuring the success of decision outcomes have found little difference in actual performance across genders but significant differences in perceived or expected performance across genders. This suggests the so-called "gender effect" may be more of a socially constructed, rather than physiologically or psychologically mandated, phenomenon in decision making.

Negotiating and Deciding

When more than one person is involved in the role of decision maker, the probability of negotiation becomes high. The very presence of more than one person responsible for a given decision implies that the nature of the decision is such that leaving it in the hands of a single decision maker would be inappropriate. The decision most likely involves multiple viewpoints that are not in harmony with each other. Thus, the need to negotiate. A *negotiated decision* is one in which opposing perspectives or factions enter into a series of confrontations focusing on issues of ends, means, or both. A common scenario for negotiation can be found in contract talks between management and labor unions. Neither side really wants to go without a decision but both sides have an obligation to ensure the best possible deal for their constituents. Think of negotiation as a tug of war between multiple players. Each player pulls on a rope connected to one end of all other ropes. Each is trying to edge the end of the other ropes nearer to his or her position. When the negotiation is complete, the center has changed but each player has agreed to the new position.

Most important to the design of a support mechanism for MDM contexts is the need to accommodate the inevitable activities of negotiation. Issues such as organization and control of conflicting criteria and preferences, creation of equitable access to all relevant information, and support for the wide variety of possible communication structures must be addressed when deciding on an MDM support technology. Sections 6-3 and 6-4 will explore the current MDM support technologies and their characteristics.

Variables in Multiparticipant Decision Making

By now it should be clear that when two or more individuals come together for the common objective of making a decision, a series of processes unique to the MDM setting are set in motion and a complex set of variables is present. Fellers (1987) suggests that when multiple participants get together to make a decision we know "something" is going on—we just don't always know exactly what that something is. The good news is that we are beginning to get a clear picture of many of the variables and their primary relationships and, through this lens, we are beginning to gain understanding into that "something"—at least from the perspective of designing and implementing effective support technologies. Figure 6-4 contains a categorization of the variables and their relationships that must be accounted for when designing and implementing an MDM support technology.

6-3 MDM SUPPORT TECHNOLOGIES

Before we focus on the various technologies available to support multiparticipant decision making, it is important to pause briefly and consider the maturity level of this technology and its rate of growth.

In most business organizations today, when groups of executives meet, they gather in a room that is little different from the one in which their predecessors met a

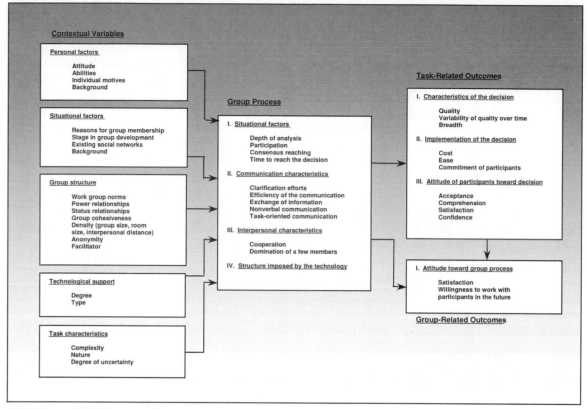

FIGURE 6-4 MDM Support Technology Variables

Source: Reprinted from *European Journal of Operational Research,* Vol. 46, Pinsonneault, A. & Kraemer, K. L., "The Effects of Electronic Meetings on Group Process and Outcomes: An Assessment of Empirical Research," 143–162, © (1990), with permission from Elsevier Science.

hundred or more years ago. Technology is evident only in the electric light, the air conditioning, and perhaps a telephone. The information available during the deliberations is combined in a few memoranda or a notebook or financial and other reports. They may receive verbal briefings made with the aid of charts or slides. However, as discussion proceeds around the table and various alternatives are considered, the decision-makers have to rely principally on what is in their heads and what has been told to them. (Gray 1981, 123)

The above description of group meetings appeared in one of the first papers on group decision support systems. Two issues are important here: (1) a great number of changes have occurred with regard to available technology, knowledge, and understanding of MDM processes and (2) the above is still quite an accurate description of a large majority of the world's organizations. The rate of maturity of multiparticipant decision making is curving upward exponentially, but the maturity level measured in terms of widespread use of support technologies is still in its infancy. In this section we will focus on the past and present state of MDM support technologies and lay the foundation for development of an understanding and vision of the next generation of MDM technologies.

Basic Concepts and Definitions

During the last two decades a variety of new terms and acronyms have evolved with regard to MDM support technologies. One problem, however, is the emergence of an equally wide variety of definitions for those new terms. Many researchers express differing views on what these definitions should be and what components they should include. Even where consensus is beginning to be reached, the definitions tend to be stated quite broadly in an effort to apply them to the myriad of situations present within an MDM context. In this text, we will adopt a simple categorization method based on a series of concentric circles for the various types of MDM support in order that no opposing perspectives will be ignored or misrepresented. The good news is that, over time, researchers and practitioners may converge on these various definitions and may use this convergence to further the maturity of multiparticipant decision making as a field. Figure 6-5 contains this author's basic categorization scheme for MDM support technologies.

Figure 6-5 depicts four basic levels of MDM technology that are congruent to the taxonomy of MDM structures outlined in section 6-1. Using this simple approach, the majority (if not all) of the present applications of MDM support technologies can be positioned. No categorization scheme is worth its salt, however, if it does not provide explicit definitions for its categories. To that end, in this text we will adopt the following definitions for the four basic levels:

1. *Organizational Decision Support System* **(ODSS).** A complex system of computer-based technologies—including those that facilitate communication—that provides support for decision makers spanning the range of organizational roles and functional levels and accommodates decision contexts that cut across organizational units (George 1991)

FIGURE 6-5 MDM Support Technology Categorization

2. *Group Support System and Groupware* **(GSS).** A collective of computer-based technologies used to aid multiparticipant efforts directed at identifying and addressing problems, opportunities, and issues (Huber, Valacich, and Jessup 1993).

3. *Group Decision Support System* **(GDSS).** A collective of computer-based technologies that are specifically designed to support the activities and processes related to multiparticipant decision making.

4. *Decision Support System* **(DSS).** A system under the control of one or more decision makers that assists in the activity of decision making by providing an organized set of tools intended to impart structure to portions of the decision-making situation and to improve the ultimate effectiveness of the decision outcome.

With the aid of the above definitions, we can begin to study and position the various types and structures of decision support technologies.

A Bit of History

The existence of specific support mechanisms for MDM activities far predates the modern terminology used to describe them. Winston Churchill's cabinet war room serves as an early example. The design of the room was notably austere, consisting of a rectangle of tables at which the principals in the British war effort sat and made their individual and collective decisions. The primary support technology consisted of the variety of maps on the walls with tacks placed at specific locations to depict the war fronts and troop deployments. New information was continually fed into this environment by staff members that worked in the outer areas surrounding this room.

By the 1960s and 1970s, many organizations were introducing new media technologies into their "war rooms." Slide projectors, overheads, and graphic depiction technologies were used to enhance the decision-making processes through standardized presentation of information and the ability to refer back to common information sources for further investigation.

The introduction of the computer during the late 1970s and early 1980s was the next logical step in the progress of MDM support. In 1971, the EMISARI system was deployed at the U.S. Office of Emergency Procedures to support the decision-making activities of close to two hundred people scattered all over the United States during periods of national emergency. Stafford Beer and a team of British programmers implemented a computer-based room in Chile during the early 1970s as well. The objective of the room was to monitor the Chilean economy in real time using a system of armchair-mounted monitors. Unfortunately, just prior to its completion, Salvador Allende, the Chilean president, was overthrown and the effort was never officially brought on-line.

Today, a number of facilities exist throughout the world that are focused on the support of group activities and MDM contexts. Many university-based facilities, such as those at the University of Arizona and the Claremont Graduate School in Claremont, California, provide a wide range of technology support and are configured to accommodate a broad range of group-related and MDM activities. Figures 6-6 and 6-7 show the physical layout of two typical facilities.

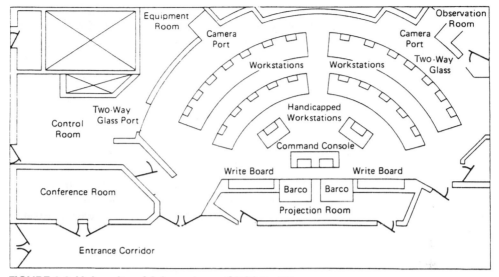

FIGURE 6-6 University of Arizona Large GDSS Facility

Source: "Group Decision Support Systems" by Gray/Nunamaker in *Decision Support Systems* 3/E edited by Sprague/Watson, © 1982. Reprinted by permission of Prentice-Hall, Inc., Upper Saddle River, NJ.

Objectives of MDM Support Technologies

We know from our prior discussion that a collective of individuals brings with it several advantages and disadvantages associated with successful decision outcomes. We can think of these advantages and disadvantages as *gains* and *losses* associated with the MDM process (Nunamaker et al. 1993). Table 6-6 summarizes the various sources of gains and losses associated with MDM activities.

The primary objective of any support technology in this realm is to apply process-related approaches in such a way that the gains are maximized and the losses are mitigated. Although that sounds simple enough, we know that the complexity of the MDM process and the multitude of variables contained therein suggest otherwise.

Four basic approaches have been identified through which MDM support can be provided: (1) process support, (2) process structure, (3) task support, and (4) task structure (Nunamaker et al. 1993). The approaches can be used either singularly or in combination depending upon the specific characteristics of the problem context.

Process support involves providing various mechanisms focused on facilitating participant interaction, communication, knowledge gathering, and memory. These mechanisms are omnipresent in current deployments of GSS and groupware applications.

Process structure focuses on mechanisms that govern the various communication activities among participants including the pattern of interaction, the timing, and sometimes even the content. The primary benefit of process structuring approaches is found in a reduction of the losses associated with the multitude of coordination problems inherent in MDM activities.

Task support involves the application of mechanisms that can select, organize, or even derive information and knowledge that is specifically relevant to the task or deci-

FIGURE 6-7 Claremont Facility

Source: "Group Decision Support Systems" by Gray/Nunamaker in *Decision Support Systems* 3/E edited by Sprague/Watson, © 1982. Reprinted by permission of Prentice-Hall, Inc., Upper Saddle River, NJ.

sion at hand. Task support enhances MDM activities through greater access to knowledge, an increase in participant synergies, and a reduction in losses associated with failure to fully analyze either the task itself or the knowledge necessary to effectively solve the problem.

Lastly, *task structure* mechanisms provide access to various techniques that assist the participants in filtering, organizing, combining, and analyzing knowledge relevant to the task or problem context—as well as in controlling when that knowledge is generated. Similar to task support, task structuring reduces the losses associated with partial problem analysis while simultaneously increasing the gains associated with improved evaluation associated with MDM processes.

Table 6-6 Sources of Gains and Losses in MDM Activities

Gains
- Collective has greater knowledge than any single participant
- Allows for synergistic results otherwise not obtainable
- Interaction stimulates the generation of knowledge or information otherwise unavailable
- Participants can improve individual performance through learning from others
- Improved evaluation over individual decision-making structure

Losses
- Relative allocation of speaking time is reduced with MDM size
- Can block the production of ideas
- Can produce information overload much faster
- Participants may not be able to remember all the contributions of others
- Pressures resulting in conformity can be exacerbated
- Can increase evaluation apprehension in participants
- Allows for "free riding" or social loafing of lazy or nonparticipative individuals
- Can promote cognitive inertia or groupthink
- Increases opportunity for socialization over goal focus
- Increases decision context coordination activities
- Can allow for partial task or knowledge analysis

Classes and Types of MDM Support Technologies

Just as we discussed in earlier chapters focusing on DSSs, the design and implementation of MDM systems must begin with a thorough understanding of the context in which the system will be used and, therefore, of the specific features necessary to support that context. As such, various classes of MDM technologies can be identified based on their intrinsic features, characteristics, and technologies or on the specifically identified needs of the MDM structure itself.

Classification by Features

Table 6-7 contains a three-level classification scheme for MDM systems proposed by DeSanctis and Gallupe (1987) that is based on the features offered in support of the multiparticipant decision-making activities. Each level contains the features associated with the previous level in addition to features specific to that level. The table shows how the features available in each of the three levels correspond to specific MDM participant needs.

The *Level 1* system is primarily intended to facilitate communication among the participants. Its main objective is to hasten and stimulate the exchange of messages and to reduce or remove the barriers to communication associated with MDM activities.

Level 2 systems are designed to reduce the uncertainty that can evolve from an MDM problem-solving activity. Both process and task structuring mechanisms are typically found in this class of MDM support. As shown in table 6-7, the Level 2 sys-

Table 6-7 DeSanctis and Gallupe MDM System Classification

MDM Level	Participant Needs	System Features
1. Reduce Communication Barriers	• Message passing among participants • Access to data files during meeting • Simultaneous display of ideas, graphs, votes, etc. to all participants • Relaxation of inhibitions to contribute • Control for free-riders • Organization and analysis of ideas and votes • Preference quantification • Agenda planning • Schedule coordination	• Electronic messaging • Computer networking • Large shared viewing screen or public display window • Anonymous contribution • Active solicitation of ideas • Summarization and tabulation • Rating/ranking scales • Agenda templates • Continuous display of progress
2. Reduce Uncertainty and Noise	• Problem structuring and solution scheduling • Uncertainty analysis • Analysis of resource allocation problems • Data analysis • Preference analysis • Structured guidance of deliberations	• Automated planning methods (PERT, etc.) • Decision tables, trees, etc. • LP and optimization modeling • Statistical tools • Subjective probability methods • MDM coordination methods (nominal, etc.)
3. Regulate Decision Processes	• Enforcement of formal decision procedures • Increased clarity of options for decision procedures • Structuring and filtering of messages to adhere to rules • Development of deliberation governance rules	• Automated procedure mechanisms • Automated advisor for providing advice regarding various approaches • Structuring and filter agents • Rule set construction and inference mechanisms

Source: Adapted from *Management Science,* "A Foundation for the Study of Group Decision Support Systems," by DeSantis, G. and Gallupe, R. B. Vol. 33, #5, pp. 589–609. Copyright © 1987.

tem contains features that focus more on analysis activities than do those contained in Level 1.

The *Level 3* system contains all of the features from the previous two levels and expands the support mechanisms through an increase in process structuring techniques intended to control participant interaction. The Level 3 system imparts a sense of rigor to the MDM activities not found in the prior two levels.

Classification by Technology

Another method of MDM system classification was proposed by Kraemer and King (1988). This approach focuses on the technologies applied in a particular MDM context. Table 6-8 contains six types of MDM support systems that can be identified using this method of classification.

In this classification the increasing use and complexity of the technologies employed establishes the boundaries for each system type. The simplest type of MDM support system using this approach is the *electronic boardroom* in which the primary

Table 6-8 Kraemer and King MDM Classification by Technology

MDM Type	Facility and Hardware	Software	Specific Considerations
Electronic Boardroom	Conference room with computer-controlled audiovisual wide-screen projection capabilities	Application for storage and retrieval of previously prepared presentations	Same time–same place synchronous interaction. Requires audiovisual technician to be present
Teleconference Room	Conference room with computer-controlled audiovisual transmission between locations	Application to control digital transmission of audio, video, and data	Same time–different place synchronous interaction. Requires teleconferencing technician to be present
Group Network	Separate office facilities connected via a computer network	Applications to allow for either real-time or asynchronous desktop conferencing and exchange of video, audio, and data	Same or different time–different place interaction with one participant serving as coordinator or chair
Information Center	Conference room with video projector for wide-screen viewing. Individual computers with display terminals	Applications for database management, statistical analysis, graphics generation, and word processing	Same time–same place interaction. Requires specialists in modeling and specific application software to be present
Collaboration Laboratory	Conference room with electronic whiteboard and networked computers	Applications for collaborative interaction and information exchange	Same or different time–same place interaction. Requires MDM process facilitator to be present
Decision Room	Conference room with video projector for wide-screen viewing and networked computers	Applications to support brainstorming, topic commentary, voting, modeling, decision analysis, collaborative interaction, and data exchange	Same or different time–same place interaction. Requires MDM process facilitator to be present

Source: Adapted from *ACM Computing Surveys 20,* No. 2, "Computer-Based Systems for Cooperative Work and Group Decision Making" by Kraemer, K. F., and King, J. L. Copyright © 1988.

technology is used in support of audiovisual and multimedia activities. The highest level of system is the *decision room* in which sophisticated computer technologies provide support for virtually all MDM activities and needs. Such systems provide tools to support such activities as brainstorming, analysis of issues, commentary, and consensus assessment or voting. Table 6-9 contains a list of the various decision support processing mechanisms that are commonly found in a modern decision room MDM system.

Collaborative Support Technologies

The trend toward collaboration in the modern organization is accelerating daily. This trend is fueled by a number of sources including the proliferation of networks that facilitate widespread connectivity. Another source is found in the increased global competition facing the world's organizations. The economic pressures common in the operation of a firm in a competitive setting is yet a third force moving the workplace into a collaborative posture. Finally, as organizations strive to take advantage of new technologies that offer greater efficiency and effectiveness, they are finding that their mainstay hierarchical infrastructures are no longer adequate. As such, the businesses of tomorrow are reinventing themselves through the use of, and to facilitate the use of, *groupware*.

Groupware

The term *groupware* refers to a particular type of MDM support technology that is specifically focused on issues related to collaborative processes among people. In one sense, groupware is people. It is a tool that, when deployed and used appropriately, positively impacts the way people communicate with each other, resulting in improvements in the way people work and the decisions people make.

The concept of groupware is really a simple computer-based extension of the traditional tools of the workplace. One of the key elements of success in any organization is the development and preservation of *organizational memory*. The knowledge gained in the process of conducting business must somehow be captured and stored in a manner that affords ease of access for present and future decisions. The tools and stores of organizational memory can be seen throughout the workplace: people, policy

---

Table 6-9 Decision Room MDM Support Functions

- Electronic brainstorming
- Topic commentary
- Issue analysis
- Voting and preference indication
- Policy formation
- Stakeholder analysis
- Organization of ideas
- Evaluation of alternatives
- Survey and questionnaire creation and administration
- Multiple-format file readers
- Participant dictionary
- Enterprise analysis of decision outcome on organization
- MDM session management

Source: Adapted from Vogel et al. (1989).

and procedure manuals, bulletin boards, newsletters, filing cabinets, in and out boxes, planning boards, and computers.

Currently, the competition among groupware competitors is strong with only a handful of major players gaining measurable ground. The current market leaders include

- Lotus Notes and Domino—Lotus Development Corporation
- Microsoft Exchange—Microsoft Corporation
- GroupWise—Novell Corporation
- Oracle Office—Oracle Corporation
- Team Office—ILC, Inc.
- Collabra—Netscape Corporation

Figure 6-8 shows a typical desktop view in the groupware application Lotus Notes and figure 6-9 shows the various components and functions contained within the Notes groupware messaging system.

The major groupware applications are in a constant state of flux with regard to their various features and components. In addition, the manufacturers are all jockey-

FIGURE 6-8 Lotus Notes Groupware Typical Desktop Layout

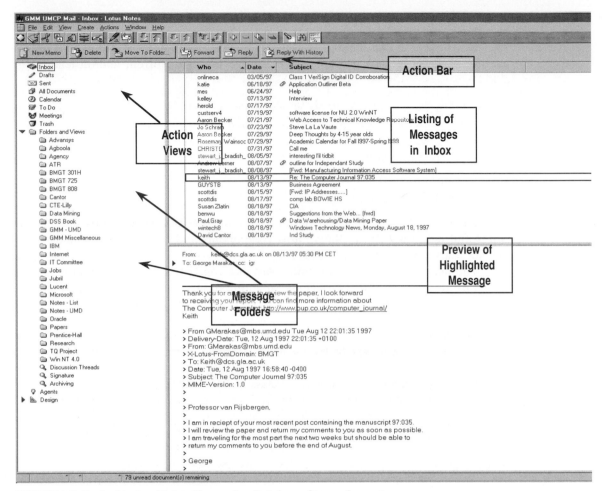

FIGURE 6-9   Typical Lotus Notes Messaging Database Screen Layout

ing to create alliances with one or more members of the competition in an effort to "freeze out" the remainder. For instance, in late 1997 Microsoft entered into an agreement with Lotus to package the Microsoft Internet product Internet Explorer 4.0 with all future versions of Notes. In doing this, Microsoft may have reduced its effectiveness in the groupware wars (Lotus had significantly more market share in this area than Microsoft) but improved its position as the leading vendor in Internet browsing (Microsoft and Netscape were in direct competition in this area).

Groupware products have evolved in response to the ever-increasing speed with which decisions must be made and business must be conducted. This speed requires immediate, simultaneous, and complete access to the organizational memory by workers at all levels of the organization. The many functions and classes of groupware products have been specifically designed to facilitate access to organizational memory using a variety of approaches. Ellis, Gibbs, and Rein (1991) proposed a six-part classification scheme for groupware based upon the type of directed support provided to the organization. Table 6-10 shows this method of classification.

Messaging Systems   The first level of classification focuses on groupware technologies that facilitate the movement of messages. The most common example of this class is *electronic mail* or *e-mail*. A text-based message along with any *attachments* (file and/or graphical inclusions) can be composed and routed to any number of recipients anywhere in the world in a matter of seconds. Unlike the traditional paper-based mail (now referred to as "snail mail"), geophysical location of the recipients is no longer an important factor with regard to delivery. Just as e-mail can be composed and sent from anywhere in the world, it can also be received from anywhere access to an Internet-connected computer can be found. The informality, speed, availability, and ease of use associated with e-mail makes it ideal for the questioning and advice-seeking activities associated with decision making. E-mail allows an individual within an organization to cast a wide net in search of specific elements of organizational memory.

     This class of groupware supports only *asynchronous* communication. This means that the sending of a message is not in any way associated, or synchronized, with the receiving of that message. The asynchronous nature of this communication system necessarily limits its application to certain problem-solving contexts but it is nonetheless quite useful in the early stages of decision support by helping multiple individuals become aware of the need for a decision and by facilitating the early acquisition of information and knowledge necessary to make that decision.

Conferencing Systems   The second class of groupware overcomes the asynchronous limitation of messaging systems by facilitating an electronic version of the typical face-to-face meeting. The greatest advantage associated with *conferencing systems* is that they eliminate the requirement for same-place communication during multiple real-time interactions. Each participant using a conferencing system can be in a convenient location while communicating with others in a synchronous manner. The media available for such conferences can be audio, video, or both. In addition, the environments in which this communication can take place range from a specially equipped meeting room to an individual's private workspace. The advent of *desktop teleconferencing* technology allows for the participants to both see and hear each other while simultaneously allowing them the use of their computers for presentation of graphics, deployment of analysis tools, or sharing of data or applications.

Collaborative Authoring Systems   This level of groupware allows multiple participants to collaborate either synchronously or asynchronously on the creation and revi-

Table 6-10 Groupware Classification

• Messaging systems	• Group decision support systems
• Conferencing systems	• Coordination systems
• Collaborative authoring systems	• Intelligent agent systems

sion of a common document or set of documents. Activities such as segment revision, commenting, formatting, and development of tables and graphics can be conducted by a group of individuals and the outcome can be immediately seen by all other participants. In addition, each individual's activities can be recorded for later review and deadlines associated with forthcoming events can be transmitted to the proper individuals, thus facilitating the management of the decision-making process.

Group Decision Support Systems   The key characteristic defining this level of groupware technology is its focus on the objective of directly assisting multiparticipant decision making. As previously discussed, a GDSS can facilitate the generation of ideas, commentary, analysis, and consensus.

Coordination Systems   Coordination systems are intended to facilitate the integration of participant activities associated with attainment of the objective(s) of the collective. For instance, a coordination system may inform one participant of the degree of completion of other activities and suggest that completion is sufficient for commencement of the next stage. Likewise, it may be used to inform a participant that his or her work is due or overdue. A common activity associated with coordination systems is referred to as *workflow management.* The facilitation of document routing, approvals, multilevel data collection, and information transfer are all activities associated with workflow management.

Intelligent Agent Systems   The final class of groupware technology employs some form of artificial intelligence to carry out a series of steps associated with a particular task. Functions available through intelligent agent systems range from a simple filter that determines the appropriate electronic filing folder for a new e-mail message to more complex "personal assistants" that can schedule meetings, forward messages, or perform background tasks associated with MDM processes. This area of groupware is still in its early stages of development but it nonetheless promises to be a significant factor in MDM support environments. We will explore the technology of intelligent agents in greater detail in chapter 15.

Forces Driving Groupware Development

Industry analysts claim that groupware will be a multibillion-dollar market before the year 2000. These claims are based on a series of forces and motivations that are driving the migration toward groupware technologies. Table 6-11 lists a number of factors relevant to the mass adoption of groupware application environments.

One important observation concerning the forces listed in table 6-11 is that none of them is directly driven by decision-making activities. They are more focused on generalizable organizational processes and activities. This suggests that groupware exists more as infrastructure than as targeted decision support systems. Implicit in this is the need for organization-wide decision support and, thus, the need for infrastructure to support these initiatives.

Table 6-11 Forces in Favor of Groupware Adoption

- Increased cost control
- Increased productivity
- Improved customer service
- Support for total quality management (TQM) activities
- Reduced number of meetings
- Increased automation of routine work-flow processes
- Desire to extend the organization to include both supplier and customer
- Need to integrate geophysically dislocated teams

- Increased competitive advantage through faster time to market
- Need for better global coordination
- Creation of services that differentiate the organization
- Leveraging of professional expertise and knowledge
- Availability of widespread network infrastructures (i.e., Internet, WWW)
- Improved price/performance ratios of both hardware and software necessary
- Increased use of ad hoc teams

Source: Adapted from Coleman and Khanna (1995).

6-4 MANAGING MDM ACTIVITIES

There are leaders and there are followers. This allows for those who wish to lead to come forward and accept the responsibilities of leadership. Further, this allows those who prefer to be led to assemble before the leader and await the orders of the day. The problem with this evolutionary approach to coordination is that it is ad hoc and often inappropriate for the situation. When multiple individuals come together for the purposes of making a decision, the nature of that decision often guides the structuring of the collective and, thus, guides the selection of an appropriate coordination method. Table 6-12 lists several common MDM coordination methods.

The list of approaches in the table is by no means comprehensive and variations of variations are constantly being tested, refined, and deployed. The more common approaches are those that have been found to be effective over multiple trials and have become refined with regard to the contexts in which they are deemed most appropriate.

Nominal Group Technique

Developed by Van de Ven and Delbecq (1971), the *nominal group technique* is most appropriate in a consensus context such as group or committee structures. The approach requires each participant to perform his or her activities using the following procedure:

Table 6-12 Common MDM Coordination Methods

- Nominal group technique
- Delphi technique
- Arbitration

- Issue-based information system
- Nemawashi

1. Each participant writes down his or her opinions and ideas relating to what the decision or choice should be.

2. Using a round-robin approach, each participant presents the ideas on his or her list. Each idea is recorded in a summary list using a flip chart or whiteboard so that all participants can view the list as it develops. At this point, no discussion regarding the desirability of the idea presented is conducted.

3. After all ideas are presented and listed, the participants ask questions of each other for clarification of any of the alternatives on the list.

4. Each participant votes on each idea in the list using a predetermined scale or ranking system. The votes are tallied and the collective's choice is revealed.

The nominal group technique can be performed in a nonautomated fashion as described in the list of steps or it can be easily computerized so that the entire process is managed and conducted electronically.

Delphi Technique

The *Delphi technique* (Lindstone and Turoff 1975) is similar to the nominal group technique with the primary difference being that the participants using Delphi never actually meet. The steps associated with the Delphi approach are as follows:

1. Assemble MDM members based upon expertise in the problem context.

2. Send a survey instrument to all members to collect their views regarding the decision at hand.

3. Organize and analyze the survey results.

4. Send a second survey instrument to each member along with a summary of the results obtained from the first questionnaire. Ask the members to consider the summary results and to fill out the second survey instrument after this activity. Should a particular member's view still be significantly different than the majority, he or she should include an explanation of the rationale behind the different position. This explanation should be forwarded to all other MDM members.

5. Repeat steps 2 through 5 until a consensus is reached among the members. Should no consensus emerge within an established time limit, the most preferred choice becomes the final decision.

We will explore nominal group technique and Delphi again in chapter 15 when we focus attention on methods of fostering creative thinking in an MDM setting.

Arbitration

Arbitration is most appropriate where the members of the MDM are in conflict or represent opposing factions. The process begins with a series of bargaining interactions in which the participants attempt to find some mutually agreeable alternative. All participants have previously agreed that should such a solution not be reached within a specified time period, the formal arbitration process will begin and they will abide by its outcome. If this occurs, an outside party serves as the arbitrator and selects an alternative that he or she deems most appropriate. This selection is not limited to those alternatives under debate but can come from the set of all possible alternatives. The arbitrator can use whatever method or criteria for selection deemed appropriate. A modified form of this approach allows for each participant to submit a final offer to the arbitrator. The arbitrator is then limited to the selection of one of the submitted offers.

Issue-Based Information System

The *issue-based information system* approach (IBIS) is a structured argumentation method that dictates the pattern of arguments and counterarguments among the MDM members (Kunz and Rittel 1970). An IBIS is represented as a graph containing nodes and links to depict the various issues, positions, and arguments. The creation of an IBIS begins with the selection of a root issue node. Then, the various position nodes corresponding to the alternative solutions available to solve the problem are linked to the root issue. Each position node is evaluated based upon the validity and strength of the argument nodes linked to it. The degree of agreed acceptance for the strength of one of these arguments is used as the basis for selection of a final alternative.

It can be easily seen that the IBIS approach could be implemented electronically using the concept of hypertext linking. The issue net could be constructed so that the various argument nodes are linked by hypertext to their respective position nodes; clicking on a position node would reveal the basis for the argumentation in support of it. Using this approach, the various arguments could be electronically categorized based on content, and their strength and validity could be rated using a predetermined scale or ranking system for easy tabulation and selection.

Nemawashi

Introduced briefly in chapter 2, the *nemawashi* approach is widely used in Japanese organizations as a method for managing the MDM process. Using nemawashi, the participants perform the following steps:

1. Once a problem context has been identified, one or more members of the MDM is designated as coordinator(s). The coordinator(s) selects the remaining participants in the MDM process and begins soliciting their views regarding the decision at hand. The number of participants can range from a select few to literally dozens.

2. Based upon the solicited views of the members, the coordinator(s) constructs a choice set. Experts are then asked to specify criteria for evaluating the items contained in the choice set and to rate each of the alternatives with respect to their chosen criteria.

3. The coordinator(s) selects a candidate alternative based on the results obtained in step 2.

4. The selected alternative is presented in an informal document that is circulated to all of the MDM members. Using both persuasion and negotiation, the coordinator(s) seeks consensus among the members. This consensus-seeking may require substantial alterations to the document or even a return to step 3 to select another candidate choice.

5. Once consensus or possibly impasse is reached, the coordinator(s) prepares a formal document containing the details of the selected alternative and begins circulating the document among the members. The document is first presented to the member at the lowest level in the organization and continues through the members until it is pre-

sented to the senior participant. Each member, upon being presented with the document, affixes a personal seal indicating that it has been examined and is supported. Should a member have a strong objection to the document, the personal seal is affixed upside down. The decision is approved if a sufficient number of properly oriented seals are affixed to it. Sufficiency, in this case, differs from organization to organization or even from one project to the next.

Nemawashi techniques are not particularly well suited to MDM structures such as groups or hierarchical teams because of the diverse levels of organizational authority among the members. Nonetheless, under the proper conditions, the nemawashi approach can result in a high degree of buy-in and support for decisions that affect multiple levels of organizational members.

6-5 THE VIRTUAL WORKPLACE

In closing our discussion of MDM activities and support technologies, we need to extend our vision to include the changes taking place within the organization as a result of the introduction of these technologies. The most prevalent change is that of the *virtual office*. Consider the following:

> With its dimpled aluminum facade and TV-screen-shaped windows, Pittsburgh's Alcoa Building once exemplified the power and pizazz of the classic corporate skyscraper. When it went up in the 1950s, 2,000 company employees streamed into this 31-story tower every morning, each to work in a private 12-foot by 15-foot office.
>
> But go looking for Aluminum Company of America Chief Executive Paul H. O'Neill in his office these days and you discover that he doesn't exactly have one. The executive suite has no permanent walls or doors. All of Alcoa's senior executives work in open cubicles and gather around a "communications center" with televisions, fax machines, newspapers, and tables to encourage impromptu meetings. O'Neill's own favorite hangout is the kitchen, where he and his staff nuke food, huddle, and talk work. "It's like being at home in your kitchen and sitting around the table," he says happily. . . . Privacy is being replaced with productivity, hierarchy with teamwork, and status with mobility. . . . Work anywhere, anytime is the new paradigm. . . . The need for speed makes it imperative for employees to team up and share information. (Hamilton, Baker, and Vlasic 1996)

Numerous worldwide organizations are trading in their real estate for technology due to the advent of collaborative technologies. The ability to coordinate the activities of a large body of participants engaged in a complex web of activities from anywhere in the world is driving the rapid shift in paradigm. In short, work is becoming a thing you do rather than a place you go to. Implicit in this is the need to understand the effects of this change on the nature of individual and MDM decision processes. The near-term results, however, indicate significant increases in employee productivity over the traditional work environment. Proctor & Gamble's new $280 million, 1.3 million-square-foot facility in Cincinnati, Ohio, was entirely designed and constructed to serve as a collaborative product development environment. Major architectural changes such as conversation-promoting escalators instead of conversation-inhibiting elevators were used throughout. Corridors were made significantly wider and equipped with strategically placed sofas to allow workers to stop for a quick chat. The traditional office approach was completely replaced with open cubicles, huddle rooms, and central whiteboards that can convert scribblings into e-mail. Early results suggest that the building configuration has contributed to productivity increases of 20 to 30 percent by facilitating immediate data sharing and thus allowing higher-quality decisions to be made in less time.

There are still many unknowns and probably more than a few rough spots associated with this shift to the virtual workplace. Most notably, the biggest changes brought about by the virtual workplace may manifest themselves more culturally and sociologically rather than technologically. Furthermore, given the speed at which our technology is changing, what makes sense today could be eclipsed by a more effective approach tomorrow. Nonetheless, the era of the "corporate edifice complex" is ending and the advent of collaborative and MDM support technologies has enabled it to be replaced with a new era of workspaces that work.

6-6 CHAPTER SUMMARY

This chapter explains the concept of group decision support. Many of the decisions faced in today's workplace are being made more and more by multiple individuals rather than by a single person. Although the multiparticipant approach carries with it several advantages, it also brings several disadvantages and problems to the decision process.

Using the variety of available MDM support technologies, managers can carefully manage the multiparticipant decision maker activities throughout the organization and can be more aware of the potential problems of MDMs so that the benefits from support of the group effort can be realized.

Key Concepts

- The definition of multiparticipant decision making (6-1)

Multiparticipant decision making is an activity conducted by a collective entity composed of two or more individuals and characterized in terms of both the properties of the collective entity and of its individual members.

- Collaborative structure versus noncollaborative structure: (6-1)

Collaborative structure

  Group: Multiple decision makers with complete interaction

Noncollaborative structure

  Team: Single decision maker with no participant interaction

  Committee: Single decision maker with complete participant interaction

- Four basic types of communication networks: (6-1)

  Highly centralized:

  1. Wheel network
  2. Chain network

  Highly decentralized:

  3. Circle network
  4. Completely connected network

- The problem with groups (6-2)

  Size: As the MDM size increases, the individual satisfaction decreases

  Groupthink: Groupthink results in the relative ineffectiveness of the MDM at best.

  Other sociological issues

    Conflict: Conflict can result in the reduced effectiveness of MDM choice outcomes.

    Participant anonymity: Participant anonymity is used to control sources of potential conflict and in support of other MDM processes.

    Gender differences and similarities: Most studies focusing on measuring the success of decision outcomes have found significant differences in perceived or expected performance across genders.

- Negotiating and deciding: A negotiated decision is one in which opposing perspectives or factions enter into a series of confrontations focusing on issues of ends, means, or both. (6-2)

- Variables in multiparticipant decision making: (6-3)

  Four basic levels of MDM support technologies

    Organizational decision support system (ODSS)

    Group support system and groupware (GSS)

    Group decision support system (GDSS)

    Decision support system (DSS)

- MDM classification by features: (6-3)

  Level 1—to reduce communication barriers

  Level 2—to reduce uncertainty and noise

  Level 3—to regulate decision processes

- MDM classification by technology (6-3)

  Electronic boardroom

  Teleconference room

  Group network

  Information center

  Collaboration laboratory

  Decision room

- The definition of groupware (6-3)

  Groupware is a particular type of MDM support technology that is specifically focused on issues related to collaborative processes among people.

- The six-part classification scheme for groupware: (6-3)

  Messaging systems

Conferencing systems

Collaborative authoring systems

Group decision support systems

Coordination systems

Intelligent agent systems

- Common MDM coordination methods: (6-4)

Nominal group technique

Delphi technique

Arbitration

Issue-based information system

Nemawashi

- The virtual workplace: This is the term applied to an office with open cubicles, huddle rooms, and central whiteboards that can convert scribblings into e-mail. (6-5)

Questions for Review

1. Define the term *multiparticipant decision maker* (MDM).
2. List and briefly describe four basic types of communication networks in group interactions.
3. What are some of the effects associated with MDM size?
4. What is "groupthink"? Provide an example of a groupthink situation.
5. What is a negotiated decision? Briefly describe it.
6. Describe the support functions of a typical MDM decision room.
7. Define groupware. Where is it applicable?
8. List and briefly describe the various classifications of groupware.
9. List and briefly describe the common MDM coordination methods.
10. What are some of the differences between the traditional office and virtual office?

For Further Discussion

1. Analyze the leading groupware systems in the market. Describe their main components and compare their functionality.
2. List some methods to control sources of potential conflict in support of MDM processes.
3. Compare the group, team, and committee decision structures. What are the similarities and differences among them? Where might each structure be appropriate or inappropriate?
4. Interview someone from an organization that is using a groupware technology. Identify the various costs and benefits associated with its use.
5. Which MDM coordination methods do you use most often? Why?

CHAPTER

7

Executive
Information Systems

Learning Objectives

■ Understand the definition of an executive information system (EIS)

■ Realize the two design requirements of an EIS and its fluidity

■ Understand the drill down capability of an EIS

■ Learn the history of the EIS

■ Be familiar with executive activities and their basic categories

■ Learn the various types of information needed by top executives

■ Be familiar with executive information determination methods

■ Gain an understanding of EIS hardware and software components

■ Become familiar with the categories of the current EIS technologies

■ Comprehend a development framework for the EIS

■ Understand some limitations and pitfalls of the EIS

■ Learn the conditions of transformation in executive decision making

■ Gain an understanding of the potential features of current and future EISs

AlliedSignal

The president of AlliedSignal's aerospace sector, along with the more than five hundred other AlliedSignal employees, can now access all their desired business information in just seconds. Less than two years ago, however, they would have had to wait for days to get many of the business reports they needed—if they could get them at all.

AlliedSignal is a $12 billion worldwide manufacturer of aerospace and automotive components and specialty materials such as fibers, chemicals, plastics, and circuit board laminates. With Dan Burnham, president of Allied's aerospace division, as the catalyst, AlliedSignal recently implemented an enterprise-wide EIS that has completely changed the way its employees use information.

Burnham wanted to access information such as the top ten customers by business unit, net sales and income by customer or product line, and unit sales by foreign versus domestic or military versus commercial. All this was available at the unit level, but it had never been collected at the sector level. Other information Burnham wanted had not even been generated by the units. "To compute a cost of quality," Burnham says, "we had to call each unit, ask what their rework dollars were, and then merge it with other data."

The biggest hurdle in getting information to Burnham's desktop in Torrance, California, was distribution. Dozens of division executives at remote sites needed to contribute information that could be collated quickly into a single system.

Allied adopted Comshare Corporation's Commander OLAP to develop a system prototype of the information Burnham requested. In just thirty days, the system was ready to be demonstrated to Allied's financial executives. Three months later, Allied developers installed the first EIS on Dan Burnham's desktop. Then, after a month of training sessions and fine-tuning based on user reactions, they rolled out the system to the desktops of more than 150 people at fifteen different sites.

Many of the initial users were executives responsible for providing information to the president's EIS. But at least one person from each site was assigned to be a technical support specialist. After the initial installation, emphasis was placed on refining the system to be useful to everybody, not just the president. Initially, the division directors saw the system simply as a mechanism for sending information to Burnham. But the members of the development team knew the EIS wouldn't flourish unless it helped all involved do their jobs.

PROTOTYPING WAS THE KEY

The Allied development team was wary, however, of expanding the system through conventional development methods that required defining up-front system specifications. They decided that the most productive way to get value to the end users was to build a number of things fast, get them into their hands, then solicit feedback and make the changes they requested. In that way, the system would be based on practical feedback rather than theoretical specifications. They were able to adopt this flexible development model in part because Commander could accommodate such rapid application updates. Commander's reliability was also critical to the rapid prototyping development process. With this development approach, usage of the EIS has grown dramatically. In eighteen months, the aerospace sector's 150-user EIS became a 500-user system spanning all three AlliedSignal sectors.

One of the first applications developed within the EIS was an aircraft delivery forecast application using Comshare's Windows-based Prism. "We track information on every aircraft that will be built in the world for the next ten years," explains Burnham. "We know all the manufacturers, the engine builders and the suppliers, and we can slice and dice the information a thousand different ways."

Since the initial rollout of the system, users have inundated the EIS development team with new ideas for applications and it has literally implemented every one of them. The development group can be this flexible because the tools it uses are similarly flexible. Commander provides the group with a broad range of capabilities that allows it to be very flexible in fulfilling customer needs.

When all the initial EIS functions are complete, more than 750 AlliedSignal employees will be using the system in all three company sectors as well as at corporate headquarters. But despite this phenomenal growth, the development team at Allied still considers the EIS to be in its infancy. People are just starting to see the possibilities of the system.

The CEO of today's organization is not so far removed from his or her predecessors of decades before. Information has always been the mainstay necessity in the executive suite and the majority of an organization's resources allocated to the executive branch is deployed in an effort to gather and maintain that information. The character of the information needed by the CEO has not changed that much either. Top executives generally need information that is much broader than that required by middle or line management. What has changed, however, is the speed with which this vital information is being generated and the speed with which the CEO needs access to it. The typical DSS designed to focus on providing support for a particular problem or decision context, that works so effectively at the line and middle management levels of the firm, cannot provide the diversity of information access and decision support needed by top management. To address the unique information needs of the CEO a particular class of decision support technologies has emerged. This chapter will focus on the information needs of the top executive and the architecture of the *executive information system* (EIS) used to address those needs.

8-1 WHAT EXACTLY IS AN EIS?

Definitions and Characteristics

In basic terms, an EIS is a special type of DSS that is uniquely designed to facilitate the analysis of information critical to the overall operation of an organization and to provide an arsenal of tools that can support the strategic decision-making processes conducted by top executives. More specifically, an EIS can help a CEO get an accurate and almost immediate picture not only of the operations and performance of the organization but of the activities of its competitors, customers, and suppliers as well. An EIS performs these functions by constantly monitoring both internal and external events and trends and then making this information available to the top executive in a manner that best suits the needs of the moment. An EIS can provide a wide range of summarization or detail at the convenience of the executive. For example, a CEO can use the EIS to quickly view sales activity categorized by product, region, subregion, month, local market, or any number of other methods of organization. Simultaneously, the CEO can also monitor the sales activity of the firm's competitors in much the same way. This high degree of summarization can be used to get a quick, comparative snapshot of what's going on in the company and/or the market. Should this snapshot reveal some discrepancy, unusual variance, or anomaly, the executive can *drill down* into the data to display a greater level of detail. This process of decomposition can continue until the individual transaction level is reached, if necessary, to provide the CEO with the information required to explain the variance and to decide on a course of action. The design of an EIS combines access to a wide variety of information sources with a mechanism for relating and summarizing those sources. It also provides the user with the tools necessary to examine and analyze the gathered information so that a swift, yet well-informed, decision can be made. Regardless of the context in which the EIS is deployed, all have certain characteristics in common. Table 7-1 contains a summary of common characteristics associated with all EIS technologies.

Building upon the common EIS characteristics and the various definitions offered in the literature on EISs, we will adopt the following definition in this text: An EIS is *a computer-based system intended to facilitate and support the information and*

Table 7-1 Common Executive Information System Characteristics

- Used directly by top-level executives
- Tailored to individual executive users
- Designed to be easy to operate and require little or no training to use
- Focused on supporting upper-level management decisions
- Can present information in graphical, tabular, and/or textual formats
- Provides access to information from a broad range of internal and external sources
- Provides tools to select, extract, filter, and track critical information
- Provides a wide range of reports including status reporting, exception reporting, trend analysis, drill down investigation, and ad hoc queries

decision-making needs of senior executives by providing easy access to both internal and external information relevant to meeting the stated goals of the organization. Throughout the literature on this subject, the terms *executive information system* and *electronic support system* (ESS) are used interchangeably, though often ESS is used to connote a system of much broader capabilities than an EIS. With the advent of distributed groupware technologies and improvements in existing decision-making and information-gathering technologies this distinction is rapidly becoming blurred. For our purposes, we will use the term EIS to refer to all executive support systems regardless of content or specific target.

At this stage of our discussion it is not particularly important to position various EIS structures within a taxonomy or categorization scheme (although we will ultimately do just that). What is important, however, is to realize that EISs differ considerably in both scope and purpose and, therefore, like DSSs, must be designed and implemented for a particular executive environment and must be based on a particular executive's information needs. Because both of these design requirements are extremely fluid, the EIS must be considered to be an evolutionary tool in an organization and therefore requires a significant commitment to its ongoing support and development.

A Typical EIS Session

To better understand the unique nature of an EIS, let's walk through the activities in a typical EIS session. The session might begin with a report of the organization's financial and business situation. This report would contain several graphics of sales revenues by region or categorical costs of goods sold, but it would also have a section displaying the value of key performance indicators ranging from typical financial ratios such as assets-to-liabilities to more targeted indicators such as the average waiting time for customers accessing telephone support services. The body of the report may use arrows or color to highlight those measures that are going up, staying steady, or declining. Other colors or graphics may be used to indicate those measures that have transcended some predetermined operating range or threshold. At a quick glance, the executive can form an overall assessment of the organization's state of being.

After reviewing the summary information, the executive may notice a color-coded trend indicator that appears troublesome. Let's say the current ratio appears to be declining unusually fast. The executive will use the *drill down* capabilities of the EIS to explore the underlying data used to compile the current ratio. In this case, the drill down feature would bring up screens listing asset and liability categories separately. If this level of disaggregation does not give the executive the answer, additional drilling down may be warranted. Drilling down further on assets may reveal itemized dollar figures for cash, inventories, receivables, and other specific assets. This process can occur until the level of detail is sufficient to reveal the root of the change in the ratio.

The *drill down* capability of an EIS is one of its most important characteristics. This process of decomposition can be selected and controlled by the executive and can be different for every situation. The executive merely selects the level of detail deemed necessary for the situation at hand using a keystroke or mouse click on the interface to bring forth the story behind the information displayed. By going down one layer from a summary of companywide sales to regional sales, for instance, an executive might learn that a slump in a product category can be attributed to a specific area of the country. Continuing to drill down in the specific region may reveal a lack of promotion. Drilling down in the other regions where sales are good may indicate that sales expectations were actually exceeded wherever distributors have advertised the product properly.

Drilling down through the data allows the executive to seek solutions to problems by employing a "top-down" analysis. The EIS summary highlights potential problem areas and the drill down feature allows for further structured investigation. This leads to better decisions, more successful solutions, and better management performance.

What an EIS Is Not

One additional issue of importance is the acknowledgment of what an EIS is not. The organizational EIS is not a panacea or substitute for other forms of information technologies and computer-based systems. Transaction-processing systems (TPS), the core management information systems (MIS), and the individual DSS and MDM support systems are all still vital elements in bringing relevant information to the various levels of a modern organization. The EIS actually feeds off of the various information systems within an organization for its internal information needs and then attaches itself to external information sources as necessary to fill in the bigger picture.

Along these same lines, an EIS does not (and above all, should not) turn the executive suite into a haven for computer techies and geeks. The well-designed EIS should have as its hallmark an interface that is intuitive, flexible, and easily managed by the nontechnical user. In this regard, the EIS should be positioned and viewed by senior management as more of a trusted confidant or assistant who can be easily called upon and relied upon when and where necessary.

7-2 SOME EIS HISTORY

The term *executive information system* was coined at the Massachusetts Institute of Technology (MIT) in the late 1970s. The first EISs were developed by a few organizations in private industry that were willing to take rather large risks in return for the significant competitive advantage perceived to be associated with the use of an EIS. The "coming out" party for the EIS is historically associated with the publishing of a *Harvard Business Review* article by Rockart and Treacy (1982) entitled "The CEO Goes On-Line." This article vividly describes the emergence of the computer in the executive suite—often assumed to be the last bastion of successful resistance to the computing technology monster. While many were skeptical of the widespread acceptance of this new organizational tool, the skeptics were soon silenced. By the mid-1980s, several vendors such as Pilot Software (Command Center) and Comshare (Commander EIS) were making huge inroads into large corporations by providing relatively easy application environments for EIS development that included easy screen design, flexible interface design, preprogrammed access to electronic news sources, mechanisms to facilitate widespread data importation, and a wide variety of easy-to-use analytical tools. A study conducted in 1985 by MIT's Center for Information Systems Research revealed that approximately one-third of the major U.S. corporations had some form of EIS either installed or under installation.

As excitement and support for EIS technology grew throughout the 1980s and early 1990s, new vendors and products emerged that increased the scope of available information sources and analytical techniques and allowed for the EIS to be used at other levels of the organization besides the executive suite. Modern EISs contain a wide variety of data including mission-critical business processes, research and development efforts, customer-related information, financial activity, and, of course, external data to support the necessary environmental scanning activities. Today's generation of EISs is aimed at a much broader audience than in the past and the available applications transcend the boundaries of typical corporate hierarchies. The adoption of an EIS is not without risk, but the number of success stories associated with EIS development and use suggests that the risks are well worth the benefits.

To fully understand and appreciate the value and power of an EIS we must first understand and appreciate the unique information needs of its users. Section 7-3 will focus on the issues surrounding the information needs of the CEO.

7-3 WHY ARE TOP EXECUTIVES SO DIFFERENT?

To help answer this question we must begin by defining who top executives are and what constitutes their realm of activities. There is no generalizable definition for the term *executive* and its application varies from organization to organization. As with other such constructs that lack a focused definition, executives tend to be defined by their common characteristics. Table 7-2 lists several commonalties associated with the executive branch of management.

Executive Information Needs

To fully appreciate the information needs of any decision support system user, we must begin by gaining an understanding of what the nature of the work is and what

Table 7-2 Common Characteristics of Executives

- They manage entire organizations or autonomous subunits
- They are enterprise-oriented in their thinking
- They possess the broadest span of control in the organization
- They are future-oriented and focus on strategic horizons rather than day-to-day activities
- They are responsible for establishing policies
- They represent the organization and its interactions with the external environment
- Their actions can have considerable financial, human, and business consequences
- They must concern themselves with a wide range of internal and external issues

Source: Adapted from Watson, Houdeshel, and Rainer (1997).

the various tasks associated with the process look like. In the design of an EIS, the unique nature of the target user makes this understanding essential for success.

From your first management class, you learned that all managers perform five basic functions: *planning, organizing, staffing, directing,* and *controlling.* You may also recall that while all managers may perform tasks within each of these functions, they do not spend equal time on all areas. One method of differentiating the various managerial roles within the hierarchy of an organization is to categorize them by frequency of function. The nature of work at the top executive level suggests that executives spend more time focusing on *planning* and *controlling* than managers at other levels of the firm. Specific tasks at the executive level include such activities as management and operational control, strategic planning, negotiation, and disturbance management. Studies by Rockart (1979) and Jones and McLeod (1986) have focused on the identification of the specific tasks performed by top executives and the frequency of their occurrence. In these studies, executives were asked to keep careful track of every activity they performed during the course of their work over an extended period. In addition, they were asked to indicate the sources of information they used during the conduct of each activity and the relative importance of that activity. The results suggest that executive activities can be divided into five basic categories. Figure 7-1 shows these activities and their relative frequency of occurrence.

Disturbance Management

The word *disturbance* may belie the real nature of tasks contained in this area. When something unexpected occurs, particularly something that could have a materially negative impact on the financial health of the organization, the immediate attention of executives and the deployment of resources are usually warranted. In times of disturbance, all other executive activities are usually subordinated to those directly related to the crisis. Furthermore, disturbance management activities may require around-the-clock attention during the early stages of the crisis and may continue for

FIGURE 7-1 Frequency of Executive Activities

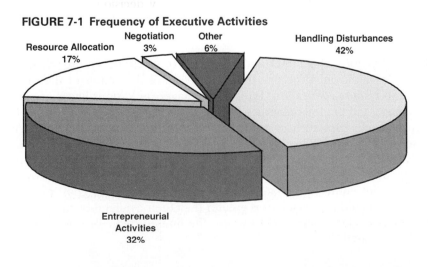

weeks or months before the disturbance is fully managed and under control. As you can see by the figure, the majority of executive time is spent in some form of disturbance management activity.

The events following the May 11, 1996, crash of ValuJet Flight 592 are a vivid example of disturbance management activities. ValuJet President Lewis Jordan was immediately thrust to the forefront of media attention and was charged with the responsibility of representing ValuJet in press conferences, internal and external investigations, and public relations activities, as well as the preparation for the inevitable mire of legal proceedings to come. FAA scrutiny caused so many disruptions in ValuJet's schedule that Jordan was faced with the decision to cut its schedule in half so its planes could be inspected in a more orderly fashion. What Jordan called "unprecedented regulatory and media scrutiny" was immediately focused on the airline. Jordan said ValuJet was subjected to four years' worth of inspection in four weeks.

Jordan then decided to add a "safety czar" and began upping quarterly bonuses to employees despite a less-than-stellar first quarter. "It's clear we're going to forgo a significant amount of revenue," Jordan said. "And we're going to forgo the opportunity to carry a number of people, but we have said we're putting safety first." In the end, Jordan predicted that "we will weather this just fine." In fact, these actions were serious efforts to reclaim public confidence and build employee morale.

Entrepreneurial Activities

These activities fall under the general heading of strategic planning tasks. Executives spend a significant portion of their time focusing on the selection, design, and implementation of improvements and projects intended to improve performance and initiate controlled change within the organization. In most cases, the *entrepreneurial* activities of an executive are triggered by real or perceived changes in the external environment. Executives must focus their attention on understanding the dynamic forces in their markets and the global environment and must use the information gathered to predict changes that can be viewed as opportunities to the firm. Because of the risk associated with making such predictions and the subsequent commitment of present and future resources to projects intended to take advantage of environmental changes, executives must spend a large percentage of their time in this area.

Allocation of Resources

In one form or another and regardless of where in the organizational hierarchy the actual deployment occurs, top executives are the center of the universe when it comes to *resource allocation*. Typically, managers at various levels are given authority to manage and deploy resources from a predetermined allocation and based upon a control mechanism such as a budget or operational plan. The authority to deploy those resources and the various behind-the-scenes activities to obtain them is normally performed by top executives. Organizational resources include more than just dollars, however. They also include people, equipment, plant and warehouse space, and all other entities associated with reaching the strategic goals of the firm. In general, the demand for resources is greater than their availability and, as such, top executives must decide where and to whom the limited cache of organizational resources will be allocated.

Negotiation

Executives are charged with the responsibility of representing the organization in both internal and external disputes. Typically, this role involves the resolution of disputes and conflicts and, thus, involves a significant amount of *negotiation* among the parties. Internal disputes can occur when functional areas within the organization disagree on an issue of procedure or span of authority. In such cases, top executives must facilitate the resolution of the dispute through negotiation among the principal members of the firm that are directly affected by the conflict. External disputes occur when the perspectives of one or more constituencies outside the organization are in conflict with the actions of the firm. Such situations include hostile acquisitions, strikes and labor disputes, shareholder relation issues, and government investigations. Despite the relatively small amount of time spent by executives on these activities (only 3 percent as shown in figure 7.1), the need for rapid information and decision support may be as critical here as it is during times of disturbance or crisis. Further, situations can occur that require an almost simultaneous conduct of the primary areas of executive actions.

In late 1997, United Parcel Service (UPS) truck drivers went on strike as a result of a vote by the members of the Teamsters Union. The fifteen-day standoff cost UPS over $500 million and was characterized by periods of literally around-the-clock negotiations by both sides. During this time, the need for rapid and accurate information was vital to the successful resolution of the dispute. In addition, the UPS executives had to divide their time between activities of negotiation and activities related to disturbance management. Every minute they spent in attempting to resolve the strike was also a minute spent in managing the crippled operations of the organization. Because of the nature of the dispute, the consequences of the various outcome scenarios had to be analyzed with regard to their impact on the availability of present and anticipated resources, the overall strategic plan, and, thus, the future of the company.

Types and Sources of Executive Information

Executive Information Types

We know from past discussion that decisions come in many forms and the information necessary to make a particular decision carries with it certain attributes relevant to the problem context. In addition to the variance in attributes associated with certain types of information, the relative importance of those attributes varies with regard to management level. Table 7-3 lists the various common attributes of information and compares their relative importance to lower- and higher-level managers.

Given the relevance of the various information attributes, it seems reasonable to expect that the kinds of information sought by executives and their sources may also be uniquely identifiable. Rockart (1979) made several observations concerning the various types of information needed by top executives:

1. Cost accounting systems that relate revenues and expenses to specific functions and operational areas are more useful to top executives for tracking critical success factors than the more traditional financial accounting systems.

2. Externally obtained information about markets, customers, suppliers, and competitors is of extreme value in determining strategy.

Table 7-3 Differences in Information Attributes between Management Levels		
Information Attribute	*Lower-Level Management*	*Top Executive Management*
Accuracy	High	Low
Timeliness	High	Low
Scope	Narrow	Broad
Time horizon	Past and present	Future
Relevance	High	Low
Level of detail	High	Low
Summarization	Low	High
Orientation	Internal	Internal and external
Source	Written	Verbal and graphical
Quantifiability	High	Low

Source: Adapted from Watson, Houdeshel, and Rainer (1997).

3. Top executives require information that is typically spread across several computer systems and is located throughout the organization.

4. Top executives rely on both objective and subjective assessments of issues internal and external to the organization.

5. High-level executives use information focused on current results and short-run performance levels.

6. Top executives require information that is often both short-term and extremely volatile.

Executive Information Determination and Sources

Given the unique characteristics of executive information needs, we need mechanisms for determining and satisfying those needs in a given situation. Rockart (1979) identified five basic methods for such determination. Table 7-4 lists these methods in order of increasing formality and level of detail.

By-Product The *by-product method* expends the least amount of effort of any of the identified approaches to determining the information needs of top executives. The primary level of support comes from traditional TPSs and other MISs that summarize

Table 7-4 Methods for Determining Executive Information Needs
• By-product method
• Null method
• Key indicator method
• Total study method
• Critical success factors method

and aggregate the various informational by-products of the current operations of the organization. Using this method, exception highlighting is limited to those areas with predefined ranges of values or easily summarized historical data. The delivery mechanism for this method is primarily through a collection of on-line or hard-copy reports and summaries.

Null   Using the null approach, no formal effort is made to supply the executive with desired information. The reasoning is that the information needs of executives are so dynamic and fluid that the predefined reports generated by typical information systems are not very useful. In contrast to the by-product method, the null approach involves the constant, but informal, collection of mostly subjective information from trusted sources via "word of mouth." This method was made famous by Peters and Waterman (1982) in their classic book *In Search of Excellence,* where they discussed the philosophy of Hewlett-Packard executives using the term "management by walking around." The null method relies on the spontaneous exchanges and discoveries that take place during informal tours of an organization. Although this method recognizes the value of subjective information, it ignores the value of more objective information such as that obtained though computer-based information systems.

Key Indicator   This method for determining executive information needs is based on three basic notions:

1. The health of an organization can be determined by comparison to a set of key financial indicators.
2. Organizations can be managed based on exception reporting where only those areas operating outside of a preestablished set of norms are of interest.
3. Technology is available to allow for flexible display of key indicator information in graphical form.

The first notion requires the identification of relevant financial indicators such as internal financial ratios, production levels, revenues and expenses, and market share. Once these indicators are identified, information about each of them is collected on a continual basis and used to make adjustments or decisions critical to the ongoing success of the organization.

The second notion suggests that a range of operational values and norms can be accurately established in such a way that the concept of "no news is good news" becomes operational. Top executives monitor only that information that reflects an out-of-nominal condition and gather additional information as a basis for making decisions intended to correct the condition.

The third notion requires the information to be made available in graphical rather than tabular form. Using this approach, the executive can more easily "see" the exceptional condition and respond to it more rapidly than would be expected through analysis of tabular data.

Total Study   The total study approach gathers information from a sample of top executives in the organization concerning the totality of their information needs. Following these interviews, system developers make a comparison between the stated needs of the executives and the present information capabilities of the organization's computer systems. Where voids can be identified, the developers create new subsystems to create the missing information. This method, while more comprehensive than its predecessors, is nonetheless both expensive and somewhat problematic with regard to its ability to meet the needs of any single executive well. As such, this method, while intuitively attractive, has not manifested itself as a practical approach to EIS design.

Critical Success Factors The fifth and most comprehensive of the approaches identified by Rockart seeks to overcome the various weaknesses associated with the other methods. Regardless of the nature of the organization, certain areas of activity, called critical success factors (CSF), exist in which satisfactory results will ensure the health and competitiveness of that organization. According to Rockart, CSFs are those things that simply must be done right if the organization is to be successful. Similar to the key indicators approach, this method requires information on the identified CSFs to be constantly gathered and supplied to top executives. This information is used as the basis for decisions affecting the organization.

The primary method for establishing the CSFs of an organization is through structured interviewing of the top executives of the firm. Following this, CSFs are further refined through a series of facilitated collaborative sessions where the executives discuss the goals and objectives of the firm, the CSFs related to those goals, and just how they might be measured. Given your knowledge of MDM structures from chapter 6, what might be an appropriate structure for such collaborative sessions?

Of the five approaches identified and discussed any or all of the last three methods could easily serve as the basis for the design of a computer-based EIS. In the next section, we will look at the various components of a typical EIS and explore several available application environments used in their design and implementation.

7-4 EIS COMPONENTS

Many organizations are still evolving from their "big iron" days of the mainframe to the more flexible and functional client/server environment. In many cases, this evolution can be credited with enabling the relative ease of development and implementation of computer-based decision support technologies (as well as many other organizational information systems). Several companies have marked the end of this transition in their environments to develop and deploy their first EIS.

The client/server architecture allows for rapid additions and modifications to be incorporated into business applications and facilitates the widespread access and dissemination of disparate databases located throughout the globe. While several of the early EIS products were originally developed for use in a high-powered computing environment, all of the currently marketed products are targeted at the client/server platform and are designed to be deployed in a variety of settings (local, mobile, Internet access, etc.). Several of the specific benefits of the client/server architecture are as follows:

1. **Multiple views of geographically dispersed data** residing on corporate computer platforms ranging from mainframes to personal computers (PCs) regardless of data format

2. **Reduction of investment costs** in new computer hardware and physical plant

3. **Establishment of a flexible platform** that can change and adapt to the dynamic needs of the organization

4. **Facilitates management using "real-time" data** resulting in faster, more informed decisions and providing a competitive advantage resulting from the reduced decision time

5. **Facilitates the use of information as a competitive weapon** through the easy creation of "strategic" applications that can reveal the "hidden treasures" within an organization's data

Figure 7-2 illustrates a typical EIS implementation within an organization's client/server environment.

Hardware Components

The EIS does not require any unique computing hardware or peripherals other than those typically found in a modern client/server environment. The important considerations regarding sufficient RAM memory, hard drive space, removable storage, high-speed graphics, data access, large display terminals, and multimedia capabilities rele-

FIGURE 7-2 Typical Client/Server Architecture for EIS Implementation

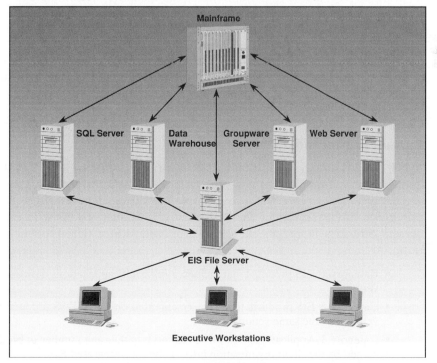

vant to any client-side setup are equally relevant in an EIS environment. A key issue, however, is to be sure that the components of the EIS optimize and conform to the organizational computing resources as well as adapt to the legacy, or existing system, data. The executive is, in many cases, the user that will require the most support in terms of both training in the early stages and modifications in the later ones. The system must be configured so that the organization's resources and capabilities with regard to providing such support are well matched. Otherwise, a disgruntled executive will result and the benefits surrounding the EIS will never be realized.

Software Components

In contrast to the rather "generic" nature of the hardware components of an EIS, the software components are normally highly specialized and designed to meet the specific needs of specific users. The trend toward open, modular development environments, however, has made the concept of an "off-the-shelf" EIS a reality. Many vendors are offering general-purpose EIS application environments that contain the features and capabilities most often required in a typical EIS. These general-purpose environments allow for the addition and integration of a wide variety of add-on packages from third-party vendors that permit the EIS designer to easily customize the application to meet the specific needs of the executive user group. More recently, EIS applications have begun to emerge that are built around groupware packages that provide additional collaborative features in addition to the standard EIS functions. Two such examples are *GroupSystems* from Ventana Corporation and *Lotus Notes* from Lotus Development. GroupSystems can facilitate the complete design and ongoing maintenance associated with an EIS and Notes can be used as either a partial integration to an existing EIS system or as a total EIS software development platform.

Suffice it to say that the individuality in an EIS comes from the software component rather than from the hardware. Regardless of the specific needs of the executive, all EIS systems tend to possess many commonly requested features and functions. Table 7-5 lists the various common features and functions of a modern client/server-based EIS.

Current EIS Technologies

The EIS marketplace contains a variety of offerings that provide EIS designers with application environments ranging from off-the-shelf solutions to highly customizable and proprietary systems. When considering the various EIS offerings, the components previously discussed render them all relatively similar. To assist in categorizing the current offerings, Dobrzeniecki (1994) proposed a three-tiered functional categorization:

- Category 1: EIS products that include a full set of applications developed by the same vendor
- Category 2: EIS products that are implemented on top of DSS products previously developed by the same vendor
- Category 3: Applications that serve to bind together any number of products currently owned by the client organization into a cohesive, integrated EIS

Table 7-5 Common Features and Functions of Modern EIS Applications

- Status access, drill down, exception reporting, trend analysis, and ad hoc queries/reports
- Multiple user interfaces
- Multiple search engines and algorithms
- Graphical user interface (GUI) navigation (pull-down menus, pop-up lists, etc.)
- Multiple output channels (screen, hardcopy, transparency, etc.)
- Seamless integration with commercial office suites
- Integrated DSS
- Widespread access to external databases and information repositories
- Data management capabilities
- Multidimensional data mining and visualization
- Electronic messaging
- Calendaring and scheduling
- Open architecture
- Online, context-sensitive help mechanisms
- Screen design templates and wizards
- Application design shells
- Multilevel access control security
- Backup and recovery functions
- Usage monitoring

To be considered an EIS, the software application product(s) should address the needs of the executive in the following areas:

- *Office support*

  Provide e-mail services and access to intracompany and external industry news services

  Support common office automation functions including word processing, calendaring and scheduling, address book, and to-do list

- *Analytical support*

  Provide unstructured system query support

  Provide DSS assistance and capabilities

  Provide graphic output of trends, key indicators, summary documents, and exception reporting

  Provide key word searching, drill down capability, and text-based explanations or help systems

- *Customization*

  Allow for flexible modification to report formats, graphic style and type, and menu content

- *Graphics*

  Provide a full range of graphic generation and display options

- *Planning*

  Provide project management and scheduling functions

- *Interface*

   Provide user-friendly, easy to learn and use data navigation modes
- *Implementation*

   Provide cost-effective integration with organizational computing resources

   Provide training and long-range technical support

   Allow for remote access capability

   Provide data security features

The EIS commercial marketplace is constantly changing with new vendors and applications emerging on an almost daily basis. A section has been included at the end of this chapter that contains a fairly comprehensive listing of the major EIS products currently available and provides short descriptions of each along with sample screenshots of several of the more popular offerings.

7-5 MAKING THE EIS WORK

In one sense, building an EIS is much like building any other type of modern information system. A structured development approach needs to be followed, requirements need to be gathered, prototypes developed, logical models revised, cost analyses performed, and the final system needs to be implemented. In another sense, the unique character of an EIS indicates that we still have much to learn about successfully building one. For some developers, their next EIS project will also be their first. They will be thrust into the realm of executives: A world where success has often been realized without a computer, time and patience may be both precious and limited, the problems are often unstructured, and computer literacy and acumen may vary considerably. Furthermore, the physical considerations associated with building an EIS, such as determining the hardware, finding and accessing the necessary data, and integrating the system into the existing computing infrastructure, also contribute to the uniqueness of the challenge. Top this all off with political issues such as middle management's fear that "Big Brother will be watching" and it becomes easy to see why building a successful EIS may be one of the most formidable development efforts analysts and developers will ever face. This section focuses on many of the issues surrounding these challenges.

An EIS Development Framework

Numerous researchers and practitioners have focused their efforts on studying and refining our understanding of the processes associated with building and implementing a successful EIS. Watson, Rainer, and Koh (1991) provide a touchstone to this ongoing investigation with their EIS development framework. A development framework provides the terminology, concepts, and guidelines necessary for building a system; it is somewhat analogous to a generic instruction manual or road map. Their framework is divided into three major components: (1) *the structural perspective,* where the key elements that are critical to EIS development and their relationships are delineated, (2) *the development process,* where the dynamics and interactions of the necessary activities are identified, and (3) *the user-system dialog,* the interface that directs the system's actions, presents the output, and provides the user with the tools to use the system effectively. A detailed discussion of this framework is beyond the scope of this text; however, we will briefly discuss the three components and their importance to a successful EIS. Figure 7-3 illustrates the elements contained in the structural perspective and their relationships to the EIS.

Structural Perspective

In this component, the focus is on people and data as they relate to the EIS. Key players such as the sponsors or advocates of the system, the user group, the developers and designers, personnel from the various functional areas within the organization, and any vendors and consultants associated with the system are identified and positioned. In addition, the various sources of internal and external data are identified and positioned. Finally, an acknowledgement of the various forces and pressures either driving or affecting the successful development of the system is included. The structural perspective provides a model for understanding the relationships among the various elements and their potential interaction during the various phases of development of the EIS.

EIS Development Process

The *development process* builds upon the elements and their relationships contained within the structural model and adds a time dimension to the framework. In this component, the various activities and sequences of events are delineated and ac-

FIGURE 7-3 Structure Perspective of EIS Development Framework (from Watson, Rainer, and Koh 1991)

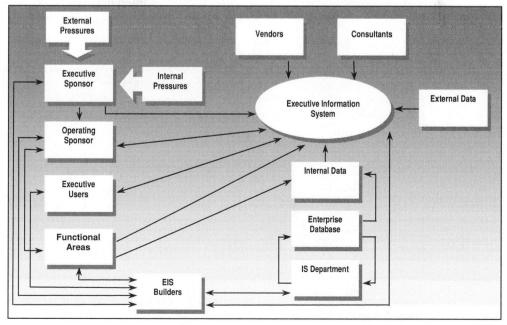

tual project management issues relating to time, critical path, and milestones are established. Figure 7-4 illustrates the various phases of the EIS development process.

User-System Dialog

This component of the framework is where we can see the most commonalties between the design and development of an EIS and other related tools such as DSS or MDM systems. The *dialog system* contains an *action language* where the various commands and elements of manipulation are contained and processed. With this language the user is directed in how to use the system. The action language element can be thought of as the incoming communication channel from the executive to the EIS.

In contrast, the dialog component also contains a *presentation language* that serves as the EIS counterpart to the action language. The outflow of information and the form in which this information is presented is guided and dictated by the presentation language component. Characteristics typical of this component include textual, graphical, and tabular formats, voice annotation, and audio and video capabilities.

The third element in this component is the *knowledge base*. Covered in greater detail in chapter 1, the knowledge base is the sum of what the executive knows about using the system and all of the support mechanisms designed to assist in its use. Experience shows that executives simply do not read documentation (unlike you or I, of course). Because of this, the knowledge base must provide the executive with a consistent and context-dependent help system if the EIS is to be used effectively.

The intention of the development framework is to provide boundaries and guidelines for development of an EIS. In addition to the component elements of the

FIGURE 7-4 EIS Development Process

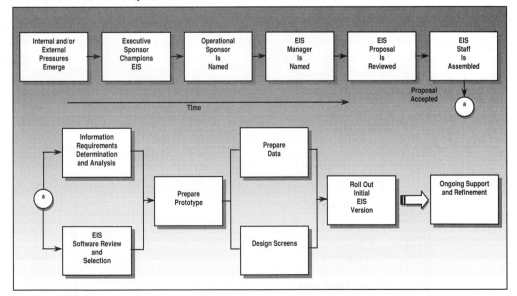

Source: Building Executive Information Systems & Other Decision Support Applications by Watson, Houdeshel, and Ranier. Copyright © 1997 by John Wiley & Sons. Reprinted by permission of John Wiley & Sons, Inc.

framework, however, Watson, Singh, and Holmes (1995) offer two additional considerations when designing and developing an EIS. First, the EIS must be easy to use. The authors state that "because of the nature of the executive user, the system has to go beyond user friendly and be 'user intuitive' or even 'user seductive.'" Second, the EIS must have an acceptably fast response time. Some designers have attempted to establish a quantifiable benchmark minimum for response time of five seconds or less. Watson, Singh, and Holmes suggest, however, that executive tolerance for response time will vary depending upon the nature of the inquiry; ad hoc queries will elicit greater tolerance for response than simple scanning of prefabricated analyses. The authors cite an unnamed EIS developer who defined acceptable EIS response time when moving from screen to screen as "the time it takes the executive to turn a page of *The Wall Street Journal.*"

Some EIS Limitations and Pitfalls to Avoid

The development and implementation of an EIS brings significant benefits to an organization, and its potential for improving both competitive advantage and performance is a driving factor in its increasingly widespread popularity. Its benefits are not without some caveats, however. Here, we summarize several of the limitations and caveats associated with EIS development.

Cost

Watson, Rainer, and Koh (1991) conducted a survey of organizations using EISs and found the mean development cost to be $365,000. A breakdown of this figure revealed an allocation for software of $128,000, hardware costs of $129,000, personnel costs of $90,000, and the remainder allocated to training. In this same survey, they found the mean annual operating costs for an EIS (including ongoing upgrade and enhancement) to be in excess of $200,000. The majority of this annual operating cost was allocated to personnel and additional training. In other words, the benefits derived from an EIS are costly and the cost of maintenance of the system after development can easily exceed the original development costs over the life of the system. The decision to adopt an EIS into an organization must be made with the understanding that the ongoing commitment of significant organizational resources is critical if the expected benefits are ever to be realized.

Technological Limitations

The essence of an EIS resides in its ability to bring all of the dispersed data and information necessary to make executive decisions into the executive suite and contain it in a easy-to-use system. The myriad of data sources necessary to accomplish this and the wide variety of media in which they can reside poses a formidable technical challenge for the EIS designer. To accomplish this seemingly magical feat, developers may need to learn new file structures, data formats, and programming languages as well as enlist the services and support of a variety of data providers and other MIS personnel.

To add to the technical issues facing the EIS designer, the seamless integration of the EIS into the existing computing infrastructure of the organization poses a challenge. As discussed previously, many organizations are still immersed in the transition from older "big iron" environments to the client/server architecture. The presence of this dynamic in the environment must be accounted for in the initial design stages of an EIS. The momentum of this change can often dictate the platform and software selected to design and deploy the EIS. Nonetheless, the EIS must be able to access the data during their residence in the legacy system and during their transition to the more modern computing environments.

Organizational Limitations

Aside from the technological issues facing the EIS designer, we must also consider those of an organizational nature. These issues can often be more complex and, thus, more difficult to address than the technical limitations. Millet and Mawhinney (1992) suggested three main categories of potential negative impacts of an EIS on organizations: (1) *biased agendas and time orientations,* (2) *loss of managerial synchronization,* and (3) *organizational destabilization.*

Agendas and Time Biases   Despite the EIS designer's goal of providing the executive with a total information and decision-making package, the system is usually only a part (albeit often a large one) of the totality of information that an executive should ideally consider in making the critical strategic decisions of an organization. The EIS provides information associated with the measurable aspects of the organization and the environment. The less quantifiable aspects of the problem context most often must be obtained from sources other than the EIS. As such, the EIS represents only part of the executive's total agenda. It may become easy to be overreliant on the EIS, thus focusing the executive's attention on that which can be measured rather than that which is both relevant and necessary. This form of information channeling can cause an executive's agenda to be biased toward a superficial analysis of the environment.

Another potential pitfall associated with EIS use is rooted in the nature of the EIS itself. Because of its ability to produce relevant information with greater frequency and with greater accuracy and depth than an executive is accustomed to, he or she may be lured into concentrating on the more short-run, lower-level decisions within the organization, thus losing focus on decisions having to do with the bigger picture. An EIS can promote a more micromanagerial approach to conducting business and this can disrupt the activities of middle- and lower-level managers. Simply knowing that the top executives can monitor their every move via the drill down capabilities of the EIS can force a shifting of time orientation. The lower-level managers will begin to turn their attention to decisions with shorter time horizons in an effort to create improvement in the more closely monitored aspects of their work, thus losing their focus on more long-term performance issues.

Managerial Synchronization   This issue is an extension of the time and agenda issues just discussed. The various managerial processes of an organization not only must be carefully delineated and effectively allocated but also must be coordinated or synchronized toward reaching the goals of the firm. One method of accomplishing this is through the establishment of a periodic reporting mechanism. Such an approach serves to orchestrate the shared review of key indicators and critical success factors across managerial levels. While most EISs can, and do, produce a variety of periodic reports, they can also be used extensively to produce on-demand, ad hoc reports. A heavy reliance on ad hoc reports can sometimes disrupt the stable and well-established reporting cycles within an organization that have been designed to synchronize management activities. The important point here is that while ad hoc reporting is a valuable tool in the executive's EIS arsenal, it must not be used as a replacement for the more stable periodic reporting systems.

Destabilization   By returning to our oft-used cache of airplane metaphors the issue of destabilization can be better understood. The physics associated with flying an airplane are in constant flux across the three dimensions of altitude, forward motion, and direction. A pilot must respond to changes in each of these dimensions with the intention of reaching a goal such as increasing altitude or changing direction while simultaneously performing actions that return the aircraft to stable flight following the attainment of the goal. If the pilot overreacts to a particular short-term flux in one or more of the flight dimensions, the aircraft may destabilize and require additional, more focused actions to take place. The point is, the concept of stability is better thought of as an average of conditions over time. The key to stability is not simply to effect an average, however, but to effect an average that is based on as small a variance in change as possible. In the organizational setting, the executive must be positioned to decide rather than to simply react. The fast responses to spur-of-the-moment inquiries made by an executive to an EIS can provide the ability to react swiftly to changes in the operating range of the organization. It is important, however, that such fast responses do not encourage the executive to react too swiftly by making adjustments to the organization that are too frequent or too strong. Such overreactions by executives can destabilize an otherwise stable organization in much the same manner as an overreactive pilot can destabilize an otherwise smooth-flying aircraft.

Failure Is Not an Acceptable Alternative

As with any development effort, there is the possibility of partial or total failure for a particular EIS. An EIS failure occurs when the development effort fails to produce a working system or when the installed system fails to be usable or deliver the desired benefits. Crockett (1992) clearly demonstrated that an EIS development effort that fails to satisfy its targeted users can be a severe setback not only for the organization but for the individuals involved. Competitive edge and opportunity can be lost, many people will be disappointed, careers will undoubtedly be adversely affected, and most important, the organization will likely become reluctant to engage in any future EIS development efforts. As *Apollo 13* Flight Director Gene Kranz put it, "Failure is not an option." Table 7-6 lists many of the factors identified by Crockett that can contribute to the failure of an EIS.

Prevention of EIS failure is not a topic that is readily prescriptive in nature. The need for broad-based executive support for the project is essential, however. Training and regular communication among all the participants are also key elements to success. Finally, being aware of the various factors that can contribute to EIS failure and paying constant attention to minimizing those factors are both important steps toward the successful implementation of an EIS within today's organization.

Table 7-6 Factors Contributing to EIS Failures

- Management failures (lack of support, loss of interest, unwillingness to train)
- Political problems (middle management resistance, lack of resource commitment)
- Developer failures (slow development, inadequate needs analysis, doubtful data integrity)
- Technology failures (inadequate speed or capacity, insufficient functionality)
- Costs (development, training, political)
- Time (development, training, maintenance)

7-6 THE FUTURE OF EXECUTIVE DECISION MAKING AND THE EIS

The future of EIS technology and, thus, executive decision making is one where several conditions will merge to transform the technology. Some of these conditions are fairly easy to predict because they exist today, whereas others have yet to manifest themselves. Nonetheless, we will spend some time looking forward to see what the EIS of the future will be.

Conditions of Transformation

Increased Comfort with Computing Technology

One current condition that will continue is the comfort with technology that executives are developing. In the early years of EIS development, a significant roadblock to the acceptance of the technology was executives' lack of comfort and experience with hands-on use of computers. This roadblock has been significantly reduced through an increased focus on training combined with the growing realization that information systems like EISs are valuable to the organization. Furthermore, the executive suite is becoming younger. New leaders are emerging who have grown up in the age of technology and have developed an understanding of and comfort level with computer-based systems that facilitates their exploitation throughout the organization. As the resistance to computers dissipates, new and more powerful EIS systems will emerge.

Broadening of Executive Responsibilities

The organization will continue to flatten and rightsize. These conditions will create a leaner, more flexible and responsive structure but will also increase the worker-to-executive ratio. Most of the reduction in force will come from staff and middle management levels and the future executive will have direct contact with and responsibility for a much broader span of personnel. We can assume that EIS technology will come to the forefront in facilitating the management of this flatter organizational structure.

The boundaries of the organization will also continue to expand. Markets are now global and the competition for market share, natural resources, and labor will continue to escalate. With this will come continued increases in regulation driven by social and environmental concerns. The scope of responsibility of the executive will clearly include these increasing complexities, and the need for accurate, more diverse, and immediate information will continue to grow. Conditions such as these point to an increased reliance on EISs.

The EIS of Tomorrow

The trend toward the integration of applications and technologies into seamless enterprise-wide systems bodes well for the future of executive information systems. Technological and conceptual advances in telecommunications, information systems, and decision support systems will all contribute to new EIS features and potentially new and more powerful EIS applications. Watson, Houdeshel, and Rainer (1997) suggest that the EIS of the future may become an *executive intelligence system.*

The Intelligent EIS

The numbers of data provided to the executive are literally overwhelming. Even with an EIS, there is the constant potential for information overload. Artificial intelligence (AI) can perform some of the data screening for the executive, reducing the amount of time spent searching for relevant data.[1]

The inclusion of voice input capabilities promotes the use of AI. Executives are accustomed to delivering verbal instructions, and voice input would reduce both the data entry time and the potential for errors committed by the executive. Properly deployed, voice input and output would clearly add greater flexibility to the EIS and allow for further understanding and comprehension of information. Voice command software is available today, but it is still in a relatively primitive form for effective use. The current state of speech recognition system technology, therefore, limits the use of voice input as an interface. Nonetheless, voice annotation technology has already demonstrated its value in increasing comprehension while reducing the need for page after page of reports. As the challenges related to voice recognition technology begin to dissolve the advent of the intelligent voice-controlled EIS will occur.

Managing the large storage requirements for voice handling is one of the major hurdles to overcome in voice technology. Physically storing a system that can recognize all the language instruction, accents, and other natural speech phenomena takes huge amounts of magnetic or optical storage space and has proven difficult. In addition, the technology necessary to overcome issues associated with speaker-dependent recognition is still in its infancy. Current systems require the user to "train" the system by participating in a rather protracted preparation exercise. The user is prompted to speak a series of words, phrases, syllables, and numbers repeatedly while the application creates a voice fingerprint for the user. Although this method dramatically increases recognition rates (currently as high as 99.7 percent with the Kurzweil Voice Plus system) it is nonetheless tedious and extremely time consuming, two conditions that are antithetical to the nature of executives. Several speaker-independent recognition technologies are currently under development, however, and when refined, will become an immediate enhancement to current EIS systems.

---

[1] We take a detailed look at artificial intelligence technologies in chapters 8, 9, and 10.

Another branch of AI is expert systems (ESs). An ES can be used within an EIS to assist the user with appropriate model selection to analyze a problem. Based on rules provided to the ES, the ES can instruct the user on which model would best fit the problem context. An ES is similar to an EIS in that they both contain components that manipulate data. They differ in the way knowledge is maintained, however. An EIS uses predefined models and associated algorithms whereas an ES operation is based primarily on heuristics. We will explore the topic of expert systems further in chapters 8 and 9.

The Multimedia EIS

A data-based component is necessary within an EIS for retrieving, analyzing, manipulating, and updating files. A multimedia database management system (MMDBMS) can increase the future EIS user's resources to manipulate text, voice, and images effectively within an integrated database structure. MMDBMSs provide the traditional benefits of a database management system as well as concatenation of voice, transformation of information, rotation of images, scaling of objects, and merging of various data types. The problem with these systems, especially for the executive user, is the complex interface. As the functionality of these systems continues to increase, more applications for their use will be developed. Combine more applications with an easy-to-use system and an opportunity for a competitive advantage develops.

The Informed EIS

We know that most of the decisions made by executives require some element of external data. Those decisions of a strategic nature require significant access to data about the market, the environment, the economy, regulatory and technological changes, and the competition. While access to external data via an EIS is not new, the degree to which the EIS will be able to manipulate and assemble those data will be.

There are literally thousands of private sector and government-maintained databases currently in existence with the present volume expected to double by the turn of the century. The information in these databases is available but the scanning, filtering, and extraction tools that allow for efficient and effective use of those data are still being refined. The challenge for the next generation of EIS designers will be to integrate data access tools into the applications that will allow the EIS to systematically find and organize the necessary information for the executive from the world's data stores and to deliver it to the EIS desktop in a manner that allows it to be readily understood and applied.

The Connected EIS

The modern-day emergence of the Internet and the World Wide Web has facilitated the electronic interconnection of companies to their customers and suppliers. The addition of web-centric groupware technologies such as Lotus Notes has furthered this move toward mass interconnectivity. One massive current development is the dawning of electronic commerce (e-comm). Firms are using the Internet to advertise and communicate new product developments to both current and future customers. Virtual markets are emerging and Internet-based commerce and finance is a reality.

With the widespread availability of high-bandwidth communications media, a logical extension of this interconnectivity frenzy would include the executive suite. The EIS of tomorrow may allow for controlled access by a variety of stakeholder groups, such as key suppliers, customers, stockholders, and partners, to that part of the EIS that is important to the conduct and maintenance of a particular relationship. This sharing of resources and information will serve to strengthen the relationship between the parties while simultaneously facilitating the coordination of the relationship and the building of a common knowledge base. This concept is simply an electronic extension of today's account manager concept. The EIS of tomorrow will not eliminate the need for human relationship management, but it will serve as a valuable resource for improving the relationship building and maintenance processes.

7-7 CHAPTER SUMMARY

Despite the increasing awareness of the value of information to the successful implementation of organizational strategy, the concept of the executive information system is still in its infancy. As new decision support and information gathering technologies emerge, new and more robust EIS designs will be manifest as well. Regardless of the power, however, the purpose of tomorrow's EIS will be the same as today: to provide senior managers with the information they need about their operating environment, internal operations, industry knowledge and events, markets, customers, and suppliers. The future EISs will be bigger and more powerful and will surely differ in the scope of data sources available to them, but their purpose will be unwavering. The EIS will be a common weapon found in every executive suite in the Information Age.

Key Concepts

- To address the unique variety of information needs of the CEO, a particular class of decision support technologies has emerged: executive information systems (EISs).
- Definition of an EIS (7-1)

  An EIS is a computer-based system intended to facilitate and support the information and decision-making needs of senior executives by providing easy access to both internal and external information relevant to meeting the stated goals of the organization.
- Design requirements of an EIS (7-1)

  An EIS must be designed and implemented for a particular executive environment.

  An EIS must be designed and implemented based upon a particular executive's information needs.

  Because both of these requirements are extremely fluid, the EIS must be considered to be an evolutionary tool in an organization and requires a significant commitment to its ongoing support and development.
- Drill down capability (7-1)

  The drill down capability of an EIS is a process of data decomposition that is selected and controlled by the executive and will be different for every situation. This feature of an EIS allows the executive to seek solutions to problems by employing a "top-down" analysis and a structured investigation.

- Executive activities (7-3)

By gaining an understanding of the unique nature of work at the top executive level, we can fully appreciate the information needs of top executives. Executive activities can be divided into several basic categories:

Disturbance management

This activity requires the immediate attention of executives as well as the deployment of resources to an unexpected occurrence, particularly one that could have a materially negative impact on the financial health of the organization.

Entrepreneurial activities

These activities are strategic planning tasks that are usually triggered by real or perceived changes in the external environment. Executives must focus their attention on understanding the dynamic forces in the markets and the global environment and must use the information gathered to predict changes that can be viewed as opportunities to the firm.

Allocation of resources

The authority to deploy resources and the various activities to obtain them is normally performed by top executives. Moreover, top executives must decide to whom and where to allocate the organizational resources because, in general, the demand for resources is greater than their availability.

Negotiation

Executives are charged with representing the organization in both internal and external disputes. This role involves the resolution of disputes and conflicts and involves a significant amount of negotiation among the parties.

- Given the relevance of the various information attributes to management levels, we can identify the various types of information needs by top executives. (7-3)
- Executive information determination and sources (7-3)

By-product

The primary support comes from traditional processing systems (TPSs) and other management information systems (MISs) that summarize and aggregate the various information by-products of the current operation in the organization.

Null

The null approach involves the constant, but informal, collection of mostly subjective information from trusted sources via "word of mouth." This method relies on the spontaneous exchanges and discoveries that take place during informal tours of an organization.

Key indicator

Top executives monitor only that information that reflects an out-of-nominal condition and gather additional information as a basis for making decisions intended to correct the condition.

Total study

The total study approach gathers information from a sample of top executives in the organization concerning the totality of their information needs.

Critical success factors

The information on the identified critical success factors (CSFs) is constantly gathered and supplied to top executives. This information is used as the basis for decisions affecting the organization.

- Client/server architecture allows for rapid additions and modifications to be incorporated into business applications and facilitates the widespread access and dissemination of disparate databases located throughout the globe. (7-4)
- EIS components (7-4)

   Hardware components

   The hardware components of the EIS should be optimized with and conformed to the organizational computing resources as well as adapted to the legacy data. Also, the system must be configured with the organization's resources and capabilities so that support is provided to both train executives and facilitate their modifications.

   Software components

   The individuality of an EIS comes from the software component rather than from the hardware. The software components of an EIS are normally highly specialized and designed to meet the specific needs of specific users.

- An EIS development framework (7-5)

   The development framework provides the terminology, concepts, and guidelines necessary for building an EIS. It can be divided into three major components:

   Structural perspective

   The structural perspective provides a model for understanding the relationships among the various elements and their potential interaction during the various phases of development of the EIS.

   EIS development process

   The development process builds upon the elements and their relationships contained within the structural model and adds a time dimension to the framework.

   User-system dialogue

   Action language:

   The various commands and elements direct users how to use the system. It is the incoming communication channel from the executive to the EIS.

   Presentation language:

   It serves as the EIS counterpart to the action language. The outflow of information and the form in which this information is presented are guided and dictated by this component.

   Knowledge base:

   The knowledge base is the sum of what the executive knows about using the system and all of the support mechanisms designed to assist in its use.

- Two considerations of designing and developing an EIS: (7-5)

   The EIS must be easy to use.

   The EIS must have an acceptably fast response time.

- EIS limitations (7-5)

   Cost

   The benefits derived from an EIS are costly and the cost of maintenance of the system after development can easily exceed the original development costs over the life of the system.

   Technological limitations

   The myriad of data sources necessary to accomplish the functionalities of an EIS and the wide variety of media in which they can reside pose formidable technical challenges for the EIS designer.

Organizational limitations

Biased agendas and time orientations:

This form of information channeling can cause an executive's agenda to be biased toward a superficial analysis of the environment. Also, an EIS can serve to promote a more micromanagerial approach to conducting business, which can serve to disrupt the activities of middle- and lower-level managers.

Loss of managerial synchronization:

A heavy reliance on ad hoc reports can sometimes serve to disrupt the stable and well-established reporting cycles within an organization that have been designed to synchronize management activities.

Organizational destabilization:

The fast response to spur-of-the-moment inquiries may cause the executive to react too swiftly by making adjustments to the organization that are too frequent or too strong. Such overreactions by executives can destabilize an otherwise stable organization.

- Failure is not an option (7-5)

An EIS development effort that fails to satisfy its targeted users can be a severe setback not only for the organization but for the individuals involved.

- Prevention of EIS failure (7-5)

Broad-based executive support for the project is needed.

Training and regular communication among all the participants is a key element to success.

Be aware of the various factors that can contribute to EIS failure and pay constant attention to minimizing those factors.

- Conditions of transformation in executive decision making (7-6)

Increased comfort with computing technology

Broadening of executive responsibilities

- The EIS of tomorrow (7-6)

The intelligent EIS

Artificial intelligence (AI) can perform some of the data screening for the executive, reducing the time spent searching for relevant data.

The multimedia EIS

A multimedia database management system (MMDBMS) can increase the EIS user resources to manipulate text, voice, and images effectively within an integrated database structure.

The informed EIS

The challenge for the next generation of EIS designers will be to integrate data access tools into the applications that will allow the EIS to systematically find and organize the necessary information for the executive from the world's data stores and to deliver it to the EIS desktop in a manner that allows it to be readily understood and applied.

The connected EIS

With the widespread availability of high-bandwidth communications media, a logical extension of this interconnectivity frenzy would include the executive suite. The EIS of tomorrow will serve as a valuable resource for improving relationship building and maintenance.

Questions for Review

1. Define executive information system.
2. List the two EIS design requirements.
3. Describe the drill down feature of an EIS.
4. Is the organizational EIS a substitute for other forms of information technology and computer-based systems? Why or why not?
5. List and briefly describe executive activities.
6. List and briefly describe the five basic methods for executive information determination.
7. What is the primary method for establishing the CSFs of an organization?
8. What are the benefits of client/server architecture?
9. Depict the key consideration of the computing hardware environment for developing and deploying an organizational EIS.
10. List and briefly describe the categories of the current EIS technologies.
11. Describe the components of an EIS development framework.
12. Identify the three basic components of the user-system dialog.
13. List and briefly describe several EIS limitations.
14. Explain the three main categories of potential negative impacts of an EIS on organizations.
15. How can the failure of an EIS implementation project be prevented?
16. Describe the conditions of transformation in executive decision making.
17. Briefly describe the EIS of tomorrow.

For Further Discussion

1. Analyze an EIS application in the market. Describe its drill down capability and how this functionality helps executives.
2. Review the categories of executive activities and the information needs for the activities in each category. Relate these to a fast-food company. How about a service organization?
3. Find and study a case of disturbance management in an organization. How can an EIS support the executives in this case?
4. Assume you and your team are the top executives of an insurance company. Identify the information you need through key indicator and critical success factors approaches.
5. Review the areas of support that should be provided by an EIS application. Analyze an EIS application product in the market. Describe its functionalities based on these areas of support.
6. Assume you and your team are assigned to develop an EIS for your organization. Design the EIS using the development framework. Identify the factors that may cause the failure of this project. How can you and your team prevent the failure?
7. Use a common development platform such as Excel or Access to develop a prototypical EIS for your department at work or at school. Use color to highlight exceptions where ap-

propriate and include models for forecasting and prediction. Prepare a report that outlines the steps you took in the development of the system and the problems you encountered during its design.

8. It appears that the EIS is no longer being used exclusively in the executive suite of large organizations. The system is rapidly diffusing down in the organization to all levels of management. Discuss why this phenomenon is occurring and make suggestions about how this diffusion may be facilitated by senior management.

9. Analyze the types of information you use in your daily tasks. Using the various categories of information discussed in this chapter, outline the types you regularly use. Do you see any patterns of information types in your daily activities? Could you benefit from a "personal EIS"?

EIS Product Offerings and Descriptions

(adapted from Dobrzeniecki 1994)

This section contains a listing of many of the DSS application software offerings and their descriptions. This list is by no means comprehensive, as DSS products are constantly being introduced, repackaged, and redesigned. It should, however, serve as an effective overview of the various products available and their respective capabilities.

Category 1 Software

Pilot Decision Support Suite — Pilot Software, Inc.

The Pilot Decision Support Suite is unlike other decision support products. It offers a truly comprehensive solution with predictive data mining, high-performance OLAP, and flexible visualization in an open, plug-and-play architecture, which is fast to implement, easy to modify, and supports analysis anywhere.

Pilot Designer, the application design environment of the Pilot Decision Support Suite, is the industry's leading solution for rapid data access and visualization. Supporting Windows 95 graphical user interface standards and a Visual Basic scripting language, Pilot Designer delivers a complete suite of dimensional objects for customizing desktop applications, building libraries, and extending existing analyses. Its tool set helps to create a variety of visual decision support applications ranging from simple executive information system front ends to complex OLAP applications. With Pilot Designer, decision makers at all levels of an organization have unparalleled access to data, wherever the data elements reside. And they get that information through a wide variety of powerful graphic formats, which combine tabular, geographical and graphical data, text, images, audio, and video.

Commander — Comshare, Inc.

Comshare was a pioneer in the EIS business on mainframe computers along with Pilot Software. According to a market study performed by IDC Research, Comshare owns 60 percent of the EIS market by revenue. Comshare's product Commander is known as the prototypical PC-based EIS.

FIGURE 7-A1 Pilot Designer Application Design Environment

Comshare's latest release is the Commander Prism spreadsheet software allowing Microsoft Windows users to view, analyze, and manage large data sources, and build and maintain detailed enterprise models. The Commander product offers several important features that contribute to its popular success. First, Commander is compatible with Lotus 1-2-3 files. This is the spreadsheet product with which most executives have experience and where most have their data stored. The user interface to Commander can be achieved through either touch screen, mouse, or keyboard. Commander uses pictures to display financial and operating data. It also uses changing colors to highlight variances and exceptions in the data reports. The software has the ability to "drill down" to deeper levels of detail either by allowing users to navigate through the data on their own or by using predefined search paths. Other features include simplified access to electronic mail and external information systems such as on-line news services and bulletin boards.

In addition to the Commander EIS product, Comshare also markets a decision support system product. Its DSS product is referred to as System W. System W was developed for use in management accounting applications, such as budgeting, financial consolidation, corporate planning, modeling, and forecasting. Comshare was an $85-million company in 1989. This was largely due to a successful migration of its EIS and DSS products.

FIGURE 7-A2 Pilot Internet Publisher

Destiny — IBM

IBM Corporation offers an EIS custom-design service that allows individual users to receive and analyze only the information they need from different areas of their corporate-wide information systems. The product this service is marketed under is called Destiny. This product features a single host repository, which stores both scanned images and voice messages. The repository acts as an information warehouse for text, images, voice, and raw data. One interesting feature of this product is the "briefing book," which contains several folders of information on key areas. Destiny can be developed to meet a customer's EIS needs on a variety of IBM hardware platforms. Destiny integrates with IBM's office system products. The user interface is either a touch screen or a mouse.

DrillDown — Specialized Systems and Software

DrillDown was developed by Specialized Systems and Software to work strictly with database files from Ashton-Tate's dBase software, but it is also able to view translated Lotus 1-2-3 files without the need for macro programming. DrillDown is especially appropriate for companies using Lotus 1-2-3 as their database, since it can group and total records that share common characteristics. This practice is usually referred

FIGURE 7-A3 Commander by Comshare

to as "rolling up" the data. For example, DrillDown has the ability to roll up a flat file of invoice records to show aggregate sales by individual product. Selecting a certain product in that list itemizes the product's sales by the next field the user selects (e.g., according to region). A second selection within the eastern region may explode the view into sales by individual salespeople for the region and for that product.

The software quickly finds data through the creation of search templates that, once defined and saved, can be reused repeatedly by untrained users, even as the data change. DrillDown is a simple and inexpensive data viewer, designed mainly to help novices analyze database information. The software provides rudimentary charting and has no live linking capability to external data.

Executive Information System 10.1 — Marcam Corporation

Executive Information System is based on Trinzic Corporation's Forest and Trees product. It provides executives with a powerful view of corporate database information. The presentation of the information can be customized according to the needs of the executive. Marcam's EIS product provides drill down capability, performance indicator tracking, and alarm triggering of potential problems. The Executive Information System is an element of Marcam's manufacturing maintenance application software, PRISM Maintenance.

FIGURE 7-A4 Commander by Comshare

Hyperion — IMRS, Inc.

IMRS develops enterprise level financial management applications for client/server environments. It designs products specifically for network (i.e., local access networks [LANs]) implementation with the intention of providing many users fast access to centrally stored corporate data. Hyperion is one the company's key products and is a financial information management application that operates in the Microsoft Windows environment. Other products include Fastar and IMRS OnTrack.

Hyperion provides corporate reporting capabilities using the Windows graphical environment. It operates as a client/server application. Hyperion delivers up-to-date corporate information by combining a high-performance server database with the Windows user interface. Using this approach, Hyperion allows simplified data collection, data analysis, and presentation of business and financial reports.

MasterCEO — Management Systems Associates, Inc. (MSA)

MasterCEO from Management Systems Associates is an integrated EIS tool for the MSA Confidence Healthcare information system. This product provides access to patient-care information, receivables, occupancy, outpatient visit, and other statistics. The text and graph tools present clear pictures of the corporate status to upper management. This EIS tracks indicators that are established using both budget and industry standards.

PRISM Maintenance — Marcam Corporation

PRISM Maintenance is the title for Marcam's family of manufacturing application software. PRISM was designed to help manufacturers monitor and track their maintenance operations. This package is particularly suited for the continuous process industries, such as pharmaceutical, paper products, or similar batch-type manufacturing environments. The modules of the PRISM software allow complete tracking of the manufacturing process and maintenance operations from customer order to product delivery.

Teamwork Enterprise Intelligence System II — Health Care Microsystems, Inc.

Teamwork EIS II is designed to provide managers, at all levels, a variety of detailed information to support the decision-making process. This product supports approximately 100 to 200 people, where a traditional EIS caters to 8 to 10 people. Teamwork EIS II is designed not only to integrate data from a variety of sources and systems but to work as a tool in the total quality management (TQM) processes. It can be customized to an individual corporation's needs, and users can further modify the system after implementation. Teamwork integrates with other databases and has the ability to access data directly from SQL-compatible databases. This product operates on stand-alone PCs, LANs, DEC hardware, and various IBM equipment platforms.

The Alternative View — Gerber Alley

Introduced in 1991 as the EIS component of Gerber Alley's Precision Alternative Hospital Information System (HIS), this product can be used in the Windows or Hewlett-Packard New Wave environments. The Alternative View operates on either a single, stand-alone executive workstation or via a LAN. The tool set included allows users to customize prepackaged formats according to individual needs. This flexible software is limited only by users' development ingenuity. The graphical interface is a mouse.

Category 2 Software

Executive Decisions — IBM

Executive Decisions was introduced in May 1989 by IBM Corporation and first released in September 1989. The product is a graphically based, touch screen system designed for top executives who need easy access to critical data. The product was aimed specifically at chief executive officers.

Executive Decision is part of IBM's Office-Vision family and complies with the systems application architecture (SAA) developed by IBM. SAA provides a common user access (CUA) standard for graphical user interfaces and a cooperative architecture to access information stored on local area networks as well as host-based and PC-based information. This product can be run on platforms using the following IBM operating systems: MVS, VM, and OS/2 EE. Depending upon the success of the product among users, IBM Corporation also plans to support IBM's AS/400 environment. Executive Decision requires an IBM PS/2 Model 70 or 80 running OS/2 EE 1.1, working in conjunction with an IBM System/370 running the VM operating system.

IBM Data Interpretation System — IBM

The IBM Data Interpretation System was first released in September 1989. It is designed as a graphically based decision support system that allows managers to access, analyze, and manipulate data through a mouse interface. Aimed at managers in corporate finance, marketing, and planning departments, this package requires an OS/2 EE, and four PS/2s combined with a System/370 running relational databases.

Express/EIS — Information Resources, Inc.

Express/EIS allows users to work with less-structured data by tracking, organizing, analyzing, and exchanging information interactively throughout the organization. Multiple graphical data presentations within the software support features such as intelligent exception reporting and drill down capability. Drilling down allows users to navigate through the underlying data via user-specific criteria. The software also features the capability for users to automatically identify and highlight the "news in the data," customizing reports to user requirements. Express/EIS combines the ease of use typically found in executive information systems with the analytical power common to many decision support systems.

Express/EIS includes a fourth-generation language with statistical and mathematical functions, a multidimensional database, and a data dictionary. With these tools, users have the flexibility to ask new questions not included during the EIS development to provide "on-the-fly" analysis. This is not a feature found in many other executive information system tool kits. Express/EIS capabilities include data querying, report writing, and graphics contained right within the software. Express/EIS uses 3270 terminal emulation protocols to have applications access host databases including IBM's DB2.

Forest & Trees — Channel Computing

Forest & Trees operates in the Windows or DOS environment. The software can read a wide variety of standard PC database, spreadsheet, and structured ASCII file formats. Further, the software provides icon-based access to live data from Lotus 1-2-3 files and other sources. Forest & Trees generates SQL queries and dynamic data exchange (DDE) requests so that developers can create views and "picks & clicks" that let users choose the data links and presentation formats. The "query assist" feature lets users investigate data in informal queries. The software offers drill down capability, conditional color coding, and alarms. Forest & Trees excels at *ad hoc* queries and at identifying and tracking key data items. Forest & Trees has low maintenance requirements once an EIS is built because the software is designed to extract data from other applications.

Executive Eagle — Transitions Systems, Inc.

Executive Eagle was designed to integrate information from Transition Systems' clinical and financial mainframe-based product lines and other data sources. Executive Eagle is a PC-based system that can be customized to meet individual needs. Several of the features that provide this customization include the "corporate browser," which allows quick overview of specific data sets, and "fact book," a file folder that tracks success factors, graphs, exception reporting, and other information to avoid having to regenerate them later for comparison. The modeling and planning features allow users to input detailed assumptions of future trends and view them in graphical form. The exception reporting feature permits users to perform "what-if" analyses. Executive Eagle operates on IBM compatible microcomputers.

Smartview — Dun and Bradstreet Software

Smartview is an EIS driven by a decision support database comprising case-mix analysis, procedure-level cost accounting, and clinical productivity analysis. Smartview is workstation-based with the user interface either through a touch screen or mouse. This product allows customized views of information, highlighting and integrating critical success factors, and provides drill down capability.

Category 3 Software

EIS ToolKit — Ferox Microsystems, Inc.

EIS ToolKit is based on Encore Plus, Ferox Microsystems' EIS product. EIS ToolKit is a fully customizable add-on module that allows nonprogrammers to build sophisticated EISs. The systems built using ToolKit have the capability to provide executive exception reporting, drill down capability, real-time forecasting, and trend analysis. EIS ToolKit can be used "as is" or customized for specific users' needs.

EIS Pak — Microsoft, Inc.

EIS Pak is a set of tools designed to speed development of EISs by using Microsoft Excel and other mainstream applications. EIS Builder is an add-in development tool aimed at helping developers rapidly create Excel-based enterprise applications without writing macro code. EIS Builder provides graphical query and analysis. It also has the ability to exchange data with external databases and applications. EIS Pak uses the functionality built into Microsoft Windows applications to simplify advanced analytical charting and text-formatting functions. This product is marketed as capable of meeting the needs of department-level managers. Additional features of EIS Pak include video and sample applications as well as an EIS development guide.

Hospital Executive Information System — Global Software, Inc.

Developed by Global Software, this PC-based product operates in a Windows environment. The user interface is mouse driven. The software allows access and analysis of strategic, tactical, operational, and financial data. It can be integrated with a variety of non-Global applications, such as spreadsheets, database applications, desktop publishing, and external sources (Dow Jones news retrieval, CompuServe). The software allows security system limits to be incorporated, limiting access to predetermined information. This limits users to a slice of the EIS data that is important to them.

IMRS OnTrack — IMRS, Inc.

IMRS markets several financial management applications. IMRS OnTrack is a visual information access software product. It is a network-based business information management package that takes advantage of network platforms to deliver comprehensive and timely information to executives, managers, and analysts. OnTrack provides users with comprehensive but concise information. The software presents data in high-level summary format and allows the user to drill down to access any level of detail desired. Presentation graphics include the option to view reports larger than the computer screen by scrolling. Reports can be enhanced by dynamically incorporating text and comments into the data and graphics.

MAXPAR — Maximus, Inc.

MAXPAR was specifically designed for use in the health care field. It is a PC-based product written in "C" language and operates under UNIX or DOS, with a local area network version also available. MAXPAR utilizes data downloaded from a mainframe or departmental computer systems to create and update the EIS internal database at the PC. Having access to corporate financial, productivity, and employee data identifies for executives productive, cost-efficient programs and practice patterns.

Media — Info Innov, Inc.

This is a Microsoft Window-based EIS product. Media provides powerful drill down capabilities from an interface built around key data items. Media extracts data needed from other applications in the form of structured ASCII files and compiles the necessary data into a proprietary database. This method requires a higher level of maintenance to support the EIS than many other software products. The trade-off is higher maintenance but superior drill down and data-analysis capabilities.

Quantum — HBO & Company

Quantum is the consolidation of EIS applications previously offered by HBO and its subsidiary, Healthquest. This product provides quick implementation and portability among IBM, DEC, and HP platforms. Quantum operates on a IBM PS/2 or Macintosh PC connected by a local area network to the host machine. The user interface for this product is through a mouse, touch screen, or keyboard. Quantum offers a library of seventy management report applications that were developed using Pilot Software's EIS tools. The reports use "time series" technology to view underlying trends. The system accesses a set of relational tables and keeps data in a single repository on the host so that users all see the same data. The product integrator feature allows users to interface with an array of source systems on a wide variety of hardware.

EIS Software: Implementation and Development

DSS Executive — MicroStrategy, Inc.

DSS Executive is MicroStrategy's design tool for developing EIS applications. All the advanced reporting capabilities of DSS Agent, their DSS development tool, are available in DSS Executive to create briefing books, dynamic newspapers, and sequential reporting tools.

FIGURE 7-A5 MicroStrategy's DSS Executive

Time Base — Pilot Software, Inc.

Time Base is a multidimensional data management and analysis system with a time-series capability. This allows users to show trends and restate EIS results according to different time periods. Pilot Software's EIS solution for LANs is the combination of the Lightship, Lightship Lens, and Time Base products.

PowerPlay — Cognos

PowerPlay 2.0 is an alternative to executive information systems. PowerPlay is a data exploration and display tool for managers. It is a personal productivity tool with a "hook" to corporate data. PowerPlay can operate in the Microsoft Windows and Hewlett-Packard HP New Wave environments. The emphasis of this product is report generation and drill down capabilities. External information can be input as single, structured ASCII files. This EIS requires high maintenance because required data are extracted from the ASCII files and compiled into a proprietary database. The trade-off is higher maintenance but superior drill down and data-analysis capabilities.

Excel (Spreadsheet) — Microsoft, Inc.

Excel is a high-powered spreadsheet product attempting to meet business information needs with its information manipulation "bells and whistles." Some features include statistical data analysis, database development, import/export capability to other software, and presentation graphics. IBM Corporation has indicated that it will pro-

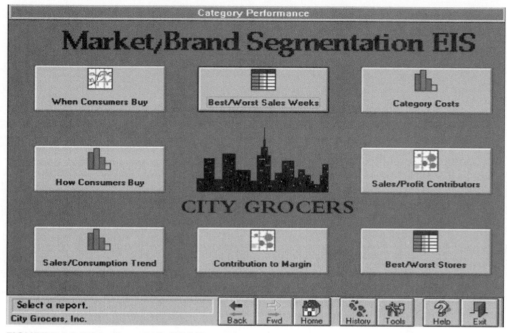

FIGURE 7-A6 MicroStrategy's DSS Executive

vide support for a gateway from Excel spreadsheets to the AS/400 minicomputer. This will provide a means to exchange data across computer hardware platforms.

Lotus 1-2-3 (Spreadsheet) — Lotus Development Corporation

EIS programs interface to Lotus 1-2-3 spreadsheets by attaching snapshots of 1-2-3 worksheets to various reports. The EISs compile disparate data and let users work through various levels of detail to find information. The EISs combine spreadsheet data with data from other sources and display them in an easy-to-understand format. An EIS may use 1-2-3 as the front end to examine vast quantities of business data and take advantage of computer users' familiarity with the 1-2-3 format.

According to research conducted in 1991 by International Data Corporation, Framington, Massachusetts, 65 percent of companies surveyed use spreadsheets in their executive decision-making systems, either as part of a larger system or standing alone; in 1991 12 percent use systems installed by an EIS vendor.

Many companies are piecing together executive information systems out of common products, such as spreadsheets. Lotus 1-2-3 files are compatible with Commander, Pilot Lightship, Forest & Trees, DrillDown, and Information Advisor EIS software products.

Lotus 1-2-3 is not a database manager and therefore does not function well as an EIS data repository. The worksheets grow to a point where they become slow and unwieldy. A better solution is to translate the spreadsheets into products such as SQL Server, dBase, Paradox, or Oracle. Many companies are currently in this position. They are searching for the right products to make the transition that will not limit their development of a full EIS in the future.

Lotus 1-2-3 for Windows can be used as an EIS front end. Using SmartPak, a new 1-2-3 add-in product, users can modify Lotus menus and customize dialog boxes to create a simple EIS within a spreadsheet.

NotesWare EIS — NotesWare, Ltd.

Decision Support from NotesWare is an enterprise information system written in the Lotus Notes development environment. It brings together information from multiple sources and then facilitates analysis and reporting in any format required. Decision Support uses a simple point-and-click interface, allowing users to see standard reports and analyses, drill down for greater detail, or create *ad hoc* queries. Key features of NotesWare EIS include powerful authoring tools for design of screens, menus and submenus, a query wizard for swift, intuitive access to SQL/ODBC databases, a script wizard for complete or partial function automation, desktop integration with leading spreadsheets (Lotus 1-2-3, Excel, Quattro Pro, and OLAP), and multidimensional data support, allowing drill down and cut/slice by and through dimensions.

Performance Advisor — SRC Software

This is a high-end financial report generator that is invoked from Lotus 1-2-3 as a series of menus. Performance Advisor adds menus, functions, and methods that ac-

FIGURE 7-A7 NotesWare Chart Window

cess outside data for analysis and reporting. This product draws data from mainframe or other financial systems to create flexible reports.

Information Advisor — SRC Software

Information Advisor is used in conjunction with Lotus 1-2-3 files as a front end to Performance Advisor reports. This add-on feature provides a mechanism for novice users to explore existing reports.

CHAPTER

8

Expert Systems and Artificial Intelligence

Learning Objectives

- Define expert system and artificial intelligence

- Describe the several different reasoning processes used by humans

- Describe the methods available to create a computer-based reasoning system

- Explain the concepts and structure of expert systems

- Understand the predesign activities associated with building an expert system

- Learn how to evaluate an expert system

Expert Systems Assist in Fraud Detection

Expert systems can be developed for fraud detection—to put up a red flag for suspicious circumstances. Investigators can then spend time on the highlighted items to stop fraud before it gets out of hand.

A wide variety of industries including banks, insurance companies, and the U.S. government are using expert systems to detect fraud. Medicare billing fraud, health and property insurance fraudulent claims, credit card fraud, and fraudulent foreign currency exchange are just some of the transactions that can be reviewed by expert systems.

In the expanding world of digital commerce, the magnitude of transactions makes it difficult for humans to carefully review all the data for fraud, given that a majority are legitimate and need timely service. Indeed, part of the problem is that customers expect fast service now that they are accustomed to what computers have done to speed up transactions.

PROPERTY AND CASUALTY INSURANCE CLAIMS

Claims adjusters are under great pressure to process claims quickly, a task that is not getting easier for them as the number of exaggerated losses and bogus claims has skyrocketed in the last few years. According to industry estimates, 10 to 15 percent of all claims are fraudulent. The use of the telephone and the computer, instead of personal contact, to gather information has accelerated the fraud problem. Now claims adjusters must determine liability, estimate damages, and deal with false or padded claims in a cost-efficient and timely manner.

Extra investigation of a suspicious claim adds expense and delays settlement, but inaction could result in payment of a fraudulent claim and the potential for inviting future bogus claims. It is a difficult dilemma for even the most seasoned claims adjuster as most claims have some suspicious elements. The difficulty is in determining which claim is most appropriate for denial.

To add insult to injury, identifying a fraudulent or exaggerated claim is only half the problem. Defending the claim denial against lawyers and a jury is the real challenge. This is time consuming, expensive, and exposes the insurer to the potential assessment of punitive damages if the court case is lost.

Enter the expert system (ES) as part of the solution to the property/casualty insurance fraud problem. Claims information can be closely examined by an expert system, which can identify and red flag various kinds of fraud. With the help of an ES, adjusters can adopt the outlook of automatically questioning suspicious claims.

AN EXPERT SYSTEM FOR AUTO BODILY INJURY CLAIMS

Correlation Research, Inc., of Needham, Massachusetts, has a prototype model of an expert system that contains useful data obtained in conjunction with the Massachusetts Automobile Insurers Bureau. Key variables were collected on claim fraud indicators and what actions were taken by the insurer to counter fraud. By having the claims adjuster answer 10 to 15 questions on each claim the system can assign a "suspicion score" to each auto bodily injury claim. The score can be used to screen claims and determine what action to take on each one. Actions might involve paying the claim quickly, getting a second medical opinion, or gathering more information.

This expert system is still evolving but can greatly speed up the decision on how to handle each claim. The database grows as a volume of claims are processed by the expert system—it stores claim characteristics, resulting score, and resulting outcome of how the case was settled. Eventually the expert system will be custom tailored for fraud classifications and cost-effective claim handling. The core data needed on each claim may change over time as new ways to make bogus claims are discovered. The cost of gathering information must be balanced against its value to the expert system and to the insurance company.

PUBLIC CONCERN

The public are not as sympathetic to insurance companies as they were twenty years ago. They are demanding that insurance regulators control fraud and not pass the cost of paying false claims on to customers via rate hikes. As a result of public concern, many insurance companies have expert systems using their own database of claim information. What is even more exciting, the National Insurance Crime Board is considering creating an expert system—it could be gigantic given the volume of its National Data Base Services program. This on-line program would be used by 150 insurance companies, 10 state insurance fraud bureaus, and more than 20 law enforcement agencies.

MEDICAL BILLING FRAUD

Medical billing fraud and abuse can be partially discovered with an expert system. Claims auditing software available in expert systems will flag suspicious claims for a real human expert to review manually. These expert systems look for fraud that is a result of the codes used for medical diagnoses and procedures. Misuse of the codes could increase a doctor's Medicare reimbursement. In 1992 health care billing fraud amounted to $84 billion—10 percent of the 1992 U.S. expenditure on health care.

CREDIT CARD FRAUD

Banks are also using expert systems. In 1993 Canada Trust Bank installed Trinzic Corporation's knowledge-based Aion Development System to monitor credit card transaction patterns. It was so successful Canada Trust no longer uses reports from MasterCard International.

Data are reviewed every night and every two hours during the business day for deviations from a customer's normal purchase pattern. A score is assigned to the transaction based on how likely it is to be fraudulent. Suspicious scores are routed to the bank's fraud department for a closer investigation. In this way the bank can investigate almost immediately every suspicious transaction. Due to sheer volume this would be impossible using manual labor. Timeliness is the key to preventing further fraud.

FOREIGN CURRENCY EXCHANGE FRAUD

Banks have also put expert systems to work watching over currency exchange transactions. New York's Chemical Bank has designed an expert system it calls Inspector. It continuously monitors foreign currency exchanges at Chemical Bank offices around the world. Any questionable transaction is flagged so a human foreign currency expert can review the deal.

Inspector is a great time saver, an important attribute because Chemical Bank handles over $1 billion a day in foreign currency transactions. One fraudulent transaction could cost the bank millions.

MORE IN THE FUTURE?

Expert systems have found a home in the world of fraud detection. The true potential for expert systems will be realized when they can all be linked so that the full picture can be monitored. With this approach, fraudulent transactions that cross over several insurance companies or banks will be noticed. Expert systems can serve as the watchdog of business transactions. Their vigilance can give human experts time to make personal investigations of suspicious events while the rest of our business deals are quickly and efficiently handled.

8-1 THE CONCEPT OF EXPERTISE

Danish physicist Niels Bohr once defined an expert as one "who has made all the mistakes which can be made in a very narrow field." While this may be a bit of an exaggeration, it nonetheless frames the realm of an expert. To make all the mistakes possible within a given knowledge domain, one must experience all there is to experience. Thus, given enough information about a particular problem scenario, an expert usually can determine the appropriate solution with a high degree of reliability and with a measurable degree of efficiency over those with less domain experience. Although this may seem rather intuitive and self-explanatory, the question of just how an expert arrives at an effective solution with such efficiency still remains. The answer to this question is found in the field of *logic*.

Logical theorem proving is a method of establishing the truth or falsity of particular assertions. It is based on the premise that all information within a particular knowledge domain is related to all other information in that domain in some manner. Given this, facts or observations about a new scenario within that domain must "fit together." This requirement of fit allows logical processes such as *deduction* and *inference* to be used to arrive at a conclusion about the problem under study. Experts use this concept of information fit within a specific knowledge domain to arrive at their decisions.

Of all the situations you can conceive of, whether they involve data interpretation, optimization, planning, diagnosis, or social behavior, most can be expressed in terms of rules. If we think of problem solving as a set of IF-THEN rules, we can begin to see how the experts perform their "magic." They use logic to derive new information from the existing information to arrive at a conclusion. By using the concept of information fit, they can construct an efficient inquiry process to collect the information necessary to create a fit, and thus arrive at a conclusion. As a simple example, consider the following:

KNOWN INFORMATION

- John is Sam's son.
- John is the eldest child.
- Mary is Sam's daughter.
- John and Mary's mother is named Anna.
- Sam has been married to Anna for fifty years.

DERIVED INFORMATION

- IF John is Sam's son, THEN John must be a boy.
- IF Mary is Sam's daughter, THEN Mary must be a girl.
- IF John and Mary have the same mother, THEN John and Mary are brother and sister.
- IF Sam and Anna have been married for fifty years, then John and Mary are their children by either birth or adoption.

The previous example uses the concept of information fit and rules to obtain new information that was not specifically available. Logic suggests that the derived information must be true if the known information is true. From this, we can collect enough information to make a decision fairly quickly because we know which specific pieces of information are necessary to make the decision. It should be easy to see that by using these concepts—i.e., information fit and seeing a problem context as a set of rules—a computer application could be developed to serve as the "expert" in a problem-solving activity.

Expert Systems and Artificial Intelligence

The term *expert system* (ES) is used to describe a computer-based application that employs a set of rules based upon human knowledge to solve problems that require human expertise. Expert systems imitate reasoning processes based on the concept of information fit used by human experts in solving specific knowledge domain problems. A nonexpert can use an ES to improve his or her abilities to solve complex problems by simulating a dialog with experts in a particular field. Experts can use an ES to simulate a highly knowledgeable assistant. Most commonly, an ES is employed to allow for the propagation of scarce expert resources throughout an organization to increase the consistency and quality of problem-solving activities.

An ES functions as an expert primarily through techniques developed in the field of *artificial intelligence* (AI). AI research focuses on understanding how humans think, reason, and learn and can be thought of as an intersection between computer science and cognitive psychology. From this understanding, AI seeks to discover and develop practical mechanisms that enable computers to simulate the reasoning processes performed by humans in solving a particular problem. Rich and Knight (1991) define AI as "the study of how to make computers do things which, at the moment, people do better" (p. 3). Although these AI mechanisms are not yet identical to those of humans, they can produce results that are quite similar, and thus useful, to those produced by human decision makers.

In this chapter, we focus on the importance of expert systems and artificial intelligence in the context of decision making and problem solving. We will explore their history, structure, and underlying concepts to better understand their present stage of development and application as well as their potential for future use. Finally, after a brief focus on their benefits and limitations, we will have laid the necessary groundwork to proceed to chapter 9, where we take a detailed look at knowledge and the method by which it can be "captured" and harnessed in an ES.

A History of ESs and AI

The roots of ESs and AI can be traced back to the mid-1950s and the work of the RAND-Carnegie team. Herbert Simon and Alan Newell of the Carnegie Institute of Technology (now Carnegie-Mellon University) and J. C. Shaw of the RAND Corporation conducted an ambitious series of investigations into the development of computer-based reasoning systems. Their first system, the *Logic Theorist,* used the concept of *reverse reasoning* to solve simple problems in propositional calculus using a small set of axioms as a knowledge base. Reverse reasoning begins with the original problem statement and then decomposes, or breaks down, the problem into a series of smaller subproblems that can be solved individually. By the late 1950s, the team had embarked on an even more ambitious project that resulted in the development of the *General Problem Solver* (GPS) system. The GPS, unlike the Logic Theorist, was able to solve problems in a wide variety of problem contexts using general reasoning methods and techniques. The GPS was capable of solving problems of elementary logic, chess, and even high school algebra word problems. It was the first effective development of a system that used a general approach to problem solving.

By the early 1960s, the basic building blocks for ESs were emerging. Minsky and McCarthy, at the Massachusetts Institute of Technology, invented the programming language LISP, which is a dominant language used in the development of AI-based systems. At this same time, DENDRAL, an ES capable of inferring a structure of molecules by mass spectrography data, was developed at Stanford University. This was a time of rapid advancement of ES technology and a period during which much of the knowledge necessary to build the industrial ESs of the next decade was formulated.

During the 1970s, expert systems were developed by industry to serve a variety of needs including diagnosis, perception, instruction, learning, theorem proving, game simulation, and pattern and speech recognition. Major organizations including Digital Equipment (with its XCON and XSEL computer configuration ESs), Xerox, IBM, General Electric (with CATS-1, a diesel locomotive troubleshooting ES), General Motors, and Texas Instruments, among many others, embraced and advanced the state of AI and expert systems into its modern-day form. Today, literally thousands of ESs are in operation worldwide and a prosperous market for ES development applications has emerged.

8-2 THE INTELLIGENCE OF ARTIFICIAL INTELLIGENCE

As stated previously, AI is focused on understanding how people reason and think and then translating that understanding into computer systems that can perform the same actions. To better understand how AI performs this translation we need to look first at the human side of the equation.

How Do People Reason?

The scope of this text precludes a thorough discussion of human reasoning processes. An entire field, cognitive psychology, has evolved to focus on the complex processes and conditions that affect human reasoning and response. Nonetheless, we can identify several specific reasoning processes used by humans that are easily translated into the realm of expert systems and artificially intelligent computers.

Categorization

The most common process associated with human reasoning is that of *categorization*. When we identify a piece of information as important enough to remember, we categorize it according to one or more characteristics or criteria. These categories are "stored" in our memory as a loose set of hierarchies where lower-level pieces of information can "inherit" characteristics from a higher-level category. Figure 8-1 illustrates this concept of categorization.

Depending upon the level of detail represented by a particular piece of information, categorization can allow us to reason to a higher level of abstraction. For example, it is logical to reason that if cars are ground-based vehicles and buses are ground-

FIGURE 8-1 Example of Concept of Categorization

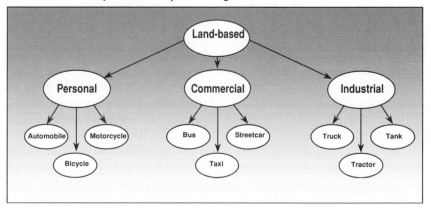

based vehicles, then they must both transport people in a similar fashion. Similarly, categorization can allow for reasoning to a lower level of abstraction with greater detail, such as reasoning that if ground-based transportation used to transport people has wheels then cars must have wheels. Categorization allows for rules to be derived from the relationships among the categories.

Specific Rules

Another method by which humans reason is by the application of known rules. If a particular rule, or set of rules, is known to exist and be true, then we can use that knowledge to reason our way through a problem context associated with the rules. For example, if we know that a red traffic light means that vehicles facing that light must stop and we know that failure to stop at a red traffic light will result in getting a traffic ticket (or worse), then we can reason that if the light is red we should stop (unless, of course, we want a ticket). Another form of rules used for reasoning are known laws. Tax laws allow us to reason whether a particular expense is allowable as a deduction and, if it is, how much of it can be applied. Humans make use of rules by cascading them into a reasoning process that allows for reliable conclusions to be reached.

Heuristics

We explored the topic of heuristics in chapter 3, where we discussed decision processes. Heuristics are yet another way in which humans can reason. Such rules of thumb can be translated or captured for use. Examples such as "If the meal includes red meat, then choose the red wine" or "If the Chicago Bulls are playing at home, they will be favored to win" are heuristics that have been captured and framed as rules. Despite the lack of formality associated with a heuristic we know that searches and decisions using well-formed heuristics can often reduce the time necessary to reach a solution.

Past Experience

Reasoning by *past experience* incorporates components and activities from both categorization and heuristics. This method can be thought of as a metacategorization whereby humans look at the whole of a situation and attempt to compare it to situations they have experienced in the past. If enough characteristics or sequences of events can be matched up, the necessary actions can be reasoned based upon what was done in the past. A common example of reasoning by past experience is found in the use of business cases as study tools in undergraduate and graduate courses. A business case recounts the activities of one or more people or organizations with regard to a particular situation. In addition to detailing the sequences of events and decisions made during the course of the situation, the business case has the advantage of also being able to record the outcomes of the decisions and use the concept of "20-20 hindsight" to review the appropriateness of those decisions. Humans reason in exactly the same manner. If the current situation appears similar to a situation I experienced in the past, and I know what I did in that situation that worked, I can reason that a similar action will be appropriate under the present conditions. Reasoning by this method makes some rather large assumptions—such as history will repeat itself and the present situation really is similar in most respects to the past situation. If these assumptions are valid, however, reasoning by past experience can be an effective decision-making method.

Expectations

One final method of human reasoning is through *expectation*. Once we have experienced a particular situation or phenomenon enough, we begin to expect it to appear in a certain manner or under a predictable set of conditions. If this occurs as we expect, then we can reason that all is well or that nothing is out of order. If, however, our expectations are not met, we can reason that something has occurred to change the expected set of conditions.

The people we see and work with every day have unique characteristics and traits that are displayed so regularly that we come to expect their presence. We often encounter a coworker who does not appear to act within the bounds of our expectations and we respond with observations such as "You are not yourself today," or inquiries such as "Is something bothering you today?" Reasoning by expectation is simply a form of pattern recognition. We expect a certain pattern and when it is not present, a series of events and inquiries are triggered to determine the reasons for the differences. Note that while similar in nature, reasoning by expectation differs from that of past experience because our expectations are formed via repetitive interaction with a similar set of conditions. Past experience rarely involves multiple experiences of similar scenarios.

As you can see, each of these methods employed by humans during the course of reasoning can be framed in terms of rules or patterns that can be recorded in such a way that they can be automated or mechanized. It is this characteristic of human reasoning processes that allows for the development of computers that "reason."

How Do Computers Reason?

The methods employed by AI system designers to create a reasoning system using a computer are based on the very same processes and mechanisms used by humans. A "reasoning" computer is provided with a set of automated models that simulate each of the main reasoning approaches found in human cognition.

Rule-Based Reasoning

An AI reasoning system uses rules in much the same manner as we do. In fact, the most common form of expert system is one that employs a technique known as *rule-based reasoning*. The process is one whereby the computer is given the characteristics of the problem space in the form of input values. It then uses the rules contained within its *knowledge base* to methodically change the state of the problem space to the desired condition. Each rule is composed of two parts: (1) the *operator* that performs the state change and (2) the *conditions* that determine when an operator may be executed. This rule composition takes the form of an IF-THEN statement as shown here:

IF condition **THEN** operator

If a condition is found to be logically true, then the operator becomes an acceptable action to take and the rule is said to have *fired* or *instantiated*. If the condition is logically false, then the operator is ignored and the next rule is accessed. This process continues until either the problem space reaches the desired condition or the rules in the knowledge base are exhausted.

Using a formal set of rules, several types of knowledge can be encoded. For example, *inferential knowledge* can be represented as rules. This type of knowledge is one whereby a conclusion is reached as a result of one or more premises (facts) being established.

IF	*premise(s)*	**IF**	road is under construction
THEN	*conclusion*	**THEN**	caution is necessary

A second form of knowledge that can be encoded in a set of rules is *procedural knowledge.* Here, the conditions take the form of a stated situation and the operator becomes an action to take when the stated situation is logically true.

IF	*situation*	**IF**	speed > 55 mph
THEN	*action*	**THEN**	issue speeding ticket

The action portion of a procedural knowledge rule can perform any relevant action including calling another rule to test the situation further.

IF	*situation*	**IF**	speed > 55 mph
THEN	*new rule*	**THEN**	check road conditions
IF	*situation*	**IF**	road is under construction
THEN	*action*	**THEN**	double speeding violation

A third form of rule-encodable knowledge is *declarative knowledge.* This form is constructed from antecedents and consequents. If the antecedent (condition portion of the rule) is found to be logically true, then the consequent (operator) must also be true.

IF	antecedent	**IF**	found guilty of speeding
THEN	consequent	**THEN**	driver must pay fine[1]

Despite its similarity to human rule-based reasoning, rule formalism in an AI-based system is not without certain disadvantages. Foremost, as the number of rules within the knowledge base grows, the processing efficiency decreases unless some formal structure (such as grouping of rules) is imposed. In addition, it is difficult to encode explicitly static knowledge about objects using an IF-THEN construction. For that type of knowledge an AI-based system must use a different mechanism similar to the human cognitive activity of categorization.

Frames

The concept of *frames* was first proposed by Marvin Minsky (1975) as a logical extension of a knowledge encoding formalism known as a *semantic net.* In a semantic

---

[1] My thanks to Dr. Madjid Tavana for the helpful suggestions regarding this section.

network, concepts or entities are represented as nodes and the arcs connecting the nodes represent their relationships. Figure 8-2 illustrates the concept of a semantic net.

The extension of semantic nets to frames created an object-oriented view that allowed knowledge to be partitioned into discrete structures having individual properties. These discrete structures, called *slots,* can be thought of as similar to fields in a database or categories in your mind. Collectively, the slots within a frame are used to describe the nature of the object stored within the frame:

> A frame is a data-structure for representing a stereotyped situation like being in a certain kind of living room or going to a child's birthday party. Attached to each frame are several kinds of information. Some of this information is about how to use the frame. Some is what to do if these expectations are not confirmed. (Minsky 1975, 211)

Frames are simply representations of stereotyped situations or objects that are typical of some category. Each category has certain characteristics that can be inherited by each member of the frame. Figure 8-3 contains an example of a portion of a frame representation for marketable securities.

In addition to slots, which represent the various attributes associated with the object frame, other component elements of frames are important to identify. For example, within each slot is contained one or more *facets*. These facets describe any data or specific procedures associated with the slot. Several types of facets exist including *cardinality* (single or multiple values), *value type* (numeric, text, logical, etc.), and *allowable values*. In addition, one important element in the frame system is the *default value*. If no attribute is directly assigned to a particular slot, then the default value is automatically assigned. For example, a frame for life insurance policies is likely to have a slot for "date_of_issuance." If this slot is empty when the frame is saved, then the default value may be the current date. By having default values for slots, the system is assured of always having sufficient information upon which to base a decision.

Another important type of facet is called the *daemon* (pronounced "demon"). A daemon is a short procedure that can be triggered whenever a slot is created, modified, or even accessed. Three common daemons in a frame system are the following:

FIGURE 8-2 Example of a Semantic Network

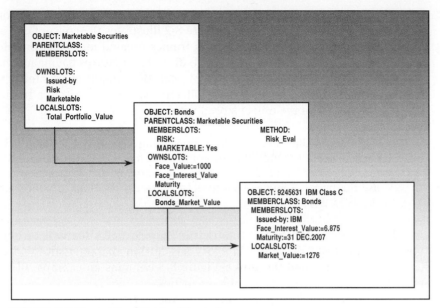

FIGURE 8-3 Example of Frame Hierarchy

1. *If modified.* This procedure daemon will execute whenever the value of the slot is modified. A common use for this daemon is to record the date, time, and user identification associated with a slot modification.

2. *If deleted.* This daemon executes whenever a value is deleted from a slot. Uses for this procedure may be as in 1 above or to prompt the user with a message box of some kind.

3. *If necessary.* This procedure may execute during a problem-solving session to supply some additional value that is needed but not existent in the frame.

The frame concept allows for two types of objects to be represented: *classes* and *instances.* As discussed above, objects represented by frames contain slot values that can be inherited down the frame hierarchy. The frame hierarchy is organized by two constructs: *subclass links* (IS-A) and *membership links* (INSTANCE-OF). The membership links serve as a classification mechanism and the subclass links serve as a taxonomic mechanism.

This mechanism of inheritance is subdivided into information types based upon the generalizability of the attribute. If an attribute can be inherited by any member of the class it is stored in a *member slot.* The attributes associated with the specific object represented by a frame are stored in *own slots.* Finally, any attributes that exist that cannot be inherited and must be only associated with that particular object frame are stored in a *local slot.*

It should be easy to see that the concept of frames is highly analogous to the human reasoning method of categorization. As with rules, however, frames have their limitations. Most notable among them is that frames allow for the representation of descriptive object-oriented information but are not very useful for storing information of a more situational nature. For these instances, AI-based systems employ a mechanism that simulates the human process of reasoning by past experience.

Case-Based Reasoning

Case-based reasoning is built upon the premise that humans use an analogical or experiential reasoning approach to learn and to solve complex problems. The idea, much like its human counterpart, is to adapt solutions of similar problems to the problem at hand. The process of case-based reasoning involves two primary steps: (1) find those cases in storage that have solved problems similar to the current problem and (2) adapt the previous solution(s) to fit the current problem context. Figure 8-4 contains a flow diagram of the solution structure in case-based reasoning.

One of the most critical steps in the process is the location and retrieval of one or more relevant cases from the case library. This is accomplished through a complex set of *case indices* that are used to efficiently search and retrieve cases that are most similar to the current problem. Each potential case is compared to the present problem using a set of *similarity metrics* that measures the degree of similarity between the selected case and the current one. Once this has occurred, the contained solutions are analyzed and adapted to the new situation. This process of adaptation consists of a series of modifications to the parameters of the old solutions to fit the new problem context. Finally, the new solution is tested and, if successful, is added to the case library. If, however, the test fails, then the adaptation process must be revised or a new set of cases must be retrieved.

Case-based reasoning is most useful in knowledge domains where precedence-based reasoning is appropriate. Domains such as medical diagnosis, audit, legal, and claims settlement are common areas for case-based reasoning.

Pattern Recognition

This AI mechanism is most analogous to the human reasoning process of expectations. *Pattern recognition* includes both visual and audio patterns. As with humans, the degree to which a computer can exhibit intelligent behavior through a pattern

FIGURE 8-4 Nominal Process in Case-Based Reasoning

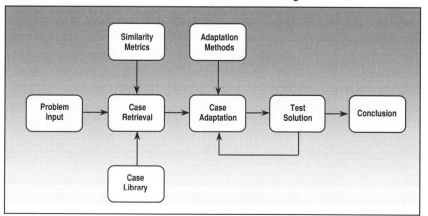

recognition system is a function of its ability to perceive its environment and surroundings. If the computer is limited to keystrokes and mouse or trackball movements then its perceptual abilities are also limited to those realms. If, however, additional hardware and software are employed to allow the computer to detect sounds and to sense patterns or shapes, then an entirely new realm of possibilities for simulating intelligent behavior manifests itself. Advanced pattern recognition systems can detect a specific human voice, a fingerprint, or even identify a person by his or her photographic or video image. Although early pattern matching mechanisms suffered from both speed and resource intensity issues, recent application of new programming algorithms has allowed for the increase in pattern recognition reliability and practicality.

Rete Algorithm   One such recent development is known as the Rete algorithm. This algorithm for pattern recognition can handle pattern matching that involves several thousand working memory elements and rules without any severe resource requirements or unacceptable performance losses. This clever algorithm makes use of the fact that the contents of working memory do not change drastically after each rule application but rather exhibit only minor changes from the previous pass. Specifically, the Rete algorithm figures out which rules from the prior cycle did not fire, which rules from the prior cycle will not fire in the next cycle, and which rules from the prior cycle that did not fire will most likely fire in the next. Using this method, the algorithm avoids performing a pattern recognition cycle from scratch each time it must cycle through the rules. It does this by maintaining an internal representation of the state of each rule in working memory and uses that representation as the basis for repeating the cycle during each subsequent pass until the pattern is matched.

Currently, pattern recognition systems are being marketed to allow for voice-driven commands, voice dictation, computer-generated voice response, photographic analysis and pattern matching, and signature verification systems. This area of AI research has the greatest potential for impact on the design of tomorrow's expert systems.

Other Forms of Artificial Intelligence

Although the expert system remains at the forefront of widespread application of AI-based systems, there are several other examples of AI investigation that bear mentioning. They are not yet as well-developed as the ES, but each has the potential to be a major contributor to the intelligent system of tomorrow. We will take a brief look at each of these developmental AI systems.

Machine Learning

Machine learning involves AI-based mechanisms that allow computers to "learn" from past experiences using examples and analogies. The outcome of machine learning results in a modification of the programmed behavior of the computer or one or more modifications to the stored knowledge the computer program is designed to act upon. Two well-known areas of machine learning research and application are *neural networks* and *genetic algorithms*.

Neural Networks   This branch of AI-based systems is focused on creating computer-based mechanisms that simulate the learning processes in the human brain. The human brain consists of thousands of networks of highly interconnected nodes called neurons. Each neuron performs a discrete computation at any given moment, the results of which are transmitted to other neurons along a neural pathway. A single human neuron can send results to as many as 10,000 other neurons as signals to the inputs of other neurons in the form of voltages. These signals can either inhibit other neurons from sending signals or excite them into signals to other neurons on the pathway. This process results in the storage of voltage in certain neurons and not in others. Through a repetitive process of firing and storing voltage, the human neural system learns and adapts to its environment.

In much the same manner, a computer-based neural net uses a series of interconnected mathematical processing elements, also called *neurons,* that look for patterns in a set of examples and learn from those examples by adjusting the weighted value of the neuron's connection to other neurons. This constant flux in interconnectivity produces specific output patterns much like the human brain. Training the neural net involves the input of numerous related examples followed by feedback on its success or failure in classifying them.

Genetic Algorithms   Originally proposed by John Holland while working at MIT in the 1940s, the term genetic algorithm (GA) applies to a set of adaptive procedures used in a computer system that are based on Darwin's theory of natural selection and survival of the fittest. Following Darwin's suggestion that species adapt to changes in their environment in an effort to become more dominant, GAs "reproduce" themselves in various recombinations in an effort to find a new recombinant that is better adapted than its predecessors. One major advantage to GAs is that they can be used to examine complex problems without any assumptions of what the correct answer or solution should be. GAs are already being used in conjunction with neural nets and expert systems to solve problems in areas such as scheduling, design, and marketing. We will explore GAs, neural nets, their components, and their application in detail in chapter 10.

Automatic Programming

This area of AI investigation involves mechanisms that automatically generate a program to carry out some prescribed task. Using this approach, a person who is not a programmer can describe the nature of the task and the specific characteristics and behaviors the program should exhibit to the system without actually knowing how to write the program. The automatic programming software takes this description as input and generates the desired program. Currently, automatic programming is most often used in managerial settings for the generation of programs that produce various reports for decision making.

Artificial Life

Artificial life (AL or Alife) is the term used to describe a relatively new AI-based focus that studies "natural" life by attempting to recreate biological phenomena from scratch within computer-based systems. In contrast to the traditional analytic approach of the life sciences of "taking apart" living organisms to see how they work, AL related problems: object descriptions and relationships, problem-solving behaviors, constraints, heuristics, and uncertainties. The success of an ES relies to a great extent on the completeness and accuracy of its knowledge base. If there is incomplete, inconsistent, or inaccurate information in the knowledge base, no matter how efficiently the other components of the ES operate, the ES will simply arrive at an incomplete or erroneous answer at an extremely fast pace.

A distinction must be made between the concepts of *data* and *knowledge* when discussing the content of an ES knowledge base. One suggestion is that if we are prepared to trust a clerk or an automatic process to collect the desired materials then the materials in question are data. If, however, we must look to an expert to provide the desired material, then we are talking about knowledge. In other words, a collection of data representing facts is a database. The collection of an expert's set of facts and heuristics is a knowledge base. As opposed to a database, a knowledge base contains information at a much higher level of abstraction. As discussed above, the knowledge base is the containment for the rules, frames, semantic nets, scripts, cases, and pattern-matching information necessary for problem-solving within the ES's knowledge domain.

The Inference Engine

If we think of the knowledge base as the brains of the outfit then the *inference engine* (IE) becomes the brawn. It is here that the processing in an ES occurs and that the knowledge is put to work to produce solutions. The inference engine performs deductions or inferences based on rules or facts. In addition, it is capable of performing inexact or *fuzzy* reasoning based on probability or pattern matching. The basic process of the IE is called a *control cycle*. Three steps can be identified in an inference control cycle: (1) *match* rules with given facts, (2) *select* the rule that is to be executed, and (3) *execute* the rule by adding the deduced fact to the working memory.

The essence of the operation of an IE is based on a famous rule of deductive inference known as *modus ponens*, which says that if A is true and A implies B (A → B) is true, then B is true. Consider the following:

1. When Mark knows there is a clothing sale, he always buys clothes.

2. Mark knows about the clothing sale at the mall.

3. Therefore, Mark buys clothes.

The counterpart rule of deductive reasoning, *modus tollens*, states that if we are given the implication that A implies B (A → B) is true, and that B is false, then we can conclude that A is also false:

1. If the sun is shining tomorrow, then we will go swimming.

2. We will not be swimming.

3. Therefore, the sun must not be shining.

An IE uses two basic procedures for applying the two rules of deductive reasoning and for drawing appropriate conclusions: *chaining* and *resolution*.

Chaining

Chaining is a simple method used by most IEs to produce a line of reasoning. Using this method the set of rules is organized in a recursive manner so that a fact concluded by one rule is used as the premise for the next. Two types of chaining based upon the direction of the search process are possible in an ES: forward and backward.

Let's investigate how these two procedures work. Consider the following set of rules from a knowledge base:

Step	Rule Base	Workspace
(1)	R1: IF A and B THEN D	A, B
(2)	R2: IF B THEN C	D
(3)	R3: IF C and D THEN E	C, D
(4)		E

In *forward chaining,* the inference engine begins with the initial content of the workspace and proceeds toward a final conclusion through a series of inference control cycles. During each cycle, the IE will search the knowledge base for a rule whose premises create a match with the true facts contained in the workspace (step 1). Once found, the antecedent conditions of these rules can be considered as satisfied, the rules can be executed, and the deduced facts will be added to the workspace (step 2). The control cycle of *match-choose-execute* is then repeated and additional facts are added to the workspace (step 3). Once the match cycle exhausts the candidate rules in the knowledge base the process ends and the workspace contains the conclusions drawn. This method of reasoning is also referred to as *data driven* since the process involves a movement from data to goals.

The second method of chaining, *backward chaining,* causes the IE to work backward from the goal to be proven to the necessary data within the workspace to prove it. Backward chaining can be thought of as a form of hypothesis testing where the conclusion is proposed and then the data are "collected" to determine support for the hypothesis. Using the same knowledge base as before:

Step	Rule Base	Workspace
(1)	R3: IF C and D THEN E	C, D
(2)	R1: IF A and B THEN D	A, B
(3)	R2: IF B THEN C	

In backward chaining, the IE starts with goal E and then looks to the knowledge base to determine support for the goal. The IE finds that rule R3 concludes with goal E and selects that rule (step 1). Once R3 is selected, the IE can place its premises, C and D, into the workspace (step 2). The next control cycle proceeds to look first for a rule that concludes with C and then one with a conclusion of D. Through rule R1, the IE determines that for D to be true, A and B must also be true. Looking to the workspace, the IE finds A and B stored as true facts (step 3) and concludes support for D as well as C (via rule R2). Backward chaining is also referred to as a *goal-directed* search because the process starts with a final goal and works backward through the subgoals to the supporting data.

The choice to use backward or forward chaining depends on two primary factors: *expert reasoning mode* and *efficiency*. The way in which an expert reasons in a particular domain, the *expert reasoning mode,* can serve to dictate the appropriate process. If the expert normally uses problem reduction techniques as a search method, then backward chaining becomes appropriate. If, however, efficiency is an issue because there are a large number of goals compared to the amount of input data, or known facts, then forward chaining becomes more appropriate. Regardless of the technique employed, however, both methods allow for a logical path to be followed through a knowledge base and toward a satisfactory conclusion. Table 8-3 illustrates the use of both methods in determining the best way to fly from one point to another.

The Blackboard Workspace

The *blackboard* provides the ES user with an area of working memory to use as a workspace for the various components of the ES. It can be thought of as a sort of electronic scratchpad or notebook where calculations are performed and intermediate hypotheses and decisions are stored during the problem-solving process. Through the blackboard system, the ES can communicate candidate solutions or request additional input. For example, in the diagnosis of a trauma patient in an emergency room, the knowledge base of the ES includes all the rules and reasoning processes related to emergency room trauma treatment. The attending physician using the system will enter all of the symptoms and vital signs of the patient into the ES. This initial information will be stored in the blackboard. After initial rule selection and hypothesis testing, the ES may suggest that some additional tests be performed. These requests for information are also stored temporarily in the blackboard workspace. When the results of the additional tests are entered, the reasoning process will continue until a conclusion is reached. Once the system has completed its work, the blackboard area is "erased" and is ready for the next problem-solving session.

8-4 DESIGNING AND BUILDING EXPERT SYSTEMS

Expert System Shells

During the 1980s, perhaps the greatest single challenge to AI research was the development of general-purpose tools for building expert systems quickly and inexpensively. This challenge was met by developing systems that had reasoning mechanisms

Table 8-3 Examples of Backward and Forward Chaining

- *Situation.* You wish to fly from Washington, D.C., to San Diego. Unfortunately, all direct flights are booked, so you will have to accept a connecting flight if you are to get to San Diego.
- *Backward chaining.* You could check the flights arriving in San Diego and see which cities they are arriving from. Then you could look up the flights arriving in those cities and so forth until you find Washington, D.C.
- *Forward chaining.* You could check the flights departing Washington D.C. and find their destination cities. Then look up the flights leaving those cities and so forth until you find a flight to San Diego.

Source: Adapted from Liebowitz (1990).

that were independent of the problem domain, allowing a generic system to be employed with all the problem-specific knowledge contained within the knowledge base. These generic systems were called *expert system shells.*

One of the earliest successful ES shells was EMYCIN—a general problem processor oriented toward certain types of diagnosis problems. Also developed during this same period were two more generalizable ES shells called OPS5 and ROSIE. Both of these shells used forward chaining as their primary search technique and allowed the developer to create a set of program statements that described the flow of reasoning to be followed during a problem-solving session. Although quite cumbersome by today's standards, these shells were a giant step forward from programming an entire ES from scratch using LISP or PROLOG.

Modern ES shells typically contain two primary modules: a *rule set builder* and an *inference engine.* The former is used by the developer to assist in constructing the initial knowledge base and the latter serves as the vehicle for reaching conclusions. More recently, the concept of an integrated ES environment has emerged. In these systems, a wide variety of knowledge management tools, such as hypertext, graphics, bulletin boards, and messaging, are incorporated along with the fundamental rule-based approach to create expert systems that go beyond the boundaries offered by more traditional systems. With each refinement, AI moves a step closer to the ultimate goal of a truly context-independent problem solver.

Building an Expert System

A bit of creative daydreaming should convince you that the scope of managerial application for expert systems is virtually infinite. Despite this, however, the targeted nature of an ES requires that the scope and boundaries of its application be clearly identified prior to its design. One method for accomplishing this is to identify the type of tasks the ES will be expected to perform. A typology of ES tasks is provided in table 8-4.

Since the 1970s, several methods have been devised and proposed with regard to the process associated with the design and implementation of intelligent computer-based systems such as an ES. Gerrity (1971) suggested that the key problems in the

---

Table 8-4 A Typology of Expert System Tasks

- *Interpretation.* Use sensor data to infer situation descriptions and meaning
- *Prediction.* Forecast from past and present the likely consequences of given situations
- *Diagnosis.* Infer faults and malfunctions based on observation and interpretation of data
- *Planning.* Design actions and plans to achieve stated goals
- *Design.* Configure object specifications for satisfying particular requirements
- *Prescription.* Prescribe remedies and solutions for malfunctions
- *Monitoring.* Compare signals and observations to expected outcomes
- *Control.* Govern overall system behavior
- *Instruction.* Diagnose, prescribe, and guide user behavior

Source: Adapted from Hayes-Roth, Waterman, and Lenat (1983).

process were methodological rather than technological. The essence of Gerrity's approach to design is to emphasize both a descriptive model of the system based on the identifiable system boundaries and a normative model based on the stated system goals and then try to close the gap between the two models until a satisfactory and functional design is reached.

In 1978, Keen and Scott Morton extended Gerrity's approach by suggesting that the first step in any intelligent system design must be the establishment of a sociopolitical climate for change and commitment. Once this is accomplished the key to success in the project is the identification of the ES problem and the *seizing of the ES opportunity*.

ES opportunities exist in a variety of locations and sizes throughout the organization. The key is for managers to develop an awareness of such opportunities. Managers not only must look for areas where an ES could serve to propagate scarce organizational expert resources but must also be tuned in to situations where an ES might serve to enhance the role of an expert by providing necessary assistance. Such situations can free up a human expert to concentrate on other aspects of the job and thus improve productivity. In short, any activity where human experts are overburdened, undersupplied, expensive, or for the most part unavailable are prime candidates for an ES opportunity. Table 8-5 lists several such candidate situations.

Predesign Activities

The actual process of design and implementation of an ES is not unlike that of other forms of DSSs, or for that matter, other information systems. As such, we will address the common analysis, design, and implementation components associated with all DSS development in chapters 13 and 14. However, there are several activities that must be performed prior to formal design that are unique to expert system development.

Finding the Experts   Probably the most important step in successfully designing an ES is the selection of the expert or group of experts that will contribute knowledge to the knowledge base. Logically enough, no expert—no expert system. It is important that the expert be clearly informed of the time commitment associated with the ES development effort. He or she must be willing to participate in the project from start to finish and to expend a significant amount of time and energy in its early stages. It is also important that the expert fully understands the value of the

---

Table 8-5 Candidate Situations for ES Opportunities

- Need for diagnosis of a problem situation or variance (audit, troubleshooting, etc.)
- Need to understand the nature of a given situation
- Need to predict the outcome of a current or future event
- Need to control or govern a particular activity or process
- Need to prescribe a solution or course of action
- Need to evaluate and assess a prior event or process

---

proposed system to the organization in terms of productivity, performance, and quality. At the same time, the system must be positioned to enhance the role of the expert rather than supplant it. An expert who is either unmotivated or threatened by the proposed system, or both, is unlikely to contribute usefully to its successful outcome.

The Development Team   As stated above, ES development has much in common with other IS development projects, but there are some unique issues to address. Given this, it is essential that the development team chosen to design and build the system be familiar with the realm of expert systems. The developers should have a functional understanding of the knowledge domain for which the ES is being built. In some cases, one or more members of the development team may also be serving as an expert in the construction of the knowledge base. Quite often, the team is divided early in the process into smaller groups that focus on specific aspects of the system. Some members of the development team will be assigned to the construction of the rule set, others will be focused on the user interface, while still others will play a unique role in the ES design process by serving as knowledge engineers (KEs). The KEs are the team members who work directly with the experts to extract and organize the body of knowledge that must be contained in the knowledge base. This knowledge-gathering process is both complex and tedious and requires several unique skills on the developer's part. We will explore the issues associated with the knowledge acquisition and engineering process in the next chapter.

The Application Development Tool   In a conventional IS design project, it is not normally necessary to select an application development tool or language platform in the early stages of development. The focus must first be on the development of a logical model that describes "what" the system will do. The development language is more of a component of the physical solution that focuses on "how" we are going to do it. In the case of ES design, however, it is important that the development tools be determined early on. The iterative nature of prototyping, reviewing, and refining the ES during development makes the selection of the development tool an important predesign decision. The tool must complement the skills of the development team and must provide the appropriate functionality for the problem domain being modeled. Furthermore, the ideal tool is one where a number of expert system projects can be supported rather than just the current one. Implicit in this is the desire for the development tool to enhance the productivity of the development team while remaining both flexible and versatile.

Hardware Selection   Again, contrary to most other system development efforts, the selection of the ES hardware platform should be made prior to design. The selected platform must not only support the final ES product and allow for its growth but ideally it should support the selected ES development tool as well. In this way, the prototypes generated during the development process will perform exactly the same in the final product and no changes in functionality or performance will be incurred due to a change in hardware platform after development.

8-5 EVALUATING THE BENEFITS OF EXPERT SYSTEMS

Given the successful development and implementation of an expert system, a number of benefits can be realized. Their achievement, however, is not without significant effort and can only be brought about if the expectations of the user in terms of system functionality are met. Several criteria exist that can assist the ES user in evaluating the quality and functionality of a new expert system. Table 8-6 outlines eight basic criteria for evaluation.

Assuming the system meets the criteria set out in table 8-6 and is accepted by its user community, a number of significant operational benefits to the organization can, and do, emerge.

Expert System Benefits

Increased Timeliness in Decision Making

Sometimes it seems that the availability of a given key piece of information is often inversely related to the immediacy of its need. While experts in virtually all knowledge domains are relatively abundant, they are rarely standing next to you, or are even in the same building with you when you need one. Expert systems serve as viable solutions to this problem in knowledge domains where expert advice and input are needed on demand. Unlike human experts, an ES can be on duty twenty-four hours a day and will never grow weary or become ill. Furthermore, depending upon the scope of knowledge covered by the ES, it can be simultaneously available to many different managers who require additional advice or expertise with regard to related but distinct problem contexts.

Increased Productivity of Organizational Experts

Depending upon the nature of the knowledge domain, a resident expert's time can be in high demand. Because the demands on an organization's expert generally are not made in any prioritized fashion, it is often the case that while the expert is busy consulting with other members of the firm on an issue of moderate operational value, an issue of relative urgency is waiting for his or her attention. The introduction of an ES can offer useful input to those situations of less urgency and, thus, can in-

---

Table 8-6 Criteria for Evaluation of an Expert System

- The system should be responsive and easy to use.
- The design and functionality should conform with current diagnostic standards.
- The system should be able to function with incomplete knowledge.
- The user should always control the consulting process.
- The explanatory facility should be clear and user-friendly.
- The knowledge base should contain generally accepted knowledge.
- The system should be independent of any geographical constraints.
- The system should allow for integration with all other current information systems.

crease the overall productivity of the resident experts by allowing them to focus on the most challenging organizational problems. Furthermore, this off-loading of day-to-day consultation activities can free up time for the expert to pursue activities of a more creative nature with associated benefits to the organization. Finally, the ability to replicate the ES in multiple organizational sites throughout the world allows for a cost-effective method for all managers to benefit from the input of an expert to their decision-making activities.

Improved Consistency in Decisions

Yet another expected benefit associated with an ES is the increased uniformity of input to decisions and, thus, the increased consistency in decision outcomes. An expert system does not suffer from the same biases and cognitive limitations as its human counterpart and, therefore, cannot suffer from lapses of memory or attention to detail. Also, an ES lacks any form of political motivation that could enter into a human expert's analysis of a situation. Although such analysis is most likely still required, it is appropriately left in the hands of the decision maker and is divorced from the foundational information used to guide the final decision.

Improved Understanding and Explanation

In much the same manner as a human expert, an ES can provide its user with an explanation for the line of reasoning used during the process of solving a problem. This ability allows the decision maker to critique the expert's thought processes and to decide on the validity (or lack thereof) of the rationale behind the conclusion reached. More often than not, however, the decision maker uses this explanation to further his or her understanding of how an expert arrives at a particular conclusion given a set of initial facts. This increased understanding of the details of a reasoning process can enhance the decision maker's understanding not only of the decision at hand, but of the overall domain knowledge as well.

Improved Management of Uncertainty

Experts must be able to cope with uncertainty in their analysis of a problem. The existence of uncertainty is ubiquitous in all decision-making contexts and an expert must be able to provide a measure of uncertainty (i.e., a degree of confidence) in all advice given in response to a problem. Expert systems are also quite capable of dealing with the uncertainties of conclusions and this characteristic is yet another way of distinguishing ESs from other traditional IS applications. The method by which an ES handles uncertainty is called *fuzzy logic*. We will explore this area of intelligent systems in conjunction with our focus on neural nets in chapter 10.

Formalization of Organizational Knowledge

By incorporating the reasoning processes and rules used by an expert within a particular knowledge domain into an ES, an organization begins the process of codification of its knowledge. The very process of knowledge acquisition allows for a detailed inspection of the organization's approaches to problem solving and thus allows for a better understanding of how the organization's problems are actually solved. Long after the human expert has left the organization, the knowledge acquired during the development process remains available to future managers as well as the next generation of experts.

Problems and Limitations Associated with Expert Systems

Despite their widespread acceptance and clear potential for benefiting an organization, expert systems have several limitations that must be acknowledged and dealt with. Table 8-7 lists several factors and problems that must be overcome with regard to ES design, deployment, and use.

In addition to the issues listed in table 8-7 one should note that an ES is not infallible. Much like its human counterpart, it can and does make mistakes. Because the rule set is simply a model based upon the combined knowledge and reasoning processes of several experts and because each of those experts is subject to error, the ES is also subject to erroneous conclusions. In fact, because we are modeling knowledge rather than exactly mirroring it, the ES has a greater propensity for error than a human expert. The XCON system, developed by Digital Equipment Corporation to assist sales representatives in assembling bids for complex computer configurations is considered one of the most successful ES projects in industry. It is often used as an example of a fully developed, mature expert system. Yet, despite its fame and maturity, the XCON system is unable to fulfill about 2 percent of the configurations presented to it. The real question here is whether an organization can become comfortable with giving responsibility for solving complex problems to a computer program known to be fallible. As technology advances, however, it is expected that these error rates will decline and the reasoning methods will significantly improve. Time will tell.

Another method of identifying an expert system's limitations is to analyze each of the tasks commonly associated with an ES in relation to the specific difficulties encountered with each task. Table 8-8 uses the typology of tasks presented in table 8-4 and lists several limitations associated with each.

Common Expert System Technologies

Since the emergence of the expert system, its growth has been significant both in terms of numbers of systems and diversity of vertical market application. A section has been included at the end of this chapter that lists and briefly describes many of the

---

Table 8-7 Limitations Associated with Expert Systems

- The needed knowledge is not always available.
- Experts use common sense. Programming common sense is not yet a reality.
- Expertise is difficult to extract and encode.
- Experts can recognize a problem outside the knowledge domain much faster than an ES.
- Expert systems cannot eliminate the cognitive limitations of the user.
- An ES is functional only within a narrow knowledge domain.
- Expert vocabulary is often limited and not easily understood by others.
- Human experts adapt to their environments naturally whereas an ES must be explicitly updated.
- An ES has a limited sensory experience compared to human experts.

Table 8-8 Limitations Associated with Common ES Task Categories

Task	Problems
Interpretation	Data may be noisy or missing
	Data may be inaccurate
Prediction	Must allow for contingencies and uncertainties
Diagnosis	Multiple symptoms can confound diagnosis
Planning	Multiple alternatives with complex scenarios exist
Design	Conflicting constraints and interaction exist among subdesigns
Prescription	Multiple problems may exist
Monitoring	Error conditions and nominal expectations are often context-specific
Control	Often requires interpretation based on common sense

more popular and successful commercial ES deployments. Though not comprehensive, this list is representative of the state of the art and should provide you with a good start in exploring the diverse applications available through intelligent computer systems.

8-6 CHAPTER SUMMARY

The chapter illustrates the concept of the expert system and its primary method of creation, artificial intelligence. We focused on the significance of both subjects as they relate to the processes of decision making and problem solving.

We looked at the methods available to create a computer-based reasoning system through discussion of human reasoning processes, and we clarified the concepts and structure of expert systems. We also focused on the predesign activities associated with building an expert system. From this focus, we developed a greater understanding of the limitations associated with an ES and, therefore, how to evaluate it. In the next chapter, we will introduce the methods by which expert knowledge is "captured" and stored in an expert system.

Key Concepts

- The definition of expert system: (8-1)

  A computer-based application that employs a set of rules based upon human knowledge to solve problems that require human expertise

- The primary method by which an ES functions as an expert is through techniques developed in the field of artificial intelligence (AI). (8-1)

- AI is focused on understanding how people reason and think and then translating that understanding into computer systems that can perform the same actions. (8-2)

- There are several specific reasoning processes used by humans that are easily translated into the realm of expert systems and artificially intelligent computers: categorization, specific rules, heuristics, past experience, and expectations. (8-2)

- The methods employed by an AI system designer to create a reasoning system using a computer are based on the following processes and mechanisms: rule-based reasoning, frames, case-base reasoning, and pattern recognition. (8-2)

- The definition of machine learning: (8-2)

  Machine learning involves AI-based mechanisms that allow computers to "learn" from past experiences using examples and analogies.

- Two well-known areas of machine learning research and application are neural networks and genetic algorithms. (8-2)

- The main difference between a DSS and an ES is in the ES's containment of real knowledge acquired from experts in the application domain. (8-3)

- The basic architecture of an ES associated with the user environment is the user interface, the inference engine, and the knowledge base. (8-3)

- Contrary to most other system development efforts, the selection of an application development tool or language platform and the selection of the ES hardware platform should be made prior to design. (8-4)

- If the expectations of the user in terms of system functionality are met, a number of significant operational benefits to the organization can emerge. (8-5)

- An ES is not infallible. Much like its human counterpart, it can, and does, make mistakes. (8-5)

Questions for Review

1. Define each of the following terms:
   expert system
   artificial intelligence
   facets
   daemon
   machine learning
   neural network
   knowledge base
   expert system shells
   blackboard workspace
   artificial life

2. What is rule-based reasoning?

3. What are frames? Describe how they work.

4. What is pattern recognition?

5. List and explain the different types of human reasoning processes.

6. What is the main difference between a DSS and an ES?

7. Describe the basic architecture of an expert system.

8. What part of an ES's architecture most often contributes to the success or failure of the ES?

9. Explain why it is important in the case of ES design to determine the development tools prior to design.

10. What are the benefits of expert systems?

11. Describe the problems and limitations associated with expert systems.

12. Discuss the criteria for evaluation of an expert system.

For Further Discussion

1. Choose a system using ES technology to support problem solving and describe its benefits and limitations.

2. What kind of organizations do you think need to use the ES most to help make decisions and solve problems? How does it help?

3. You are about to buy a car. Using a rule-based reasoning technique, describe how you make your decision.

4. Identify the differences between two well-known areas of machine learning research and application, neural networks, and genetic algorithms, and give some example systems of each.

5. Analyze the design of the user interface in an ES application. Discuss the reasons why you think it is a good (or bad) design.

Listing of Past and Present Expert System Technologies

DENDRAL (1965–1983)

The DENDRAL project was one of the earliest expert systems. DENDRAL began as an effort to explore the mechanization of scientific reasoning and the formalization of scientific knowledge by working within a specific domain of science, organic chemistry. Another concern was to use AI methodology to better understand some fundamental questions in the philosophy of science, including the process by which explanatory hypotheses are discovered or judged adequate. After more than a decade of collaboration among chemists, geneticists, and computer scientists, DENDRAL had become not only a successful demonstration of the power of rule-based expert systems but also a significant tool for molecular structure analysis, in use in both academic and industrial research labs. Using a plan-generate-test search paradigm and data from mass spectrometry and other sources, DENDRAL proposes plausible candidate structures for new or unknown chemical compounds. Its performance rivals that of human experts for certain classes of organic compounds and has resulted in a number of papers that were published in the chemistry literature. Although no longer a topic of academic research, the most recent version of the interactive structure generator, GENOA, has been licensed by Stanford University for commercial use.

META-DENDRAL (1970–1976)

META-DENDRAL is an inductive program that automatically formulates new rules for DENDRAL to use in explaining data about unknown chemical compounds. Using the plan-generate-test paradigm, META-DENDRAL has successfully formulated rules of mass spectrometry, both by rediscovering existing rules and by proposing entirely new rules. Although META-DENDRAL is no longer an active program, its contributions to ideas about learning and discovery are being applied to new domains. Among these ideas are the following: induction can be automated as heuristic search; for efficiency, the search can be broken into two steps—approximate and refined; learning must be able to cope with noisy (unfiltered or unhomogenous) and incomplete data; and learning multiple concepts at the same time is sometimes inescapable.

MYCIN (1972–1980)

MYCIN is an interactive program that diagnoses certain infectious diseases, prescribes antimicrobial therapy, and can explain its reasoning in detail. In a controlled test, its performance equaled that of specialists. In addition, the MYCIN program incorporated several important AI developments. MYCIN extended the notion that the knowledge base should be separate from the inference engine, and its rule-based inference engine was built on a backward-chaining, or goal-directed, control strategy. Because it was designed as a consultant for physicians, MYCIN was given the ability to explain both its line of reasoning and its knowledge. Because of the rapid pace of developments in medicine, the knowledge base was designed for easy augmentation. And because medical diagnosis often involves a degree of uncertainty, MYCIN's rules incorporated certainty factors to indicate the importance (i.e., likelihood and risk) of a conclusion. Although MYCIN was never used routinely by physicians, it has substantially influenced other AI research. MYCIN has led to work in TEIRESIAS, EMYCIN, PUFF, CENTAUR, VM, GUIDON, and SACON, all described below, and to ONCOCIN and ROGET.

TEIRESIAS (1974–1977)

The knowledge acquisition program TEIRESIAS was built to assist domain experts in refining the MYCIN knowledge base. TEIRESIAS developed the concept of meta-level knowledge—that is, knowledge by which a program can not only use its knowledge directly, but can examine it, reason about it, and direct its use. TEIRESIAS makes clear the line of reasoning used in making a diagnosis and aids physician experts in modifying or adding to the knowledge base. Much of this was incorporated into the EMYCIN framework. The flexibility and understandability that TEIRESIAS introduced into the knowledge base debugging process have been models for the design of many expert systems.

EMYCIN (1974–1979)

The core inference engine of MYCIN, together with a knowledge engineering interface, was developed under the name EMYCIN, or "Essential MYCIN." It is a domain-independent framework that can be used to build rule-based expert systems for consultation problems such as those encountered in diagnosis or troubleshooting. EMYCIN continues to be a primary example of software that can facilitate building expert systems and has been used in a variety of domains, both medical (e.g., PUFF) and nonmedical (e.g., SACON). The system has been widely distributed in the United States and abroad and is the basis for the Texas Instruments software system called Personal Consultant.

PUFF (1977–1979)

The PUFF system was the first program built using EMYCIN. PUFF's domain is the interpretation of pulmonary function tests for patients with lung disease. The program can diagnose the presence and severity of lung disease and produce reports for the patient's file. Once the rule set for this domain had been developed and debugged, PUFF was transferred to a minicomputer at Pacific Medical Center in San Francisco, where it is used routinely to aid with interpretation of pulmonary function tests. A version of PUFF has been licensed for commercial use.

CENTAUR (1977–1980)

The CENTAUR system was designed to experiment with an expert system that combines both rule- and frame-based approaches to represent and use knowledge about medicine and medical diagnostic strategies. For purposes of comparison, CENTAUR was developed for the same task domain as PUFF, interpretation of pulmonary function tests. CENTAUR performed well, demonstrating the effectiveness of this representation and control methodology.

VM (1977–1981)

The Ventilator Manager (VM) program interprets on-line quantitative data in the intensive care unit (ICU) and advises physicians on the management of postsurgical patients needing a mechanical ventilator to help them breathe. Although based on the MYCIN architecture, VM was redesigned to allow for the description of events that change over time. Thus, it can monitor the progress of a patient, interpret data in the context of the patient's present and past condition, and suggest adjustments to therapy. VM was tested in the surgical ICU at Pacific Medical Center in San Francisco. Some of the program's concepts have been built directly into more recent respiratory monitoring devices.

GUIDON (1977–1981)

GUIDON is an experimental program intended to make available to students the expertise contained in EMYCIN-based systems. GUIDON incorporates separate knowledge bases for the domain itself and for tutoring, and engages the student in a dialogue that presents domain knowledge in an organized way over a number of sessions. Using the MYCIN knowledge base as the domain to be taught, work in GUIDON explored several issues in intelligent computer–assisted instruction (ICAI), including means for structuring and planning a dialogue, generating teaching material, constructing and verifying a model of what the student knows, and explaining expert reasoning. Although GUIDON was successful in many respects, it also revealed that the diagnostic strategies and some of the medical knowledge that were contained implicitly in the MYCIN rules had to be made explicit in order for students to understand and remember them easily. As a result, a new expert system, NEOMYCIN, has been developed.

SACON (1977–1978)

SACON was implemented as a test of the EMYCIN framework in an engineering context. SACON advised structural engineers on the use of MARC, a large structural analysis program, and has served as a prototype of many advisory systems.

MOLGEN (1975–1984)

The MOLGEN project has applied AI methods to research in molecular biology. Initial work focused on acquiring and representing the expert knowledge needed to design and simulate experiments in the domain. This led to the development of UNITS, described below. The second phase of research resulted in two expert systems, representing distinct approaches to the design of genetic experiments. One system used "skeletal plans," which are abstracted outlines of experiment designs that can be applied to specific experimental goals and environments. The other system was based on planning with constraints, in which planning decisions are made in the spaces of overall strategy, domain-independent decisions, and domain-dependent laboratory decisions, and the interaction of separate steps or subproblems of an experiment constitute constraints on the overall problem. These two systems were later synthesized into a third system, called SPEX. Current work, known as MOLGEN-II, is investigating the process of theory formation in molecular biology.

UNITS (1975–1981)

The frame-based UNITS system was developed in the MOLGEN project as a general-purpose knowledge representation, acquisition, and manipulation tool. Designed for use by domain experts with little previous knowledge of computers, it provides an interface that allows the expert to describe both factual and heuristic knowledge. It contains both domain-independent and domain-specific components, including modified English rules for describing the procedural knowledge. UNITS has been licensed by Stanford University for commercial development.

AM (1974–1980)

The AM program explored machine learning by discovery in the domain of elementary mathematics. Using a framework of 243 heuristic rules, AM successfully proposed plausible new mathematical concepts, gathered data about them, noticed regularities, and, completing this cycle, found ways of shortening the statement of those hypotheses by making new definitions. However, AM was not able to generate new heuristics. This failing was found to be inherent in the design of AM; related work on discovering new heuristics was done as part of EURISKO.

EURISKO (1978–1984)

A successor to AM, EURISKO has also investigated automatic discovery, with a particular emphasis on heuristics, their representation, and the part played by analogy in their discovery. Several hundred heuristics, mostly related to functions, design, and simulation, guide EURISKO in applying its knowledge in several domains. In each domain, the program has three levels of tasks to perform: working at the domain level to solve problems; inventing new domain concepts; and synthesizing new heuristics that are specific and powerful enough to aid in handling tasks in the domain. EURISKO has been applied to elementary mathematics; programming, where it has uncovered several LISP bugs; naval fleet design, where it has reigned undefeated in the Traveller Trillion Credit Squadron tournament; VLSI design, where it has come up with some novel and potentially useful three-dimensional devices; oil-spill cleanup; and a few other domains.

RLL (1978–1980)

RLL (for Representation Language Language) is a prototype tool for building customized representation languages. RLL is self-descriptive—that is, it is itself described in terms of RLL units. It has been used as the underlying language for EURISKO and other systems.

Contract Nets (1976–1979)

The Contract Nets architecture is an early contribution to work on computer architectures for parallel computation. Recently, it has received much attention in the emerging literature on multiprocessor architectures for symbolic computation. In the Contract Nets architecture, problem solving is distributed among decentralized and loosely coupled processors. These processors communicate about task distribution and answers to subproblems through an interactive negotiation analogous to contract negotiation in the building trades: The "contract" is given to the processor that can handle the task at the lowest system cost, and failure to complete a task results in its reassignment to another processor.

CRYSALIS (1976–1983)

The CRYSALIS project explored the power of the blackboard model in interpreting X-ray data from crystallized proteins. The overall strategy was to piece together the three-dimensional molecular structure of a protein by successively refining descriptions of the structure. Although the knowledge base was developed for only a small part of the problem, the blackboard model with its hierarchical control structure was shown to be very powerful for solving such highly complex problems. Results from CRYSALIS are currently being incorporated in other KSL work and have contributed to improved models of control.

AGE (1976–1982)

The AGE (for Attempt to GEneralize) project sought to develop a software laboratory for building knowledge-based programs. AGE-1, the knowledge engineering tool that resulted, is designed for building programs that use the blackboard problem-solving framework. It can aid in the construction, debugging, and running of a program. AGE-1 has been used in a number of academic laboratories and for various applications in industry and the defense community.

QUIST (1978–1981)

QUIST combines AI and conventional database technology in a system that optimizes queries to large relational databases. QUIST uses heuristics embodying semantic knowledge about the contents of the database to make inferences about the meanings of the terms in a query. It reformulates the original query into an equivalent one whose answer can be found in the database more efficiently. Then conventional query optimization techniques are used to plan an efficient sequence of retrieval operations.

GLisp (1982–1983)

GLisp is a programming language that allows programs to be written in terms of objects and their properties and behavior. The GLisp compiler converts such programs into efficient LISP code. The compiler has been released to outside users, along with the GEV window-based data inspector, which displays data according to their GLisp description. GLisp is now being distributed from the University of Texas.

XCON 1980 to Present

XCON is probably one of the most famous of all expert systems due to its enormous success. Developed by Digital Equipment Corporation, XCON manages the complex process of configuring the variety of specifications associated with typical customer orders for Digital's products. Before XCON, the configuration of Digital's systems was performed manually by a team of highly skilled computer professionals. Despite their skills, the manual configuration process often resulted in configuration errors or incomplete orders. Following the installation of XCON, however, configuration orders attained an accuracy level of 98 percent compared with 65 percent using the previous manual system. Initial cost savings due to XCON were estimated to be in excess of $15 million with later estimates soaring as high as $40 million per year. XCON is still operational today and remains one of the greatest single success stories in the history of expert systems.

CHAPTER

9

Knowledge Engineering and Acquisition

Learning Objectives

- Understand the concept of knowledge engineering and how it is distinct from traditional IS development

- Compare a decision support system with an expert system

- Provide an overview of the methods and tools used in knowledge engineering today and provide a glimpse of how these will evolve in the future

- Understand the basis of knowledge and distinguish it from data and information

- Conceptualize the views of knowledge under three different perspectives: representation, production, and states

- Comprehend the sources of knowledge and be able to classify different types of knowledge

- Identify various methods of knowledge acquisition and management

DSS MINICASE

Robotrader and Christine's Brain

BACKGROUND

In the early 1990s, the director of research at the British investment house Pareto Partners Ltd. started searching for technical partners to help Pareto automate the stewardship of at least some of the $17 billion in funds it manages. Because financial and military decision makers both face information overload and emotional stress, the partnership of Pareto and the Hughes Electronics Corporation—a missile maker, robot designer, and spy satellite pioneer—became an obvious match.

THE DEVELOPMENT OF ROBOTRADER

In 1993, Christine Downton, an experienced analyst who had studied the trading markets for over twenty years, flew out to Hughes Research Laboratories in Malibu, California, to "upload" her knowledge of the world's bond markets into a machine. The man at Hughes assigned to squeeze out Downton's experience was Charles Dolan, who has a Ph.D. in computer science from UCLA.

Dolan's approach to AI is a mixture of traditional symbolic logic and newer connectionist theories, which proceed from the assumption that intelligent behavior emerges out of an artificial "neural net." Dolan's view is that the two are part and parcel of each other—that within the brain's networks of neurons there is structure and that this structure is the embodiment of symbols. He tries to create such "knowledge spaces" on the computer, based on the symbolic structures that have been laboriously built into the "wetware" of his willing subjects.

To do this, Dolan developed a system Hughes calls MKAT (Modular Knowledge Acquisition Toolkit)—software tools for extracting and encoding human expertise. MKAT has been used to "knowledge engineer" military skills such as how tank commanders plan an assault on an enemy position. Because knowledge engineering means cross-examining the expert's thought processes, it often exposes charlatans. Christine Downton, however, is no charlatan. Although Dolan and his Hughes team had become highly proficient at knowledge engineering, it still took a grueling series of sessions with Downton spread over eighteen months to get a fair sample of those processes, with Dolan switching from tool to tool to try to mimic the complex trains of thought Downton often described.

The result is a set of two thousand rules called the Global Bond Allocation Strategy. Using electronic market data feeds, the system takes in around eight hundred items of economic information—things like countries' public sector and current account deficits, inflation rates, money-supply figures, and so on. After crunching through millions of permutations, it spits out conclusions as a series of recommendations, such as selling holdings in Denmark and buying bonds in Germany. The recommendations are passed to a flesh-and-blood Pareto trader, who then makes the deals.

Pareto is devoted to a "quantitative" approach to trading whereby all the trading and investment is done using simplified models of what is happening, rather than feelings and theories about why. As such, it seemed natural for Pareto to turn to AI, and AI fit into the firm easily. Robotrader produces recommendations, as any of Pareto's other models do, for which its traders must then find the best market price. It does so at a far more sophisticated level, to be sure, but it is fulfilling the same basic function.

THE ROBOTRADER

So how has Robotrader performed? As of the end of 1997, Robotrader was looking after US$200 million worth of funds that are mostly highly diversified portfolios with relatively low risk levels. The system produces returns of around 3 percent above a bond market benchmark—the kind of workmanlike performance that large pension funds seek. The returns are not stunning. But then, Robotrader isn't being asked to be stunning; the low risk levels are part of its (reprogrammable) parameters. And they are all the program's own work. Downton resists any temptation to override the system's recommendations, especially when the markets are volatile.

Downton modestly says that no human could process the volume of information that the machine sucks up. Because of this, she believes that AI systems will one day lead to radical downsizing in the upper-middle ranks of the finance industry. The functions people perform and for which they charge huge margins will be picked off and automated. The Internet will hasten the process, delivering sophisticated services directly to the consumer. Downton and the rest of the Pareto-Hughes team believe that their artificial intelligence trading system, Robotrader, is one of the first concrete steps toward a shakeout of the financial industry precipitated by new technology.

—Yu-Ting "Caisy" Hung

Simultaneous to the development of the first expert system by Feigenbaum and his colleagues at Stanford came the emergence of a new role in systems analysis, the *knowledge engineer* (KE):

> The knowledge engineer practices the art of bringing the principles and tools of AI research to bear on difficult application problems requiring experts' knowledge for their solution. The technical issues of acquiring this knowledge, representing it, and using it appropriately to construct and explain lines-of-reasoning, are important problems in the design of knowledge-based systems. . . . The art of constructing intelligent agents is both a part of and an extension of the programming art. It is the art of building complex computer programs that represent and reason with knowledge of the world. (Feigenbaum 1977, 1015)

Although the concept of knowledge engineering can be thought of as a special form of systems analysis, the goals of the two are nonetheless the same. Both knowledge engineers and systems analysts seek to create a thorough specification of an information system that can be successfully implemented. The process of knowledge engineering, however, differs in one key aspect from traditional IS development: The problem context of an ES is unique to the ES and seeks to emulate human expert problem solving. In this sense, each ES is a one-of-a-kind system and its success is predicated on the skill of the KEs to extract that which is deeply hidden in the mind of a human expert. From this perspective, we can see that the KE needs to have a high degree of domain knowledge combined with a broad set of system development skills. We can also see why Feigenbaum calls knowledge engineering an art.

Gaines (1995) points out that expert system research is rightfully recognized as having made a significant contribution to information technology. Despite this contribution, however, it would be disappointing if, in common with many ventures in artificial intelligence research in the past, ES research fails to provide any insights into the nature of human knowledge processes. What is expertise, why do we value it, how does it arise, what are the underlying social, psychological, and logical processes, what role does it play in the dynamics of the human species, and so on? The notion of expertise is central to the professions, career structures, the health care system, the educational system, and so on. It is at the core of the way in which our society functions, and it is the basis on which individuals are valued in that society.

From the narrow point of view of information technology, computer and communications systems at the very least *support* the dynamics of expertise in our society even if they do not as yet effectively emulate or replace expertise. A reasonable model of expertise would be valuable in the development of such technology, and various tacit models of expertise are implicit in existing developments. As technology develops and society changes, it would be useful to have an overall model of humanity that contains its processes and products. Such a model would provide some basis for understanding who we are, where we are going, the interplay of our psychology, culture, and technology, and the effect upon all these of personal, societal, and technical choices that are open to us. This long-term objective is assuming short-term significance as the goals of knowledge-based systems research have advanced from emulating the expertise of individuals to emulating that of organizations through enterprise modeling (Petrie 1992).

In this chapter, we will explore many of the key issues and elements of knowledge engineering and acquisition as they relate to the design and development of an expert system. First, however, we must establish a foundation of understanding with regard to the key construct of *knowledge*.

9-1 THE CONCEPT OF KNOWLEDGE

In this, the dawn of the digital era, we are constantly being barraged with reports of the importance of *knowledge* and *information* with respect to the struggle for global competitive advantage and economic success. Drucker (1993) considers knowledge to be the key resource of tomorrow's organization:

> The knowledge society will inevitably be far more competitive than any society we have yet known—for the simple reason that with knowledge being universally accessible, there will be no excuse for nonperformance. There will be no "poor" countries. There will only be ignorant countries. And the same will be true for companies, industries, and organizations of all kinds. It will be true for individuals too. (p. 80)

Although the terms *data, information,* and *knowledge* are assumed to have commonsense meanings, quite often their distinction is not well understood and, thus, they are inappropriatcly used interchangeably. If we are to engineer knowledge, we must be clear on exactly what it is we are engineering.

What Exactly Is Knowledge?

We can look in any good dictionary and find definitions for the three primary constructs of human thought and reasoning, but to more fully understand how they relate to one another we must understand their evolution.

More than twelve millennia were required for humanity to evolve from oral to written communications. The early stages of this evolution were marked by the emergence of counting. As early as 3100 B.C., we find evidence of an evolutionary process beginning with notched-stick tallies and incised tablets and moving to abstract numerals, ideographic writing, and phonetic coding. Once revealed, writing dominated human communications for the next forty-five hundred years. By the middle of the fifteenth century there were more than thirty thousand books in Europe. By the year 1500, less than fifty years after the invention of the printing press, there were morc than eight million books. This dawning of the "age of growing abundance of data"[1] is where we first see the importance of fully understanding the distinctions between the constructs of human thought and reasoning.

The scope of this section precludes a thorough identification and listing of all of the philosophical perspectives and definitions of data, information, and knowledge. As such, we will establish our definitions within the confines of this text and leave the debate surrounding the various nuances of meaning to those better equipped. For our purposes, we will adopt the following definitions:

1. ***Data***. Facts, measurements, or observations with or without context. An example of data without context is 60, 62, 66, 72. The same data with context might be the height in inches of Laura, Samantha, John, and Kristine, respectively. The validity and the effectiveness of data are determined primarily by the data's accuracy.

2. ***Information.*** Data organized in such a manner as to be useful and relevant to a problem solver in making decisions. The key criterion in evaluating information is its usefulness. Information can also be thought of as an event rather than an entity. As such, information "occurs" when a decision maker peruses and understands some structured collection of data.

---

[1] I must offer my thanks to Jacek Kryt from Ryerson Polytechnic University in Toronto for coining this phrase and offering it up as an explanation for our current state of cognitive affairs.

3. *Knowledge.* The application of a combination of instincts, ideas, rules, procedures, and information to guide the actions and decisions of a problem solver within a particular problem context. In this sense, knowledge is an interpretation made by the mind. Success in explaining the interactions of the problem context is a key element in evaluating the validity of knowledge.

From the above definitions, two additional points can be inferred. First, information is personal. One person's information is another person's data. Second, knowledge is not static and, therefore, must change as the environment of the decision maker changes. Knowledge useful in one paradigm or historical era may be completely useless in another. As such, an ES is only useful when its knowledge base contains knowledge from the current paradigm. We could develop an ES to assist doctors during the Civil War in treating the wounded using the knowledge of that era, but its usefulness would be negligible in today's sophisticated medical environments.

Knowledge Perspectives

The branch of philosophy known as *epistemology* deals with the characterization of knowledge as an entity. Although a comprehensive analysis of the nature of knowledge from an epistemological perspective is far beyond our scope, we can nonetheless scratch the surface by reviewing a few basic concepts related to the knowledge construct.

For our purposes it will be helpful to understand the various perspectives regarding what knowledge is. In this regard, three predominant perspectives can be identified: (1) *representation,* (2) *production,* and (3) *states.*

Knowledge as Representation

This perspective of knowledge embodied as a usable representation of something was advanced by Newell (1982). He suggested that if a system contains a knowledge representation, such as a model or rule set, of "something . . . , then the system itself can also be said to have knowledge, namely the knowledge embodied in that representation about that thing" (p. 89). It must be noted, however, that this perspective differentiates between the knowledge itself and the representation of that knowledge. The book you are reading is not knowledge but rather a representation of it. If you were unable to read the English language, then the symbols and patterns that serve to communicate such thoughts would be unusable by you and the representation of knowledge embodied herein would also become useless. The point is that knowledge as representation is only of value if the form of representation is such that it can be understood and made useful.

Another important characteristic of this perspective is the distinction made between the knowledge representation and the processing required to apply it to a given problem context. Newell suggests that "knowledge cannot so easily be seen, only imagined as the result of interpretive processes operating on symbolic expressions" (1982, 89). In other words, a system, such as a DSS or ES, must possess not only the knowledge representations necessary to solve a particular problem but also the ability to process that knowledge in the form in which it is represented. Implicit here is the notion that each form of knowledge representation in a system will require a complementary knowledge-processing mechanism.

Knowledge as Production

Theorists holding this view see knowledge as a set of stocks or inventories in which items are transferred from one stock to another based on process or external event. The production perspective suggests that learning is a form of knowledge production and that knowledge is "manufactured" as well as acquired. Here, we find the process of decision making to be fueled by knowledge stocks that are either held in reserve until needed or manufactured on demand. This highly metaphoric perspective, while limited in its ability to explain a number of cognitive behaviors, is nonetheless useful in conceptualizing the design of a computer system intended to support a decision-making activity.

Knowledge as States

The third way of viewing knowledge, offered by van Lohuizen (1986), regards knowledge as a set of six hierarchical states. Table 9-1 lists these six states in order of increasing relevance. Each of the knowledge states can be used to generate a different, more relevant state of knowledge. Problem-solving activities such as gathering, analyzing, evaluating, weighing, synthesizing, and selecting all play a role in the conversion of knowledge from one state of relevance to a higher state. Further, as the state of knowledge is increased, the chance for information overload is diminished and the quality of the knowledge is extended. The highest state of knowledge, the decision, implies an end to the process of state conversion and a realization of the objective or goal of the conversion process.

Where Does Knowledge Live?

It will be helpful to this discussion to characterize knowledge by means of the sources of knowledge available to the decision maker. Both internal and external sources of knowledge exist and are necessary to the generation of a successful solution product. Further, the acquisition of knowledge from external sources may be either active or passive; that is, knowledge can be acquired either through active communication and messaging between the decision maker and the environment or it may be acquired through simple observation and unobtrusive gathering methods.

Internal sources of knowledge are tapped through knowledge derivation activities. The decision maker must use the existing knowledge of the problem context as a basis for deriving new knowledge through inference, logic, or process of elimination. The decision as to which source or combination of sources to use in solving a particular problem is based on the limits of time, economic resources, and cognitive limitations associated with the problem context. In addition, the decision maker must assess the potential trade-off between the reliability of knowledge acquired internally or ex-

Table 9-1 The Six States of Knowledge		
1. Data	**2.** Information	**3.** Structured information
4. Insight	**5.** Judgment	**6.** Decision

ternally and the costs and cognitive strain associated with that knowledge. Although it may be easy and inexpensive to acquire a piece of knowledge, its reliability may be such that we may choose to expend greater resources to derive it.

A Taxonomy of Knowledge

Before we can move on to our primary topic of interest, the acquisition and management of knowledge in an ES, we must focus on one remaining issue: the classification of types of knowledge. It seems intuitive to assume that not all knowledge is the same and that a classification scheme would be useful in both organizing the knowledge for storage as well as identifying the appropriate type of knowledge to apply in a given situation. To satisfy this need, we will adopt the taxonomy of knowledge advanced by Holsapple and Whinston (1988). In this classification, three primary and three secondary types of knowledge are identified. Table 9-2 lists the types of knowledge within this taxonomy and several examples of each.

The three primary types of knowledge in the taxonomy not only serve as the fundamental inputs and processes associated with problem solving but are also associated with the ability of a decision maker to recognize the need or opportunity to initiate decision-making activities. *Procedural knowledge* may be used to analyze *descriptive knowledge,* and *reasoning knowledge* can be employed to either govern the analysis or determine the usefulness and applicability of its outcomes.

The secondary knowledge types can be thought of as peripheral influences on the core process of decision making. Each of the secondary types provides the decision maker with additional channels of inference and knowledge derivation that can "feed" the processes associated with the primary types of knowledge. Suffice it to say that an effective decision maker (or an effective DSS) must be capable of managing each of the six types of knowledge.

9-2 KNOWLEDGE ACQUISITION FOR EXPERT SYSTEMS

The essence of knowledge engineering is the process of knowledge acquisition (KA). Here, knowledge is elicited from experts in a specific domain, gathered, organized, and

---

Table 9-2 Taxonomy of Knowledge Types

Primary
- *Descriptive.* Data, information, descriptions of past, present, and future situations
- *Procedural.* How to do something
- *Reasoning.* Codes of conduct, regulations, policies, diagnostic rules

Secondary
- *Linguistic.* Vocabulary, grammar, knowledge of gestures
- *Assimilative.* Permissible contents, retention cycles, relevancy filters
- *Presentation.* Modes of communication, graphing, messaging, inverse of linguistic knowledge

---

formalized with the goal of transforming it into a computer-usable representation. The KA process is a complex one that requires a thorough understanding of the various channels and mechanisms for transfer of information from one human being to another. Numerous methods and approaches to KA have been offered and, to date, no completely generalizable method exists. In this text, we will explore the various steps and processes associated with the more common approaches in an effort to construct a usable prescriptive framework for KA. Figure 9-1 provides a graphical view of the psychological and computational foundations associated with knowledge engineering.

At the top left of the figure is the person regarded as capable of expertly performing some task in some domain. At the top right is the computer regarded as capable of emulating the performance of that task in that domain. The arrow from person to computer indicates that an objective of knowledge acquisition research is to support the required expertise transfer from the person to the computer. The lower portion of the figure illustrates the interplay between the tools employed by the KE and the psychological and computational models developed to represent the knowledge and process contained within the mind of the expert.

FIGURE 9-1 Conceptual Model of Knowledge Engineering Process

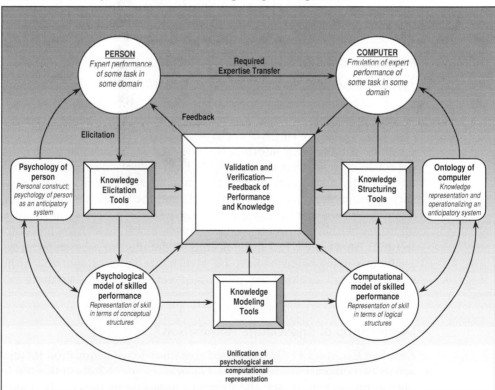

Source: Adapted from Gaines, B. R., and Shaw, M. L. G. *Knowlege Acquisition Tools Based on Personal Construct Psychology,* copyright © 1995, Knowledge Science Institute. Used with permission.

Modeling the Task

Regardless of the approach, most methods begin with the development of a model of the task or problem domain for which the ES will be designed and built. The primary functions of the *task model* are to fully define the task under study, assist in the selection of the expert(s), establish the user characteristics and performance criteria for the system, and function as an interpretive framework for protocol analysis of the experts' responses. The task model can be thought of simply as a general competence model of how a typical expert might perform the task or solve the problem of interest. The initial task model represents a decomposition of the task or problem into subtasks and a specification of the flow of control and information between the subtasks. As additional empirical data become available to the KE, the task model will be further developed from its first-order form.

In addition to the task model, a general *domain description* must be generated. This description, usually synthesized from domain-related reference documents or textbooks, consists of both the vocabulary of the domain and the relevant theories and methods associated with the domain. In addition, the general characteristics of the users within this domain must also be included in this description. An explication of both the competence level of the users and their various roles within the task or problem-solving context must be formulated. Finally, an evaluation of the potential costs and benefits associated with the development of an ES must be performed at this stage.

Modeling the Performance

Performance modeling utilizes models, hypotheses, and cognitive analysis techniques to elicit the real problem-solving knowledge from experts. The primary vehicle by which this process occurs is through verbalization by the expert, often referred to as *protocol reporting*. The KE elicits knowledge from the expert using verbalization schemes ranging from informal interviewing techniques to highly structured protocol schemes. Following each round of knowledge acquisition, a model of the knowledge is constructed and reviewed by the expert for clarity and accuracy. Any necessary modifications are made by the KE and the process is repeated. The knowledge acquisition and performance-modeling process proceeds until all case situations identified within the problem space have been "solved" from a protocol perspective. In other words, the KE continues until all detailed step-by-step traces of the expert's problem-solving behavior have been verbalized and categorized within the problem space. We will explore the process of verbal protocol analysis in further detail shortly.

Dimensions of Knowledge Acquisition

Kim and Courtney (1988) proposed that knowledge acquisition methods be classified across two dimensions: *strategic* and *tactical*. Figure 9-2 illustrates the features of each dimension. As you can see, the *strategic* dimension focuses on the specific method that drives the KA process, whereas the *tactical* dimension is concerned with the specific technique used to extract the expert's knowledge.

FIGURE 9-2 Knowledge Acquisitions Dimensions

Source: Adapted from Gaines, B. R., and Shaw, M. L. G. *Knowledge Acquisition Tools Based on Personal Construct Psychology,* copyright © 1995, Knowledge Science Institute. Used with permission.

KE-Driven

Within the strategic dimension, *knowledge engineer–driven* acquisition is considered the most common approach. In this method, the KE interacts directly with the expert and seeks to model both the task knowledge and the performance knowledge about the domain. Good communication skills along with patience, persistence, empathy, and a reasonable level of intelligence are all important contributors to the success of this process. The primary KA techniques employed using this approach include interviewing, protocol analysis, and the repertory grid method, among others.

Expert-Driven

In this approach to KA, the expert encodes his or her own expertise and knowledge and enters it directly into the computer system. In effect, the expert is serving two roles: expert and KE. Although the potential for loss of clarity exists (due primarily to the lack of an autonomous KE forcing clarification on key issues), this technique can be useful if the expert can assure the performance of the final model through some independent assessment method. Visual modeling is the primary technique used to construct domain models when using this approach. That technique allows the expert to visualize real-world problems and to manipulate their elements using a graphical entity representation.

Machine-Driven

This field within AI focuses on machine learning (covered in greater depth in chapter 10) and works to develop and refine *machine-driven* approaches to KA. The current technology is exploring the use of inductive inference engines to extract the knowledge from a set of example cases presented to the computer. The cases, their solutions, and the various attributes that were considered during the problem-solving activity are processed using a computerized algorithm designed to infer rules. Although still in its earliest stages of development, this method promises to become a significant contributor to the next generation of intelligent computer problem solvers.

Knowledge Acquisition Techniques

Hayes-Roth (1985) proposed that KA occurs in five general stages (see figure 9-3). Each stage is intended to structure the performance of certain activities on the part of the KE and to prepare the "deliverables" from that stage to be used as input in the next. For example, the requirements derived from the activities in the *identification* stage become the input to the activities and processes contained within the *conceptualization* stage.

Figure 9-3 clearly illustrates the recursive nature of the general KA process. Once an initial cycle of the process has been completed, a series of refinements, redesigns, and reformulations require the KE to revisit various stages of the process until all of the requirements and elements of knowledge have been identified and correctly modeled. This process of recursion can be quite lengthy and tedious and requires constant attention to detail on the part of the KE if it is to be successful. It is, however, a necessary approach to ensure that the totality of the knowledge domain is captured.

Throughout the KA process, the knowledge engineer must use a variety of elicitation techniques to gather the expert's knowledge. In the next section, we will explore three of the most common techniques employed using the KE-driven approach discussed above.

Interviewing Techniques

The interview is probably the most widely used and familiar of all KA techniques. Although simple and relatively easy to perform, interviewing is as much an art as it is a skill and it requires a significant amount of preparation if useful results are to

FIGURE 9-3 Five General Stages of Knowledge Acquisition

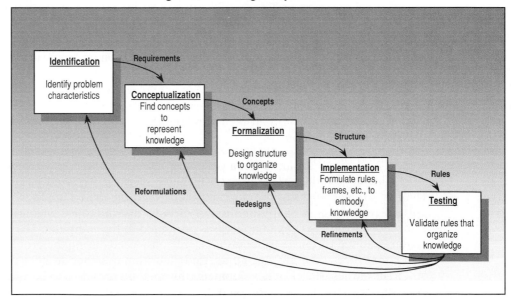

be obtained. Although a wide variety of interviewing techniques have been identified, two common classifications have emerged: *structured* and *unstructured.*

Unstructured Interviews   This type of interviewing technique can best be thought of as normal conversation. The KE engages the expert in conversation with no specific objective or goal in mind and follows a line of inquiry that is driven primarily by the responses provided by the expert to previous questions. The KE may choose to prepare a list of topics to discuss but no formal preparation is performed. The essence of unstructured interviewing is a constant addressing and probing scheme. Topics are addressed in either a breadth-first or depth-first manner and then the KE uses probing questions to guide the conversation in whatever direction is deemed necessary to fill in the details of a particular dimension. This form of interviewing is best used in the early stages of KA and is essentially an exploratory pass at the knowledge domain in preparation for a more detailed analysis.

Structured Interviews   In contrast to the unstructured interview technique, structured interviews require a significant up-front investment in planning and organizing the topics to be discussed and the sequence and construction of questions to be used. Properly performed, structured interviewing can elicit detailed insight into the expert's knowledge base and can generate the necessary clarifications, explanations, justifications, and consequences for each case solution to be encoded into computer-usable form. The steps associated with the structuring of an interview involve the selection and organization of topics, the generation of specific sets of questions and lines of inquiry, and the determination of the relationships between the questions and lines of inquiry and the various case solutions under investigation. In this sense, structured interviewing becomes more of an interrogation than a conversation, in which the content of the questions are focused on specific pieces of information or lines of reasoning. It has been shown, however, that the semantic construction of the questions (the way in which the questions are formed) asked of the expert can also have a significant effect on the efficiency of the process and the degree of accuracy of the response (Marakas and Elam 1997).

General Interviewing Techniques   Regardless of the degree of structuredness chosen for the interview process, several basic tips and techniques can be employed. To begin with, the interviewer needs to start with a few boring but important points—the name and position of the person being interviewed, the date of the interview, the place of the interview, and the main subject of the interview. Also, he or she should try not to ask questions that simply get a yes or no answer, particularly if the chosen interview approach is unstructured. Such questions are called close-ended questions. Unless the objective of the question is to get the expert simply to verify a previously obtained fact, the open-ended question form is preferable. Open-ended questions generally create a more uninhibited, "stream-of-consciousness" atmosphere that promotes increased detail in the expert's responses.

Whenever possible, questions should be phrased in a stand-alone manner by avoiding the *double question:* "Is this a step you commonly perform and is it normal to do it in this way?" Generally speaking, the expert will tend to focus on the answer to the last question first and will not give a thorough answer to the first part of the compound inquiry. In addition, the interviewer should try to avoid framing questions as either leading or hypothetical. In the former case, a question such as "Do you agree that this is the most appropriate way to perform this task?" places the expert in a position of either providing a simple affirmative, thus limiting the level of detail in the response, or having to justify a negative response, thus placing the expert in an unnecessarily defensive position. In the latter case, a question such as "Suppose you didn't possess this level of knowledge—would you still be able to perform this task?" places the expert in a frame of mind that is, most likely, irrelevant to the task under study and, thus, yields little useful knowledge. Finally, as with any KA activity, the interviewer should take the time to plan ahead. Table 9-3 contains the common elements that should be included in a preinterview checklist.

Benefits and Limitations of Interview-Based KA   Although interviewing remains the most common method of knowledge elicitation and provides many clear benefits, we must be cognizant of its limitations as well. Interviewing is most effective in the early stages of KA, where the basic structures of domain knowledge are identified, and in the final stages, where the contents of the knowledge base are refined and finalized. The technique is less effective during the phases where performance knowledge must be acquired. In general, information acquired through interviewing is inherently general, imprecise, incomprehensive, and often inconsistent. Because of the lack of common or definitive structure to the technique, the analysis of the information derived is often problematic. Finally, despite its advantages, interviewing is both time consuming and tedious. Regardless of these caveats, however, interviewing remains an important tool in the KA process.

Verbal Protocol Analysis

Most of the information necessary to model the knowledge of an expert is found in the myriad of cognitive processes he or she uses to solve a particular problem or perform a specific task. The true structure of that information is known only to the individual expert and is still beyond the understanding of even our most talented cognitive and behavioral scientists. Our problem is that we need not only to retrieve that knowledge but also structure it in a manner that is usable by a computer. This *representation mismatch* is one of the most difficult problems faced by the KE.

One method of KA that has been used successfully to reduce the difficulties associated with representation mismatch is *protocol analysis*. A protocol is a

---

Table 9-3 Basic Preinterview Checklist

- Decide what you need to know.
- Ask yourself why this information is needed.
- Determine that an interview is the best method for obtaining this information.
- Determine the appropriate degree of structure for the interview.
- Consider the method by which the answers to your questions will be coded and analyzed.

---

record or some form of documentation of the step-by-step information processing and decision-making behavior employed by an expert during a specific task. In most cases, protocols are recorded on audiotape while the expert is actually performing the task or while the expert is attempting to visualize its detailed performance. These tapes are then transcribed and used by the KE to construct a rule set and an accurate performance model of the expert's actions and behavior. There are several approaches to the collection of protocols including retrospective, introspective, interpretative, and concurrent. However, the concurrent approach, or "thinking aloud," has emerged as the most popular and useful; therefore, we will limit our focus to this method.

A concurrent protocol is collected by asking the expert to think aloud, or verbalize, his or her thoughts while simultaneously performing a task. Figure 9-4 contains a sample listing of a set of eight task instructions given to an expert and the resulting verbal protocols obtained during the performance of each task.

Originally proposed by Ericsson and Simon (1984), this verbal protocol analysis can tap directly into the detailed process information contained in the mind of the expert and can closely reflect the true cognitive processes taking place:

> We claim that cognitive processes are not modified by these verbal reports, and that task-directed cognitive processes determine what information is needed and verbalized. . . . the performance may be slowed down, and the verbalization may be incomplete, but . . . the course and structure of the task-performance will remain largely unchanged. (p. 215)

Limitations of Verbal Protocol Analysis   As with any KA technique, certain benefits and limitations can be associated with this protocol. First, although verbal protocols do provide a dense trace of the expert's cognitive behavior, they do not provide all the necessary details for modeling, and, therefore, additional techniques must be employed. In addition, it is important that the setting for a concurrent protocol session be as close to the natural setting for the task as possible. Also, certain task conditions must be present for the concurrent session to yield useful results. Table 9-4 lists these necessary task conditions.

Finally, for a complete protocol to be obtained it is vitally important that no interruptions occur during the process. The KE should not make any inquiries of the expert until the verbalization has been completed.

Repertory Grid Method

Kelly (1955) is credited with providing the KE with yet another powerful technique for knowledge gathering, the *repertory grid method* (RGM). Kelly conceived of humans as "personal scientists," each with his or her own personal model of the world. The scientist classifies and categorizes knowledge and perceptions and seeks to predict and control events by forming theories and testing hypotheses. Kelly refers to this conceptualization of human thinking as *personal construct theory.* Each personal scientist's model of the world is made up of individual personal constructs and the RGM serves as a useful way to elicit and record them. Figure 9-5 illustrates Kelly's conceptualization of a typical repertory grid.

1. First of all, write down the name of a subject or author of particular interest to you (a new name if this is the second time you are performing this task Now try to a book on this topic that you would find of interest and briefly write down the name of it.
2. You have heard that Isaac Asimov has written a book on Halley's comet. Check if it is in the library and if you find it, write down the title and location code?
3. Now check if Isaac Asimov has any books in the library from his Foundation series of books. If so write down the number of items in this series that the library keeps?
4. You want to find the UDC code on hazardous substances so that you can browse through the shelves on that and similar topics. Try to find a book on this subject and write down the code.
5. You are looking for a book on pop art, preferably a dictionary. If you find one that matches the description, what is the publisher's name and year of publication?
6. You receive a telephone message to find a book by Sidney Siegell on non- parametric statistics. What is the ISBN number of this book?
7. For the book 'Fishes of the World', check and write down how many copies have not been lent out?
8. You have a friend interested in music, decor and dolls. You want to buy her an encyclopaedia on one of the topics but with not too many pages. Find a suitable book to buy for them?

Key:

?=user query	!=problem	=useful feature
@=assistance given	results of search= 7	achievement=50%

```
T1      Keyword'7
        Shorter versions'many
        ! Some words in German.
        ? How to get to next page.  Gave up 0%
T2      ?How to get back to main menu.
        ! Help not helpful.
        @Assistance given.
        Looked at TIPS
        _Suggested search by author.
        ! Wanted boolean to cut down
        Scanned list.
        Found details 100%
T3      Back to author list.
        _Able to step through details.
        _'v' to narrow search.
        Found book and checked number of copies.
        ! Didn't expect 'u' to get loan details.
        Found number copies of 100%
T4      ! Selected subject no. option but did
        not help to locate a UDC.
        _ Got keyword list.
        ! Selected numbers but delimited with '+'.
        _ Help useful.
        ! Pressed 'Enter' and lost search.
        Restarted search, got list and found subject code 100%
T5      ? Still not sure of option to get back.
        ? Wondered if can enter 2 keywords.
        _ Entered one and found item  100%
T6      Entered incorrectly spelled name.
        Couldn't find book.
        ! Entered 2 worded title but got long list based on one.
        Tried another word but gave up  0%
T7      Entered word in title.
        ? Confused by order alphabetical based strictly on first word.
        ! Pressed enter in error and exited search. Re-entered and
        found number of copies.  100%
T8      ? 's' didn't take to top level.
        ? Entered keyword but confused by context selection.
        ?  Difficult to distinguish book types.
        Entered word from title and got long list.
        ! Wanted to enter two words.
        Found book, partially satisfied  50%
```

FIGURE 9-4 Sample Expert Task List and Protocols

Using the RGM, the expert is presented with objects from the knowledge domain grouped into triplets. The expert is asked to compare the elements of each set to each other and identify one or more distinguishing features that separate any two elements from the third. Each successive set is analyzed in this way until all object sets have been distinguished both within and across the entire set of objects. A numeric scale is used to identify the ranking or final grouping of each construct for subsequent

Table 9-4 Necessary Task Conditions for Successful Concurrent Protocols

- The sample of cases employed must be highly representative of the task under study.
- Each task must have a clearly defined conclusion or point of completion.
- The task must be able to be completed in one protocol session.
- All data must be presented to the expert in a familiar form.
- A test case should be given to the expert prior to the collection of protocols so that he or she may become familiar and comfortable with the verbalization process.

analysis. Once the grid has been elicited and finalized, it can be thought of as a representation of the expert's personal model of the domain.

The RGM can also be used to infer similarities in construct beliefs held by multiple experts. Referring to figure 9-5, if one takes a particular concept somewhere in the lattice and a set of individuals asserted to fall under that concept, then each distinction that may be made about individuals falling under that concept forms the rows of a matrix; the individuals form the columns and the constraints applying to a particular indi-

FIGURE 9-5 Typical Structure of a Repertory Grid

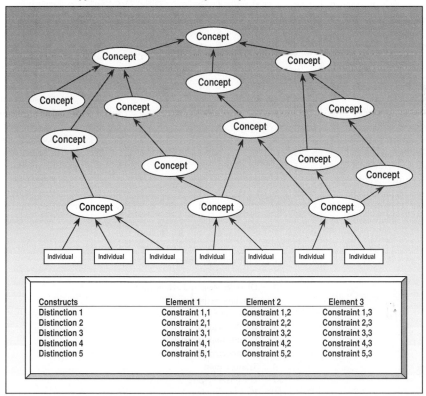

Constructs	Element 1	Element 2	Element 3
Distinction 1	Constraint 1,1	Constraint 1,2	Constraint 1,3
Distinction 2	Constraint 2,1	Constraint 2,2	Constraint 2,3
Distinction 3	Constraint 3,1	Constraint 3,2	Constraint 3,3
Distinction 4	Constraint 4,1	Constraint 4,2	Constraint 4,3
Distinction 5	Constraint 5,1	Constraint 5,2	Constraint 5,3

vidual relative to a particular distinction form the values in the matrix. In simple applications of the repertory grid, these constraints are taken to be the values or beliefs of the individuals on the roles corresponding to the distinctions.

Figure 9-6 shows a basic repertory grid elicited from a geographer about spatial mapping techniques. The mapping techniques used as elements are listed as column names at the bottom. The poles of the constructs elicited are listed on the left and the right as row names. The ratings of the mapping techniques (on a scale of 1 to 9) along the dimensions of the constructs form the body of the grid. For example, "probability mapping" is rated 8 on the dimension "qualitative and quantitative–quantitative," which means that it is construed as primarily "quantitative." Note that the predicates defined by the pole names may through their linguistic labeling indicate that they themselves are compounds of more primitive predicates. The grid is the starting point for analysis and refinement, not necessarily in itself a conceptual structure but rather a set of data that must be accounted for by any conceptual structure developed. Techniques such as *multidimensional scaling* or *cluster analysis* can then be used to further

FIGURE 9-6 Example of Repertory Grid Analysis for Spatial Mapping Techniques

		1	2	3	4	5	6	7	8	9	10	11	12		
Qualitative and quantitative	1	8	8	6	9	1	9	8	8	9	4	4	4	1	Quantitative
Local	2	9	9	6	3	5	1	9	9	1	4	4	4	2	Global
Autocorrelation not considered	3	1	1	5	4	7	2	3	1	2	9	9	9	3	Autocorrelation considered
Doesn't honor datapoints	4	2	1	3	5	9	9	1	1	9	8	7	7	4	Honors datapoints
Multiple variables considered	5	9	9	9	9	9	9	9	1	9	9	9	9	5	One variable considered
Mathematical curve fitting	6	4	4	8	9	9	1	2	4	9	5	8	8	6	Doesn't fit mathematical curve
Nonparametric	7	9	8	6	1	1	3	6	8	3	8	8	1	7	Parametric
Interval or ratio data	8	9	1	1	5	5	1	1	1	1	1	1	1	8	Nominal data
Requires periodicities	9	6	6	9	9	9	9	1	6	9	9	9	9	9	Doesn't require periodicities
Doesn't fit a trend	10	9	9	1	1	8	1	7	9	1	6	1	1	10	Fits a trend to the data
Heavy computing load	11	7	6	7	8	9	4	4	5	3	1	2	3	11	No computing load
Assumes isotropic surface	12	1	1	4	3	8	9	1	1	9	7	6	6	12	Assumes anisotropic surface
Not as susceptible to clusters	13	8	8	6	9	3	4	7	8	5	1	2	2	13	Susceptible to clusters
Doesn't incorporate geologic model	14	2	2	3	1	9	1	2	2	1	6	6	6	14	Incorporates geologic model
Interpretive	15	9	9	5	9	1	7	9	9	7	3	4	4	15	Representative
Not very important	16	4	5	2	1	9	1	1	6	7	8	9	9	16	Very important
Not very effective	17	4	5	3	1	9	2	4	6	7	9	8	8	17	Very effective
Not widely used	18	3	8	7	5	9	3	3	4	6	2	2	1	18	Widely used
		1	2	3	4	5	6	7	8	9	10	11	12		

1 Probability mapping
2 Trend surface analysis
3 Distance weighted averaging
4 Proximal mapping
5 Hand contouring
6 Bicubic splines
7 Double fourier series
8 Most predictable surface
9 Triangulation
10 Universal kriging
11 Punctual kriging
12 Nonparametric kriging

analyze the grid and identify subtle similarities and differences among the constructs and their elements. The grid of figure 9-6 is a typical one based on Kelly's original specification. Later developments allow structural relations between elements and between constructs to be specified, and the ratings to be extended to more complex constraints. Most recently, several computer programs have emerged that automate the use of the RGM for knowledge-gathering activities.

Benefits and Limitations of the Repertory Grid Method   When a KE is faced with the task of modeling knowledge for a well-structured problem space, the RGM is a good choice for elicitation. Domains requiring diagnosis, classification, elicitation of traits, and building of relationships are all good candidates for the RGM. Grid techniques are not well suited, however, for problems of design and planning where unique solutions are derived from components of the problem (Klein and Methlie 1995). This is because the RGM does not lend itself well to the elicitation of either deep knowledge or performance knowledge.

Multisource Knowledge Acquisition

Up to this point, we have discussed methods by which knowledge is acquired from a single expert. Although it is conceivable that a knowledge base could be effectively populated by a single "master of the domain," it is more likely that multiple sources will be necessary to fully acquire and model the reasoning processes and rules associated with a given problem context. This becomes especially true when faced with the development of an ES where expertise is not particularly well defined or when the development effort is intended to proliferate an expert resource in certain mission-critical environments. In these cases, KA activities must be conducted with multiple sources.

The processes and techniques described so far are applicable in a multiple-expert project, with several important differences. Most notably, when using a single expert there is no chance of unresolved ambiguity or difference of opinion. When multiple experts are used there are often conflicting views and opinions that must be resolved. Those conflicts are to be expected given the level of subjective reasoning and heuristics that exist in a typical knowledge domain. In addition, because experts may follow different lines of reasoning in solving a particular problem, this discord can manifest itself in the form of conflicting solutions to the problem. In an effort to minimize such situations, several methods have been developed to integrate the knowledge from multiple sources. We will briefly review two of the more common approaches to integration.

Consensus

Using techniques and facilities similar to those employed during group decision-making scenarios (see chapter 6), consensus among multiple experts can often be achieved in those areas where conflicting views exist. By providing each expert with the judgments and opinions of the others, each can review and revise his or her perspective based on this information. The consensus method may not be able to resolve all sources of conflict, but it is successful in a wide variety of scenarios.

Meta-Analysis

This technique takes a more statistical and quantitative approach than the consensus method and is most useful when expertise involves numerical values such as the assessment of probabilities. Here, the KE uses the individual assessments of the experts to develop a group probability fashioned as a weighted aggregation of its individual components. Also, numerous statistical methods exist in the domain of multiple-criteria decision making that may be useful in resolving multiple-source conflict.

9-3 VALIDATING AND VERIFYING THE KNOWLEDGE BASE

Once the knowledge has been "captured" by the KE, it must be evaluated for usability and accuracy. Two specific issues that must be addressed in this regard are the *validity* of the knowledge and the *verification* of the knowledge base construction. In many cases, these two issues can be addressed at one and the same time and, often, while other knowledge acquisition processes are taking place.

The two terms *validation* and *verification* are often used interchangeably and inappropriately. Validation is that part of the evaluation process that focuses on the *performance* aspects of the knowledge base. In other words, validation is concerned with whether we have built a system that performs with an acceptable level of competence and accuracy. In contrast, verification is concerned with whether the system we have built conforms to its original specifications. Verification answers the question "Did we build the right system?"; validation provides the answer to the question "Did we build the system right?" Although the process of verification simply involves comparing each of the original system specifications to the final implementation, the process of knowledge validation can involve a variety of tests and control tasks. Table 9-5 lists many of the various validation techniques and measures that may be necessary in the final stages of KA.

It is important to note that a knowledge base can be logically correct without being valid. Validation is a measure of how well the knowledge base conforms to the knowledge domain that has been modeled. In this sense, validation of the knowledge base is a concept external to the system itself—it is an expression of the degree to which the system is a true representation of reality.

Of the many ways the validity of the knowledge base may be disproved, experience has identified three primary types of faults: (1) *factual faults*, where an assertion does not correctly represent its associated fact, (2) *inferential faults*, where a rule does not correctly represent the domain knowledge, and (3) *control faults*, where the rules are contextually correct but have an undesirable control behavior on the conclusion.

9-4 CHAPTER SUMMARY

To fully appreciate the complexities associated with capturing knowledge from experts and encoding it into a computer-based system requires a thorough understanding of the differences between the concepts of data, information, and knowledge. The

4. When knowledge is viewed as production, how are the banks of knowledge built upon or improved?

5. What are the six states of knowledge, and how are they transformed into more relevant states in the decision-making process?

6. What are some limiting factors in the information-gathering process?

7. Compare primary and secondary types of knowledge and describe how they are related.

8. What are the primary functions of the task model?

9. Define a "domain description."

10. What is the primary vehicle for obtaining problem-solving knowledge from experts?

11. When does the knowledge acquisition and performance-modeling process end?

12. Compare and contrast the two dimensions of knowledge acquisition.

13. Compare KE-driven KA with expert-driven KA. Discuss the advantages and disadvantages of each method.

14. What kind of knowledge can be gained from open-ended questions compared with close-ended questions?

15. What is the objective of concurrent protocol analysis and how does that analysis work?

16. What are the benefits and limitations of the repertory grid method of knowledge gathering?

17. How do the consensus and meta-analysis techniques of KA avoid conflict?

18. Define *validity* and *verification* in the context of the knowledge base.

19. What are the three primary challenges to obtaining valid knowledge?

For Further Discussion

1. Interview an expert in a discipline that interests you. Ask her to identify a decision she makes regularly and attempt to document her specific thinking process and assumptions as she decides on a conclusion. Do you think a computer could be taught to consider and make this decision?

2. What are the benefits and limitations of structured versus unstructured interviewing techniques? Describe situations where each would be the preferred technique.

3. Describe an area of personal expertise. How did you acquire your knowledge in this area?

4. Some people feel that expert systems will one day make expert knowledge in some areas a commodity. Explain how you agree or disagree with this claim.

5. Discuss reasons why expert knowledge acquisition and modeling is so difficult and complex.

6. Most experts have mixed feelings and reactions regarding the knowledge acquisition process and goals. Some are proud and honored to be acknowledged and mined as an expert, whereas others claim their decision-making processes are much too complex to model and mimic. As an expert, how would you feel if you were approached by a KE?

CHAPTER
10
Machines
That Can Learn

Learning Objectives

■ Understand the types of problems that lend themselves to the application of machine learning systems

■ Understand the basics of how fuzzy logic processing employs set membership and how linguistic ambiguity can be modeled

■ Understand the strengths and limitations of fuzzy logic systems

■ Understand the basic concepts and components of artificial neural networks and their structures

■ Understand the strengths and limitations of neural computing

■ Understand the basic components and functioning of genetic algorithms

■ Be able to determine what type of intelligent system is best suited to different kinds of problems

Chase Manhattan Bank Credit Scoring System

In 1985, Chase Manhattan Bank began a search for new quantitative techniques to assist senior loan officers in forecasting the creditworthiness of corporate loan candidates. Chase established a thirty-six-member internal consulting organization called Chase Financial Technologies to oversee the development of pattern-analysis network models for evaluating corporate loan risk.

The resulting models, called the Creditview system, perform three-year forecasts that indicate the likelihood of a company being assigned a Chase risk classification of *good, criticized,* or *charged-off.* In addition to the overall forecast, Creditview provides a detailed listing of the items that significantly contributed to the forecast, an ES-generated interpretation of those items, and several comparison reports.

Creditview models run on a Chase Financial Technologies host computer. A user system resides at each user's PC and communicates with the host through telephone lines. In addition, conventional financial statement analysis may be performed using Chase's Financial Reporting System, an independent financial spreading and analysis package. The Financial Reporting System also resides on the user's PC and permits a company's standard financial statements to be accessed and displayed.

The "secret" to the success of Chase's analysis systems lies with an embedded pattern-analysis technology that provides the ability to construct a hybrid neural network, if enough high-quality historical data are available. Each hybrid net represents a separate "model" produced by the pattern-analysis module. The PLCM (Public Loan Company Model), the first model implemented at Chase, derives from Chase's extensive loan history of large, publicly-traded companies and their past financial data. (Chase has both publicly- and privately-owned corporations in its base of clients and prospects).

The historical data analyzed by the pattern-analysis module to produce forecasting models consist of a large collection of data units. Each data unit contains as much as six years of consecutive financial data for a particular company, corresponding industry norms, and the company's status three years after the last year of data. (The last of the six years is called the "year of the data unit.") The data unit's status is the company's rating—G stands for good, C stands for criticized, and X stands for charged-off. The system uses these data to construct a large set of candidate variables that may or may not indicate a company's future financial condition. These variables become the basis for forming patterns.

A pattern is fundamentally a statement about the value of a particular financial variable or set of variables. A very simple pattern may have the following form: $C1 < V1 < C2$, where $V1$ is a financial ratio or variable and $C1$ and $C2$ are constants. For example: $1.75 <$ quick ratio < 2.00 could be a simple pattern. Typically, patterns are more complex; they have several elements of this kind and are combined by using *and, or,* and *not.* This example could be one of a small complex pattern:

$$C1 < V1 < C2$$

$$V2 < C3$$

$$C4 < V3 < C5 \text{ and } C6 < V4 < C7$$

$$C8 < V5 < C9$$

where all the Cs are constants and Vs financial variables or ratios. Candidate variables are arranged into thousands of complex patterns and analyzed by the system to produce an optimal set of variables and patterns that form a pattern network called the Forecaster. The criteria for selection of patterns are as follows:

- *Score.* The score (as observed in the historical data) measures the ability of the pattern to differentiate between the categories *good, criticized,* and *charged-off*—in other words, the ability of the pattern to classify correctly.
- *Complexity.* Complexity is a measure of how complicated the pattern is (in terms of number of variables), simple patterns within it, and the amount of historical data it satisfies.
- *Spuriousness.* A measure of the likelihood that the pattern's score (how well it predicts) is due solely to chance.

These statistics are used to evaluate the predictive power of the patterns and to ensure that whatever predictive power is uncovered is not by chance. To each pattern and status a probability (called the "precision") exists that a data unit corresponding to the pattern will have that status. The system uses a proprietary network-balancing technique that selects the patterns for the network to maximize precision and minimize bias.

The benefits of this system to Chase are obvious. Chase can now identify the strengths and vulnerabilities in the financial structure of an obligor and forecast the impact of these factors on the firm's financial health three years into the future. The savings associated with being able to "predict the future" are a key element in the longevity of Chase Manhattan Bank.

Adapted from NIBS Pte, Ltd. (1996), www.singapore.com/products/nfga.

The advent of the digital computer has brought with it a general misconception that the majority of information processing at any given moment in our world is being carried out by an automated device. The ubiquitous nature of the computer has allowed us to forget about the most complex and powerful information processing device on earth: the human mind. If we look at cybernetics and other disciplines that form the basis of information science, we see that the true nature of information processing is rooted in the actions of living creatures as they struggle to survive and adapt to their environments. Viewed in this light, the information being processed by today's computers can be seen as accounting for only a small part of the total. Extending this, we can begin to seriously consider the development of information processing devices that mimic the structures and operating principles found in humans and other living creatures.

    Neural computing and the development of *artificial neural networks* (ANNs) is one of the new multidisciplinary fields of research that has evolved in response to the attractiveness of digital information processors that can simulate the human brain's potential for solving ill-structured business problems. Neural computing involves processing information by means of changing the states of networks formed by interconnecting extremely large numbers of simple processing elements that interact with one another by exchanging signals. This interconnection approach to information processing is a direct simulation of the way the human brain processes information and learns. This chapter will introduce the concept of *machine learning* by focusing attention on specific methods such as neural computing and genetic algorithms and will discuss numerous applications and domains in which such systems play an integral part.

    Up to this point, we have been quite successful in developing our understanding of how knowledge can be modeled as rules and relationships contained within the traditional notions of set membership and, thus, stored within the digital realm. As a preface to our focus on machine learning, however, we need to develop a better understanding of the way the human brain actually works. The world of human thought and reasoning is a world of vagueness, linguistic ambiguity, and fuzzy descriptions.

10-1 FUZZY LOGIC AND LINGUISTIC AMBIGUITY

Fuzzy logic is a relatively recent alternative to the traditional notions of set membership and logic that has its origins in ancient Greek philosophy and its applications at the leading edge of AI research (Brule 1985). It is a method of reasoning that allows for the partial or "fuzzy" description of a rule. Combining this approach to reasoning with the realm of digital processors has resulted in a class of computer applications that can "learn" from their mistakes and can "understand" the vagaries commonly found in human thought.

Linguistic Ambiguity

Our language is replete with vague and imprecise concepts. While sometimes a rule is clear-cut, at other times it is difficult (if not impossible) to describe things in terms of well-defined distinctions. Take, for example, the phrase "Dan is very tall," or the phrase "It is extremely hot today." Statements such as these are commonplace in our daily interactions and are representative of a reasoning process of measurable complexity. Yet the translation of these statements into ones of "greater precision" often causes them to lose some of their semantic richness and meaning. For example, the statement, "The current temperature is 97.65 degrees Fahrenheit" does not explicitly state that it is hot, and the statement "The current temperature is 1.1 standard deviations above the mean temperature for this geographic region at this time of the year" is also fraught with many linguistic difficulties. Would it still be hot today if the current temperature was 1.099 standard deviations above the mean? Do I need to know precisely where I am at in the world to determine whether or not it is hot today?

The point is that our language has evolved to allow for the conveyance of meaning through semantic approximation rather than precise content. We are quite comfortable with adjectives of categorization that describe *intelligent* people, *midsize* automobiles, *tall* buildings, and *powerful* computer systems, among many others. This method of categorization provides us with a simple means of expression for general terms and allows us to interpret these generalizations based upon the context in which they are made. While quite useful to humans, these context-based meanings do not lend themselves to the common rule-based or case-based codification schemes necessary for inclusion in an expert system knowledge base. Fuzzy logic, however, is quite adept at supporting reasoning about these kinds of situations because it focuses on gradation rather than precise distinction.

The kinds of categorizations we often use to describe something do not have precise boundaries. Rather, the categories often encompass a range of values. For example, the term *highly skilled* encompasses a range of values that is context-specific. If the context is a group of elementary school students playing baseball and one of the young students tends to hit the ball farther than anyone else, she may be referred to as "highly skilled." If, on the other hand, this same student were to be placed in a major league baseball game, the term highly skilled (as it directly relates to her) would no longer be applicable. The "truth" of these categorizations can be thought of as varying much like a light does with a dimmer switch. If the switch is completely off, then there is 0 percent agreement concerning the categorization. If the switch is completely on, then there is 100 percent agreement; there also exists, however, an infinite number of gradations in between.

If we think of the world in terms of the degree to which something is a member of a category or set we can see how fuzzy logic could be used to express many problem contexts. A verbal protocol obtained from the operator of a production line might come in the form of "When the line gets *near* capacity, I begin to *slow* the feed." Converting this into a set of precise rules could prove problematic, if not impossible. With fuzzy logic, however, rules such as these are completely acceptable and quite easy to accommodate.

The Basics of Fuzzy Logic

Fuzzy logic is based on an approach to logic that dates back to the days of Plato. Its primary distinction from the early conceptualizations of the world by Aristotle and others is that it defines truth to be a value that is contained within the set of values ranging from [0.0, 1.0] with 0.0 representing absolute *Falseness* and 1.0 representing absolute *Truth*. It is important to note that fuzzy logic does not mean vague answers but, rather, precise answers that vary mathematically within a given range of values. Fuzzy logic can deal with any degree of precision from the input data and can react just as precisely in returning the results.

Rather than carry around a lot of mathematical baggage, however, let's develop our understanding of fuzzy logic using an example that is commonplace. Consider the phrase "Dan is very tall." From this phrase we can infer that there exists a subset of all people that are classified as tall and Dan is contained within that subset. Further, we can infer that Dan is considered to be an extreme value within the subset of tall people because his membership within the subset is further qualified by the adjective *very*. By formally defining the fuzzy subset TALL_PEOPLE we can answer the question "to what degree is person *x* tall?" To accomplish this, we must assign a degree of membership in the fuzzy subset TALL_PEOPLE to every member of the set ALL_PEOPLE. The easiest way of doing this is by creating a membership function based on a person's height. Figure 10-1 illustrates this membership function and shows the shape of a graph of the derived function.

    Using the derived membership function for the fuzzy subset TALL_PEOPLE, we can compute values that represent the degree of tallness for any member of the set ALL_PEOPLE. Table 10-1 contains some tallness values for a sample of people drawn from the set. It can be seen from the figure that a "precise" mathematical value for degree of tallness has been assigned to each person sampled. Using this approach,

FIGURE 10-1 Membership Function for Inclusion in Subset TALL_PEOPLE

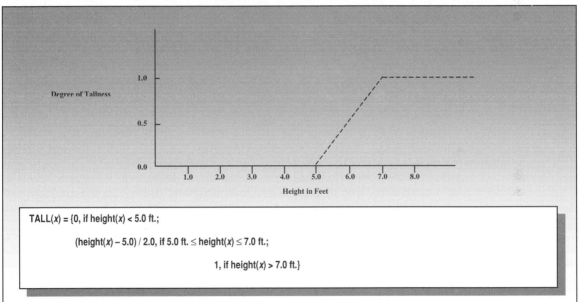

$$\text{TALL}(x) = \{0, \text{ if height}(x) < 5.0 \text{ ft.};$$

$$(\text{height}(x) - 5.0) / 2.0, \text{ if } 5.0 \text{ ft.} \leq \text{height}(x) \leq 7.0 \text{ ft.};$$

$$1, \text{ if height}(x) > 7.0 \text{ ft.}\}$$

Table 10-1 Sample Values Obtained from Tallness Function

Person	Height	Degree of Tallness
Tom Thumb	2'10"	0.000
Mugsy Bogues	5'3"	0.125
Albert Einstein	5'5"	0.208
Thomas Edison	5'10"	0.417
Michael Jordan	6'6"	0.750
Kareem Abdul-Jabbar	7'2"	1.000

a rule for determining tallness could be constructed in the form of a "tallness algorithm" that could be contained within a knowledge base for an ES. By developing a network of these algorithms, a complex set of categorizations can be analyzed and a high level of reasoning can be brought to bear on a given problem context. This is the essence of fuzzy logic reasoning in the development of expert systems and the focus of this chapter: *machine learning*.

It is important to note, however, that membership functions are rarely as simple as the one used in our example. Often, they involve degrees of membership in multiple subsets based on multiple criteria. For instance, a membership function for the subset TALL_PEOPLE may depend not only on physical height but on chronological age, as well (He's tall for his age). In fact, it is not uncommon for a particular membership function to contain elements from a wide variety of criteria and populations. The complexity of such functions is significant and requires a deep level of understanding in sophisticated mathematical concepts to be fully appreciated. This level of understanding is best left to the computer scientists who will build these systems for use by the managerial community. Important here, in the realm of management, is the notion that fuzziness can be codified and that the linguistic ambiguities so commonplace in human interaction can be modeled and systematized in an intelligent computer system.

Fuzziness versus Probability

Before we move away from the concept of fuzzy logic, one last point needs clarification. There often arises confusion between the concept of *fuzziness* and that of probability. Both operate over the same continuous numeric range and at first glance have similarities in the interpretation of their values: 0.0 representing False (or nonmembership) and 1.0 representing True (or membership). However, there are some fundamental differences between fuzziness and probability.

To fully understand these differences, consider, again, our statement "Dan is very tall." Let's assume that by using our membership algorithm, we assign a degree of tallness value to the statement of 0.80. From this, we can render the statement symbolically as follows:

$$m\text{TALL\_PEOPLE}(\text{Dan}) = 0.80$$

where m is the membership function operating on the fuzzy subset of TALL_PEOPLE.

From a probabilistic approach, we might interpret the degree of tallness value to mean "There is an 80 percent chance that Dan is tall." Conversely, the fuzzy logic approach would yield a statement corresponding to "Dan's degree of membership within the set of tall people is 0.80." The semantic difference between these two statements is significant. The first statement supposes that Dan is or is not tall; it is just that we have only an 80 percent chance of knowing which set he is in. By contrast, the fuzzy statement supposes that Dan is "more or less" tall. In other words, probability deals with the likelihood that something has a particular property, whereas fuzzy logic deals with the degree to which a particular property is present in something. In the former, we are guessing about the presence of a property; in the latter we are assuming the presence of a property and comparing its strength relative to all other members of the set. With probability, we can only determine membership in a set, but with fuzzy logic, we can determine where on the continuum of membership a particular set member resides.

Advantages and Limitations of Fuzzy Logic

The truly nice thing about rules is that they allow you to state relationships very generally and compactly, as associations (Dhar and Stein 1997). On the other hand, they do not require you to be as precise as mathematical models. This is good because we know that the complexity of a system increases when variables begin to interact in a nonlinear fashion. The acknowledged modern-day "father of fuzzy logic," Lotfi Zadeh, suggests that "as complexity rises, precise statements lose meaning and meaningful statements lose precision." Fuzzy rules offer an attractive trade-off between the need for accuracy, compactness, and scalability as reasoning systems and processes within a particular knowledge domain become more complex. Fuzzy rules generalize the concept of categorization because, by definition, the same object can belong to any set to a certain degree and can belong to multiple sets as necessary. In this sense, fuzzy logic eliminates the problems associated with borderline cases: where the value 1.1 causes a rule to fire but the value 1.099 does not. The net result is that fuzzy logic tends to provide greater accuracy than traditional rule-based systems when continuous variables are involved. In this section, we explore the key benefits derived from the use of fuzzy logic along with identifying several limitations to its use that must be both acknowledged and understood.

Advantages of Fuzzy Systems

Fuzzy logic systems have been utilized in a wide variety of applications and they can be found in many facets of business and society. Their use in microprocessor-based appliances and products is pervasive and their value has already been proven beyond doubt. Regardless of the application or context, fuzzy logic offers several generalizable advantages and benefits over traditional rule-based logic.

Modeling of Contradiction   Fuzzy logic allows for the modeling and inclusion of contradiction within a knowledge base. Fuzzy rules can be completely contradictory and yet exist in complete harmony. Compared to traditional logic where opposing instructions would result in an inability on the part of the computer to resolve the contradiction, fuzzy logic imparts a certain degree of tolerance to such ambiguities and thus, compromise is allowed. For example, by allowing for membership in multiple sets, a six-foot-tall person might be simultaneously assigned a degree of membership in the set TALL_PEOPLE of 0.80, a degree of membership of 0.45 in the MEDIUM_PEOPLE set, and a value of 0.01 in the SHORT_PEOPLE set. Using fuzzy logic, the designer has complete control over the accuracy of a given conclusion or reasoning process by simply increasing or decreasing the number of rules required and the degrees of sensitivity to membership allowed.

Increased System Autonomy   The rules contained within the knowledge base of a fuzzy system can function completely independently of one another. In a traditional rule-based system, if a single rule is faulty, it can result in outcomes ranging from erroneous conclusions to complete inability of the system to resolve. In a fuzzy system, however, one rule could be faulty and the others will "compensate" for the error. Fuzzy systems actually change the common trade-off relationship between system robustness and system sensitivity. Unlike conventional rule-based systems, properly constructed fuzzy systems actually increase in sensitivity as the robustness of the system is increased. Fuzzy rules will continue to "work" even in circumstances where the whole system is completely changed.

Limitations to Fuzzy Systems

Despite its advantages, fuzzy reasoning presents certain limitations to both the KE and the end user. Its application cannot be construed to be universally better than traditional reasoning methods and, as with all forms of problem-solving strategies, it must be carefully assessed in terms of its appropriateness to a given problem context.

Obstacles to System Verification   Fuzzy reasoning can become an obstacle to the verification of a system's stability or reliability. Under situations of high complexity, it may become impossible to know if the correct rules are firing. Further, the redefinition of membership associated with fine-tuning a fuzzy system has no set guidelines or prescriptions that are easily followed. As a result, designers may find it difficult to determine whether their actions are serving to improve the system or are resulting in a move away from a better solution. One response to this limitation is the use of simulation in the verification of a fuzzy system. Results of multiple simulations can be used to analyze small refinements in set memberships and their relative sensitivities to outcomes derived from the system.

Fuzzy Systems Lack Memory   Basic fuzzy reasoning mechanisms cannot learn from their mistakes and possess no memory. As such, fuzzy logic is not yet capable of optimizing the efficiency of a system. Presently, there exists no precise mathematical method of verifying the correctness of a fuzzy system. Furthermore, the high degree of complexity of a given situation that can be modeled using fuzzy reasoning can result in a literal simultaneous firing of rules. This phenomenon is referred to as fuzzy set saturation. This means that the fuzzy set gets so full of inferences that consequent fuzzy sets are overloaded. The end result is that the entire system loses the information provided by the fuzzy rules and the entire fuzzy region begins to "balance itself" around its mean value. The answers to this constant retention of all rules and inferences and the problems of saturation are being addressed by developing systems that can learn from their mistakes and can "learn to forget" information that is no longer applicable to the problem context. Such systems are the next topic of our focus in this chapter: neural networks.

10-2 ARTIFICIAL NEURAL NETWORKS

Artificial neural networks (ANNs) were first proposed in the early 1940s at the University of Chicago as an attempt to simulate the human brain's cognitive learning processes. Within the last decade, ANNs have found considerable application in numerous domains such as business and finance due to their ability to model complex, yet poorly understood, problems for which sufficient data can be collected. Their capacity to learn has often resulted in solutions that are superior to those achieved using traditional statistical or mathematical methods.

ANNs[1] are simple computer-based programs whose primary function is to construct models of a problem space based upon trial and error. Conceptually, the process is easily described: A piece of data is presented to a neural net. The ANN "guesses" an output and then compares its prediction with the actual, or correct, value presented as a form of feedback. If the guess is correct, then the network performs no further action. If, however, the prediction is incorrect, then the network analyzes itself in an effort to figure out which internal parameters to adjust to improve the quality of the prediction. Once these adjustments are made, the net is presented with another piece of data and the process is repeated. Over time, the ANN begins to converge on a fairly accurate model of the process.

Fundamentals of Neural Computing

To better understand how the ANN "learns" from experience, we must begin with an understanding of the biological principles that underlie both human neural processes and artificial neural computing.

The Human Brain

The basic processing element in the human nervous system is the *neuron.* Our nervous system is made up of a network of these interconnected nerve cells that receive information from various sensors, such as our eyes, ears, skin, and nose, that are positioned at various places along the network. Figure 10-2 provides a simple representation of a single human neuron and its component parts.

As shown in the figure, the human neuron is composed of a nucleus and connectors called *dendrites* that are responsible for providing input signals to the neuron and *axons,* which carry away the output of the neuron to other parts of the network. The transmission of signals from one neuron to another occurs at the *neural synapse* via a complex chemical process in which specific substances, called *neurotransmitters,* are released from one side of the synaptic junction. The effect is to raise or lower the electrical potential inside the body of the neuron. If the electrical potential within a specific neuron reaches a certain threshold, a pulse is sent down the axon and the neuron cell is said to have "fired." These bursts of electricity that occur when a neuron fires are used to transmit information along the network to other neurons. Conceptually speaking, the larger the burst of electricity at the synapse, the more important the information contained within.

Information received at a neuron can have one of two effects: It can either *excite* the cell or it can *inhibit* it. If the neuron is excited, it will immediately fire and pass its information along the network to the other neurons. If the neuron is inhibited, however, it will not fire, in effect suppressing the flow of that information along the net-

---

[1] The terms *artificial neural network, neural network, network,* and *net* will be used interchangeably throughout this chapter.

FIGURE 10-2 Typical Human Neuron Cell

work. Through this process, each neuron processes the incoming raw input and then determines whether it is important enough to pass along.

The synaptic connections that exist among the neurons can be strengthened or weakened as a result of the passing of time or the gaining of experience. Strengthening of the connection results in learning, whereas the lack of use of a connection over time results in forgetting. This dynamic process results in the establishment of new responses to new stimuli, modifications to existing stimuli, and the complete removal of unused responses.

Putting a Brain in a Box

Following a biological metaphor, the ANN involves an interconnected system of nodes called *neurodes* that are associated with one or more *weighted connections* that are equivalent to human neural synapses, inside the memory of a digital computer. The ANN is constructed of multiple layers with the connections running between the layers. Figure 10-3 shows a simple ANN.

As shown in the figure, the ANN is composed of three basic layers. The layer that receives the data is referred to as the *input layer* and the layer that relays the final results of the net is called the *output layer*. The internal layer, also referred to as the *hidden layer,* is where the processing and transformation of the input signal takes place and where the type of output signal is determined. The hierarchical network dynamics among the neurodes are determined by a mathematical combination of the weight of each input to the neurode and the threshold parameters associated with that neurode. As each pass of the net is made, these weights are adjusted in response to the feedback received by the net regarding the accuracy of its last output. Over time, these weights are adjusted to allow for an accurate transformation of the input data. Learning, in a neural network, results from this adjustment of weights.

Inside the Neurode

Figure 10-4 shows the component parts of a typical neurode. The basic structure consists of a set of weighted input connections, a bias input, a state function, a nonlinear transfer function, and an output connection. We will explore each of these primary components and their functions in greater detail.

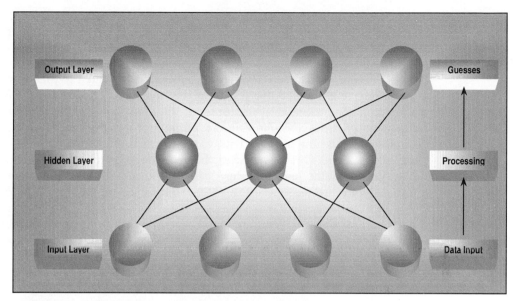

FIGURE 10-3 A Typical Neural Network Configuration

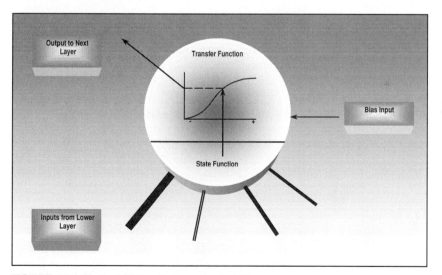

FIGURE 10-4 Typical Neurode Component Structure

Weighted Inputs   As shown in the figure, each of the inputs to a neurode is a connection from a lower layer of the network. The neurode can, and usually does, have multiple inputs each with its own associated weight or importance. In the figure, we depict the relative weights of each of the inputs by varying the thickness or style of the line representing that input. The thickness of the line is proportional to its weight or importance. A hollow line indicates a negative weight. The weight of an input determines how much importance it will have in terms of its contribution to the output of the neurode. Because all of the weights are added together inside the neurode, the more important inputs will be those with larger weights and the lesser contributors will be those with the smaller weights.

The Bias Input   The bias input is not normally connected to the network and is assumed to have an input value of 1.0 for the state function. Its purpose is to allow for the individual adjustment of the firing threshold of the neurode to facilitate the final adjustment of the ANN following the learning process. Under normal circumstances the bias input is not used and its value to the state function remains a constant throughout the network. If, however, the need for adjustment of a specific neurode becomes necessary, the bias input for that neurode can be set within a range of -1.0 to 1.0 to allow for the appropriate "bias" to be imparted to the transfer function.

The State Function   The state function, although conceivably a mathematical algorithm of any form or complexity, is typically a simple summation function. Its purpose is to consolidate the weights of the various inputs to the neurode into a single value that can be passed to the transfer function for processing. The value obtained by the state function determines the degree of impact the combined inputs will have on the transfer function and, thus, on the final output of the neurode. Figure 10-5 illustrates this process.

The Transfer Function   As implied by its name, the primary purpose of the transfer function is to serve as the vehicle by which the summed information is passed on as output. It performs this function, however, in a rather unique manner. Referring to fig-

FIGURE 10-5 Relationship between State Function Value and Transfer Function Value

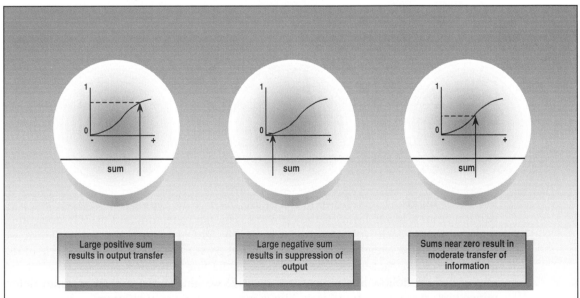

| Large positive sum results in output transfer | Large negative sum results in suppression of output | Sums near zero result in moderate transfer of information |

ure 10-5, note that the value of the output (and ultimately the threshold at which the neurode will fire) is not linear with respect to the summed inputs. The transfer function acts metaphorically like a dimmer switch for turning the neurode on and off.

Note that in the figure we have chosen to depict the transfer function in the shape of the typical *logistic function*. The logistic function is characterized by its "lazy S-shaped" form. Transfer functions can be either continuous (as shown in the figure) or discrete (such as a series of "on" or "off" ranges of values) and can take any appropriate mathematical form. While the logistic function is the most commonly used, another popular transfer function is the *radial basis function*, which takes on a more bell-shaped form. The important issue, here, is that the transfer function must impart a sense of nonlinearity between the summed inputs and the resultant output.

Training the Artificial Neural Network

The process of *training* a neural net to associate certain input patterns with correct output responses involves the use of repetitive examples and feedback, much like the training of a human being. The operation begins by setting all of the connection weights in the net to small random values. This allows for the net to begin with no specific "memory" or imprint. Next, the net is presented with a single data example drawn from a training set with known outputs. The net processes this example and then provides a "guess" at the answer based on the example provided.

As you can probably imagine, the first guess provided by the net is usually incorrect. This is because the weights for each of the input connections are not yet set correctly. However, just as humans can learn from their mistakes, so can ANNs. Once the example data are processed, the ANN compares the results of its calculations with the feedback received regarding the desired, correct output and records that comparison in a *training record*. If the calculation performed by the net compares favorably with the feedback, then no action is necessary. If, however, the guess is deemed incorrect when compared to the feedback, the net begins an iterative process of making small adjustments to the input weights of certain neurodes in an attempt to bring its own output more in line with the feedback. Figure 10-6 illustrates this iterative adjustment process.

The actual process by which the net determines an appropriate adjustment to each input weight is a complex mathematical procedure. Essentially, however, it can be thought of as a form of sensitivity analysis in which the size of the error is determined and an adjustment is made to see how much effect (and in what direction) the change has on the size of the error. This process continues for each hidden layer in the network until all neurodes have been subjected to the sensitivity analysis and the net is ready for another trial.

Sending the Net to School — ANN Learning Paradigms

The actual procedure used by a neural network to find the appropriate weight settings is referred to as its *learning paradigm*. Again, much like the ways in which humans can acquire knowledge and learn, learning paradigms for ANNs can be loosely classified into those that are largely *unsupervised* and those that are *supervised*.

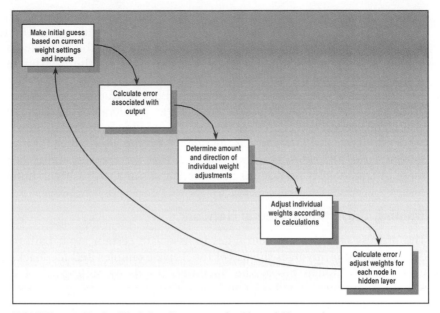

FIGURE 10-6 Typical Training Sequence for Neural Networks

Unsupervised Learning Paradigms

While a wide variety of specific unsupervised learning paradigms have been developed in response to particular problem context needs, all of them possess the same basic characteristics and approaches. As such, we will limit our discussion to the general characteristics of all unsupervised learning methods.

The unsupervised nature of an unsupervised learning paradigm simply means that the ANN has been provided with the input data and examples but not with any feedback in the form of desired results. To effect its learning process, an unsupervised net begins by developing *clusters* of the training records it generates based upon similarities it detects in the data examples. The net continues to process data examples, create a training record, and then re-cluster the records until a set of definable patterns begins to emerge. With each successive pass, the net finds a pattern that is more closely matched with the input data than any of the others. Over time, the net refines this pattern recognition until the difference between the input and the output patterns for the training set reach a close approximation of each other.

One way to envision the unsupervised learning process is to imagine a scenario in which you present a group of strangers with a stack of randomly ordered photographs of different situations and ask each of them to classify the photos in some way. Without any specific instructions regarding the method of classification, each stranger will probably choose an approach that is unique and one that is based upon some common characteristic contained within each picture. One stranger might set up a classification based upon the type of scene (indoor, outdoor, day, night, landscape, portrait, etc.). Another may classify the pictures according to the situation depicted (people interacting, pictures of machines, pictures of natural settings, etc.). Yet another may choose to classify the pictures according to their specific photographic characteristics (black-and-white, color, glossy, matte, etc.). Although each grouping would be logical from a given perspective, the relationships among the photos would be different from one grouping to the next. By comparing the relationships within each group, as well as the relationships *across* groups, we might begin to discover new relationships that were not discernable in any of the previous clusters.

The unsupervised learning paradigm for an ANN works in much the same manner as the situation just described. The net is unsupervised with respect to what it is supposed to discover or conclude. As such, it is left to its own devices to find relationships among the input data examples and use those relationships to create accurate output. Using this approach, a neural net can begin to "specialize" its learning with respect to a specific dimension of the data. A more "organized" form of this approach to the discovery of relationships will be the focus of chapter 12: *data mining and visualization.*

Supervised Learning Paradigms

In contrast to the unsupervised approach, the most common *supervised learning paradigm* is called *back propagation.* Here, the net receives an input example, generates a guess, and compares that guess to feedback containing the desired results. In this sense, the ANN is being "supervised" by the feedback, which shows the net where the mistakes are being made and how the answer should look. The name of this technique is based on the fact that the algorithm used to adjust the neurode weights *propagates* some measure of the calculated error between the guess and the feedback *back* through the various layers of the network in the direction of the input layer. The most common form of the back propagation algorithm uses a sum-of-squared-errors approach to generate an aggregate measure of the difference error. Following this, a progressive adjusting of the weights along the network is conducted to bring the network "closer" to the correct response. This adjustment process is based on a combination of the calculated error measure and an adjustment increment established by the net trainer. This adjustment increment, or *learning rate,* is a specification of how much adjustment should occur in each training session. If too large a learning rate is specified, then the net may constantly "overshoot" its optimized weights and never reach the desired level of accuracy. If, conversely, the learning rate is specified in too small an increment, the net may take a long time to reach the desired level of accuracy, if at all.

As with most of the inner workings of an ANN, the mathematics are complex and require a high level of understanding to successfully construct a working ANN. For those with a flair for the calculus, an appendix to this chapter is provided that further describes the mathematical foundations of the back propagation algorithm. For the rest of you, suffice it to say that understanding exactly how it works is not as important as understanding how, and under what conditions, the technology should be applied. Therefore, we turn our attention to some of the advantages and disadvantages that must be acknowledged in the application of neural computing technologies.

Benefits and Limitations Associated with Neural Computing

One of the most obvious benefits of neural computing is the ability to obtain inferential insights not readily available through the use of other knowledge-based techniques and technologies. In addition to this, however, ANNs provide several other advantages over more traditional problem-solving systems. Table 10-2 lists several of those benefits.

A key advantage to ANNs is the elimination of the need for direct input from domain experts. In some cases, soliciting knowledge from a domain expert may be too costly in terms of either economic resources or time involved. In other cases, an expert simply may not exist. Our forays into diverse knowledge domains framed within the physical, biological, and social sciences can often venture beyond the bounds of domain experts. In these cases, ANNs provide a valuable vehicle for the discovery of new relationships and knowledge that is beyond the capabilities of other problem-solving and support technologies.

Another unique advantage of ANNs is their inherent ability to deal with noisy or incomplete data sets. Most often, the availability of clean, high-quality data sets is limited, if not nonexistent, and the problem solver is faced with analyzing data that are poorly distributed and inconsistent. The structural nature of ANNs makes them better suited to deal with such data than more traditional statistical or AI methods. Because each of the neurodes looks at only a small portion of the problem and the neurodes and layers are positioned to look at each of these small elements from different angles, ANNs can often reconstruct missing or corrupt data by inferring what the data "should" look like and then using that inference as an input to its current guess. Such inferences can be modified as necessary along with the weights for each input as the network seeks to reduce the error associated with previous training sessions.

Along these same lines, the ability of an ANN to look at small parts of a large and complex problem also makes it uniquely capable of scaling up as necessary to accommodate problems of increased complexity. Intuitively, more complicated problems can be solved by adding more hidden layers to the network, thus increasing the ability of the network to use the output of neurodes in lower layers and allowing for a greater number of neurodes to interact. In this way, many complicated, highly nonlinear relationships and processes can be modeled effectively.

We must be prepared, however, to acknowledge that these advantages and benefits associated with neural computing do not come without a price. Table 10-3 lists several of the limitations and drawbacks associated with application of neural computing techniques to a problem context.

Table 10-2 Benefits Derived from Neural Computing

- Avoidance of explicit programming and detailed IF-THEN rule base.
- Reduced need for expensive or limited availability experts.
- ANNs are inherently adaptable and do not require update when inputs change.
- Elimination of need for redefined knowledge base.
- ANNs are dynamic and continue to improve with use.
- Ability to process erroneous, inconsistent, or even incomplete data.
- Allows for generalization from specific information context.
- Facilitates the creation of abstractions from diverse data sets.
- Allows for the inclusion of "common sense" into the problem-solving domain.

Table 10-3 Limitations to Neural Computing Techniques

- ANNs cannot "explain" their inferences.
- The "black box" nature of ANNs makes accountability and reliability issues difficult.
- The repetitive training process is often extremely time consuming.
- Highly skilled machine learning analysts and designers are still a scarce resource.
- Neural computing technologies generally push the limits of existing hardware.
- ANNs require that a certain amount of faith be imparted to the final output.

ANNs are often successfully applied in finding solutions to complex problems involving pattern recognition and nonlinear relationships because of their unique ability to find subtle relationships within data sets. Unfortunately, however, once such subtleties are revealed, the ANN has no mechanism for explaining or justifying them. The fact that an ANN can effectively differentiate items based on inherent, yet latent, characteristics within the data set does not mean that such differentiation is based on the desired set of discriminating characteristics. In fact, it is possible for the ANN to develop an understanding and ability to discriminate between patterns contained within the noise in the data rather than in the data itself.

One famous example of this comes from the military. A neural net was developed for the purpose of distinguishing between pictures containing specific military armaments and those without such elements. In the early training sessions, the net was presented with two sets of photographs: one containing combat tanks and one without any tanks in the pictures. Each of these pictures were converted to machine-readable format and presented to the net for training. Within a relatively short number of passes, the net displayed an excitingly high degree of discrimination between the pictures containing combat tanks and those without. To ensure the success of the training, a new set of photographs were digitized and presented to the net for analysis. The excitement from the training session soon turned to disappointment when the net failed to correctly discriminate the desired elements. An inspection of the training set quickly revealed the problem: The photographs containing tanks were all taken on sunny days, whereas the photos without the tanks were taken on generally overcast days. The net had learned to discriminate between sunny and overcast days rather than to identify images of combat tanks.

The evolution of neural computing and machine learning techniques is rapidly accelerating with new approaches emerging each day that are intended as improvements over the current methods. One such improvement over "conventional" neural computing techniques is the subject of our next discussion.

10-3 GENETIC ALGORITHMS AND GENETICALLY EVOLVED NETWORKS

Recall from our discussion of bounded rationality and optimization in chapter 3 that man, although desiring the optimal solution, tends to satisfice and accept a solution of lesser quality than optimum. While Simon's explanation of this suggests that optimization is a laudable, yet unattainable, cognitive goal, we nonetheless continue our quest for the best possible solution to our daily problems. We know there exists an optimal, very best solution to our problem, if we could only find it.

The Concept of Optimization

The goal of any problem solver is to arrive at a solution that effectively solves the problem within the constraints (perceived or real) imposed on the problem context. This suggests that for a given problem context and set of constraints, there exists an optimal solution based on some predetermined measure of goodness. Although Simon's position on optimizing versus satisficing holds true from a human cognition perspective, there are situations where optimization is not only desirable, but attainable as well. The field of management science has dealt successfully with the development of mathematical techniques intended to derive optimal solutions under a given set of often complex constraints. Such techniques are useful in making the best of an imperfect situation by taking the fullest advantage of the limited resources available to the problem. The advent of the computer, combined with these mathematical optimization models, has further extended our ability to find the best solution available. Our problem is that as we get more proficient and capable of solving increasingly complex problems, we also develop an appetite for achieving optimal solutions to even more complex problems and constrained contexts. This cycle of complexity has identified a need for innovative methods of deriving such optimal solutions.

Consider the traveling salesman problem from chapter 3. Recall that one of the problems was to determine the number of unique routes without visiting any city along the route more than once. We determined that the need to visit ten cities yielded a total of 181,440 unique routes.[2] Assuming we have a relatively powerful computer that can evaluate one million (10^6) unique routes per second, we could perform an *exhaustive search* of the problem space in approximately 0.18 seconds—not much time considering the potential return in the form of efficient performance and cost savings. If, however, our zeal for this newfound optimization power suggests that we might want to increase the size of the problem, our limitations for exhaustive search will soon be revealed. By increasing the number of cities to twenty-five, we also increase the number of unique routes to 3.10×10^{23} possibilities. No problem, though. We have a computer that will figure out the optimal route based on the constraints we have placed on the solution. Unfortunately, however, our computer, operating at a speed of one million evaluations per second, will require just a bit longer to process the twenty-five-city problem. At that rate, it will take it somewhere around ten billion years to perform an exhaustive search and determine the optimal solution.[3] It would appear that conventional approaches to optimization do have their limits.

Recall further from the traveling salesman problem that we found that a heuristic approach to the solution resulted in a pretty good outcome with a minimum of ef-

---

[2] Using the formula 0.5(number of cities − 1)!

[3] Assuming 365.25 days per year: 3.10×10^{23} unique routes would require approximately 8.62×10^{13} hours to solve. This approximates to 9,830,411,719 years.

fort. Such techniques have found their way into the realm of machine learning and one such method, the *genetic algorithm,* is finding widespread acceptance and application.

Introduction to Genetic Algorithms

Similar to the conceptual foundations of ANNs, genetic algorithms (GAs) have their basis in biological theory. In contrast to the neuroscience roots of ANNs, however, GAs find their roots in Darwin's evolutionary theories of natural selection and adaptation.

The theory of natural selection offers some compelling arguments that individuals with certain characteristics are better able to survive and pass on those characteristics to their offspring. A genetic algorithm is an elegantly simple, yet extremely powerful, type of optimization technique based on the ideas of genetics and natural selection. Originally developed by John Holland at MIT during the 1940s, the essence of a GA is a set of adaptive processes that mimic the concept of "survival-of-the-fittest" by regenerating recombinants of the algorithm in response to a calculated difference between the network's guess and the desired solution state. The power of a GA lies in the fact that as members of the population mate, they produce offspring that have a significant chance of retaining the desirable characteristics of their parents, perhaps even combining the best characteristics of both parents. In this manner, the overall fitness of the population can potentially increase from generation to generation as we discover better solutions to our problem. The primary advantage of a GA over conventional unsupervised neural networks is its ability to overcome the combinatorial limitations associated with the development of complex ANNs with intricate combinations of performance criteria.

The Concept of Natural Selection

To better understand the fundamentals of GAs, we must first understand the theoretical foundation upon which they are built. The primary problem faced by all organisms found in nature is that of survival. Those that come up with successful solutions will survive and those that fail to solve the problem will become extinct. The Darwinian approach to the evolution of species suggests that those organisms that survive have done so by adapting themselves to the conditions within the environment that will best support them and by insulating themselves from those environmental factors that can do them the most harm. It is this adaptation to the environment that serves as the basis for the development and use of genetic algorithms.

Basic Components of Genetic Algorithms

In keeping with its root biological metaphor, the GA's smallest unit is called a *gene.* The gene represents the smallest unit of information in the problem domain and can be thought of as the basic building block for a possible solution. If the problem context were, for example, the creation of a well-balanced investment portfolio, a gene might represent the number of shares of a particular security to purchase. If the problem context focused on the traveling salesman problem, the gene might represent one of the cities that must be visited on a route. Continuing with the metaphor, a series of genes that represent the components of one possible solution to the problem is referred to as a *chromosome*. Figure 10-7 illustrates examples of chromosome strings that might be found in a typical GA.

The chromosome is represented in computer memory as a bit string of binary digits that can be "decoded" by the GA to determine how good a particular chromosome's gene pool solution is for the given problem. The decoding process simply informs the GA what the various genes within the chromosome represent. For the traveling salesman problem, for example, the decoder would know how to convert the genes into cities along the route. This representation of the solution as a bit string is probably the only significant limitation with regard to the application of a GA to a problem context. For the GA to be effective in reaching a solution to the problem, the solution must be able to be represented as a digital bit string.

Figure 10-8 illustrates the basic processes associated with the operation of a GA.

Initialization   The first step in the creation of a GA is the development of an initial population of chromosomes that are possible solutions to the problem under investigation. This population of initial genetic structures should be constructed in such a way that it represents solutions that are randomly distributed throughout the solution space.

Evaluation   In the evaluation stage, each chromosome is decoded by the decoder function and evaluated using a fitness function to determine which genetic structures are good and which are not so good. The fitness function is analogous to an objective function commonly found in optimization techniques such as linear programming. The function represents some constraint or requirement to minimize or maximize the use of some resource. In the traveling salesman example, typical fitness functions might include requirements to minimize time en route, minimize fuel or travel expense, and maximize individual city contact time.

Figure 10-9 illustrates the decoding process using a binary chromosome that represents the cities along a route, their distances from a home base, and the desired con-

FIGURE 10-7 Examples of Genetic Algorithm Chromosome Strings

Well-balanced investment portfolio chromosome:

   {100 300 1000 1000 500 . . . 200 1500}

The decoding function for this chromosome interprets this to mean:

   Buy 100 shares of Stock A, 300 shares of Stock B, . . . etc.

Traveling salesman city routing problem:

   {Miami Newark Chicago Denver Phoenix . . . Dallas}

The decoding function for this chromosome interprets this to mean:

   Start in Miami, go to Newark, go to Chicago, . . ., go to Dallas, return to start}

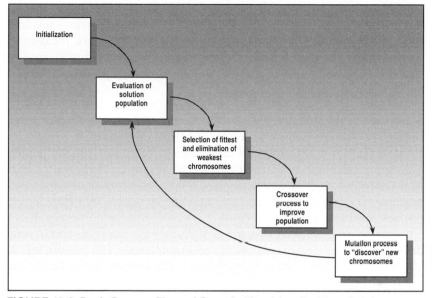

FIGURE 10-8 Basic Process Flow of Genetic Algorithm Problem Solving

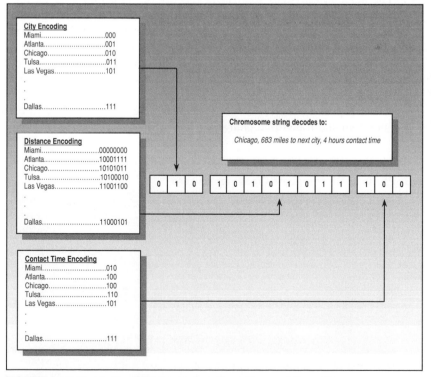

FIGURE 10-9 Example of Chromosome Encoding and Decoding

tact time in each. Thinking in terms of the problem domain, the decoder function and the fitness function are the only two GA components that are specific to the problem context. As such, the GA can be altered with respect to how it ranks solutions simply by changing the nature of the fitness functions. Additionally, the same GA can be used to solve a wide variety of problems simply by changing the decoder function and the fitness functions to those relevant to the new problem domain.

Selection   Once the initial pool of chromosomes is evaluated by the fitness function, the GA experiments with new solutions by iteratively refining the initial solutions so that those with the best fit are more likely to be ranked higher in the overall evaluation of solutions. In essence, the GA begins to "experiment" with the existing set of chromosomes by combining and refining the genes contained within each chromosome. The objective is to produce new chromosomes that form a new generation of possible solutions to evaluate.

In the first step, *selection*, the GA chooses the fittest species to remain and reproduce within the population of solution chromosomes. The poorer, less fit solutions are eliminated. The most common method for this evolution is called *fitness proportional selection*. In its simplest form, this method determines the relative fitness of each chromosome to all the other chromosomes in the current generation. If chromosome A is determined to be twice as fit as chromosome B, then chromosome A is given twice the chance of survival as chromosome B. The fittest evolve and the weaker species "die off." The selection process weeds out the poorer solutions and passes the remaining chromosomes on to the crossover process.

Crossover   Continuing the refinement process, the crossover phase involves the exchange of gene information between two selected chromosomes. Figure 10-10 illustrates this activity in which a portion of one chromosome crosses over into another chromosome and vice versa.

The purpose of the crossover operation is to allow the GA to create new chromosomes that share positive characteristics while simultaneously reducing the preva-

FIGURE 10-10 Chromosome Crossover Process

lence of negative characteristics in an otherwise reasonably fit solution. This is analogous to the concept of "strengthening the breed" in the field of biogenetics.

One important limitation in the crossover phase, however, is that it can only rearrange gene information that already exists within the population of chromosomes. For example, in our traveling salesman problem, if we fail to include a city, or a specific characteristic, in the original population, then that value will never become a part of any solution set and, thus, will never be swapped into a better solution chromosome. Just as in nature, however, GAs have a mechanism for spontaneous evolution of new genetic code.

Mutation   The final step in the refinement process is mutation. The mutation phase randomly changes the value of a gene from its current setting to a completely different one. Figure 10-11 shows the mutation of a chromosome.

The majority of the mutations formed by this process is, as is often the case in nature, less fit rather than more so. Occasionally, however, a highly superior and beneficial mutation will occur. Mutation provides the GA with the opportunity to create chromosomes and information genes that can explore previously uncharted areas of the solution space, thus increasing the chances for the discovery of an optimal solution. In conformance with the natural laws, however, mutation is normally set to a very low frequency of occurrence and is primarily used to ensure that the probability of searching any point within the solution is never zero.

Benefits and Limitations Associated with Genetic Algorithms

Despite the power of genetic algorithms, there are some precautions that must be taken when setting up or coding a GA problem. Several parameters exist that can have a significant effect on the speed with which an optimal solution is discovered.

One of the most important parameters in this regard is *population size*. The ideal number of initial solution chromosomes is based on a trade-off between time to carry out the processes and degree of diversity in the solution population. Wayner (1991) has provided evidence that, for most problems, a population size of ten appears to be

FIGURE 10-11 Chromosome Mutation Process

optimal. Fewer than ten chromosomes causes excessive failures to reach a solution and greater than ten increases the process time with no measurable advantage.

One of the advantages noted in using GAs to solve complex problems also can be attributed to population size. GAs tend to zero in on a solution much faster than a neural network and generally are highly predictable in their process time. Since the GA is always following the same steps, the total process time is based upon the number of chromosomes in the initial solution population and the number of generations that is chosen to run. A reasonably accurate prediction of time to solution can be derived by multiplying the time necessary to evaluate a single chromosome by the number of chromosomes, and then multiplying that result by the number of generations.

Other parameters that can have a direct effect on the efficiency of the GA are the processes of crossover and mutation. Mutation should be used judiciously to ensure that duplication of solution space members can never occur. Crossover must be set such that an appropriate number of new recombinants can be evaluated without wasting the resources allocated to the GA. If no crossover is conducted, then no new structures will ever become available for evaluation. If all chromosomes in the population are subjected to crossbreeding, then good genes will begin to disappear along with the bad ones. Heuristically speaking, it is recommended that 90 percent of the chromosome population be subjected to crossover with mutation occurring less than 5 percent of the total evaluation time.

The greatest advantage that GAs have for solving complex problems lies in their ability to "stretch" themselves across a vast solution space in search of the optimal solution. Further, because all initial populations are composed of possible solutions, GAs generally come up with a proposed optimal solution based on the initial population. In other words, with the application of a GA to an optimization problem, you are usually guaranteed to find at least some reasonable solution. In many cases, the proposed solution will be superior to any that were used to seed the initial chromosome population.

Recall from our discussion of Simon and the concept of satisficing that humans are willing to settle for a suboptimal solution as long as it is a good one and meets their criteria for successful outcome. The processes of nature and the evolutionary processes of living organisms tend, also, to conform more to Simon's theories than to those of optimization. It is unimaginable that any population of human species will ever yield a single member that possesses the vision of a Thomas Edison, the charisma and empathy of a Princess Diana, the intellect of a Carl Sagan, *and* the athletic prowess of a Michael Jordan. We accept the fact that the evolution of our species will be suboptimal and we must also accept the fact that the solutions we derive will also be suboptimal. The important issue is that the evolution of species appears to be constantly improving and is, for the most part, responsible for improvements in quality of life within the species. Likewise, the generation of a suboptimal solution that shows improvement over prior solutions is also beneficial to the advancement of our understanding of complex problems and to our abilities to deal with them. In this regard, GAs play an important part in the decision challenges facing tomorrow's manager.

Another significant benefit associated with the application of genetic algorithms is that they can be used to solve problems that we have no clue how to solve. If we can describe the components of a reasonably good solution and provide a fitness function that is usable by the GA, we can derive one or more solutions that would otherwise be unattainable. This ability to "invent" solutions makes GAs more attractive than conventional expert system applications, where a great deal of explicit knowledge about the domain must exist. In other words, GAs do not need to know how to solve a problem but simply need to know a good solution when one presents itself.

One final advantage associated with GAs is that their power does not result from a complex algorithmic perspective, but rather from a relatively simple and widely understood set of concepts. This increases the potential for widespread acceptance of a GA approach across an organization composed of individuals without a deep technical background. Almost everyone has had at least one class in biology and the concept of survival-of-the-fittest is used in almost every knowledge domain. The familiarity with the underlying concepts of genetic algorithms makes their acceptance and credibility relatively easy to establish over other machine learning and AI-based techniques.

10-4 APPLICATIONS OF MACHINES THAT LEARN

Machine Learning Application Domains

Table 10-4 contains a brief listing of the types of problem contexts in which machine learning systems such as neural networks and genetic algorithms have been successfully applied. Although it is not intended to be comprehensive, the list's diversity illustrates the wide variety of problems and domains in which AI-based systems can be useful.

A number of developmental projects involving ANN technology have been publicized in the media. For example, Nippon Steel Corporation has built a blast furnace operation control support system that makes use of ANNs. The neural network employed in this system has been equipped with functions that enable it to learn the relationship between sensor data and the eight kinds of temperature distribution patterns known from experience to pertain to the overall operation of blast furnaces, and to instantaneously recognize and output that pattern that most closely approximates sensor data input into the system. The neural network learns very quickly and achieves a better than 90 percent pattern recognition ratio following learning. Because this system has been performing extremely well during operational testing, Nippon Steel is planning to introduce it into other aspects of its operations in addition to blast furnace control, to include the diagnosis of malfunctions and other control processes.

A second example is the experimental work started by Daiwa Securities Company and NEC Corporation on applying neural network technology to the learning and recognition of stock price chart patterns for use in stock price forecasting. NEC had already developed neural network simulation software for use on its EWS 4800 series of workstations, and, by limiting stock price chart pattern learning to a few dozen major stocks, has improved the accuracy of this software's forecasting capabilities. Based on these results, the Daiwa Computer Services Company (DCS), an information processing subsidiary of the Daiwa Securities Group, transferred the NEC system to its supercomputer and taught it to recognize the stock price chart patterns for 1,134 companies listed on the Tokyo Stock Exchange. DCS has since put this system to good use in the performance of stock price forecasting.

Table 10-4 Typical Applications of Machine Learning Systems

- Predict staffing requirements at different times of the year and for different conditions.
  Brooklyn Union Gas Corp predicts in advance the number of crew members who will be needed for service calls based on the time of year, predicted temperature, and day of the week.
- Predict which job a job applicant is best suited for.
- Predict which customers will pay their bills.
- Spot odd trading patterns.
  This is how Ivan Boesky, the rogue trader, was caught.
- Predict the properties of chemical mixtures.
- Diagnose diseases.
  A neural net has been developed that outdid an expert system in diagnosing smell disorders.
- Predict the stock market, futures markets, and the like.
- Flag faulty parts on an assembly line.
- Regulate industrial processes using inputs from sensors at different points in the process.
- Classify medical ailments (such as hearing losses), living things, and cells (as cancerous/noncancerous).
- Predict pollution based on the composition of trash coming into an incinerator.
- Predict sales and/or costs.
- Predict a company's corporate bond rating.
- Appraise real estate.
- Predict the outcome of sports events (such as horse racing).
- Predict solar flare activity.
- Predict the length of survival for medical patients with certain ailments.
- Recognize welds that are most likely to fail under stress in nuclear containments.
- Test beer.
  Anheuser-Busch identifies the organic contents of its competitors' beer vapors with 96 percent accuracy.
- Predict which prison inmates could benefit from less expensive alternative programs.

Yet another recent example is the project at Mitsubishi Electric, where neural network technology has been combined with optical technology to achieve the world's first basic optical neurocomputer system capable of recognizing the twenty-six letters of the alphabet. The system comprises a set of light-emitting diodes (LED) that output letter patterns as optical signals, optical fibers, liquid crystal displays (LCD) that display letter patterns, and light-receiving devices that read these letters. This system is capable of 100 percent letter recognition even when slightly misshapen handwritten letters are input.

A fourth example is a development project for a facilities diagnosis system that employs a neural network system commenced by the Nippon Oil Company in cooperation with CSK Research Institute. This project is attracting considerable attention as it is the first time research has been carried out on applying neural network systems to facilities diagnosis. Initially, the project will be aimed at developing a diagnosis system for pump facilities that employs vibration analysis. Nippon Oil operates a total of fifteen hundred pumps at its Negishi Oil Refinery in Yokohama, Kanagawa Prefecture, alone and must retain large numbers of experienced personnel to maintain these pumps. The company decided to apply neural network technology to pump facilities diagnosis operations with the ultimate goal of saving labor.

Bond rating is another successful ANN application domain. Bond rating refers to the process by which a particular bond is assigned a label that categorizes the ability of the bond's issuer to repay the coupon and par value of that bond. Thus, for example, the Standard and Poor's organization might assign a rating varying from AAA (very high probability of payment) to BBB (possibility of default in times of economic adversity) for investment grade bonds. The problem here is that there is no hard-and-fast rule for determining these ratings. Rating agencies must consider a vast spectrum of factors before assigning a rating to an issuer. Some of these factors, such as sales, assets, liabilities, and the like, might be well defined. Others such as willingness to repay are quite nebulous. Thus, a precise problem definition is not possible.

Still other areas where machine learning systems are regularly applied are credit scoring and target marketing. Credit scoring is used to screen an applicant for credit cards based on known facts about the person applying. These facts usually include such things as salary, number of checking accounts, and previous credit history. Large banks and other lenders lose millions each year from bad debts. Even a small increase in the ability to predict accurately which accounts will go unpaid can result in hundreds of thousands of dollars saved each year for large lenders. To help fight this problem, major banks and finance companies are actively pursuing new technologies and systems that can aid in credit prediction.

Machine learning applications also serve to address a long-standing problem in advertising. For years, advertising agencies and other companies have been trying to identify and sell to target, or specific, markets. For example, a company selling life insurance might send out an advertisement enclosed in a monthly credit card bill. What the company would like to be able to do is to send out a small percentage of these advertisements to consumers and keep information on what type of person responds. Once the company has data on who responded, it can then build a predictive model to analyze potentially good customers. Thus, a life insurance company may be able to save money by only sending out advertisements to a select one million credit card holders who are more likely to buy life insurance, rather than to all credit card holders. Successful target marketing can save large companies hundreds of thousands of dollars each year.

The statistical-based hybrid neural network at Chase Manhattan Bank, discussed in the minicase at the beginning of this chapter, is one of the largest and most successful AI applications in the United States. It addresses a critical success factor in the bank's strategic plan: reducing losses on loans made to public and private corporations. Most of Chase's business for corporations involves assessing their creditworthiness. Chase loans $300 million annually and has long searched for tools to improve loan assessment. This assessment allows Chase to mitigate risk and seek out new business opportunities. Financial restructuring deals are promising business opportunities for the bank.

Many recent studies and success stories have been reported in various international conferences and academic and professional journals and magazines. An exam-

FIGURE 10-A2 The Evolving Network Population

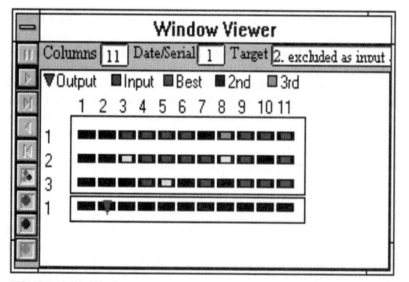

FIGURE 10-A3 The Input Combination and Forecast Horizon Searched by GA

FIGURE 10-A4 Rescaled Range Analysis to Determine the Hidden Cycles

FIGURE 10-A5 Correlation Analysis to Identify Leading Indicators

FIGURE 10-A6 The Learning process with the Histograms

FIGURE 10-A7 The Main Chart with a User-Friendly Interface

Powerful and Unique Features

- Reads various file formats including MetaStock, CSI, Computrac, FutureSource, ASCII, and VisuaData, displayed in its built-in spreadsheet.

- GENETICA Net Builder, which searches for the best input data combination and forecast horizon, and builds the best forecaster networks.

- Rescaled range analysis and Hurst exponent to unveil hidden market cycles and check for predictability.

- Correlation analysis to compute correlation factors to analyze the significance of input indicators.

- Weight and AEI (accumulated error index) histograms to monitor learning process.

Back Propagation Algorithm

The primary objective of a back propagation algorithm is the minimization of error between the output of a neural network and the true solution contained within the training data record.[4]

Assuming a logistic transfer function, we can update the weight, ω_{ij}, from a given node, n_i, to the current node, n_j, as follows:

$$\omega_{j(t+1)} = \omega_{j,t} + (\lambda)(\varepsilon\omega_{ij})(n_i)$$

where λ is the learning parameter, the subscript t refers to the number of times the net has been updated, and $\varepsilon\omega_{ij}$ is the sensitivity of node n_j to the change in the weight ω_{ij}.

Recall that the total input to a given neurode is described as

$$s_j = \sum n_i\omega_{ij}$$

where s_j represents the sum of all inputs to the neurode, n_i is the output from the ith neurode in the previous layer, and ω_{ij} is the weight of the input connection between the ith neurode in the previous layer and the current neurode.

The result of this summation is passed to a nonlinear transfer function to yield the total output n_j, of neurode j. Typical of the transfer function forms used is the *logistic function,* shown as

$$n_j = \frac{1}{1 + e^{-sj}}$$

With these equations in place, we can determine the overall error for a single pass of the ANN using the following steps:

- Calculate the (RMS) error, E, for the output layer as

$$E = \frac{1}{2}\sum_{\text{output}}(n_j - d_j)^2,$$

  where d_j is the desired output for output neurode j.

- Calculate the error term for each output neurode and determine the sensitivity of the error terms to changes in neurode output:

$$\varepsilon o_j = \frac{\partial E}{\partial n_j},$$
$$\varepsilon o_j = (n_j - d_j).$$

- Determine the relationship of change between input and output:

$$\varepsilon s_j = \frac{\partial E}{\partial n_j},$$
$$\varepsilon s_j = \frac{\partial E}{\partial s_j}\frac{dn_j}{ds_j},$$
$$\varepsilon s_j = \varepsilon o_j n_j(1 - n_j).$$

---

[4] This section was adapted from Dhar and Stein, 1997.

- Next, we calculate how much to adjust each weight, w_{ij}, from a given neurode on the layer below the current layer, n_i, to the current neurode, n_j:

$$\varepsilon\omega_j = \frac{\partial E}{\partial \omega_{ij}},$$

$$\varepsilon\omega_{ij} = \frac{\partial E}{\partial s_j}\frac{ds_j}{d\omega_{ij}},$$

$$\varepsilon\omega_{ij} = \varepsilon s_j n_i.$$

- We continue this operation on the neurodes in the hidden layers by summing all the contributions of inputs to the errors of the hidden neurodes in the lower layers. The variable εh replaces the variable εo from the previous equations to differentiate the error of the output layers from that of the hidden layers:

$$\varepsilon h_i = \frac{\partial E}{\partial n_i},$$

$$\varepsilon h_i = \sum_j \frac{\partial E}{\partial s_i}\frac{\partial s_j}{\partial n_i},$$

$$\varepsilon h_i = \sum_j \varepsilon s_j \omega_{ij}.$$

Using this approach, we can back propagate the error recursively through the entire ANN with all the weights being adjusted to minimize the overall error of the net.

11

The Data Warehouse

Learning Objectives

- Explain the goal of the data warehouse and its characteristics

- Explain the differences between an operational data store, a data mart, and a data warehouse

- Describe briefly each interconnected element in the data warehouse architecture

- Describe the role of metadata in the data warehouse

- Describe the components of the metadata

- Identify the challenge of implementing a data warehouse

- Describe the various data warehouse technologies and the future of data warehousing

Capital One

As a result of mass customization, the credit card industry has been transformed from a one-size-fits-all market into a microsegmented market offering thousands of product configurations tailored to the individual. Capital One, one of the top ten U.S. credit card issuers, was founded on the premise that the credit card business is really an information business and that mass customization is the key to growth and profitability.

Capital One uses information technology to implement a scientific testing approach to targeting profitable business. A strategy is formulated by mining behavioral data from the data warehouse. The target population is segmented and a test cell is established. The test cell is then exposed to the strategy and the results are recorded. An integrated economic evaluation is performed to judge the profit potential of the strategy. The results of the evaluation may lead to a larger scale rollout, a modification and retesting, or a rejection of the strategy. No matter what the outcome, the data collected from the test become part of the data warehouse for use in evaluating future strategies.

DATA VOLUME

The numbers of data needed to support Capital One's marketing efforts are enormous. The granularity of the segmentation being performed requires all data to be available at the individual account level. Also, the sophistication of the predictive models used requires low levels of transaction detail with a substantial set of measures. With approximately nine million active accounts, four thousand products, and twenty thousand tests, some with up to eight years of history, the raw data available are well over a terabyte.

Complex segmentation can potentially require many steps to execute. Each step creates interim files, which need to be stored as input to subsequent steps. With dozens of analysts doing thousands of tests every year, the disk space needed to support analyst work areas accounts for over five hundred gigabytes of storage. Analysts have access to large amounts of table space where they create new tables potentially containing millions of rows. Mass updates on these tables are routine because of the complex nature of the segmentations being performed.

DATA STRUCTURE

Rarely do analysts at Capital One ask the same questions twice. The lack of a consistent access path to the data makes it almost impossible to utilize standard DSS architectures such as star schemas. Stars require the users to restrict their questions to be framed around predetermined dimensions. With rich sources of data available to the analysts, the number of candidate dimensions would be physically impossible to implement given today's technology.

Most data are stored in slightly de-normalized relational formats at a very low level of granularity. There are very few prebuilt aggregations for the same reason that stars are not effective. The analysts pay for the flexibility of the data structures by having to endure longer query turnaround times and more complex query syntax.

DATA WAREHOUSING PRODUCTS

Most data warehouse tools on the market today do not support the mass customization environment. On the data acquisition side of data warehousing, most tools available cannot handle the complex integration of disparate, large-volume data sources. As the tool offerings continue to address the more sophisticated environments, this situation will improve. But for now, companies like Capital One are forced to build tools in-house.

DATA WAREHOUSING TALENT

Finding the right type of IT professional who can thrive in Capital One's unique culture is a constant challenge. The key characteristics of a successful data warehouse technician include a good balance of business and technical understanding, the ability to be a team player, and a great deal of flexibility. The demand for these types of resources seems endless and makes recruiting data warehousing talent a top priority.

Data warehousing is much more than an IT project for companies embracing the concept of mass customization. Armed with a data warehouse filled with quality information, Capital One has used mass customization techniques and scientific testing methods to expand its customer base from one million to nearly nine million in eight years.

Mass customization is the ultimate use of data warehousing, making it an integral part of the business process. Just like a muscle, a data warehouse increases in strength with active use. With each new test and each new product, valuable information is added to the data warehouse, allowing the analyst to learn from the successes and failures of the past.

During the 1980s, businesses and industries all over the globe participated in a "frenzy" of automation. Almost literally, if it moved, it was computerized. In this regard, the office became the new frontier for analysts and software engineers much as the factory floor had been in the decade prior. This overwhelming concentration on the automation of business processes appeared to offer organizations the opportunity to improve from within and to realize the benefits associated with such improvement through increased profits and reduced costs. Although many mission-critical business processes were improved during this period, the support of decision making throughout the organization remained focused on the operational and functional levels of the firm. Basic stock reports gushed out of the organization's information systems at alarming rates on a daily, weekly, and monthly basis. Often, the data used to construct these recurrent emanations were too old, too detailed, too aggregated, or uninte-grated. In some cases, the use of such reports led to negative consequences seemingly greater than if no information had been used. Simultaneous to this "rain" (or reign, in some cases) of data was the ever-narrowing window of time to market and to respond to changes in global environments. By the end of the 1980s, it became clear to most or-ganizations that if they were to identify a single key to survival in the 1990s and be-yond, it would be the ability to analyze, plan, and react to changing business condi-tions in a much more rapid fashion. To accomplish this, management at all levels of the firm would need more and better information.

Despite this growing need for more information, every day organizations large and small created billions of bytes of data about all aspects of their business—millions of individual facts about their customers, products, operations, and people without any formalized initiative beyond the transaction level to organize it. For the most part, these data were literally "locked up" in a thousand computer systems and were, metaphorically speaking, "data in jail."

It is estimated that only a small fraction of the data that are captured, processed, and stored in the enterprise is ever actually made available to executives and decision makers. The concept of the *data warehouse* (DW) is part of the response by informa-tion technology to meet this identified need. It is an elegantly simple concept that, over time, has the potential to evolve into a significant contributor to the success and stability of an organization in the global marketplace. The essence of the data ware-house concept is a recognition that the characteristics and usage patterns of opera-tional systems used to automate business processes and those of a DSS are fundamen-tally different but, nonetheless, symbiotically linked (Kelly 1994). The data warehouse provides a facility for integrating the data generated in a world of unintegrated infor-mation systems. A functional DW organizes and stores all of the available data needed for informational, analytical processing over a historical time perspective. It is the goal of the DW to reintegrate the data generated by a myriad of internal and external in-formation systems to create a sense of unity about the data without surrendering their natural complexities.

11-1 STORES, WAREHOUSES, AND MARTS

The concept of the data warehouse is brand new and, as such, in a state of flux with re-gard to standardization of terms and definitions. Some definitions focus on data, while others refer to people, software, tools, and business processes. The acknowledged fa-ther of data warehousing, W. H. Inmon, has provided a clear and useful definition of the DW concept, in terms of measurable attributes, that will serve our purposes in this text:

> The data warehouse is a collection of integrated, subject-oriented databases de-signed to support the DSS (decision support) function, where each unit of data is non-volatile and relevant to some moment in time. (Inmon 1992a, 5)

Inmon's definition of a DW makes two implicit assumptions: (1) the DW is physically separated from all other operational systems and (2) DWs hold aggregated data and transactional (atomic) data for management separate from those used for on-line transaction processing.

The requirement of a separate environment for the DW is an essential element in the concept. In most cases, the systems employed in an operational environment are inadequate, in many respects, with regard to decision-making and analysis. Primarily, the type, quantity, and quality of the data contained in such environments are not well suited to historical analysis. Warehouse data must be consistent, well integrated, well defined, and most important, time stamped. In addition, the need to merge a wide variety of internal and external environments with an equally wide variety of access methods suggests the need for separate DW systems. Table 11-1 contains a comparison between operational versus data warehouse charactcristics.

The blue-collar, distribution-channel metaphor of a "warehouse for data" extends itself easily to the primary components of a complete data warehouse environment. While the focus of this chapter is on the warehouse itself, we must briefly exam-

Table 11-1 Operational Data Store and Data Warehouse Characteristics

Characteristic	*Operational Data Store*	*Data Warehouse*
How is it built?	One application or subject area at a time.	Typically multiple subject areas at a time.
User requirements	Well defined prior to logical design.	Often vague and conflicting.
Area of support	Day-to-day business operations.	Decision support for managerial activities.
Type of access	Relatively small number of records retrieved via a single query.	Large data sets scanned to retrieve results from either single or multiple queries.
Frequency of access	Tuned for frequent access to small amounts of data.	Tuned for infrequent access to large amounts of data.
Volume of data	Similar to typical daily volume of operational transactions.	Much larger than typical daily transaction volume.
Retention period	Retained as necessary to meet daily operating requirements.	Retention period is indeterminate and must support historical reporting, comparison, and analysis.
Currency of data	Up-to-the-minute; real time.	Typically represents a static point in time.
Availability of data	High and immediate availability may be required.	Immediate availability is less critical.
Typical unit of analysis	Small, manageable, transaction-level units.	Large, unpredictable, variable units.
Design focus	High-performance, limited flexibility.	High flexibility, high-performance.

Source: Adapted from Bischoff and Alexander (1997).

ine three additional components of the DW environment: the *data store,* the *data mart,* and the *metadata.*

The Data Store

The *operational data store* (ODS) is the most common component of the DW environment. Its primary day-to-day function is to store the data for a single, specific set of operational applications. Its function within the DW environment, however, is to feed the data warehouse a stream of desired raw data.

The data organization within an ODS is generally subject oriented, volatile, and current (or near current) with common focuses being on customers, products, orders, policies, claims, and so forth. Normally, the ODS is fed by one or more legacy systems and the DBMS associated with such systems serves to cleanse, transform, and integrate the data into homogenous records of transactions or instances of occurrence. Although the data within an ODS lend themselves favorably to analysis performed by one or more of its legacy systems, the data generally do not integrate easily with data from other, nonrelated systems. Nonetheless, many data stores (both internal and external to the organization) may be drawn upon to feed the organizational data warehouse for the purpose of analysis.

The Data Mart

Although the concept of a central aggregation of disparate, yet relevant, data is appealing, the costs associated with such aggregation across an entire organization may be prohibitive. The need for certain types and sources of aggregated data may exist only within certain business units within the firm and the specific needs of each unit may be tangential to those of the others. An alternative being adopted by many firms is a lower-cost, scaled-down version of the DW called the *data mart.*

The data mart is often viewed as a way to gain entry into the realm of data warehouses and to make all the mistakes on a smaller scale. Further, vendors of data warehousing applications have found it easier to deal directly with a small group of isolated users than with the IS department of an entire organization. Although the concept of the "mini-mart" is both appealing and useful, a single caveat regarding its proliferation must be acknowledged: Without careful planning from an enterprise-wide perspective, the data mart can become an isolated island of information that will be inaccessible to others in the firm. Assuming the data marts are constructed within the bigger picture of an enterprise-wide system, they can serve as a targeted and less costly method of gaining the advantages associated with data warehousing and can be scaled up to a full DW environment over time.

The Metadata

One additional component of the DW environment is called the *metadata.* Legacy systems generally do not keep a record of characteristics of the data, such as exactly *what pieces of data exist, where they are located, where they came from,* and *how they can be accessed.* The metadata are simply data about data—that is, information that is kept about the warehouse rather than information kept within the warehouse. We will cover metadata in detail in section 11-3.

The Data Warehouse Environment

Figure 11-1 illustrates the flow of data within an organization and the position of the components of the DW environment with regard to other information systems.

As shown in the figure, the organization's legacy systems and the relevant data stores of external systems are the core sources of data for the data warehouse and data mart. During the transfer of data from the various data stores, a process of cleansing and transformation occurs that is intended to result in a uniformity of the DW data. Simultaneously, the metadata are collected and associated with the DW data so that potential users can determine the source and general characteristics of the DW data. Finally, the DW or data mart may be employed to create one or more personal data warehouses intended for isolated analysis. In the following sections, we will explore the details of the processes and architectures typically associated with a data warehouse environment.

Characteristics of a Data Warehouse

So far we have established the reasons why data warehousing is an important innovation in decision support and we have formally defined the DW to be

FIGURE 11-1 Organizational Data Flow and Data Storage Components

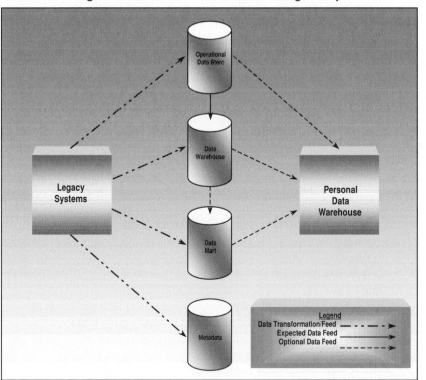

- Subject oriented
- Data integrated
- Time variant
- Nonvolatile

Table 11-2 summarizes the essential characteristics of the DW and provides a brief description of each.

Subject Orientation

The first feature of the DW is that it is oriented toward the major subjects of the organization. This is in clear contrast to the more functional orientation of the various applications associated with the firm's legacy systems. Figure 11-2 illustrates this contrast in orientations.

As illustrated by the figure, the operational world of the organization is typically designed around processes and functions such as inventory or human resources, each of which have specific data needs with most of the data elements local to that process or function. The DW, on the other hand, contains data that are primarily oriented to decision making and, as such, are organized more around the major subject areas relevant to the firm, such as customers or vendors.

This distinct subject orientation results in several specific differences between typical applications and the data warehouse. For example, while design activities in the application world must be equally focused on both process and database design, the DW world is primarily void of process design (at least in its classical form) and tends to focus exclusively on issues of data modeling and database design.

Another specific distinction can be found in the characteristics of the data contained within the DW. Operational data are normally stored in the form of an ongoing relationship between two or more tables that is based on some established business rule such as "Each order must be related to one and only one customer." This business rule creates a relationship between the table containing instances of orders and the table containing instances of customers. One entry in the customer table may be related to many entries in the order table, whereas one entry in the order table will al-

---

Table 11-2 Characteristics of a Data Warehouse

- *Subject orientation.* Data are organized based on how the users refer to them.
- *Integrated.* All inconsistencies regarding naming convention and value representations are removed.
- *Nonvolatile.* Data are stored in read-only format and do not change over time.
- *Time variant.* Data are not current but normally time-series.
- *Summarized.* Operational data are mapped into a decision-usable format.
- *Large volume.* Time-series data sets are normally quite large.
- *Not normalized.* DW data can be, and often are, redundant.
- *Metadata.* Data about data are stored.
- *Data sources.* Data come from internal and external unintegrated operational systems.

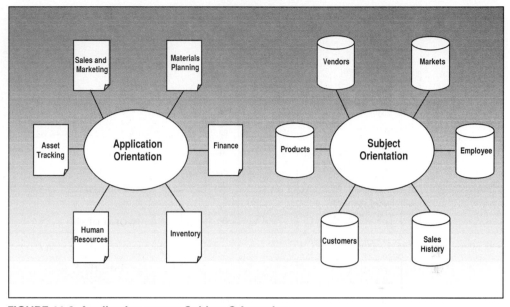

FIGURE 11-2 Application versus Subject Orientation

ways be related to only one entry in the customer table. In contrast, data in the DW span a range of time and, as such, many business rules (and correspondingly, many data relationships) can be represented in the DW between two or more tables (Inmon 1992a).

Data Integrated

According to Inmon (1992b), the very essence of the DW environment is that the data contained within the boundaries of the warehouse are integrated. This integration manifests itself through consistency in naming convention and measurement attributes, accuracy, and common aggregation. Figure 11-3 illustrates the sharp contrast between the lack of integration found within the operational application environment and that of the DW environment.

Consistent Naming and Measurement Attributes   One of the "freedoms" associated with application design has always been the selection of a naming convention for variables, both as they are represented in the data dictionary and as they appear on the screen. The frequent exercise of this freedom has made the inconsistency of applications throughout an organization legendary. For example, the typical data element of gender can (and has) been encoded in operational applications in a myriad of ways. In one application, the variable may be represented as M or F. In another application, the designer may choose to represent it numerically with 1 or 0, or 1 or 2, or possibly 0 or 1. In yet another, the representation may be as an x and a y. As long as these representations are "understood" by their respective applications and users then no serious problems will occur. However, when the databases associated with these dissimilar ap-

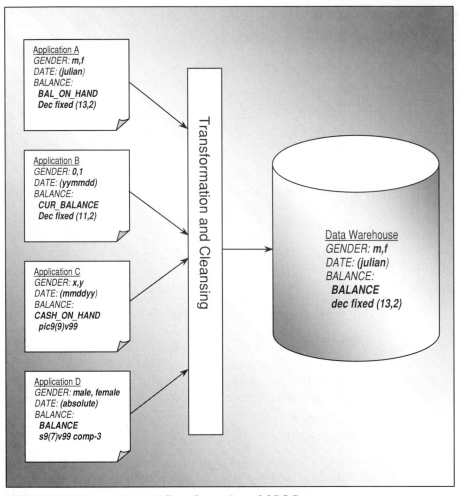

FIGURE 11-3 Integration and Transformation of ODS Data

plications are loaded into the data warehouse, a decision as to what naming convention will be adopted must be made and a transformation process based on that naming convention must be effected. Using this example, it doesn't particularly matter how gender is represented in the DW as long as it is represented in a consistent and integrated manner. To assure this consistency, each source of data must have an associated conversion process that "scrubs" the data into a converted state.

Another result of the need for integrated data is the establishment of a common unit of measure for all synonymous data elements from dissimilar databases. This common measurement must not only serve to integrate the variety of measuring attributes being loaded into the DW but must also create a globally acceptable unit of measure for the final data. In one database, an employee's term of employment may be represented in weeks, whereas in another it may be represented in months or years and decimal years. Just like the conversion of data element names to a common convention, units of measure must also be converted as the data are loaded into the warehouse. This conversion, while serving to standardize the unit of measure, must also create a standard that is universally acceptable to the decision makers and DSS technologies that will use the DW. In some cases, it is an easy decision as to how to represent a particular measurement. Temperature, for instance, will typically be a choice between the Fahrenheit, Celsius, or Kelvin scales. The decision will depend on the intended use of the data. In other cases, however, the decision may be constrained by a wide variety of intended uses for the data element in question. In these cases, it may become necessary to convert the data to some "non-standard" unit of measure that will allow for the most flexible conversion schema to be employed. In the case of employee tenure, the conversion to a unit of days of employment during data loading of the DW may turn out to be the most flexible choice because this unit will allow easy conversion to any desired output. To extend this concept further, the needs analysis for this data element may suggest that it would be better to not store the length of employee service but, rather, to store the initial date of employment. In this way, a single mathematical process could be employed to convert the data to whatever unit of measure was deemed most desirable at the moment.

Whatever the issue, the data must be stored in the DW in an integrated, globally acceptable manner. It is important to the success of a DW that the DSS analyst be allowed to focus on the use of the data contained in the warehouse rather than on issues of credibility or consistency.

Time Variant

In an operational application system, the expectation is that all data within the database are accurate as of the moment of access. When a customer service representative for your credit card company checks on your current balance, his expectation (and yours) is that the value returned will be accurate as of that moment. It would not be particularly useful for the credit representative to tell you that your balance was $459.00 as of three weeks ago. In the realm of data warehouses, however, data are simply assumed to be accurate as of some moment in time and not necessarily "right now." Typically, the data are assumed to be accurate at the moment they were loaded into the DW. In this regard, data within a data warehouse are said to be *time variant*.

The time variance of the warehouse data manifests itself in a variety of ways. Typically, the time horizon for the data in the warehouse is long—from five to ten years. In contrast, the typical operational environment time horizon is much shorter—anywhere from current values to sixty to ninety days. The level of performance associated with high-volume transaction processing necessitates the shorter time horizons in operational applications. In DW environments, however, the desire is generally to analyze data over longer time periods in an effort to reveal trends and temporal relationships.

Another place where DW data display time variance is in the structure of the record key. Every primary key contained within the DW must contain, either implicitly or explicitly, an element of time (day, week, month, year, etc.). In an explicit representation, the time unit may be concatenated (appended) to the primary key (i.e., *CUST-ORDER+0992,* where the second part of the key reflects month and year). In other cases, the time element will be implicitly stated, such as a file that is always loaded at the end of a month or quarter and is named for its associated time period. Regardless of the method employed, every piece of data contained within the warehouse must be associated with a particular point in time if any useful analysis is to be performed with it.

Yet another aspect of time variance in DW data is that, once recorded, data within the warehouse cannot be updated or changed. In this regard, warehouse data can be thought of as a series of sequential photographs. Using this metaphor, an inaccurate snapshot may be replaced by an accurate one, but once the accuracy of the photos is ascertained, they cannot be altered.

Nonvolatility

In keeping with the restriction of not changing or updating the data contained in a DW, it makes sense that the typical activities of *inserts, deletes,* and *changes* performed regularly in an operational application environment are completely nonexistent in a DW environment. There are only two data operations ever performed in the data warehouse: *data loading* and *data access.*

This simplicity of data operations creates some extremely powerful differences between operational processing and processing in a DW environment. The design issues in a typical operational application must focus on issues of data integrity and update anomalies. Complex processes must be coded to ensure that the data update processes occur in a manner that allows for high integrity of the final product. Such issues are of no concern in a DW environment because data update is never performed. Liberties in the design of the DW databases can be taken to allow for optimal access to the data that could never be allowed in an operational environment. Recall from your study of database design the need to place data in a normalized form to ensure a minimal redundancy.[1] In this regard, the third normal form eliminates any derived data elements, such as those that can be calculated. In an operational application database, a designer would never store the total for a particular order. If this data element is desired it can be easily calculated upon retrieval of the order. In the world of data warehouses, however, designers might actually find it useful to store many such calculations or summarizations not found in the operational data. For example, it might be useful to include weekly or monthly sales figures obtained by aggregating the daily sales figures found in the operational database.

Along with the simplicity of processing in a DW environment comes a relative simplicity in the necessary technology. In the operational realm, the technologies necessary to support issues of transaction and data recovery, roll back, and detection and remedy of deadlock are quite complex. In the realm of data warehouses, all this is quite unnecessary.

Issues of Data Redundancy

The lack of relevancy in the DW environment of issues such as data normalization, that are so important to the reduction of data redundancy in the operational realm, may suggest the prospect of massive data redundancy within the data warehouse and be-

---

[1] If you find this confusing, any good textbook on introductory database design should clear up the turmoil.

tween the operational and DW environments. Inmon (1992a) points out that, counter to that first impression, there is actually a minimum of redundancy between the data in the operational application databases feeding the DW and warehouse itself. Several points bear out the truth of this assertion.

First, consider that the data being loaded into the DW are filtered and "cleansed" as they pass from the operational database to the warehouse. Because of this cleansing, numerous data that exist in the operational environment never pass to the data warehouse. Only the data necessary for processing by the DSS or EIS are ever actually loaded into the DW. Also, the DW contains a great deal of summarized data that are never reflected in the operational data store.

Consider also that the time horizons for warehouse and operational data elements are uniquely different. Data in the operational environment are very fresh whereas warehouse data are generally much older. When viewed from a time horizon perspective, there is little opportunity for overlap or redundancy between the operational and data warehouse environments.

Finally, recall that the data being loaded into the DW often undergo a radical transformation as they pass from the operational to the DW environment. Because of this transformation and alteration, most of the data that ultimately reside in the data warehouse are not the same data that once resided in the operational environment (at least not from a data integration perspective).

Given these factors, Inmon suggests that data redundancy between the two environments is a rare occurrence with a typical redundancy factor of less than 1 percent.

11-2 THE DATA WAREHOUSE ARCHITECTURE

A *data warehouse architecture* (DWA) is a method by which the overall structure of data, communication, processing, and presentation that exists for end-user computing within the enterprise can be represented. Figure 11-4 illustrates the various interconnected elements that serve to make up the DWA.

Operational and External Database Layer

The *operational and external database layer* represents the source data for the DW. This layer comprises, primarily, operational transaction processing systems and external secondary databases. The goal of the data warehouse is to free the information that is locked up in the operational databases and to mix it with information from other, often external, sources. An additional objective of the DW is to have a minimal impact on the performance and operation of the systems found in this layer. In other words, the addition of the necessary extraction software to this environment should go unnoticed in terms of performance of the operational applications whose databases are being accessed.

Increasingly, large organizations are acquiring additional data from outside databases. The ubiquitous nature of the Web and the Internet has made it easy and economical for firms to access and incorporate such data into their DW. Data related to demographic, econometric, competitive, and purchasing trends are typically found in

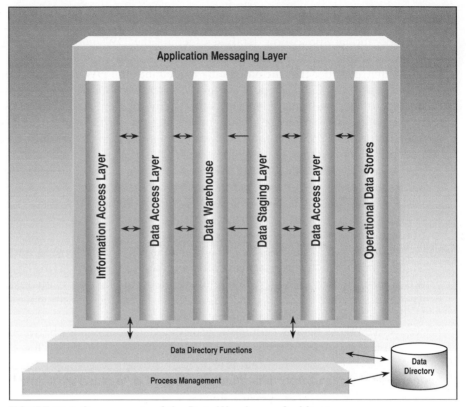

FIGURE 11-4 Components of the Data Warehouse Architecture

public- or subscriber-access databases via the Internet. These data are treated in the same manner as the ODS data and, following extraction and conditioning for consistency, are loaded into the data warehouse.

Information Access Layer

The *information access layer* of the DWA is the layer that the end user deals with directly. In particular, it represents the tools that the end user normally uses day to day to extract and analyze the data contained within the DW. At this layer are found the hardware and software involved in displaying and printing reports, spreadsheets, graphs, and charts for analysis and presentation. The information access layer is where the DSSs that have been designed to use the DW data and to support the various categories and types of decision making throughout the organization are located.

Data Access Layer

As shown in figure 11-4, the *data access layer* serves as a sort of interface or middleman between the operational and information access layers and the data warehouse itself. This layer spans the various databases contained within the DW and facilitates common access by the DW users. But not only does the data access layer span multiple databases and file systems on the same hardware, it also spans the wide variety of manufacturers and network protocols as well. One of the keys to a successful DW is to provide end users with *universal data access*. This means that, theoretically at least, end users regardless of location or information access tool should be able to access any or all of the data in the enterprise that are necessary for them to do their job. It is the role of the data access layer to make this happen.

Metadata Layer

In order to provide for universal data access, it is absolutely necessary to maintain some form of data directory or repository of metadata information. As discussed briefly in section 11-1, *metadata* are data about the data stored within the DW. Examples of metadata include the directory of where the data are stored, the rules used for summarization and scrubbing, or possibly records of where the operational data came from.

Process Management Layer

The *process management layer* focuses on scheduling the various tasks that must be accomplished to build and maintain the data warehouse and data directory information. This layer can be thought of as the scheduler or the high-level job control for the many processes (procedures) that must occur to keep the DW up to date. Tasks such as periodic download from identified operational data stores, scheduled summarization of operational data, access and download of external data sources, and update of the metadata are typical of those performed at this layer of the DWA.

Application Messaging Layer

The *application messaging layer* has to do with transporting information around the enterprise computing network. This layer is also referred to as the "middleware," but it can typically involve more that just networking protocols and request routing. Application messaging, for example, can be used to isolate applications, operational or informational, from the exact data format on either end, thus facilitating a seamless interface between the uniqueness of a particular data format and the specific format requirements of the analysis tool being used. This layer can also be used to collect transactions or messages and deliver them to a certain location at a certain time. In this sense, the application messaging layer can be thought of as the transport system underlying the DW.

Physical Data Warehouse Layer

The *physical data warehouse layer* is where the actual data used for decision support throughout the organization are located. In some cases, one can think of the DW simply as a logical or virtual view of data. This is because, as we will see shortly, in some instances the data warehouse may not actually store the data accessed through it.

Data Staging Layer

The final component of the DWA is the *data staging layer.* Data staging (sometimes referred to as *copy* or *replication management*) includes all of the processes necessary to select, edit, summarize, combine, and load data warehouse and information access data from operational and/or external data bases.

Data staging often involves complex programming, but increasingly vendors are marketing data warehousing tools intended to reduce the complexities associated with this process. Data staging may also involve data quality analysis programs and other such filters that identify patterns and data structures within existing operational data.

Data Warehousing Typology

As mentioned above, although the data warehouse may appear to be the source of data for various organizational analysis initiatives and decision-making activities, it may not physically be the location of the data being accessed. While numerous hybrid mechanisms exist to structure a DW, three basic configurations can be identified: *virtual* or *point-to-point, central,* and *distributed* data warehouses.

In preface to an overview of each configuration it must be noted that there is no one best approach to configuring a DW schema. Each option fits a specific set of requirements, and a data warehousing strategy may ultimately include all three options.

The Virtual Data Warehouse

A *virtual* or *point-to-point* data warehousing strategy allows the end users to access the operational data stores directly using tools enabled at the data access layer. This approach provides the ultimate in flexibility as well as the minimum amount of redundant data that must be loaded and maintained; however, it can also put the largest unplanned query load and performance degradation on operational application systems.

Virtual warehousing is often an initial strategy in organizations where there is a broad but largely undefined need to get at operational data by a relatively large class of end users and where the likely frequency of requests is low. Virtual data warehouses often provide a relatively low-cost starting point for organizations to assess what types of data end users are really looking for.

The Central Data Warehouse

Central data warehouses are what most people think of when they are first introduced to the concept of a data warehouse. The central data warehouse is a single physical database that contains all of the data for a specific functional area, department, division, or enterprise. This warehousing approach is often selected where there is a common need for informational data and there are large numbers of end users already connected to a central computer or network. A central data warehouse may contain data for any specific period of time and usually contains data from multiple operational applications.

The central data warehouse is real. The data stored in the DW are physically located in and accessible from one place and must be loaded and maintained on a regular basis. This configuration is the most common of the three basic types and is becoming the de facto standard for DW implementation due to the wide variety of construction and manipulation tools being offered.

The Distributed Data Warehouse

A *distributed data warehouse* is just what its name implies: a data warehouse the components of which are distributed across a number of different physical databases. Increasingly, large organizations are pushing decision making down to lower and lower levels of the organization and in turn pushing the data needed for decision making down (or out) to the LAN or local computer serving the local decision maker. Many older DW implementations use the distributed approach because initially it was easier to create several small data warehouse databases than to facilitate one all-encompassing one. The advent of modern DW implementation and management applications, however, has reduced the need for multiple or distributed DWs.

11-3 DATA HAVE DATA — THE METADATA

Just What I Need — More Data!

The real problem with *metadata* is that the name suggests some high-level technological concept that requires far too much cognitive energy to discuss and understand. With the emergence of the DW as a primary decision support resource, metadata are now considered as much of a resource of the organization as the business data they describe.

The standard definition of metadata is "data about data." Although this definition has a comforting Zen-like quality to it that makes for a great slogan, it leaves a lot to be desired with regard to providing any useful description. For example, how can we add meaning to data by associating that data with more data? To answer this question we must first understand the primary concept upon which metadata are built.

The Concept of Abstraction

To understand metadata, we must focus on a relatively simple concept of general semantics called the *chain of abstraction*. For example, a sofa is a fairly concrete entity. Any particular sofa has a multitude of descriptive characteristics: It is made of wood, cloth, steel, and leather; it has two arms and a back; it is a particular shape or style; it has several cushions; and so on. We can abstract from that sofa, and others we encounter, to the word "sofa." In other words, by using the word "sofa," we can describe a wide variety of specific sofas; in fact, we can describe all sofas ever made. Moving from describing a particular sofa to representing all sofas by using a single word is but one step in the chain of abstraction. We can take further steps. For instance, we could describe the *word* "sofa" and all the other words we know by the word "word." There really exists no limit to the chain of abstraction for anything provided the level of abstraction we use conveys some useful meaning.

Software is simply a link in the chain of abstraction. The word "sofa" that you are reading now, if stored in a computer, would be represented by a string of magnetic flux changes on the oxide surface of a hard disk or as minute pits in the surface of a compact disk. So would a source code statement such as this:

LET CHECK_BALANCE = CHECK_BALANCE + CREDIT − DEBIT.

The source code statement, in turn, is an abstraction of a banking transaction, which is an abstraction of a bank, which is an abstraction of an industry, which is an abstraction of an economy, which is . . . well, you see where this is going.

Metadata are simply abstractions from data. They are high-level data that provide us with concise descriptions of lower-level data. The world is full of metadata—consider these examples:

- Author, title, ISBN number, and publisher
- Headlines of stories in a paper
- The business definitions for all data elements in the DW
- Road maps
- Data flow diagrams in a CASE tool's repository

The Key to the Data

Metadata are essential ingredients in the transformation of raw data into knowledge. For example, metadata in the form of a field definition tell us that a given stream of bits is a customer's order number, part of a bit-mapped graphic, or the name of a word processing document we just created. Should the metadata get mixed up or out of alignment, none of the data will make sense. The order number won't match any of our orders; the document we created will not be retrievable; even the graphic will not look quite the way it should, though depending upon how jumbled the metadata get, our eyes may not detect the difference.

It may be helpful to think of metadata as "tongs" with which we can handle raw data (APT 1996). Without metadata, the data are meaningless. We do not even know where they are or what percentage to take. Take away data definitions, and how could we query a database? All we could hope to recover would be a string of ones and zeroes. In the early days of commercial computing, each application created and handled its own data files. Because the files' metadata were embedded in the application's data definitions, no application could make sense of another application's files. When databases were introduced, one of the greatest advantages they brought was that the metadata were stored in the database catalog, not in the individual programs. There was one version of the truth, and that was held in the database.

The Metadata in Action

Assume for the moment, that while exploring our organization's data warehouse we find three unique sets of data:

1. 615397 8350621 885214 0051023 6487921
2. A Garrison Group report dated 9/11/96 states that the Asian market for machine tools expanded by 33 percent in 1995
3. Leading sports marketing firms: IMG 45 percent, SportStarz 33 percent, Legends, Inc. 16 percent

How much can we learn from these data?

In the first case, the answer is "absolutely nothing." The numbers may be sales figures for a department or region, the population of European cities, or maybe the number of blood cells in a set of samples. The numbers could even represent a sequence of machine code for a computer. These data are typical of tabular data found in a relational database. There are, however, two specific ways to assign meaning to the data: *from the context* or *from the metadata*. In the former case, these numbers are the result of a query on a given table so we already know their meaning. In the latter, if we associate a metadata description with the data, it will tell us the name of the table and possibly a great deal more.

Example 2 appears to be more straightforward. It is free text, and seems to be self-descriptive. One small point, however: The date shown is ambiguous. Does "9/11/95" mean September 11, 1995 (U.S. convention) or November 9, 1995 (British convention)? In this case, the metadata serve to clear up the confusion by indicating that all dates are displayed using "MM/DD/YY."

The third example contains some metadata: We know the data represent leading sports marketing firms. What we don't know is what the percentages represent, what time period is referred to, how the data were collected, or even the source of the information. Without sufficient metadata, the data element in the example is rendered useless.

These examples demonstrate the importance of metadata in the DW environment. Here, data analysts and executives are looking for useful facts and correlations that they will recognize when they find them—and often, not before. Routine applications are of no use to them: They need to get in among the data, and to do so successfully, they need to understand their structure and meaning. Passengers on a train do not need a map, although a timetable may prove useful. A driver setting out by road across a foreign country to an unknown village, though, would be very unwise to set out without a complete set of large-scale and small-scale maps (APT 1996). A data warehouse without adequate metadata is like filing cabinets stuffed full of paper, but void of any folders or labels. Try finding anything useful in that!

Consistency — Avoiding Many Versions of the Truth

Unreliable or missing metadata lead to untenable situations where one business unit reports that overall corporate profits are up 15 percent, while another business unit says they are down 10 percent. Each functional area is using its own numbers, collected in accordance with its own procedures and interpreted by its own applications. This "algorithmic differential" often results in organizational decision making lapsing into a morass of politics and personalities.

Unlike the individual ODSs established for the benefit of a specific business unit or department, the data warehouse is set up for the benefit of business analysts and executives across all functional areas of the organization. If they need metadata—and they do—then it is the job of the warehouse support staff to make sure they get that information. In this regard, the DW support staff can be thought of as librarians. If you need help finding what you are looking for, they are there to guide you. If you require no assistance, then you are free to browse at your convenience.

In a DW environment, both the data and the metadata are in a constant state of update. Organizational decision makers are constantly on the lookout for new and interesting patterns in the data and this can lead them to investigate and compare information from all corners of the enterprise and beyond. It can also lead to requests for new data sets, which must be replicated from operational application systems or imported from external sources. With each new addition to the DW, the warehouse's metadata map has to be extended to embrace it.

Agreeing on One Version of the Truth

Not only must warehouse administrators keep up with ever-changing data definitions and requests for new and disparate data sets, they must also agree on a single version of the truth. In the corporate world, it is often quipped that if the revenues for which credit was claimed by all the department managers were totaled, the resulting sum would exceed the organization's actual revenue by several hundred percent. In aggregating the myriad of data elements necessary for a useful data warehouse, the metadata must be organized in such a way that accurate and useful comparisons across time and sources can be effected. The greatest challenge faced by developers and maintainers of a DW is the task of ensuring the integrity and accuracy of the data contained within.

11-4 INTERVIEWING THE DATA — METADATA EXTRACTION

General Metadata Issues

Inmon (1992b) suggests that, regardless of the specific nature of a given query to the DW, several general pieces of information, derived from the metadata, are important to all decision makers. Table 11-3 lists the generic information essential to using data from a DW.

Data warehouse metadata are really not all that different in kind from operational database metadata, although DW metadata are *versioned* in order to permit historical analysis. This means that the DW metadata must be tagged with some information that lets the user know the general conditions under which the DW data were

---

Table 11-3 General Metadata Issues Associated with Data Warehouse Use

- What tables, attributes, and keys do the data warehouse contain?
- Where did each set of data come from?
- What transformation logic was applied in loading the data?
- How have the metadata changed over time?
- What aliases exist and how are they related to each other?
- What are the cross-references between technical and business terms?
- How often do the data get reloaded?
- How many data elements are there in the DW? (assists in avoiding the submission of unrealistic queries)

collected. When collection methods or conditions change, then the metadata version must change as well. In this regard, we can think of metadata versioning as meta-metadata.

Components of the Metadata

Collecting the right metadata at the right time is a foundational requirement for a successful DW implementation. Although specific metadata considered useful for one DW may not be useful to another, several categories of general metadata exist that can commonly be expected to be found in a typical DW environment.

Transformation Mapping

Transformation mapping metadata records how data from operational data stores and external sources are transformed on the way into the warehouse. As the individual data elements from these sources are mapped to the existing DW structures, this mapping should be collected and maintained as metadata. With the advent of modern data warehouse development tools, the mapping process has become virtually indistinguishable from the process of transformation. Table 11-4 lists several of the types of mappings that must be available as metadata.

Extraction and Relationship History

Whenever historical information is analyzed, meticulous update records must be kept. Often a decision maker will begin the process of constructing a time-based report by reviewing the *extraction history* because any changes to the business rules must be ascertained in order to apply the right rules to the right data. If sales regions were reallocated in 1994, then the decision maker will know that results from before that date may not be directly comparable with more recent results.

In addition to the extraction metadata, information regarding the various *relationships* contained within the DW must be maintained. Data warehouses often implement data relationships in a different way than operational application databases. Metadata pertaining to related tables, constraints, and cardinality must be maintained, together with text descriptions and ownership records. This information and the his-

---

Table 11-4 Typical Mapping Metadata

- Identification of original source fields
- Simple attribute-to-attribute mapping
- Attribute conversions
- Physical characteristic conversions
- Encoding/reference table conversions
- Naming changes
- Key changes
- Values of defaults
- Logic to choose from among multiple sources
- Algorithmic changes

---

tory of changes to it can be of significant value to decision makers when performing analysis with multiple aggregations of data.

Algorithms for Summarization

A typical data warehouse contains a wide variety of lightly and heavily summarized data, as well as fully detailed records. The *summarization algorithms* applied to the detail data are of importance to any decision maker analyzing or interpreting the meaning of the summaries. This metadata can also save time by making it easier to decide which level of summarization is most appropriate for a given analysis context.

Data Ownership

Operational data stores are often "owned" by particular business units or divisions within an organization. In a data warehouse environment, however, all data are stored in a common format and are normally accessible to all. This makes it necessary to identify the originator of each set of data, so that inquiries and corrections can be made to the proper group. It is useful to distinguish between "ownership" of data in the operational environment and "stewardship" in the data warehouse. The administrators of the DW are responsible for the collection, summarization, and dissemination of warehouse data and in this regard are the caretakers or stewards of the data. The administrators of the source ODS, however, are responsible for the accuracy of the transaction-level data and are the actual owners of the data.

Patterns of Warehouse Access

It is often desirable to record patterns of access to the warehouse for the purpose of optimizing and tuning DW performance. Understanding what tables are being accessed, how often, and by whom can alert the DW administrators to ways of improving or simplifying the queries being performed by the end users. Less frequently used data can be migrated to cheaper storage media, and various methods can be employed to accelerate access to the data that are most in demand. Further, the identification and recording of queries that have been written can be a valuable resource to the organization because it can facilitate the reuse of queries. Instead of spending the time to figure out how to construct a new query, a decision maker can simply access a repository of past queries and choose the one that most closely resembles the immediate need.

Additional Common Metadata

In addition to the major categories of metadata discussed above, several other less common, yet equally important, categories of metadata can be identified. The existence of each of these *miscellaneous metadata* components is often context-specific or organization-dependent. When needed for analysis, however, the miscellaneous metadata are as important as the more common categories.

One important member of this class of metadata are the *logical business data models*. It is often important to understand the logical model that defines the entities, relationships, and rules that exist in a particular business environment where data have been obtained. Building a data warehouse without including the source data models is both dangerous and prone to error. When the source data model is available, metadata describing the mapping between the data model and the physical design can be retrieved, thus allowing for any ambiguities or uncertainties to be resolved.

Another category of metadata that can make the warehouse much more user-friendly is the recording of *aliases*. By allowing a table to be queried by "Units produced by each region" rather than "REG_MFG_STATS," the use of aliases makes both the construction and subsequent interpretation of a query more understandable. Aliases are also useful when different business units have the freedom to use their own names to refer to the same underlying data. Careful tracking of aliases for data elements is an important part of the DW metadata.

Development status metadata are yet another important source of information to the DW user. Often, parts of the same data warehouse may be in various stages of development or completion. Status information can be used to convey information to the decision maker regarding, for example, the tables being accessed by a certain query. Such tables might be classified as *in-design, in-test,* or *inactive.*

Finally, *volumetric metadata* can be stored to inform users as to the exact volume of data they are dealing with, so that they may have some idea how much their queries will cost in terms of time and resources. Volumetrics often include such information as number of rows, table growth rate, usage characteristics, indexing, and byte specifications.

11-5 IMPLEMENTING THE DATA WAREHOUSE

The challenge of providing access to the aggregated data of an organization is not a new one. The 1970s saw the advent of the *information center,* an ill-fated concept requiring both a dedicated high-powered computer and a severe resource drain in terms of hardware, software, and personnel. The 1980s brought with it the emphasis on data reengineering using the extended relational model. This, too, was fraught with complexities and severe performance degradation issues. The 1990s answer appears to be the data warehouse. If we are to avoid the problems of the past and realize the successes assumed to be associated with total access to data, IT management and organizational data warehouse champions must not only understand what needs to be done, but also just how to do it.

Denis Kozar (1997), vice president of Enterprise Information Architecture for Chase Manhattan Bank, has assembled the "seven deadly sins" of data warehouse implementation. Each of these errors can result in the failure of an otherwise valuable data warehouse initiative. Table 11-5 lists the "seven deadly sins" of data warehousing.

Sin #1: "If You Build It, They Will Come"

Kozar suggests that the first of the seven sins is one of blind faith. This is the failure to recognize the importance of developing a clear set of business objectives for the data warehouse prior to its construction. A successful data warehouse plan is one in which the needs of the entire enterprise are considered and a documented set of requirements is developed to guide the design, construction, and rollout of the project. The data warehouse cannot simply be built in the hope that someone will find a use for it.

Table 11-5 The Seven Deadly Sins of Data Warehouse Implementation

1. "If you build it, they will come"
2. Omission of a data warehouse architectural framework
3. Underestimating the importance of documenting all assumptions and potential conflicts
4. Abuse of methodology and tools
5. Abuse of the data warehouse life cycle
6. Ignorance concerning the resolution of data conflicts
7. Failure to document the mistakes made during the first DW project

Sin #2: Omission of an Architectural Framework

One of the most important factors in a successful data warehouse initiative is the development and maintenance of a comprehensive architectural framework. Such a framework serves as the blueprints for construction and use of the various DW components. Issues such as the expected number of end users, the volume and diversity of data, and the expected data-refresh cycle, among many others, must be considered (and reflected) in the DW architecture.

Sin #3: Underestimating the Importance of Documenting Assumptions

The assumptions and potential data conflicts associated with the DW must be included in the architectural framework for the project. They must be ascertained and codified within the document as early in the project as possible to ensure their reflection in the final product. Several questions must be answered during the requirements phase of the project that serve to reveal these important underlying assumptions about the DW. How much data should be loaded into the warehouse? What is the expected level of data granularity? How often do we need to refresh the data? On what platform will the DW be developed and implemented? Accurate answers to questions such as these is essential to the success of a data warehouse project.

Sin #4: Failure to Use the Right Tool for the Job

The design and construction of a data warehouse is, in many ways, much different than the construction of an operational application system. Because of this, a different set of tools must be employed in a DW project than those typically found in an application development effort.

Data warehouse tools can be categorized into four discrete groupings: (1) *analysis tools*, (2) *development tools*, (3) *implementation tools*, and (4) *delivery tools*. Within each of these categories are specialized tools designed specifically to accommodate the unique design activities associated with data warehouse development.

Analysis Tools   The tools in this category assist in the identification of data requirements, the primary sources of data for the DW, and the construction of the data model for the warehouse. Modern CASE tools are a typical member of this category. Another analysis tool is the code scanner. These applications scan source code for file or database definitions and data usage identifiers. This information helps to build the initial data model for the warehouse by determining the data requirements contained within the source ODS.

Development Tools   This class of tools is responsible for data cleansing, code generation, data integration, and loading of the data into the final warehouse repository. These tools are also the primary generators of metadata for the warehouse.

Implementation Tools   This category contains the data acquisition tools used to gather, process, clean, replicate, and consolidate the data to be contained within the warehouse. In addition, information storage tools from this category may be employed to assist in loading summarized data from external data sources.

Delivery Tools   Delivery tools assist in the data conversion, data derivation, and reporting for the final delivery platform. This category includes specific tools for querying and reporting and the generation of and access to data glossaries intended to provide end users with the ability to identify what data are actually contained within the warehouse.

Sin #5: Life Cycle Abuse

This sin is the failure of the DW developers to realize the differences between the data warehouse life cycle (DWLC) and the traditional system development life cycle (SDLC) methodologies. Although similar, these two approaches differ in one critical aspect: The DWLC never ends. The life cycle of a data warehouse project is a continuous, ongoing set of activities that flow from initial investigation of DW requirements through data administration and back again. Typically, as each phase of the DW is completed, a new one is started due to new data requirements, additional user groups being identified, and new required sources of data. The DW developers must realize that the project must never end if the warehouse is to remain a viable source of decision-making support.

Sin #6: Ignorance Concerning the Resolution of Data Conflicts

The justification for a new data warehouse initiative is often predicated on the need for greater quality data for decision making within the organization. While this is a laudable objective for a DW project, it is simply the tip of the iceberg with regard to actually putting the warehouse into operation. People and organizations tend naturally to be highly protective and territorial when it comes to their data and associated applications. As a result, a great deal of often tedious analysis must be conducted to determine the best data sources available within the organization. Once these systems have been identified, the conflicts associated with disparate naming conventions, file formats and sizes, and value ranges must be resolved. This process may involve working with the data owners to establish an understanding with regard to future planned or unplanned changes to the source data. Failure to allow sufficient time and resources to resolve data conflicts can stall a warehouse initiative and result in an organizational stalemate that can threaten the success of the project.

Sin #7: Failure to Learn from Mistakes

The ongoing nature of the DWLC suggests that one data warehouse project simply begets another. Because of this, careful documentation of the mistakes made in the first round will directly impact the quality assurance activities of all future projects. By learning from the mistakes of the past, a strong data warehouse with lasting benefits can be built.

11-6 DATA WAREHOUSE TECHNOLOGIES

The real dream of anyone who has suffered through the pre-development-tool days of data warehousing is that someday we will be able to place an order with Wile E. Coyote's favorite supplier, Acme. Seconds later, we will receive a big wooden crate with "Acme Data Warehouse" stenciled on the side with everything we need inside, including batteries.

That day may actually come, but current data warehouse products are still quite a ways from the "Acme" ideal. Today organizations have very little choice but to buy bits and pieces of very complex hardware and software from a number of vendors. Vendors, analysts, and pundits are fond of directing attention away from the product side of data warehouse technologies, wielding platitudes like a bullfighter's red cape. A typical sales pitch by a DW vendor might include "A data warehouse is an architecture, not a product," or "It's a process, not a place," or even something such as "It's 90 percent expertise, 10 percent technology." The translation for all this rhetoric is simple: Good luck making all this stuff work together!

To build a data warehouse that works, developers have to be even more resourceful than a cartoon coyote when it comes to architecture, process, expertise, and dozens of other abstractions. But that, in itself, may still not be enough to guarantee a successful DW environment. The DW investment must be ensured with a thorough evaluation process that probes the promises and pitfalls of integrating data warehouse tools offered by the leading DW vendors.

No one currently offers an end-to-end data warehouse solution, but several companies such as SAS, IBM, Software AG, Information Builders, and Platinum are moving toward that goal, albeit often with glacial momentum. For instance, here is an example of the type of challenges facing one of the current key data warehouse vendors: IBM.

IBM's premier offering, Visual Warehouse, offers good integration if you run under OS/2 but is much less flexible under other leading operating system platforms such as Windows NT and Novell. In addition, Visual Warehouse is, as yet, unable to manage databases beyond the LAN environment. Larger, more robust databases built around DB/2 Parallel Edition, DB2 MVS, and the new AS/400 parallel database (all IBM offerings) have yet to be accommodated by IBM's leading DW product. Although the company claims it is vigorously working on the problems, it is unwilling to offer any specific time horizons that fall within the current millennium. In other words, even the vendors are having trouble making all this work together in harmony.

The good news is that the marketplace is bursting with vendor offerings in the data warehouse arena and, given the plenitude of choices, an organization is likely to find the technology it needs to embark on a DW initiative. The bad news is that the constant state of flux and the high cost of operations make it difficult for the smaller players to stay afloat in this fiercely competitive marketplace, and, as such, the leader board changes daily. Table 11-6 contains a fairly comprehensive listing of the current data warehouse offerings (at the time of this writing, at least).

Table 11-6 Leading Data Warehouse Vendors and Products

DW Vendor	Product Offering(s)
Actuate Software	Report Server, Reporting System, Web Agent
Andyne Computing	GQL, PaBLO, Text Tool
Angoss Software	KnowledgeSEEKER
Aonix	Nomad
Applix	TM1 Server, TM1 Client, TM1 Perspective, TM1 ShowBusiness
AppSource	Wired for OLAP
Arbor Software	Essbase, Essbase Web Gateway
Attar Software	XpertRule Profiler
Belmont Research	CrossGraphs
Brio Technology	BrioQuery Enterprise, brio.web.warehouse
Business Objects	BusinessObjects, BusinessMiner
Carleton	Passport
Cognos	Impromptu, PowerPlay, Scenario
CorVu	Integrated Business Intelligence Suite (IBIS)
Computer Associates	CA-LDM, CA-OpenIngres, Visual Express
Concentric Data Systems	Arpeggio
Data Distilleries B.V.	Data Surveyor
Data Junction	Data Junction, Cambio
Data Management Technologies	Time Machine, RQA-Remote Query Accelerator
DataMind	DataMind
Digital Equipment	Alpha Warehouse
Dimensional Insight	CrossTarget
Enterprise Solutions	InfoCat
European Management Systems	Eureka
Evolutionary Technologies International	ETI-Extract
Harbor Software	HarborLight
Hewlett-Packard	Intelligent Warehouse
Holistic Systems	HOLOS
Hyperion	OLAP, Spider-Man
IBM	Data Propagator, DB2 Database Server, Enterprise Copy Manager, Data Hub for OS/2, Data Hub for Unix, Flow-Mark, DataGuide, Application System, Visualizer family, Intelligent Decision Server, Query Management Facility, Intelligent Miner

(continued)

Table 11-6 Continued

DW Vendor	Product Offering(s)
Informatica	PowerMart
Information Advantage	DecisionSuite, WebOLAP
Information Builders	EDA/Copy Manager, Focus Fusion, Focus Six EIS Edition
Information Discovery	Data Mining Suite
Informix Software	OnLine Dynamic Server-Unix, OnLine Dynamic Server-Windows NT, New Era ViewPoint OnLine Extended Parallel Server, MetaCube, MetaCube Warehouse Manager
InfoSAGE	DECISIVE
Innovative Group	Innovative-Warehouse
Integral Solutions Limited	Clementine
Intersolv	DataDirect Explorer, SmartData
Intrepid Systems	DecisionMaster
IQ Software	IQ/SmartServer, IQ/Objects, Intelligent Query, IQ/Vision
Kenan Systems	Acumate ES
Liant Software	Relativity
Lingo Computer Design	Fiscal Executive Dashboard
Logic Works	Universal Directory
Mayflower Software	Sentinel, Information Catalog
Mercantile Software Systems	IRE Marketing Warehouse
MathSoft	Axum
Microsoft	Microsoft SQL Server
NCR	Teradata
NewGeneration Software	NGS Managed Query Environment
Oberon Software	Prospero
Oracle	Oracle8, Discoverer/2000, Oracle Express Server
Pilot Software	Decision Support Suite, Command Center
Pine Cone Systems	Data Content Tracker
Platinum Technology	InfoRefiner, Info Transport, Fast Load, Data Shopper, InfoReports, Object Administrator, Query Analyzer, Report Facility (PRF), InfoBeacon, Forest & Trees
Postalsoft	Postalsoft Library products
Powersoft	InfoMaker
Praxis International	OmniLoader
Precise Software Solutions	Inspect/SQL

(continued)

11-7 THE FUTURE OF DATA WAREHOUSING

It is both highly likely and highly desirable that as the data warehouse becomes a mature part of an organization's decision support infrastructure it will blend into the fabric of the organization and be as anonymous as the data communication network used to move data from place to place. In other words, once the problems currently associated with an inability to access corporate data are completely resolved, an increased

Table 11-6 Continued

DW Vendor	Product Offering(s)
Prism Solutions	Prism Warehouse Manager, Prism Change Manager, Prism Directory Manager
Progress Software	EnQuiry
QDB Solutions	QDB/Analyze
Red Brick Systems	Red Brick Warehouse 5.0, Red Brick Data Mine Option, Red Brick Data Mine Builder, Red Brick Enterprise Control & Coordination
Reduct Systems	DataLogic/R
ReGenisys	extract:R
Sagent	Sagent Data mart
SAS Institute	SAS Data Warehouse, Warehouse Administrator, SAS System, SAS/MDDB
Seagate Software IMG	Crystal Reports, Crystal Info
SelectStar	StarTrieve
ShowCase	STRATEGY
Siemens-Pyramid	Smart Warehouse
Silicon Graphics	MineSet
Smart Corporation	Smart DB Workbench
Software AG	Intelligon, Passport, SourcePoint, Esperant, ADABAS
Softworks	metaVISION
Spalding Software	DataImport
Speedware	Esperant, EasyReporter, Media
SPSS	SPSS
Sterling Software	Vision:Journey
Sybase	Sybase SQL Server 11, Sybase IQ, Sybase MPP
Syware	DataSync
Tandem	Tandem NonStop
Thinking Machines	Darwin
Torrent Systems	Orchestrate
Trillium Software	Trillium Software System
Visual Numerics	PV-Wave
Vmark Software	uniVerse, DataStage
Wincite Systems	WINCITE
WizSoft	WizWhy

effort to find new ways to utilize those data will emerge. This new focus will bring with it several new challenges. This final section will identify several of these challenges facing data warehousing in the future.

Regulatory Constraints

The power associated with the ability to analyze and extract information from large volumes of disparate data has given rise to the passing of legislation that seeks to protect individuals from abuse by government or commercial entities that have large volumes of data concerning those individuals. Increased fears over covert and overt invasions of privacy will continue to escalate and the ease with which external data sources can be accessed will decline. This tightening of security will require a concerted effort on the part of all users of data sources to craft a workable set of rules and guidelines that will allow for the privacy of individuals to be maintained while simultaneously facilitating the use of large data sets for meaningful analyses.

Storage of Unstructured Data

Currently the modern data warehouse is limited to storage of structured data in the form of records, fields, and databases. Unstructured data, such as multimedia, maps, graphs, pictures, sound, and video files, are rapidly increasing in importance throughout organizations. The need to store, retrieve, and combine these new data types will require a new and expanded data warehouse architecture and interface. In the DW environment of tomorrow, a user may be searching for relationships between different types of products. The DW will contain not only structured data for such analysis but may also allow for the scanning and analysis of the contents of images and audio and video files to facilitate the establishment of such relationships. To bring this level of use and functionality to fruition, vendors of DW applications and tools face a number of technological and practical challenges yet to be explored. Issues including how to manage the storage and retrieval of unstructured data and how to search for specific data items must be addressed and resolved if the DW of tomorrow is to accommodate the technology and data being generated today.

The World Wide Web

As with everything it comes into contact with, the WWW will undoubtedly have a significant impact on data warehousing. The ability to access and transfer large numbers of data relatively easily and economically will make the Internet and the Web ideal vehicles to integrate external data into the warehouse environment. As this happens, issues of data integrity, accuracy, and quality will have to be addressed and resolved. It is conceivable that third-party enterprises will evolve whose sole purpose is to evaluate and rate the quality and integrity of external data sources. Those quality ratings could be used to determine the degree of value to be placed on the integration of a particular source of external data into the data warehouse. Equally conceivable is the use of the quality rating to determine the price to be paid for access to such data; the higher the quality rating, the higher the price.

11-8 CHAPTER SUMMARY

Due to the overwhelming concentration on the automation of processes by business and industry, organizations, no matter how large or small, create enormous numbers of data every day. The biggest problem with this is the difficulty in integrating data generated in a world of unintegrated information systems. With data warehousing comes the ability to ask questions of the data that were previously unaskable and to discover new relationships contained within the data that were previously undiscoverable. The concept has served to reintegrate the data generated by the wide variety of internal and external information systems. In the next chapter, we will build upon our understanding of data warehousing by focusing our attention on methods intended to "mine" the hidden resources contained within the data.

Key Concepts

- The data warehouse is "a collection of integrated, subject-oriented databases designed to support the DSS function (decision support), where each unit of data is non-volatile and relevant to some moment in time" (Inmon 1992a, 5). (11-1)
- The operational data store's function is to store the data for a single, specific set of operational applications. (11-1)
- The data mart is often viewed as a way to gain entry to the realm of data warehouses and to make all the mistakes on a smaller scale. (11-1)
- Characteristics of a data warehouse: (11-1)

  Subject orientation

  Integrated

  Nonvolatile

  Time variant

  Summarized

  Large volume

  Not normalized

  Metadata

  Data sources

- The data warehouse world is primarily void of process design (at least in its classical form) and tends to focus exclusively on issues of data modeling and database design. (11-1)
- There are only two data operations ever performed in the data warehouse: data loading and data access. (11-1)
- A data warehouse architecture is a method by which the overall structure of data, communication, processing, and presentation that exists for end-user computing can be represented. (11-2)
- Three data warehousing typologies: (11-2)

  Virtual data warehouse (point-to-point data warehouse)

  Central data warehouse

  Distributed data warehouse

- Metadata are simply abstractions from data. They are high-level data that provide us with a concise description of lower-level data (data about data). (11-3)
- The "seven deadly sins" of data warehouse implementation. (11-5)

Questions for Review

1. Define each of the following terms:
   Data store
   Data mart
   Metadata
   Subject orientation
   Data integrated
   Time variant
   Nonvolatile
   Chain of abstraction
   Transformation mapping

2. What unique benefits does a data warehouse provide for management at all levels of the firm?

3. What is a data warehouse? How is it better than traditional information-gathering techniques?

4. Describe the data warehouse environment.

5. What are the characteristics of a data warehouse?

6. List and explain the different layers in the data warehouse architecture.

7. What are metadata? Why are metadata so important to a data warehouse?

8. What are the "seven deadly sins" of building a data warehouse?

For Further Discussion

1. The WWW contains a vast amount of information about data warehousing and is, in fact, a data warehouse itself. Viewing the WWW from the perspective of a data warehouse, describe and identify the various warehouse components and consider how an organization might harness the power of the WWW as a useful data warehouse.

2. Proponents of data warehousing state that the concept is highly generalizable and can be used by any industry or knowledge domain. Think of several industries where data warehousing could be useful in improving the management of information. Can you think of any industries where data warehousing would not be applicable?

3. Find an organization in your area that is employing the concept of data warehousing. If possible, have a talk with the warehouse administrator about the trials and tribulations faced during the design and implementation of the warehouse. How did he or she deal with the problems? What problems still exist today?

4. Metadata are everywhere. Find a database of information around your school, work, or home and identify as many pieces of metadata as you can.

CHAPTER

12

Data Mining and
Data Visualization

Learning Objectives

■ Understand the concept of data mining (DM)

■ Realize the evolution of decision support activities from verification to discovery

■ Understand the concept of on-line analytical processing (OLAP) and its rules

■ Learn the two approaches used to conduct multidimensional analysis of data—multidimensional OLAP (MOLAP) and relational OLAP (ROLAP)—and explore the different situations suited for MOLAP and ROLAP architectures

■ Be familiar with the four major categories of processing algorithms and rule approaches used to mine data: classification, association, sequence, and cluster

■ Gain an understanding of current data mining technologies including statistical analysis, neural networks, genetic algorithms, fuzzy logic, and decision trees

■ Learn the general process of knowledge discovery through examples

■ Understand the current limitations and challenges to data mining

■ Understand the history of data visualization and how it can help with decision-making activities

■ Realize the typical applications of data visualization techniques

■ Review several current "siftware" technologies

The National Basketball Association Gets a "Jump" on Data Mining

Anyone who follows professional basketball knows that the Dallas Mavericks are green, and that's not just one of the colors in their uniforms. Like many NBA franchises, the Mavericks are experiencing the growing pains associated with developing young players and building a winning professional basketball program. They aren't likely to earn an NBA championship anytime soon. Assistant coach Bob Salmi knows this.

But he also knows that by the time Michael Jordan retires from the Chicago Bulls, at least 10 NBA teams will have assembled lineups of comparable talent— including, he hopes, the Mavericks. Given this relatively level playing field, how can a coach create a competitive advantage for his team?

One way is with information—specifically, the information gleaned through Advanced Scout, a data mining application for postgame analysis created by IBM for the NBA to showcase the use of the technology in professional sports.

Salmi uses Advanced Scout to mine for patterns in coaching data, such as winning player combinations. Advanced Scout is synchronized with digital video that is time-stamped by a uniform time clock that tabulates all the statistics— such as rebounding, matchups, and scoring—for all NBA games. Once a seemingly successful pattern is discovered, a coach can cue up the digital video to view additional factors that contributed to those combinations: what plays were run, how they were executed and defended, what other players were involved, and so on.

The data mining approach to postgame analysis is much less time consuming than the old manual method of jotting down stats with pencil and paper and forever rewinding the videotape. That process greatly relied on guesswork and a coach's intuition, and often took all night. In contrast, Advanced Scout allows for analysis to be performed in the few hours it takes to fly to the location of the next game.

Advanced Scout is based on a data mining technique written in C++ called attribute focusing, which looks for "interesting" patterns and statistical correlations. The key characteristic of the attribute focusing technique is that it is designed for use by lay people, or "domain experts," rather than professional data analysts. The attribute focusing technique's emphasis on the nontechnical user differentiates it from other methods—such as neural networks, decision trees, and regression analysis—typically used in data mining applications like category management, market-basket analysis, and sequence analysis. The complexity of most software tools for these applications makes them better suited to analysts.

Currently, the NBA is mining data on a per-season basis, but now that coaches have two seasons' worth of experience under their belt, they are ready to expand to historical statistical data, going back with Advanced Scout a number of years. Then coaches can use the results not only for postgame analysis but also for contract negotiations with players.

That perspective was clearly illustrated during the 1997 NBA play-off series between the Orlando Magic and the Miami Heat. Like Bob Salmi, Orlando Magic assistant coach Tom Sterner has worked with Advanced Scout since its beginnings. The Heat eventually won the best-of-five series in a hotly contested fifth game. But without Advanced Scout's data mining, it would likely have ended in a three-game Heat blowout.

"We were beaten so badly in games 1 and 2 at Miami—99-64 in game 1 and 104-87 in game 2," Sterner recalls. "After game 2, we ran our analysis and watched the tape to determine what happened. Advanced Scout gave us some interesting pieces of data."

First, Advanced Scout revealed that the starting backcourt combination of Orlando Magic players Anfernee "Penny" Hardaway and Brian Shaw were −17 in game 2. (Basketball coaches use a plus/minus system based on how many points are scored by or against a team while players are on the court as one indicator of the relative performance of a player or combinations of players.) It also revealed that in the same game the combination of Shaw and point guard Darrell Armstrong—a backup player who usually saw little game time—was +6. Moreover, the combination of Armstrong and Hardaway was +14.

Sterner's conclusion, based on Advanced Scout's analysis: Use Armstrong more in game 3 at Orlando. The results were stunning. "In game 3, with about six or seven minutes left to go in the half, we were down 20 points again," he says. "We brought Darrell into the game, and by the end of the half we were tied, 42-42. By the end of the game, we had won, 88-75. Penny Hardaway had scored 42 points, and Armstrong scored 21. Most importantly, we avoided elimination."

"The coach needs to determine how the information relates to his team— his insight is the art," says Sterner. "Why is Phil Jackson of Chicago successful? Michael Jordan sure helps. But the human element in every team is still important to the success of the team.

"Talent goes a long way to winning. If you have more talent than your opponent, you'll win. When your talent equals theirs, then the competitive edge could be the technology you use to prepare for the game."

Also reinforced is the business case for data mining. A more competitive game is money in the bank for professional sports teams.

"Our fans' faith in the team was restored, and we played two more home games than anybody expected," Sterner says. "That's worth millions of dollars" in terms of the gate, TV advertising, even concession sales. "It's a snowball of positive effects."

askibm@vnet.ibm.com

12-1 A PICTURE IS WORTH A THOUSAND WORDS

The title of this section is, admittedly, an old cliché. We use it often when we need to point out that by looking at something, we can derive more information than by reading or talking about it. Symbolically that may be true, but if it were literally true, I could deliver this book to you in somewhere around 350 pictures and the same message would be delivered as well (if they were the right pictures).

It seems reasonable to assume that a cliché is not intended to be universally applicable but rather applicable under a given set of circumstances. There are times when we find it more useful to articulate with words things that are difficult to express with pictures alone. There are other times when we might use words for making an inquiry so that we may discover something new that is best represented by a picture. In still other situations, a picture is the only method by which certain information can be transmitted effectively (or even at all).

In this chapter, we will explore the new realm of *data mining* and *data visualization*. With the realization of the data warehouse comes the ability to ask questions of the data previously unable to be asked and to discover new relationships contained within the data previously undiscoverable.

What Is Data Mining?

By its simplest definition, *data mining* (DM) is the set of activities used to find new, hidden, or unexpected patterns in data. Using information contained within the data warehouse, data mining can often provide answers to questions about an organization that a decision maker had previously not thought to ask.

An increasingly common synonym for data mining techniques is *knowledge data discovery* (KDD). This more descriptive term applies to all activities and processes associated with discovering useful knowledge from aggregate data. Using a combination of techniques including statistical analysis, neural and fuzzy logic, multidimensional analysis, data visualization, and intelligent agents, KDD can discover highly useful and informative patterns within the data that can be used to develop predictive models of behavior or consequences in a wide variety of knowledge domains.

For example, from using KDD techniques we know that left-handed women tend to buy right-handed golf gloves. This pattern relates a customer's attributes to product sales. It is also known that AT&T's stock price predictably rises at least 2 percent after every three-day slump in the Dow Jones Industrial Average. One can think of several uses for this single piece of information (I know I can).

Another example of KDD at work is the relation of product consumption habits to each other: Men who buy diapers also buy beer; people who buy scuba gear take Australian vacations; people who purchase skim milk also tend to buy whole wheat bread. Finally, the minicase at the beginning of this chapter clearly demonstrates how data mining can be used to assist in play selection in the National Basketball Association. This is just a small sampling of the types of patterns that can be found using KDD techniques. The myriad of potential patterns, however, dictates the need for a wide variety of KDD approaches and technologies to assist in finding them.

Verification versus Discovery

In the past, decision support activities were primarily based on the concept of *verification*. In this sense, a relational database could be queried to provide dynamic answers to well-formed questions. The key issue in verification is that it requires a great deal of a priori knowledge on the part of the decision maker if a suspected relationship is going to be verified by the query. An industry that has made extensive use of verification querying is the gaming, or casino, industry. The host of the casino can use a database of customer characteristics to develop a unique set of classifications for customers. He or she can then enter a new customer's observable or known characteristics into a query to assist in classifying the customer as a high roller, a souvenir buyer, a ticket purchaser, or any number of other categories related to casino services. Although this approach requires the casino host to manage a large volume of known relationships contained within the database, the ability to categorize a new customer has proven highly profitable.

As casinos embrace more sophisticated computer technologies, the concept of verification has evolved into one of *discovery*. By using *siftware,* software that is specifically designed to find new and previously unclassified patterns in data, the casino host can discover new patterns and classifications of customer spending habits that allow for the effective targeting of casino services and events to a specific group of customers.

It is easy to see the vast potential for decision support activities in virtually any domain using KDD. As with any technology, if we are to use KDD effectively, we must first understand the foundations upon which it is based. Therefore, our exploration of the new world of data mining must begin at the beginning: the conception of on-line analytical processing.

12-2 ON-LINE ANALYTICAL PROCESSING

In 1993, E. F. Codd, the acknowledged father of relational databases, introduced the term *on-line analytical processing* (OLAP). Codd suggested that the conventional relational database used for transaction processing had reached its maximum capability with regard to the dimensionality of the views of the data available to the user. He concluded that operational data and operational databases were simply not adequate for answering the types of questions typically posed by managers (a view held by members of the DSS and EIS communities for many years prior to Dr. Codd's revelation). From this conclusion, Codd developed a set of twelve rules for the development and use of multidimensional databases that were intended to facilitate decision makers within an organization in freely manipulating their enterprise data models across many simultaneous dimensions. Table 12-1 summarizes Codd's twelve rules for OLAP.

To date, it does not appear that any implementations exist for which all the rules are strictly obeyed. It has been argued, in fact, that it may not even be possible to implement all twelve rules simultaneously (Gray 1997). More recently, the term *OLAP* has come to represent the broad category of software technology that enables decision

Table 12-1 Codd's Twelve Rules for OLAP

1. Multidimensional view
2. Transparent to the user
3. Accessible
4. Consistent reporting
5. Client-server architecture
6. Generic dimensionality
7. Dynamic sparse matrix handling
8. Multiuser support
9. Cross-dimensional operations
10. Intuitive data manipulation
11. Flexible reporting
12. Unlimited levels of dimension and aggregation

makers to conduct a multidimensional analysis of consolidated enterprise data. Along with this, two new terms have been coined to represent the specific approach used to conduct the analysis: (1) *multidimensional on-line analytical processing* (MOLAP) and (2) *relational on-line analytical processing* (ROLAP).

Multidimensional OLAP — MOLAP

Analyzing data across multiple dimensions is much easier to visualize than to describe. Figure 12-1 shows how sales data might be analyzed across the dimensions of time, product, and market region.

FIGURE 12-1 Multidimensional Analysis of Data

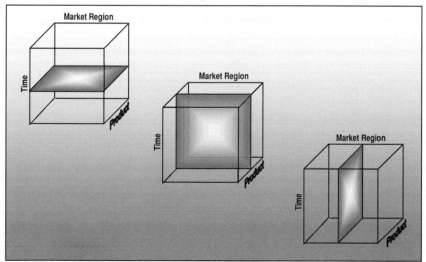

As the figure shows, the data can be viewed as though they were stored in a three-dimensional array, or cube, with each side of the cube representing a single dimension. The intersecting cells of the three dimensions contain the actual data of interest and each of the dimensions can contain one or more members. For example, the market region dimension might have *north, south, east, west,* and *central* as its members and the product dimension would contain members representing each of the products being sold. The members of the time dimension could be *months, quarters, years,* or *specific fiscal periods* that represent particular sales cycles.

While three dimensions of analysis may be useful in a limited setting, most multidimensional analysis is conducted using many more than three dimensions. In fact, MOLAP organizes and analyzes data as an *n-dimensional cube.*[1] The MOLAP cube can be conceptually thought of as a common spreadsheet with two extensions: (1) support for multiple dimensions and (2) support for multiple concurrent users.

In a *hypercube,* the data are stored as a multidimensional array where each cell in the array represents the intersection of all of the dimensions. Using this approach, any number of dimensions may be analyzed simultaneously and any number of multidimensional views of the data can be created. In such a design, however, many cells in the hypercube may not have a value. For example, if the hypercube is analyzing a sales system across *product, region, time, sales volume,* and *ratio of actual versus budgeted sales,* it is conceivable that not all products will have been sold in all stores or regions during any given time period. In general, as the number of dimensions of the hypercube increases, so does the number of potentially empty cells. This phenomenon, called *sparcity,* can significantly increase the storage requirements of a MOLAP hypercube by requiring that storage space be allocated to all cells rather than only to those containing a value. New products are emerging, however, that incorporate special physical storage techniques such as data compression and complex indexing mechanisms that can serve to reduce the negative impact of sparcity and thus ensure the fast access to datacube cells.

One of the current limits to MOLAP is with regard to scalability. Although it is very good at handling summary data it is not particularly well suited to handling large numbers of detailed data. Currently, MOLAP architectures are limited to data warehouses under approximately fifty gigabytes. To accommodate data sets larger than the current limitations and to address issues of scalability, the database world is, once again, embracing the relational model as an alternative approach to MOLAP.

Relational OLAP — ROLAP

In ROLAP, the multidimensional database server is replaced with a large relational database server. This "super" relational database will contain both detailed and summarized data, thus allowing for "drill down" techniques to be applied to the data sets. In those cases where a specific needed summarization is not contained within the database, the ROLAP client tool will build it dynamically. The use of a ROLAP ap-

---

[1] The term *cube* is used to describe the *n*-dimensional space occupied by the data. Once the number of dimensions increases beyond three, however, it is no longer a cube in the geometric sense. A data cube with more than three dimensions is often referred to as a hypercube.

proach is a trade-off between flexibility or scalability and performance. On the plus side, ROLAP implementations have robust administration tools and open SQL interfaces that allow vendors to build tools that are both portable and scalable. The minus side is that ROLAP requires a significantly large number of relational tables to handle the massive volume of data and dimensional relations. This situation manifests itself in significantly degraded performance over MOLAP implementations due to the extreme processor overhead needed for table joins and index processing.[2]

One method being employed to reduce the processing overhead associated with ROLAP is the de-normalization of the tables into a *star schema*. Figure 12-2 illustrates this approach to data organization.

At the center of a star schema is a central *fact table*. This table contains numerical measurements that exist at the intersection of all dimensions. If any combination of dimensions does not yield a value, then no zero value is stored. The facts in the central fact table represent quantities of data that can be aggregated without losing their meaning and need to be described by more than two dimensions (Inmon, Welch, and Glassey 1997). The purpose of a central fact table is to streamline the processing associated with access to the facts contained within the fact table.

Surrounding the central fact table are the *dimension tables*. These tables serve to describe or categorize the data contained in the fact table. The key of the central fact table is a concatenated (compound) key made up of the keys from all of the dimension tables. This results in a row in the fact table for every unique combination of the domains of all the keys of all of the dimension tables (whew!). The bottom line is that using this approach, multidimensional analysis can be performed on data sets larger than the current fifty-gigabyte limit imposed on MOLAP implementations. ROLAP architectures are especially well suited to those situations where dynamic access to combinations of summarized and detailed data is more important than the performance gains offered by the MOLAP approach using only summarized or preconsolidated data.

12-3 TECHNIQUES USED TO MINE THE DATA

With the popularity of data mining growing at a lightning-fast pace, the cadre of new and innovative techniques to mine the warehouse data is burgeoning. Many of the new techniques are refinements of previous methods, and some can truly be classified as major innovations. Because of a lack of standardization across vendors, however, innovations in data mining are often limited to a particular vendor platform and, thus, cannot be used across the board to advance the state of the art. Rather than concentrate on vendor-specific techniques and mining methods, we will focus on developing an understanding of the basic categories of mining techniques currently in use. Re-

---

[2] A *table join* is a basic database operation that links the rows, or records, of two or more tables by one or more columns in each table. *Index processing* involves the creation, maintenance, and use of a lookup table that relates the value of a field in an indexed file to its record in that file. This allows for a lookup to be performed on a field value other than the primary key. Both of these operations require significant amounts of processing power, especially for large databases.

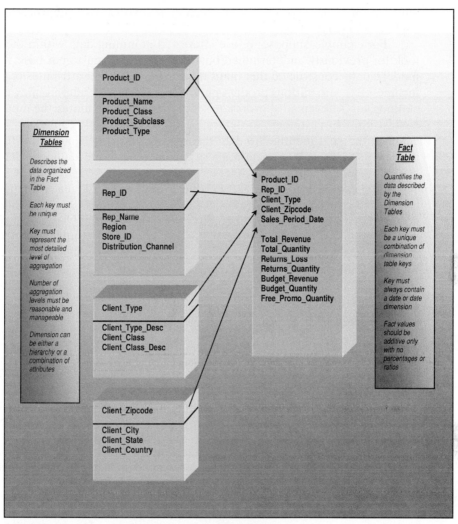

FIGURE 12-2 Typical Star Schema Data Organization

Source: Managing the Data Warehouse, by Inmon, Welch, and Glassey, copyright © 1997 by John Wiley & Sons. Reprinted with permission of John Wiley & Sons, Inc.

gardless of the specific technique, data mining methods may be classified by the function they perform or by the class of application they can be used in. Using this approach, four major categories of processing algorithms and rule approaches emerge: (1) *classification,* (2) *association,* (3) *sequence,* and (4) *cluster.*

Classification

The *classification* approach includes those mining processes that are intended to discover rules that define whether an item or event belongs to a particular subset or class of data. This category of techniques is probably the most broadly applicable to different types of business problems. The technique involves two subprocesses: (1) *building a model* and (2) *predicting classifications.*

For example, suppose we are interested in mining data within the warehouse to look for previously undetermined buying patterns in a customer base. A classification model can be constructed that maps the various customer attributes (e.g., age, gender, income, etc.) with various product purchases (e.g., luxury automobiles, concert tickets, clothing, etc.). Given an appropriate set of predicting attributes, the model can be used against a list of customers to determine those most likely to make a particular purchase in the next month. The data records isolated by the classification model could then be used to feed a selection query against a customer database that could generate a targeted promotional contact or mailing list.

Other typical questions of classification include "Which households will likely respond to a forthcoming direct mail campaign?"; "Which stocks in this portfolio will go up after the next major stock market correction?"; and "Which insurance claims currently under process are most likely fraudulent?" By building and refining a predictive model of the business problem, data mining classification methods can often provide useful and highly accurate answers to questions such as these.

Generally speaking, classification methods develop a model composed of common IF-THEN rules.[3] Because the idea is to gain insight into probable members of a class, the standard approach to determining whether a specific rule is satisfied is relaxed to allow for three possible conditions and, thus, three possible subclasses:

1. ***Exact rule.*** Permits no exceptions—that is, each **IF** object is an exact element of the **THEN** class. This approach creates the highest probability class of members: 100 percent probability.

2. ***Strong rule.*** Some exceptions allowed but an acceptable range of exceptions is prescribed. This approach creates a subclass of strong probability members: 90 to 100 percent probability.

3. ***Probabilistic rule.*** Relates the conditional probability $P(\textbf{THEN}|\textbf{IF})$ to the probability $P(\textbf{THEN})$. This approach creates a measured probability subclass of members: X percent probability.

Association

Techniques that employ *association* or *linkage analysis* search all details or transactions from operational systems for patterns that have a high probability of repetition. This approach results in the development of an associative algorithm that includes the rules that will correlate one set of events or items with another set of events or items. Patterns derived from the algorithm are generally expressed such as "Eighty-three percent of all records that contain items A, B, and C also contain items D and E." The specific percentage supplied by the associative algorithm is referred to as the *confidence factor of the rule.* Associations can involve any number of items on either side of the rule.

A common example of the use of association methods is *market basket analysis.* Using a linkage approach, a retailer can mine the data generated by a point-of-sale

---

[3] See chapter 8 for a review of rule-based reasoning.

system such as is typically a part of the price scanner you are familiar with at the grocery store. By analyzing the products contained in a purchaser's basket and then using an associative algorithm to compare hundreds of thousands of baskets, specific product affinities can be derived. Example outcomes of an association method might be "Twenty-nine percent of the time that the brand X blender is sold, the customer also buys a set of kitchen tumblers," or "Sixty-eight percent of the time that a customer buys beverages, he or she also buys pretzels." This type of information can be used to determine the location and content of promotional or end-of-aisle displays (such as a ten-foot-high display of pretzels at the end of the aisle where the beverages are sold). While common associations such as yogurt and skim milk or wine and cheese are relatively intuitive, data mining using a linkage approach can find less obvious, yet nonetheless useful, associations such as men who buy diapers also buy beer (really, this is true).

Sequence

Sequencing or *time-series analysis* methods are used to relate events in time, such as the prediction of interest rate fluctuations or stock performance, based on a series of preceding events. Through this analysis, various hidden trends can be discovered that are often highly predictive of future events.

Common applications of sequence analysis methods can be found in the direct mail industry. Sequences are often analyzed as they relate to a specific customer or group of customers. Using this information, a catalog containing specific product types can be target mailed to a customer associated with a known sequence of purchases. For example, a known buying sequence might be that parents tend to buy promotional toys associated with a particular movie within two weeks after renting the movie. This sequence would suggest that a flyer campaign for promotional toys should be linked to customer lists created as a result of movie rentals. Another sequential pattern might be the determination of a set of purchases that frequently precedes the purchase of a microwave oven. By monitoring buying patterns of customers, particularly using credit card transactions, highly targeted mailing lists can be generated to focus promotions and marketing campaigns on those customers most likely to be persuaded to buy.

One additional technique within this class focuses on the determination of *similar sequences.* In a typical sequential analysis, the output is a pattern representing a sequence of events over time. In a similar sequential analysis, however, the goal is to find groups of timed sequences. One of the most common examples of this approach is a large retailer using a similar sequence approach to find unrelated departments with similar sales streams. This information can be used to determine more profitable promotions, customer flow, or store layouts. Similar sequence techniques have also been successfully used in investment portfolio balancing by identifying stocks or securities with similar price movements.

Cluster

There are some cases where it is difficult or impossible to define the parameters of a class of data to be analyzed. In these cases, *clustering* methods can be used to create partitions so that all members of each set are similar according to some metric or set of metrics. A cluster is simply a set of objects grouped together by virtue of their similarity or proximity to each other. For instance, a clustering approach might be used to mine credit card purchase data to discover that meals charged on a business-issued gold card are typically purchased on weekdays and have a mean value of greater than $250, whereas meals purchased using a personal platinum card occur predominately on weekends, have a mean value of $175, and include a bottle of wine more than 65 percent of the time.

Clustering processes can be based on a particular event, such as the cancellation of a credit card by a customer. By analyzing the characteristics of members of this class, clustering might derive certain rules that could assist the credit card issuer in reducing the number of card cancellations in the future.

Data Mining Technologies

By now you should begin to realize the potential power of data mining with regard to providing new answers to old questions and to the development of new knowledge and understanding through discovery. The types of questions that can be asked and answered are unlimited and the methodologies used to answer these questions are diverse and growing in number. Just as there are many techniques available to assist in mining the data, there are numerous technologies that can be deployed in building the mining models. Most of these technologies have been covered in greater detail in other chapters of the text but, for purposes of continuity, they are mentioned briefly again here.

Statistical Analysis

Statistical analysis, despite requiring specialized capabilities to truly grasp all its importance, is the most mature of all data mining technologies and is the easiest to understand. If 69 percent of people who purchase product X using a credit card also purchase product Y, and product Y never sells independently, then it is relatively easy to build a model predicting product Y sales with an accuracy of 69 percent. Of greater interest, of course, is to be able to predict the sales of product X.

At this point, the traditional statistical analysis methods and data mining methods begin to diverge. Traditional statistical modeling techniques such as *regression analysis* are fine for building linear models that describe predictable data points; however, complex data patterns are often not linear in nature. Further, traditional statistical methods can frequently be negatively affected or problematic if the data are not well described by a linear model or if the data set contains a large number of outliers.[4] Although they are beyond the scope of this text to discuss or enumerate, suffice it to say that data mining requires the use of statistical techniques capable of accommodating the conditions of nonlinearity, multiple outliers, and nonnumerical data typically found in a data warehouse environment.

---

[4] An *outlier* is a data point that is unusually distant from the mean of the data set. In some cases, an outlier may represent simply an extremely low probability data point. In other cases, it may be an indicator of a more complex relationship than is currently being modeled or assumed.

Neural Networks, Genetic Algorithms, and Fuzzy Logic

As discussed in chapter 10, *neural networks* are an attempt to mirror the way the human brain works in recognizing patterns by developing mathematical structures with the ability to learn. In this way it is possible to develop nonlinear predictive models that "learn" by studying combinations of variables and how different combinations affect data sets. Machine learning techniques, such as genetic algorithms and fuzzy logic, have the remarkable ability to derive meaning from complicated and imprecise data and can extract patterns from and detect trends within the data that are far too complex to be noticed by either humans or more conventional automated analysis techniques. Because of this ability, neural computing and machine learning technologies have broad applicability to the world of data mining and, thus, to a wide variety of complex business problems.

Decision Trees

Recall from our discussion of problem-structuring tools in chapter 5, *decision trees* are a conceptually simple mathematical method of following the effect each event, or decision, has on successive events. For example, in a simple decision tree involving the decisions associated with performing an activity indoors or outdoors, if "indoors" is selected from the initial choice set, then the next decision will more likely be something like "upstairs/downstairs" than "sun/shade." By continually breaking data sets into separate, smaller groups, a predictive model can be built. Decision trees are often used in data mining applications to assist in the classification of items or events contained within the warehouse.

The Knowledge Discovery Search Process

While there are no rules for mining a data warehouse and each inquiry must be considered individually, there are, nonetheless, some guidelines that can be established. Table 12-2 contains the sequence of events that describes a generic data mining "expedition."

Table 12-2 General Process of Knowledge Discovery

- Select a topic for study: Develop an understanding of the business problem.
- Identify a target data set(s): Determine what data are relevant for study.
- Clean and preprocess the data: Identify missing data fields, data noise, etc.
- Build a data model: Use the mining software to construct a mathematical model "explaining" the varying impacts of the inputs on the outputs.
- Mine the data: Search for patterns of interest (not all patterns identified by the model will be "interesting").
- Interpret and refine: Review the results of the initial mining and use the results to refine the model, as necessary, to gain additional insight into identified patterns of interest.
- Predict: Use the refined model to predict the output for a set of inputs where the output is not yet known.
- Share the model: Once validated, make the model available to other warehouse users.

One way to better understand the data mining process is to actually see it in operation. Although we can't do that completely within the pages of a book, we can look at examples of some queries that might be constructed during a typical data mining session.

For example, a typical model-building SQL statement might take the following form:

```
CREATE MODEL promo_list
income character input,age integer input . . . respond character output)
```

Note the similarity of the **CREATE MODEL** statement to the standard SQL **CREATE TABLE** statement. Data mining software designers have done this intentionally because the newly created model is actually the same as a table or a view available for subsequent SQL processing. The **CREATE MODEL** statement above creates a model that will relate various *inputs,* such as level of income (*high, mid,* or *low*) and age, to a desired *output,* such as a direct mail response rate (respond = *yes* or *no*). Bear in mind that this example is purposely simplistic and that there is no practical limit on the number or type of inputs that could be considered. A real application would typically include from several dozen to a hundred or more such attributes.

To provide the model with a data set to process it is simply a matter of inserting the data into the model using a standard SQL statement such as:

```
INSERT INTO mail_list SELECT income,age, respond
FROM client_list,
WHERE mail = "Q2_Southeast"
```

This process automatically creates additional views of the model table that can be used for understanding the relationships and predicting future outcomes (**mail_list_UNDERSTAND and mail_list_PREDICT** tables). Once the model is built, it represents the best information the decision maker has about the profile of people who respond to the organization's direct mail campaigns. To view the information generated by the model, a SQL statement is constructed to select from the table:

```
SELECT * FROM mail_list_UNDERSTAND
      WHERE input_column_name = "income" and
      input_column_value = "high" and
      output_column_name = "respond"
      and output_column_value = "yes"

ORDER BY importance, conjunctionid
```

In order to generate a mailing list for a new regional promotion in Miami, a SQL statement could be constructed to access the PREDICT table for just the records where a positive response is predicted:

```
SELECT name FROM client_list,mail_list_PREDICT
WHERE city = "Miami" AND respond = "yes"
```

Notice that the model and its associated views, once created, are treated simply as tables in the database. They can be viewed and joined as appropriate to deliver the most benefit from the data mining process. Also, the model tables are available to anyone with access to the warehouse and the ability to generate SQL, not just the person who created them. Other users may choose to use this model as a template, but modify it slightly for their custom use. Although the actual process is much more involved than this example, the same basic steps are followed and the same types of SQL statements are constructed.

12-4 CURRENT LIMITATIONS AND CHALLENGES TO DATA MINING

It is important to remember that despite the potential power and value of data mining to the business world, it is still a new and underdeveloped field. Most current developers of commercial data mining products are relatively small and generally have their products purchased or licensed by larger, more established software vendors for incorporation into existing software products. Significant limitations currently face the advancement of data mining products. Several of these challenges are identified in this section.

Identification of Missing Information

Until such time as data mining becomes commonplace and legacy application databases are replaced by newer "warehouse friendly" databases, warehouse designers will continue to be faced with the conversion of data from an ODS into a homogenous form for the warehouse. This transformation, albeit quite thorough and technologically sophisticated, cannot as yet detect whether the original data set contains the necessary elements for effective mining. For example, the data contained in an ODS are normally not inclusive of domain knowledge. In other words, not all knowledge about a particular application domain is present in the data. We know from past discussion that the data within an ODS are normally limited to those which are needed by the operational application associated with that database. Even though application-relevant queries can be successfully made on the data, more generalizable queries may not be possible. Data mining applications need to include mechanisms for "inventorying" the data sets so that a determination of sufficiency in attributes can be made prior to loading the data into the warehouse. For instance, if it is known that decision makers may wish to diagnose potential cases of malaria from a patient database, it is also known that all patient data sets loaded into the warehouse must include the patient's red blood cell count. Without these data, no diagnosis can be effectively made.

Data Noise and Missing Values

Virtually all operational data bases are contaminated to some degree by errors. Data attributes that rely on subjective measurements or judgments can give rise to errors so significant that some examples may even be misclassified. When error exists in either the values of the attributes or the classification of data, we refer to this as *data noise*. Mining applications must begin to address the problem of data noise as it can have a debilitating effect on the overall accuracy of rules generated from the data. Currently, data mining systems are limited to the treatment of noise via statistical techniques that rely on known distributions of data noise. Future systems must incorporate more sophisticated mechanisms for treating missing or noisy data that include *inference of missing values, Bayesian techniques for averaging over the missing values,* and other methods of data inference.

Large Databases and High Dimensionality

Operational databases are inherently large and dynamic; their contents are ever changing as data are added, modified, or removed. Rules derived from a data set at one moment in time may become less accurate as the data change. This need for timeliness of the data creates a parallel need for increased dimensionality of the data for purposes of discovery. In other words, to ensure that discovered patterns are not "local" to a given time period, data patterns must be constantly updated by an ever increasing set of time-sensitive data values. This creates a problem space of significant breadth and depth that requires increasingly greater computing power to search. The spiraling nature of this problem must be addressed by future discovery applications that can parse up the problem space into smaller more manageable chunks without losing any of the intrinsic attributes of the data contained therein.

12-5 DATA VISUALIZATION — "SEEING" THE DATA

Data visualization is the process by which numerical data are converted into meaningful images. The raw data may come from any number of different sources, including satellite photos, undersea sonic measurements, surveys, or computer simulations, to name just a few. Typically, these sources create data that are difficult to interpret because of the overwhelming quantity and complexity of information and the embedded patterns. The human brain is capable of processing a significant amount of visual information, instantly recognizing millions of different physical objects. Data visualization techniques are intended to assist in analyzing complex data sets by mapping physical properties to the data, thus taking advantage of human visual systems. Reflectance and other lighting effects, color, direction and size of shadows, relative sizes of and distances between objects, speed, curvature, and transparency are just a small sample of the characteristics that are often used to help visualize data.

For example, table 12-3 contains an example of some real-life weather balloon data. As you can see, our ability to extract any useful information from looking at the numbers is virtually nonexistent.

Using a data visualization technique that allows for the creation of a three-dimensional model of the sensor data reveals the shape in figure 12-3. The various shadings contained within the figure indicate relative degrees of thunderstorm activity with the darkest portions of the figure indicating the most violent storm activity.[5]

---

[5] Normally data visualization images are rendered in color so that colors, rather than shades of gray, can be used as data value indicators. Because we are limited to a grayscale medium for this text, we will determine data values using relative shades of gray.

Table 12-3 Sample Weather Sensor Data

Offset	X	Y	Z	Vector
0.000000	−17.833000	6.661000	0.011000	−0.118000
0.000000	−17.773001	6.683000	0.015000	−0.122000
0.000000	−17.673000	6.718000	0.009000	−0.143000
0.000000	−17.563999	6.757000	0.008000	−0.163000
0.000000	−17.461000	6.802000	0.011000	−0.165000
0.000000	−17.375000	6.865000	0.012000	−0.149000
0.000000	−17.297001	6.940000	0.009000	−0.127000
0.000000	−17.239000	7.016000	0.010000	−0.114000
0.000000	−17.200001	7.091000	0.018000	−0.116000
0.000000	−17.170000	7.167000	0.030000	−0.133000
0.000000	−17.169001	7.256000	0.050000	−0.148000
0.000000	−17.187000	7.345000	0.064000	−0.152000
0.000000	−17.226000	7.429000	0.074000	−0.153000
0.000000	−17.290001	7.509000	0.088000	−0.152000
0.000000	−17.375999	7.583000	0.106000	−0.146000
0.000000	−17.488001	7.645000	0.112000	−0.145000
0.000000	−17.620001	7.692000	0.118000	−0.156000
0.000000	−17.768000	7.724000	0.126000	−0.158000
0.000000	−17.931000	7.737000	0.133000	−0.143000
0.000000	−18.106001	7.736000	0.128000	−0.134000
0.000000	−18.284000	7.719000	0.121000	−0.132000
0.000000	−18.450001	7.688000	0.121000	−0.129000

FIGURE 12-3 Data Visualization of Weather Sensor Data Depicting Storm Cell Activity

The ability to create multidimensional structures and models from raw data is one of the most important innovations in the realm of decision support technologies. In this section we continue our discussion (begun in section 12-2) of multidimensional analysis and examine the visualization of data across *n* dimensions.

A Bit of History

The early concepts of data visualization originated in the statistical and scientific disciplines. Most of the early work involved a series of two-dimensional analyses of multidimensional or multivariate data sets. Such analyses involved the use of static images and graphs that could then be sequenced to effect a quasi-layering of the data across dimensions.

Much of the advancement in data visualization can be credited to the National Center for Supercomputing Applications (NCSA) at the University of Illinois at Champaign-Urbana. One of the first practical applications of multidimensional data analysis was the Los Angeles smog project conducted by NCSA. By creating a computer animation of smog data superimposed over a three-dimensional map of the Los Angeles basin, NCSA was able to pinpoint locations of major contributors to pollution and to accurately predict smog levels and movement over a wide area of the basin.

Some of the newest developments in data visualization have come from the work conducted at Xerox PARC in the area of virtual reality. Three-dimensional visualization programs allow the user to "fly through" large data sets, view the data from infinite angles, and examine and rearrange virtual object representations of the data interactively. Military and industrial simulations are two examples of the practical application of these innovative data analysis methods. Computers can be used to display realistic visuals of tank combat in urban areas or large tankers docking in busy harbors, thus allowing for learning through experience and avoiding the messy cleanup associated with mistakes made during the early phases of training.

Human Visual Perception and Data Visualization

If you were to go outside right now, your sense of vision would immediately detect a variety of objects—automobiles, buildings, people, trees, dogs—all organized in a neatly coherent and meaningful framework. Your brain would be processing all of these objects by assembling edges, movements, and distances into multidimensional wholes for which you would seamlessly retrieve identities and labels. This apparently effortless processing is both continuous and subconscious.

Data visualization is so powerful not only because the human visual cortex dominates our perception but because the process of converting objects into information occurs so quickly. Using data visualization, massive amounts of information can be presented, thus accelerating the identification of hidden patterns contained within the data. Stop for a moment and contrast how easily you processed the image presented in figure 12-3 with how difficult it was to process the rows and columns in table 12-3, and you will immediately realize the value of data visualization as an analytical tool.

Applying the old adage of a picture being worth a thousand words, we may better come to appreciate the value of data visualization by simply looking at several examples of complex data sets from a variety of knowledge domains represented in visual form.

The graphic in figure 12-4 represents a model of a dynamic data set related to the connectivity, relative throughput, and usage of a private global computer network. The lightest shaded lines connecting the nodes indicate the lowest values of throughput and the darkest shades indicate the highest values. The relative vertical size of each of the ground-based and satellite-based nodes represents the current number of active processes or users accessing that node. While this figure is a static representation of network activity, these data could be easily converted into a dynamic animation of the network, which would allow analysts to see patterns of usage over time and indications of peak or overload conditions at a given node.

Figure 12-5 is a static screenshot of an interactive visualization of the multiple variables affecting the monitoring of a natural gas pipeline. The underlying map and pipeline network diagram shows each of the compressor stations, with the total flow through each station represented by the height of each station. Although not easily detectable in grayscale, the large station in the foreground indicates an alert condition (shown in bright red in a color rendering), in this case highlighting a station with a particularly high flow volume. Drill down permits the operator to explore the situation—pointing to a station elicits a pop-up text report of all the underlying data, or pop-up charts and graphs, or detailed graphics, such as the state of each turbine within the station, shown as small, light-colored bars on top of the station.

The visualization in figure 12-6 shows the benefit that three-dimensional representation can have on the most mundane printed reports. Instead of seeing just a yield

FIGURE 12-4 Data Visualization of Global Private Computer Network Activity

FIGURE 12-5 Natural Gas Pipeline Analysis

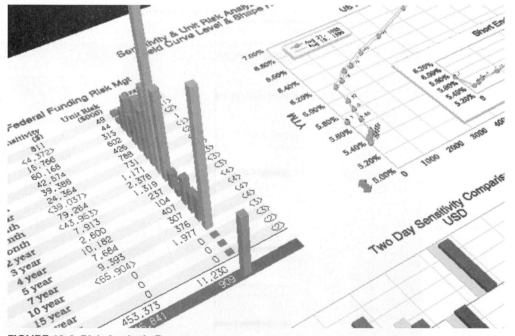

FIGURE 12-6 Risk Analysis Report

curve and the overnight impact on the portfolio, the manager is enticed by an interactive yield curve to partake in "what-if" interactions, without having to wait for reports detailing various scenarios.

If you have ever received one of those telephone survey calls around dinnertime or during the most exciting part of a televised sporting event or movie then you know how annoying they can be. Your opinions are, nonetheless, important and the process of polling is often quite expensive. But often, the subject of the poll, while interesting to the pollster, is not something you are particularly interested in, and the pollster must randomly call thousands of homes until enough interested parties have expressed their opinions. Using data visualization, however, a polling application could be developed that would allow people to participate on only those issues that they feel strongly about. Consider the following scenario: A new poll question is advertised on TV or radio with a 1-800 phone number. Interested voters call the 1-800 number and press 1, 2, or 3 based on whether their vote is *yes, no,* or *other.* A database correlates the votes and can even verify through caller identification that no originating phone number votes twice. The data visualization application converts the collected opinion data into a three-dimensional map of the calling area and depicts the frequency of answers as different shaded vertical bars (such as illustrated in figure 12-7). The user clicks on the area that he or she is interested in to see the results in that area and can successively click until he or she gets down to poll results by districts.

FIGURE 12-7 Interactive Telephone Polling Discovery

Geographical Information Systems

A *geographic information system* (GIS) is a special-purpose digital database in which a common spatial coordinate system is the primary means of reference. Comprehensive GISs require a means of (1) *data input,* from maps, aerial photos, satellites, surveys, and other sources, (2) *data storage,* retrieval, and query, (3) *data transformation,* analysis, and modeling, including spatial statistics, and (4) *data reporting,* such as maps, reports, and plans.

Many people have offered a definition of GIS. In those definitions emphasis is placed on various aspects of the GIS. Some miss the true power of the GIS—that is, its ability to integrate information and to help in making decisions—but all include the essential features of spatial references and data analysis.

For the purposes of this text, we define a GIS as follows: a system of hardware, software, and procedures designed to support the capture, management, manipulation, analysis, modeling, and display of spatially-referenced data for solving complex planning and management problems.

In other words, a GIS is both a database system with specific capabilities for spatially referenced data and a set of operations for working with those data.

Spatial Data

Spatial data are elements that can be stored in map form. These elements correspond to a uniquely defined location on the Earth's surface. There are three basic components to spatial data: *points, lines,* and *polygons.*

- *Points.* Points are single locations in two- or three-dimensional space. Example: The dot representing a city on a map of the United States.
- *Lines.* Lines can be isolated, within a tree structure, or elements of a network structure. Example: River or road systems.
- *Polygons.* Polygons can be isolated, adjacent, or nested. Example: State boundaries or contour lines on a map.

Attribute Data

Along with spatial data, a GIS must be able to handle *attribute data* as well. Simply put, attribute data are the description of the spatial data seen on a map. For example, a map of Pittsburgh, Pennsylvania, will have corresponding "attribute" data that describe it such as elevation numbers, land use designations, and boundary information. This information is usually kept in tabular form, managed as a normal database. If something on that map changes (for example, city zoning areas), the attribute data can be modified, and the map will reflect the changes.

The GIS is often referred to as the "spreadsheet of the 1990s." As the computer spreadsheet changed the way people organized and used information in the 1980s, so is the GIS doing the same thing today, though in a much more powerful way. The GIS facilitates wise use of limited resources by clarifying characteristics and patterns over space.

Examples of decision-making scenarios where a GIS may be appropriate include the following:

- Does it make sense to put a megamall here?
- Should legislative district boundaries go here or there?
- Do we expand the existing airport here or build a new one there?
- Will there be enough schools for students here in ten years?
- Which pockets of endangered environment should we protect?
- What is the impact of waste facilities on local health patterns?
- Where might restocking of native species be environmentally wise?
- Are we adequately prepared to service the local and surrounding population in the event of various possible disasters?

Applications of Data Visualization Techniques

We live in an age of fierce competition and ever-increasing needs for more and faster information. The power of data visualization is one response to meeting these needs and it appears that its value is generalizable across a wide variety of application domains. Currently, industries ranging from banking, where data visualization is used in credit scoring and risk analysis, to government, where data visualization is used in fraud analysis and drug enforcement, are making effective use of available data visualization techniques and applications.

Table 12-4 contains a brief listing of typical data visualization business applications.

12-6 SIFTWARE TECHNOLOGIES

Although the market is in a constant state of flux with the entry and exit of data visualization product vendors on a daily basis, a number of vendors have begun to establish a stronghold in the marketplace and appear to be developing a significant brand loyalty among their customers. This next section briefly outlines the characteristics of several of the more prominent players in the field.

Red Brick

Red Brick has a number of cases to present in support of the use of its data mining technology, two of which are H.E.B. and Hewlett-Packard.

H.E.B., of San Antonio, Texas, (sales of approximately $4.5 billion, 225 stores, 50,000 employees) was able to bring about a category management application from design to rollout in under nine months because it kept the requirements simple and had database support from Red Brick and server support from Hewlett-Packard Company.

Previously, the marketing information department would take ad hoc requests for information from users, write a program to extract the information, and return the information to the user a week or so later—not timely enough for most business decisions and in some cases not what the user really wanted in the first place.

The organization implemented a change to category management in 1990. The category manager is characterized as the "CEO" of the category with profit and loss

Table 12-4 Typical Applications of Data Visualization Techniques

Retail Banking
- Customer/product cross-selling analysis
- Electronic banking management
- Credit risk
- Product pricing strategy

Government
- Budget analysis
- Resource management
- Economic analysis
- Fraud detection and drug trafficking analysis

Insurance
- Asset/liability management
- Actuarial modeling
- Workflow management and analysis

Health Care and Medicine
- Claims analysis
- Patient behavior analysis
- Therapy analysis

Telecommunications
- Call-center management
- Network operations management
- Service policy analysis
- Market analysis
- Loading pattern analysis

Transportation
- Yield analysis
- Asset utilization
- Fleet management

Capital Markets
- Risk assessment
- Derivatives trading
- Institutional sales systems
- Retail marketing

Asset Management
- Portfolio performance analysis
- Asset allocation
- Portfolio optimization

responsibilities, final decision over which products to buy and which to delete, and where the products are to be located on the shelves. The category manager also decides which stores get which products. Although H.E.B. stores are only within the state of Texas, it is a diverse market where some stores near Mexico have 98 percent Hispanic customers while suburban Dallas stores may have only 2 percent Hispanic customers. The change to category management centralized all merchandising and marketing decisions, removing these decisions from the stores.

As category managers built up their negotiating skills, technical skills, and partnering skills over three years, the need for more timely decision support information grew. An enterprise-wide survey of users to determine requirements took until September 1993. The final system was delivered in March 1994 and the application has been up and running without problems since then. The company maintains two years of data by week, by item (257,000 universal product codes, or UPCs), and by store. This is about 400 million detail records. Summary files are only maintained by time and total company, which can be an advantage.

The goal was to have all queries answered in four seconds, but some trend reports dealing with large groups of items over long time periods take thirty to forty seconds. The users are not always technically oriented, so the design is intentionally simple. The system is ad hoc to the extent that the user can specify time, place, and product.

H.E.B. feels that category managers are now making fact-based decisions to determine which products to put in which stores, how much product to send to a store, and the proper product mix. Historically, buyers usually were promoted from the stores and had considerable product knowledge, whereas now category managers are coming from other operational areas such as finance and human resources. This is possible because the system gives people with limited product knowledge the equivalent of years of experience.

Another example of Red Brick technology in the marketplace can be found at Hewlett-Packard, a premier global provider of hardware systems. HP is known for manufacturing high-quality products, but to maintain its reputation it depends on delivering service and support through and after product delivery.

The Worldwide Customer Support Organization (WCSO) within Hewlett-Packard is responsible for providing support services to its hardware and software customers. For several years, the WCSO has used a data warehouse of financial, account, product, and service contract information to support decision making. WCSO Information Management is responsible for developing and supporting this data warehouse.

Until 1994, WCSO Information Management supported business information queries with a data warehouse architecture based on two HP3000/Allbase systems and an IBM DB2 system. This was a first attempt at collecting, integrating, and storing data related to customer support for decision-making purposes. As WCSO users increasingly relied upon the data warehouse, they began to demand better performance, additional data coverage, and more timely data availability.

The warehouse architecture did not keep pace with the increased requirements from WCSO users. Users wanted to get information quickly. Both load and query performance were directly impacted as more data were added. WCSO decided to investigate other warehouse alternatives with the aim of finding a new data warehouse that would significantly improve load/query performance, be more cost effective, and support large amounts of data without sacrificing performance.

HP chose to use Red Brick software on an HP9000 and the project began with the consolidation of the existing three databases into a single data warehouse named Discovery. This downsizing provided significant cost savings and increased resource efficiencies in managing and supporting the warehouse environment. Today, Discovery supports approximately 250 marketing, finance, and administration users in the Americas, Europe, and Asia-Pacific regions. They pull query results into their desktop report writers, load information into worksheets, or use the data to feed executive information systems. User satisfaction has risen dramatically due to Discovery's vastly improved performance and remodeled business views.

Oracle

For large-scale data mining, Oracle on the SP2 offers its users robust functionality and excellent performance. Data spread across multiple SP2 processor nodes are treated as a single image affording exceptionally fast access to very large databases. Oracle Parallel Query allows multiple users to submit complex queries at the same time. Individual complex queries can be broken down and processed across several processing nodes simultaneously. Execution time can be reduced from overnight to hours or minutes, enabling organizations to make better business decisions faster.

Oracle offers products that help customers create, administer, and use their data warehouse. Oracle has a large suite of connectivity products that provide transparent access to many popular mainframe databases and allow customers to move data from legacy mainframe applications into the data warehouse on the SP2.

Some of the examples of its technology at work are as follows:

- John Alden Insurance, based in Miami, Florida, is using Oracle Parallel Query on the SP2 to mine health care information and it has seen orders-of-magnitude improvements in response time for typical business queries.

- ShopKo Stores, a $2-billion, Wisconsin-based mass merchandise chain that operates 128 stores throughout the Midwest and Northeast, chose the SP2 to meet its current and projected needs for both data mining and mission-critical merchandising applications.

- Pacific Bell and U.S. West, both telecommunications providers, are using the Oracle Warehouse, introduced in 1995, to improve their ability to track customers and identify new service needs. Pacific Bell's data warehouse provides a common set of summarized and compressed information to base decision support systems. The first system is designed to analyze product profitability, and similar decision support systems are in development for marketing, capital investment, procurement, and two additional financial systems.

- U.S. West has implemented a warehousing system to analyze intra–area code calling data from its three operating companies. Running Oracle7 Release 7.2 on a nine-CPU symmetric multiprocessing system from Pyramid, U.S. West's initial centralized architecture supports use by twenty executives and marketing specialists. The next phase will deliver warehouse access to more than four hundred service representatives, which will ultimately be expanded up to forty-five hundred service representatives.

Informix — Data Warehousing

As a major player in the field of data mining, Informix has a number of success stories. For example, Associated Grocers, one of the leading cooperative grocery wholesalers in the northwest United States, with revenues of $1.2 billion, is replacing its traditional mainframe environment with a three-tiered client/server architecture based on Informix database technology. The new system's advanced applications have cut order-fulfillment times in half, reduced inventory carrying costs, and enabled the company to offer its 350 independent grocers greater selection at a lower cost.

In 1991, Associated Grocers embarked on a phased transition from its mainframe-based information system to open systems. The company initially used IBM RS/6000 hardware, and has since included Hewlett-Packard and NCR. In evaluating relational database management systems, Associated Grocers developed a checklist of requirements including education/training, scalability, technical support, solid customer references, and future product direction.

After selecting Informix as its companywide database standard, Associated Grocers then assembled the rest of its system architecture using a three-tier model. On tier one, the "client" presentation layer, graphical user interfaces are developed using Microsoft Windows and Visual Basic. Tier two, based on Hewlett-Packard hardware, runs Micro Focus COBOL applications on top of the OEC Developer Package from Open Environment Corporation. This helps Associated Grocers develop DCE-compliant applications. The third layer, the data layer, is the INFORMIX-OnLine database.

Associated Grocers' pilot Informix-based application provides real-time inventory information for its deli warehouse. In the past, merchandise was received manually, and pertinent product information was later keyed into Associated Grocers' financial system. In contrast, the new system recognizes merchandise right at the receiving dock. Handheld radio frequency devices allow merchandise to be immediately scanned into the Informix database. Product is assigned to a warehouse location and its expiration date is noted. When orders are filled, products with the earliest expiration dates are shipped first.

An extension to the deli warehouse system is a new postbilling system, which is the ability to separate physical and financial inventory. Previously, merchandise could not be released for sale until the financial systems had been updated, which typically occurred over night. The new Informix-based system allows for immediate sale and distribution of recently received merchandise.

A third Informix-based application enables Associated Grocers to sell unique items economically—that is, slow-moving merchandise that is ordered monthly versus daily. Rather than incurring the high cost to warehouse these items, Associated Grocers created a direct link to outside specialty warehouses to supply the needed items on demand. Independent stores simply order the merchandise from Associated Grocers. The order goes into Associated Grocers' billing system, then gets transmitted to the specialty warehouse, which immediately ships the merchandise to Associated Grocers. The specialty items are loaded onto Associated Grocers' delivery trucks and delivered along with the rest of an independent store's order.

Sybase

As testimony to the interest and activity in data warehousing, recent surveys (conducted by Meta Group, Inc.) show that more than 70 percent of Fortune 1000 companies have data warehousing projects budgeted or under way at an average cost of $3 million and a typical development time of six to eighteen months.

Conventional warehousing applications today extract basic business data from operational systems, edit or transform them in some fashion to ensure their accuracy and clarity, and move them by means of transformation products, custom programming, or "sneaker net" to the newly deployed analytical database system. This extract, edit, load, query, extract, edit, load, query system might be acceptable if business life were very simple and relatively static, but that is not the case. New data and data structures are added, changes are made to existing data, and even whole new databases are added.

Sybase Warehouse WORKS was designed around four key functions in data warehousing:

- Assembling data from multiple sources
- Transforming data for a consistent and understandable view of the business
- Distributing data to where they are needed by business users
- Providing high-speed access to the data for those business users

The Sybase Warehouse WORKS Alliance Program provides a complete, open, and integrated solution for organizations building and deploying data warehouse solu-

FIGURE 12-8 Typical Sybase Data Warehouse Development Screen

tions. The program addresses the entire range of technology requirements for data warehouse development, including data transformation, data distribution, and interactive data access. The alliance partners have made commitments to adopt the Warehouse WORKS architecture and APIs, as well as to work closely with Sybase in marketing and sales programs.

Silicon Graphics

The advances in data analysis realized through breakthroughs in data warehousing are now being extended by new solutions for data mining. Sophisticated tools for three-dimensional visualization, coupled with data mining software developed by Silicon Graphics, make it possible to bring out patterns and trends in the data that may not have been realized using traditional SQL techniques. These "nuggets" of information can then be brought to the attention of the end user, yielding bottom-line results.

Using fly-through techniques, the user can navigate through models on consumer purchasing and channel velocity to follow trends and observe patterns. In response to what the user sees, he or she can interact directly with the data, using visual computing to factor critical "what-if" scenarios into your models. By making it possible to go through many such iterations without resorting to overburdened IS staff for analytical assistance, the user can eliminate days—even months—from the review process.

IBM

IBM provides a number of decision support tools to give users a powerful but easy-to-use interface to the data warehouse. IBM Information Warehouse Solutions offers the choice of decision support tools that best meet the needs of the end users in keeping with their commitment to provide open systems implementations.

IBM has announced a Customer Partnership Program to work with selected customers to gain experience and validate the applicability of the data mining technology. This offers customers the advantage of IBM's powerful new data mining technology to analyze their data looking for key patterns and associations. For example, Visa and IBM announced an agreement in 1995 signaling their intention to work together. This will change the way in which Visa and its member banks exchange information worldwide. The proposed structure will facilitate the timely delivery of information and critical decision support tools directly to member financial institutions' desktops worldwide.

IBM Visualizer provides a powerful and comprehensive set of ready-to-use building blocks and development tools that can support a wide range of end-user requirements for query, report writing, data analysis, chart/graph making, business planning, and multimedia database. As a workstation-based product, Visualizer is object-oriented and that makes it easy to plug in additional functions such as those mentioned. And Visualizer can access databases such as Oracle and Sybase as well as the DB2 family.

There are a number of other decision support products available from IBM based on the platform, operating environment, and database with which you need to work. For example, the IBM Application System (AS) provides a client/server architecture and the widest range of decision support functions available for the MVS and VM environments. AS has become the decision support server of choice in these environments because of its capability to access many different data sources. IBM Query Management Facility (QMF) provides query, reporting, and graphics functions in the MVS, VM, and CICS environments. The Data Interpretation System (DIS) is an object-oriented set of tools that enable end users to access, analyze, and present information with little technical assistance. It is a LAN-based client/server architecture that enables access to IBM and non-IBM relational databases as well as host applications in the MVS and VM environment. These and other products are available from IBM to provide the functions and capabilities needed for a variety of implementation alternatives.

12-7 CHAPTER SUMMARY

"Seeing" the data is becoming a major component in decision support and the formation of organizational strategies. The coming "Age of Information" will bring with it increased demands on organizing and using the multitude of information and knowledge resident within a typical organization, and the discovery of hidden structures and patterns within that information will be a key activity. Through this technology we will fundamentally transform our understanding of the concept of information from its present form of "something we need to know" into its future form of "something we could otherwise never have known."

- -

Key Concepts

- Data mining (DM) is the set of activities used to find new, hidden, or unexpected patterns in data. A synonym for data mining techniques is knowledge data discovery (KDD). (12-1)
- On-line analytical processing (OLAP). This category of software technology enables decision makers to conduct multidimensional analysis of consolidated enterprise data. There are two approaches to conduct the analysis: (12-2)

Multidimensional OLAP (MOLAP)

MOLAP organizes and analyzes data as a hypercube, an n-dimensional cube, which allows a number of dimensions to be analyzed simultaneously and any number of multidimensional views of data to be created. Although MOLAP is good at handling summarized data, it is not particularly well suited to handling large amounts of detailed data.

Relational OLAP (ROLAP)

In ROLAP, the multidimensional database server is replaced with a large relational database server. ROLAP architectures are especially well suited to those situations where dynamic access to combinations of summarized and detailed data is more important than the performance gains offered by the MOLAP approach using only summarized or preconsolidated data.

- Categories of processing algorithms and rule approaches: (12-3)

Classification

By building and refining a predictive model of the business problem, data mining classification methods can often provide useful and highly accurate answers.

Association

By searching all details or transactions from operational systems, an associated algorithm that includes the rules that will correlate one set of events or items with another can be developed.

Sequence

Sequencing and time-series analysis are used to relate events in time and, therefore, discover hidden trends for predicting future events.

Cluster

By creating clusters of data according to some metric or set of metrics and analyzing the characteristics of members in the class, clustering might derive certain rules.

- Data mining technologies (12-3)

Statistical analysis

Data mining requires the use of statistical techniques capable of accommodating the conditions of nonlinearity, multiple outliers, and nonnumerical data typically found in a data warehouse environment.

Neural networks, genetic algorithms, and fuzzy logic

By utilizing these machine learning techniques to derive meaning from complicated and imprecise data, patterns and trends within the data can be extracted and detected.

Decision trees

By continually breaking data sets into two separate smaller groups, a predictive model can be built. This technique is often used in data mining applications to assist in the classification of items or events contained within the warehouse.

- General process of knowledge discovery (12-3)

1. Select a topic for study.
2. Identify a target data set.
3. Clean and preprocess the data.
4. Build a data model.
5. Interpret and refine.
6. Predict.
7. Share the model.

- Current limitations and challenges to data mining (12-4)

Identification of missing information

Even with thorough and sophisticated technologies, we cannot yet detect whether the original data set contains the necessary elements for effective mining. Therefore, data mining applications need to include mechanisms for "inventorying" the data set so that a determination of sufficiency in attributes can be made prior to loading the data into the warehouse.

Data noise and missing values

Currently, data mining systems are limited to the treatment of noise via statistical techniques that rely on known distributions of data noise. Future systems must incorporate more sophisticated mechanisms for treating missing or noisy data.

Large databases and high dimensionality

This ensures that discovered patterns are not "local" due to the constant update of the data by an ever increasing set of time-sensitive data values.

- Data visualization (12-5)

Data visualization is the process by which numerical data are converted into meaningful images. The ability to create multidimensional structures and models from raw data can assist in analyzing complex data sets by mapping physical properties to the data, thus taking advantage of human visual systems. The identification of hidden patterns contained within the data can be accelerated.

Questions for Review

1. Define data mining.
2. Describe the evolution of decision support activities from verification to discovery.
3. What is on-line analytical processing (OLAP)?
4. Explain the concept of multidimensional on-line analytical processing (MOLAP).
5. Describe how relational on-line analytical processing (ROLAP) works.
6. Compare the two approaches to conducting OLAP analysis. What are the differences between them?
7. Explain the technique of classification for mining data.
8. How does the association technique apply to data mining?
9. List and briefly describe several data mining technologies.
10. List and briefly describe the knowledge discovery search process.
11. What are the current limitations and challenges to data mining?
12. What is data visualization?

For Further Discussion

1. After gaining an understanding of the evolution of decision support activities from verification to discovery, find an example of this evolution and what makes it possible.
2. Analyze a data mining product utilizing the concept of OLAP in the market. Describe which approach(es) and technique(s) it applies and how it works.
3. Analyze a data mining product in the market. Identify the benefits of this product and discuss its limitations.
4. How can data visualization help in decision making?
5. Compare the siftware technologies discussed in section 12-6. What are their common characteristics? What are the differences among them?

13

Designing and Building Decision Support Systems

Learning Objectives

- Grasp the two basic DSS development strategies

- Comprehend the various approaches to DSS analysis and design

- Understand the DSS development process (DDP)

- Learn the differences between the traditional system development life cycle (SDLC) approach and the DDP

- Be familiar with the process of prototyping

- Grasp the two basic kinds of prototypes: throwaway prototypes and iterative prototypes

- Understand the benefits and limitations of prototyping

- Gain an understanding of the skill set needed by DSS developers

- Learn the concept of end-user computing

- Learn the advantages and risks of end-user DSS development

- Understand the criteria for selection of DSS development tools

Rapid Prototyping the Allkauf Information System

During the summer of 1994, the management of the German retail chain All-kauf decided to implement a companywide executive information system. Er-hard Jusche, managing director of the Allkauf Group explains: "In the past we have worked very successfully—using our experience and intuition. Now we want to use modern technology to create an easily accessible information base for present and future generations of management." Understanding the needs of its customers is a top priority for Allkauf. This includes knowing exactly what product is sold in which store and when. The company's new EIS would have to deliver that kind of information within five seconds!

Allkauf owns and operates a chain of seventy-five superstores each with more than sixty-five thousand square feet of shopping area stocked with more than eighty thousand different products. Because of the company's size, the task of collecting and integrating the enormous amount of information needed for the EIS was monumental. One of the key requirements for the new system was rapid response time. The size, complexity, and requirements of this system made it clear from the beginning that only the latest technology would do: client/server architecture, multiuser facilities, Windows, multidimensional modeling facilities, and full EIS functionality. When Allkauf went into the marketplace to look for a vendor that could meet all of its system needs at once, it soon found out that such a vendor was a scarce commodity. Only two vendors were able to meet the stringent demands of the new system, and Allkauf finally selected Comshare.

The Allkauf information system (AIS) is designed to cover three functional areas: standard reporting, exception reporting, and ad hoc analysis. Among the three primary functions, ad hoc analysis is considered to be the most important because Allkauf wants all of its users to be able to analyze any data according to their individual needs.

The AIS was built using a step-by-step "evolutionary prototyping" approach. Two Allkauf analysts developed the first application in only one month. This first system component monitors sales results using dynamic reporting by directly accessing the data held on the company's OLAP server. Data can be represented in tables or in graphics, sorted and color coded, and users can drill down by line item. One of the primary requirements of the system was met, too: Response times for queries are typically under five seconds.

The second module, the short-term income statement, was up and running by the middle of March 1995. The third module contained all of the statistical information on all items on sale in all superstores and was initially intended for use by the thirty members of the central buying department. The most significant feature of this application is a single dimension with close to 200,000 item members. Only Comshare's new Essbase version 4.0 was able to meet this requirement. This version was scheduled for release in March 1996. In the meantime, Allkauf developed three less challenging applications using the existing Essbase version.

The use of an evolutionary approach to development produced prototypes that users were able to respond to very quickly, and, therefore, developers were able to modify them to meet the needs of the users. Allkauf analysts believe that a more structured approach, such as a typical life cycle method, would not have added materially to the quality of the system and, more important, would have delayed the availability of the three primary modules. It is important to note, however, that Allkauf employs a highly structured development approach for all of its major transactional information system development projects.

Using the AIS, Allkauf can support its business much more effectively and save valuable time in business analysis. Allkauf management is convinced that it has chosen exactly the right time to gain a competitive advantage using its EIS.

We are now at the point in our journey into the world of decision making and decision support where, for a brief instant, we must turn our attention to the technology itself. One of the most challenging problems associated with the DSS is its design and implementation. This chapter will focus on the complexities and design issues regarding the construction of a modern DSS, and chapter 14 will look at the various issues surrounding the implementation of a DSS and its integration into the organization.

From past discussion, you are aware of a wide variety of decision support systems, each with its own set of tools, assumptions, and underlying models. While the "generic" DSS can be described in terms of a generalized set of components (see chapter 1), the physical manifestation of the final product will necessarily possess characteristics and functionality unique from all other systems (no matter how similar). Because there is no one best DSS, it stands to reason that there is no one best way to design and build one. Some DSS projects can be completed in a matter of days whereas other systems can take years to develop and implement. Still others are never truly finished but, rather, exist in a dynamic state of refinement and modification.

Recent studies of DSS development methodologies (Arinza 1991; Saxena 1992) have identified more than thirty different approaches to the design and construction of DSS technologies. We will not look at each and every defined methodology currently in use, but we will, nonetheless, present a variety of strategies that embody the spirit and complexity of the domain of DSS design. Most important, the premise of this chapter and the next is that despite the outward similarities between a DSS and an organizational application system, the design and implementation processes for each are decidedly different. To demonstrate this, we begin with an overview of the basic strategies associated with DSS development.

13-1 STRATEGIES FOR DSS ANALYSIS AND DESIGN

Basic DSS Development Strategies

From the many different approaches to DSS development, two common strategies can be identified: (1) programming a customized DSS and (2) employing a DSS generator. Each approach is unique and the choice of which one to adopt is often contingent on the organizational setting or problem context. In fact, it is quite possible for a complex DSS undertaking to use both approaches in combination during the various design stages of the project. We will briefly explore the two strategies below and will look in greater detail at the various tools used in each later in the chapter.

Programming a Customized DSS

This strategy employs either a general-purpose programming language (GPL) such as PASCAL or COBOL or a fourth-generation language (4GL) such as Delphi or Visual C++. Although early DSS designs were built using the GPL approach, most modern systems use a combination of 4GL and modeling applets to boost programmer productivity and decrease development time and effort. Despite the advent of specialized applications intended to support the DSS development process, a large organizational DSS intended to interface with a variety of existing operational systems is usually built using a commercial programming product to allow for the development of "one-of-a-kind" interfaces and conduits between the DSS and the other organizational applications.

Employing a DSS Generator

A *DSS generator* is an application system that eliminates the need for programming thousands of individual instructions or code in the design and construction of a DSS. One of the most common forms of DSS generator is an electronic spreadsheet such as Excel, Lotus 1-2-3, or Quattro Pro. Literally thousands of individual and organizational DSS applications have been developed and implemented using this form of DSS generator as the basic development foundation. Several commercial add-ins such as @RISK, a sophisticated probability assessment tool, are available to assist in the development of various types of DSS analysis mechanisms using an electronic spreadsheet as the primary DSS generator. More sophisticated generators such as MicroStrategy's DSS Architect (see figure 13-1) allow the designer increased flexibility over the conventional spreadsheet. While considerably more efficient than using the programming language approach, the DSS generator strategy is nonetheless limited in its flexibility and level of complexity compared to 4GLs or other available strategies.

One recent improvement in this area is the advent of *domain-specific DSS generators*. Such systems are designed to assist in the generation of a highly structured DSS intended for use within a specific functional area. Examples of domain-specific DSS generators include SAS for complex statistical applications and Commander FDC for financial analysis.

The DSS Analysis and Design Process

A number of analysis and design approaches exist that can be applied to the process of DSS development. Here we explore each of the common processes in some detail and offer several comparisons between the methods in an effort to identify their contributions and limitations within a DSS development setting.

System Development Life Cycle

A common perspective with regard to system design and development is found in the *system development life cycle* (SDLC) approach. The SDLC portrays the

FIGURE 13-1 MicroStrategy's DSS Architect

process as a series of recursive phases, each with its own set of required inputs, activities, and outputs. Figure 13-2 illustrates the various phases and the recursive nature of the SDLC.

In the *problem definition* phase, analysts assess the nature of the organization's problem and develop documentation describing the problem context and the organizational environment. Once that has been completed, a *feasibility analysis* is performed to assess whether the problem context outlined in the previous stage can be effectively addressed by one or more applications integrated into an information system. Activities during this stage include conversion of the existing physical system into a series of logical models to look at the embedded processes in an implementation-independent manner. Initial determinations of feasibility with regard to available technologies, human and economic resources, and political and regulatory constraints are conducted during this phase.

During *systems analysis,* the analysts focus on the determination, collection, and documentation of specific requirements for the new system. Based on these requirements, the *design* phase involves the creation of a detailed model of the various system component processes and data elements as well as of the interactions and interrelationships among them. Modifications are made to the resultant logical model so that the identified requirements of the new system are reflected and any weaknesses in the old system are improved or completely eliminated. During the *programming* phase, the logical model for the new system is converted into a physical system via the development and acquisition of software and hardware necessary to meet the needs of the system's users. Following the *testing* phase, where the final system is put through a series of trial runs to ascertain its performance relative to the stated requirements, the *implementation* of the system takes place and the final installation activities are performed. Once the system is operational, the *maintenance* phase begins. Here various

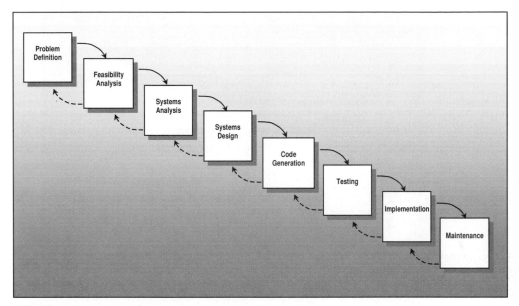

FIGURE 13-2 Classical System Development Life Cycle

refinements and incremental enhancements are applied to the operational system to effect performance and functionality improvements to the production system.

ROMC Analysis

An alternative to the SDLC approach is ROMC analysis (Sprague and Carlson 1982). This approach focuses the analysis effort on developing understandings of representations (R), operations (O), memory aids (M), and controls (C).

Using this approach to DSS design, the analyst characterizes the various *representations* available for use as methods of communication between the DSS user and the DSS application. Examples of representations include graphical displays, charts, tables, lists, stock reports, input forms, and menus, among many others.

In *operations* analysis, the analyst is focused on identifying those activities necessary for the DSS to perform or facilitate the generation and delivery of the various representations contained within the system. Such activities include the interpretation, production, and packaging of relevant knowledge contained within the DSS.

Memory aids are those components intended to provide support to the use of the various identified representations and operations. Examples of memory aids include databases, workspaces or blackboard systems, and embedded triggers intended to alert DSS users of the need to perform specific operations relevant to the task at hand.

Finally, *controls* are mechanisms that help the DSS extract or synthesize a particular decision-making process from the myriad of available representations, operations, and memory aids. Examples of controls include mechanisms to assist the user in submitting specific requests or queries to the DSS, functions that assist the user in tailoring the DSS to his or her unique problem-solving style or tendencies, and modules that assist the user in learning to use specific elements within the DSS via examples rather than trial-and-error discovery.

Functional Category Analysis

Yet another methodology for the design of a DSS is *functional category analysis* (Blanning 1979). This method focuses on the identification of specific functions necessary for the development of a particular DSS from a broad list of available functions including *selection, aggregation, estimation, simulation, equalization,* and *optimization.* Table 13-1 lists the various functional categories and provides a brief description of each.

Functional category analysis allows for the organization of the key functions of the proposed DSS into a useful arrangement, thus allowing the DSS designer to perform a more focused and detailed analysis.

DSS Development Process — DDP

Despite the many similarities between the design and construction of an organizational DSS and that of transactional application systems, the unique nature of the semistructured or unstructured problems that are typical of the objective for developing a DSS dictates that an equally unique approach to design be employed. Often the specific information needs of managers in a given problem context are not clear in the early stages of DSS design and thus are not easily identified. To facilitate the collection of DSS requirements and functions a process involving a heavy emphasis on prototyping is employed. In this section, we identify a general process of system development that is tailored to the special needs and challenges of the DSS designer. Because each DSS design project will be unique, however, not all activities identified may be performed. A simple DSS project may allow for a reduced approach involving only the

Table 13-1 Functional Category Analysis

Functional Category	Activities Performed
Selection	Locating knowledge within the knowledge base for presentation or use as input to the new knowledge derivation process
Aggregation	Creation or derivation of summary statistics such as averages, subtotals, frequencies, and groupings
Estimation	Creation or derivation of model parameter estimates
Simulation	Creation or derivation of knowledge regarding expected outcomes or consequences of specific actions within the organizational environment
Equalization	Creation or derivation of knowledge regarding the conditions necessary to maintain equilibrium or consistency within the problem context
Optimization	Derivation of knowledge regarding what set of parameters serve to maximize or minimize a given performance measure within a set of defined constraints

essential activities of DSS design, whereas a more complex project may involve all of the outlined activities and phases of the process. For our purposes, however, we will discuss the *DSS development process* (DDP) in terms of a generalized set of activities and phases of development that are typically associated with DSS design. Figure 13-3 illustrates the phases contained within the process.

The first step in DSS development is the formal identification and recognition of a problem context requiring decision support. Recall from chapter 3 that problems manifest themselves as a collection of symptoms. The totality of symptoms identifies the underlying problem and, thus, the opportunity for decision support.

Opportunities for decision support can manifest themselves in many ways. In addition to support for identified problems within the organization, a DSS can be employed to assist in the discovery of new knowledge that can advance the competitive position of the firm or improve its ability to reach a specific market segment. Using the data mining and visualization techniques discussed in chapters 11 and 12, a manager may be able to identify buying patterns in isolated segments of the market that can be exploited into increased market share for the firm. In another situation, the use of a DSS may serve to facilitate the discovery of organizational problems that would otherwise go undetected, such as embezzlement or theft. These examples show that the manager must be constantly alert for opportunities to use decision support in the course of daily activities throughout the organization.

FIGURE 13-3 Generalized DSS Development Process

Identification of DSS Objectives and Resources

Once the opportunity for decision support has been identified, the specific objectives and key decisions to be supported by the DSS must be described. In addition, a determination of available resources including hardware, software, current technology, and available knowledge must be made. During this phase, the designer must carefully identify the general objectives of the DSS. These objectives should serve to clarify the function of the proposed DSS with regard to the various types of knowledge to be managed, the capacity of knowledge to be made available to the decision maker, and the general performance characteristics of the system. In addition, the types of support to be made available to the user by the DSS must be specified. Here the designer must determine exactly what role the DSS will be expected to play within the identified problem context. Table 13-2 lists several general types of support a DSS can provide.

Along with the identification of the objectives for the proposed DSS must come the methods by which those objectives will be evaluated in terms of success. Specific and objective standards of performance must be established. For example, consider the following set of objectives:

- Improve the quality of decisions made within the organization
- Improve the quality of a particular raw material by more than 12 percent
- Reduce the nominal decision time for a particular analysis activity by 10 percent
- Increase the market share for product X

Despite the apparent value of each of the stated objectives to the firm, only two of them represent objectives that can be accurately assessed. The first and last goals are stated in such a way that they cannot be objectively assessed. The first example, the improvement of decision quality within the organization, is a lofty and laudable goal, but it cannot be determined without first identifying the criteria for a quality decision. Even so, one might argue that if any improvement in decision quality, however minuscule, is realized via the DSS, the objective will have been reached. In this case, the investment of one million dollars for the development of a DSS that results in an improved decision quality netting the organization ten cents would be sufficient evidence of goal attainment. Try and sell that concept to your boss.

The same problem exists with the last of the four stated objectives. Any increase in market share for product X would be sufficient to satisfy the goal. The second and

---

Table 13-2 Types of Support Provided by a DSS

- Identify the need for decisions
- Identify specific problems that require attention
- Solve or assist in solving problems
- Help compensate for cognitive limitations of human decision makers
- Provide assistance in the form of advice, analysis, or evaluation
- Enhance user creativity, imagination, or insight
- Facilitate interactions in multiparticipant decision maker settings

third objectives, however, are stated in such a way that they allow for the objective assessment of not only the value of the goal but whether or not it has been achieved. Although some objectives are necessarily difficult to quantify or are seemingly intangible, the ultimate success of a DSS development project rests on the establishment of explicit goals and the methods intended to be employed in their assessment.

System Analysis

The activities of this phase of the DSS development process are intended to result in a detailed set of requirements for the DSS. According to Holsapple, Park, and Whinston (1993) three primary categories of system requirements for the DSS can be established: (1) *functional requirements,* (2) *interface requirements,* and (3) *coordination requirements.*

Functional Requirements   This set of specifications for the DSS focuses on its capacity for the storage, recall, and production of knowledge useful to the problem context. An example of this type of requirement might be the capability of a particular DSS to store a variety of product sales projections, recall specific components or characteristics of one or more projections, and estimate the effect on sales volume of one or more changes to the underlying assumptions or variables contained therein.

Interface Requirements   The heart and soul of a DSS is arguably related to the quality and usefulness of its interface. The *interface requirements* focus on the communication capabilities of the DSS. During this phase, the designer must determine the various channels and methods of communication that will be made available to the DSS user and the conditions under which they will be made available. Menuing, report structures, command interface, and output formats are all identified during this phase of the development process. In addition, the developer must identify the various types of requests that might be made of the DSS by the decision maker and the appropriate types of responses the DSS must be able to make as a result.

Coordination Requirements   In addition to establishing the specific functions and communication mechanisms associated with the proposed DSS, the designer must determine the *coordination requirements.* These include the timing of events associated with the decision-making process, the facilitation of access to relevant information, and the integration of various modeling tools contained within the DSS. An example of a coordination requirement might be the necessity for one event to have occurred before another action can be initiated (for instance, sales projections for prior fiscal periods would need to be updated to actual figures before initiating a future projection process).

System Design

The determination of specific physical components, structure, and development platforms is made during the *system design* stage of the DSS development process. One of the primary activities in this phase is the selection of a set of development tools to be used in the construction of the DSS. Once the development tools have been determined, a design can be created that takes advantage of the specific strengths and features of those tools while simultaneously avoiding known weaknesses associated with the platform. We will take a closer look at the various development tools and platforms available for DSS design later in this chapter.

System Construction

During the *system construction* phase, the designer uses an iterative prototyping approach that allows for small, yet constant, refinements to be made to the system based on feedback received from testing and user involvement. This process of refinement is continuous during this phase and often results in significant changes to the initial design specifications. Each iteration of the prototype is intended to provoke the DSS user into verbalizing needs and desires not yet reflected in the design. In addition, the prototype can be used to incrementally determine the various requirements associated with interconnecting the DSS with other existing organizational application systems. We will focus on the activities associated with prototyping later in this section. For now, know that the design phase often represents the majority of the effort and time associated with the development of an organizational DSS.

System Implementation

The goal of the *system implementation* phase is to test, evaluate, and deploy a fully functional and documented DSS. This phase includes an all-important final determination and evaluation of the degree to which the DSS meets the users' needs. As in the design phase, modifications may be necessary to fully realize the potential of the DSS and to fully implement the identified objectives of the decision makers. Also performed during this phase is the training of the DSS user group with regard to specific capabilities, functions, and structure of the system. Users are also trained in methods associated with maintenance and refinement of the system over time. At the conclusion of this set of development activities, the organization has a fully deployed and functional decision support system tailored to the specific needs and characteristics of the problem context. Following this, the final step in the process, *incremental adaptation,* can be initiated.

Incremental Adaptation

This final stage in the DSS development process is a never-ending revisiting of the activities of the earlier stages in an effort to enhance the capabilities of the DSS based on knowledge gained as a result of its use. Over the operating life of an organizational DSS, new needs manifest themselves and many innovative functions are developed in response to those needs. In addition, as technology changes in the environment, the desire to incorporate those changes and improvements into the DSS may result in the development process starting again on a major revision to the existing design. As you can see, the development of a DSS is truly an evolutionary and living process that can, and should, result in a highly effective support mechanism for organizational decision making.

SDLC versus DSS Development Process

We have identified several general approaches to the design and development of a DSS that range from highly staged and structured to highly iterative and unstructured strategies. To further understand the need for a unique development process in the design of a DSS, we must look at the two extremes of the development strategy continuum, the SDLC and the DDP, in greater detail.

The SDLC has evolved out of the decades of experience analysts and developers have had with computer-based information systems. The sequential and structured nature of the process is one of its primary strengths in that it provides a vehicle for programmed problem solving while simultaneously minimizing the inherent biases and cognitive limitations associated with human problem-solving activities. The life cycle approach to system development is characterized as a *top-down* design philosophy. This implies that the exact needs and specifications of the system are determined first and then followed by the design and construction of a system that meets those exact needs. Practicing analysts are quick to point out, however, that the SDLC is an idealized abstraction of the actual process and that often a more iterative *bottom-up* design approach may become necessary to facilitate the development of a particular system or component. Nonetheless, its strength is clearly in its simplicity and ability to impose necessary structure on the design process. The SDLC has proven over time to be the single most useful approach to the development of computer-based information systems. It is, however, this very strength that renders it inadequate for the effective design and construction of an organizational DSS.

The underlying cause for this inadequacy is related to the stated objective of a DSS: the providing of support for semistructured problem contexts. The use of the SDLC presumes that the structure of the problem to be solved or the nature of the problem context in which the DSS will operate is fully known and identifiable prior to the initiation of the design phase. In most system projects where the SDLC is appropriately employed, the problem context, managerial preferences, decision-making processes, and environmental conditions are, for the most part, identifiable and largely static. While the initial activities in the SDLC approach are associated with the gathering of knowledge by the analysts, it is nonetheless assumed by the process that such knowledge is readily available and in a form that allows for its gathering and categorization into a set of system requirements. This assumption is simply untenable within the realm of DSS design and construction. The lack of understanding on the part of the DSS designer is only one variable in the development equation. More often than not, the problem context, the managerial preferences, the decision-making processes, and the environmental conditions are also unknown to the user and tend to vary greatly throughout the development process. This "mental migration" of system requirements commonly (and necessarily) associated with the development of a DSS is counter to the assumptions of convergence commonly associated with the life cycle approach:

> Over time the initially unstructured or semi-structured planning issue that originally motivated the DSS project migrates in the minds of both the user and the DSS designer. This occurs when the traditional life-cycle design methodology begins to enforce premature closure on the original problem definition so that the specifications can be "frozen." The resulting DSS system design, therefore, also tends to migrate over the developmental time interval. (Moore and Chang 1983, 184)

It follows that the design of a DSS requires a process uniquely constructed to allow for the largely evolutionary design approach necessary in DSS development. This approach involves a heavy emphasis on the activity of prototyping.

Prototyping

The *prototyping* approach is a common and increasingly popular method of system development. Although opinion differs regarding the appropriate use of prototyping as part of a life cycle approach, the use of iterative, or evolutionary, prototyping in the design and construction of a DSS appears to be an expedient and efficient method of "hitting the moving target" of DSS user requirements. Although no commonly prescribed methodology for prototyping exists, several researchers (Courbon, Grajew, and Tolovi 1980; Henderson and Ingraham 1982) have offered a useful description of the task sequence associated with developing an iterative prototype.

The early stages of the prototyping approach contain several similarities to the classic SDLC methodology. The primary differences begin to occur following the initial gathering of requirements and the development of the first round of prototypes. Once the first prototype is in place, a repetitive and incremental process begins in which increasingly smaller, but constant, changes are made to the prototype until a stable system exists that accurately reflects the needs and desires of the DSS users. This process requires a significantly higher level of interaction between the analyst and user, and the nature of the cooperation between the two is generally more intense than in an SDLC-based design effort. This cooperative effort is characterized by a repetitive shift in responsibility throughout the project. While a particular iteration of the prototype is being constructed, the analyst is bearing the bulk of the responsibility and the users are not directly involved. When the iteration is complete and ready for preview, however, the DSS users bear the bulk of the responsibility of determining what's good, what's bad, and what needs to be added or removed from the functionality of the system. Contrary to the user's more passive or reactive involvement in the SDLC approach, the DSS user is an integral and active part of the usability and evaluation activities during DSS development. In addition, both parties cooperate in the identification and location of additional data needed for input to the DSS during this iterative activity. Once completed, the prototyping approach supplies a highly specific application usable in a very narrow problem context and often by a very few decision makers or problem solvers.

Throwaway versus Iterative Prototypes

Two basic kinds of prototypes can evolve from the development process. The *throwaway prototype* is for demonstration purposes only and is discarded after its usefulness as a demonstration tool is depleted. The advantage to developing a throwaway prototype lies with the increased speed—compared to a life cycle approach—with which a quasi-functional application can be put before the user and with the relative cost savings associated with development. By reducing the time necessary to develop a working version of the project, the value of the application can be demonstrated to senior management and financial supporters much earlier in the project. This expediency can often aid in securing the long-term support of the necessary entities so vital to the successful implementation of the DSS application. Moreover, the cost of development, in the early stages at least, is significantly lower than with an SDLC design effort. This is because the initial success of the application can be more readily determined early in the prototyping process. If, for whatever reason, the developer is unable to design and implement the DSS with the currently available technologies and development tools, the plan can be more easily reconsidered and revised earlier in the design process.

The alternative to the throwaway system is the development of an *iterative prototype* (also referred to as an *evolutionary prototype*). Rather than being discarded following demonstration, the iterative prototype is redeveloped and continually refined until it completely satisfies the requirements and needs of the DSS users, and then any necessary integration with other existing organizational systems is performed. In other words, the prototype "evolves" into the final production system. Unlike the throwaway system, the iterative prototype is a much more complex and formidable design effort. In both types, however, the basic process of development remains the same. The requirements of the system, often inexplicable or even initially unknown to both the user and the analyst, are eventually discovered, documented, and embedded in a fully operational DSS.

Benefits and Limitations of Prototyping

As stated previously, the prototyping approach to the design and construction of a DSS appears to be superior to the more conventional life cycle process. Several clear benefits can be identified with the adoption of this design approach. The significant reduction in development time and generally lower cost compared to an SDLC approach makes prototyping an attractive alternative in today's fast-paced managerial environment. In addition, the immediate nature of user response and feedback regarding system functionality can often result in a greater degree of support from senior management because it can more easily see the advantages of the project to the firm. Finally, the iterative nature of the prototyping process, at least theoretically, promotes an increased user understanding of the system and its range of capabilities.

Many of the strengths and benefits associated with the prototyping approach can also contribute to its limitations. Although the SDLC approach is admittedly slower and more cautious than a pure prototyping process, that increased caution often contributes to a greater attention to detail with regard to the development of comprehensive documentation and a more thorough understanding of the system's benefits and corresponding costs. In addition, a prototype development process increases the likelihood that system maintenance will be more difficult than in a comparable SDLC-based system. This is because the focus of both the users and the analyst in a prototyping effort is on the immediate functionality and ease of use of the DSS rather than on ancillary issues such as ease of maintenance, detailed documentation, or adherence to formal design standards. These limitations are not insurmountable, however, and can be effectively managed by a heightened awareness of and diligent attention to the need for accurate and timely documentation and, more recently, through the use of development tools specifically intended to facilitate the DSS design effort.

13-2 THE DSS DEVELOPER

Developers of decision support systems are often as diverse as the systems they create. The skills and backgrounds of DSS developers range from the experienced professional analyst to the novice first-time developer. Within the population of experienced professionals is an equally broad spectrum of experience ranging from analysts who specialize in the development of DSS applications to those who, while experienced in the development of organizational systems, have not had any experience in the design of a DSS application. In contrast to the professional DSS developer who is formally trained in either computer science or business information systems, the novice developer is typically a managerial decision maker within the organization who perceives the need for computer-based support in a onetime or recurrent problem context. He or she is rarely trained in the formalities and complexities of systems analysis and design and may very well be experiencing the development process for the first time. Novice developers do possess one significant advantage over the formally trained and more experienced analysts, however: They have a more intimate knowledge of what they want the DSS to accomplish and, with the right set of tools, can take advantage of the synergy associated with the developer and the user being the same person.

Necessary Skill Set

Regardless of the DSS developer's experience or organizational role, several key skills are essential to the success of the endeavor. As you will see, the professional developer has an advantage over the novice with regard to possession or attainment of certain of these skills, but the novice may have an edge over the professional in other areas. For example, as discussed above, the novice may have the advantage of knowing exactly what functions are expected of the system, whereas the professional must work to extract that understanding from the DSS users. Conversely, the professional is more likely to be able to respond to the complexities of tool selection and system design more readily than a novice developer who has had no formal training in these subjects. In the following subsections, we briefly outline and discuss the skill set needed by the developer for a successful DSS design effort.

Understanding the Problem Domain

Of utmost importance to the development of any organizational application, especially one intended for decision support, is a thorough understanding of the problem domain. In some cases, the necessary level of understanding may approach that of domain expertise, while in other situations, a more general knowledge of the problem domain is sufficient. The problem-centric nature of a DSS, however, demands that both the developer and the user be more than conversant in the specific characteristics unique to the problem context of interest. The DSS developer must possess not only the knowledge to develop the computer-based application but also a knowledge of the details surrounding the problem under study. A DSS developer with expertise in the medical profession may be valuable in the development of a system to support initial trauma center decisions regarding patient care but probably will not be effective in the development of a product allocation DSS for a consumer manufacturing firm.

Understanding Specific User Requirements

Just as the designer must understand the problem context, he or she must also understand the needs of the DSS users. This understanding encompasses both the functions of the proposed system as well as the specific interface requirements for communication with the system. Getting the DSS users involved early in the analysis and design of the system is necessary for the designer to develop this skill.

Understanding the Available Development Technologies

The combined skills and knowledge of the analyst and DSS users serve to determine the final selection of a DSS development tool or platform. A number of technologies exist to provide a basis for DSS development. The broader the range of familiarity and knowledge the developer has with such technologies, the more likely that the most appropriate one will be selected. For example, a spreadsheet may be an appropriate platform for building a DSS intended to provide "what-if" analysis, whereas a rule management platform may be more suitable when designing a DSS to assist in determining the most appropriate corrective action in a complex manufacturing process. Still other situations may call for development of a system around a case-based reasoning engine. The greater the familiarity with the intricacies of the technology, the greater the chances of successful tool selection and, thus, the greater the chances for successful DSS development.

Access to Appropriate Knowledge

Even the most experienced and skilled DSS developer must still be able to identify, locate, and represent the relevant knowledge appropriate for decisions made in the specific problem context for which the DSS is being developed. In many instances, activities with regard to the identification and location of the relevant knowledge are equally shared by the analyst and the DSS users, but the burden of accurate representation of that knowledge falls almost exclusively on the developer. The DSS user can only confirm that the knowledge is appropriately represented by thoroughly testing each iteration of the DSS. This necessary skill is closely aligned with the need for a thorough understanding of the problem domain. A developer who is not familiar with a specific problem domain may not be aware of the existence of knowledge in the form of specific procedures or modeling techniques relevant to the DSS. In such cases, the developer may either waste time and resources by "reinventing the wheel" or may design a less effective system.

End-User DSS Development

The novice DSS developer belongs to a growing and diverse population of individuals actively engaged in the activity referred to as *end-user computing.* End users are those individuals who fall outside the confines of the formally defined IS department or function within an organization. The realm of end-user computing includes, among others, those people who use electronic mail in the daily course of business, people who regularly use word processors to develop documents, and people who take on the role of developer by designing and implementing a computer-based information system, such as a DSS. End-user DSS developers are those individuals who build computer-based systems either to solve organizational problems or to assist in the pursuit of decision-making activities.

The population of end-user developers is made up of individuals playing a variety of organizational roles and possessing a variety of computer skill levels. End users are found at all levels of the organization, from the shop floor to the executive suite, and in all functional areas, from accounting to marketing to materials planning. In addition, their experience and skill level associated with developing and using a DSS are equally as diverse, ranging from a first-time user to the department computer guru. Comparable to this diversity is the range of applications developed by end users and the degree of formality associated with the chosen development methodology.

Because the typical end-user developer lacks formal training in system development methods, most end-user-developed applications tend to evolve from a relatively informal, often ad hoc process. While this informality poses no serious problem in a small and isolated DSS development project, it can result in serious negative consequences when applied to a large and complex DSS development effort. Without the rigor and discipline of a formal design methodology, complex DSS development projects can fall prey to defects related to a lack of direction, divergence of system objectives, and inexactitude of system requirements and specification.

Advantages of the End-User-Developed DSS

The most obvious advantage gained from end-user DSS development is a major reduction in delivery time of the application. Assuming the end user possesses the skills necessary to complete the project successfully, the delay often experienced in getting the information systems department actively involved in a development effort can be avoided. The DSS project can be initiated literally overnight and, depending upon the complexity of the design, can be completed within the span of a few hours to a few weeks. As you know, the value of a DSS lies solely with its effectiveness in supporting a successful decision process. The faster the DSS can be put into operation, the faster the organization can realize the benefits it provides.

Another major benefit of end-user development is the elimination of the time-consuming process of gathering and formalizing the end-user specifications for the system. Users are often unable to verbalize their needs with the same degree of clarity with which they can envision them. In end-user development, the analyst and the user are the same person. This facilitates the rapid transfer of envisioned needs and requirements into a working prototype. The end user may not be adept at explaining what is needed but she will undoubtedly know it when she sees it.

A third benefit of end-user DSS development is in the reduction of implementation problems following the design phase of the project. Often the same issues of communication that existed between the analyst and the users with regard to gaining an understanding of the complexities of the system are found during the implementation training process. Not only does the analyst have a difficult and time-consuming task of identifying and formalizing the users' needs during the requirements gathering phase of the project, but he or she must transfer the operational aspects of the new system back to the end users during the implementation phase. In the case of end-user development, the user is immediately and intimately familiar with the operation of the DSS and can proceed from development to operation and use with a minimum of effort and time.

The final advantage of end-user DSS development is a consequence of the previous three that we have identified: lower cost of development. The reduction in time and organizational resources associated with end-user development often translates into huge cost savings for the organization. This, combined with the increased speed with which the benefits of the operational DSS can be realized makes the concept of end-user DSS development an attractive alternative to the more conventional analyst-user life cycle approach.

Risks in End-User DSS Development

Along with the advantages of end-user DSS development come certain inherent risks that must be carefully managed if a successful DSS project is to be realized. The most obvious concern is that the final product will lack the necessary quality to make it a reliable and useful decision aid. End users often ignore or bypass conventional control mechanisms and testing procedures intrinsic to formal, structured development methodologies. This lack of rigor during the development process can often lead to serious deficiencies and sometimes catastrophic consequences. Something as simple as a formula in a spreadsheet that fails to accurately account for all subtotals in a grand total can result in the loss of millions of dollars if it is not detected during a testing phase and the users rely on the results provided by the DSS in their decision making. In other cases, deficiencies in the functionality of the DSS can go undetected during the development process and can manifest themselves at the most inopportune moments during a crucial decision-making activity.

Another common risk associated with end-user development is the lack of quality documentation. Professional developers lament the tedium of documentation but realize the importance of the process and the necessity for accuracy and thoroughness. End users may acknowledge the importance of accurate and thorough documentation but they rarely demonstrate their concerns by actually doing it. The focus of the end user is on completion of the application and documentation is, more often than not, an afterthought (if a thought at all). As long as the same individual that developed the system uses the system, the lack of comprehensive documentation is not a major problem. In some cases, however, an end-user DSS can evolve into an integral part of a functional area's decision processes. Should the developer leave the organization, the knowledge associated with the internal workings of that system generally leave as well. Years later, when a modification to the otherwise reliable DSS becomes necessary, it is suddenly discovered that no one in the organization can decipher the source code sufficiently to make the necessary changes. At this point, the organization is faced with either not making the desired improvements or changes or starting the development effort from scratch and designing a new DSS that incorporates the necessary functions (and, one would hope, is well documented).

A third area of concern is the potential lack of necessary security measures built into the system due to the end user's lack of familiarity with proper application security controls. In most cases, this poses little threat to the integrity of the organizational data because the typical end-user-developed DSS is a stand-alone application that is used only by a select few members of the organization. In some cases, however, the end-user-developed application may need to access data from one or more organizational data stores. When this occurs, the end-user application becomes a direct conduit to not only the organization's proprietary data but, in some cases, to other operational application systems as well. By failing to impart the same level of security and control to the end-user-developed application that is typically included in a more formally designed and developed system, the end user potentially leaves an unlocked door that can be used to gain access to proprietary and, otherwise, secure organizational data and information.

These risks we have discussed (and many others we have not) can be effectively managed so that the expected benefits associated with end-user development can be realized. A novice developer, despite his or her lack of formal training, can still acquire an understanding of the important elements of good design and can develop an attitude of professionalism that will increase the prospects of a successfully developed and implemented DSS.

The management of risk in end-user development is the subject of extensive research in both academic and applied realms. Frameworks have been developed to focus attention on the proper application of security and control (Walls and Turban 1992), on overall risk reduction techniques (Alavi and Weiss 1986), and on specific error-location and reduction techniques in spreadsheets (Galletta et al. 1996). Figure 13-4 contains a model of factors that influence risk in end-user-developed applications

FIGURE 13-4 Factors Influencing Risks and Outcome Characteristics of End-User Developed Applications (adapted from Janvrin and Morrison 1996, 348)

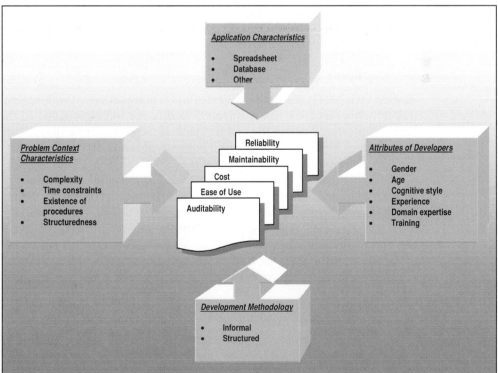

that can be useful in developing guidelines for end-user development activities within an organization.

More recently, organizations have been addressing the risks associated with end-user development through internally developed education programs. The concept of the *information center* (IC) arose to address the need for end-user support in the design and development of computer-based applications. Often associated with the MIS department of an organization, the IC exists to assist the end user with issues of project selection, scope, and selection of appropriate development tools. In addition, the IC can serve as a resource for technical assistance for the end user while still encouraging the creativity and autonomy generally associated with end-user development projects. The existence of an information center within an organization is a sign of a strong commitment to end-user computing and application development.

13-3 TOOLS FOR DSS DEVELOPMENT

As DSS implementation within the modern organization becomes more and more common, it brings with it the advent of new and more powerful DSS development tools. Tools for specific decision support techniques such as spreadsheet management or text management are now commonly found on most business-computing desktops. Multiple technique development tools that incorporate two or more design capabilities such as spreadsheet, text, and graphical presentation techniques are also becoming increasing available. Finally, highly sophisticated DSS development tools, referred to as *DSS generators,* also exist to facilitate the development of equally sophisticated and complex DSS applications. We will examine the various tools and methods of classifying them in this section.

Development Tool Classification

A wide variety of classification schemes and frameworks exist with regard to DSS design and development tools. Some methods classify the tools according to the development techniques offered by the tool. Others look at the specific role played by the tool during the course of DSS development. Still others focus on the type of interfaces generated by the tool. A thorough understanding of the various available DSS development tools can provide both the experienced professional and the end-user developer with a better chance of choosing the most appropriate development platform for the task at hand.

A common, and easily generalizable, classification scheme for DSS development tools was proposed by Sprague and Carlson (1982). Figure 13-5 illustrates this hierarchical classification scheme.

The development tools are classified according to three levels of technology: (1) DSS primary development tools, (2) DSS generators, and (3) specific DSS applications.

DSS Primary Development Tools

As implied by their name, the *primary development tools* are the lowest level of DSS development technology. In this category, we find the programming languages, code and text editors, graphics development applications, and database query mecha-

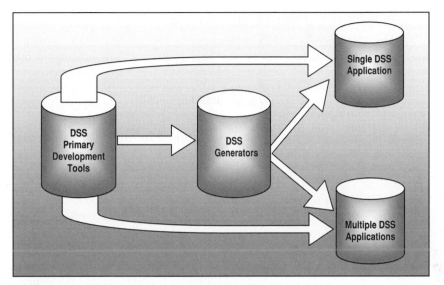

FIGURE 13-5 DSS Development Tools Classification

nisms employed during the development of either a DSS generator or a specific DSS application. A detailed discussion of these elements is beyond the scope of this text but a great deal of literature exists regarding the programming of DSS applications if one needs additional information (see, for example, Lotfi and Pegels 1996; Sprague and Carlson 1982).

DSS Generators

According to Sprague and Carlson's classification, a *DSS generator* is a "package of hardware/software which provides a set of capabilities to build specific DSS[s] quickly and easily" (1982, 10). A wide variety of commercially available DSS generators can be found ranging from Microsoft's Excel, a spreadsheet package found on most business-computing desktops, to highly sophisticated, and often expensive, applications such as MicroStrategy's DSS Agent. Regardless of the level of sophistication, however, all DSS generators possess integrated and diverse functionality including decision modeling, report design and generation, presentation graphics, and basic database management capabilities.

The main advantage of DSS generators over primary DSS development tools is convenience. Issues such as integration among the tools, access to multiple tools, import and export of data, and nonstandardized command structures across tools are all eliminated with the use of a DSS generator. The tight integration among the various functions of the DSS generator allows for the developer to concentrate on the design process rather than on getting two tools to work together or transfer data.

One important item to note about DSS generators is that their name is not completely accurate. In most cases, a DSS generator does not actually "generate" anything. Rather, it is simply an integrated set of tools and functions that assists in the design and implementation of a DSS. In reality, the true "DSS generator" is the developer.

Specific DSS Applications

The third level of DSS technology is the *specific DSS application*. In certain knowledge domains, decision makers face problems that, although semistructured, are widely experienced and generalizable across a large set of scenarios. In these cases, a commercially developed DSS application can be acquired rather than internally developed. One example of this type of problem context is the use of DSSs in the medical profession. While each specific situation encountered by a medical professional is unique, the vast knowledge base of medicine is for the most part generalizable across the human race. Because of this, adoption of a commercially available DSS that can assist in diagnosis or treatment of medical conditions or illnesses is a more expedient, economical, and reliable way to acquire the necessary decision support than internal DSS development using a generator.

Referring again to figure 13-5, we can see that the relationships between the three elements of the classification are not strictly hierarchical in nature. DSS tools can be used to construct a DSS generator, which can be used to develop a single DSS, or possibly many different DSS applications. Those same tools can be used to directly develop a specific DSS application. Likewise, a commercial DSS generator can be acquired by an organization that can develop a wide variety of specific DSS applications. The choice of sequence depends on the specific needs of the decision maker and on the nature of the problem context.

Development Tool Selection Criteria

The evaluation of whether to use a selected set of primary DSS development tools or to acquire an existing DSS generator is a complex decision in its own right and often involves a significant amount of research and analysis. A number of criteria must be considered when making the decision to build from scratch or buy a commercial development generator. Table 13-3 contains a brief listing of the various criteria that are important in the selection of a DSS generator.

Within each of these categories are numerous questions that must be answered before deciding to acquire the DSS generator. Does the data management system allow for creation of individual or personal databases? Does the user interface generator provide support for a wide variety of input and output devices? What are the ongoing maintenance and upgrade costs associated with a particular vendor's applica-

---

Table 13-3 Selection Criteria for DSS Generators

- Data management functions
- Model management functions
- User interface capabilities
- Compatibility and degree of connectivity
- Available hardware platforms
- Cost
- Quality and availability of vendor support

---

tion? What technical support is available for this application? Remember that the realm of decision support is complex, varied, and often unpredictable in terms of specific needs. The DSS generator must allow for the broadest possible spectrum of development support to achieve the necessary economies of ownership and to ensure long-term usefulness.

13-4 CHAPTER SUMMARY

The design and development of a DSS is a significant undertaking that can result in huge benefits to the organization if done right. The selection of the development tools, methodology, and the gathering of requirements are all precursors to a successful DSS development effort. Designing and constructing the DSS are only half the battle, however. Once the system is complete, it must be fully implemented and integrated into the organization if any of its benefits are to be realized. We will focus on the issues of DSS implementation in the next chapter.

Key Concepts

- Basic DSS development strategies (13-1)

  Program a customized DSS

  This strategy employs either a general-purpose programming language (GPL) or a fourth-generation language (4GL).

  Employ a DSS generator

  This strategy employs application systems that eliminate the need for programming thousands of individual instructions or code in the design and construction of a DSS.

- DSS analysis and design process (13-1)

  System development life cycle (SDLC)

  The SDLC portrays the analysis and design processes as a series of iterative and recursive phases, each with its own set of required inputs, activities, and deliverables. These processes are problem definition, feasibility analysis, systems analysis, systems design, code generation, testing, implementation, and maintenance.

  ROMC analysis

  This approach focuses on the analysis effort developing understanding of representations (R), operations (O), memory aids (M), and controls (C):

  Representations: The analysis focuses on characterizing the various representations available for use as methods of communication between the DSS user and the DSS application.

  Operations analysis: The analysis is focused on identifying those activities necessary for the DSS to perform or facilitate the generation and delivery of the various representations contained within the system.

  Memory aids: Memory aids are the components intended to provide support to the use of the various identified representations and operations.

Controls: Controls are mechanisms that help the DSS extract or synthesize a particular decision-making process from the myriad of available representations, operations, and memory aids.

Functional category analysis

Functional category analysis focuses on the identification of specific functions necessary for the development of a particular DSS from a broad list of available functions including selection, aggregation, estimation, simulation, equalization, and optimization.

- DSS development process (DDP) (13-1)

The development of a DSS employs a unique approach because of its nature of dealing with semistructured or unstructured problems.

Problem diagnosis

The first step in DSS development is the formal identification and recognition of a problem context requiring decision support.

DSS objectives and resources

During the problem definition phase, the specific objectives of the DSS and key decisions to be supported by the DSS must be carefully identified. Further, specific standards of performance must be established and detailed in a manner that allows for an objective assessment of their attainment.

System analysis

Within this phase, a detailed set of requirements for the DSS is generated:

Functional requirements

Interface requirements

Coordination requirements

System design

During the system design stage of the DSS development process, the determination of specific physical components, structure, and development platforms is made.

System construction

During the system construction phase, the designer uses an iterative prototyping approach that allows for small, yet constant, refinements to be made to the system based on the feedback received from testing and user involvement.

System implementation

The goal of the system implementation phase is to test, evaluate, and deploy a fully functional and documented DSS.

Incremental adaptation

The final stage in the DSS development process is a never-ending revisiting of the activities contained within the earlier stages in an effort to enhance the capabilities of the DSS based on experiences and knowledge gained as a result of its use.

- The prototyping process requires a significantly higher level of interaction between the analyst and user, and the nature of the cooperation between the two is generally much more intense than in an SDLC-based design effort. (13-1)

- Contrary to the user's more passive or reactive involvement in the SDLC approach, the DSS user is an integral and active part of the usability and evaluation activities during DSS development. (13-1)

- Two basic kinds of prototypes (13-1)

  Throwaway prototypes

  The throwaway prototype is intended for demonstration purposes only and is discarded after its usefulness as a demonstration tool is depleted. The advantages of using throwaway prototypes include the increased speed over a life cycle approach, the expediency of gaining long-term support, and the lower cost in the early stage.

  Iterative prototypes (evolutionary prototypes)

  The iterative prototype is redeveloped and continually refined until it completely satisfies the requirements and needs of the DSS users, and then any necessary integration with other existing organizational systems is performed.

- Benefits of prototyping (13-1)

  The significant reduction in development time and generally lower cost over an SDLC approach make prototyping an attractive method in today's fast-paced managerial environment.

  The more immediate nature of user response and feedback regarding system functionality can often result in a greater degree of support from senior management.

  The iterative nature of the prototyping process promotes an increased user understanding of the system and its range of capabilities.

- Limitations of prototyping (13-1)

  Because a slower and more cautious pace lends itself to a greater attention to detail with regard to the development of comprehensive documentation and a more thorough understanding of the system's benefits and corresponding costs, a pure prototype process may lose this benefit.

  A prototype development process increases the likelihood that system maintenance will be more difficult than in a comparable SDLC-based system.

- Necessary skill set for the DSS developer (13-2)

  Understand the problem domain

  Understand the specific user requirements

  Understand the available development technologies

  Have access to appropriate knowledge

- End-user computing (13-2)

  End-user computing refers to the involvement of end users in the development of a computer-based system. End-user DSS developers are those individuals who build computer-based systems either to solve organizational problems or to assist in the pursuit of decision-making activities. The identifiable characteristics of the population of end-user developers are the wide variance in organizational role and individual computer skill level.

- Advantages of an end-user-developed DSS (13-2)

  A reduction in delivery time of the application.

  The elimination of the time-consuming process of gathering and formalizing the end users' specifications for the system.

  The reduction of implementation problems following the design phase of the project.

  Lower cost of development due to the reduction in time and organizational resources associated with the development of the system.

- Risks of end-user DSS development (13-2)

  The final product will lack the necessary quality to make it a reliable and useful decision aid.

  The final product will lack quality documentation.

  The potential lack of necessary security measures built into the system due to the end user's lack of familiarity with proper application security controls.

- DSS development tool classification (13-3)

  The DSS primary development tools

  The primary development tools are the lowest level of DSS development technology, such as programming languages, code and text editors, and graphics development applications.

  The DSS generators

  A DSS generator is a "package of hardware/software which provides a set of capabilities to build specific DSS[s] quickly and easily." The main advantage of DSS generators over primary DSS development tools is convenience.

  The specific DSS applications

  In certain knowledge domains, because the problems faced by decision makers are widely experienced and generalizable across many scenarios, a commercially developed DSS application may be preferable to one that is internally developed.

Questions for Review

1. What are the two basic strategies for DSS analysis and design?
2. Explain *domain-specific DSS generators*.
3. List and briefly describe the processes of the system development life cycle (SDLC) approach.
4. Describe the functional category analysis approach. What is its most significant benefit?
5. During the system analysis phase of the DSS development process, what kinds of requirements should be identified?
6. Describe the major task(s) of the system design and construction phases of the DSS development process.
7. What are the strengths and weaknesses of the traditional SDLC approach?
8. What is prototyping?
9. List and briefly describe the two kinds of prototypes. Compare their advantages and limitations.
10. Compare the SDLC and the DDP in terms of user roles and the level of user involvement.
11. List and briefly describe the benefits and limitations of prototyping.
12. What skills are necessary to be a DSS developer?
13. Explain the concept of end-user computing.
14. Identify the advantages and risks of end-user DSS development.
15. Classify the DSS development tools.
16. How do you evaluate the selection of DSS development tools?

For Further Discussion

1. Use the ROMC analysis approach to analyze a DSS development project.
2. Why do we need a unique development approach to the DSS other than the traditional SDLC?
3. Discuss the importance of quantifying DSS objectives.
4. Compare DDP with SDLC. Discuss the major differences between these two system development approaches
5. Discuss the diversity of the DSS developers within organizations and the effects of this diversity.
6. Observe a decision-making process in an organization you are familiar with. Assume that you are developing a DSS for this process. List your considerations for selecting the development tool(s).

Implementing and Integrating Decision Support Systems

Learning Objectives

- Understand that the essence of implementation is the introduction of change

- Learn several theoretical models of change

- Based upon the sources of project initiation, identify the six patterns of implementation

- Gain an understanding of the frameworks for system evaluation: overall software quality, attitudinal measures of success, technical measures of success, organizational measures of success

- Learn how to measure user satisfaction toward a DSS

- Understand the four categories of measurement in a generalized framework to measure the success of a DSS: system performance, task performance, business opportunities, and evolutionary aspects

- Comprehend the risk factors in DSS implementation projects

- Learn how to formulate possible implementation strategies for dealing with identified risk factors

- Understand the importance of integration

- Learn the concepts behind global DSS integration

- Recognize the factors that can result in resistance to changes associated with a new system

DSS MINICASE

3Com ASSIST Customer Service Web Site

3Com Corporation has a problem its competitors envy. Since the company's founding in 1979, sales have skyrocketed to nearly $2.3 billion in 1996. As one of the data networking industry's largest and fastest growing companies, 3Com serves more than thirty-two million users in thirty-two countries worldwide.

One critical corporate challenge is how to provide an ever-expanding customer base with the world-class *anytime, anywhere* global support that is the company's hallmark. After the number of its customer support personnel more than doubled over the last few years, 3Com concluded that ongoing staff expansion is not a viable long-term customer service strategy.

"We can't continue hiring at the present rate, or our support organization will outgrow the company," Bob Noakes, manager, Internet commerce marketing, says. "To preserve our quality of product support, we need to give customers alternative and equally satisfactory ways to resolve problems without calling us."

SPEEDING PROBLEM RESOLUTION

To create more options for product support, 3Com decided to enhance its customer service offering on the World Wide Web. The Web's tremendous round-the-clock accessibility worldwide makes it an unparalleled vehicle to enhance customer service. 3Com is a key player on the Internet, able to connect millions of people worldwide with its Internet access solutions. Still, 3Com believes there is much it can do to enhance its Web offering. The company's initial Web technical support had no information and customers relied on search mechanisms to find solutions on their own.

To bring intelligence to its Web site, 3Com adopted Inference Corporation's CBR technology. By merging existing support information with CBR, 3Com created an interactive troubleshooting tool with hot links that gives customers step-by-step guidance to problem solving. Anyone with a Web browser can access the service regardless of the user's operating platform.

MINIMUM DEVELOPMENT AND MAXIMUM BENEFIT

3Com ASSIST was built using Inference's CasePointÆ WebServer, Windows NT version; CBR Express; CasePoint; CBR Tester; and CBR Search Engine for Windows. Inference's CBR software uses an approach similar to a doctor's medical diagnosis. The computer system is given details of a series of cases illustrating common problems, together with the accepted path to resolve them. When a caller has a query, the software leads the user through a series of questions and answers to identify a solution.

PUTTING KNOWLEDGE TO WORK

3Com is known for the superior quality and reliability of its network adapters, the interface devices that connect computers to networks. The EtherLink III adapter is 3Com's highest volume product, accounting for roughly 40 percent of the company's business.

The company has sold more than thirty-two million EtherLink IIIs, and although only a low percentage require support, that number is nonetheless large and growing. Because the product generates the highest volume of customer support calls, Noakes expects that its inclusion on 3Com ASSIST will make a substantial contribution to the company's call avoidance strategy.

The 3Com Impact External Digital Modem is a new, not highly complex, product, that had a high percentage of calls per shipment initially. "The modem's ISDN technology is unfamiliar to many users, and we're also dealing with less sophisticated customers," Noakes says. "3Com ASSIST is an ideal way to reduce calls per shipment."

QUICK RESOLUTION

"By putting a tool to resolve problems directly in our customers' hands, we expect to promote call avoidance," Noakes says. "Equally important, we hope to turn the information we receive from customer inquiries into self-help."

3Com hopes that half the people using products supported by 3Com ASSIST will be able to resolve their problems on the Web. Customers can avoid waiting and solve their own problems.

After starting with two product lines this year, 3Com plans to expand 3Com ASSIST in 1998 to include more products. "One goal is to be better at capturing information when customers call," Noakes says. As 3Com ASSIST goes forward, the company will work on integrating CBR with other methods to capture information. "Since CBR is OLE compliant, we expect to integrate the system with Clarify, multimedia, other databases, online documentation and marketing information."

Check out how 3Com Corporation has integrated Inference's CBR technology into 3Com ASSIST by visiting http://infodeli.3com.com/wcp/ profile1.htm.

Inference, CasePoint, CasePoint Search Engine, CasePoint WebServer, CBR Express, CBR Express Tester, and CBR Generator are trademarks of Inference Corporation.

14-1 DSS IMPLEMENTATION

For All the Marbles . . .

You are already aware of the need for a unique approach to the design and construction of a DSS. Equally important is the complex process of implementing the DSS and integrating it into the organization. This is probably the most important step in the entire DSS design process because without successful implementation, the greatest DSS ever created will go unused or perhaps even unnoticed. The implementation process is, metaphorically speaking, "for all the marbles."

The nineteenth-century author Washington Irving once observed:

> There is a certain relief in change, even though it may be from bad to worse; as I have found in travelling in a stage-coach, that it is often a comfort to shift one's position and be bruised in a new place.

Implementation is, in fact, the introduction of change. Although it is often referred to as if it were an "event"—as in "When we implement the system . . ." or "Following implementation . . ."—it is more accurately thought of as a set of activities that are focused on the successful introduction of the DSS into the organizational environment. As such, the position of the implementation phase in a classic SDLC model is somewhat misleading. By the end of this chapter, you will see that implementation is truly a dynamic activity that actually occurs throughout the entire development process and simply completes itself during what we are calling the implementation phase of the project. Contrary to the other steps in the DSS development process where each phase marks an initiation of a set of activities, the implementation phase marks a completion of activities. Further, following Irving's observations about riding in stagecoaches, successful DSS implementation may require a series of incremental shifts within the organization that, at the time, may be painful to some while a relief to others.

Introducing Change into the Organization

A rich and extensive literature exists that discusses the subject of change—its characteristics, the steps to take to achieve it, and the ways to measure its success. Pervasive in this literature is the recognition that the process by which the change is introduced is, in many cases, more important to its acceptance and success than the nature of the change itself. Although numerous models of change have been advanced, two elegantly concise ways of describing the process can be found in the *Lewin-Schein theory of change* and the *Kolb-Frohman change model*. We will briefly explore the components of each of these approaches in an effort to understand the concept of change.

The Lewin-Schein Theory of Change

According to the Lewin-Schein theory of change (Schein 1956), the process of change occurs in three basic steps:

1. *Unfreezing.* The creation of an awareness of the need for change and a climate receptive to change.
2. *Moving.* The changing of the magnitude and/or direction of the forces defining the initial need for change through the development of new methods and the learning of new attitudes and behaviors.
3. *Refreezing.* Reinforcement of the desirable changes that have occurred and the establishment of a maintainable and stable new equilibrium.

As you can see, the Lewin-Schein theory is simultaneously both structured and fluid: structured in the sense that the description of the three steps implies a specific order of events deemed necessary for successful implementation, and fluid in the sense that the activities within each of the steps are dynamically related to the nature of the change, the magnitude of the change, and the environment within which the change is taking place. This theory of change was directly applied by Zand and Sorensen (1975) in a study focusing on a large sample of projects associated with the implementation of a variety of management science methods within organizations. The researchers found that success in handling the issues encountered at each step in the process was strongly correlated with the overall success of a given project. Table 14-1 lists the key issues identified by Zand and Sorensen at each stage of the change model.

Kolb-Frohman Model

In contrast to the Lewin-Schein model is a slightly more elaborate offering by Kolb and Frohman (1970). This model of change contains seven steps and is considered to be more normative than that of Lewin-Schein. The essence of the Kolb-Frohman model is the assumption that successful implementation depends on a specific pattern of actions between the users and analysts. An empirical study by Ginzberg (1975, 1976) applied this model of change in the development of a series of hypotheses suggesting a strong relationship between the degree to which issues were successfully resolved at each of the seven stages and the overall success of the implementation process. His results suggested that projects that conformed closely to the normative Kolb-Frohman process showed a significantly greater degree of success than those projects that measurably deviated from the model. Table 14-2 lists the seven phases of the model and provides a brief explanation of the activities within each phase.

The purpose of reviewing these two accepted theories of change is to develop an understanding of the change process as it occurs during a typical DSS implementation. The models are not intended to be prescriptive but, rather, are intended to serve as a descriptive framework within which the implementation process can be conducted.

Patterns of Implementation

Alter (1980) suggests that the initial impetus behind the development of a DSS can be categorized in the following terms: (1) *user stimulus,* (2) *managerial stimulus,* or (3) *entrepreneurial stimulus.*

As the first two category names imply, the stimulus for a DSS project can result from the perceived needs of the users or the perceived needs of management. The third source assumes one or more persons from inside or outside the organization makes an effort to sell the organization on the idea of developing a DSS. Building upon these three sources of initiation, Alter has identified six generic DSS implementation patterns differing in terms of degree of user initiation, degree of mandated use, and degree of user participation in the design and development. Each scenario is descriptively named to suggest its underlying characteristics. Figure 14-1 illustrates Alter's six generic implementation patterns.

"Join Hands and Circle Round"

This is the ideal and most commonly employed scenario, according to the normative literature and reported empirical findings on implementation. Assuming all other factors remain the same, higher levels of user initiation and user involvement in a DSS development project are associated with higher probabilities of success. In this scenario, it is assumed that no obvious solution can be determined in advance and that the

Table 14-1 Favorable and Unfavorable Forces during Stages of Lewin-Schein Change Model

Stage of Change	Favorable Forces	Unfavorable Forces
Unfreezing	• Top managers felt the problem was important to the company. • Top management became involved. • Unit management recognized a need for change. • Top management initiated the project. • Both top management and unit management were both open and candid during discussion. • Unit managers were willing to revise some of their initial assumptions.	• Unit managers were unable to state their problems clearly. • Top management felt the overall problem was too big. • Unit management felt threatened by the project. • Some unit management resented the project. • Unit management lacked confidence in the analysts. • Unit managers felt they were capable of handling the project alone.
Moving	• Unit management and analysts gathered data jointly. • All relevant data were accessible and available. • New alternatives were devised. • Unit management reviewed and evaluated all alternatives. • Top management was advised of options. • Top management participated in the development of a solution. • All proposals for solutions were improved sequentially.	• Analysts were often not effective in educating unit management. • Unit management did not participate in the development of new solutions. • Unit management often did not fully understand the proposed solution of the analysts. • Analysts felt the project was concluded too quickly.
Refreezing	• Unit management tried the solution. • Frequency of utilization demonstrated the superiority of the new solution. • Analysts initiated positive feedback after early adoption and use. • Final solution was widely accepted after initial success. • Unit management expressed satisfaction with the new solution.	• Analysts did not try to support new managerial behavior after the solution was used. • Analysts did not try to reestablish stability after the solution was used. • Results were often difficult to quantify or measure.

Source: Reprinted from "Theory of Change & Effective Use of Management Science," by Zand, Dale E., and Sorenson, Richard E., published in *Administrative Science Quarterly,* Vol. 20, #4, by permission of Administrative Science Quarterly.

Table 14-2 The Kolb-Frohman Normative Model of Change in System Development	
Scouting	User and designer assess each other's needs and abilities to see if there is a match. An appropriate organizational starting point for the project is selected.
Entry	User and designer develop an initial statement of the goals and objectives. Commitment to the project is developed. User and designer develop a trusting relationship and a "contract" for conducting the project.
Diagnosis	User and designer gather data to refine and sharpen the definition of the problem and goals for the solution. User and designer assess available resources (including commitment) to determine whether continued effort is feasible.
Planning	User and designer define specific operational objectives and examine alternative ways to meet these objectives. Impacts of the proposed solutions on all parts of the organization are examined. User and designer develop an action plan that takes account of the solutions' impacts on the organization.
Action	User and designer put the "best" alternative into practice. Training necessary for effective use of the system is undertaken in all affected parts of the organization.
Evaluation	User and designer assess how well the goals and objectives (specified during the diagnosis and planning stages) were met. User and designer decide whether to work further on the system (evolve) or to cease active work (terminate).
Termination	User and designer ensure that "ownership" of and effective control over the new system rest in the hands of those who must use and maintain it. User and designer ensure that the necessary new patterns of behavior have become a stable part of the user's routine.

Source: Reprinted from "An Organizational Development Approach to Consulting" by Kolb and Frohman, Sloan Management Review, 1970, by permission of publisher. Copyright © 1970 by Sloan Management Review Association. All rights reserved.

user is ready to become involved in a cooperative problem-definition and problem-solving endeavor.

"Service with a Smile"

Here the user is simply looking to buy a product rather than a service. The form and content of the product are relatively clear-cut and predetermined. The main goal in this scenario is the completion of the DSS to specifications within the time and budget constraints set forth. Similar to "Join Hands and Circle Round," the degree of user initiation is quite high. In contrast to the previous scenario, however, the degree of user participation in development is relatively low.

"Do-It-Yourself Kit Salesman"

As shown by the figure, the degree of user initiation in this implementation scenario is small but the degree to which adoption is voluntary is relatively high. This scenario is an effort to convert a low-initiation, low-participation situation into a more favorable one. In this case, the user must be convinced that the DSS is necessary to the success of the firm and must be encouraged to participate in its development.

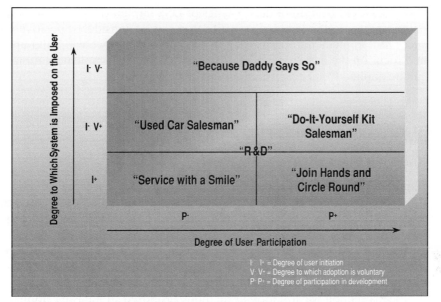

FIGURE 14-1 Six Generic DSS Implementation Patterns (Adapted from Alter, S. L. 1980. *Decision Support Systems: Current Practices and Continuing Challenges.* Reading, MA: Addison-Wesley.)

"Used Car Salesman"

This common scenario is characterized by a consultant or salesman attempting to sell the need for a DSS to the user. It is not unusual for this situation to yield significant benefits to the organization because many successful innovations often originate outside the settings in which they are applied. This same scenario, however, has a comparatively high risk of implementation difficulties stemming from the external initiation of the project.

"Because Daddy Says So"

The fifth implementation situation is also considered a common one in which the senior management of the firm mandates the development and use of a DSS. Despite its commonplace occurrence, this scenario is considered to be the least effective method of introducing decision support technologies into an organization. Without sufficient user initiation and support, the DSS will never become satisfactorily institutionalized so that its value can be fully realized.

"R&D"

The sixth and final scenario identified by Alter lies squarely in the middle of all the others and suggests that the results of an internally initiated research and development effort can emerge into the regular implementation stream through any of the other five scenarios.

The identification of the six types of DSS implementation situations allows us to gain insight into the types of activities that can be considered positive steps toward a successful implementation project. In the next section, we will build upon this insight and focus on the development of a framework for DSS implementation strategies that can be applied to specific situations and development needs.

14-2 SYSTEM EVALUATION

Knowing Success When You See It

Implicit in the process of implementation is the goal of success. If the implementation is a success then the effort is deemed worthy and sufficient. If, on the other hand, the implementation is viewed as a failure, then it is quite possible that nothing of the project can be salvaged and the question of what went wrong becomes the focus of all participants. Although the goal of success may be implicit, the measure of success remains less than clear. Just exactly what constitutes the successful design and implementation of a DSS? How do the designer and the users know success when they see it? In this section we will look at methods proposed to measure implementation success and several indicators of success that have resulted from various implementation research efforts.

Frameworks for System Evaluation

Success is a somewhat elusive construct. One person's measure of success may be another's minimum acceptable level of expectation. Although there exists no generalizable set of standards for measuring the success of a DSS implementation, unless a set of localized standards is developed it will be difficult, if not impossible, to determine the degree of success of the project. A number of approaches to measuring success have been advanced in the literature, each with its own set of unique criteria.

Overall Software Quality

Boehm et al. (1978) proposed a framework for measuring success that focuses on the characteristics, or quality, of the software. Table 14-3 lists the elements identified in this framework and provides brief descriptions of each of the specific measures.

Dickson and Powers (1973) suggested a more macro set of criteria in the form of specific quantitative measures:

- Ratio of actual project execution time to estimated project time
- Managerial attitudes toward the system
- Ratio of actual cost to develop the project to the budgeted costs
- The degree to which managers' needs are satisfied
- Impact of the project on the computer operations of the firm

It can be seen by a close consideration of the criteria proposed by Dickson and Powers that success, from their perspective, appears to be more related to efficiency than effectiveness (recall chapter 3). But even though efficiency may be an important

Table 14-3 Characteristics of Software Quality

Portability	Degree of platform or device independence: Software can be executed on a variety of hardware configurations.
Reliability	Degree of completeness: All of the software components are present and each is fully developed.
	Degree of accuracy: Software outputs are sufficiently precise to satisfy their intended use.
	Degree of consistency: Software contains uniform notation, terminology, and symbology within itself, and its content is traceable back to the requirements.
Efficiency	Degree of device efficiency: Software fulfills its purpose without waste of resources.
	Degree of accessibility: Design of software facilitates the selective use of its components.
Human-Engineering	Degree of communicativeness: Software facilitates the specification of inputs and provides outputs whose form and content are easy to assimilate and which are useful.
Testability	Degree of structuredness: Software possesses a definite pattern of organization of its independent parts.
Understandability	Degree of self-descriptiveness: Software contains enough information for the reader to determine its objectives, assumptions, constraints, inputs, outputs, components, and status.
	Degree of conciseness: No excessive information is presented.
	Degree of legibility: Software function and those of its component statements are easily discerned by reading the documentation or code.
Modifiability	Degree of augmentability: Software easily accommodates expansions in data storage requirements or component computational functions.

Source: Reprinted from *Characteristics of Software Quality,* © 1978, by permission of Barry Boehm.

element in measuring success, it must be subordinated to effectiveness if the goals of the project are to be realized.

Attitudinal Measures of Success

Another approach to the assessment of DSS design and implementation success is by measuring the attitudes of the users of the system with regard to various aspects of its use. One common approach is to focus on the degree to which the system is actually used by the intended user group. Measures such as the number of inquiries made during a given period or the number of accesses of the system during a specific set of activities have been suggested as possible success measures. While initially attractive, primarily due to the ease with which they can be obtained, such measures fail to account for whether system use is mandated by the organization or whether alternative decision support mechanisms are available to the users. If use is mandated, then measuring the number of times the system is accessed does not necessarily indicate the success of the system. Furthermore, if no alternative decision support mechanisms exist for a particular problem context, then access of the system may be a measure of its being "better than nothing" rather than true user preference. To avoid the problems associated with directly measuring system use while still attempting to measure the users' attitudes toward a given system, the concept of *user satisfaction* was proposed.

The logic behind user satisfaction as a measure of success is that the users will view a DSS as favorable if they perceive it to be effective in supporting the decision-making process. The more effective the system appears to be, the more satisfied the users will be with the system. Ives, Olson, and Baroudi (1983) developed a concise forty-item measure of user satisfaction that synthesizes the work of several researchers in this area. Although this is a popular measure and appears to be reliable across various projects, its use in the context of a DSS development effort can be problematic. DSS users tend to base their responses to the questionnaire on their most recent experience with the DSS rather than on their overall experience with the system. Contrary to a typical organizational application where one experience is very similar and easily generalizable to all others, the interaction with a DSS is not nearly as predictable. Because of this, measures of user satisfaction may vary greatly over time with regard to a particular DSS.

An alternative to measuring user satisfaction was proposed by Davis (1989). He used Likert scales[1] to measure attributes of two constructs associated with success: (1) *perceived usefulness* and (2) *perceived ease of use*. The former construct focuses on the attitudes of the user with regard to the degree to which the system is perceived to bring utility or value to the activity within which it is used. The latter focuses on the degree to which the users of the system perceive the tool to be easy to use. The distinction between these two constructs can be illustrated with a simple example. Suppose you are faced with the task of removing a large tree from the middle of an otherwise barren field. One tool you might consider is a bulldozer, and another is a chain saw. The bulldozer may actually elicit a higher degree of *perceived usefulness* over the saw because it could easily push the tree over in one motion and move it out of the way with little effort. The chain saw, however, for a variety of reasons, may elicit a higher *perceived ease of use* over the bulldozer. Factors ranging from familiarity with tool use, accessibility, environmental constraints, and other such issues can result in one tool being perceived easier to use in spite of it being perceived as less useful. The key measure of DSS success using Davis's approach is for the system to elicit both a high degree of perceived usefulness and a high degree of perceived ease of use. Table 14-4 lists several elements contained within each of the two constructs as they relate to DSS development and implementation.

Technical Measures of Success

A third approach to measuring DSS success is to determine whether the system does what it is supposed to do. In this regard, the technical functionality of the system

---

[1] A Likert-type item consists of a single statement followed by a usually five-point choice with each choice phrased to indicate that the choices are equally distant from each other. For example: strongly agree, agree, no opinion, disagree, strongly disagree.

Table 14-4 Characteristics of Davis's Success Measures

Perceived Usefulness	Perceived Ease-of-Use
• Increases user productivity • Enhances choice effectiveness • Improves choice performance • Increases ease with which choices can be made	• Increases user understanding of interaction with system • Increases overall flexibility of system • Facilitates steeper learning curves • Increases likelihood of skilled application of system

is used to determine system success. One advantage to focusing on the technical aspects of the system is that, for the most part, they are easily measured and readily accessible. For example, assuming the existence of a documented set of user requirements for the DSS, the degree to which the system accomplishes its original objectives, such as providing useful advice, may be an acceptable measure of DSS success. Another measure of success in this realm might be the number of DSS features consistent with the stated information needs of the users. Still another measure might be the adequacy of advice or explanations provided to the user during a specific problem-solving activity or, quite possibly, the number of cases submitted to the DSS for which no advice was offered. In the case where an expert system is a component of a DSS, technical success may be measured by comparing the advice offered by a live expert to that of the DSS when both are presented with an identical problem. Depending on the nature of the problem context, technical measures of success may be adequate to determine the overall success of the DSS implementation project.

Organizational Measures of Success

A final category of success measures focuses on the degree to which the system meets or exceeds certain organizational needs or expectations. For example, the direct payoff to an organization from its use of a particular DSS, either through cost reductions, increased revenues, or both, may be a useful measure of DSS implementation success. Ratios of direct benefits to direct costs are also commonly used to determine issues of organizational success.

Meador, Guyote, and Keen (1984) proposed a set of conditions for which organizational appropriateness and, thus, DSS success can be ascertained. Table 14-5 lists these criteria for DSS success.

Measuring DSS Success

One thing is clear regarding the question of what constitutes success and what criteria should be used to determine its degree: All of the ways in which success can be addressed are important to some aspect of the DSS implementation. That being the case, we can incorporate the various approaches to measuring success into a generalizable framework for DSS evaluation. Klein and Methlie (1995) have suggested a framework for evaluating a DSS that contains four categories of measurement. Table 14-6 contains the four categories and the various measures of success within each.

Table 14-5 Criteria for a Successful DSS

- Improves the way decision makers think about problems.
- Fits well with the organization's planning methods.
- Fits well with the political approach to decision making within the organization.
- Results in alternatives and choices that are implemented.
- Is considered both cost-effective and valuable relative to its development costs.
- Is expected to be used for a measurable period of time.

Table 14-6 A Framework for DSS Success Evaluation

System Performance
- Efficiency and response time
- Data entry
- Output format
- Hardware
- Usage
- Man-machine interface

Task Performance
- Decision-making time, alternatives, analysis, quality, and participants
- User perceptions of trust, satisfaction, usefulness, and understanding

Business Opportunities
- Costs of development, operation, and maintenance
- Benefits associated with increased income and reduced costs
- Value to the organization of better service, competitive advantage, and training

Evolutionary Aspects
- Degree of flexibility, ability to change
- Overall functionality of the development tool

Source: Adapted from Klein and Methlie (1995).

System Performance

The first of Klein and Methlie's categories focuses on the quality of the computer system. Issues such as system response time, availability, usage time, reliability, and quality of system support, among others, are identified and measured. These measures can be obtained using a variety of methods including direct observation, event logging, and attitude or perceptual construct surveys. As discussed previously, the overall quality of the performance of the DSS is often highly correlated to the acceptance of the system by its users.

Task Performance

This category of assessment takes a micro focus on performance and addresses issues related to the functionality of the DSS within the specific problem context for which it was developed. Ideally, a DSS is intended to provide the support that will result in an improved decision outcome. Unfortunately, however, the degree of uncertainty associated with a typical semistructured or unstructured decision context makes a focus on the quality of the outcome somewhat untenable in terms of performance evaluation. This is because once the decision has been made, the outcome is often out of the control of the decision maker. We can agree that a high-quality decision does not necessarily result in a high-quality outcome. Furthermore, a high-quality outcome can occur by chance, even in the face of a poor-quality decision. The point is that we assume a relationship between the quality of the decision made and the quality, or desirability, of the outcome realized. As such, we measure task performance by focusing on that which we can control (decision quality) instead of that which we cannot (outcome quality). Decision quality can be assessed in terms of time spent in the decision process, number of alternatives evaluated, and span of information searched. Additionally, qualitative measures dealing with trust or confidence, satisfaction, and understanding can also be included in this measure.

Business Opportunities

Klein and Methlie's third category measures the DSS's effect on certain organizational factors. The development and implementation of a DSS normally requires a significant commitment of organizational resources represented by both dollars and time. The effects of that commitment can be used to determine the level of success achieved in this area. This category is primarily quantitative in nature and includes measures focusing on increases in revenue, cost reductions, increases in training effectiveness, increases in competitive advantages, and changes in productivity, among many others.

Evolutionary Aspects

How well the DSS adapts to changes within the problem context and environment is the focus of this fourth category of performance measurement. Inherent in providing support to ill-structured decisions and problem-solving tasks are the changes that can occur in the users' decision-making behavior, the problem characteristics, and circumstances under which the decision must be made. The ability of a DSS to adapt to these dynamics is often a function of the original development tool selected and the ability of the user to make necessary changes to data or models. Despite the highly qualitative nature of this measurement category, perceptions of flexibility and adaptability can speak to one aspect of the overall performance quality of a DSS.

Risks in DSS Implementation Projects

Recall from chapter 5 that risk is a concept rooted in probability assessment. Often one cannot know the exact probability of one or more negative events occurring during the course of a project, nor can one ever be sure that all possible negative outcomes have been identified and assessed. So the bad news is that we cannot completely determine the scope of the possible risks and their exact probabilities of occurrence. However, the good news is that any identification of potential risk and any quality assessment of probability will directly contribute to an increase in the quality of the DSS implementation effort and, thus, the success of the project. To perform a risk assessment in any environment, one needs simply to know what risks are possible and to attempt to determine conditions that suggest an increased likelihood of failure.

Alter (1980) has identified eight basic clusters of risk factors that can be used to assist in determining the degree of uncertainty during the DSS implementation process. Table 14-7 lists each of these clusters of risk factors, its effect on the project, and the typical way in which it presents itself.

DSS Implementation Strategy

Once a thorough risk analysis has been conducted using the factors outlined in table 14-7, the next step is to formulate possible strategies for dealing with either the identified risk factors themselves or their expected consequences.

As with any organizational application development project, the choice of implementation strategy is based on a series of considerations. In the case of selecting an appropriate DSS implementation strategy, the choice will depend on determinations of resource requirements and availability, likelihood of successful completion of the project, and the specific situational constraints associated with a specific strategy. Alter (1980) has identified four general categories of DSS implementation strategies, each with its own set of unique characteristics and situational constraints. Table 14-8 summarizes the four strategies and lists several situations where each would be considered appropriate.

It is important to note that the various strategies contained within the framework are not meant to be universally useful. For example, while the strategy of avoiding change may minimize difficulties in implementing a new DSS, it may not be a viable strategy if the primary objective of the new DSS is to foster or promote change. In other words, the selection of an implementation strategy is a function of the stated objectives of the system and of the environmental characteristics in which it will be implemented.

In the next section, we turn our attention away from the big picture of DSS implementation to the more focused but equally important activities of system integration. Without an effective integration of the DSS into the existing application infrastructure of the organization, the odds are significantly less that the DSS will become an institutionalized component of the organization's daily decision processes.

14-3 THE IMPORTANCE OF INTEGRATION

The Organization That Decides Together . . .

In some cases, a DSS may be developed and implemented in a manner such that it requires no special access or interface to other organizational applications and simply operates as a stand-alone decision support tool. With the increasing popularity of expert systems, executive information systems, and data mining applications, however, the isolated DSS is becoming virtually extinct. The costs associated with the development of an organizational DSS dictate that the widest possible community of decision makers have access to the technology. Furthermore, the growing need for multiple and

Table 14-7 DSS Implementation Risk Factors

Risk Factor	Problem	Typical Situation	Result
Nonexistent or unwilling users	Lack of commitment to use the system	System not initiated by potential users and developed without their participation	Disuse; uneven use; lack of impact
Multiple users or implementers	Communication problems; inability to incorporate interests of many people	System involving voluntary use by many individuals or coordination among many people	Uneven use
Disappearing users, implementers, or maintainers	No one available to use or modify the system	Worst case: System is the vehicle of a person who leaves, or system initiator leaves before system is installed	Reduced use or disappearance of the system
Inability to specify purpose or usage pattern	Overoptimism on part of system designer and advocates	Assumption that non-computer personnel will figure out how to use the system	Disuse
Inability to predict and cushion impact	Lack of motivation to work or change work pattern without receiving benefits	No benefits from the system to people in the "feeder role"; forced changes in organizational procedures	"Why bother" syndrome; fear and/or annoyance
Loss or lack of support	Requirements for funding; obstruction by uncooperative people	Lack of budget to run system; lack of management action to use system effectively	System death or disuse
Lack of experience with similar systems	Unfamiliarity leading to mistakes	Developing an innovative system aimed at substantive change rather than automation per se	Technical problems; bad fit of solution and problem; misuse or disuse of system
Technical problems and cost-effectiveness	Cost of maintaining or improving system	Advocacy situation: No adequate way to estimate value of system either before or after potential improvements	Failure of system to meet needs; either limps on or is discarded

Source: Adapted from Alter, S.L. 1980. *Decision Support Systems: Current Practices and Continuing Challenges.* Reading, MA: Addison-Wesley.

disparate sources of information requires the modern DSS to be "connected" in some manner to a large population of existing applications and data stores. It is this connectivity or *integration* of the DSS into the existing organizational computing infrastructure that is the subject of this discussion.

Integrating the DSS into the organization simply means that the new application is merged into the existing computing infrastructure in a way that gives the appearance of a seamless architecture to the user. This appearance of one agency rather than separate hardware, software, communications, and data access contributes significantly

Table 14-8 DSS Implementation Strategies

Implementation Strategy	Typical Situation or Purpose	Pitfalls Encountered
1. Divide the project into manageable pieces	To minimize the risk of producing a massive system that doesn't work.	
Use prototypes	Success of the effort hinges on relatively untested concepts. Test these concepts before committing to a full-fledged version.	Reactions to the prototype system (in an experimental setting) may differ from reactions to the final system in day-to-day use.
Use an evolutionary approach	Implementer attempts to shorten feedback loops between self and clients and between intentions and products.	Requires users to live with continuing change, which some may find annoying.
Develop a series of tools	To meet ad hoc analysis needs by providing databases and small models that can be created, modified, and discarded.	Limited applicability. Expense of maintaining infrequently used data.
2. Keep the solution simple	To encourage use and to avoid scaring away users.	Although generally beneficial, can lead to misrepresentation, misunderstanding, and misuse.
Be simple	Not an issue for inherently simple systems. For other systems or situations, it may be possible to choose between simple and complicated approaches.	Some business problems are not inherently simple. Insisting on simple solutions may result in skirting the real issue.
Hide complexity	The system is presented as a "black box" that answers questions using procedures not presented to the user.	Use of "black boxes" by nonexperts can lead to misuse of the results because of misunderstanding of the underlying models and assumptions.
Avoid change	Given a choice of automating existing practice or developing new methods, choose the former.	New system may have little real impact. Not applicable to efforts purporting to foster change.
3. Develop a satisfactory support base	One or more components of the user-management support base is missing.	Danger that one support-gaining strategy will be applied without adequate attention to others.
Obtain user participation	The system effort was not initiated by users. The usage pattern is not obvious in advance.	With multiple users, difficulty of getting everyone involved and incorporating everyone's interests. With sophisticated models, reduced feasibility of user participation in model formulation and interpretation.
Obtain user commitment	The system has been developed without user involvement. The system is to be imposed on users by management.	It is difficult to obtain commitment without some kind of quid pro quo or demonstration that the system will help the user.

(continued)

Table 14-8 Continued

Implementation Strategy	Typical Situation or Purpose	Pitfalls Encountered
Obtain management support	To obtain funding for the continuation of the project. To obtain management action in forcing people to comply with the system or to use it.	Management enthusiasm may not be shared by users, resulting in perfunctory use or disuse.
Sell the system	Some potential users were not involved in system development and do not use it. System is not used to full potential by the organization.	Often unsuccessful unless real advantages can be convincingly demonstrated.
4. Meet user needs and institutionalize system	A system is to have many users in an ongoing application.	Because strategies under this heading are somewhat incompatible, emphasis on one may exclude another.
Provide training	The system is not designed in close cooperation with all potential users.	Frequent difficulty in estimating the type and intensity of training that is needed. Initial training programs often require substantial reformation and elaboration.
Provide ongoing assistance	The system is used by an intermediary rather than a decision maker. The system is used with the help of an intermediary who handles the mechanical details.	If the system is used by an intermediary, the decision maker may not understand the analysis in sufficient detail.
Insist on mandatory use	The system is a medium for integration and coordination in planning. The system purports to facilitate the work of individuals.	Difference between genuine use and halfhearted submission of numbers for a plan. Difficulty in forcing people to think in a particular mold.
Permit voluntary use	Avoid building resistance to a hard sell by allowing voluntary use.	Generally ineffective unless the system meets a genuine felt need or appeals to an individual user intellectually or otherwise.
Rely on diffusion and exposure	It is hoped that the enthusiasts will demonstrate the benefits of a system to their colleagues.	Ineffective; perhaps as much an excuse for lack of positive action as it is a real strategy.
Tailor systems to users' capabilities	Users differ in their ability and/or propensity to use analytic techniques.	Not clear how to do so. In practice, systems seem to be built to users' requirements, not their capabilities.

Source: Adapted from Alter, S.L. 1980. *Decision Support Systems: Current Practices and Continuing Challenges.* Reading, MA: Addison-Wesley.

to the perception by the users of ease of use and usefulness so important to the success of a DSS implementation.

Another important benefit associated with integration comes from the various synergies created from having simultaneous access to multiple decision support and development tools that facilitate the movement of models and data between the various applications. Once the decision maker is provided with a wide variety of integrated tools and support mechanisms, he or she can focus attention on using each of the tools to reach a specific objective within the problem context. Instead of having to divert effort away from the problem at hand in order to achieve some application-related objective such as the transfer of data from one DSS to the next or the modification of a model in one application using a tool contained in another, the decision maker can concentrate on solving the problem of importance to the organization.

Types of Integration

Two general categories of DSS integration can be identified: (1) functional integration and (2) physical integration.

In *functional integration,* the various decision support functions of the DSS are integrated and linked to those of the existing infrastructure. This linking includes providing common menu access, inter- and intra-application transfer of data and tools, and a common application interface at the same desktop client or workstation. In this way, single or multiple users can have access to all available organizational decision support mechanisms and resources on demand.

Physical integration involves the architectural bundling of the hardware, software, and data communication characteristics associated with the new DSS into the existing set of physical systems. In many cases, physical integration begins before the DSS is even designed because the need for integration with the existing infrastructure will, in some cases, determine which DSS development tools to employ and which software platforms to adopt for development.

The activities of both physical and functional integration are often quite technical and tend to be unique to each organizational environment. Because of this, any detailed discussion is beyond the scope of this text and is best left to the computer scientists that have devoted themselves to understanding the inner world of the machinery. For our purposes, it is sufficient to realize the importance of integrating the DSS into the existing arsenal of computing applications and to further realize the complexities associated with accomplishing this necessary objective.

A Model for Global DSS Integration

A number of models have been proposed that focus on the integration of DSS, ES, and EIS systems into existing computing architectures. Each of the models has its own approach; for example, some are problem driven, some application driven, and some function driven. Furthermore, each proposed model of integration contains its own set of terms and titles ranging from *management support system* (MSS) to *expert support system* (ESS) to *intelligent decision support system* (IDSS). Regardless of the approach, however, the common bond among all of these proposed models of integration is the global connectivity and access to all organizational communication channels and decision support mechanisms. Figure 14-2 depicts a generalized global integration concept for decision support within an organization.

Resistance and Other Completely Normal Reactions

One of the most common problems faced during the implementation and integration of virtually any computer-based information system, including a DSS, is the resistance by certain individuals or groups to the changes associated with the new system. The most important thing to realize about user resistance to new systems and resistance to change in general is that it is a normal and, in some cases, healthy human response.

Change tends to disrupt a person's frame of reference, particularly if it appears to suggest a future where lessons learned from past experiences will not hold true, or will be potentially unreliable. Technological change can be the most pervasive and the most formidable faced by the typical organizational member. Resistance to change is often most noticeable when such change is viewed as a crisis or a response to an emer-

FIGURE 14-2 Generalized Globally Integrated DSS (adapted from Min and Eom 1994).

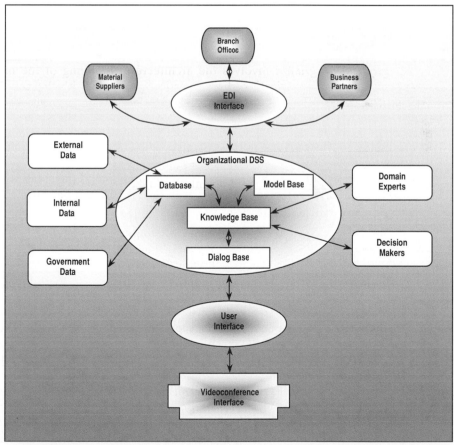

gency. In the case of an impending new DSS, which may not be completely understood or which may appear to require significant effort to master, users may react in several ways. They may simply deny the change. They may actually distort information about the new system so that they convince themselves and others that the new system will not really affect the status quo. In other cases, however, they may engage in efforts, either overt or covert, to derail the new system, thus eliminating the source of the undesirable change (Marakas and Hornik 1996). The importance of effective integration to the reduction of resistance to change cannot be overstated. No matter how important the new system is to the attainment of organizational objectives, resistance to change can result from a number of factors:

- ***Self-interest.*** When users have achieved status, privilege, or self-esteem through effective use of an old system, they will often see the new system as a threat. If the plan threatens paid overtime by serving to reduce effort in a particular problem context, users may fear the impact on their bank balance.
- ***Fear of the unknown.*** Users may be uncertain of their ability to learn new skills, their aptitude with new systems, or their ability to take on new roles.
- ***Conscientious objection or differing perceptions.*** Users may sincerely believe that the new system either is inappropriate or will be ineffective. They may view the situation from a different viewpoint, or they may have aspirations for themselves or the organization that are fundamentally opposed to those of the designers of the new system.
- ***Suspicion.*** Users may not trust the new system or the advocates of the development project.
- ***Conservatism.*** Organizations or factions of people within them may simply be opposed to change. This can result from a feeling that everything is OK, from being out of touch with customers, from lack of exposure to better ways of doing things, or from slowness of decision making.

Table 14.9 lists several potential resisters to a new DSS application within the organization.

The important point here is that if we can understand the roots of possible resistance to change, we can plan for it and overcome it before it becomes a significant obstacle.

Table 14-9 Potential Resisters to DSS Implementations

- ***Managers.*** Some may fear loss of job through automation or loss of importance.
- ***Users.*** Some may resist any form of computerization and others may experience difficulties adapting to user-DSS interfaces.
- ***IS personnel.*** Some may fear loss of power if technologies reside outside their sphere of control or influence.
- ***Experts.*** Some may fear a loss of importance or complete loss of job.
- ***Nonexperts.*** Some may fear inability to be recognized in an environment dependent upon decision support technologies.
- ***Unions.*** Resistance to change is often an effective vehicle to increase membership.

14-4 CHAPTER SUMMARY

With this chapter, we have completed the cycle started in chapter 1. The implementation of the organizational DSS is as important, if not more so, as the design of the application itself. Organizations must be aware of the importance of committing sufficient resources to the implementation and integration processes to ensure a successful, and useful, DSS project. In the remaining two chapters, we will look at two supplementary issues related to decision support within the modern organization: the role of creativity in decision making and the future of DSS technologies.

Key Concepts

- DSS implementation (14-1)

  Implementation is the introduction of change. It is a set of activities that are focused on the successful introduction of the DSS into the organizational environment.

- Models of change (14-1)

  The Lewin-Schein theory of change

    According to this theory, the process of change occurs in three basic steps: unfreezing, moving, and refreezing. Success in handling the issues encountered at each step in the process has been strongly correlated with the overall success of a given project.

  The Kolb-Frohman change model

    This model contains seven steps and is considered to be the most common. The essence of this model is the assumption that the probability of successful implementation will depend on a specific pattern of actions between the users and analysts. Researchers have shown that projects that conformed closely to the normative Kolb-Frohman process showed a significantly greater degree of success than those projects that measurably deviated from the model.

- DSS development project initiation sources (14-1)

  The initial impetus for the development of a DSS can be categorized in terms of three potential sources:

    User stimulus

    Managerial stimulus

    Entrepreneurial stimulus

- DSS implementation patterns. The six generic DSS implementation patterns differ in terms of degree of user initiation, degree of mandated use, and the degree of user participation in the design and development. (14-1)

  Join Hands and Circle Round

    This scenario is considered to be the ideal situation. It is assumed that no obvious solution can be determined in advance and that the user is ready to become involved in a cooperative problem-definition and problem-solving endeavor.

  Service with a Smile

    In this situation, the form and content of the solution is relatively clear-cut and predetermined. The degree of user initiation is quite high; however, the degree of user participation in development is relatively low.

Do-It-Yourself Kit Salesman

This scenario is an effort to convert a low-initiation, low-participation situation into a more favorable one. In this case, the user must be convinced that the DSS is necessary to the success of the firm and must be encouraged to participate in its development.

Used Car Salesman

This scenario is characterized by a consultant or salesman who attempts to sell the need for a DSS to the user. It has a comparatively high risk of implementation difficulties stemming from the external initiation of the project.

Because Daddy Says So

This situation is a common one in which the senior management of the firm mandates the development and use of a DSS. It is considered to be the least effective method of introducing decision support technologies into an organization.

R&D

This scenario suggests that the results of an internally initiated research and development effort can emerge into the regular implementation stream through any of the other five scenarios.

- The identification of the six types of DSS implementation situations allows us to gain insight into the types of activities that can be considered positive steps toward a successful implementation project. (14-1)

- Frameworks for system evaluation (14-2)

Overall software quality

The measuring of success focuses on the quality of the software.

Attitudinal measures of success

The measuring of success focuses on the attitudes of the users of the system with regard to various aspects of its use.

Technical measures of success

The measuring of success focuses on determining whether the system does what it is supposed to do. In this regard, the technical functionality of the system is used to determine system success. The advantages of this method are that the technical functions are easily measured and accessible.

Organizational measures of success

The measuring of success focuses on the degree to which the system meets or exceeds certain organizational needs or expectations.

- Measurement of user satisfaction (14-2)

The logic behind user satisfaction as a measure of success is that the user will view a DSS as favorable if it is perceived to be effective in supporting the decision-making process. The more effective the system appears to be, the more satisfied the user will be with the system.

- A generalized framework for DSS success evaluation (14-2)

System performance

In this category, the quality of the computer system becomes the focus. The overall quality of the performance of the DSS is often highly correlated to the acceptance of the system by its users.

Task performance

> This category of assessment takes a micro focus on performance and addresses issues related to the functionality of the DSS within the specific problem context for which it was developed.

Business opportunities

> This category measures the factors that contribute to the organizational aspects of the DSS.

Evolutionary aspects

> The degree to which the DSS adapts to changes within the problem context and environment is the focus of this category of performance measurement.

- Eight basic clusters of risk factors in DSS implementation projects (14-2)

  Nonexistent or unwilling users

  Multiple users or implementers

  Disappearing users, implementers, or maintainers

  Inability to specify purpose or usage pattern

  Loss or lack of support

  Lack of experience with similar systems

  Technical problems and cost-effectiveness

- Four general categories of DSS implementation strategies (14-2)

  Divide the project into manageable pieces

  Keep the solution simple

  Develop a satisfactory support base

  Meet user need and institutionalize system

- The selection of an implementation strategy is a function of the stated objectives of the system and of the environmental characteristics in which it will be implemented. (14-2)

- The importance of integration (14-3)

  The costs associated with the development of an organizational DSS dictate that the widest possible community of decision makers has access to the technology.

  The growing need for multiple and disparate sources of information requires the modern DSS to be "connected" in some manner to a large population of existing applications and data stores.

  The integrating of the DSS into the organization contributes significantly to the perception by the users of ease of use and usefulness, factors that are important to the success of a DSS implementation.

  Having simultaneous access to multiple decision support and development tools can facilitate the movement of models and data between the various applications.

- Types of integration (14-3)

  Functional integration

  > In functional integration, the various decision support functions of the DSS are integrated and linked to those of the existing infrastructure.

  Physical integration

  > Physical integration involves the architectural bundling of the hardware, software, and data communication characteristics associated with the new DSS into the existing set of physical systems.

- Global DSS integration (14-3)

Global DSS integration is the creation of a global connectivity and access to all organizational communication channels and decision support mechanisms.

- Several factors can result in resistance to changes associated with the new system: (14-3)

Self-interest

Fear of the unknown

Conscientious objection or differing perceptions

Suspicion

Conservatism

Questions for Review

1. Describe the relationship between system implementation and change.
2. Describe the Lewin-Schein theory of change and its characteristics.
3. What are the seven steps of the process of change in the Kolb-Frohman model?
4. What are the possible sources of initial impetus for the development of a DSS?
5. Briefly describe the basic concept Alter used for classifying implementation patterns. What is the value of this classification?
6. List and briefly describe the six generic DSS implementation patterns.
7. List and briefly describe the frameworks for system evaluation.
8. What are the various methods of measuring user satisfaction?
9. What are the differences between the evaluation of system performance and the evaluation of task performance?
10. Describe the generalized framework for DSS success evaluation introduced in this chapter.
11. Identify the risk factors in DSS implementation projects.
12. List and briefly describe the types of integration.
13. Is resistance to change natural? Why or why not?

For Further Discussion

1. Observe the implementation of a DSS in an organization you are familiar with. Identify its pattern of implementation.
2. Use the generalized framework for DSS success evaluation to evaluate the success of a DSS implementation project in an organization you are familiar with.
3. Discuss the considerations for formulating and selecting implementation strategies.
4. Discuss the importance of integration.
5. Study a successful case of system integration. Describe the type(s) of integration used. Discuss the impacts of resistance to changes associated with the new system.

15

Creative Decision Making and Problem Solving

Learning Objectives

- Learn three perspectives on the theory of creativity: psychoanalytical, behavioral, and process

- Understand five basic categories of ways of thinking: logical, lateral, critical, opposite, and groupthink

- Comprehend why it is important for decision makers to impart intuition and creativity to the decision process

- Be familiar with the categories of creative problem-solving techniques and their basic concepts

- Learn the basic concept of intelligent agents (IAs)

- Be familiar with the characteristics of intelligent software agents

- Learn the types of problems intelligent agents can solve

- Become familiar with future applications of intelligent software agents

Fishing for New Ideas

Marsh Fisher has been captivated by creativity since 1964 when he first attended a writing class at UCLA. Much to his amazement, he discovered that he lacked the ability to ad-lib and generate ideas as quickly as his fellow students. As he drove home, however, he would think of a funny idea and wonder why he could not think of those same ideas in class. As Fisher pursued the elusive ability to make creative connections, he realized that his own production of creative ideas was limited primarily by his memory abilities and the variety of associations that were generated by his life experience.

In general, the human mind is much better at recognizing information than recalling it. This is one reason multiple choice tests can be so much easier than essay exams. Fisher believed that his limitations to recall and to make a variety of associations were roadblocks that might be overcome with the help of computer software. Therefore, when he retired as cofounder of Century 21 Real Estate Corporation in 1977, he devoted himself full-time to developing a software package that would help people generate ideas by expanding their limited memory capabilities, helping them make associations, and asking probing questions.

Through his years of studying the creative process, Fisher concluded, "Creativity is about as magical as the skill required to add two plus two. Both can be taught and learned. And the more one practices any discipline, the more proficient one becomes."

The software package that resulted from his research is IdeaFisher: a twenty-five-megabyte associative database (compressed to seven megabytes) designed to stimulate thinking about virtually any subject and capable of being tailored by the user to include industry- or product-specific terms and links. IdeaFisher contains two databases that are linked in a unique manner to perform these tasks. The first database, the QBank, contains nearly six thousand questions organized to clarify problems, modify ideas, and evaluate solutions. The second, the IdeaBank, contains more than seventy thousand idea words and nearly eight hundred thousand associated links. It is somewhat analogous to a huge free-associated thesaurus.

The psychological foundation of IdeaFisher rests on the principles of association, memory retrieval, and the use of analogy and metaphor. Thinkers interact with and use the idea words to stimulate ideas and associations in their own memory banks. New connections and associations are stimulated and a tremendous number of ideas can be generated in an extremely short period of time.

IdeaFisher speeds up the creative process by mimicking the way the human mind organizes and remembers experiences through the formation of associations to link words and concepts together. These idea associations invoke different mental images about the subject being considered, thus stimulating new viewpoints and ideas. Further, these associations can be used to generate ideas for new products or services, new markets or uses for existing products or services, advertising or promotional campaigns, special events or programs, training programs, presentations, stories or scripts, and corporate or product names.

A typical example of the use of IdeaFisher comes from Jim Shenk, manager of contracts and program management with CEC Instruments in San Dimas, California, who used the software to facilitate a strategic planning process. "We needed to do some strategic thinking for the division so we used IdeaFisher to help guide us through the process. The first thing it does is ask the questions that are so obvious that you usually don't ask them . . . and, all too often, don't really know the answer to . . . such as "What business are we in?" and "Why do our customers buy from us?" As noted earlier, IdeaFisher offers nearly six thousand questions to help stimulate thinking.

"We asked ourselves a lot of questions and the answers began to lead us toward an opportunity. We have been heavily dependent on the aerospace industry and this opportunity helped us create a market outside that industry, in the commercial aviation market."

"I've also used the software to help set up a mission statement and for understanding what our business is all about. It was extremely helpful for thinking through those questions. I also use the Strategic Planning Module, which has a lot of interesting questions specifically organized for planning, as well as the Presentation Planning Module." (There is also a Business and Grant Proposal Module available.)

It is important to remember that IdeaFisher does not create anything for you. It's not like a spreadsheet or a database program that will produce something. IdeaFisher just helps stimulate your own thinking and keeps you focused on questions that most of us tend to think are too obvious to even be considered. In actual fact, we can't answer many of those questions because we really have not thought about them . . . and when we do think about them enough to answer them, we find they lead us in directions that we might not have discovered before.

"IdeaFisher is a great way to find a hundred new ideas . . . even if you reject ninety-nine of them, so what? If you get one that's usable or opens up a new opportunity, it makes the process worthwhile," says Shenk.

Clayton Lee, Houston-based inventor of the Orbiter, an impact-free trampoline treadmill, used IdeaFisher to reduce the unit cost of an add-on to the Orbiter . . . from $2,000 a unit to approximately $100 per unit. The vast reduction in cost opened up new markets. Said Lee, "IdeaFisher puts more thinking back into the marketplace. It helps develop our minds, which is something we've forgotten how to do. Thinking is no longer an elective skill."

Ron Sargent, a fluid engineer who designed the first cruise control for GM, the Porta Potti, and the Dancing Waters at Disney World's EPCOT Center, states, "We look at IdeaFisher almost as an open-ended platform, an AutoCAD for creativity."

IdeaFisher is a powerful thinking tool that has been used in a wide variety of ways. In addition to the previous examples, IdeaFisher has been used to write sermons, design tapestries, develop university courses, create product names, and invent a tree shaker modification for the orchard industry. It has even played a part in Vice President Al Gore's reinventing government project where it was used by the Department of Commerce in a series of focus group meetings to help transform complaints into suggestions.

Despite the advances in artificial intelligence and computer-based decision support mechanisms, we still are faced with making certain underlying assumptions about the human decision-making process that are just that: assumptions. For example, in the context of decision models, we are often faced with the assumption that all alternative courses of action are known to the decision maker or are easily ascertained. In most unstructured problem contexts, however, this assumption is simply untenable. We know we must generate new ideas if an acceptable alternative is to be realized. Often this new idea generation is something that just happens during the normal course of problem solving. In other words, there are some things that we know are happening but we just do not fully understand their role in either the process or outcomes. One of these is the role of *creativity* in decision making. In this chapter, we will explore the concept of creativity and identify what is currently known about its role in managerial decision making. Through this investigation we will begin to see why the study of creativity is becoming increasingly important in the field of DSSs.

15-1 WHAT IS CREATIVITY?

One way to think about creativity is as an ability to see the same things as everyone else but to think of something different. Creativity is a concept that has summoned almost as many definitions of itself as it has resulted in new ideas. From philosopher to layman, each person seems to have his or her own definition of what creativity is. Often the definition takes the form of "I don't really know what it is, but I know it when I see it." No matter the origin or focus of the definition, however, all seem to agree that creativity involves the ability to generate novel and useful ideas and solutions to problems and challenges.

Creativity involves the translation of our unique gifts, talents, and vision into some form of external reality that is both new and useful. Often creativity can involve the combining of existing objects intended for one purpose into a new object intended to serve a completely different purpose. When NASA realized the need to develop a low-friction coating for spacecraft heat shields to keep astronauts from burning up when reentering Earth's atmosphere, someone else saw the same coating as a way to solve the problem of eggs sticking to the frying pan: Teflon. When astronaut James Lovell and the crew of *Apollo 13* were faced with literally running out of oxygen while trying to get themselves and their crippled spacecraft back to Earth from the Moon, creativity helped them and their team figure out how to use unrelated components from the lunar lander to fashion a carbon dioxide filter for the command module so they could recycle their oxygen. When the wine press and the die punch were developed in the seventeenth century, their respective inventors saw devices useful for making wine and for manufacturing castings for metal parts. Gutenberg, on the other hand, saw the same objects as the parts necessary to build a printing press capable of mass-producing manuscripts. Lucky for us that he did, too. Imagine reading this textbook on handwritten scrolls!

Creativity is an important element in the generation of new ways to do old things and ways to do things yet undone, and these new alternatives are essential to achieving the competitive edge so necessary to success and survival in the world's markets. Because a DSS is intended to support the decision-making process and an essential element in that process is the creative generation of new ideas, it makes perfect sense that the two concepts should be entwined.

Theories of Creativity

The origins of creative thought have been the source of debate among psychologists for decades. From this debate, a wide variety of theories have emerged to explain why some people seem to be more creative than others.

The *psychoanalytic perspective* maintains that creativity is a preconscious mental activity. In other words, creative thinking occurs in our subconscious thoughts and, as such, is not directly accessible to our conscious thoughts. In contrast, the *behavioral perspective* argues that creativity is nothing more than a natural response to stimuli within our individual environments and that certain combinations of stimuli can lead to more creative behavior than other combinations. A third perspective, the *process orientation view,* sees creativity as a property of a thought process that can be acquired and improved through instruction and practice. Recent studies have indicated that individual creativity is not as strong a function of individualized traits such as inventiveness or independence as had been thought and can, therefore, be learned and improved. This suggests that the potential for creative thinking exists to a greater or lesser degree in everyone (Marakas and Elam 1997). This has led to an influx of commercial products into the realm of the DSS intended to foster and enhance creativity in decision makers and organizational problem solvers at all levels of the firm.

It is generally agreed that to "teach" creativity, one must break down rigid thinking that serves as a barrier to the generation of new ideas. In this regard, the enhancement of creativity is a process of change. By eliciting and facilitating different ways of thinking, creativity can be enhanced and new ideas can be generated.

Different Ways to Think

When we think about a particular problem context, the way in which we conduct our thinking can have a significant effect on the generation of alternatives or the selection of an appropriate alternative from a choice set. Using a common classification scheme, five basic categories of ways of thinking can be identified: (1) logical, (2) lateral, (3) critical, (4) opposite, and (5) groupthink.

Logical Thinking

One way to think about a problem is for the decision maker to build on his or her experimental and analytical abilities. *Logical thinking* is perhaps the most common, most widely used, and most often recommended approach to solving a problem.

This method of thinking is rooted in the model-building and quantitative methods of management science and is an integral part of the design and development of a computer-based DSS.

Lateral Thinking

Lateral thinking was originally identified by Edward de Bono (1970), a British physician and psychologist, as a method of providing an escape from conventional "vertical" lines of thought. The method is based upon the premise that the human mind naturally processes and stores information in accordance with a specific pattern of thought and action. Because of this logical categorization process, the mind becomes hindered in any attempt to change these recognized patterns of thought. Lateral thinking disrupts these patterns through the introduction of discontinuity. Table 15-1 compares the characteristics of conventional vertical thinking with those of a lateral thinking process.

Three major activities are available to promote lateral thinking processes: (1) *awareness*, (2) *alternatives*, and (3) *provocation*.

Awareness   The activities in this category are intended to redefine and clarify current ideas. Before any new ideas can be generated or any old ideas rejected, the range of current ideas must be fully identified and understood. Activities such as the direct identification of the dominant ideas in the problem context, a review of com-

Table 15-1 Comparison of Characteristics of Vertical and Lateral Thinking

Vertical Thinking Process	*Lateral Thinking Process*
Concerned with stability and the identification of absolutes for judging various relationships.	Concerned with both change and movement and with trying to find new ways to look at things.
Seeks to find the "right" answer by using YES/NO justification at each step of the process.	Avoids looking for the absolute "right" or "wrong" answer and focuses attention on what is different.
Analyzes ideas with regard to their probability of success.	Analyzes ideas with regard to how they might be useful in generating new ideas.
Strives for continuity of process by logically proceeding from one step to the next.	Constantly strives for the introduction of discontinuity by encouraging illogical jumps from one step to another.
Rejects any information not considered to be immediately relevant and selectively chooses what to consider in the generation of new ideas.	Chance intrusions are welcomed and nothing is considered irrelevant.
Focuses primarily on the obvious and tends to progress using established patterns of thought.	Focuses on progress via avoidance of the obvious.
Guarantees that at least a minimally acceptable solution will be found.	Increases the odds that a new or innovative solution will be found but avoids making any guarantees.

mon boundaries of the problem space, and identification of typical assumptions made about the problem are all necessary to promote the awareness required to think laterally. The important thing to note here is that awareness activities are intended only to identify current ideas and not to evaluate them. The process of evaluation comes later.

Alternatives   In this second category of activities, a conscious effort is made to produce as many different ways as possible of looking at the problem context. The object is to provide the decision maker with as wide a variety of approaches as possible without regard to which one might be the best. To facilitate this, an alternative can be generated using any number of assumptions without further justification of those assumptions. This flexible form of problem analysis allows the decision maker to become free of the boundaries of traditional justification of assumptions and focus attention on the "what if we could do it this way" part of alternative generation. Using techniques such as rotation of attention (looking at the problem from a different perspective), establishment of a quota of alternatives (forcing the generation of a given number of choices), and problem fractionation (breaking the problem into random subdivisions without regard to logical boundaries), the decision maker can begin the process of generating new ways of doing old things.

Provocation   The activities in provocation are intended to assist directly in the development of new ideas. The primary objective of provocation is to introduce discontinuity into the thought process by forcing a change in the way the problem is looked at. Change from both within the problem context and external to the problem context can be provoked. Change from within can be introduced by looking at the problem using a *reversal* or backward approach. For example, suppose we are faced with a situation where parking meters are being used to discourage local commuter parking in a particular area. Reversal of the problem context would require analysis from the perspective of encouraging parking. From this perspective, we might suggest providing any out-of-town shopper with a ticket to park for free one day each week while shopping. This solution could result in an increase in out-of-town shoppers parking near the retail areas and, thus, the discouragement of parking by daily commuters. In lateral thinking, it is not so much the correctness of the reversal that is important, but rather the simple fact that the perspective is reversed.

Another method of change from within is to employ *exaggeration*. In contrast to a reversal, the direction of change is one of increasing the characteristics and boundaries of the problem rather than simply reversing them. For example, suppose our problem is one of quality control of several products manufactured by our production facilities. Exaggeration could be used to view the problem as if every product we made were faulty. In looking at the problem from that perspective, we might discover new and innovative ways of completely redesigning the production facility to improve the quality of all of our products.

Change from outside the problem context can also be used to provoke lateral thinking. The most common method of introducing change from outside the problem context is to use *analogies*. By translating the problem into a completely different context, developing and refining solutions for it, and then translating those solutions back into the original problem context, new and creative alternatives can often be discovered. Let's look at an example.

Suppose our problem is to find a way to conserve the water used during a waste disposal process. The current process simply allows the soluble waste products to collect in a container of water and then they are periodically flushed away into a sewer or other carry-off with the water. The water facilitates the movement of the waste through the carry-off and into a more permanent collection point. The problem is that because the water is mixed with the waste product, the permanent collection facility must be large enough not only to accommodate the volume of waste we generate but also to accommodate the volume of water we use to move it. We need an analogy to view this problem in a new way.

One analogy to our problem might be to compare it to how logging operations use rivers to transport their cut trees to convenient loading points. The loggers simply push the cut trees into the river and then let the current of the river move the logs down to a collection point where the logs can be loaded onto trucks for transportation to a sawmill. When the logs are collected, the vehicle by which they were transported (the water in the river) is left behind to be used again by other natural processes such as rain and irrigation. The reason this can occur is because the logs are not soluble in water and therefore are never really mixed with the water. This lack of solubility allows for the items being transported and the vehicle of transport to be easily separated upon reaching the desired destination. What if we did this same thing with our solid waste? By using a liquid to transport the waste that does not allow the waste material to dissolve, say oil, we can transport the waste to its collection point, recover the oil, and recycle the whole process, thus eliminating the need to store both the waste product and the oil. Voilà, introduction of change from without.

Critical Thinking

This method of thinking takes the position that there exist certain elements within a problem context that are most critical to the significance of any solution outcome. Given this, by focusing on the critical elements only, a solution can be crafted that will have an immediate and measurable impact on the problem. One common approach to problem solving based on the *critical thinking* method is called the *Pareto Law* (also commonly referred to as the *80-20 rule*). Figure 15-1 illustrates a hypothetical Pareto distribution of parts of a product in relation to their individual cost.

As can be seen in the figure, 80 percent of the cost of the product is represented by only 20 percent of the parts used to manufacture it. If we wish to control the production costs for this product, we could control 80 percent of the costs by focusing our attention on only a certain number of critical parts of the product representing only 20 percent of the total parts. We could, therefore, design a system that continuously monitors this 20 percent while managing the remaining 80 percent of the parts using some form of exception reporting or control. Critical thinking allows for the partitioning of any problem into important and unimportant elements.

Opposite Thinking

Opposite thinking is a method of problem solving whereby the decision maker simply takes the perspective of someone other than herself. This is a form of "standing

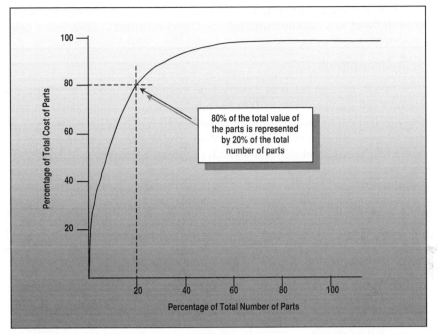

FIGURE 15-1 A Pareto Distribution of Parts Necessary to Build a Product

in another's shoes." Using this method, a decision maker can often gain insight into why a particular problem exists in the first place. Consider the following problem:

> Lynne is probably the most valuable member of the software development staff at Trident Software. It seems as if whenever a big job comes along that looks as though it can't be solved, Lynne comes to the rescue with the perfect cost-effective solution for the client. The company has finally gained the attention of a major client that it has been trying to get business from for several months. A large part of this opportunity must be attributed to the successes Lynne has engineered with two of the client's biggest competitors. The client wants to schedule planning meetings during the last two days of next week and cannot offer much flexibility in scheduling due to some previous government commitments. Lynne insists that she cannot be available on those days. When pressed for a reason, she reveals that next week is the first anniversary of her father's passing and she needs to be with her mother in Indiana. Lynne acknowledges the importance of the meetings but remains firm in her position that she must be with her mother on those specific days. If Trident wants the business, they must be able to meet next week and they must be able to deliver Lynne for the meetings. Got any ideas?

One way of looking at this problem is to look at it from Lynne's perspective rather than from Trident's. Lynne believes her mother will be comforted by her presence and feels obligated to spend time with her mother during this period. Logically speaking, Lynne is not so concerned about being in Indiana as she is in being with her mother. Standing in her shoes, the answer begins to become clear. Why not bring

Lynne's mother to her instead of Lynne going to her mother's? When asked, Lynne sees the win-win situation and agrees. Opposite thinking can often produce new perspectives and, thus, new solutions.

Groupthink

Since *groupthink* was covered in a detailed manner in chapter 6, we will not spend much time on it here. It bears a brief mention in this context, however, because despite its negative connotations, it does represent an alternative way of thinking and can be used effectively to achieve group involvement in activities such as idea generation and brainstorming (discussed later in this chapter).

Intuition?!

Although not the same as creativity, *intuition* has often been identified as an important element in creative decision making and problem solving. Managers that can harness their intuitions can often respond more quickly to a given situation and apply both experience and judgment. Consider the following example:

> In Marseilles, France, . . . a suspect on board a fishing vessel was thought to be smuggling heroin. Unfortunately, when the naval patrol boarded the vessel, they could not find any drugs. As the naval patrol prepared to depart, one officer noticed that the boat's concrete ballast was located in the front of the ship rather than at its normal position in the center. When the ballast was examined, the patrol discovered that it was hollowed out and contained the largest cache of heroin ever found. The intuition of the naval officer helped solve the problem. (Rowe and Boulgarides 1994, 172)

In the realm of DSS design, mechanisms must be developed to allow the decision maker to impart intuition to the decision process as a supplement to other problem-solving resources, including creativity.

15-2 CREATIVE PROBLEM-SOLVING TECHNIQUES

A review of the literature on the subject of creative problem solving will quickly suggest that there are probably as many different techniques in existence to apply to a problem-solving context as there are problems that need solving. VanGundy's *Techniques of Structured Problem Solving* (1988) contains over a hundred detailed techniques for fostering creativity in a wide variety of problem contexts. This is both good news and bad news to the DSS designer: good news in the sense that if there is a need to enhance or foster creative thinking under a given set of circumstances, there is most likely a specified method for accomplishing it; bad news in that because the nature of DSS design and use is to support semistructured problem contexts, deciding which creative problem-solving techniques to incorporate into the design becomes a major decision in and of itself. But there is more good news: The vast majority of creative problem-solving techniques applicable in an electronic decision support mechanism can be categorized into an easily manageable taxonomy consisting of three basic categories: (1) *free association,* (2) *structured relationships,* and (3) *group techniques.*

Free Association Techniques

The techniques in this category are all focused on a single goal: divergent thinking and the generation of ideas. Of the several principles that guide the techniques of *free association,* probably the most important is to *defer judgment.* Divergent idea generation relies on the complete suspension of analysis and judgment. If each time an idea is generated it must be fully analyzed and judged, then the number of possible alternatives to consider will be significantly reduced and the odds of generating a new and innovative solution to the problem will be diminished.

Additional principles guiding the techniques in this category include the assumptions that *quantity begets quality, the crazier the better,* and *to combine is to improve.* The first maxim simply assumes that with deferred judgment, more ideas will emerge, and with more ideas, the laws of probability suggest that more quality ideas will be part of the set. The second principle suggests that divergent thinking requires a certain propensity for risk taking. Conservative and cautious thinking approaches generally do not yield breakthrough ideas. The third principle calls for not only a generation of completely divergent ideas but the combination of divergent concepts and ideas into new and improved ones, as well. In 1912, a magazine advertisement for the new Oldsmobile quotes Mr. Olds himself as saying, "I do not believe that a car materially better will ever be built." What a visionary Mr. Olds must have sounded like at the time. Fortunately for us, however, a few people since 1912 have managed to combine ideas and improve somewhat on Mr. Olds's 1912 prognostication.

Brainstorming

Probably the most common free association technique used in the DSS realm is that of *brainstorming.* This method has proven to be extremely effective at both the individual and group levels at generating a long list of ideas quickly and efficiently. Building upon the principles outlined above, brainstorming techniques focus on quantity and variety and require the deferment of all judgment, criticism, and analysis until the list of ideas is completed. Although the process typically leads to an initially overwhelming number of alternatives, the process of culling the list down to a more manageable size is normally accomplished with limited effort. Brainstorming can be conducted either individually or collectively and can be unstructured or structurally facilitated. In a multiparticipant setting, brainstorming can often stimulate the phenomenon of *idea hitchhiking,* where one idea leads to another and then another with each subsequent iteration becoming more refined and, often, more implementable. Most important, brainstorming can be easily incorporated into a DSS as either a part of a guided process or a stand-alone module that can be adopted as desired by the users. In a DSS setting, additional features such as list combining, ranking, and culling can also be built into the system to facilitate the brainstorming activity.

A number of commercial products intended to facilitate the idea generation and brainstorming functions are beginning to emerge. One of the most successful products in this arena is IdeaFisher (see the minicase at the head of this chapter), which contains an associative lexicon of the English language and can easily and quickly create thousands of cross-references and word associations intended to facilitate idea generation. Figure 15-2 contains examples of typical screen layouts in Idea-Fisher.

Another highly successful electronic brainstorming product is contained within the Ventana Corporation's GroupSystems product. While marketed as a GDSS product (see chapter 6), the brainstorming facilities included in the product are considered some of the most sophisticated free association tools available. Figure 15-3 contains examples of screens from GroupSystems.

FIGURE 15-2 Screenshots from IdeaFisher

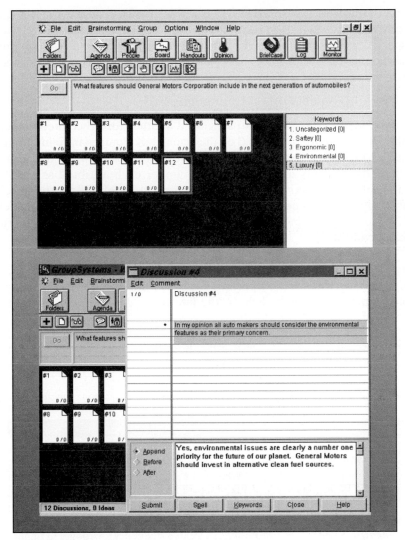

FIGURE 15-3 Screenshots from GroupSystems

Structured Relationships

In this category of creative problem-solving techniques the focus is on the generation of new ideas via a process whereby two or more objects, products, ideas, or concepts are *forced* together or combined to produce new objects or ideas. Although it is generally the case that elements related to each other will tend to produce practical ideas more than unrelated elements, such ideas also tend to be more mundane and less unique than those produced from unrelated elements.

Osborn's Idea Checklist

A classic technique that falls into this category uses checklists that cover many potential perspectives and sources of creative solutions to problem contexts. The best known example of this approach is Osborn's (1963) *73 Idea-Spurring Questions*. The questions require the user to transform the decision context into a variety of new perspectives and shapes, thus forcing a new formulation and combination of the elements contained within. Table 15-2 contains a complete list of Osborn's transformation questions.

Morphological Forced Connections

Koberg and Bagnall (1976) suggested another forced connection technique that emphasizes the morphological (i.e., the science of changes in living things) attributes of design problems. The technique requires the user to write down attributes of a problem, list as many alternative options under each attribute as possible, and then consider all possible combinations and permutations of the alternatives. The analysis is most appropriately performed in a matrix format and can be easily delivered via a DSS. Table 15-3 contains an example of a morphological analysis for a drug smuggling problem context.

NASA has made extensive use of morphological forced connection modules in many of its DSSs used to support the establishment of scientific objectives for space exploration activities. Action phrases such as "Measure the tidal deformations in . . ." are combined with targets such as "the interior of Jupiter" to create a possible scientific objective.

The real value of a forced connection technique lies not in its ability to find all possible combinations but rather in its ability to create a framework within which all possible combinations exist and can be selectively screened to determine the most appropriate candidates.

Table 15-2 Osborn's 73 Idea-Spurring Questions

- *Put to other uses.* New ways to use as is? Other uses if modified?
- *Adapt.* What else is like this? What other ideas does this suggest? Does the past offer a parallel? What could I copy? Whom could I emulate?
- *Modify.* New twist? Change meaning, color, motion, sound, odor, form, shape? Other changes?
- *Magnify.* What to add? More time? Greater frequency? Stronger? Higher? Longer? Thicker? Extra Value? Plus ingredient? Duplicate? Multiply? Exaggerate?
- *Minify.* What to subtract? Smaller? Condensed? Miniature? Lower? Shorter? Lighter? Omit? Streamline? Split up? Understate?
- *Substitute.* Who else instead? What else instead? Other ingredient? Other material? Other process? Other power? Other place? Other approach? Other tone of voice?
- *Rearrange.* Interchange components? Other pattern? Other layout? Other sequence? Transpose cause and effect? Change pace? Change schedule?
- *Reverse.* Transpose positive and negative? How about opposites? Turn it backward? Turn it upside down? Reverse roles? Change shoes? Turn tables? Turn other cheek?
- *Combine.* How about a blend, an alloy, an assortment, an ensemble? Combine units? Combine purposes? Combine appeals? Combine ideas?

Source: Osborn, A.O., (1963). *Applied Imagination.* Reprinted with permission from the publisher, The Creative Education Foundation Press, 1050 Union Road, Buffalo, NY 14224.

Table 15-3 Example of a Morphological Analysis Grid for Drug Smuggling

Problem Components	Component Alternatives	
Type	A. Cocaine	B. Heroin
	C. Amphetamines	D. Marijuana
Source	E. Thailand	F. Local sources
	G. Turkey	H. United States
Importation method	I. Air	J. Sea
	K. Courier	L. Produced locally
Distribution method	M. Large-scale, highly organized	N. Hobby
	O. Small-scale, poorly organized	
Sponsors	P. Organized crime	Q. Triad
	R. Political terrorists	S. Individual

Possible morphological connections include:

- Cocaine (A) from the United States (H) produced locally (L) and distributed on a large-scale, highly organized (M) basis by organized crime (P).
- Heroin (B) from Turkey (G) imported by air (I) and distributed on a small-scale, poorly organized (O) basis by an individual (S).

Analytic Hierarchy Process

It is often difficult to conceptualize all the different elements that make up a decision. Because of this, failing to include one or more elements, or including elements that are not important in the decision, is a common error. In addition, the cognitive energy necessary to prioritize decision elements may make it difficult to keep track of all previous priority rankings and may lead to inconsistent priority judgements. In an attempt to counter these problems, a methodology was developed by Thomas Saaty at the University of Pennsylvania in the early 1980s called the analytic hierarchy process (AHP).

The AHP is a mathematically based theory and comprehensive methodology for use in decision making, employing two key aspects:

1. Data from the various variables that make up the decision
2. Judgments of these variables from decision makers

AHP provides support to the decision-making process by allowing decision makers to organize and evaluate the relative importance of selected objectives and the relative importance of alternative solutions to a decision. AHP allows for a way to measure the consistency of judgments and to reevaluate these judgements if inconsistency is deemed a problem. Finally, this methodology provides a theoretical grounding for consistent decision making.

To determine the best overall action to take, AHP requires the following steps:

1. The structuring of a decision into a hierarchical model
2. Pairwise comparisons of all objectives and alternative solutions

First, as stated previously, every AHP decision begins with a model in the form of a hierarchy. The general form of the model is composed of four elements:

1. *Goal.* The goal of the decision
2. *Criteria.* Sometimes called the objectives; the elements that comprise the goal
3. *Subcriteria.* The lowest level; the elements that make up the criteria under which they fall (the node directly above)
4. *Alternatives.* The different solutions or choices that are available

Decomposing a decision into this format allows decision makers to focus on each and every part of a complex problem.

Once the model is built, the next step is to evaluate the elements by making pairwise comparisons. A pairwise comparison is the process of comparing the relative importance, preference, or likelihood of any element with respect to the element in the level above. Comparisons are usually top-down, both across nodes and within nodes. Consider the following examples:

1. Is criterion 1 more preferable/important/likely than criterion 2, with respect to the goal?
2. Is subcriterion 1 more preferable/important/likely than subcriterion 2, with respect to criterion 1, with respect to the goal?

Because we are seldom consistent when making comparative judgements, AHP assumes that there will always be inconsistency in judgements. AHP attempts to measure this via a mathematical formula called an *inconsistency ratio,* where a value of 1.0 is considered complete consistency, less than 0.10 is considered tolerable consistency, and a value greater than 0.10 suggests a need to reexamine the judgments made with an eye toward improving consistency.

After all preferences are recorded, and are of sufficient consistency, data corresponding to the *subcriteria* are introduced into the model. This process of prioritizing the alternatives is referred to as *synthesis.*

By taking these two elements—(1) consistent preferences and (2) data on subcriteria—AHP generates the global weights of the nodes by combining the local priorities throughout the entire model. Via synthesis, we arrive at the overall priorities of the alternatives, thus providing decision makers information on which alternative is the best choice.

An example of an AHP decision hierarchy is demonstrated with the following situation: The objective is to decide whether to admit an applicant to an MBA program. To begin with, the decision must be broken down into its constituent elements. The applicant's academic, professional, and personal credentials are the main components upon which the admission decision will be made. These components represent the decision criteria. Under each of these criteria are the subcriteria: the elements that make up their respective criteria. For example, the essence of an applicant's academic credentials are the overall undergraduate GPA, major GPA, GMAT score, quality of the undergraduate institution, and so on. Finally, the alternatives are the range of possible choices: in this case, the range of possible applicants. Each alternative, or applicant, will provide the data for each subcriterion, in order to conduct synthesis. By performing the complete set of pairwise comparisons and ranking the alternatives based upon this method, AHP can assist the decision maker in reaching a ranking that reflects the relative contribution of each of the subcriteria to the final decision and applicant selection.

Group Techniques

As the name implies, this category of creative techniques is focused on enhancing and fostering creativity within a multiparticipant problem-solving context. A key element present in these techniques is the improvement of group interaction. The assumption is that participants in a problem-solving exercise will naturally create synergies that generate creative ideas if they are stimulated into some form of regular and flexible interaction. Once the interaction is initiated, the process tends to build upon itself and creative ideas begin to be generated.

Nominal Group Technique

Delbecq, Van de Ven, and Gustafson (1975) are credited for developing a widely used and highly successful group interaction mechanism known as the *nominal group technique* (NGT). This technique builds upon the concept of brainstorming in a multi-participant setting and may use a variety of media, including paper-based, verbal, and electronic, to facilitate the activity.

The name describes how the process works. It is a process for a group of people who become a group in name only (hence the name, nominal group) when they are using the technique. The purpose of NGT is to eliminate social and psychological dynamics of group behavior that tend to inhibit individual creativity and participation in MDM contexts. While the group uses the technique, they avoid the normal problems of a few individuals doing all the talking, the rest listening, and very few people taking the time to actually think about the issue at hand. Individuals can be more creative and everyone is given a structured opportunity to participate. This helps to overcome the common problems often encountered in small group meetings organized for the purpose of generating ideas, planning programs, and problem solving. Table 15-4 lists each step of NGT.

Delphi

Recall that in chapter 6 we briefly mentioned the MDM technique called *Delphi*. This technique was developed at the RAND corporation (a well-known think tank of the 1950s and 1960s) to elicit expert opinion on how many Soviet atomic bombs it would take to do a specified amount of damage to various locations throughout the United States. It has been used by a number of research groups as well as many business groups and private corporations within a DSS setting including Bell Canada, Honeywell, AT&T, Owens-Corning, General Dynamics, TRW, Skandia Insurance Company, Weyerhaeuser, and Imperial Chemical, among many others.

A key element in the Delphi technique that separates it from NGT is that the participants are all anonymous and, in most cases, are widely geographically dispersed. The Delphi questionnaires are generally presented to the members of a group in the form of carefully prepared written questions, although oral questions are sometimes used. The questions normally require subjective estimates, assessments, or projections by the group members.

Table 15-4 Nominal Group Technique

Silent Generation of Ideas in Writing
- Provides time to think
- Provides a creative setting
- Provides focus and uninterrupted thought
- Encourages each member to search for ideas
- Avoids competition and status differences
- Avoids conformity pressures
- Avoids evaluation and closure
- Avoids polarizing on ideas

Recorded Round-Robin Listing of Ideas on Chart
- Structures equal sharing and participation
- Encourages problem identification
- Encourages each member to build on other member's ideas
- Depersonalizes ideas
- Tolerates conflicting ideas
- Reinforces concentration: hear and see ideas
- Provides written permanence

Discussion and Clarification of Each Idea on Chart
- Each idea is as important as another
- Equal time to each idea
- Clarifies ideas

Preliminary Vote on Priorities
- Provides focus on important issues
- Structures equality in choices
- Allows a "trial run"
- Avoids a premature decision
- Avoids dominance by strong members

Discussion of Preliminary Vote
- Clarifies misunderstandings
- Encourages minority opinions
- Promotes "criticizing" ideas on wall—not people
- Provides preparation for decision

Final Vote on Priorities
- Structures an independent judgment from each member
- Provides closure
- Promotes sense of accomplishment
- Motivates involvement in future phases of planning and problem solving
- Provides a written record of the ideas generated

The first round of questionnaire responses are then analyzed, usually statistically (e.g., average, variance, median, quartile, range). The result of this analysis plus the respondents' initial estimates are then provided as feedback to the original participants, who are then requested to reevaluate their estimates and revise them if appropriate, knowing the group's response.

Several iterations of the above process are conducted until convergence (in the form of decreasing variance) of response is noted.

Studies have shown that a Delphi-developed consensus is more effective and more accurate than a consensus developed through verbal interaction. The reasons for this relate to the domination of the opinions of certain personality or authority types in face-to-face group dynamics; those opinions that dominate are not necessarily the most correct. The quiet, reflective mood of the Delphi results in better projections than the noise of a meeting. Also, the Delphi is generally a more efficient use of the time of a group of experts and can be easily incorporated into a DSS.

The operating assumption of the Delphi technique is that those respondents whose original projections involved less confidence will be more inclined to revise their response, knowing the group's response, than those whose estimates involved more confidence or knowledge.

15-3 INTELLIGENT AGENTS IN DECISION SUPPORT

Although creativity remains one of the last bastions of human cognitive endeavors, the concept of *intelligent agents* (IAs) is an emerging technology that is rapidly finding its way into all computer-related realms, including that of the DSS, by facilitating users in the delegation of work to a computer. IA technology is truly a glimpse into the future of DSSs and tomorrow's problem solving because intelligent agents are capable of performing many of the necessary decision support tasks formerly designated as uniquely human activities. They help do things like find and filter information, customize views of information, and automate work. In this next section we will summarize the characteristics that differentiate agents from other software, examine several proposed classification schemes for intelligent agents, and identify several current intelligent agent technologies that can be used to add agents to new or existing DSS applications.

What Exactly Is an Intelligent Agent?

We have seen throughout this text that the pace and complexity of decision making and problem solving in tomorrow's organization are truly increasing. However, ease of use has not kept pace with the tremendous amount of advanced function now available. The result is that DSS applications are becoming more and more daunting for beginning, and even veteran, users. The information and processing that should be available are simply not accessible.

In our lives, when we find ourselves in a position where time and activities overtake us, we seek help in the form of assistants—people who take care of things we could do ourselves but prefer not to. In the DSS world, intelligent agents play the role of such assistants. IAs function by allowing users to delegate their work to the agent software. IAs are useful in automating repetitive tasks, assisting the user in remembering critical dates or events, or intelligently summarizing complex data. More important, just like their human counterparts, intelligent agents can learn from the user and even make recommendations to you regarding a particular course of action.

As with any cutting edge technology, the formal definition of the concept tends to be both varied and custom tailored to the definer's specific vision of the technology. The world of intelligent agents has spawned numerous early definitions and conceptualizations, each with its own unique perspective on just what an IA is, or should be. Table 15-5 summarizes the current range of definitions for intelligent agents, their sources, and basic assumptions.

A review of the various definitions shown in table 15-5 reveals two subtle commonalties: (1) *an agent is one who acts, or who can act* and (2) *an agent is one who acts in place of another person with permission from that person.* Building upon these two common characteristics of intelligent agents, Franklin and Graesser (1996) have offered a formal definition of intelligent software agents that embodies the essence of the prior definitions and to which we will subscribe in this text:

> An autonomous agent is a system situated within and a part of an environment that senses that environment and acts on it, over time, in pursuit of its own agenda and so as to effect what it senses in the future.

This definition is broad enough that it avoids the restrictive, targeted nature of other definitions while simultaneously offering a useful boundary within which to explore the realm of intelligent software agents and their use. Within the context of the DSS, we believe that the concept of the IA should be focused enough to define a specific mechanism for analyzing systems such as semistructured problem spaces, but at the same time be expansive enough, as necessary, to allow for creative and innovative uses for the technology. In this sense, not every program is an agent. Intelligent software agents are, by definition, computer programs, but a computer program must possess several unique characteristics to be classified as an agent.

Characteristics of Intelligent Software Agents

Table 15-6 contains a listing of the various identifying characteristics of intelligent software agents that serve to differentiate them from other computer-based programs.

Autonomy

An agent must display a measure of autonomy from its user. In other words, once initiated it has control over its own actions. This is good because when you delegate something to your agent, you expect it to have the independence to work on your request no matter what happens around it. To this end, a software agent must be able to display a certain level of spontaneous execution and preemptive or independent action with the intent of benefiting its user. In this respect, IAs differ from other computer programs, which tend to respond only to direct manipulation and otherwise function without any awareness of the conditions in which they are operating.

Table 15-5 Summary of Current Definitions of Intelligent Software Agents

Agent Name	Agent Definition
MuBot Agent	Represents two orthogonal concepts: the agent's ability for autonomous execution and the agent's ability to perform domain-oriented reasoning.
AIMA Agent	Anything that can be viewed as perceiving its environment through sensors and acting upon that environment through effectors.
Maes Agent	Autonomous agents are computational systems that inhabit some complex dynamic environment and act autonomously in this environment, and by doing so realize a set of goals or tasks for which they are designed.
KidSim Agent	A persistent software entity dedicated to a specific purpose. "Persistent" distinguishes agents from subroutines; agents have their own ideas about how to accomplish tasks, their own agendas. "Special purpose" distinguishes them from entire multifunction applications; agents are typically much smaller.
Hayes-Roth Agent	Intelligent agents continuously perform three functions: perception of dynamic conditions in the environment; action to affect conditions in the environment; and reasoning to interpret perceptions, solve problems, draw inferences, and determine actions.
IBM Agent	Intelligent agents are software entities that carry out some set of operations on behalf of a user or another program with some degree of independence or autonomy, and, in doing so, employ some knowledge or representation of the user's goals or desires.
Wooldridge-Jennings Agent	A hardware or (more usually) software-based computer system that enjoys the following properties: • *Autonomy.* Agents operate without the direct intervention of humans or others and have some kind of control over their actions and internal state. • *Social ability.* Agents interact with other agents (and possibly humans) via some kind of agent communication language. • *Reactivity.* Agents perceive their environment (which may be the physical world, a user via a graphical user interface, a collection of other agents, the Internet, or perhaps all of these combined) and respond in a timely fashion to changes that occur in it. • *Proactiveness.* Agents do not simply act in response to their environment; they are able to exhibit goal-directed behavior by taking the initiative.
SodaBot Agent	Software agents are programs that engage in dialogs and negotiate and coordinate transfer of information.
Foner Agent	Agents collaborate, are autonomous, trustworthy, and degrade gracefully in the face of communications mismatch.
Brustoloni Agent	Autonomous agents are systems capable of autonomous, purposeful action in the real world.
FAQ Agent	Agents possess attributes of autonomy, goal orientation, collaboration, flexibility, self-startedness, temporal continuity, character, communicativeness, adaptiveness, and mobility.

Table 15-6 Common Characteristics of Intelligent Software Agents		
Autonomy	Cooperation	Graceful degradation
Personalizability	Risk and trust	Anthropomorphism
Discourse	Domain	Mobility

An agent must be relatively reactive. That is, an IA must sense changes in its environment and respond in a timely fashion. This characteristic of agents is also at the core of delegation and automation. Just as you tell your assistant, "When *x* happens, do *y,*" an agent is always waiting for *x* to happen! Finally, in order to carry out the wishes of the user, all agents must be continuously operational, even when the user is gone.

Personalizability

The whole point of an IA is to enable a user to perform a task, such as information gathering or data analysis, better than he or she could do alone. Because each decision maker is unique and each problem context is different from the last, an IA must be educable in the task at hand and in how to perform it. The characteristic of *personalizability* is displayed by a *learning agent* that can acquire the necessary information it needs to function, in part, by initially monitoring the actions of its user.

Discourse and Cooperation

To ensure that an IA shares the agenda of its user and can carry out the task in the manner desired, some form of *discourse* or two-way feedback is required. This discourse allows both entities to make their intentions and abilities known to the other and, through this feedback, agree on something resembling a contract about what is to be done, by whom, and when.

In addition to feedback or discourse with the user, IAs may need to invoke one or more additional IAs to help them accomplish a task. In this sense, an IA must possess the ability, when necessary, to interact and communicate with other related IAs. To this end, some IAs are considered "social." That is, they interact, or communicate with other agents. This communication could be by proprietary means, or it could be through some common language standard.

Risk, Trust, and Domain

Implicit in the concept of an intelligent agent is the notion of delegation. If we do not trust the entity to carry out the task that we have delegated to it, then we are faced with performing the task ourselves. Even if we have the required level of trust in the agent, by delegating responsibility for a task to an external agent we expose ourselves to the risk that the agent will do something wrong. The use of intelligent software agents requires a balance between the risks associated with relinquishing control of an operation and our level of trust in the technology. This decision requires the user to possess a reasonably accurate mental model of not only what the agent will do (hence, the level of trust we ascribe to it) but also the problem context and domain of interest (hence, the degree of risk associated with an error on the part of the IA).

Having knowledge of the domain within which the IA will reside and operate is an important element in the successful employment of IAs. If the domain is a localized decision simulation then the degree of trust associated with employing the agent does not need to be very high and the associated degree of risk is likely to be quite low. If, on the other hand, the agent is being deployed in a domain where its responsibility includes monitoring the position of the control rods in a nuclear reactor and notifying its user when a certain set of conditions exists, then the degree of trust needed in the IA is, by necessity, quite high and the level of risk associated with its use is also substantial. In these cases, the use of IAs must be accompanied by additional control mechanisms intended not only to back up the IA but to monitor its performance as well.

Graceful Degradation and Cooperation

The characteristic of *graceful degradation* is a key element that serves to differentiate an IA from a simple computer program. This concept is closely related to the concepts of risk, trust, and domain discussed above. In the event that the agent has difficulty communicating with its user (even in situations where one or the other party may not realize it) or is experiencing a domain mismatch (one or both entities are simply out of their element and, again, may not realize it), the agent should be able to complete a portion of the task assigned instead of simply failing to operate. In situations where the use of IAs is appropriate, completion of a portion of the task is generally a better outcome than failing to run at all.

Anthropomorphism

This characteristic of IAs is the subject of great debate. *Anthropomorphism* is the ascription of humanlike characteristics to an otherwise nonhuman entity. The practice is evident in a wide variety of common situations, such as the assumption that a watercraft is female in gender ("She's a fine craft") or that computers are interactive social entities ("My system has a virus and it infected the whole lab"). In the case of IAs, anthropomorphism is a commonly employed, but nonessential, characteristic. Some agents strive to be believable, in that they are represented as an entity visible or audible to the user, and may even have aspects of emotion or personality. Software agents are often designed to display humanlike tendencies and actions in situations where possible interaction with users other than the agent owner might be desirable. One such example of the use of anthropomorphism in the design of IAs is the concept of an *avatar*.

An avatar is defined as an embodiment or concrete manifestation of a principle, attitude, view of life, or the like. In a virtual reality environment (VRE), your avatar is your signature, your trademark, and the symbol of your physical presence. Users with IAs that work within a VRE may have hundreds of avatars: some are idiosyncratic, some are pictographic, some iconoclastic, but, typically, most of the enduring avatars have been those associated with recognizable symbols of popular culture—cans of Spam, Winnie the Pooh, or Tarzan. As avatars grow more common and complex, and more ambitious in terms of their ability to do things—to simulate conversational exchange, to exhibit dynamically generated behaviors—we will rely more and more upon visualization skills to establish on-line identity. The design challenges here are considerable: strategic, visual, conceptual, choreographic.

Mobility

Some agents are mobile and, when necessary, can move from machine to machine or across different system architectures and platforms. Agents that move can get closer to data they may need to process and, moreover, they can do so without network delays. A *transportable agent* is a program that can migrate from machine to machine in a heterogeneous network. The program chooses when and where to migrate. It can suspend its execution at an arbitrary point, transport to another machine, and resume execution on the new machine. The agent can perform arbitrarily complex processing at each machine in order to ensure that the message reaches the intended recipient. Figure 15-4 illustrates an example of a mobile agent carrying a mail message.

Transportable agents have several advantages over the traditional client/server model.

- *Efficiency.* Transportable agents consume fewer network resources because they move the computation to the data rather than the data to the computation.
- *Fault tolerance.* Transportable agents do not require a continuous connection between machines.
- *Convenient paradigm.* Transportable agents hide the communication channels but not the location of the computation.

FIGURE 15-4 Illustration of a Transportable Mail Agent

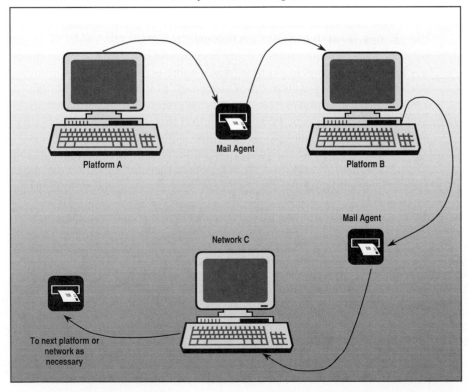

Platform A

Mail Agent

Platform B

Mail Agent

Network C

To next platform or network as necessary

• ***Customization.*** Transportable agents allow clients and servers to extend each other's functionality by programming each other.

Classification of Intelligent Agents

Intelligent software agents can be classified according to several subsets of properties and characteristics. While all agents must possess the characteristics of *reactivity, autonomy, goal orientation,* and *temporal continuity,* other characteristics allow for their classification in either a hierarchical or categorical manner.

Hierarchical Classification of Intelligent Agents

Franklin and Graesser (1996) proposed a "biological" metaphoric classification scheme for IAs that takes the form of a tree with "living creatures" at the root and individual species at its leaves. Figure 15-5 contains this hierarchical classification scheme.

Categorical Classification of Intelligent Agents

Another method of classification of IAs is *organizational versus personal* agents (also referred to as public, or shared, versus private agents) where the differentiation is based on whether the agent is executing a business process or task on behalf of an organizational application or on behalf of a specific user. Personal agents are more prevalent in today's DSS environments but the deployment of organizational IAs is

FIGURE 15-5 Franklin and Graesser Hierarchical Classification of Intelligent Agents

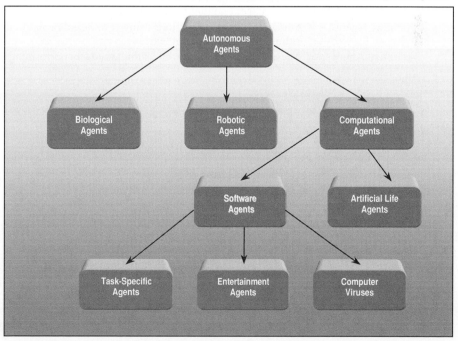

escalating. The pervasive nature of collaborative technologies such as Lotus Notes makes the use of organizational agents for tasks such as e-mail sorting and filtering or document workflow management increasingly desirable.

Brustoloni (1991) offered a method of classifying IAs based on a three-way categorization into *regulation agents, planning agents,* and *adaptive agents.* Table 15-7 provides a brief description of each category of agent within this classification method.

Yet another classification method for agents was proposed by Lee, Cheung, and Kao (1997). This method classifies IAs according to their level of intelligence and power. Table 15-8 contains the Lee, Cheung, and Kao taxonomy of software agents.

The Types of Problems Intelligent Agents Can Solve

To increase our understanding of IA technology, we can examine some of the various practical problems that intelligent agents can help to solve. The list of problems discussed in this section is not meant to be exhaustive, but rather illustrative of general types of problem contexts in which deployment of IAs may be useful.

Consider the following: Corinne is up to her neck in information. Her position as a researcher for a small but rapidly growing retail industry consulting firm is both exciting and challenging. She is regularly asked to gather information on a wide variety

Table 15-7 Brustoloni Taxonomy of Software Agents

Classification	Definition
Regulation Agent	Reacts to each sensory input as it comes in and always knows what to do. This agent neither plans nor learns.
Planning Agent	Performs planning functions using case-based or randomizing algorithms. This agent cannot learn.
Adaptive Agent	These agents can learn while simultaneously performing planning.

Table 15-8 Lee, Cheung, and Kao Taxonomy of Software Agents by Level of Intelligence

Intelligence Level	Definition
Level 0	Agents retrieve documents for a user under straight orders. The user must specify the exact location of the desired documents. Example: typical web browser.
Level 1	Agents conduct a user-initiated search activity. Agent can match user-supplied key words with indexed information. Example: Internet search agents (i.e., Yahoo, Alta Vista, etc.).
Level 2	Agents maintain profiles on behalf of their users. Agents can monitor various information sources and notify user whenever relevant information is located or new information is discovered. Example: Web-Watcher.
Level 3	Agents learn and deduce from user-specified profiles to assist in the formalization of a query or target search. Example: DiffAgent.

of subjects relevant to the firm's clients and to "keep her eyes open" for new developments in areas that relate to projects the firm is currently working on. Although Corinne really enjoys the "thrill of the hunt" for information related to a new project, she often finds herself swamped with data that seem to take forever to wade through to find what she refers to as "the keepers." An even bigger problem is the constant struggle to meet the mandate of "keeping her eyes open" for important events. She just knows that a better way has to exist. Maybe she needs to hire some help.

Corinne could benefit enormously from the employment of several IAs to assist her in her daily work. Her daily task of wading through information to find the "keepers" is tenable when there are only a few pieces of data, but as the number of data grows, and as the rate of arrival of new data also grows, the task rapidly becomes daunting and untenable. Intelligent agents could be used to help solve this problem by customizing information to Corinne's preferences, thus saving her time in handling it and sorting through it.

What about her problem of keeping up with current events? These events could be real world events like competitive announcements or emergencies, or they could be computer events like a new version of a design document becoming ready. Regardless of the nature of the event, intelligent agents can help solve this problem by continuously monitoring various information sources for key words that indicate the arrival of an event that may be of interest to one of Corinne's clients or relevant to one or more of the firm's projects. When an event of interest occurs, the agent could notify Corinne, download appropriate documents to a specified location, schedule a meeting with a specified group of people, or all of the above.

IAs are currently being employed in a wide variety of organizational situations. Imagine a customer help desk where an IA can take the basic parameters of a customer's problem and use them to retrieve relevant technical documents from a database for use by the support personnel. The point is that the business value of delegating intelligent agents to handle these, and many other, types of problems is that you get the right information at the right time, without having to do it all yourself or rewrite the base applications.

The Future of Intelligent Software Agents

It is quite possible that intelligent software agents will be one of the most important advancements in the DSS environment in the next decade. It is expected that by the year 2000, virtually every significant computer-based application will have some form of agent-enablement (Janca 1996). Several reasons can be cited for this conclusion:

1. Desktop applications are becoming extremely "feature rich." Because of this, users can master only a small part of their capabilities. IAs can mask the complexity of new applications and help the user accomplish what he or she wants.

2. Sources and volumes of information are burgeoning. IAs can help do the data mining and can assist in locating the most productive data mines.

3. The current bandwidth limitation in the realm of decision support exists between the tip of the user's nose and the surface of the computer screen. Greater computing bandwidth means more data can get to the user more quickly, but the user still has a limited cognitive processing capacity and a limited number of hours in the day available to

work. IAs can work around-the-clock and can help manage the data flow by filtering and sending only that information *the user* considers essential.

4. Client desktops and servers are now getting powerful enough to support the deployment of multiple IAs to help users and processes easily.

5. The rapid increase in the use of the Internet and WWW is creating a much more complex computing environment. This new environment is commonly referred to as "network computing," which implies that we are moving from a world of simple connections (i.e., a terminal-to-a-host, or a client-to-a-server) to a more complex world of multiple servers and services interconnected like a highway network. In this new environment, everything is available, but changes occur by the second and the decision maker has to figure out how to find out about them. IAs can create a cohesive whole out of this seemingly random mess.

6. Both academic and commercial research are now beyond the point of mere theory in their understanding of IAs, and experimental systems are freely available and in use on the Internet.

7. Large custom applications, such as Lotus Notes, are significantly agent-enabled, further broadening the experience base.

As of this writing, there are more than fifty commercial vendors currently offering agent-enabled software and services. Their products are spread across virtually every application area, including Internet applications. The present challenge is to make it easy to add intelligent agents to *any* application, new or existing. The important point is that IAs are not a concept of the future; they are in use today helping make applications easier to use and their usage is increasing rapidly.

15-4 CHAPTER SUMMARY

Creativity, intuition, and innovativeness are all components of the decision-making process that we have yet to fully understand. It is important, however, that we realize their value in contributing to effective solutions and that we design our support mechanisms to embrace and enhance their contribution. From research, we know that human creativity can be supported by computer-based systems and that the use of intelligent agents can both extend our reach and relieve us of many tasks, allowing us to spend more time developing the creative side of our solutions and allowing intuition to permeate the process.

Key Concepts

- Creativity (15-1)

  Creativity is an ability to see the same things as everyone else but to think of something different. It involves the ability to generate novel and useful ideas and solutions to problems and challenges.

- Theories of creativity (15-1)

  Psychoanalytical perspective

  Creativity is a preconscious mental activity. Creative thinking occurs in our subconscious thoughts and is not directly accessible to our conscious thoughts.

  Behavioral perspective

  Creativity is a natural response to stimuli within our individual environments. Certain combinations of stimuli can lead to more creative behavior than other combinations.

  Process perspective

  Creativity is a property of a thought process that can be acquired and improved through instruction and practice.

- Ways of thinking (15-1)

  Logical thinking

  This method of thinking is rooted in the model-building and quantitative methods of management decision science and is an integral part of the design and development of a computer-based DSS.

  Lateral thinking

  This method of thinking is based upon the premise that the human mind naturally processes and stores information in accordance with a specific pattern of thought and action. Lateral thinking disrupts these patterns through the introduction of discontinuity. Three major activities are available to promote lateral thinking processes: awareness, alternatives, and provocation.

  Critical thinking

  By focusing on certain critical elements within a problem context, a solution can be crafted that will have an immediate and measurable impact on the problem.

  Opposite thinking

  Opposite thinking is a method of problem solving whereby the decision maker simply takes the perspective of someone other than herself. This is a form of "standing in another's shoes."

  Groupthink

  Groupthink is an alternative way of thinking and can be used effectively to achieve group involvement in activities such as idea generation and brainstorming.

- In the realm of DSS design, mechanisms must be developed to allow the decision maker to impart intuition to the decision process as a supplement to other problem-solving resources, including creativity. (15-1)

- Creative problem-solving techniques (15-2)

  Free association techniques

  The techniques in this category are all focused on a single goal: divergent thinking and the generation of ideas. Several principles guide the techniques of free association:

  1. Defer judgment.
  2. Quantity begets quality.
  3. The crazier the better.
  4. To combine is to improve.

  The most common free association technique used in the DSS realm is brainstorming.

Structured relationships

> These techniques focus on the generation of new ideas via a process where two or more objects, products, ideas, or concepts are forced together or combined to produce new objects or ideas. Two common techniques in this category are Osborn's idea checklist and the morphological forced connection technique from Koberg and Bagnall.

Group techniques

> These techniques focus on enhancing and fostering creativity within a multiparticipant problem-solving context. The assumption is that participants in a problem-solving exercise will naturally create synergies that generate creative ideas if they are stimulated into some form of regular and flexible interaction. Common techniques in this category include the nominal group technique and the Delphi technique.

- Intelligent agent (IA) (15-3)

According to Franklin and Graesser (1996), "An autonomous agent is a system situated within and a part of an environment that senses that environment and acts on it, over time, in pursuit of its own agenda and so as to effect what it senses in the future."

- The concept of intelligent agents is an emerging technology that facilitates users in the delegation of work to a computer. Intelligent agents are capable of performing many of the necessary decision support functions formerly relegated to human beings. (15-3)

- Two common characteristics of intelligent agents: (15-3)

An agent is one who acts, or who can act.

An agent is one who acts in place of another person with permission from that person.

- Characteristics of intelligent software agents (15-3)

Autonomy

Personalizability

Discourse

Cooperation

Risk and trust

Domain

Graceful degradation

Anthropomorphism

Mobility

- Transportable agents have several advantages over the traditional client/server model: (15-3)

Efficiency

Fault tolerance

Convenient paradigm

Customization

- Classification of intelligent agents (15-3)

Hierarchical classification

> Hierarchical classification is a "biological" metaphoric classification scheme for IAs that takes the form of a tree with "living creatures" at the root and individual species at its leaves.

Organizational versus personal agents

> This classification is based on whether the agent is carrying out a business process or task on behalf of an organizational application or on behalf of a specific user.

Brustoloni taxonomy of software agents

This classification is based on a three-way categorization of IAs into regulation agents, planning agents, and adaptive agents.

Lee, Cheung, and Kao taxonomy of software agents

This method classifies IAs according to their level of intelligence and power.

Questions for Review

1. What is creativity? Try to explain it from different perspectives.
2. Explain the basic concept of logical thinking.
3. Describe the basis of lateral thinking.
4. List and briefly describe the three major activities in promoting lateral thinking processes.
5. What approaches can utilized to provoke changes in lateral thinking?
6. List the major principles of free association techniques.
7. Briefly describe the major concept of a structured relationship technique in problem solving.
8. Describe the primary assumptions of nominal group technique in problem solving. What are the benefits of using this technique?
9. What is an intelligent agent?
10. Identify and discuss two characteristics of intelligent agents.
11. What is a learning agent?
12. Explain why graceful degradation of an IA is important.
13. What are the advantages of transportable agents over the traditional client/server model?
14. List and briefly describe the methods of classifying IAs.

For Further Discussion

1. Discuss the importance of creativity and intuition in decision making.
2. Study a case where the critical thinking approach (e.g., the Pareto law) can be utilized in solving problems. Describe how it can be applied in the process of problem solving.
3. Find a problem occurring in an organization you are familiar with. Briefly describe the problem. Use the technique of brainstorming to find the solutions.
4. Use a structured relationship technique to solve the problem identified in the previous question.
5. Analyze an intelligent software agent in the market. Characterize its functionality. Discuss the types of problems it can solve.
6. Discuss why it is important for the user of intelligent software technology to maintain a balance between the risks of IA use and the trust the user has for the IA.
7. Information about IAs is plentiful on the WWW. Find some Web sites that discuss the use of IAs. Hint: try Firefly, IBM, or BargainFinder.

16

Decision Support in the Twenty-First Century

Computers in the future may weigh no more than 1.5 tons.
— *Popular Mechanics,* FORECASTING THE RELENTLESS MARCH
OF SCIENCE AND INNOVATION, 1949

I have traveled the length and breadth of this country and talked with the best people, and I can assure you that data processing is a fad that won't last out the year.
— THE EDITOR IN CHARGE OF BUSINESS BOOKS FOR PRENTICE HALL, 1957

We are at the end of our journey (at least for now). This only means that you have gained a sufficient understanding of the application of current decision support technologies to use them effectively during the course of your managerial activities. The journey continues, however, because even as you read this text new and innovative DSS technologies are emerging that will require acceptance and assimilation by managers into their world. This is one of the first problems we must address.

There is a common and natural hesitation on the part of managers to squarely confront the central, long-term challenge facing an organization: the formidable nature of emerging technologies. Recent history has made it evident that discounting the future can be very costly. Over the long-term, new technologies will arise and take hold. These innovations will lead to novel products and processes, sometimes supplanting entire industries or creating whole new businesses. Coping with the continual flow of new technologies is a monumental task that decision makers will face in the next century. If the organization is to benefit from the increased power that new decision support technologies have to offer, managers must seize upon the opportunities these technologies present, while simultaneously guarding against the pitfalls they bring with them.

The objective of this final chapter is to provide a glimpse into the future of decision making and DSS-related technologies. To be sure, this is a formidable task. One only has to recall the abundance of futuristic technologies we see in the latest offerings from Hollywood to understand the size of this undertaking. Some of these prototypes of tomorrow have gradually materialized, but the majority remains the pursuit of forerunning researchers and inventors. This is the result of a fundamental problem, as described by John Rennie, editor-in-chief of *Scientific American,* that "most technology predictions . . . are simplistic and hence, unrealistic." He goes on to point out that externalities such as market forces, government policies, socioeconomic conditions, whims of fashion or fad, and even the vagaries of the human nature all contribute to whether a technological innovation can blossom to its fruition and diffuse into the lives of the ordinary you and me. This important and insightful point should not be lost on those who populate the realm of decision making.

In this chapter, the author's intention is not to perform the impossible: to predict that which is unpredictable. The objective is to focus on emerging trends and innovations in decision support technology and to explore the possible changes in the way we think and solve problems that may result from these innovations. Important to note is that this chapter will not provide an exhaustive peek into the future of the DSS but, rather, will attempt to provoke each of you into exploring the possibilities that you will assuredly experience in the next millenium.

16-1 WHERE WE ARE AND WHERE WE HAVE BEEN

> I think there is a world market for maybe five computers.
> —THOMAS WATSON, CHAIRMAN OF IBM, 1943

> 640K ought to be enough for anybody.
> —BILL GATES COMMENTING ON THE TYPICAL AMOUNT
> OF PERSONAL COMPUTER MEMORY, 1981

No successful look into the future can be accomplished without some grounding in the current state of affairs. We, therefore, begin our prognostications with a look at the wide variety of domains in which DSS technology has been effectively integrated and applied within the modern organization.

DSSs have been successfully applied to a wide variety of problems. Application domains where DSSs have played an important part include urban traffic management, health care and medical diagnosis, environmental planning, farming, forestry, and agriculture, among many others. The following sections outline further only a very few of the myriad of important areas of DSS application.

Environmental Decision Making and Impact Assessment

Environmental decision support systems (EDSSs) have been developed that can be used to assess the impact of natural resource development. There are also several commercial systems available that are being used for environmental monitoring and impact assessment. One major area of application is in the field of *water resource management.* DSSs to support water reservoir decision analysis have been developed by several organizations (both government and commercial) and tools to support water delivery maintenance and planning have been in use since the late 1980s. DSSs that can assist decision makers in the planning of complex irrigation systems have also been developed.

Agriculture

Irrigation systems are primarily deployed in an effort to improve food production in a region suffering from a lack of natural water supply for crops. However, irrigation management is only one application related to agriculture that has been supported using DSS technology. DSSs focusing on the overall improvement of agricultural production processes have been developed along with DSSs intended to assist in the identification of disease and treatment decisions related to both crops and agricultural animals. The use of such systems has made a major contribution to the world's food resources and is playing a major part in the agricultural development of third world countries.

Forestry

Several DSSs have been developed that can be used to assist forestry- and natural resource–related decision making. For example, a DSS called TEAMS is in use as a tactical planning system to aid forest managers in developing site-specific treatment schedules. Reforestation problems and financial issues related to forest management are also being assisted by domain-specific DSSs. Most recently, a DSS was developed that embeds a linear programming model to evaluate New Zealand forests that were privatized by the government.

Manufacturing

Deciding on appropriate levels of investment in industrial and manufacturing enterprises can be a difficult undertaking. DSSs have become ubiquitous elements in the realm of industrial investment decisions. Further, DSSs have been found useful in environments that have adopted industrywide analysis and planning techniques such as MRP (materials requirements planning) and MRP II (manufacturing resource planning). Numerically controlled machine tools is but one area where computer-based decision support and artificial intelligence systems are being used successfully in manufacturing.

Medicine

Recall from chapter 8 that DSS and expert system technologies such as MYCIN and DENDRAL have been mainstays in the medical profession for many years. More recently, DSSs to support hospital services planning, such as patient loads and staffing forecasts, have been developed in response to the importance and burgeoning cost of these services. A wide variety of medical decision making is currently being supported by DSS technologies. For example, a DSS to assist in the development of proper nutritional balance for diets is being marketed commercially. Other uses of DSSs by the medical profession include tropical disease diagnosis, simulation of epidemics, and creation of pharmaceutical interaction scenarios.

Organizational Support

Numerous examples of DSS applications in support of common organizational decision-making activities can be found. Specific instances of these applications include DSSs that assist in the assessment of risk in international investments, DSSs that provide guidance for decisions involving the management of assets and liabilities, and DSSs that participate in the development of organizational investment strategies and capital budgeting decisions. It is commonly accepted that the use of a DSS can improve the organizational decision maker's capabilities by improving his or her ability to visualize pertinent financial data.

This list of current DSS application areas is by no means exhaustive. The list does, however, illustrate both the scope of and interest in practical applications of DSS technologies. The next section will begin our discussion of the future of DSSs and the succeeding sections will address the future of IT-related technologies: expert systems and executive information systems.[1]

16-2 THE FUTURE OF DECISION SUPPORT SYSTEMS

> But what . . . is it good for?
> —ENGINEER AT THE ADVANCED COMPUTING SYSTEMS DIVISION
> OF IBM ON THE MICROCHIP, 1968

> This "telephone" has too many shortcomings to be seriously considered as a means of communication. The device is inherently of no value to us.
> —WESTERN UNION INTERNAL MEMO, 1876

One ultimate mission of tomorrow's DSSs will be to apply information technologies to enhance the productivity of information workers in the new "Information Age" in dealing with problems that vary in complexity and structure. Alvin Toffler (1970) warned of an impending flood of information so severe that people would become paralyzed and unable to choose between options. The problem of information overload is a reality; it is estimated that the numbers of data collected by a typical modern organization double every year. Given that a typical knowledge worker can only effectively analyze about five percent of those data, the need for support in the area of decision making appears to be ever-present. In this regard, a number of challenges face the DSS designers and users of tomorrow.

---

[1] Many of the predictions set forth in these sections have been built upon the work of Kersten and Meister (1993) and Dobrzenieki (1994).

DSS Integration

As discussed in chapter 14, one of the major challenges facing DSS use is one of integration—there must be a common dialog interface throughout the organization to allow users to easily and effectively access all available information resources. The window of connectivity between the DSS and the various operational data stores should be transparent and enable the integration of various architectures and platforms on which separate resources might reside. In this regard, the *graphical user interface* (GUI) should be standardized so that all applications and data are compatible and easily accessible. This type of standardization is the primary reason for the worldwide adoption of Microsoft Windows and its related products. A major problem in DSS development, however, is the lack of appropriate GUIs to help integrate the various architectures and platforms. From the perspective of the typical decision maker, the GUI can be a determining factor as to whether the DSS will succeed or fail when it comes to implementing the system in the work environment.

In this regard, the concepts of information representation must be addressed by DSS designers and users. What forms of information representation will be required to face the problems and decisions of tomorrow? Will we continue to rely on traditional reporting formats like charts, maps, or diagrams? Will we need new types of graphics such as dynamic graphical models and reports that allow for multidimensional representations?

The integration of components of expert systems and other AI approaches with organizational DSSs has been a major focus as of late. The knowledge base becomes a form of database or model base, the inference engine can be viewed as a knowledge base management system, and the language system of the ES is now effectively a part of the DSS dialog system. One of the challenges for the future will be to introduce even tighter integration between the DSS and the organizational applications, thus extending the "IQ" of the DSS and the decision maker even further.

DSS Connectivity

Connectivity is becoming an extremely important aspect of the next generation DSS, especially with regard to communications. Although our present ability to connect desktop clients through LANs (local area networks), WANs (wide area networks), and gateways is an important first step, the next challenge is clearly the standardization of communication protocols, communication channels, bandwidths, and data transfer rates to facilitate the increasing demands for interchange of large data sets, graphical databases, digital images, and video.

The ability to connect to other networks is important to the organization because it provides a diverse and global source for resources. The major drawback here is the potential security problems attributable to open network links through insecure gateways. One way to minimize these potential security issues is the standardization of communication protocols so that these disparities are minimized.

DSSs in Document Processing

Improvements in the access and management of organizational document resources in addition to organizational and external data are essential to the future strength and effectiveness of the DSS. New search and structuring technologies, such as concept retrieval, hypertext, and multimedia, are under development by both research and commercial efforts with an eye toward creating effective enabling technologies. Probably the single greatest manifestation of this effort is the recent emergence and burgeoning growth of groupware products such as Lotus Notes. The world is rapidly getting connected and this bodes well for the emergence of the next round of decision support tools.

The proper representation of knowledge will enable systems to better mimic experts, and this ability will translate into competitive gains—especially so if the expert systems are used in critical areas where profit margins are very high. Access to documents from widespread and diverse sources with the use of quick search algorithms will also serve to enhance organizational competitiveness. Ensuring that communications are upgraded so that the DSSs can interface with the Internet and WWW will enable organizations to remain abreast of emerging technologies and innovations in decision making and thereby maintain their competitive edge in the emerging electronic marketplace.

Virtual Reality in a DSS Environment

Virtual reality (VR) technology enables an individual to become actively immersed in a simulated environment. This offspring of computer graphics will rely increasingly on the development of more sophisticated hardware and software programs as efforts intensify to make the environments more "real." VR presentation environments range from theater style viewing on large screens to computer monitor displays to helmets equipped with stereoscopic screens and headphones. The experience is multisensory: sight, sound, and touch are the most common. The technology facilitates the viewer's understanding of interrelationships among contextual elements and provides a means by which the viewer can learn to respond effectively and efficiently to the available data.

Scope of Impact

It is predicted that VR will have a dramatic impact on such diverse areas as manufacturing, education and training, medical interventions, military preparedness, and entertainment. For example, engineers engaged in computer-aided design (CAD) will be able to interact with their designs for the early detection of design flaws that are not obvious with current technologies until prototype construction. Impact on the educational system could be significant. People tend to learn more easily through experiential exercise rather than through memorizing rules. VR offers such a tool. Many types of training could be carried out efficiently and effectively through VR. The potential for high economic returns based on VR research and development is encouraging entrepreneurial activity, and giants such as Boeing and AT&T are investing millions.

Areas of Concern

VR environments may be so enticing as to become addictive to viewers. A more insidious side effect could be that certain users would be incapable of distinguishing between reality and virtual reality, leading to actions that could be dangerous to themselves or others. Likewise, VR could be used to manipulate users as well. U.S. congressional hearings, chaired by Al Gore in 1991, concluded that the United States is not investing sufficiently in VR. It has been called the "manifest destiny for computers," but the issues of control and manipulation may lead to the need for a code of ethics for cyberspace.

16-3 THE FUTURE OF EXPERT SYSTEMS AND ARTIFICIAL INTELLIGENCE SYSTEMS

> Everything that can be invented has been invented.
> —CHARLES H. DUELL, COMMISSIONER, U.S. OFFICE OF PATENTS, 1899

> Professor Goddard does not know the relation between action and reaction and the need to have something better than a vacuum against which to react. He is clearly no expert and seems to lack the basic knowledge ladled out daily in all high schools.
> —*New York Times* EDITORIAL ABOUT ROBERT GODDARD'S REVOLUTIONARY ROCKET WORK, 1921

There are two primary issues that must be addressed regarding the future of expert systems: (1) *future AI requirements for intelligent databases* and (2) *knowledge management.*

Artificial Intelligence Requirements for Intelligent Database Systems

The advancement of expert systems in the realm of decision making will require a significant focus on the development of database systems that can contain and manage agents of artificial intelligence. The concept of intelligent database systems (IDSs) can be best illustrated by drawing an analogy to a typical health care system. In this domain, the health care providers such as doctors, nurses, and medical technicians can be considered analogous to software intelligent agents, each with individual and shared knowledge and reasoning abilities and assigned to provide the best possible care for patients. The level of care they can deliver, however, is often dependent upon the complex relationships concerning authority, roles, and responsibilities encountered by these agents as they interact and cooperate with one another. In other words, the knowledge possessed by these agents can only be effectively applied within the rules and regulations defined by the health care environment itself.

Applying this same logic to the domain of expert systems and intelligent software agents, the ability for two or more agents to cooperate intelligently to achieve a common goal evokes the problem of *interoperability*. The advent of an IDS will provide systems support for interoperability (management and access to shared and private objects). The development of such systems might include the integration of AI knowledge representation and reasoning with database data models and processing to produce a super object model. The problems or tasks within the domain will then be solved or executed by agents cooperating to determine the best solution using the available resources.

Although the concept of intelligent software agents attached to expert systems is attractive, distributing such work across multiple domains will require the system to possess a variety of knowledge and associated reasoning capabilities much more powerful than today's systems. This knowledge and reasoning capability will be characterized by the nature and amount of knowledge and reasoning required, the degree of distribution and sharing among the system's agents, and the precision and completeness of, as well as the means for, acquisition, augmentation, and learning of domain-related knowledge. The representation, modeling, controlling, and managing of large volumes and differing data types of persistent, shared, distributed knowledge and associated reasoning clearly pose major challenges for intelligent database systems.

One promising response to that challenge that is currently under development is the *high-performance storage system* (HPSS). A HPSS is software that provides hierarchical storage management and services for very large storage environments. The technology may be of particular use in those situations such as management of large rule sets having present or future scalability requirements that are very demanding in terms of total storage capacity, file sizes, data rates, number of objects stored, and number of users. A central technical goal of HPSS is to move large files between storage devices and parallel or clustered computers at speeds many times faster than today's commercial storage system software products, and to do this in a way that is more reliable and manageable than is possible with current systems. HPSS is the result of a collaborative effort by leading U.S. government supercomputer laboratories and industry to address very real, very urgent, high-end storage requirements.

Knowledge Management

In anticipation of the increased size and usefulness of tomorrow's expert systems, questions surrounding issues of maintenance and management begin to surface. Central to these issues is improvement with regard to methods of gathering and acquiring expert knowledge and ensuring that the knowledge base contains the most current information available. Currently research is focusing on several potential approaches to extend and capture knowledge for an ES. The first method involves software engineering practices that are used for large conventional programs for the maintenance of the knowledge base. The second builds support for rules into an efficient system for managing large relational databases. The problem of scaling, however, occurs when there is a need to compute a million rules over several million pieces of data. To overcome the problem of scaling in this context, systems must be designed is such a way that the rule support mechanisms are tightly coupled within the DBMS, thus allowing the rules to be used efficiently for large applications, integrity control, referential integrity, transition constraints, and protection.

A third potential approach is to use the declarative form of rule specification so that ES implementers have some form of abstract standard that will detail and define the type of answers from the knowledge base. The problem here is to find knowledge representation that is declaratively well founded and procedurally effective. Finally, a promising approach focuses on the depth and breadth of knowledge. The advent of a deep knowledge base for an expert system facilitates the possibility of solving complex search problems. A system possessing broad (general) knowledge combined with a variety of specific concepts and situations could easily provide support for multiple problem context generalization and analogy. Together with suitable procedures for deployment and use, such an ES should be able to address different subject areas, understand English-like statements, and possibly learn to enhance its own problem-solving capabilities.

Advancements in Knowledge Acquisition and Representation

In conjunction with the intelligence component of an expert system, mention must also be made of the future of knowledge acquisition and representation. We know from chapters 8 and 9 that the modeling of expert behavior is a complex and often difficult task. Not all knowledge can be captured by production rules; knowledge can exist through causal information or mathematical relationships as well. The ultimate design goal for expert system knowledge acquisition in the next century will be to design systems that allow experts to encode their own knowledge directly into the computer, thus removing the role of the knowledge engineer from the knowledge acquisition phase. This may be a difficult goal to achieve in the near future, however, because the functioning of the knowledge engineer is currently understood as more of an art than a science. The current state regarding the transfer of knowledge involves asking the expert to introspect about the decision-making process, and such translations still involve codifying experiences based on sensations, thought, memories, and feelings. We are not yet capable of building a system that can handle the complexities of those concepts. But we most likely will be soon.

In the near future, however, there will be increased focus on improving the processes by which expert knowledge is coded into machine language by knowledge engineers because the current procedures only try to mimic expertise as well as possible. In this regard, a number of questions must be answered. Will direct interaction between the expert and the ES be more productive than acting through the knowledge engineer? Can we capture and represent knowledge that can be applied to a variety of problem domains? Can multiple sources of knowledge be captured and incorporated in a single ES so that they are able to interact with other expert systems tools with respect to the problem domain? Finally, can we automate the knowledge acquisition process using technologies such as machine learning?

16-4 THE FUTURE OF EXECUTIVE INFORMATION SYSTEMS

> There is no reason anyone would want a computer in their home.
> —KEN OLSON, PRESIDENT, CHAIRMAN, AND FOUNDER
> OF DIGITAL EQUIPMENT CORPORATION, 1977

> Drill for oil? You mean drill into the ground to try and find oil?
> —DRILLERS WHO EDWIN L. DRAKE TRIED TO ENLIST
> IN HIS PROJECT TO DRILL FOR OIL, 1859

The advancement of executive information systems, to date, has depended upon the continued successful migration away from mainframe computer systems. This trend has helped to eliminate the need for executives and senior managers to learn different computer operating systems and has additionally served to substantially reduce the costs of EIS implementation. This "downsizing" of computers in terms of operational footprint does not mean that greater demands for processing power will not be made with regard to tomorrow's EIS. Future executive information systems will be based on super personal computers that dynamically organize and integrate a wide variety of existing and future software application packages into a useful EIS. An additional impetus will be not only to provide a system that supports senior executives but to satisfy the information needs of middle management as well. In this sense, the EIS of tomorrow may be more appropriately called an *organizational information system* (OIS).

Several functions just now appearing will become commonplace in the future OIS. One recent addition is the inclusion of a module to perform *visual information access and analysis* (VIAA). VIAA modules provide access to both organizational and external information through visual screens that combine text, numerical data, graphical data, and images. The visual screens provide users quick and easy access to data, improving their decision-making capabilities.

An OIS that employs VIAA modules can be thought of as the second generation of executive information systems, taking advantage of the profound increases in information processing speed and capability found in the latest personal computers or workstations. The typical EIS and the OIS differ in several respects, however:

- *Originally the EIS was designed for senior executives.* OIS systems will be designed for use by all levels of company personnel.

- *Even modern EISs typically operate in closed, proprietary systems,* where the output to the user is dependent on the weakest component of an integrated set of organizational systems. For example, the overall system may have excellent graphics capabilities and be based upon a powerful fourth-generation language but be linked to one or more legacy database systems. As manufacturers begin to provide solutions to the conversion of data from older legacy applications and databases, users will be able to "snap together" products from different software vendors to form a complete OIS solution. This approach will allow the "best-of-breed" components to be integrated into a customized product based on individual end user and organizational needs.

- *Many older generation EISs still limit user access to preprocessed data only.* OIS applications will enable users to access real-time data instantly regardless of its location. Improvements in data conversion based on current standards such as dynamic data exchange (DDE) will allow OIS applications to reflect automatically the most current information when the underlying data or images change. This will provide users at all levels of the organization with fast access to the most up-to-date data available.

Many EIS software vendors are already incorporating VIAA functions into their next generation of products. The latest EIS software developments are responding to the changing needs of their users and making the systems accessible to many different layers of management within a company. The abilities to access data already stored and to incorporate the best features of other software applications are beginning to be recognized by the software developers as the means to increase their customer base. As new products are developed and the customer base is broadened to several management layers within a company, the gap between the EIS and other computer-assisted analysis tools, such as the DSS, will become blurred and narrow.

This trend toward the integration of all organizational applications and technologies makes the future very promising for executive information systems. A vast number of technological and conceptual advances in information systems as well as in the telecommunications area suggest that the realization of a truly functional OIS is not far in the future.

16-5 SOME FINAL THOUGHTS ON THE FUTURE OF DSS TECHNOLOGIES

So we went to Atari and said, "Hey, we've got this amazing thing, even built with some of your parts, and what do you think about funding us? Or we'll give it to you. We just want to do it. Pay our salary, we'll come work for you." And they said, "No." So then we went to Hewlett-Packard, and they said, "Hey, we don't need you. You haven't even made it through college yet."

—STEVE JOBS, FOUNDER OF APPLE COMPUTERS, INC.

We don't like their sound, and guitar music is on the way out.

—DECCA RECORDING COMPANY REJECTING THE BEATLES, 1962

The future of a technology-dependent activity such as decision making cannot be easily envisioned without simultaneously looking at the future of the technology upon which it depends. This final section will focus on several issues regarding the future of computing technologies and their relationship to decision support.

Who Will Lead Us into the Future?

In January 1996, a summit conference was held for top IT suppliers. The 150-plus invited attendees represented top corporate, marketing, and sales executives of such companies as IBM, Microsoft, Compaq, Intel, AT&T, Sony, and NEC.

During the conference, attendees were polled for their opinions on a variety of industry issues, using a groupware-like "instant polling" technology. The two questions yielding the most intriguing responses were the following:

1. Who do you believe will be the IT industry's most influential supplier in the year 2000?
2. Who do you believe will be the most influential supplier in 2005?

Not surprisingly, the leading response for the year 2000 was Microsoft Corporation. The turn of the century was, after all, just three and a half years away at that point. The general consensus among the attendees was that regardless of how Microsoft responds to the countless global changes being led by the emerging Internet, it will still influence a large portion of the marketplace as a residual effect of its current market position. The most interesting outcome, however, was the consensus among the group regarding the question about 2005: Far and away, the top vote getter was "a supplier that does not yet exist."

If the response to the second question seems unexpected, it certainly shouldn't. Since the advent of the personal computer, the dynamics in the computer industry in terms of leadership have been volatile. The now ubiquitous Microsoft (arguably the most influential member of the computer industry today) was essentially nonexistent prior to the introduction of the PC, and seven of the top twenty North American computer suppliers today did not exist before the introduction of the PC. If the Internet continues to impact the global marketplace as it has to date, the conditions are highly favorable for a major supplier displacement.

When you look closely, the responses from the summit attendees were almost clairvoyant. The results of this poll suggest that a good number of computer industry leaders clearly see the changes being brought about by the Internet and sense how vulnerable their positions potentially are in the forthcoming period of major growth and change.

The Silicon Revolution

One major driving force behind technology change, to date, has been the advancements in processor speeds and capabilities brought about by the research and development efforts of the semiconductor industry. A current state-of-the-art silicon chip smaller than the size of your thumbnail contains the equivalent complexity of a comprehensive road map of the entire United States—including every interstate, every street, and every alley. Furthermore, this same thumbnail-size chip has the capacity to route traffic on this electronic "highway system" in a trillionth of a second.

Today's microprocessors are more powerful than those made yesterday, and those available next year will undoubtedly dwarf today's capacity. The raw power of silicon technology doubles every eighteen months. This observation was first made by Gordon Moore, cofounder of Intel, over three decades ago and it is now known as Moore's Law. Based on this law, we can safely predict that by the year 2004 silicon chips will be in production containing over a billion transistors. A chip of this capacity is capable of meeting the needs for forty-two central office telephone switches!

In 1992, the Semiconductors Industries Association sponsored the development and publication of a "national road map" for semiconductor technology. The essence of the road map is a series of three-year interval projections of successfully smaller and more powerful devices with each generation of memory devices approximately four times greater in density than those of the previous generation. By the year 2007, it is estimated that the typical RAM memory chip will contain sixteen gigabytes of memory and the typical CPU chip will operate in excess of one thousand megahertz compared to today's standards of sixteen megabytes and three hundred megahertz respectively.

Bandwidth Is Almost Free

Simultaneous to the advancements of silicon technology with respect to increases in storage capacity and processing power, we see vast increases in the capabilities of various communications media including glass fibers, copper wires, and wireless communication systems. Scientists at Fujitsu and elsewhere have already demonstrated the ability to send data over a single strand of glass the diameter of a human hair at a speed of one trillion bits per second. At this speed, every word from every issue of the

New York Times, since it was first published, could be sent to a new location in just under one second.

As bandwidth increases, the cost of sending information drops proportionately. Some have argued that in the future communication costs will be so cheap that it won't even be cost-effective to meter them. Some future-thinking communities have already taken an aggressive stance to ensure their participation in the communications revolution. All residents of Glasgow, Kentucky, for example, have access to the Internet at speeds of two million bits per second for a flat rate of $11.45 per month. This service is provided by Glasgow's *power* company, a local municipal utility that has expanded its services from providing power to also providing cable TV and broadband digital communication services. America's power companies have already installed so much fiber-optic cable that they have the capacity to be the second largest provider of telecommunications should they choose to.

Network Power Grows, Too

Advances in the technologies of computers and bandwidth have combined to feed energy into the digital hurricane: the Internet. The Internet is a network of networks—a dynamic, vast communication system built from the bottom up. All participants on this network have agreed on a simple set of protocols that define how data are to be formatted and routed from one place to the next. As a result of these simple rules, the Internet is capable of displaying incredibly complex behavior, including its capacity to grow without collapsing under its own weight. The Internet is currently doubling in size every year. Homes, schools, businesses, libraries, and museums are connected to the Net, and each new connection adds value to the whole. This added value was first expressed by Bob Metcalfe, inventor of the Ethernet, who observed that the power of a network increases by the square of the number of users. This statement is now known as Metcalfe's Law and it, in combination with Moore's Law, forms the foundation of the communication revolution we are now experiencing.

The impact of the World Wide Web on decision making is likely to be profound. Unlike the Internet, which is doubling in size every year, the WWW is doubling its size approximately every ninety days. In 1996, the U.S. Postal Service delivered over 185 billion pieces of first-class mail. In that same year, the Internet handled over one trillion e-mail messages. The Web has democratized the publishing and accessibility of information in ways unanticipated even a few years ago. As FCC Chairman Reed Hundt has said, "The communication age is connected to the greatest revolution in the history of information since the invention of the printing press." Some have suggested that the Industrial Revolution increased productivity fiftyfold. In the twenty-five years since the invention of the microprocessor, computer power has increased by a factor of more than one thousand. This is the equivalent of almost one Industrial Revolution per year! Now that's progress!

Dreams Are Becoming Realities

It has always been fashionable for technologists to look out into the future and to dream about the events of tomorrow. The world of decision making will change as rapidly as the technology and world around it changes, and, because of this relationship, we can look at the velocity of technological change and use it as a basis for envisioning what problem solving will be like in the next century. What were once dreams are now the clear realities of the future. Let's look at some of the expected technological developments that could affect decision making in the year 2000 and beyond.

By the year 2000, it is expected that the world chess champion will be a computer. Chess has endured through the years as a measure of a man's ability to reason and to strategize into the future. Although IBM publicly announced, following its recent limited triumph over the reigning chess champion, Gary Kasparov, that it no longer intends to pursue the development of a chess-playing computer, the near-term improvements in decision support algorithms will most likely result in a computerized chess champion.

By 2005, translating telephones will emerge that will allow two people anywhere on the globe to speak to each other even if they do not speak the same language. This same core technology will be used to create practical speech-to-text translators that will convert speech into visual displays. Telephones will be able to be answered by an intelligent telephone answering machine that will converse briefly with the calling party to determine the nature and priority of the call.

Within the first decade of the next century, computers will come to dominate the educational environment. Courseware will exist that will be intelligent enough to understand and correct any inaccuracies in the conceptual model of a particular student. Multimedia technologies will allow students to interact with simulations of the systems and the personalities from past history they are currently studying. This same intelligent technology will be used to create human biochemical simulators that will facilitate the design and testing of advanced medicines and pharmaceuticals. And somewhere between the year 2020 and the year 2070 a computer will pass the Turing test, thus marking the dawning of human-level intelligence in a machine.[2]

16-6 CHAPTER SUMMARY

This chapter, for that matter this entire text, was intended to whet the appetite of the reader rather than satisfy it. We are no longer entering the age of information—we are in it. The management of knowledge and the decisions of tomorrow represent new horizons and the challenges that come with such adventures. The purpose of management in the next century will be refocused from productivity of the firm to productivity of the firm's knowledge. Drucker is correct in identifying knowledge as the key organizational resource of the next century. The world's organizations will compete on a playing field of knowledge competency and the successful managers will be those who can harness the power of technology to support the complex problems that will have to be solved. The challenge is yours.

---

[2] The Turing test was invented by Alan M. Turing (1912–1954) as a method to determine the degree of humanlike intelligence displayed by a computer. An interrogator is connected to one person and one machine via a terminal and, therefore, cannot see either counterpart. The interrogator's task is to find out which of the two candidates is the machine and which is the human by asking each of them questions. If the interrogator cannot make a decision within a certain time (Turing proposed five minutes, but the exact amount is generally considered irrelevant), the machine is declared to be intelligent.

Heavier-than-air flying machines are simply impossible.

—Lord Kelvin, president, Royal Society, 1895

If I had thought about it, I wouldn't have done the experiment. The literature was full of examples that said you can't do this.

—Spencer Silver, 3-M Corporation, the discoverer
of the unique adhesives used on Post-it notes

APPENDIX
A

Decision Style Inventory III

DECISION STYLE INVENTORY INSTRUCTIONS

1. Use *only* the following numbers to answer each question:
   - 8   when the question is *most* like you.
   - 4   when the question is *moderately* like you.
   - 2   when the question is *slightly* like you.
   - 1   when the question is *least* like you.

2. Each of the numbers must be inserted in the box below the answers to each question.

3. You may only use the 8, 4, 2, and 1 *once* for each question.

4. For example, the numbers you might use to answer a given question could look as follows: 8 1 4 2.

5. Notice that each number has been used only once in the answers for a given question.

6. In answering the questions, think of how you *normally* act in a situation.

7. Choose the *first* response that comes to your mind when answering the questions.

8. There is no time limit in answering the questions, and there are no right or wrong answers. You can change your mind.

9. Your responses reflect how you *feel* about the response to the questions and what you *prefer* to do, *not* what you think is the right thing to do.

	I	*II*	*III*	*IV*
1. My prime objective is to:	Have a position with status	Be the best in my field	Achieve recognition for my work	Feel secure in my job
	☐	☐	☐	☐

Source: Decision Style Inventory III and Scoring Information adapted from Rowe, A. J. and Boulgarides, J. D., (1994), *Managerial Decision Making,* Englewood Cliffs, NJ: Prentice-Hall. Used by permission, © 1985, all rights reserved.

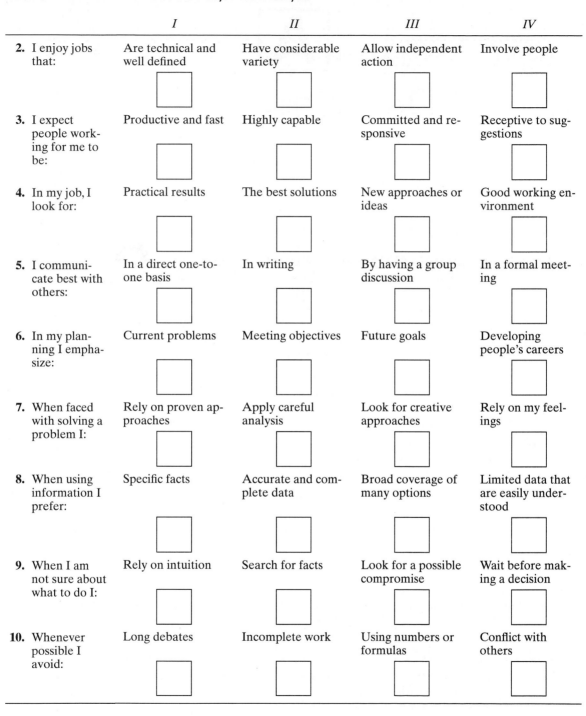

	I	*II*	*III*	*IV*
2. I enjoy jobs that:	Are technical and well defined ☐	Have considerable variety ☐	Allow independent action ☐	Involve people ☐
3. I expect people working for me to be:	Productive and fast ☐	Highly capable ☐	Committed and responsive ☐	Receptive to suggestions ☐
4. In my job, I look for:	Practical results ☐	The best solutions ☐	New approaches or ideas ☐	Good working environment ☐
5. I communicate best with others:	In a direct one-to-one basis ☐	In writing ☐	By having a group discussion ☐	In a formal meeting ☐
6. In my planning I emphasize:	Current problems ☐	Meeting objectives ☐	Future goals ☐	Developing people's careers ☐
7. When faced with solving a problem I:	Rely on proven approaches ☐	Apply careful analysis ☐	Look for creative approaches ☐	Rely on my feelings ☐
8. When using information I prefer:	Specific facts ☐	Accurate and complete data ☐	Broad coverage of many options ☐	Limited data that are easily understood ☐
9. When I am not sure about what to do I:	Rely on intuition ☐	Search for facts ☐	Look for a possible compromise ☐	Wait before making a decision ☐
10. Whenever possible I avoid:	Long debates ☐	Incomplete work ☐	Using numbers or formulas ☐	Conflict with others ☐

	I	II	III	IV
11. I am especially good at:	Remembering dates and facts	Solving difficult problems	Seeing many possibilities	Interacting with others
12. When time is important I:	Decide and act quickly	Follow plans and priorities	Refuse to be pressured	Seek guidance and support
13. In social settings I generally:	Speak with others	Think about what is being said	Observe what is going on	Listen to a conversation
14. I am good at remembering:	People's names	Places we met	People's faces	People's personalities
15. The work I do provides me:	The power to influence others	Challenging assignments	Achievement of my personal goals	Acceptance by the group
16. I work well with those who are:	Energetic and ambitious	Self-confident	Open-minded	Polite and trusting
17. When under stress I:	Become anxious	Concentrate on the problem	Become frustrated	Am forgetful
18. Others consider me:	Aggressive	Disciplined	Imaginative	Supportive
19. My decisions typically are:	Realistic and direct	Systematic or abstract	Broad and flexible	Sensitive to the needs of others
20. I dislike:	Losing control	Boring work	Following rules	Being rejected

INSTRUCTIONS FOR SCORING THE DECISION STYLE INVENTORY

1. Total the points in each of the four columns—I, II, III, IV.

2. Total the sum of these four numbers. The sum of the four columns should be 300 points. If your sum does not equal 300 points, check your addition and that you have not repeated any numbers for a given question.

3. Place your scores in the appropriate box—I, II, III, IV in the figure below.

4. Refer to chapter 2 for a more detailed description of the four quadrant characteristics.

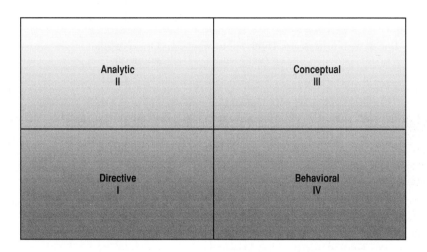

References

Chapter 1

Alter, S. L. 1980. *Decision Support Systems: Current Practices and Continuing Challenges.* Reading, MA: Addison-Wesley.

Anthony, R. N. 1965. *Planning and Control Systems: A Framework for Analysis.* Boston: Harvard University Graduate School of Business Administration.

Donovan, J. J., and S. E. Madnick. 1977. Institutional and Ad Hoc Decision Support Systems and Their Effective Use. MIT Working Paper No. C15R-27, Cambridge, MA.

Gorry, G. A., and M. S. Scott Morton. 1989. "A Framework for Management Information Systems." *Sloan Management Review* 13(1):49–62.

Little, J. D. 1970. "Models and Managers: The Concept of a Decision Calculus." *Management Science* 16(8):B466–85.

Silver, M. S. 1991. "Decisional Guidance for Computer-Based Decision Support." *MIS Quarterly* 15(1):105–22.

Simon, H. A. 1960. *The New Science of Management Decision.* New York: Harper & Row.

Chapter 2

Barnard, C. I. 1938. *The Functions of the Executive.* Cambridge, MA: Harvard University Press.

Miller, G. A. 1956. "The Magical Number Seven, Plus or Minus Two: Some Limits on Our Capability for Processing Information." *Psychological Review* 63(2):81–97.

Myers, I. B. 1962. *Manual for the Myers-Briggs Type Indicator.* Princeton, NJ: Educational Testing Services.

Rowe, A. J., and J. D. Boulgarides. 1994. *Managerial Decision Making.* Englewood Cliffs, NJ: Prentice Hall.

Chapter 3

Adams, J. L. 1979. *Conceptual Blockbusting: A Guide to Better Ideas.* 2d ed. Stanford, CA: Stanford Alumni Association.

Beach, L. R., and T. R. Mitchell. 1978. "A Contingency Model for the Selection of Decision Strategies." *Academy of Management Review* (July):439–50.

Clemen, R. T. 1991. *Making Hard Decisions: An Introduction to Decision Analysis.* Belmont, CA: Duxbury Press.

Clough, D. J. 1984. *Decisions in Public and Private Sectors.* Englewood Cliffs, NJ: Prentice Hall.

Delbecq, A. L. 1967. "The Management of Decision-Making within the Firm: Three Strategies for Three Types of Decision-Making." *Academy of Management Journal.*

Etzioni, A. 1967. "Mixed-Scanning: A 'Third' Approach to Decision Making." *Public Administration Review* 27(5):385–92.

Geoffrion, A. M., and T. J. Van Roy. 1979. "Caution: Common Sense Planning Methods Can Be Hazardous to Your Corporate Health." *Sloan Management Review* 20(4):31.

Harrison, E. F. 1995. *The Managerial Decision-Making Process.* Boston: Houghton Mifflin Co.

Katona, G. 1953. "Rational Behavior and Economic Behavior." *Psychological Review* 60:313.

Keen, P. G., and M. S. Scott Morton. 1978. *Decision Support Systems: An Organizational Perspective.* Reading, MA: Addison-Wesley.

Lindblom, C. E. 1959. "The Science of 'Muddling Through.'" *Public Administration Review* 19(spring):113–27.

Miller, G. A. 1956. "The Magical Number Seven, Plus or Minus Two: Some Limits on Our Capability for Processing Information." *Psychology Review* 63(2):81–97.

Mintzberg, H. 1973. *The Nature of Managerial Work.* Englewood Cliffs, NJ: Prentice Hall.

Saaty, R. W. 1987. "The Analytic Hierarchy Process—What It Is and How It Is Used." *Mathematical Modeling* 9(3–5):161–76.

Simon, H. A. 1960. *The New Science of Management Decision.* New York: Harper & Row.

Sprague, R. H., Jr., and E. D. Carlson. 1982. *Building Effective Decision Support Systems.* Englewood Cliffs, NJ: Prentice Hall.

Thompson, J. D. 1967. *Organizations in Action.* New York: McGraw-Hill.

Tversky, A. 1972. "Elimination by Aspects: A Theory of Choice." *Psychological Review* 79:281–99.

———. 1973. "Availability: A Heuristic for Judging Frequency and Probability." *Cognitive Psychology* 5:207–32.

Tversky, A., and D. Kahneman. 1974. "Judgment under Uncertainty: Heuristics and Biases." *Science* 185:1124–31.

Zanakis, S. H., and J. R. Evans. 1981. "Heuristic Optimization: Why, When, and How to Use It." *Interfaces* 11(5):84–92.

Chapter 4

Bowers, D. G., and S. L. Seashore. 1966. "Predicting Organizational Effectiveness with Four Factor Theory of Leadership." *Administrative Science Quarterly* 11(September):238–63.

Culnan, M. J., and B. Gutek. 1989. Why Organizations Collect and Store Information. In *Information Systems and Decision Processes,* edited by E. A. Stohr and B. R. Konsynski. Los Alamitos, CA: IEEE Computer Society Press.

Deal, T. E., and A. A. Kennedy. 1982. *Corporate Cultures.* Reading, MA: Addison-Wesley.

Gore, W. J. 1964. *Administrative Decision Making: A Heuristic Model.* New York: Wiley.

Harrison, E. F. 1995. *The Managerial Decision-Making Process.* Boston: Houghton Mifflin Co.

Mintzberg, H. 1985. "The Organization as a Political Arena." *Journal of Management Studies* 21(2):133–55.

Pascale, R. T., and A. G. Athos. 1981. *The Art of Japanese Management.* New York: Simon and Schuster.

Patz, A. E., and A. J. Rowe. 1977. *Management Control and Decision System.* New York: Wiley.

Peter, L. J., and R. Hull. 1969. *The Peter Principle.* New York: Morrow.

Peters, T. J., and R. H. Waterman, Jr. 1982. *In Search of Excellence.* New York: Harper & Row.

Robbins, S. P. 1990. *Organization Theory: Structure, Design, and Applications.* 3d ed. Englewood Cliffs, NJ: Prentice Hall.

Schein, E. H. 1985. *Organizational Culture and Leadership.* San Francisco: Jossey-Bass.

Stohr, E. D., and B. R. Konsynski, eds. 1992. *Information Systems and Decision Processes.* Los Alamitos, CA: IEEE Computer Society Press.

Swanson, E. B., and R. W. Zmud. 1989. ODSS Concepts and Architecture. In *Information Systems and Decision Processes,* edited by E. A. Stohr and B. R. Konsynski. Los Alamitos, CA: IEEE Computer Society Press.

Zaleznick, A. 1970. "Power and Politics in Organizational Life." *Harvard Business Review* (May–June):101–09.

Chapter 5

Beyth-Marom, R. 1982. "How Probable is Probable? A Numerical Translation of Verbal Probability Expressions." *Journal of Forecasting* 1:257–69.

Clemen, R. T. 1991. *Making Hard Decisions: An Introduction to Decision Analysis.* Belmont, CA: Duxbury Press.

Davis, M. W. 1988. *Applied Decision Support.* Englewood Cliffs, NJ: Prentice Hall.

De Finetti, B. 1964. La Prévision: Ses Lois Logiques, Ses Sources Subjectives. Translated by H. E. Kyburg. In *Studies in Subjective Probability,* edited by H. E. Kyburg, Jr., and H. E. Smokler (New York: Wiley). First published in *Annales de I'Institut Henri Poincaré* 7 (1937):1–68.

Golub, A. L. 1997. *Decision Analysis: An Integrated Approach.* New York: Wiley.

Howard, R. A. 1988. "Decision Analysis: Practice and Promise." *Management Science* 34(6):679–96.

Howard, R. A., and J. E. Matheson. 1968. An Introduction to Decision Analysis. In *Readings on the Principles and Applications of Decision Analysis.* Stanford, CA: Decision Analysis Group, SRI International.

Savage, L. J. 1954. *The Foundations of Statistics.* New York: Wiley.

Watson, S. R., and D. M. Buede. 1987. *Decision Synthesis: The Principles and Practice of Decision Analysis.* Cambridge: Cambridge University Press.

Chapter 6

Bavelas, A. 1948. "A Mathematical Model for Group Structures." *Applied Anthropology* 7:16–30.

Coleman, D., and R. Khanna. 1995. *Groupware: Technology and Applications.* Upper Saddle River, NJ: Prentice Hall.

DeSanctis, G., and R. B. Gallupe. 1987. "A Foundation for the Study of Group Decision Support Systems." *Management Science* 33(5):589–609.

Ellis, C. A., S. J. Gibbs, and G. L. Rein. 1991. "Groupware: Some Issues and Experiences." *Communications of the ACM* 34(1):38–59.

Fellers, J. W. 1987. "Skills and Techniques for Knowledge Acquisition." Indiana University Working Paper Series.

George, J. F. 1991. "The Conceptualization and Development of Organizational Decision Support Systems." *Journal of Management Information Systems* 8(3):109–25.

Gray, P. 1981. The SMU Decision Room Project. In *Transactions of the First International Conference on Decision Support Systems,* edited by D. Young and P. G. W. Keen. Providence, RI: The Institute of Management Sciences.

Hamilton, J., S. Baker, and B. Vlasic. 1996. "The New Workplace." *Business Week,* 29 April.

Harrison, E. F. 1986. *Policy, Strategy, and Managerial Action.* Boston: Houghton Mifflin Co.

———. 1995. *The Managerial Decision-Making Process.* Boston: Houghton Mifflin Co.

Holsapple, C. W. 1991. "Decision Support in Multiparticipant Decision Making." *Journal of Computer Information Systems* (summer):37–45.

Homans, G. C. 1950. *The Human Group.* New York: Harcourt, Brace & Co.

Huber, G. P., J. S. Valacich, and L. M. Jessup. 1993. A Theory of the Effects of Group Support Systems on an Organization's Nature and Decisions. In *Group Decision Support Systems: New Perspectives,* edited by L. M. Jessup and J. S. Valacich. New York: Macmillan.

Janis, I. L. 1982. *Groupthink.* 2d ed. Boston: Houghton Mifflin Co.

Kraemer, K. F., and J. L. King. 1988. "Computer-Based Systems for Cooperative Work and Group Decision Making." *ACM Computing Surveys* 20(2):115–46.

Kunz, W., and H. Rittel. 1970. Issues as Elements of Information Systems. Working Paper No. 131. University of California–Berkeley, Center for Planning and Development Research.

Leavitt, H. 1951. "Some Effects of Certain Communication Patterns on Group Performance." *Journal of Abnormal and Social Psychology* 46.

Lindstone, H., and M. Turoff. 1975. *The Delphi Method: Technology and Applications.* Reading, MA: Addison-Wesley.

Marakas, G. M., and J. T. Wu. 1997. A Taxonomy of Multiparticipant Decision Structures. University of Maryland Working Paper Series in Information Systems.

Nunamaker, J. F., Jr., A. R. Dennis, J. S. Valacich, D. R. Vogel, and J. F. George. 1993. Group Support Systems Research: Experience from the Lab and the Field. In *Group Decision Support Systems: New Perspectives,* edited by L. Jessup and J. Valacich. New York: Macmillan.

Shull et al. 1970. *Organizational Decision Making.*

Van de Ven, A. H., and A. L. Delbecq. 1971. "Nominal Versus Interacting Group Processes for Committee Decision Making." *Academy of Management Journal* 14:129–39.

Vogel, D. R., J. F. Nunamaker, Jr., W. B. Martz, Jr., R. Grohowski, and C. McGoff. 1989. "Electronic Meeting Systems Experience at IBM." *Journal of Management Information Systems* 6(3):25–43.

Vroom, V. H., and P. W. Yetton. 1973. Leadership Behavior on Standardized Cases. Technical Report No. 3. New Haven, CT: Yale University Press.

Chapter 7

Crockett, F. 1992. "Revitalizing Executive Information Systems." *Sloan Management Review* 38(summer):17–29.

Dobrzeniecki, A. 1994. Executive Information Systems. IIT Research Institute White Paper Series.

Jones, J. W., and R. McLeod. 1986. "The Structure of Executive Information Systems: An Exploratory Analysis." *Decision Sciences* 17(2):220–49.

Millet, I., and C. H. Mawhinney. 1992. "Executive Information Systems—A Critical Perspective." *Information and Management* 23(1):83–93.

Peters, T., and R. Waterman. 1982. *In Search of Excellence.* New York: Harper & Row.

Rockart, J. F. 1979. "Chief Executives Define Their Own Data Needs." *Harvard Business Review* (March–April).

Rockart, J. F., and M. E. Treacy. 1982. "The CEO Goes On-Line." *Harvard Business Review* 60(1):82–87.

Watson, H. J., G. Houdeshel, and R. K. Rainer, Jr. 1997. *Building Executive Information Systems and Other Decision Support Applications.* New York: Wiley.

Watson, H. J., R. K. Rainer, and C. Koh. 1991. "Executive Information Systems: A Framework for Development and a Survey of Current Practices." *MIS Quarterly* 15(1):13-31.

Watson, H. J., S. Singh, and D. Holmes. 1995. "Development Practices for Executive Information Systems: Findings of a Field Study." *Decision Support Systems* 14(2):171–85.

Chapter 8

Berry, D. C., and D. E. Broadbent. 1987. "Expert Systems and the Man-Machine Interface Part Two: The User Interface." *Expert Systems* 4(1):18–28.

Gerrity, T. P., Jr. 1971. "The Design of Man-Machine Decision Systems: An Application to Portfolio Management" *Sloan Management Review* 12(2):59–75.

Hayes-Roth, F., D. A. Waterman, and D. Lenat, eds. 1983. *Building Expert Systems.* Reading, MA: Addison-Wesley.

Keen, P.G., and M. S. Scott Morton. 1978. *Decision Support Systems: An Organizational Perspective.* Reading, MA: Addison-Wesley.

Klein, M. R., and L. B. Methlie. 1995. *Knowledge-Based Decision Support Systems.* 2d ed. New York: Wiley.

Liebowitz, J., 1990. *The Dynamics of Decision Support Systems and Expert Systems.* Chicago: Dryden Press.

Minsky, M. 1975. A Framework for Representing Knowledge. In *The Psychology of Computer Vision,* edited by P. Winston. New York: McGraw-Hill.

Rich, E., and K. Knight. 1991. *Artificial Intelligence.* New York: McGraw-Hill.

Chapter 9

Drucker, P. F. 1993. *Post-Capitalist Society.* New York: Harper Business.

Ericsson, K. A., and H. A. Simon. 1984. *Protocol Analysis: Verbal Reports as Data.* Cambridge, MA: MIT Press.

Feigenbaum, E. 1977. "The Art of Artificial Intelligence: Themes and Case Studies of Knowledge Engineering." In *Proceedings of the Fifth International Joint Conference on Artificial Intelligence,* pp. 1014–29. Cambridge, MA: MIT Press.

Gaines, B. R. 1995. *The Collective Stance in Modeling Expertise in Individuals and Organizations.* Knowledge Science Institute. University of Calgary. <http://ksi.cpsc.ucalgary.ca/articles/Collective/> (accessed January 1998).

Gaines, B. R., and M. L. G. Shaw. 1995. *Knowledge Acquisition Tools Based on Personal Construct Psychology.* Knowledge Science Institute. University of Calgary. <http://ksi.cpsc.ucalgary.ca/articles/KBS/KER/> (accessed January 1998).

Hayes-Roth, B. 1985. "A Blackboard Architecture for Control." *Artificial Intelligence* 26:251–321.

Holsapple, C. W., and A. B. Whinston. 1988. *The Information Jungle.* Homewood, IL: Dow Jones-Irwin.

Kelly, G. 1955. *The Psychology of Personal Constructs.* New York: Norton.

Kim, J., and J. F. Courtney. 1988. "A Survey of Knowledge Acquisition Techniques and Their Relevance to Managerial Problem Domains." *Decision Support Systems* 4(October):269–85.

Klein, M. R., and L. B. Methlie. 1995. *Knowledge-Based Decision Support Systems.* 2d ed. New York: Wiley.

Marakas, G. M., and J. J. Elam. 1997. "Creativity Enhancement in Problem Solving: Through Software or Process?" *Management Science* 43(8):1136–46.

Marcot, B. 1987. "Testing Your Knowledge Base." *AI Expert* (August).

Newell A. 1982. "The Knowledge Level." *Artificial Intelligence* 18:87–127.

Petrie, C., ed. 1992. *Enterprise Integration Modeling.* Cambridge, MA: MIT Press.

van Lohuizen, C. W. W. 1986. "Knowledge Management and Policymaking." *Knowledge Creation, Diffusion, Utilization* 8(1).

Chapter 10

Brule, J. F. 1985. *Fuzzy Systems—A Tutorial.* <http://www.austinlinks.com/Fuzzy/tutorial.html> (accessed January 1998).

Dhar, V., and R. Stein. 1997. *Intelligent Decision Support Methods.* Upper Saddle River, NJ: Prentice Hall.

NIBS Pte, Ltd. 1996. *NeuroForecaster Genetica Software Package.* <http://www.singapore.com/ products/nfga> (accessed November 1997).

Wayner, P. 1991. "Genetic Algorithms." *Byte,* January, 361–64.

Chapter 11

APT Data Group. 1996. *Briefing Paper: What is Metadata?* <http://www.computerwire.com/ bulletinsuk/212e_1a6.htm> (accessed October 1997).

Bischoff, J., and T. Alexander. 1997. *Data Warehouse: Practical Advice from the Experts.* Upper Saddle River, NJ: Prentice Hall.

Inmon, W. H. 1992a. *Building the Data Warehouse.* New York: Wiley.

———. W. H. 1992b. "EIS and the Data Warehouse." *Database Programming and Design* (November).

Kelly, S. 1994. *Data Warehousing: The Route to Mass Customization.* New York: Wiley.

Kozar, D. 1997. The Seven Deadly Sins. In *Data Warehouse: Practical Advice from the Experts,* by J. Bischoff and T. Alexander. Upper Saddle River, NJ: Prentice Hall.

Chapter 12

Codd, E. F., S. B. Codd, and T. S. Clynch. 1993. Beyond Decision Support. *Computerworld,* 26 July.

Gray, P. 1997. The New DSS: Data Warehouses, OLAP, MDD, and KDD. In *Proceedings of the Americas Conference on Information Systems,* edited by J. M. Carey, pp. 917–19. Phoenix, AZ: Association for Information Systems.

Inmon, W. H., J. D. Welch, and K. L. Glassey. 1997. *Managing the Data Warehouse.* New York: Wiley.

Chapter 13

Alavi, M., and I. Weiss. 1986. "Managing the Risks Associated with End-User Computing." *Journal of MIS* (winter).

Arinza, B. 1991. "A Contingency Model of DSS Development Methodology." *Journal of MIS* (summer).

Blanning, R. W. 1979. "The Functions of a Decision Support System." *Information and Management* 2(September):71–96.

Courbon, J. C., J. Grajew, and J. Tolovi, Jr. 1980. "Design and Implementation of Decision Support Systems." 14.

Galletta, D. F., K. S. Hartzel, S. E. Johnson, J. L. Joseph, and S. Rustagi. 1996. "Spreadsheet Presentation and Error Detection: An Experimental Study." *Journal of MIS* 13(3):45–63.

Henderson, J. C., and R. S. Ingraham. 1982. Prototyping for DSS: A Critical Appraisal. In *Decision Support Systems,* edited by M. Ginzberg et al. New York: North-Holland.

Holsapple, C. W., S. Park, and A. B. Whinston. 1993. Framework for DSS Interface Development. In *Recent Developments in Decision Support Systems,* edited by C. Holsapple and A. Whinston. Berlin: Springer-Verlag.

Janvrin, D., and J. Morrison. 1996. Factors Influencing Risks and Outcomes in End-User Development. In *Proceedings of the Twenty-ninth Annual HICSS Conference,* vol. 2. Los Alamitos, CA: IEEE Computer Society Press.

Lotfi, V. and C. Pegels. 1996. *Decision Support Systems for Operations Management and Management Science.* 3d ed. Homewood, IL: Irwin.

Moore, J. H., and M. G. Chang. 1983. Meta-Design Considerations in Building DSS. In *Building Decision Support Systems,* edited by J. L. Bennett. Reading, MA: Addison-Wesley.

Saxena, K. B. C. 1992. DSS Development Methodologies: A Comparative Review. In *Proceedings of the Twenty-fifth Annual Hawaii International Conference on System Sciences.* Los Alamitos, CA: IEEE Computer Society Press.

Sprague, R. H., Jr., and E. C. Carlson. 1982. *Building Effective Decision Support Systems.* Englewood Cliffs, NJ: Prentice Hall.

Walls, J., and E. Turban. 1992. "Selecting Controls for Computer-Based Information Systems." *Accounting Management Information Systems* (October).

Chapter 14

Alter, S. L. 1980. *Decision Support Systems: Current Practices and Continuing Challenges.* Reading, MA: Addison-Wesley.

Boehm, B. W., J. R. Brown, H. Kaspar, M. Lipow, G. McLeod, and M. Merritt. 1978. *Characteristics of Software Quality.* Amsterdam: North-Holland.

Davis, F. 1989. "Perceived Usefulness, Perceived Ease of Use, and User Acceptance of Information Technology." *MIS Quarterly* 13(3):319–42.

Dickson, G., and R. Powers. 1973. MIS Project Management: Myths, Opinions, and Realities. In *Information System Administration,* edited by F. W. McFarlan et al. New York: Holt, Rinehart & Winston.

Ginzberg, M. J. 1975. A Process Approach to Management Science Implementation. Ph.D. diss. Massachusetts Institute of Technology.

———. 1976. A Study of the Implementation Process. Paper presented at Implementation II: An International Conference on the Implementation of Management Science in Social Organizations, University of Pittsburgh.

Ives, B., M. H. Olson, and J. J. Baroudi. 1983. "The Measurement of User Information Satisfaction." *Communications of the ACM* 26(10):785–93.

Klein, M. R., and L. B. Methlie. 1995. *Knowledge-Based Decision Support Systems.* 2d ed. New York: Wiley.

Kolb, D.A., and A. L. Frohman. 1970. "An Organization Development Approach to Consulting." *Sloan Management Review* 12(4):51–65.

Marakas, G. M., and S. Hornik. 1996. "Passive Resistance Misuse: Overt Support and Covert Recalcitrance in IS Implementation." *European Journal of Information Systems* 5:208–19.

Meador, C. L., M. J. Guyote, and P. G. W. Keen. 1984. "Setting Priorities for DSS Development." *MIS Quarterly* 8(2).

Min, H., and S. B. Eom. 1994. "An Integrated Decision Support System for Global Logistics." *International Journal of Physical Distribution and Logistics Management* 24(1): 3–23.

Schein, E. H. 1956. "The Chinese Indoctrination Program for Prisoners of War." *Psychiatry* 19:149–72.

Zand, D. E., and R. E. Sorenson. 1975. "Theory of Change and the Effective Use of Management Science." *Administrative Science Quarterly* 20(4):532–95.

Chapter 15

Brustoloni, J. C. 1991. Autonomous Agents: Characterization and Requirements. Carnegie-Mellon Technical Report CMU-CS-91-204. Pittsburgh: Carnegie Mellon University.

de Bono, E. 1970. *Lateral Thinking: Creativity Step by Step.* New York: Harper & Row.

Delbecq, A. L., A. H. Van de Ven, and D. H. Gustafson. *Group Techniques for Program Planning.* Glenview, IL: Scott, Foresman.

Franklin S., and A. Graesser. 1996. Is It an Agent, or Just a Program?: A Taxonomy for Autonomous Agents. In *Proceedings of the Third International Workshop on Agent Theories, Architectures, and Languages.* Springer-Verlag.

Janca, P. 1996. *Intelligent Agents: Technology and Application.* Norwell, MA: GiGa Information Group.

Koberg, D., and J. Bagnall. 1976. *The Universal Traveler.* Los Altos, CA: William Kaufmann.

Lee, J. K. W., D. W. Cheung, and B. Kao. 1997. Intelligent Agents for Matching Information Providers and Consumers of the World Wide Web. In *Proceedings of the Thirtieth Hawaii International Conference on Systems Sciences.* Los Alamitos, CA: IEEE Computer Society Press.

Marakas, G. M., and J. J. Elam. 1997. "Creativity Enhancement in Problem Solving: Through Software or Process?" *Management Science* 43(8):1136–46.

Osborn, A. F. 1963. *Applied Imagination.* 3d ed. New York: Scribner.

Rowe, A. J., and J. D. Boulgarides. 1994. *Managerial Decision Making.* Englewood Cliffs, NJ: Prentice Hall.

VanGundy, A.B. *Techniques of Structured Problem Solving.* 2d ed. New York: Van Nostrand Reinhold.

Chapter 16

Dobrzeniecki, A. 1994. *Executive Information Systems. IIT Research Institute White Paper Series.* <http://mtiac.hq.iitri.com/MTIAC/pubs/eis/eis.txt>.

Hundt, R. 1997. "The Internet: From Here to Ubiquity." *IEEE Computer* 30(10):122–24.

Kersten, G. E., and D. B. Meister. 1993. *Decision Support Systems: An Overview of Research Directions and Applications.* <http://www.business.carleton.ca/~gregory/papers/idrc_report_93/>.

Toffler, A. 1970. *Future Shock.* New York: Random House.

Index